Frommer's®
New Zealand

My New Zealand

by Adrienne Rewi

MEMORIES OF MY NEW ZEALAND RURAL CHILDHOOD ARE INDELIBLY stamped with heady days of freedom and fun: long summer holidays on hot sandy beaches, aimless bike rides down country roads, and treks through tightly woven native bush. We vanished for hours on end, our parents safe in the knowledge that a New Zealand childhood was a fine and healthy thing with few dangers. We are still a nation of people at one with the land.

We're sports mad. We're the inventors of crazy adrenalin-pumping pastimes like bungee jumping, zorb-riding, jetboating—high speed thrills born of that Kiwi ingenuity that has made us famous. We're a spirited, friendly, fun-loving lot—just watch any rugby match if you want further proof—and when you visit our quirky, geographically diverse country you'll be left awestruck.

Life is easy here; that's why I stay. I have happily settled on the South Island, where there are zero traffic jams, dramatic landscapes, and lovely cafes. That's just the beginning. Oceans, lakes, ski fields, mountains, forests, and beaches—they're all close by. Come with me to some of my favorite New Zealand places.

Whenever I want to see New Zealand at its best, I head for one of the thousands of gorgeous bushwalks that zigzag up and down the country. With huge lacy-leafed ferns closing in on the track and sunlight filtering through the **ANCIENT MOSS-COVERED TREES (left),** you can experience the tranquil back-to-nature landscapes that have made New Zealand famous.

At the risk of being cast out of my own country, I've never quite understood what all the fuss is about when it comes to rugby, but you only need to visit New Zealand during rugby season to discover just how passionate the average fan is about the national sport. **THE ALL BLACKS (above)** are the demigods of the game. When they play, the crowds reach fever pitch.

Getting up close to a sperm whale is one of the most memorable nature experiences I've had. There is something bewitching about the marine experience in the tiny seaside town of Kaikoura in the South Island. It's on the migratory path of several species of whales, teems with bird life, and seals and dolphins are a common sight. The town's eco-friendly **WHALE WATCH** (above) operation has put Kaikoura on the international map.

I don't know how many times I've stood in front of a quirky **TUATARA** (right) waiting for it to move. This stone-still reptile is native to New Zealand and is the last remaining member of an ancient group of reptiles *(Sphenodontia)* that roamed the earth at the time of the dinosaurs.

I love our fat **KERERU** (right), or wood pigeon. They're the chubbiest of birds and their beautiful iridescent green, purple, and teal-blue plumage is always a welcome sight. Once prized by Maori for their tasty meat, they're now a protected species. You'll often hear them swooping through the trees in native bush.

The **KIWI** (below) is our favorite icon, and one of the most special experiences I've had is to watch a kiwi chick hatch. You'll see this unique little bird in many guises throughout New Zealand as a design motif, in souvenir shops, on billboards, but consider yourself lucky if you get to see one in the wild.

© John Kershaw/Alamy

© Neil Farrin/JAI/Corbis

MAORI WOOD CARVING (left) is a traditional art enjoying a welcome renaissance. Every cut, every symbol tells a traditional story, and carvings are unique to their tribal roots. There's nothing quite like a **MAORI HAKA (below)**, or war dance, to make the hairs on the back of your neck stand up on end. A **MAORI MARAE (below right)** is officially "a courtyard or open meeting ground," but the word *marae* is more broadly used to describe a traditional Maori complex, with the carved meeting house or *wharenui* at the center of things. To most New Zealanders it is greenstone; to Maori it is *pounamu*. This exceptionally hard stone has been prized for centuries by Maori. For them it is endowed with symbolic status and mystical power, and treasured for its beauty and toughness. There has been a resurgence in **POUNAMU CARVING (above right)** especially on the West Coast of the South Island.

TONGARIRO NATIONAL PARK is one of my favorite places. It's wild, majestic, challenging, and at the center of it all is Tongariro and one of the country's most beautiful (and testing) 1-day walks, the Tongariro Crossing. Be prepared to be impressed by jewel-like CRATER LAKES and a volcanic landscape that will knock your socks off. © David Wall/Alamy

Frommer's®

New Zealand

6th Edition

by Adrienne Rewi

WILEY

Wiley Publishing, Inc.

ABOUT THE AUTHOR

Photojournalist **Adrienne Rewi**'s passion for words and writing has taken her throughout Asia and into almost every writing genre and every subject. When not organizing her next overseas trip, taking photographs, or writing her next book, she is based in Christchurch writing for numerous New Zealand and international magazines. She is the author of five editions of the bestselling travel guide Frommer's *New Zealand* and has published three other non-fiction titles and assorted short stories. She is a contributor to the Frommer's publication *Dream Vacations*.

Published by:

WILEY PUBLISHING, INC.

111 River St.
Hoboken, NJ 07030-5774

ISBN 978-0-470-49733-3
Editor: Hilary Achauer *with* Jennifer Reilly
Production Editor: Lindsay Conner
Cartographer: Andy Dolan
Photo Editor: Richard Fox
Production by Wiley Indianapolis Composition Services

Front cover photo: Maori statue in Picton © Braden Gunem / AGE Fotostock, Inc.
Back cover photo: Panoramic view of the Milford Sound © iStockphoto / Dean Turner

For information on our other products and services or to obtain technical support, please contact our Customer Care Department within the U.S. at 877/762-2974, outside the U.S. at 317/572-3993 or fax 317/572-4002.

Wiley also publishes its books in a variety of electronic formats. Some content that appears in print may not be available in electronic formats.

Manufactured in the United States of America

5 4 3 2 1

CONTENTS

4 SUGGESTED NEW ZEALAND ITINERARIES 70

5 THE ACTIVE VACATION PLANNER 88

6 AUCKLAND 112

7 NORTHLAND & COROMANDEL 172

15 WEST COAST & THE GLACIERS   403

16 QUEENSTOWN & ENVIRONS   428

17 DUNEDIN, SOUTHLAND & STEWART ISLAND   478

18 FAST FACTS   512

19 KIWI TERMS & PHRASES   517

INDEX   521

LIST OF MAPS

HOW TO CONTACT US

In researching this book, we discovered many wonderful places—hotels, restaurants, shops, and more. We're sure you'll find others. Please tell us about them, so we can share the information with your fellow travelers in upcoming editions. If you were disappointed with a recommendation, we'd love to know that, too. Please write to:

Frommer's New Zealand, 6th Edition
Wiley Publishing, Inc. • 111 River St. • Hoboken, NJ 07030-5774

AN ADDITIONAL NOTE

Please be advised that travel information is subject to change at any time—and this is especially true of prices. We therefore suggest that you write or call ahead for confirmation when making your travel plans. The authors, editors, and publisher cannot be held responsible for the experiences of readers while traveling. Your safety is important to us, however, so we encourage you to stay alert and be aware of your surroundings. Keep a close eye on cameras, purses, and wallets, all favorite targets of thieves and pickpockets.

FROMMER'S STAR RATINGS, ICONS & ABBREVIATIONS

Every hotel, restaurant, and attraction listing in this guide has been ranked for quality, value, service, amenities, and special features using a **star-rating system.** In country, state, and regional guides, we also rate towns and regions to help you narrow down your choices and budget your time accordingly. Hotels and restaurants are rated on a scale of zero (recommended) to three stars (exceptional). Attractions, shopping, nightlife, towns, and regions are rated according to the following scale: zero stars (recommended), one star (highly recommended), two stars (very highly recommended), and three stars (must-see).

In addition to the star-rating system, we also use **seven feature icons** that point you to the great deals, in-the-know advice, and unique experiences that separate travelers from tourists. Throughout the book, look for:

(Finds)	Special finds—those places only insiders know about
(Fun Facts)	Fun facts—details that make travelers more informed and their trips more fun
(Kids)	Best bets for kids and advice for the whole family
(Moments)	Special moments—those experiences that memories are made of
(Overrated)	Places or experiences not worth your time or money
(Tips)	Insider tips—great ways to save time and money
(Value)	Great values—where to get the best deals

The following **abbreviations** are used for credit cards:

AE	American Express	**DISC**	Discover	**V**	Visa
DC	Diners Club	**MC**	MasterCard		

TRAVEL RESOURCES AT FROMMERS.COM

Frommer's travel resources don't end with this guide. **Frommers.com** has travel information on more than 4,000 destinations. We update features regularly, giving you access to the most current trip-planning information and the best airfare, lodging, and car-rental bargains. You can also listen to podcasts, connect with other Frommers.com members through our active-reader forums, share your travel photos, read blogs from guidebook editors and fellow travelers, and much more.

The Best of
New Zealand

Back in 1979, New Zealand cartoonist and satirist Tom Scott, writing in
NZ Listener magazine, had this to say about New Zealand: "Terrible tragedy in the South
Seas. Three million people trapped alive."

The big news in 2003 was that we hit the four million population mark, and more
than half of that increase was due to immigration. (By 2009, that number climbed to 4.3
million.) Given that we have around 44 million sheep, one New Zealander still equates
to a whole lot of fresh lamb. Look beyond the farm gate, though, and you'll find we've
caught up with the rest of the world. We may bob about at the bottom of the Southern
Hemisphere, but it would be unfair to consider the country a backwater.

New Zealand continues to notch up big gains in tourism, welcoming more than two
million visitors a year, despite international upheavals like terrorist attacks, flu epidemics,
and economic downturns. Tourism is our largest source of overseas income. International
visitors contribute NZ$8.3 billion to the economy each year and the tourism sector at
large contributes NZ$19 billion to the country's economy annually. One in every 10
New Zealanders now works in the tourism industry. And we're better equipped for tourists than ever. Efficient visitor centers abound, with accommodations ranging from
budget to exclusive. You can shop 7 days a week, whoop it up at clubs and bars 24 hours
a day, or savor a glass of internationally recognized New Zealand wine in an inexpensive
cafe. You can get real coffee in as many variations as you can imagine, and New Zealand's
fresh, innovative cuisine will leave you breathless and begging for more. Even provincial
New Zealand has pulled up its socks without losing its heart. Small-town pride is beam-
ing, and farmers are turning their hands to boutique tour operations and gorgeous
restored B&Bs to supplement farm incomes, changing the whole nature of many backwater rural districts. Yet you'll still find, at its core, the very Kiwi hospitality that has
made this country famous.

You may have heard that New Zealanders are born wearing wet suits and carrying
paddles, such is their appetite for the outdoors and adventure. No part of the country is
more than 128km (79 miles) from the sea, and a coastline spread with splendid beaches
dishes up thousands of beautiful coastal walks and chances to surf and soak in the sun.

New Zealand is also a winter magnet for international skiers and is the white-knuckle
capital of the world. This is where you can push it to the limits, pit yourself against your
fears and limitations, take risk by the throat, and go for it—leaping off bridges into surging river gorges attached to a giant rubber band, or taking a stab at luging, Zorbing, sky
diving, paragliding, kayaking, white-water rafting, and jet-boating. There's no lack of
invention when it comes to adrenaline-pumping activities in this country.

But you don't have to be an extreme athlete to enjoy New Zealand. There are just as
many ways to be laid-back and indulgent—tour wineries that have stampeded their way
to the top of world ratings in record time; take in the wealth of Polynesian and Maori
culture that forms the backbone of an increasingly multicultural society; or check out the
strong historic and architectural reminders of a colonial past. There are lush gardens, art

galleries, museums, and plenty of one-off reminders that New Zealand is like no other place.

I was born in New Zealand and despite frequent trips overseas, I can't shake off the inherent sense of belonging here. This book presents "my" New Zealand. After many months traveling thousands of miles, testing mattresses, comparing prices, leaping off cliff tops (well, almost), speeding up rivers, and eating and drinking in far too many restaurants, I am more convinced than ever that New Zealand is one of the quirkiest, quaintest, craziest places on earth. It's one of the most favored destinations of the new millennium, and before you've even left here, you'll want to come back. Dip into these pages, and you'll see why.

1 THE MOST UNFORGETTABLE TRAVEL EXPERIENCES

- **Swim with Sharks:** You've got to be keen, I admit, but this can be done in perfect safety. You can come face to face with *Jaws*'s South Seas cousins in a tough metal cage in a knuckle-biting thrill just north of Gisborne. See "Gisborne & the East Cape" in chapter 10.

- **Explore a Glacial Lake:** There are few things as mind-blowing as taking a boat trip on Tasman Lake, on Aoraki/Mount Cook, sailing between towering ice cliffs and floating icebergs in total, surreal silence. It's one of only three places in the world you can do a tour like this, so don't miss it. See "Mount Cook" on p. 438 in chapter 16.

- **Whale-Watch in Kaikoura:** When a mighty sperm whale flaps its tail at you, you won't forget it in a hurry. These big sea monsters come to this particular stretch of water for a marine habitat rich in their kind of plankton. Don't be surprised to see dolphins aplenty, too. See "Marine Experiences in Kaikoura" on p. 400 in chapter 14.

- **Take the Train:** Rated one of the five most spectacular train journeys in the world, the TranzAlpine is an easy day trip that gives a dramatic introduction to the splendor of South Island landscapes. Tunnels, beech forests, viaducts, massive river gorges—they're all there for the taking. See "An Unforgettable Train Trip" on p. 385 in chapter 14.

- **Eat Bugs and Beetles at the Wildfoods Festival:** Prime yourself! You'll need culinary fortitude for this mind-boggling event—you could be served up anything from wriggling grubs to the unmentionable body parts of a number of wild and not-so-wild animals. This is the West Coast at its most rugged best. See the "Wildfoods Festival" box on p. 416 in chapter 15.

- **Stalk Kiwis at Night:** And I mean the birds! Get ready for surprises on this little southern adventure. It's the only place in the country where you can creep about lonely beaches at night with flashlights and stealth and not get arrested! At the same time, you'll be one of the lucky few who get to see a wild kiwi foraging for its supper among the seaweed. See "Making a Date with a Kiwi" on p. 509 in chapter 17.

- **Walk Around Sky Tower:** And I mean from the top, not at ground level. See how brave you really are when it comes to walking around the thin perimeter ring of one of the tallest towers in the Southern Hemisphere. The fearless will be rewarded with amazing views; the terrified can cower inside the viewing level. See "Sky Jump" on p. 142 in chapter 6.

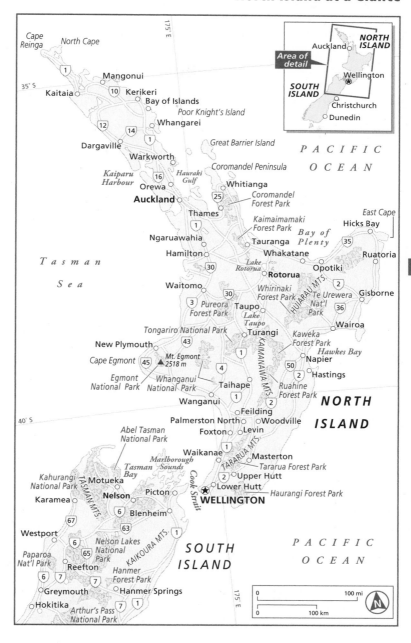

1

- **Visit a Maori Marae:** Experience the *hongi* (the formal nose-to-nose Maori greeting), see deeply moving song-and-dance performances, and eat from a traditional underground *hangi* (oven). Do this in Rotorua as part of an organized tour experience, or seek permission to visit one of the dozens of East Cape *marae* (village common). See "Rotorua" in chapter 9 and "Gisborne & the East Cape" in chapter 10.

2 THE BEST BEACHES

- **Waiheke Island's Onetangi Bay:** Stand on the bay's wide stretch of golden sand, and you can see for miles. On a clear day, throw yourself down into the sand and gaze at the steep pinnacles of Great Barrier Island and Little Barrier, off in the hazy distance. There might even be a few glimpses of the Coromandel in between deliciously warm swims. See "A Side Trip to Waiheke Island" in chapter 6.
- **Karikari Peninsula's Beaches:** This is the Far North at its subtropical best— endless sweeps of sparkling white sand lapped by crystal-clear, azure-blue waters. And from Tokerau Beach to Rangiputa to Matai Bay, you could have miles of it to yourself for beach-combing, sunbathing, and swimming (with care). See "Bay of Islands & the Far North" in chapter 7.
- **Coopers Beach:** Partly shaded by a bank of red-emblazoned pohutukawa trees, how could you not be content to stretch out here? Exercise? A walk to the water should do it! See "Bay of Islands & the Far North" in chapter 7.
- **Hot Water Beach:** Don't ask me why, or how, but if you get here 2 hours before or after low tide, you can hollow out a spot on the beach for yourself, and then wait for natural hot water to seep up through the sand. A natural spa experience without paying a cent! See "The Coromandel Peninsula" in chapter 7.
- **Mount Maunganui's Ocean Beach:** Surf, sand, and sun—some people never want more than that. Throw on a bit of suntan lotion, a pair of sunglasses, and a skimpy swimsuit, and you'll be able to mix in with the best of the bronzed bodies that make an annual pilgrimage to this perennial beach and surf favorite. See "Tauranga & Bay of Plenty" in chapter 8.
- **Kaiteriteri Beach:** Half of Canterbury makes a beeline for these blissful shores every summer. It's not expansive—in fact it's quite small, but perfectly formed nonetheless, and there's a busy vacation atmosphere with packed campgrounds and holiday houses. And with Nelson's endless hours of sunshine, who could complain about size? See "Nelson, Richmond & Motueka" in chapter 13.
- **Abel Tasman National Park's Beaches:** Bush-wrapped and locked between rocky headlands, these idyllic golden patches from Marahau north to Totaranui are accessible by sea only. That's what makes them so special. Gliding through the turquoise waters in your sea kayak, with curious seals to keep you company, you can take your pick of isolated havens. See "Abel Tasman National Park & Golden Bay" in chapter 13.

3 THE BEST ACTIVE VACATIONS

- **Scuba Diving in the Poor Knights:** Jacques Yves Cousteau rated this among the best diving spots in the world. This unique marine reserve has the best of

Area of detail

NORTH ISLAND

SOUTH ISLAND

Auckland

Wellington

Christchurch

Dunedin

New Plymouth

Cape Egmont

45

43

Mt. Egmont
2518 m

Egmont National Park

Wanganui

NORTH ISLAND

40° S

Tasman Sea

Abel Tasman Nat'l Park

Marlborough Sounds

Tasman Bay

Kahurangi National Park

Motueka

Picton

Nelson

6

WELLINGTON

Karamea

6

Blenheim

67

Westport

6

63

Nelson Lakes National Park

KAIKOURA MTS.

1

Paparoa Nat'l Park

65

Reefton

6

7

Hanmer Forest Park

Greymouth

7

Hanmer Springs

Hokitika

7

1

SOUTH ISLAND

Arthur's Pass National Park

6

73

Kaiapoi

73

Christchurch

Franz Josef Glacier

Mt. Cook Nat'l Park

Methven

75

Fox Glacier

Westland National Park

Mt. Cook
3754 m

Lake Tekapo

1

Akaroa

6

Lake Tekapo

Ashburton

Haast

Lake Pukaki

8

Timaru

Twizel

Canterbury Bight

Mount Aspiring National Park

Lake Wanaka

8

83

45° S

Milford Sound

Wanaka

Oamaru

Queenstown

Cromwell

6

85

1

Doubtful Sound

Lake Wakatipu

Alexandra

Palmerston

Fiordland National Park

Lake Te Anau

6

87

Te Anau

8

Roxburgh

94

Lake Manapouri

Dunedin

6

94

8

6

96

Gore

1

Milton

99

1

PACIFIC OCEAN

Invercargill

Foveaux Strait

Oban

170° E

Stewart Island

0   100 mi
0   100 km

THE BEST OF NEW ZEALAND

1

THE BEST ACTIVE VACATIONS

tropical currents sweeping in to make it warm and inviting for a wide variety of tropical species that aren't found anywhere else in New Zealand's waters. See "Into the Deep Blue Sea" on p. 189.

- **Blackwater Rafting in the Waitomo Glowworm Caves:** Daredevils can now go underground to leap off waterfalls; slink through dark, damp, underground waterways; rappel off Lost World rock faces; and do other things in the dark. See "Hamilton & the Waikato" in chapter 8.

- **Trout Fishing in Taupo:** They say the fish in Lake Taupo are so big that when you catch one, the lake level drops. The dozens of other rivers (especially world-renowned Tongariro) and streams in the region also have rich pickings for the fisherman. See "Taupo" in chapter 9.

- **Sea Kayaking in Abel Tasman National Park:** It takes a lot to beat this balmy little paddle into the best-preserved and most beautiful coastline of New Zealand. Keep company with nosy seal pups and dolphins; call into pristine, deserted beaches; and explore rocky headlands. See "Abel Tasman National Park & Golden Bay" in chapter 13.

- **Walking the Glaciers:** Dig out those snow boots and walking poles, add a dash of nerve and daring, and take the walk of a lifetime down Fox or Franz Josef glaciers in the deep south. And don't forget your camera so you can bring home those unforgettable views into the snow caves. See "Franz Josef & Fox Glaciers" in chapter 15.

- **Getting Wild in Queenstown:** This is New Zealand's adrenaline capital, where you get more than one chance to show how crazy you really are. There are more daredevil stunts per square inch here than anywhere else in the country. An international skiing mecca in winter, it readily transforms itself into summer madness as well. See "Queenstown" in chapter 16.

- **Walking the Fiordland Tracks:** If you fancy yourself as a multiday tramper, there's plenty to keep you out of mischief in Fiordland. This is where you get some of the best walks in the world—the Milford, the Hollyford, the Kepler, and the Routeburn tracks. See "Tramping" in chapter 5 and "Te Anau" in chapter 16.

4 THE BEST OF NATURAL NEW ZEALAND

- **Ninety Mile Beach and Cape Reinga:** From the spiritual tip of the North Island where, Maori say, the souls of the dead depart, to mountainous sand dunes, quicksand, and the broad flat stretch of Ninety Mile Beach, this is a must-see area filled with the unexpected. See "Bay of Islands & the Far North" in chapter 7.

- **Waiotapu Thermal Wonderland:** The earth's molten core hints at its artistic potential in a veritable rainbow of color and steamy chaos manifested in geysers, mud pools, hot bubbling lakes, steamy terraces, and more. A photographer's paradise, but tread carefully. See "Bubble,

Bubble, Toil & Trouble: The Geothermal Attractions" on p. 224.

- **Tongariro National Park:** Three major volcanoes dominate a rugged central plateau landscape: Ruapehu, Tongariro, and Ngauruhoe. An indomitable threesome, they're rife with Maori legend and rich in a few modern stories as well. Great for skiers, trampers, and anyone else wanting a physical challenge. See "Tongariro National Park" in chapter 9.

- **Fox and Franz Josef Glaciers:** This is one of the very few places on earth where you'll find full-fledged glaciers this close to the ocean. In a slow, ever-onward creep, they make their way from the heights of the Southern Alps down into untouched rainforest. See "Franz Josef & Fox Glaciers" in chapter 15.

- **Fiordland:** Come here on a wet day (and that's easy because this place gets the most rainfall in New Zealand), and you'll think you've stepped into the living set of *The Lord of the Rings*. This place defies all superlatives. It is the ultimate must-see. See "Te Anau" in chapter 16.
- **The Catlins Coast:** This is wild, natural New Zealand at its unspoiled best. From unique fossil forests to all manner of seabirds and mammals, native bush,

waterfalls, wild beaches, unforgettable tangles of driftwood, and a frustratingly changeable climate—the area takes a lot of beating, but the resulting dramatic impact is unforgettable. See "Dunedin" in chapter 17.

- **Ulva Island:** Tucked into Stewart Island's Paterson Inlet, tiny Ulva Island will leave you speechless with its incredible native bird life. It's wall-to-wall feathers here—and what's more, they're not afraid of humans. Don't go without your camera; you'll need evidence once you start telling friends back home about it. See "Stewart Island" in chapter 17.

5 THE BEST TRAMPS

For details, see "Tramping" in chapter 5.

- **Tongariro Crossing:** Often described as one of the best 1-day walks in New Zealand, this high-altitude hike across volcanic terrain will give you cold mountain springs, lava flows, an active crater, emerald-colored crater lakes, and unforgettable views. Ideal for the fit and enthusiastic hiker. See "Tongariro National Park" in chapter 9.
- **The Abel Tasman Coastal Track:** This is an easy 3- to 5-day walk where the guided option gives you the choice of ditching those hefty packs. From start to finish, 52km (32 miles) later, it winds in and out of gorgeous sheltered coves, golden beaches, rocky headlands, and natural unspoiled bush. See "Abel Tasman National Park & Golden Bay" in chapter 13.
- **The Heaphy Track:** No softy guided options here: You go it alone for 4 to 6 days from the junction of the Brown and Aorere rivers, across tussock-covered flats to the wild seas of Karamea on the West Coast. See "Westport & Karamea" in chapter 15.

- **The Milford Track:** The mother of them all, the Milford is one of the world's best and most-loved multiday tramps. Stretching through the best of Fiordland, this 54km (33-mile) trail follows the Clinton and Arthur valleys and crosses McKinnon Pass with views you'll never forget. See "Te Anau" in chapter 16.
- **The Routeburn Track:** Like the Milford and the Hollyford before it, this track makes its way into virgin rainforest and the sort of wild fairyland scenery where you'd expect to see elves and gnomes prancing around. See "Queenstown" in chapter 16.
- **The North West Circuit:** This is a real test for experienced trampers who think they can face 10 to 12 days walking 125km (78 miles) through bird-filled native bush, big beaches, and long stretches knee-deep in mud. I'm told the rewards are plenty. See "Stewart Island" in chapter 17.

6 THE BEST VIEWS

- **Sky Tower:** The paramount city view in not only New Zealand, but also the entire Southern Hemisphere. Once you get out of that glass-faced lift 328m (1,076 ft.) above the city, you'll know just what I mean. Fabulous 360-degree views of Auckland unfold below, and you can test your courage by walking over glass floors! See p. 141.

- **Hicks Bay:** Stop at the high point above Hicks Bay before you descend into Te Araroa to see New Zealand's largest pohutukawa tree and the East Cape Lighthouse. Resting awhile, high up between the two bays, see if you can imagine Captain Cook's expression when he first sighted the area, and his relief to be leaving again after a tragic Maori massacre in which one European was killed and eaten on his wedding night. See "Gisborne & the East Cape" in chapter 10.

- **Hastings's Te Mata Peak:** A big "sleeping giant" of a hill, 393m (1,289-ft.) high, Te Mata affords big views of endless green and brown undulations, reaching all the way to the coast. Havelock North, Hastings, and Napier all blend together below. See "Hawke's Bay" in chapter 10.

- **Wellington's Kelburn Cable Car:** Not so far above the capital's busy shopping streets, you'll be rewarded with postcard-perfect vistas of glass-faced high-rises silhouetted against the harbor. Step off the cute red cable car into the verdant acres of the Botanical Gardens and look seaward. No matter what the weather, the view is always memorable. See p. 307.

- **Queenstown's Skyline Gondola:** It's everybody's aim to get high in Queenstown one way or another. Make yours by way of a smooth gondola ride to the top of Bob's Peak. Step out into the cool, crisp, exceedingly fresh air with New Zealand's playground spread out at your feet. The Remarkables will keep the view in check, and Lake Wakatipu will be a big blue basin below. See "Queenstown" in chapter 16.

- **Nugget Point:** You may not have seen another human being for hours by the time you make your way to the lookout above Nugget Point. And once you've experienced the blissful solitude of standing on this wild, wind-swept Catlins promontory, you probably won't care if you don't see anyone for several more. Thick, swirling masses of kelp, seals, penguins, and seabirds are here by the hundreds. See "Dunedin" in chapter 17.

7 THE BEST DRIVES

- **Auckland City to Mission Bay:** This is the stuff of a weekend afternoon spin to see how the other half lives. Best done in a Ferrari, a BMW, an Audi, or an equally cool classic if you want to leave a lasting impression. Tight shorts and in-line skates do the trick just as well if you want a cheaper set of wheels. Do the cafe crawl; join the walkers, the runners, and the dog strollers; or just drool over million-dollar real estate. See "Orientation" in chapter 6.

- **Rotorua's Blue and Green Lakes:** From the stately redwood forest on the edge of town, all the way past the Blue and Green lakes to the Buried Village and Lake Tarawera and back again, you'll squeal with delight at a dozen different things. There are lots of picnic spots on the way, but the Landing Café at Lake Tarawera is a good bet if you forget the hamper. See "Rotorua" in chapter 9.

- **The Capital to Mellow Martinborough:** Once you've left the motorways behind, you'll be up and over the winding Rimutaka Hill Road in little more than 40 minutes. Then it's downhill all the way to Martinborough's enchanting pocket of prizewinning wineries. Surrender to hedonism and squander time in idyllic vineyard settings. Make the only exercise you do raising your glass, or at most a wee stroll through pretty little Martinborough Village, where cute shops await. See "A Side Trip to Wairarapa" in chapter 12.

- **Queen Charlotte Sound:** Take the scenic loop from Picton to the little fishing village of Havelock and back to Picton on the main highway. Stop and admire the bush-clad sounds and the boats, and indulge in fresh green-lipped mussels grown in these very waters at the Mussel Boys restaurant, in Havelock. It's a narrow winding road around the Sounds, so take it quietly. See "Picton & Blenheim" in chapter 13.

- **Greymouth to Westport:** Pretty, pretty, pretty! Nikau palms, native bush, tree ferns, jagged rocks, roaring surf, and the big blue Tasman Sea combine to make this a lovely half-day outing. Be sure to stop at the famous Punakaiki Pancake Rocks, where blowholes have a spectacular hissy fit as the ocean roars into, under, and around rocky caverns on the coast. See "Westport & Karamea" in chapter 15.

- **The Famous Milford Road:** Even the Wanaka-Haast road can't match the splendor of this one. It's been called one of the best drives in the world, and no amount of raving can do it justice. You really have to experience it. Virgin rainforest, mirrorlike lakes, astounding waterfalls (especially during rain), beech forest, mountains of moss, bright orange lichens, and sheer mountain faces thousands of feet high contribute to the overall picture—not to mention the slightly daunting Homer Tunnel. See "Milford Sound" in chapter 16.

8 THE BEST GARDENS

- **Hamilton Gardens:** Stretched along the banks of the Waikato River, this blissful, relatively new 58-hectare (143-acre) reserve is a lovely place to wander and picnic. Development began around 30 years ago; there's now a well-established Asian garden, English garden, herb and scented gardens, and lavish stands of trees. See "Hamilton & the Waikato" in chapter 8.

- **Eastwoodhill Arboretum:** One of the most magical places in the country, hardly a garden by normal standards, this astounding collection—the best in New Zealand—is one man's life's work and presents over 3,500 species often studied by international scientists. Go in autumn for unforgettable color displays—and bring a camera. See "Gisborne & the East Cape" in chapter 10.

- **Pukeiti Rhododendron Trust:** Here you get a world-class collection of rhododendrons, viraya, and azaleas set in a centuries-old forest near Mount Egmont—our little Mount Fuji. The gardens spread over many acres in a lovely rural setting 30 minutes from New Plymouth. See "New Plymouth: Gateway to Egmont National Park" in chapter 11.

- **Christchurch's Botanic Gardens:** Regardless of the season, this central-city acreage has plenty to offer, but it's quintessentially Christchurch when the daffodils and bluebells bloom under the huge oak trees along the Avon River and avenues of weeping cherries burst into color. This is when people think of England. See p. 376.

- **Mona Vale:** This little beauty is often overlooked in favor of the city's Botanical Gardens, but it has an intimate charm all its own. Spreading out around a stately Victorian home, these public gardens have myriad lovely features, including iris collections along stream banks, fountains, hostas by the yard, and that old favorite, the rose, which does so well in Canterbury. See "Exploring Christchurch" in chapter 14.
- **Ohinetahi:** If you're a garden fan, this is a must. Formal, architectural, and

stately are all words that instantly spring to mind. Definitely English-inspired and modeled after the best of England's stately gardens, with quirky New Zealand modifications. See "Exploring Christchurch" in chapter 14.

- **Dunedin Chinese Garden:** Here is an unexpected chance to see one of just three truly authentic Chinese gardens created outside of China. Built in Shanghai by Chinese artisans, the garden was dismantled and then shipped to Dunedin, where it was reconstructed under the supervision of Chinese craftsmen. This is a beautiful addition to this southern city's quirky list of attractions. See "Parks & Gardens" on p. 486.

9 THE BEST MUSEUMS

- **Auckland Museum:** After a very significant internal revamp, this museum is everything you'd want in a city's storehouse of treasures: fun, interactive, attractive, informative, and filled with interesting collections. Its Maori and Polynesian section, the biggest in the world, sends shivers down your spine; if you've got kids, let them loose in the Discovery Centre, where they can legally stick their fingers into just about anything. See p. 140 in chapter 6.
- **New Zealand National Maritime Museum:** At the pinnacle of New Zealand's boating history—with the America's Cup Challenge right in our backyard—the Maritime Museum is booming. Look for *KZ1* outside, and inside discover 1,000 years of the country's maritime history. See sail makers, boat builders, and wood-turners at work and take a cruise on one of the vessels. See p. 144 in chapter 6.
- **Museum of New Zealand—Te Papa Tongarewa:** One of the largest national

museums in the world, this giant new edifice on Wellington's waterfront is said to be 5 years ahead of anything else like it. Truly bicultural, it's a magical place where art and artifacts meet technological brilliance, creating riveting displays and interactive playthings for all ages. You'll find everything from a whale skeleton and a working Maori marae to art collections and virtual-reality diversions. See p. 306 in chapter 12.

- **Canterbury Museum and the International Antarctic Centre:** Although these two museums are completely separate entities located miles apart, together they present a terrific overview of life and history in Antarctica. Nowhere else in the world will you find this much gathered information about the great icy continent. There's everything from wildlife displays to human exploration accounts and a real ice chamber so you can get the feel of life in subzero temperatures. See p. 375 and p. 376 in chapter 14.

- **Auckland Museum:** This is the perfect place for an early lesson in things Maori. The recently revamped museum has the largest collection of Maori artifacts in the world. Large war canoes, meetinghouses, greenstone weapons, and feather cloaks are here. On top of that, the Manaia Maori Performance Group puts on a stunning show three times a day. See p. 140.

- **Te Puia's Whakarewarewa Thermal Reserve and New Zealand Maori Arts & Crafts Institute:** Maori guides will lead you through the thermal reserve, explaining the significance of the area to the Maori people. There's also a live song-and-dance performance, a tour of a replica Maori village, and the chance to watch working weavers and carvers in the Arts & Crafts Institute, which was set up in 1963 to foster traditional craft skills. See p. 221.

- **Tamaki Maori Village:** This re-created ancient Maori village presents Maori life as it used to be pre-European settlement. You'll tour the village with a Maori elder, learn the ancient myths, watch a traditional performance, and eat from a traditional hangi. See "Rotorua" in chapter 9.

- **Whakarewarewa Thermal Village:** This small village of just 70 or so people has a 300-year history of settlement. It's probably the only place in the world where people live in such proximity to geothermal activity and still harness the natural forces of the earth for washing and cooking. See "Rotorua" in chapter 9.

- **East Cape:** This is a remote enclave of Maori culture—one of the last places in New Zealand where the Maori language is part of everyday life. You'll find more than 100 marae scattered along the length of the East Cape Road, and if you ask permission, in most cases you'll be allowed to enter. There are numerous Maori settlements and highly decorative Maori churches. See "Gisborne & the East Cape" in chapter 10.

11 THE BEST B&Bs

- **A-Kahu** (Rotorua; © 07/347-4148): I had one of the best B&B stays in New Zealand with Kiri Atkinson-Crean and her husband Nigel Crean—a young, contemporary Maori couple, who will give you a real insight into what it means to be Maori in modern New Zealand. On top of that, their beds and rooms are divine, the food is fantastic, and there is laughter aplenty. See p. 231.

- **Booklovers Bed and Breakfast** (Wellington; © 04/384-2714): Journalist and author Jane Tolerton is a woman with a passion for history and the astonishing book collection to prove it. Her charming city villa bulges with books and her rooms are large, comfortable, and close to town. See p. 299.

- **Glendinning House** (Dunedin; © 03/477-8262): Sandy Black and Jocelyn Robinson live in an elegant brick mansion in the nicest part of town. Jocelyn, a former caterer, tempts guests with ongoing edible treats. Rooms are huge and are the perfect place to imagine life as a wealthy colonialist. See p. 493.

- **Elgin House** (Dunedin; © 03/453-0004): Roger and Carolyn Rennie have mastered the art of spoiling their guests, and their gorgeous old three-story home is riddled with character, history, charm, and hospitality. Don't miss it! See p. 492.

- **Pencarrow** (Queenstown; © 03/442-8938): You'll have to completely revise your benchmark for service and value for money after staying with Bill and Kari Moers. They give a whole new meaning to guest comforts, and I think they should give lessons to B&Bs everywhere. See p. 458.

- **Waiorau Homestead** (Wanaka; ✆ 03/443-2225): Get a taste of the country in this beautifully restored homestead, where chef Blyth Adams and his wife, Ann Lockhart, will spoil you rotten. Modern comforts prevail against a

backdrop of rural history and spectacular scenery. See p. 436.

- **Maison de la Mer** (Akaroa; ✆ 03/304-8907): If you want to know how a top B&B should be run, visit the experts. Bruce and Carol Hyland have hosted over 14,000 guests during their tenure in the hospitality industry, and their new Akaroa venture is as luscious as their last. You'd be silly to miss it. See p. 395.

12 THE BEST LUXURY ACCOMMODATIONS

- **Kauri Cliffs** (Kerikeri; ✆ 09/407-0010): I could find no fault whatsoever with this sublime northern retreat. It is, as the saying goes, "heaven on a stick," and I'm not even a golfer! The staff here are some of the friendliest in the country and the rooms—especially the bathrooms—are my idea of true luxury. See p. 184.

- **Eagles Nest** (Russell; ✆ 09/403-8333): Combine the very best of international taste with the magic of Northland's subtropical environment and a rich vein of natural energy, and you get a luxury retreat quite unlike any other in New Zealand. Daniel and Sandie Biskind have created a world-class retreat worthy of anyone's prolonged attention. See p. 184.

- **Huka Lodge** (Taupo; ✆ 07/378-5791): Exclusivity reigns supreme at this Small Luxury Hotels of the World member. International awards bounce off the walls, and guests invariably comment on rooms fit for kings. It has a supreme location beside the Waikato River just above the Huka Falls and a reputation for quality and service that seems impossible to shake. See p. 242.

- **Treetops Lodge & Estate** (Rotorua; ✆ 07/333-2066): My expectations may never be the same again after staying at Treetops. Being spoiled with one of the most gorgeous suites in the country tends to have that effect. Set in a

unique native bush environment, it's a true sanctuary that will lower your heart rate within minutes of arriving. See p. 230.

- **The Farm at Cape Kidnappers** (Hawke's Bay; ✆ 06/875-1900): Like its big sister, Kauri Cliffs, this stay richly deserves all the superlatives. It's a case of "your wish is our command" here and if you're a golfer, you'll love what is rated the 10th best course in the world outside the U.S. The cliff-edge, rural setting is to die for. See p. 269.

- **Eichardt's Private Hotel** (Queenstown; ✆ 03/441-0450): This new Small Luxury Hotels of the World member has received glowing accolades in Andrew Harper's *Hideaway Report,* and it's becoming the hotel of choice for discerning, upscale travelers. In a remodeled historic building in central Queenstown, it oozes first-class style and understated glamour. It remains one of my favorites. See p. 457.

- **Blanket Bay** (Queenstown; ✆ 03/442-9442): If you want luxury on a grand scale in a majestic setting to match, look no further than Blanket Bay. These gorgeous stone buildings marry so completely with the awesome landscape, it seems as if they were always here. Inside, you'll find an outstanding level of service and comfort. What more could you want? See p. 462.

13 THE BEST BOUTIQUE HOTELS & SMALL LODGES

- **Te Whau Lodge** (Waiheke Island; ☎ 09/372-2288): Every time I visit Te Whau I'm convinced all over again that Gene O'Neill and Liz Eglinton give you the best of everything—winning personalities, fabulous food, great rooms, and views you won't believe. There's something quintessentially Kiwi about the whole experience that I'm proud to recommend. See p. 165.

- **Ridge Country Retreat** (Tauranga; ☎ 07/542-1301): The generosity and style of rooms here leave many more expensive stays in the shade. Joanne O'Keeffe and Penny Oxnam were some of the best (and funniest) hosts on my last road trip, and I'm confident your expectations will be exceeded at every level. The food is divine! See p. 213.

- **Millar Road** (Hastings; ☎ 06/875-1977): Waking up to staggering views over vineyards, orchards, and rolling green hills is only part of the pleasure of this exquisite stay. Somewhere between lodge and B&B, these two modern, self-contained "cottages" are divine. I can't get the memory of them out of my head. It's a classy, unexpected gem filled with contemporary New Zealand art, and I know you'll want to stay at least a week! See p. 270.

- **Ohtel** (Wellington; ☎ 04/803-0600): I couldn't believe my luck when I found this small, chic, ecofriendly, waterfront hotel packed to the gills with collectible mid-century modern furniture. It's an unbeatable value, a total sensory experience, and one of my top picks for something unique and memorable. See p. 300.

- **Arrowtown House** (Arrowtown; ☎ 03/441-6008): This brand-new boutique hotel is the third brainchild of seasoned travelers and hosts alike, Steve and Jeanette Brough, who are two of the best hosts in the country. Located in a pretty, tree-lined residential street, it's an understated haven within a short walk of the village. See p. 461.

- **River Birches** (Turangi; ☎ 0800/102-025): This is one of my favorite new discoveries. Transplanted New Yorker Jason Bleibtreu and his wife Rebecca—both former journalists covering the world's hot spots—have spent years living in hotels, so they know exactly what it takes to create a restful haven. They've imbued this special place with an extra level of professionalism that's hard to fault. And the location? Right beside one of the best trout-fishing rivers in the world! See p. 245.

- **Remarkables Lodge** (Queenstown; ☎ 03/442-2720): Brian Savage and Colleen Ryan sailed the world for 10 years chartering their yacht. We can be thankful they came ashore in Queenstown and took this well-established lodge and shook it by the scruff of the neck. With new life and an understated level of class that puts it above many, it's a top retreat tucked into the foot of the very remarkable Remarkables mountains. See p. 460.

14 THE BEST RESTAURANTS

- **White** (Auckland; ☎ 09/978-2000): Named for its stunning minimal all-white interior, White is the handiwork of celebrated consulting chef Luke Mangan, who owns the award-winning restaurant Salt in Sydney. Its best feature is the Table, a big informal table for diners who like the idea of mixing with others over an outstanding meal. See p. 135.

- **The French Café** (Auckland; (C) 09/ 377-1911): This is posh-plush (in an elegant, understated kind of way) and professionalism-plus. Consistently rated one of Auckland's best and most romantic restaurants, this little den will take your taste buds to new, dizzying heights. See p. 135.

- **DINE By Peter Gordon** (Auckland; (C) 09/363-7030): This sleek, dimly lit culinary "palace" is the new playground of London/New Zealand celebrity chef Peter Gordon. Set in the new SKYCITY Grand Hotel, it's fusion cuisine at its best. Just make sure you save a few good breaths for gasping at the bill. See p. 135.

- **Logan Brown** (Wellington; (C) 04/801-5114): Located in a restored bank building on the edge of the red-light district, this restaurant is guaranteed to exceed your expectations. Consistently voted one of the capital's best eateries—for its service and its delicious focus on

top meat cuts and wild game—it shouldn't be bypassed. See p. 301.

- **Herzog** (Blenheim; (C) 03/572-8770): Expect the very best from this winery and restaurant that has been held up by New York's *Wine Spectator* for its impressive stock of around 3,200 of the world's best wines. It's a fine-dining experience you won't forget in a hurry. See p. 334.

- **Rotherams** (Christchurch; (C) 03/341-5142): Swiss-born chef Martin Weiss has mastered the art of stunning his hungry patrons. In an interior that's all about romance and special occasions, he presents meals that excel in both presentation and taste. Not to be missed—likewise the extensive wine list. See p. 372.

- **The Bunker** (Queenstown; (C) 03/441-8030): Don't start celebrating until you've actually found it and are sitting at one of its tables! Notoriously hard to find (that's part of its charm), and expensive when you get there, this hidden culinary jewel delivers on all the superlatives it receives. Make sure you hunt it down. See p. 464.

15 THE BEST SHOPPING

- **Auckland:** The whole city is a treasure-trove of shops. Try the chic fashion and design shops of High Street; international designers duty-free at DFS Galleria Customhouse; upmarket boutiques in Parnell; antiques on Manukau Road; mainstream fashion in Newmarket—plus the super-classy Nuffield Street and its top designer labels; big mall shopping at St. Luke's Shopping Centre; and fabulous specialty shops on K'Road and Ponsonby Road. See "Shopping" in chapter 6.

- **Rotorua:** A rich vein of New Zealand souvenirs runs right through the whole city, but for the best Maori arts and

crafts, look to Tamaki Maori Village. See "Rotorua" in chapter 9.

- **Wellington:** The Old Bank Building on Lambton Quay has only added to the electric atmosphere of this capital shopping area. Wander the length of the Quay for fashion, books, shoes, and more; move up through Willis Street for more of the same, and into Cuba Mall for edgy design stores and off-the-wall retail surprises. Check out Tinakori Road for a handsome cluster of boutiques. See "Shopping" in chapter 12.

- **Nelson:** Long recognized as the best region for leisure crafts shopping, greater Nelson is dotted with hundreds of pottery, craft, and jewelry studios. Find international-quality art glass at Höglund Art Glass Studio and go from there. Many craftspeople are located out in the country, so you get a bonus look at the countryside as well. See "Nelson, Richmond & Motueka" in chapter 13.

- **Christchurch:** The Arts Centre Galleria is home to about 40 crafts stores selling a wide range of goods, from sheepskin products and leather to wood-turned bowls and ceramics. More turn up for the weekend Arts Centre Market. Also in Christchurch, check out High Street for an eclectic mix of antiques, secondhand stores, cafes, and new and old clothing boutiques; Cashel Mall for fashion and design stores; Victoria Street for a whole host of new boutique stores; and Merivale Mall for upmarket fashion and specialty shops. See "Shopping" in chapter 14.

- **Hokitika and Greymouth:** Jade/greenstone/*pounamu* and gold are found in abundance in these two West Coast towns. Stores specializing in both are found side by side in both Hokitika and Greymouth. See "Greymouth & Lake Brunner" and "Hokitika: Greenstone, Glowworms & Gold" in chapter 15.

- **Queenstown:** This is the home of expensive shopping. You'll find that most things have big price tags, but the quality is invariably tops. There are leading New Zealand and international clothing labels, sheepskin products, souvenirs, leather, original arts and crafts, and masses of jewelry. See "Queenstown" in chapter 16.

16 THE BEST AFTER DARK FUN

- **Dinner on High:** Dining in Auckland's Sky Tower Observatory restaurant over 1,000 feet above New Zealand's largest city gives new meaning to the phrase "getting high." Take your pick from a terrific menu and enjoy your meal gazing out over the sparkling waters of Waitemata Harbour and the city below. Before or after dinner, make sure you take time to look through the high-powered binoculars on the Observation Deck. See "Exploring Auckland" in chapter 6.

- **Soaking Under the Stars:** What could be better than lying back in the hot, soothing mineral waters of Rotorua's award-winning Japanese Buro pools at the Polynesian Spa, set among rocks and waterfalls beside the misty Lake Rotorua, looking up at the stars? The complex has 27 pools in total (some indoors), including 13 lovely private pools. This is the perfect place to ease sore muscles after a long day exploring. See "Rotorua" in chapter 9.

- **Seeing Stars:** This is your chance to see the wonders of the Southern Hemisphere sky in a whole new way. Fresh from a major refurbishment, the Carter Observatory features exciting exhibitions and multimedia presentations that take you on an amazing interplanetary adventure. If you thought our skies were bright and starry before you went in, you'll come out with a fresh appreciation of their beauty. See "Exploring Wellington" in chapter 12.

- **Meeting the Creatures of the Night:** There's always something going on at Wellington Zoo after dark, and this could be your chance to find out which animals wake up as everyone else goes to sleep. If you time it right, you could join one of the group sleepovers (minimum numbers required); or, if you don't fancy bedding with the animals, check out the zoo's summer evening program. They often have picnic evenings with live jazz or blues to add to the entertainment. See "Exploring Wellington" in chapter 12.

- **Eating on the Move:** See the sights of Christchurch and enjoy dinner at the same time. Climb aboard the Tramway Restaurant in one of the city's beautifully restored trams and savor a four course dinner while you complete five circuits of the tramway through central city. See "Meals on Wheels" in chapter 14.

- **Art After Dark:** Enjoy one of the largest permanent art collections in New Zealand when Christchurch Art Gallery opens its doors for its weekly late night on Wednesday evenings. There are 5,500 paintings, sculptures, prints, and drawings for you to peruse, and an excellent restaurant for you to dine in before or after soaking up Canterbury culture. See "Exploring Christchurch" in chapter 14.

- **Bar Hopping:** If you're a night owl looking for a good time, strut your stuff South of Lichfield—more commonly known as SOL—a new back-alley development that features over a dozen lively themed bars and restaurants. There are lights galore, lots of music, and heaps of people.

The best time to go is after dark on a Thursday, Friday, or Saturday when there are bigger crowds. Nearby Poplar Lane is a similar, smaller development with more funky bars. See "Christchurch After Dark" in chapter 14.

- **Now Showing:** At Wanaka's Cinema Paradiso you'll get a night at the movies like no other. Think old hall, castoff armchairs, big cushions and sofas, and even an old car to give you the drive-in feel. Factor in a 30-minute cafe-snack break and you're guaranteed a unique night at the movies See "The Big Screen" in chapter 16.

- **Over the Edge:** If you ran out of time to complete a bungy jump during the day, fear not, for there's still time. At the Ledge, A. J. Hackett and his crew have created the ultimate nighttime jump. You can't see how far you're falling in the dark, so if you were too afraid to try it in daylight, maybe this is for you! You also get to enjoy a nighttime ride up to the Ledge on the gondola, so you'll have great views of all the Queenstown lights twinkling in Lake Wakatipu. See "Queenstown" in chapter 16.

New Zealand in Depth

Kia ora, welcome to New Zealand! Get used to this greeting because you're going to hear it a lot during your stay. Kia ora simply means hello in greeting, or *go well* as a farewell. The meaning will be obvious in context. (See below for more details on Maori terms you'll hear.)

Many people think we live in remote, watery isolation down here in New Zealand, and that we're overrun by 60 million sheep and rugby players as big as kauri trees. Well, for a start, sheep numbers have dropped. Current estimates are closer to 44 million, and while there are some big boys out there, they're not all 7 feet tall, wearing rugby boots and All Blacks jerseys.

New Zealand is no longer the sleepy little backwater it was back in the 1950s, although lingering pockets do exist, and you'll still find that, as incomprehensible as it seems, thousands of North Islanders have never been to the South Island and vice versa. That aside, a lot has been achieved here in a few short decades. We share in the rapid changes of the big, wide world and we celebrate the good things that progress has brought us. There have been downsides—like the brutal clearing of native forests and the lack of respect for a truly unique landscape—but we're wiser now, and we have 13 national parks protecting the most enviable slices of these little islands.

Although some still won't believe this, I'd like to clarify that New Zealand is not joined to the geographical hip of Australia. In fact, the 1,600km (990 miles) separating us account for some pretty significant differences. Australia, for instance, is vast; New Zealand is not. Australia has a very large red desert in its middle; New Zealand doesn't. And whereas Australia was settled by British convicts, we New Zealanders like to remind everyone that we started out as England's other pasture. The one irrefutable thing the two countries do share is a lively, generally good-spirited rivalry over just about everything, but especially sports.

1 NEW ZEALAND TODAY

Like any young country, New Zealand is growing rapidly and facing issues associated with progress. Urban drift accounts for 80% of the population living in towns and cities, most of which is north of Lake Taupo, with a full third of the population in the Auckland region alone. City infrastructures, transport systems, and housing developments are struggling in some cases to keep up with the pace.

Biculturalism has been the loudest catchphrase of the past decade. From the late 19th century until after World War II,

there was a marked decline in the use of the Maori language because schools insisted that only English be taught. Since the 1960s, however, there has been a growing resurgence of interest in Maori identity, language, and tradition, and many Maori are now bilingual, thanks to extensive language programs in schools.

The Waitangi Tribunal, set up by the New Zealand government in 1987 to settle unresolved issues related to the Treaty of Waitangi, has brought Maori grievances to light. Many claim their ancestors were tricked out of much of their land. Today, a good portion of that land has been returned to Maori ownership and many tribes have established lucrative business and corporate entities in the seafood, forestry, farming, and tourism industries.

Today, a combination of farming practices, growing populations, urban spread, and increasing tourism numbers are putting pressure on the land. New Zealanders have always taken pride in their "clean, green" image, but in face of evidence that suggests we may not be as clean and green as we had hoped, there are strong moves to take better care of our natural assets. Sustainability is a big issue, especially in industry and tourism.

In face of our passion for the great outdoors and our reputation for being crazy adventurers, you could be forgiven for thinking that the arts have been overlooked. Nothing could be further from the truth. The main cities—Auckland, Wellington, Christchurch, and Dunedin—all have vibrant cultural hearts; and New Zealand has given the world more than its fair share of talented artists, musicians, writers, filmmakers, and designers.

We've carved out an international reputation for much more than those hefty rugby players I talked about earlier. Maybe it's because we have always been so isolated. Maybe it's because, as a young country, we are still finding our way and still striving to prove we can foot it with the best of the Northern Hemisphere. Whatever the reason, New Zealanders are fiercely proud of their patch. Wherever else they go in the world, they invariably prove themselves as innovative, hardworking, passionate people, making their way in the wider world but always, somehow, still attached to their island roots.

2 LOOKING BACK AT NEW ZEALAND

EARLY MAORI SETTLEMENT There's more than one theory as to how New Zealand's first inhabitants settled here. The Maori legend tells of Kupe, who in A.D. 950 sailed from Hawaiiki, the traditional homeland of the Polynesians. The legend doesn't tell us exactly where Hawaiiki was located in the vast South Pacific, but present-day authorities believe it belonged to the Society Islands group that includes Tahiti.

It wasn't until the mid–14th century that Maori arrived in great numbers. These settlers found abundant supplies of seafood and berries, which they supplemented with tropical plants like taro, yams, and Kumara (sweet potato) that they'd brought along from Hawaiiki. Dogs and rats also made the voyage, and they were added to the protein source. The cultivation of these imported vegetables and animals gradually led to an agricultural society in which Maori lived in per-

manent villages based on a central *marae* (village common or courtyard) and *whare runanga* (meetinghouse). This is where the distinctive Maori art forms of woodcarving and tattooing evolved.

ABEL TASMAN & DUTCH DISCOVERY The first recorded sighting of New Zealand by Europeans occurred in December 1642. Abel Tasman, who was scouting territory for the Dutch East India Company, spied the west coast of the South Island, entered Golden Bay, and met the Maori before even reaching land. As his two ships anchored, several Maori war canoes entered the water and paddlers shouted hostile challenges. The next day, Maori attacked a cockboat, killing four sailors. Tasman fired at the retreating canoes and departed. Bad weather forced him to proceed up the west coast of the North Island. Failing to find a suitable landing spot, he sailed on to Tonga and

Fiji, and Golden Bay was known as Murderer's Bay for many years to come.

CAPTAIN COOK When Captain James Cook left England in 1768 on the *Endeavour,* he carried orders from King George III to sail south in search of the "continent" reported by Abel Tasman. If he found it uninhabited, he was to plant the English flag and claim it for the king; if not, he was to take possession of "convenient situations," but only with the consent of the indigenous people.

On October 7, 1769, Nicholas Young, son of the ship's surgeon, spotted New Zealand from his perch in the mast. Naming the headland (in the Gisborne area) Young Nick's Head, Cook sailed into a crescent-shaped bay and anchored. With the help of a young Tahitian chief, Tupea, who had sailed with the crew as a guide and interpreter, Cook tried to make contact with the Maori, but to no avail. They remained hostile and would not accept Cook's gifts, nor let him take food and water to his men.

Disappointed, Cook claimed the country for King George, and named the bay Poverty Bay because, as he noted in his journal, "it afforded us not one thing we wanted." Sailing north, he rounded the tip of the North Island and went on to circumnavigate both islands. During the next 6 months, he accurately charted the country, and missed only the entrance to Milford Sound (which is virtually invisible from the open sea) and the fact that Stewart Island was not part of the mainland.

THE BRITISH ARRIVE Sealers began arriving in 1792 and essentially stripped the South Island waters of its seal colonies. Whalers, too, discovered rich hunting grounds in New Zealand waters. Oil vats soon dotted the Bay of Islands, which provided safe harbor.

Traders and merchants, attracted by the wealth of flax, the abundance of trees for shipbuilding, and the lucrative trading of muskets and other European goods with the Maori, were little better than the sealers and whalers in respecting the country's natural resources. Great forests were felled and luxuriant bushlands disappeared as land was cleared.

The immigration of Europeans, mostly from Great Britain, had a devastating impact on Maori culture. Most destructive was the introduction of liquor, muskets, and diseases against which the Maori had no immunity. Muskets intensified the fierce intertribal warfare, eventually becoming so common that no one tribe had superiority in terms of firepower. By 1830, Maori chiefs began to realize the weapon was destroying all their tribes.

Missionaries also began to come during this period. They were responsible for putting the Maori language in writing (largely for the purpose of translating and printing the Bible), establishing mission schools, and upgrading agricultural methods through the use of plows and windmills.

Lawlessness grew along with the number of British immigrants, and harm was inflicted on both Maori and the new settlers. The missionaries complained to the British government, which was by no means eager to recognize faraway New Zealand as a full-fledged colony, having already experienced problems with America and Canada. As an alternative, the Crown placed New Zealand under the jurisdiction of New South Wales in 1833, and dispatched James Busby as "British Resident" with full responsibilities to enforce law and order. Unfortunately, he was completely ineffective.

THE TREATY OF WAITANGI Back in Britain, the newly formed New Zealand Company began sending ships to buy land from the Maori and establish permanent settlements. Their questionable methods caused increasing alarm in London. Between 1839 and 1843, the New Zealand Company sent out 57 ships carrying 19,000 settlers, the nucleus of the permanent British population.

In 1839, Captain William Hobson was sent by the government to sort out the concerns. By catering to the Maori sense of ceremony, he arranged an assembly of chiefs at the Busby residence in the Bay of Islands. There, on February 6, 1840, the Treaty of Waitangi was signed after lengthy debate. The treaty guaranteed Maori "all the rights and privileges of British subjects" in exchange for their acknowledgment of British sovereignty, while granting the Crown exclusive rights to buy land from the Maori. Many of the chiefs did not understand what they had signed. Nevertheless, 45 of them ultimately signed the treaty, and when it was circulated around the country, another 500 signed as well.

Instead of easing tensions, though, the Treaty of Waitangi ushered in one of the bloodiest periods in New Zealand's history. The British were eager to exercise their right to purchase Maori land, and while some chiefs were eager to sell, others were not. As pressures forced them to sell, the Maori revolted, and when Chief Hone Heke (the first to sign the treaty) hacked down the British flagpole at Kororareka (Russell) in 1844, it signaled the beginning of some 20 years of fierce battles. The British finally emerged the victors, but the seizure of that Maori land continues to be the subject of debate today.

FROM WAITANGI TO THE PRESENT By the time the 1860s arrived, gold had been discovered on the South Island's West Coast. The Gold Rush opened up huge tracts of Central Otago, and Cobb & Co, a stagecoach company, extended their coaching operations to link the major towns from Christchurch south. They added to that in 1866, initiating a coach service across Arthur's Pass to the gold fields of Westland. By the end of the 1860s, Dunedin was by far the largest city in the country thanks to gold wealth. Advances in rail transport flourished dur-

ing this period, and with waves of new immigrants keen to seek their fortune in the gold fields, New Zealand entered a period of lively economic activity that was to see it through the 1870s and 1880s.

Whaling, too, changed the face of New Zealand during this period. It was one of our first major industries and with the influx of international whalers came traders, missionaries, onshore whaling stations, and new housing settlements. Many whalers stayed on, leaving their ships to marry into Maori families—the fact that there are many Maori families today with Scandinavian names is part of that legacy.

In 1892, the introduction of the first refrigerated shipment of lamb to England heralded a new era in New Zealand beef and lamb exports. History was made in 1893 when New Zealand became the first country in the world to allow women to vote.

By 1914, thoughts had turned to war. One hundred thousand New Zealanders joined the Australia–New Zealand Army Corps to fight in World War I, and New Zealand lost more soldiers per capita than any other nation.

The 1930s were colored by the Great Depression, unemployment, riots and, on a happier note, the beginning of air services across Cook Strait. Our soldiers returned to battle in 1939 with the advent of World War II; and in 1947 the Statute of Westminster was adopted by the government, giving New Zealand full independence from Britain.

For many, the 1950s were a golden era. The economy had long-since settled, our men were back from war, and, for the first time, New Zealand's population hit two million. Life was easy in the '50s. Threats were few and achievements began piling up—Edmund Hillary became the first man to climb Mount Everest; we had our first royal visit when the newly crowned Queen Elizabeth stepped foot on our shores; and the Auckland Harbour Bridge heralded a new age of modernity when it opened in 1959.

It's hard to believe now, but New Zealand had to wait until the 1960s to get its first regional television—in Auckland. We didn't get color television until 1973, by which time the New Zealand population had hit three million and the Auckland International Airport had opened.

The country's economy has traditionally depended on the success of wool, dairy, and meat exports with protected, unlimited access to British markets. This changed when Britain entered the European Common Market in the 1970s. New Zealand was then forced to diversify and do business with many other countries. By the mid-1980s, meat, wool, and dairy products accounted for just under 50% of our export income.

The mid-1980s also heralded the complete deregulation of the domestic economy. It took a decade of struggle for many industries to come to terms with the changes. (This is the main reason our infamous sheep numbers dropped from 72 million in 1983 to the present low of around 44 million.) The stern belt-tightening ultimately bore fruit, however, and by 1993, the economy was flourishing. Today, forestry, horticulture, fishing, tourism, and manufacturing are the leading industries. Tourism is the country's largest single source of foreign exchange. Overall standards and the level of professionalism have improved tenfold in recent years, making New Zealand one of the ripest countries in the world for visitors.

3 ART & ARCHITECTURE

ART As a visitor viewing our museum collections and contemporary galleries, it will soon become obvious that our artistic roots are firmly embedded in a mix of European tradition and Pacific, especially Maori, influences. In some ways the two are quite different. The early European tradition favored an emblematic and literary pairing of image and poetic allusion with subject matter leaning toward the land and self-questioning. The Maori tradition of figurative imagery (traditionally expressed in carving), asserted a strong genealogical identity. While it's easy to generalize, that difference probably still holds true today for much of New Zealand's contemporary art. While Maori artists have borrowed from the European traditions (materially and stylistically), contemporary Maori art is still usually very strongly concerned with what it means to be Maori. There is often a strong reference to heritage, myths, and legends in Maori work. Maori figurative art has also been heavily inspired by the land and natural forms.

That said, Pakeha artists are also heavily inspired by the land and nature. Perhaps that goes back to our short history and our closeness to the land. It's not so long ago that we were clearing forest (150 years) and carving out new lives in these remote islands. I think most New Zealanders at some point in their lives are aware of that geographical isolation. Our country and our population are both small, so perhaps we are more keenly aware of everything that happens to the land here; and perhaps we have a subconscious awareness of just how much our survival depends on the land. It would be fair to say that New Zealand as a nation has also struggled to come to terms with its own sense of identity as it developed from a pioneering colony into a modern western nation. Nowhere is that more obvious than in our artistic expressions. Time and again, still, you will hear people here talking about "a

New Zealand identity" as if it were some mythical aspiration; yet I am firmly of the view that we already have an established New Zealand identity—especially in our art.

Among the most collectible of our contemporary artists are names like Colin McCahon (1919–87), Len Lye (1901–80), Toss Woollaston (1910–98), Rita Angus (1908–70), Philip Clairmont (1949–84), Bill Hammond (1947–), and Maori artists Ralph Hotere (1931–), Shane Cotton (1964–), Michael Parekowhai (1968–), and Robyn Kahukiwa (1938–) to name just a tiny smattering. Other important artists to look out for include Philip Trusttum, Barry Cleavin, Andrew Drummond, Tony Fomison, Neil Dawson, Seraphine Pick, Peter Robinson, Richard Killeen, Dick Frizzell, Mark Braunias, Gretchen Albrecht, and others. No matter how many I list, there will be someone equally important left out.

ARCHITECTURE When the first settlers arrived in New Zealand, the only architecture here was the *raupo* (reed) *whare* (houses) built by Maori and some ramshackle whalers' huts. It goes without saying that the British settlers quickly felled trees and began building little cottages (and later bigger houses and mansions) based on the British model. As wealth in the new colony increased, so did the stature and durability of the buildings. New Zealand's first substantial buildings were erected by missionaries in the Bay of Islands around 1814. You can still visit **Kemp House** and the **Stone Store,** both built in the Georgian style that set the tone for much that was to come.

Today in the wealthier suburbs of Auckland (Remuera, Parnell, Mount Eden, Devonport); Wellington (Thorndon, Mount Victoria); Christchurch (Fendalton, Merivale); and Dunedin (Maori Hill) you'll still find many fine large Georgian-style and Victorian homes. Christchurch

and Dunedin in particular are known for their fine Victorian Gothic architecture. Sadly, many of these houses have been pulled down to make way for the new. Large sheep and cattle stations are spread throughout the country, but the South Island is blessed with huge homesteads from this period. If you're lucky, you may get to stay in some that have been converted into lodges or upmarket bed-and-breakfast accommodations. Canterbury's **Otahuna Lodge** is one example. It is one of the finest examples of Queen Anne architecture in Australasia and has been beautifully restored and converted into one of New Zealand's finest luxury lodges. I've tried to list a number of excellent B&Bs in fine old homes throughout the guide, so if you're interested in architecture, make sure you check each chapter.

You'll also find some splendid early architecture in our churches. Throughout the country, from tiny towns to large cities, there are hundreds of examples of excellent ecclesiastical architecture well worth visiting. In the more remote areas of Northland and East Cape, you'll also find many exquisite little Maori churches. The best examples of these are **St. Faith's Church** in Ohinemutu, Rotorua, and **St. Mary's** at Tikitiki on East Cape. Both are open to the public and both feature exquisite carving and tukutuku paneling that you won't see anywhere else in the world.

Architecture buffs should also seek out Napier and the wider Hawke's Bay for one of the finest collections of Art Deco and Spanish mission architecture outside of Miami. Central Napier was rebuilt almost entirely in Art Deco style after the massive 1931 earthquake that obliterated the city. And in Oamaru in the South Island (btw. Timaru and Dunedin), you'll find an impressive collection of classical and Renaissance buildings complete with Corinthian pillars that will make you wonder if you've landed in a remote outpost of Greece.

Contemporary architecture—both domestic and commercial—is increasingly finding "a New Zealand voice." Our architecture very much follows the path of art in that regard. Yet it is said that only around 2% of New Zealanders employ an architect to design their home—it being seen as the realm of the wealthy—and many of the finest examples of modern New Zealand residential architecture are tucked away down long driveways, well away from easy public view. There are, however, many fine public buildings. Some, like the **Museum of New Zealand Te Papa Tongarewa** in Wellington and the **Christchurch Art Gallery** in Christ-church, have not been without contro-versy and detractors. But we're a small nation and too often small minds rebel against the new. Perhaps that's the way of an isolated, island nation?

Wineries, too, are at the leading edge of New Zealand contemporary architecture as increasing numbers of vineyards realize the power of individualistic branding that includes a statement winery and (often) restaurant. Fine examples include Pere-grine (Central Otago), Cable Bay (Wai-heke Island), Craggy Range (Hawke's Bay), Elephant Hill (Hawke's Bay), and Villa Maria, Oyster Bay, and Spy Valley, all in Marlborough.

4 THE LAY OF THE LAND

New Zealand is part of a fiery rim of vol-canoes that encircle the Pacific Ocean. The last large eruption occurred in 1886—Mount Tarawera near Rotorua left an estimated 150 people dead. Our most recent showoff has been Mount Ruapehu, which did its best to ruin the central North Island ski season for several years in a row in the late '90s.

Today, New Zealand bears all the fasci-nating geographical hallmarks of a tumul-tuous geologic history. It may have a reputation for being "very green," but most visitors are astonished to discover a small country of incredible geographic diversity. There are 500-million-year-old marble outcrops on the top of the Takaka Hills in Nelson, and volcanic ash and pumice have created a barren, desertlike landscape in the central North Island. Franz Josef is one of the fastest-moving glaciers in the world, and the Marlbor-ough Sounds are a labyrinth of islands and waterways. Parched tussock country and strange rocky outcrops cover Central Otago, and the Canterbury Plains spread wide and flat as evidence of prehuman glacial erosion.

Despite all this earthly fury, the land has been blessed with an endless coastline of stunning beaches—white or golden sand on the east coasts, black or gray on the west coasts. Craters have filled to cre-ate jewel-like lakes, and rivers and streams are the endless arteries and veins that feed lush flora.

FLORA & FAUNA
Fauna

For 70 million years, New Zealand has been completely separate from all other landmasses. We've been left with a few pretty strange creatures as a result: four flightless birds—the kiwi, weka, kakapo, and takahe—along with an ancient reptile (the tuatara), directly descended from the dinosaurs. The **kiwi,** of course, has been embraced as a national symbol, so much so that many New Zealanders are quite happy to be called Kiwis themselves. And that odd spiky "lizard," the **tuatara,** is being encouraged to breed itself silly in captivity to ensure it will be around for future generations to marvel at.

Apart from that, we don't have anything very exciting in the way of wildlife. New

Zealand has no native mammals. It was the first Polynesian settlers who brought in both the dog and the rat. Captain Cook then arrived with pigs, goats, fowl, and probably more rats. As more foreign animals were introduced, it became necessary to bring in other animals to control those that had become pests. We now have more than 33 introduced species of mammals, 34 species of birds, 14 species of freshwater fish, at least 1,000 species of introduced insects, plus an Australian lizard and frog or two. Unfortunately, a good many of the above are pests, especially the opossum, which eats its way through frightening quantities of our forests every night. Oddly, while we in New Zealand are busy trying to eradicate this Australian native, in Australia they are busy protecting it.

The good news is, we have no nasties—no snakes, predatory animals, or deadly critters of any kind. The only one that comes close is the **poisonous katipo spider,** which you're unlikely to even see, unless you're on the western beaches of the North Island and spot a small black spider with a bright red stripe on its abdomen. There are sometimes **sharks** in the waters around New Zealand, though, so be sure to ask the locals about this, even though shark attacks are rare.

BIRD-WATCHING Our bird life is abundant and our native birds (around 250 species) in particular are a rich lot, attracting bird-watchers from all over the world. Because of New Zealand's isolation and the evolutionary patterns that have developed here as a result, many species are found nowhere else in the world. The **bellbird,** plain of feather and easily missed, is the songster supreme. The handsome inky **tui,** with his white-tufted neck, comes a close second. The flightless **weka** is rowdy rather than tuneful, and you'll see him in the bush or poking his nose into campsites. The green-and-orange **kea** is a cheeky mountain parrot

with a reputation for mischief on the ski fields and in high-country camps. Make sure you don't leave any belongings about, as keas love to steal whatever is not locked away. This especially applies to anything shiny. They are notorious for damaging mirrors, aerials, and other attachments on vehicles; and their large, strong beaks will give you a nasty bite, so don't be tempted to feed them.

Seabirds of course abound and you'll be delighted by nesting **albatross** and **gannets,** elegant **white herons, penguins,** and many more. Keen bird-watchers have many choice spots to visit. The **Miranda Seabird Coast near Thames** on the Coromandel Peninsular is home to 8,500 hectares (21,000 acres) of tidal flats that attract millions of migratory species every year. **Farewell Spit northwest of Nelson** is another major migratory path; and **South Brighton Spit in Christchurch** attracts millions of godwits every year on their return from Siberia. You can enjoy seabird tours at **Kaikoura;** and **Otago Peninsular** is home to both albatross and penguin colonies, which you can visit. Another not-to-be-missed bird-watching location is **Okarito in the South Westland.** This is where you'll find the white heron nesting colonies. Keep in mind that the only access to these protected areas is via guided tours, which I've listed in the appropriate chapter. There are several tourism operators offering seabird tours around the peninsular coastline. **Stewart Island** is another superb destination for bird-watchers. Not only does it have a wealth of pelagic species which you can arrange to see by boat; it also has easy access to **Ulva Island,** a protected bird sanctuary that is home to several unique species. One of the delights here is the tiny native robins that are surprisingly tame and fearless. If you scratch the ground gently, they will hop right up to your feet, providing you with unforgettable photo opportunities. Stewart Island is also the only place in New

Zealand where you can join nighttime kiwi-spotting tours that take you out into the wild to see this native icon. You'll be very lucky to see a kiwi in the wild on your own, as they tend to forage deep in the bush at night, or on remote, often inaccessible beaches.

Birds are easier to spot in clearings or secondary forests than they are in primary forests. Unless you have lots of experience bird-watching, your best hope for enjoying a walk through the forest lies in employing a trained and knowledgeable guide. (By the way, if it's been raining a lot and the trails are muddy, a good pair of rubber boots comes in handy).

As with any form of bird or wildlife spotting, the standard rules apply. Here are a few helpful hints:

- **Listen.** Pay attention to rustling in the leaves; whether it's bellbirds up above or penguins on the ground, you're most likely to hear an animal before seeing one.

- **Keep quiet.** Noise will scare off animals and prevent you from hearing their movements and calls.

- **Don't try too hard.** Soften your focus and allow your peripheral vision to take over. This way you can catch glimpses of motion and then focus in on the prey.

- **Bring binoculars.** It's also a good idea to practice a little first to get the hang of them. It would be a shame to be fiddling around and staring into space while everyone else in your group oohs and aahs over a kiwi.

- **Dress appropriately.** You'll have a hard time focusing your binoculars if you're busy swatting flies. Light, long pants and long-sleeved shirts are your best bet. Comfortable hiking boots are a real boon, except where heavy rubber boots are necessary. Avoid loud colors; the better you blend in with your surroundings, the better your chances are of spotting birds.

- **Be patient.** The forest isn't on a schedule. However, your best shots at seeing birds (or other wildlife) are in the very early morning and late afternoon hours.

- **Read up.** Familiarize yourself with what you're most likely to see, and if you plan to study the birds, get a copy of *The Field Guide to the Birds of New Zealand* by Barrie Heather and Hugh Robertson. It's published by Penguin and is the only guide endorsed by the Ornithological Society of New Zealand. The same authors also produce a smaller book, *The Hand Guide to the Birds of New Zealand.* If you'd like a more colorful reference, get *Know Your New Zealand Birds* by Lynette and Geoff Moon, published by New Holland. They also produce a small, handbag-size *Photographic Guide to New Zealand Birds.*

It is also important to remember that you put yourself at grave risk by wandering off into the bush alone. You will have a much safer and more satisfying bush bird-watching experience by joining a guide who knows exactly where and when to go to find specific species. Also check at information centers for the best local knowledge of key bird-watching areas, the species you are likely to see, and tour operators or guides who can take you there.

Flora

When it comes to **flora,** we have diverse vegetation—everything from coastal grasses, moss-covered **rainforests,** and dense **primeval forests** of ancient podocarp trees to palms, lush ferns, orchids, Norfolk pines, bougainvillea, flame trees, and hibiscus. In the far north, the Waipoua Forest is home to our giant kauri trees, which are one of the oldest species in the world. Tane Mahuta, the largest of the kauri trees, is said to be over 2,000 years old. In the central North Island and throughout the mountainous regions of

Going Shopping

You won't be short of opportunities to find take-home souvenirs of your trip to New Zealand. Gift and souvenir shops abound in every city, and most major attractions, museums, and art galleries also have their own stores. Their shelves bulge with all the iconic New Zealand gifts—woolen products of every sort, from clothing to floor rugs; kiwis, sheep, and penguins in every size and shape; a growing range of excellent skin-care and cosmetic products; New Zealand–brand sports clothing; some packaged food products (chocolates, honey, sweets); and a plethora of Maori souvenirs.

For high quality, genuine Maori products, you should only purchase items from quality art galleries and gift stores, and preferably items bearing the toi iho™ trademark, which is used to promote authentic Maori crafts in New Zealand. Many Maori items on display in mainstream souvenir shops have been made *en masse* in Asia. I would suggest you purchase any Maori items from places like Auckland Museum, Te Papa in Wellington, and from authentic craftsmen in the Rotorua and Gisborne areas, so you can be sure you have the genuine article. I have also listed reputable stores in individual chapters of the guide.

Pounamu, or greenstone, is only found (in its raw state) in the South Island, so that's the best place to buy it—specifically in Hokitika on the West Coast. Again, much of the greenstone for sale in New Zealand has been imported from Asia, so make sure you purchase from top quality stores and galleries. In places like Hokitika, you can actually watch the craftsmen carving greenstone.

If you're buying New Zealand wine, ask the winery if they will pack and send your precious cargo home for you—if they don't, they will be able to recommend someone who does. That way you don't have to carry it all around the country with you. A number of wine merchants also offer this service.

Nelson is an excellent place to purchase New Zealand crafts of all kinds, especially fine handblown glass, pottery, woodwork, and jewelry. The Nelson Visitor Centre has a comprehensive guide to all local galleries and artisans, many of whom can be visited in their private studios.

If you'd like to take home some of our fine woolen casual and sports clothing, a few top names to look out for are Kathmandu, Icebreaker, Canterbury Sport, Wild South, and Untouched World. Most are available nationwide in quality stores selling New Zealand goods and/or sports clothing, but you'll find them all within reasonable proximity of each other in central Christchurch.

the South, there are tortured-looking alpine plants, brilliant lichens, beech forests, and gigantic tree ferns. Because of that same geographic isolation that shaped our bird life, 84% of New Zealand's flowering plants are found nowhere else in the world.

New Zealand is a highly productive agricultural country, and during early settlement, much of the land was developed at the expense of our unique native forests. Lush pastoral lowlands have been coaxed out of swampland; and many high country farmlands are littered with the rotting tree stumps that attest to once thriving forests.

That, inevitably, is the cost of human progress. In all, around one-third of the country's total land area has been cleared since the arrival of European settlers. In more recent decades, though, New Zealand has taken a very proactive stance toward the protection of what remains. We have 13 national parks that can never be destroyed, and these are the places you should explore to get a feel for New Zealand the way it once was. But as I will mention many times throughout this guide, treat native forest areas with great respect and never venture into them alone, or without being extremely well-equipped with food, water, warm clothing, and some sort of communication device. Many thousands of people have been lost in the bush; many have never been found again. Don't take the warnings lightly.

5 NEW ZEALAND IN POPULAR CULTURE: BOOKS, MUSIC & FILMS

Katherine Mansfield (1888–1923) put New Zealand on the literary map with her still-admired short stories set in New Zealand (though she spent most of her adult life in Europe). Among contemporary fiction writers, **Keri Hulme** won the prestigious Booker McConnell Prize for *The Bone People* in 1985; **Janet Frame** is famous for *Owls Do Cry, An Angel at My Table,* and several others; **Owen Marshall** is perhaps our finest living short-story writer; and the late **Barry Crump** is a legend of a completely unique, raw, backcountry style, having produced books like *A Good Keen Man* and *Hang On a Minute Mate.*

Top Maori writers include **Witi Ihimaera, Patricia Grace,** and **Alan Duff.** In addition, **Maurice Gee, Maurice Shadbolt, Fiona Kidman,** and **Lauris Edmond** all warrant attention.

Filmmaker **Jane Campion** attracted world attention with *The Piano,* which was nominated for nine Academy Awards. (Anna Paquin of Wellington won best supporting actress.)

Director **Peter Jackson** grabbed headlines when he secured Hollywood funding for *The Lord of the Rings,* which was filmed in 2000 with the biggest film budget ever. His *Heavenly Creatures* (1994) was the winner of the Silver Lion at the Venice Film Festival; and of course the *Lord of the Rings* trilogy went on to win a cluster of Oscars. Jackson has since added to his success with the blockbuster *King Kong.* The Weta Studios in Wellington are now a major tourism venture, and there are numerous location tours all over New Zealand.

Two of Maori author **Alan Duff's** novels have also been made into successful films; *Once Were Warriors* and *What Becomes of the Broken Hearted* shocked audiences with their true-to-life violent portrayal of Maori gang society. More recently, *Whale Rider* won international acclaim from movie audiences and, spurred on by Peter Jackson's success, we now have a thriving film industry that has given rise to many award-winning movies.

The very fact that we have such diverse landscapes within a small country has also attracted international filmmakers keen to film here. Much of *The Chronicles of Narnia: The Lion, the Witch and the Wardrobe* was filmed in the South Island; and Tom Cruise filmed *Samurai* in the North Island's Taranaki district. Indian Bollywood film crews are also regular visitors.

We've also turned out our fair share of musicians, none more famous than internationally regarded opera singer **Dame Kiri**

Te Kanawa. On the pop scene, **Crowded House and Tim Finn** had big international hits in the '80s and '90s; and today we have a slew of Auckland-based rap artists making it big. Last but not least, **Hayley Westenra** has won hearts worldwide with her pop-opera crossover albums.

6 MAORI LANGUAGE & CULTURE

The Maori language is a Polynesian dialect. It was first given a written form in the early 19th century by missionaries and British linguists. In the latter part of the 19th century, Maori were forced to adopt the English language in schools, and it wasn't until the 1960s that a strong Maori resurgence began. The **Maori Language Act** of 1987 really changed things. It made Maori an official New Zealand language along with English, and a Maori Language Commission was set up to create authentic Maori names for government departments and major organizations. Today, there are Maori radio stations and television channels, and Maori is taught in all levels of the education system.

When you visit New Zealand, you will be surrounded by things Maori: Words, place names, and many tourist ventures are all indications of this revitalized culture. No one expects you to be able to pronounce many Maori names—it's hard enough for those who have spent all their lives here—but the following tips might make it easier for you. Some Maori words are both singular and plural and require no *s*. *Maori, Pakeha,* and *kea* are all good examples (like the English words *deer* and *fish*). There are only 15 letters in the Maori alphabet: A, E, H, I, K, M, N, O, P, R, T, U, W, NG, and WH, and every syllable in Maori ends in a vowel. The vowel sounds are of great importance and when two vowels come together, each is given its proper sound. WH is usually pronounced as an F.

In the last 10 years, the inclusion of Maori words and phrases in everyday life has become increasingly common. As visitors here, you'll come across a number of words that may seem incomprehensible. *Kia ora* is probably the simplest and the most common. *Kai* (food) is also in common usage, as are *whanau* (family), *iwi* (tribe), and *tangata whenua* (literally "people of the land"—in reference to Maori).

Tourism New Zealand and many tourism operators have also adopted a number of traditional Maori values as part of their

---

Tips **A Word on Cultural Protocol**

If you want to visit a Maori marae, always make sure you ask permission first, but be aware that unless you are staying with a Maori family, or participating in a commercially run tour, you are unlikely to gain access. You must never eat, chew gum, or take food onto the premises. Some Maori will request that you take off your shoes, and some may have particular rules about visits by women during certain ceremonies. And **never** take photographs inside a meetinghouse. If you are uncertain about whether or not photographs are appropriate, just ask. In short, behavior on the marae is governed by strict protocol and you **WILL** be challenged if you ignore these rules. To save yourself and others a great deal of embarrassment, please do not offend. But don't panic; you will be instructed on the proper behavior.

Maori for Beginners

Here's a list of the most commonly used prefixes and suffixes for place names:

Ao   Cloud
Ika   Fish
Nui   Big, or plenty of
Roto   Lake
Rua   Cave, or hollow, or two (Rotorua's two lakes)
Tahi   One, single
Te   The
Wai   Water
Whanga   Bay, inlet, or stretch of water

These are other frequently used words:

Ariki   Chief or priest
Atua   Supernatural being, such as a god or demon
Haka   Dance (war, funeral, and so on)
Hangi   An oven made by filling a hole with heated stones, and the feast roasted in it
Hongi   The pressing together of noses in traditional greeting
Karakia   Prayer or spell
Kaumatua   Elder
Kereru   Wood pigeon
Kia ora   Hello, Go well
Kumara   Sweet potato
Mana   Authority, prestige, psychic force
Marae   Courtyard, village common
Mere   War club made of greenstone (jade)
Pa   Stockade or fortified place
Pakeha   Caucasian person; primarily used to refer to those of European descent
Poi   Bulrush ball with string attached, twirled in action song
Tangi   Funeral mourning or lamentation
Taonga   Treasure
Tapu   Under religious or superstitious restriction (taboo)
Tiki   Human image, sometimes carved of greenstone
Whare   House

NEW ZEALAND IN DEPTH

2

MAORI LANGUAGE & CULTURE

contemporary business practice. These include *manaakitanga* (hospitality/nurturing), *kaitiakitanga* (guardianship), *rangatiratanga* (leadership), and *kotahitanga* (unity). The two you'll come across most often as a visitor to this country are *manaakitangi*, which is an all-encompassing sense of hospitality, sharing, and welcome; and *kaitiakitanga*, which is most used (in a tourism context) in relation to the guardianship of treasures *(taonga)*, and the bounty of the land and its resources.

DINING CUSTOMS

New Zealand has not "grown up" with a long tradition of service in restaurants, so there will be times when you wonder if we even know what the word "service" means. For many young people, being a waitress or waiter is a reluctantly sought holiday job to earn money for university studies—and sadly, it often shows. However, the competitive market is forcing restaurant owners to wake up to the importance of good, friendly, smiling service, and many polytechnics now offer proper training. It is heartening to see a gradual swing toward a belief that restaurant service can be a career option, not just a long-suffering ordeal.

Service glitches are more noticeable in smaller provincial centers, and some of that can be attributed to a lack of suitable employees in the district. Areas such as the West Coast face the reality of young people moving out to the cities; and major tourist centers like Queenstown tend to have a very transient population of restaurant employees.

New Zealand restaurants are either licensed to serve alcohol or BYO (bring your own), and some are both. BYO of course is cheaper, as you don't have to pay the restaurant's surcharge on the wine. Some BYO establishments do charge a corkage fee (usually NZ$3–NZ$8) for opening the wine bottle. *Note:* BYO means wine only, not beer or any other alcoholic beverages.

New Zealand restaurants and cafes do not apply any sort of surcharge to simply sitting at a restaurant table. You are only charged for what you purchase. However, where there are outdoor cafe tables, you must purchase from the restaurant/cafe they're owned by. You cannot use this seating as a casual resting place when you get sore feet.

Most cafes and restaurants now have table service, but some smaller cafes still operate on a counter service policy, where you place your order at the counter and pay before receiving your meal.

Important note: All eateries are now smoke-free. This is a government edict, with smoking banned across-the-board in all restaurants, nightclubs, and public buildings.

Tipping is not customary in New Zealand, although I've never met a New Zealander who doesn't like a show of appreciation for good service and value. But that's relative. My policy is *don't tip for the sake of it.* You may be used to that in your own country, but I maintain that this does nothing to foster an improvement in New Zealand serving standards, which, let's face it, still need work. If you feel you've had a special dining experience and would like to reward the staff, then do so by all means, but be aware that many restaurants operate a shared tipping system, so your favorite waitress or waiter may not be the only recipient of your goodwill. She/he may have to share the goodies with others who may not deserve it—something I personally would like to see changed.

Dining hours vary from one eatery to another. Many cafes and restaurants open for coffee from around 9 to 10am and serve lunch between noon and 2 or 3pm, reverting to coffee and snack service only after that, then serving dinner from 6pm on. Others open for dinner only and that is almost always from 6pm onward.

Other than that, it's all pretty straightforward—eat and enjoy! Oh, and don't forget **New Zealand wine.** With the many international award-winners to our credit, I can assure you, you *will* be tempted!

MEALS

My best advice to anyone coming to New Zealand is to plan plenty of exercise so that you'll be perpetually hungry and therefore well able to justify every single indulgence that you're likely to be faced with. Forget restraint and prepare to be surprised by the level of sophistication of the top New Zealand dining experiences. This is a land of edible bounty—**Canterbury lamb;** Central Otago pinot noir; Bluff and Nelson oysters; Nelson scallops; Kaikoura crayfish (lobster); West Coast whitebait; South Island venison; **Marlborough green-lipped mussels;** Akaroa salmon; Stewart Island blue cod; **Central Otago cherries and apricots**—and you shouldn't miss any of it.

Within the restaurant scene itself, there has been a revolution in the last decade. Fine dining (silver service) still lingers in a few city pockets, but the upmarket trend is predominantly toward fine gourmet food in more relaxed, contemporary settings. Increasing numbers of restaurants are also sourcing fresh, local ingredients, often specific to their region and often organically grown. As farmers' markets spring up all around the country and increasing amounts of genuinely organic meat and produce become available (albeit at extra cost), chefs are able to secure the very best ingredients to ensure flavorsome, healthy menus. Most will state this on their in-house menus.

Pacific Rim has been the primary culinary influence for some time, and although many chefs have stopped using the term, preferring modern or contemporary New Zealand terminology instead, the end result is much the same—the combination of classic Pacific and Asian ingredients combined to perfection and presented elegantly. You'll be spoiled with all the choices in this category, especially in Auckland, Wellington, Christchurch, and Queenstown (in that order).

For moderately priced, casual meals, including lunches, there are now so many cafes, restaurants, and bars it seems silly to try to define what each delivers. In short, you will seldom be without a choice. Most prepare good soups, salads, and main courses based around beef, lamb, chicken, fish, and vegetarian choices. Many others specialize in counter food, rather than menu-based options, and include panini, pastries, pies, sandwiches, and salads. Just be aware that many of the more casual cafe/bar establishments offering lighter meals often turn into rowdy drinking holes after 11pm.

There are a huge number of ethnic restaurants in all the main cities—Indian, Thai, Vietnamese, Chinese, Japanese, and Korean are the most common, but you'll also come across Burmese, Afghani, Turkish, Mexican, Spanish, Italian, French, and Middle Eastern choices in Auckland, Wellington, and Christchurch. Thai, Chinese, Vietnamese, and Indian restaurants are usually the cheapest of the ethnic choices, and you'll be able to enjoy great meals for a very reasonable price.

On top of the usual restaurant and cafe experiences, you'd be doing yourself a disservice if you miss trying a few of our iconic Kiwi meals. **Fish and chips** for instance. The fish-and-chip shop is still one of the most popular takeaway choices in this country—despite the colonization of McDonald's, Pizza Hut, and other conglomerates—and you'll find a fish-and-chip shop in virtually every town and village in the country. It goes without saying that some are better than others. Many still offer the meal—deep-fried battered fish and fat potato fries—wrapped in newspaper, which is how most New Zealanders prefer them; but some have opted for fancier packaging.

The small **meat pie** is still a Kiwi favorite, too. Every dairy and service station in the country has a pie warmer and, I'm almost reluctant to report, the meat pie is famed as a hangover cure after a night of heavy drinking.

The **barbecue** is a summer favorite. Almost every family in New Zealand will probably have a barbecue at some point during the summer months. Our balmy evenings lend themselves to eating outdoors and there's nothing quite like it. It invariably includes sausages and steak—often wrapped in bread and smothered in tomato sauce—accompanied by salads. Like most things, though, the barbecue is also changing and many people now apply as much culinary invention to the once-humble barbecue as they do any meal. I have friends who stay at the beach every summer and they live off freshly barbecued fish, scallops, and crayfish (lobster) plucked straight from the ocean and enhanced with their own particular sauces and spices. It's as good as any restaurant meal.

Last but certainly not least, the traditional **Maori hangi,** where food is cooked underground, is a must-do experience while you're in New Zealand. Traditionally, it involves lighting a fire and putting large stones in the embers to heat. Simultaneously, a large pit is dug. The heated rocks are then transferred into the pit, covered with wet sacking and/or wet newspapers. Prepared lamb, chicken, pork, fish, shellfish, and vegetables (most commonly sweet potato, pumpkin, and cabbage) are wrapped in leaves, placed in flax baskets (now made of wire or mesh), and lowered into the cooking pit, covered with more newspaper and earth, and left to steam. The moist, tender, melt-in-your-mouth food is lifted a few hours later.

Hangi food is not to everyone's taste—certainly not initially. The distinctive smoky flavors are an acquired taste. If you'd like to try hangi food, ask at visitor centers for tour operators who include a hangi. You'll find this easiest in Rotorua,

where a number of hotels offer hangi meals as part of a cultural performance package. Bear in mind, though, that because of modern health and safety regulations, many hotels now prepare their hangi meals using gas-fired ovens, so the meal will lack some of the unique traditional smoky flavors that to my mind, make a hangi meal.

Other distinctly New Zealand culinary experiences include the sheer craziness of the annual Hokitika Wildfoods Festival, where the policy is "If it's not moving, it's edible" (p. 416); the numerous annual wine and food festivals; and farmers' markets held in individual provinces. All are always well-publicized at information centers.

BEVERAGES

A decade ago New Zealand's **wine** exports totaled around NZ$100 million; soon they are expected to top NZ$1 billion. That's rapid growth by anyone's standards, and as you drive around New Zealand you'll probably wonder if there'll be any farmland left without flourishing vines in another 10 years. It was a very different story 20 to 30 years ago when our nation's vineyards and wineries were restricted to a few long-standing operations in West Auckland and Hawke's Bay. That all changed in the 1990s when a British wine critic tagged New Zealand sauvignon blanc as "arguably the best in the world." Since then, the growth in the wine industry has been unbelievable. We now have 10 major winegrowing regions spanning latitudes 36 to 45 and the entire length of the country. That makes for some diverse growing conditions and some very distinct wine styles. Turns out we can just about grow anything here, although it is our pinot noir and our sauvignon blancs that have made us famous internationally. There is also growing recognition of our chardonnay, *methode traditionelle* sparkling wines, our Rieslings, cabernet sauvignon, and our merlot—all of which has cemented New Zealand's reputation as a producer of world-class wines. I have highlighted major wineries in all the wine regions throughout the guide; you'd do well to get yourself a copy of the *Classic New Zealand Wine Trail* when you arrive here. It's available from all visitor centers and is well worth your while if you enjoy wine and food.

To say that **New Zealand is a nation of beer drinkers** is an understatement. We don't use the phrase "rugby, racing, and beer" here for nothing. There was a time when the New Zealand beer scene was dominated by just one or two major breweries—Lion and DB for example—but in the last 10 years there has been a proliferation of small boutique breweries springing up all over the country. I may be wrong, but it seems to me that this has almost been in response to the astonishing growth of our wine industry; or maybe it was a backlash to the domination of the industry by a few big players. Whatever the reason, New Zealand beer drinkers are happier than they've ever been. You can travel from one end of the country to the other and never drink the same beer twice. To name just a few brewers: there's Epic Beer in Auckland; Macs in Wellington; Founders Organic in Nelson; Dux de Lux in Christchurch and Queenstown; Monteith's in Greymouth; Twisted Hop in Christchurch; Speights and Emersons in Dunedin; and Wanaka Beerworks in Wanaka. You can now do an excellent beer tour in Wellington, with one of New Zealand's top beer critics, Neil Miller, and you can visit breweries in most major centers. I have included these in the applicable chapters.

Vodka is also a word on many people's lips—specifically 42-Below Vodka, that multi-award-winning sensation that tackled the world head-on with its stunning advertising campaign. Based in Auckland,

42-Below hit the shelves around 2002 and it's been winning international awards ever since—or as their cheeky advertising campaign says, they've "had more awards for best vodka than you've had hot dates."

In the **soft drink** line (sometimes called fizzy drinks here), we've also had a flurry of recent activity. Our ever-popular Lemon & Paeroa, "World Famous in New Zealand," is part of contemporary New Zealand lore. Ever since therapeutic spring water was discovered in the little Thames Valley town of Paeroa in the 19th century, it's been a huge hit—for over 100 years. Now we have many new players bringing us a whole range of tempting new soft drink flavors—from elderberry to feijoa and guava. Most have sidestepped mass marketing and have targeted boutique delicatessen stores. That's where you'll find more new brands than I can possibly name here—all of them well worth sampling.

Coffee is the other revolution! In the last 10 years we have turned into a nation of caffeine addicts. There are numerous coffee grinding companies in most cities—Christchurch alone has close to 20—and cafes serving excellent espresso are springing up on every corner. You'll also find mobile espresso carts in all sorts of unexpected places, from sports grounds and farmers' markets to street corners and beaches. There's even one on Stewart Island. A number of national cafes have moved into franchising. Yes, we have Starbucks here, but you'll find their cafes are usually filled with tourists. Most New Zealanders prefer a different brew (more like the coffee of Melbourne and Italy) and if they're going to frequent a franchise, they're usually loyal to a New Zealand–based franchise.

Of course you'll also find some "interesting" interpretations of espresso in the provinces—not all of them drinkable—but at least they're trying. It all comes down to good espresso training and product knowledge, and sadly not all cafes have learned how important it is to invest in these. But with increasing numbers of students pouring out of our hospitality schools, we can only hope more people will take a career in coffee seriously.

Organic and fair trade coffee is also readily available in all the larger cities and towns.

Planning Your Trip to New Zealand

With so much to see and do, it's easy to feel overwhelmed and unsure about where to start your New Zealand holiday. I'm here to help—in the pages that follow, you'll find all the nitty-gritty for organizing your big South Seas excursion.

Entry into New Zealand is relatively easy compared to many other countries. You don't need to get any painful shots, and we have no unusual legalities to confuse things. That said, we are very particular about bio-security. New Zealand's economy is heavily dependent on agriculture and horticulture, so we don't want alien pests arriving. To guard against that, there are strict regulations against bringing food into this country.

You can relax on the personal safety front, too. New Zealand is generally a safe place. However, wherever there are people there is the potential for misdeeds, so be sensible, be practical, always be vigilant with belongings, and avoid going into remote areas or city back streets alone. Every year our newspapers detail at least one theft from tourist vehicles. While many of these cases are the result of unfortunate luck, many times staying safe is a matter of common sense.

I would recommend much more vigilance if you plan to hike or climb in our bush and mountain areas. It never fails to astound me when, yet again, I read of missing, or worse, deceased tourists who have gone into the mountains with very little preparation or concern for weather conditions. The outcomes are invariably unhappy. Even in summer, you need top-quality thermal gear when entering mountain areas. Never underestimate the power and changeability of mountain conditions in New Zealand and always take more gear than you think you'll need.

Beyond that, enjoy!

For additional help in planning your trip and for more on-the-ground resources in New Zealand, please see "Fast Facts: New Zealand," on p. 512.

1 WHEN TO GO

New Zealand is in the Southern Hemisphere; therefore, all seasons are the opposite of those in North America, Europe, and other Northern Hemisphere locations.

There really isn't a bad time to travel to New Zealand. Keep in mind, though, that most Kiwi families take their main annual holidays between mid-December and the end of January, which puts enormous pressure on accommodations in major summer beach destinations. During the Easter break and school holidays in April, June to July, and September to October (see "Holidays," below, for exact dates), it also pays to reserve well in advance.

Remember, too, that accommodations at ski destinations like Ohakune, National Park, Methven near Mount Hutt, Wanaka, and Queenstown fill up quickly—reserve early and be prepared to pay higher winter rates. In most other areas, though, you'll be paying lower rates during the winter months (Apr–Aug). In some summer-peak

(Tips) Dialing the Weather

In New Zealand, call **Metservice** at © **0900/999** followed by your New Zealand area code to hear the current and expected weather conditions for the region you are in. Calls cost NZ$1.30 per minute including GST. You can also visit the Metservice website, www.metservice.co.nz, for further details, or check their blog, http://blog.metservice.com, for the latest updates. Check the website for details about receiving weather updates via SMS texting at a time to suit you. Daily updates cost NZ50¢; on-demand updates cost NZ99¢. For further information, call **Metservice** toll-free at © **0800/932-843.**

areas, the winter also means that tour, lodge, and adventure operators may take advantage of lower tourist numbers and take their own holiday breaks, closing their businesses for 1- to 3-month periods.

THE WEATHER

New Zealand's climate, especially by Northern Hemisphere standards, is pretty mellow for much of the year. You'll find a far greater seasonal difference in the South Island than in the subtropical North, and don't believe anyone who says it never gets cold here or that there are no extremes. In Central Otago, winter temperatures are often 14°F (−10°C) and sometimes as low as −4°F (−20°C), with summers up to 100°F to 104°F (38°C–40°C). By comparison, the northern part of the North Island is subtropical. That means *lots* of winter/spring rain, and often daily light showers.

The west coast of the South Island can get up to 100 inches or more of rain a year on its side of the Southern Alps, while just over the mountains to the east, rainfall is a moderate 20 to 30 inches annually. Rain is also heavier on the west coast of the North Island, averaging 40 to 70 inches annually. Milford Sound, though, beats the lot; it's the wettest place in the country, with a phenomenal 365 inches of rain a year.

THE SEASONS

SPRING (SEPT, OCT, NOV) This is a beautiful time to visit—the countryside is flush with new green grass, baby lambs,

and blooming trees. Christchurch in the spring means blossoms, bluebells, and daffodils in abundance; Dunedin is a splurge of rhododendron color. The weather can still be very changeable right up to mid-October, so come prepared with light rain gear. In the South Island, it's still perfectly normal to get late snowfalls in September.

SUMMER (DEC, JAN, FEB) This is peak tourist season, so you'll pay top dollar for accommodations and airfares. Book early to avoid disappointment—this also applies to the major walking tracks, such as Milford, for which you should make bookings 6 months ahead. Beaches all over the country come alive, and boaties flock to the water. Fresh fruit are falling off the trees. (You must try Central Otago cherries and apricots; the apple district is Hawke's Bay.) And everyone should see Central Otago when the lupines are flowering, with brilliant colors etched against blue skies and golden tussock.

AUTUMN (MAR, APR, MAY) Personally, I think the best time to visit is February through April. The temperatures are pleasant (still hot in Feb in most parts), and even in April you'll be wearing summer clothes in the upper North Island. The most spectacular autumn colors are found in Queenstown, Central Otago, and Christchurch. Keep Easter and April school holidays in mind, though, when accommodations may be tight in some areas.

Temperatures reflected are daily average (°C/°F). Rainfall reflects the daily average in millimeters/inches (mm/in.) and is accurate within 1 millimeter.

	Summer	Fall	Winter	Spring		Summer	Fall	Winter	Spring
Bay of Islands					**Westport**				
Max. Temp	25/77	21/70	16/61	19/66	Max. Temp	22/72	17/63	13/55	15/59
Min. Temp	14/57	11/52	7/45	9/48	Min. Temp	12/54	10/50	5/41	8/46
Rainfall	7/0.28	1/0.44	16/0.64	11/0.44	Rainfall	12/0.48	14/0.56	15/0.6	16/0.64
Auckland					**Christchurch**				
Max. Temp	24/75	20/68	15/59	18/65	Max. Temp	22/72	18/65	12/54	17/63
Min. Temp	12/54	13/55	9/48	11/52	Min. Temp	12/54	8/46	3/37	7/45
Rainfall	8/0.32	11/0.44	15/0.6	12/0.48	Rainfall	7/0.28	7/0.28	7/0.28	7/0.28
Rotorua					**Mount Cook**				
Max. Temp	24/75	18/65	13/55	17/63	Max. Temp	20/68	14/57	8/46	14/57
Min. Temp	12/54	9/48	4/39	7/45	Min. Temp	9/48	4/39	-1/30	4/39
Rainfall	9/0.36	9/0.36	13/0.52	11/0.44	Rainfall	12/0.48	13/0.52	13/0.52	14/0.56
Wellington					**Queenstown**				
Max. Temp	20/68	17/63	12/54	15/59	Max. Temp	22/72	16/61	10/50	16/61
Min. Temp	13/55	11/52	6/43	9/48	Min. Temp	10/50	6/43	1/34	5/41
Rainfall	7/0.28	10/0.4	13/0.52	11/0.44	Rainfall	8/0.32	8/0.32	7/0.28	9/0.36
Nelson					**Invercargill**				
Max. Temp	22/72	18/65	13/55	17/63	Max. Temp	18/65	15/59	11/52	15/59
Min. Temp	13/55	8/46	3/37	7/45	Min. Temp	9/48	6/43	1/34	5/41
Rainfall	6/0.24	8/0.32	10/0.4	10/0.4	Rainfall	13/0.52	14/0.56	12/0.48	13/0.52

PLANNING YOUR TRIP TO NEW ZEALAND

3

WHEN TO GO

WINTER (JUNE, JULY, AUG) If you're a skier, you'll be heading to Queenstown, Mount Hutt, Canterbury, or the Central Plateau in the North Island—and paying top dollar for the privilege. Otherwise, if you travel elsewhere during this period, you won't need to prebook much at all (except during the July school holidays). You'll find some excellent rates—just don't expect great things from the weather.

HOLIDAYS

National public holidays include New Year's Day (Jan 1), New Year's Holiday (Jan 2), Waitangi Day (Feb 6), Good Friday (varies), Easter and Easter Monday (varies), ANZAC Day (Apr 25), Queen's Birthday (first Mon in June), Labour Day (last Mon in Oct), Christmas Day (Dec 25), and Boxing Day (Dec 26).

Regional holidays include Wellington (Jan 22), Auckland (Jan 29), Northland (Jan 29), Nelson Region (Feb 1), Otago (Mar 23), Southland (Mar 23), Taranaki (Mar 31), Hawke's Bay (Nov 1), Marlborough (Nov 1), Westland (Dec 1), and Canterbury (Dec 16). Regional holidays are always observed on a Monday. If the date lands on a Friday or weekend, the holiday is observed on the following Monday. If it falls earlier in the week, it is observed on the preceding Monday.

School holidays consist of three midterm breaks—in April, June to July, and September to October—that last for 2 weeks each, plus 6 weeks for the December holidays. Kiwi families do much of their traveling during these periods, so be sure to reserve early.

NEW ZEALAND CALENDAR OF EVENTS

More information can be found in the regional chapters that follow and by going to the Tourism New Zealand website at **www.newzealand.com**. For an exhaustive list of even more events beyond those listed here, check http://events.frommers.com, where you'll find a searchable, up-to-the-minute roster of what's happening in cities all over the world.

JANUARY

ASB Bank Tennis Classic, Auckland. International women's tennis tour event preceding the Australian Open. Attracts leading overseas players. Call ✆ **09/373-3623,** or check www.auckland tennis.co.nz. First week of January.

Heineken Open, Auckland. International Men's ATP tennis tour event for leading international players. Call ✆ **09/373-3623,** or check www. heinekenopen.co.nz. Early January.

Auckland Anniversary Day Regatta, Auckland. "The City of Sails" hosts this colorful annual sailing event, which attracts both local and international competitors and spectators. Call ✆ **0800/734-2882,** or check www. regatta.org.nz. Last Monday in January.

World Buskers Festival, Christchurch. A week of zany street entertainment provided by leading international entertainers. Call ✆ **03/377-2365,** or check www.worldbuskersfestival.com. Mid- to late January.

Wellington Cup Race Meeting, Wellington. Leading horse-racing event (galloping), held in conjunction with the National Yearling Sales. Call ✆ **04/528-9611,** or check www.trentham. co.nz. Late January.

FEBRUARY

Hawke's Bay Wine and Food Festival, Hawke's Bay. A showcase of the region's world-class wines and good food. Call ✆ **0800/442-9463** in New Zealand, or check www.harvesthawkesbay.co.nz. First week of February.

Speights Coast to Coast, South Island. A major multisport endurance race from Kumara on the West Coast to Sumner, Christchurch, featuring a 33km (20-mile) mountain run followed by a 67km (42-mile) kayak race and a 142km (88-mile) cycle dash. Call ✆ **03/326-7493,** or check www.coast tocoast.co.nz. February 5 to February 6.

Waitangi Day Celebrations, Bay of Islands. New Zealand's national day celebrating the signing of the Treaty of Waitangi. Call ✆ **09/402-7308.** February 6.

Garden City Festival of Flowers, Christchurch. Garden visits, floating gardens, and floral carpets in the "Garden City" of the South Island. Call ✆ **03/365-5403,** or go to www.festival offlowers.co.nz. Mid-February for 10 days.

Brebner Art Deco Weekend, Napier. A fun celebration of the city's Art Deco heritage that includes dancing, jazz, vintage cars, walks, and tours. Most participants dress in 1920s and 1930s fashions. Call ✆ **06/835-0022,** or check www.artdeconapier.com. Third weekend in February.

Devonport Food and Wine Festival, Devonport. Held near the Ferry Wharf in Auckland's picturesque North Shore village of Devonport, this weekend event includes jazz, classical, and opera performances. Call ✆ **09/378-9030,** or log on to www.devonportwinefestival. co.nz. Late February.

Auckland Arts Festival. An extravaganza of national and international dance, music, theater, and visual arts talent every 2 years. The next festival will be staged in 2011. Call ✆ **09/309-0101,** or check www.aucklandfestival. co.nz. Late February to March.

MARCH

Pasifika Festival, Auckland. Auckland's Pacific Island communities celebrate the largest 1-day cultural festival in the South Pacific. Not to be missed. For details, fax **09/379-2020,** or check www.aucklandcity.govt.nz/pasifika. First week of March.

New Zealand International Festival of Arts, Wellington. The largest and most prestigious event on the New Zealand arts calendar features top overseas and national artists and entertainers. A vibrant mix of all art forms, from contemporary dance to fine music and theater. Call ✆ **04/473-0149,** or visit www.nzfestival.telecom.co.nz. Beginning of March.

Ellerslie International Flower Show Christchurch, Christchurch. New Zealand's premier garden event has shifted from Auckland to Christchurch. It showcases the best of garden design over 5 days in Hagley Park. Nurseries and garden retailers also participate. Call ✆ **03/379-4581,** or visit www. ellerslieflowershow.co.nz. March 10 to March 14, 2010.

Hokitika Wildfoods Festival, Hokitika. A culinary adventure for the brave and curious, this 1-day event presents the weird and wonderful of New Zealand's wild foods, including wild pig, possum pâté, goat, various bugs and insects, honey, fish, and venison. Call ✆ **03/756-9048,** or check www.wild foods.co.nz. Mid-March.

Arrowtown Autumn Festival, Arrowtown. A week of market days, music, and street entertainment celebrating the gold-mining era. Call ✆ **03/442-0809,**

or visit www.arrowtownautumnfestival. org.nz. The week after Easter.

APRIL

Warbirds Over Wanaka, Wanaka. Now classified as one of the best Warbirds air shows in the world, it combines classic vintage and veteran aircraft, machinery, fire engines, and tractors with dynamic Air Force displays and aerobatic teams in the natural amphitheater of the Upper Clutha Basin. Call ✆ **03/443-8619,** or visit www.warbirdsoverwanaka.com. Easter weekend (in even-numbered years only).

Fletcher Challenge Forest Marathon, Rotorua. A full marathon around Lake Rotorua for serious competitors. Attracts over 500 runners. Call ✆ **07/ 348-8448,** or check www.rotorua marathon.co.nz. Late April to early May.

MAY

Bay of Islands Country Music Festival, Bay of Islands. This festival draws musicians from all around New Zealand, and there's at least one international act each year. Call ✆ **09/404-1063,** or check www.country-rock. co.nz. Second weekend in May.

JUNE

National Agricultural Fieldays, Hamilton. One of the largest agricultural shows in the world, exhibiting the best of New Zealand agriculture, horticulture, floriculture, and forestry products. Call ✆ **07/843-4499,** or visit www. fieldays.co.nz. Mid-June.

Matariki, nationwide. Matariki is the Maori New Year, which coincides with the time when the Pleiades constellation is visible. It is traditionally a time for planting new crops. Since 2000 there has been renewed interest in Matariki, and a diverse range of cultural celebrations are now held throughout the country during late May and throughout June. You'll find more information at www.matarikifestival.co.nz and www.matariki.net.nz.

JULY

Queenstown Winter Festival, Queenstown. Every year in July, Queenstown officially goes mad with a host of zany mountain events and street entertainment. Call (C) **03/441-2453,** or check www.winterfestival.co.nz. Mid-July.

Christchurch Arts Festival. Biennially in July to August, this festival showcases the best of national and international dance, music, theater, and visual arts. For more information, visit www.artsfestival.co.nz. The next festival will be in 2011.

AUGUST

Bay of Islands Jazz and Blues Festival, Bay of Islands. More than 50 jazz bands from New Zealand and overseas provide live entertainment at various places around Paihia and Russell, night and day. Call (C) **09/404-1063** in New Zealand, or go to www.jazz-blues.co.nz. Early to mid-August.

SEPTEMBER

Montana World of Wearable Art Awards, Wellington. This creative extravaganza in Wellington should not be missed. Call (C) **03/547-0863,** or go to www.worldofwearableart.com. Mid-to late September.

Alexandra Blossom Festival, Alexandra. An annual parade of floats and entertainment celebrating the onset of spring. Call (C) **03/377-2823,** or check www.blossom.co.nz. Late September to early October.

Gay Ski Week. A week of celebrations on and around the slopes. See www.gayskiweeknz.com for more information. First week of September.

OCTOBER

Kaikoura Seafest, Kaikoura. An annual celebration of the best seafood and

Marlborough and Canterbury wines, plus fun and entertainment for the entire family. Call (C) **0800/473-2337** in New Zealand, or visit www.seafest.co.nz. Early October.

Dunedin Rhododendron Festival, Dunedin. Fun-filled days highlighted by garden tours and cultural events to celebrate the city's magnificent displays of rhododendron blooms. Call (C) **03/477-1092,** or check www.rhododunedin.co.nz. Mid- to late October.

Nelson Arts Festival, Nelson. Twelve days of music, dance, theater, and street performances throughout the city. The 15th Nelson Arts Festival will be held in 2010. Call (C) **03/546-0200,** or check www.nelsonartsfestival.co.nz.

Queenstown Jazz Festival, Queenstown. Over 200 musicians attend and play in bars and restaurants in a non-stop jam session with food and dancing. Call (C) **03/442-1211,** or visit www.queenstownjazz.co.nz. Late October.

NOVEMBER

Toast Martinborough, Martinborough. An annual wine-and-food festival. Call (C) **06/306-9183,** or go to www.toastmartinborough.co.nz. Mid-to late November.

Canterbury A&P Show, Christchurch. The South Island's largest agricultural and pastoral event, which includes thoroughbred and standard-bred racing and the New Zealand Cup. Call (C) **03/343-3033,** or go to www.theshow.co.nz. Second week of November.

Southern Traverse, South Island. An adventure race for teams of three to five serious competitors through New Zealand's toughest terrain. The endurance events cover high ridges, lakes, and river crossings throughout Otago. Call (C) **03/441-8215,** or check out www.southerntraverse.com. Late November.

Nelson Jazz Festival, Nelson. A wide variety of local and national jazz bands perform in a weekend event, culminating in a special New Year's Eve concert. Call ✆ **03/547-2559,** or visit www. nelsonjazz.co.nz. Late December to early January.

2 ENTRY REQUIREMENTS

PASSPORTS

A **passport** is required for all entering visitors, and it must be valid for at least 3 months beyond your departure date from New Zealand. If you lose yours, visit the nearest consulate of your native country as soon as possible for a replacement. See "Embassies & Consulates" and "Passports" in chapter 18.

Visas are not required for stays shorter than 3 months (as long as you don't plan to study, work, or undergo medical treatment) if you're a citizen of one of the following countries: Andorra, Argentina, Austria, Bahrain, Belgium, Brazil, Brunei, Canada, Chile, Cyprus, Czech Republic, Denmark, Estonia, Finland, France, Germany, Greece, Hong Kong (if you're traveling with a Special Administrative passport or if you hold a British national passport), Hungary, Iceland, Ireland, Israel, Italy, Japan, Korea (South), Kuwait, Latvia, Liechtenstein, Lithuania, Luxembourg, Malaysia, Malta, Mexico, Monaco, the Netherlands, Norway, Oman, Poland, Portugal (Portuguese passport holders must have the right to live permanently in Portugal), Qatar, San Marino, Saudi Arabia, Singapore, Slovak Republic, Slovenia, South Africa, Spain, Sweden, Switzerland, United Arab Emirates, United States, Uruguay, and Vatican City. British citizens are allowed a 6-month stay without a visa.

If you're planning to visit for longer than is stated above, or if your country of origin is not listed, contact the nearest New Zealand embassy, consulate, or High Commission for information on the appropriate visa and an application. If you'd like to work or live in New Zealand, you can inquire at an embassy or consulate, or write to the **New Zealand Immigration Service,** P.O. Box 27-149, Wellington, NZ (www.immigration.govt. nz).

You must also have the following items before entering New Zealand: a confirmed round-trip or outward-bound ticket; enough money for your designated stay (NZ$1,000 per person per month; credit cards are accepted); and the necessary documents to enter the country from which you came or the next country on your itinerary.

CUSTOMS

WHAT YOU CAN BRING INTO NEW ZEALAND Do *not* bring any fruit or plants into New Zealand. Because of the importance of agriculture and horticulture to the economy, animal products, fruit, plant material, and foodstuffs that may contain plant or animal pests and diseases will not be allowed into the country. Heavy fines may be imposed on people caught carrying these prohibited materials. If in doubt, place all questionable items, especially fruit, into the marked bins before approaching the immigration area upon arrival at a New Zealand airport.

Firearms and weapons, unless a permit is obtained from the New Zealand police upon arrival at the airport, are not allowed. *Note:* This includes firearms intended for sporting purposes. Other prohibited items include ivory, in any form; tortoise- or turtle-shell jewelry and ornaments; medicines that incorporate musk, rhinoceros, or tiger derivatives; carvings or anything made from whalebone or bone from any other marine animal; and cat skins or coats. Certain drugs (diuretics, tranquilizers, depressants, stimulants, cardiac drugs, and sleeping pills) may not be allowed unless they are covered by a doctor's prescription. Pirated copyright goods and objectionable (indecent) articles such as DVDs and publications are also prohibited. No live animals of any kind are allowed into New Zealand without going through the legal quarantine requirements.

Customs duties are not assessed on personal items you bring into the country and plan to take with you. New Zealand's duty-free allowances are 200 cigarettes or 250 grams (about 8 oz.) of tobacco or 50 cigars; 4.5 liters of wine or beer (equivalent to six 750ml bottles); three bottles of spirits or liquor (each containing no more than 1,125ml/about 2½ pints); and goods totaling NZ$700 that were purchased for your own use or for a gift. Make sure you have receipts available for inspection. If you plan to take in anything beyond those limits, contact the embassy or consulate office nearest you *before* you arrive or check **www.customs.govt.nz**.

WHAT YOU CAN BRING HOME
Returning **United States** citizens who have been away for 48 hours or more are allowed to bring back, once every 30 days, $800 worth of merchandise duty-free. You'll be charged a flat rate of 4% duty on the next $1,000 worth of purchases. Be sure to have your receipts handy. On mailed gifts, the duty-free limit is $200. You cannot bring fresh foodstuffs into the United States; tinned foods, however, are allowed. For more information, contact the **U.S. Customs Service,** 1300 Pennsylvania Ave., NW, Washington, DC 20229 (✆ **877/287-8867**), and request the free pamphlet *Know Before You Go.* It's also available online at www.customs.gov.

Canada allows its citizens a C$750 exemption, and you're allowed to bring back duty-free one carton of cigarettes, one can of tobacco, 40 imperial ounces of liquor, and 50 cigars. In addition, you're allowed to mail gifts to Canada valued at less than C$60 a day, provided they're unsolicited and don't contain alcohol or tobacco (write on the package "Unsolicited gift, under $60 value"). All valuables should be declared on the Y-38 form before departure from Canada, including serial numbers of valuables you already own, such as expensive foreign cameras. *Note:* The C$750 exemption can be used only once a year and only after an absence of 7 days. For a clear summary of Canadian rules, write for the booklet *I Declare,* issued by the **Canada Customs and Revenue Agency** (✆ **800/461-9999** in Canada, or 204/983-3500; www.ccra-adrc. gc.ca).

U.K. citizens returning from **a non-E.U. country** have a Customs allowance of 200 cigarettes; 50 cigars; 250 grams of smoking tobacco; 2 liters of still table wine; 1 liter of spirits or strong liquor (over 22% volume); 2 liters of fortified wine, sparkling wine, or other liquor; 60cc (ml) perfume; 250cc (ml) of toilet water; and £145 worth of all other goods, including gifts and souvenirs. People 16 and under cannot have the tobacco or alcohol allowance. For more information, contact HM Customs & Excise at ✆ **0845/010-9000** (from outside the U.K., 020/8929-0152), or consult their website at www. hmce.gov.uk.

The duty-free allowance in **Australia** is A$400 or, for those 17 and under, A$200. Citizens age 18 and older can bring in 250 cigarettes or 250 grams of loose tobacco, and 1,125 milliliters of alcohol. If you're returning with valuables you already own, such as foreign-made cameras, you should file form B263. A helpful brochure available from Australian consulates or Customs offices is *Know Before You Go.* For more information, call the **Australian Customs Service** at ℂ **1300/363-263,** or log on to www.customs.gov.au.

Medical Requirements

Unless you are arriving from an area known to be suffering from an epidemic, inoculations or vaccinations are not required to enter New Zealand. If you are currently taking any prescription medicines for recognized medical conditions, it is wise to bring the dosage you'll require with you. Keep all drugs in original bottles and bring a cover letter from your doctor to show airport security staff if required. If you require needles, they'll be fine in the aircraft hold but if you need them during your flight you will need to make special arrangements.

3 GETTING THERE & GETTING AROUND

GETTING TO NEW ZEALAND

The cost of getting to New Zealand is likely to be your single biggest cash outlay, so it makes sense to shop around. Remember to check out those recommended agents and hot travel offers listed for your country of origin on the Tourism New Zealand website, **www.newzealand.com**. Also go to Air New Zealand's website at **www.airnewzealand.com** for special deals.

By Plane

From the West Coast of the United States, you can fly to New Zealand nonstop overnight; a direct flight from Singapore takes 10 hours; and a flight from eastern Australia is around 3 hours. Auckland, Wellington, and Christchurch are all serviced by major domestic and international terminals. There are also much smaller international terminals at Hamilton and Dunedin; and most cities have domestic terminals. Auckland Airport is the major hub for most airlines coming in to New Zealand, followed by Christchurch and then Wellington. If you intend to spend most of your time in the South Island, it makes sense to fly into Christchurch, but depending on your airline, you may have to fly into Auckland and then transfer to domestic flights to Christchurch, Dunedin, or Queenstown.

There are at least 20 foreign airlines flying into Auckland. The main ones providing service from the **United States** are Air New Zealand, Qantas, and British Airways.

To and from **Canada,** you can choose from Air New Zealand and Air Pacific; to and from **Europe** and the United Kingdom, Air New Zealand, British Airways, and Qantas. From **Asia,** options include Singapore Airlines, Korean Air, Japan Airlines, Malaysian Airlines, Cathay Pacific, and Thai Airways. Dubai-based Emirates Airline now flies into New Zealand as well. There are also code-sharing arrangements with Lufthansa, American Airlines, United Airlines, and several others.

The timing of your trip can have a tremendous impact on your airline costs. New Zealand's **peak season** is December through February; the **shoulder season** includes March and September through November; and the **low season** begins in April and runs through August.

To find out which airlines travel to New Zealand, please see "Airline, Hotel & Car Rental Websites," p. 515.

By Cruise Ship

In the 2007–08 cruise season (Oct–Mar), 98 cruises ships brought over 116,000 people to New Zealand. While the current global economic downturn is already impacting on those numbers (down approx. 10% in 2009), New Zealand remains a popular cruise destination with over one-third of passengers coming from the United States.

Most cruises coming to New Zealand also visit Australia and are typically 12 to 16 days in duration. New Zealand cruise ports include Auckland, Tauranga, Napier, Wellington, Lyttelton (near Christchurch), Dunedin, and Milford Sound. You can fly to Australia or New Zealand to join a cruise, or you can take a segment on a world cruise that includes New Zealand.

There are at least a dozen international cruise lines that include New Zealand on their itineraries. Contact details for the main ones are Cunard Line, www.cunard. com; Silversea Cruises, www.silversea. com; Holland America, www.holland america.com; Crystal Cruises, www.crystal cruises.com; Regent, www.rssc.com; Princess Cruise Lines, www.princess.com; P&O Cruises, www.pocruises.com; Fred Olsen Line, www.fredolsencruises.com; and Oceania Cruises, www.oceaniacruises. com.

GETTING AROUND
By Plane

A year seldom passes without some slight upheaval in New Zealand's domestic air scene. **Air New Zealand** (© **0800/737-000** in NZ, or 09/357-3000; www. airnewzealand.co.nz), with Air New Zealand Link, now dominates the airways, with **Qantas New Zealand** (© **0800/808-767** in NZ, or 09/357-8900; www.qantas. com) servicing the main centers. British-owned **Virgin Blue's** trans-Tasman flights operate under the name **Pacific Blue** (© **0800/670-000;** www.flypacificblue. com), with domestic flights between Auckland, Brisbane, Hamilton, Wellington, Christchurch, and Dunedin. **Jet Star** (© **0800/800-995;** www.jetstar.com) is another new addition to the domestic airways. It offers service between Auckland, Wellington, Christchurch, and Queens-

town. Several other smaller airlines fly internal routes, and you'll come across other aircraft willing to fly chartered routes.

If your time is limited, Air New Zealand (© 800/262-1234 in the U.S, or www.airnewzealand.com) is a good source of special deals. They regularly offer vacation packages and deals of the month, but these must be purchased outside of New Zealand.

Once you're inside the country, **Air New Zealand Grab a Seat Deals** are a fantastic option, although you need to be spending quite some time in New Zealand, as they're usually for travel 2 or 3 months in advance. They are posted online daily, and because they're limited and such amazing prices, they're snapped up fast.

By Car

I think roads in New Zealand are pretty good, but I've heard many Americans say they're terrible and that New Zealanders are aggressive drivers. I do know that traffic on New Zealand roads, especially in the South Island, is minimal compared to that found in Northern Hemisphere cities. Unfortunately, I do have to agree with the bit about aggressive drivers. The biggest dangers are excessive speed and foolhardy overtaking, so be careful of both. The New Zealand police have taken a much stronger stance against speeding drivers in recent years, so expect many more speed cameras, more police on the roads, and much higher fines for speeding.

It is also important that visitors do not underestimate travel times. Distances may seem short in kilometer terms but roads are very often winding and sometimes narrow. Time and again I hear of international visitors driving from, say, Nelson to Queenstown in 1 day, or Auckland to Wellington in 1 day. It's certainly possible, but the idea is ludicrous. If you're that short on time, you'd be better off flying between destinations because you're not doing yourselves or the country any justice. Progress can be slower than you expect.

Multilane motorways surround most of the larger cities, but most roads are dual carriageways. There are some single-lane and unsealed roads in remote areas, and these should be approached cautiously— as should all roads during the winter months when rain and ice can create treacherous surfaces.

Statistics show that in 2003, 632 drivers in New Zealand with foreign licenses were involved in nonfatal accidents and 23 in fatal crashes. Police at the scene of 85 of the nonfatal and three of the fatal crashes believed that the fact the driver was foreign was a factor in the accident. So, the message is to keep your wits about you and don't underestimate the danger just because fewer cars are on the roads.

Car parking in Auckland, Wellington, and Christchurch can be expensive and hard to find. All cities have numerous car-parking buildings, though, and these are indicated in each chapter. Street parking is metered. You pay in coins, or by using a credit card or via your mobile phone. Instructions are marked clearly on each meter. If you exceed metered times, expect to be fined heavily in the major cities. Fines usually start at NZ$40 and go up from there the longer you overstay your limit.

New Zealand roads are not tolled, with one exception—the Northern Gateway Toll Road, a new stretch of the Northern Motorway, which bypasses the town of Orewa, north of Auckland. This is a more direct route between Auckland and Northland, but as it only cuts around 10 minutes off your journey and the automated payment of tolls has been causing headaches ever since it was instigated, I would strongly advise you simply turn off the motorway and continue on the old route through pretty, seaside Orewa. The exit for

this free route on the Hibiscus Coast Highway via Orewa is clearly marked on signs above the motorway.

For those who wish to continue on the toll road, you will pay NZ$2 for a car or light commercial vehicle and NZ$4 for a heavy vehicle (exceeding about 7,700 lb. or 3.5 metric tons). Motorcycles are free. There is no additional charge for towing a trailer or caravan. The fully Electronic Toll Collection (ETC) system means tolls are collected without the need for vehicles to slow, stop, or change lanes to pay a toll; and you can pay at your convenience, either by setting up an account, via a toll-free phone number, or at one of the self-service kiosks. As a visitor to New Zealand, though, you'll be an occasional user, so you can buy single, return, or multiple trip tickets via the website www.landtransport. govt.nz/tollroad, at a service kiosk located the road, or by calling the toll-free number © **0800/402-020** between 8am and 6pm. The road is electronically patrolled and failure to pay the toll will result in fines. Again, I strongly suggest turning off the motorway and proceeding through Orewa. The way is well marked with signs.

If you plan to drive, consider joining the **New Zealand Automobile Association (AA)** while you're here. In New Zealand, call © **0800/500-213** or visit www. aa.co.nz; they have offices around the country and can give you all the details about driving in New Zealand, plus maps, that you need. AA offers excellent breakdown services and advice to drivers. If you belong to a similar organization in your home country, membership is free, so don't forget to bring along your membership card.

DRIVING RULES & REQUIREMENTS

You must be at least 21 to 25 years old to rent a car in New Zealand, and you must have a driver's license that you've held for at least 1 year from the United States, Australia, Canada, or the United Kingdom (or an international driving permit).

(Tips) **Mapping a Path**

You'll receive a set of maps when you collect your rental car; if you're a member of the Automobile Association in the United States, Australia, Britain, or other European countries, you'll have reciprocal privileges with the New Zealand AA. One of the best maps of the country is issued by the **New Zealand Automobile Association,** 99 Albert St., Auckland (© 09/966-8800; www.aa.co.nz); 343 Lambton Quay, Wellington (© 04/931-9999); or 210 Hereford St., Christchurch (© 03/964-3650). AA sells other detailed maps as well, plus "strip maps" of your itinerary and comprehensive guidebooks of accommodations (some of which give discounts to AA members). Be sure to bring your membership card from home. **Wises Mapping,** 360 Dominion Rd., Mount Eden, Auckland (www.wises.co.nz), also produces an excellent map, available at newsstands and bookshops throughout New Zealand.

Recent law changes mean all drivers, including visitors, must carry their license or permit at all times.

Remember to drive on the left and wear seat belts at all times. The open-road speed limit is 100kmph (62 mph); in towns and built-up areas, 50kmph (31 mph). Rigid speeding laws are now in place and you face heavy fines if you exceed limits. New Zealand has also tightened up its drunk-driving laws, and if you are stopped in a random police check for compulsory breath testing for alcohol, you must take the test.

CAR RENTALS Every major city has numerous rental-car companies, and international companies like Avis, Budget, and Hertz hire a wide range of vehicles. Most offer good deals that can be prebooked before you leave home. However, it pays to shop around and compare not only the prices, but also the cars. Some companies offer cheap deals, but their cars may be well over 10 years old. Most companies also require that you take out accident insurance with an insurance company authorized by them, and you generally need to be 25 to be able to rent a car in New Zealand.

Maui Rentals (© 800/351-2323 in the U.S.; www.maui-rentals.com) has vehicles that are either brand-new or less than a year old. Daily rates range from NZ$150 to NZ$400, depending on the size of the car and the time of year. The price includes GST and unlimited mileage, but insurance runs about NZ$30 extra per day. Because Maui has offices in Auckland and Christchurch, there's no extra charge for one-way trips. They also rent a range of extras like a GPS, which goes for NZ$9 per day—a very good investment, I think. Contact the local offices at 36 Richard Pearce Dr., Mangere, Auckland (© **09/255-0620;** fax 09/255-0629), or 530–544 Memorial Ave., Christchurch (© **0800/651-080** in NZ, or 03/358-4159). Both provide courtesy airport shuttle service.

Auto Rentals NZ Wide, 179 Hereford St., Christchurch (© **0800/736-893** in NZ, or 800/905-8071 in U.S.; www.autorentals.co.nz) is an established chain offering a modern fleet of cars for budget-minded travelers. They offer sedans, station wagons, and minibuses at competitive rates. They are also an accredited TranzRail booking agency and can help with interisland ferry and train bookings, accommodations, and further vehicle rentals.

Affordable Rental Cars, 48 Carr Rd., Mount Roskill, Auckland (© **0800/454-443** in NZ, or 09/630-1567; fax 09/630-3692; www.car-rental.co.nz), has daily rates on unlimited-mileage vehicles from NZ$35 to NZ$95, depending on the vehicle and time of travel. Prices include GST and insurance.

If you want to spoil yourself, try **Classic Car Touring New Zealand,** 181 Hobson St., Auckland (© **021/702-623** in NZ; www.classiccartouring.co.nz), specializing in self-drive classic cars for NZ$350 to NZ$750 per day, depending on the vehicle; or **Smartcars Luxury Car Hire,** 110 Nelson St., Auckland (© **0800/458-987** in NZ, or 09/307-3553; www.smartcars.co.nz), offering the very latest convertibles and 4×4s from Europe.

You can also rent in advance from the following: **Avis** (© **800/230-4898** in the U.S.; www.avis.com), **Budget** (© **800/527-0700** in the U.S.; www.budget.com), **Hertz** (© **800/654-3131** in the U.S.; www.hertz.com), and **Thrifty** (© **800/847-4389** in the U.S.; www.thrifty.com). Daily costs average about NZ$100 to NZ$150.

ALTERNATIVES TO RENTING A CAR
If you'll be in New Zealand for an extended period of time, it may be worthwhile to investigate the guaranteed tourist buyback plan offered by **North Harbour Hyundai,** 175 Wairau Rd., Takapuna (© **09/444-7777;** fax 09/444-7099; www.hyundainz.

co.nz). This Auckland dealership sells used Toyotas, Nissans, Hondas, and similar cars to visitors with a written agreement to purchase them back after a stipulated time period. Cars come with a nationwide warranty; the owner pays for the insurance. For an example of what to expect, **Wheels,** 376 Lincoln Rd., Christchurch (© **03/366-4855;** www.newzealandrentalcar.co.nz), has sold buyback vehicles for NZ$5,000 and bought them back for approximately NZ$3,000 after 3 months of use. (*Note:* This is only an example of a possible scenario.)

If you're staying in hostels, you'll often find car-share schemes advertised on notice boards. If you want to arrange a carpool officially, check **www.carpoolnz.org.** It puts people who need a ride in touch with those willing to give them one. The system operates throughout the country, and the person getting the ride pays a small commission and something toward gas costs, which usually works out to be about half the cost of a bus ticket.

By RV or Motor Home
If you want ultimate freedom, consider renting what we call a campervan. Both **Maui Rentals** (© **800/351-2323** in the U.S., or 0800/651-080 in NZ) and **Newmans** (© **09/302-1582** in Auckland) offer minivans and motor homes. Maui rents two-berth, four-berth, and six-berth vehicles, and you'll find their rates and special deals on their website. **Britz New**

(Tips **Taking to the Highways**

Some kind and ever-so-thoughtful person—and I think it might be someone at **Jasons Publishing** (www.jasons.com)—had the good sense to create seven marvelous highway route planners. They include *The Twin Coast Discovery Highway,* covering Northland and Auckland, and *The Pacific Coast Highway,* covering Auckland, Coromandel, coastal Bay of Plenty, Eastland, and Hawke's Bay; and the Classic New Zealand Wine Trail. These free maps detail the best features of each trip, places to stay and eat, and adventures to sample along the way. They're available at visitor centers throughout the country.

Zealand (© 0800/831-900 in NZ; www. britz.com) also has a range of excellent vehicles at good rates.

If you fancy yourself in something superfunky, opt for New Zealand's most distinctive campervans, individually painted by top New Zealand artists. You can get these from **Escape Rentals** (© 0800/216-171; www.escaperentals. co.nz), which has depots in Auckland, Wellington, and Christchurch. They offer competitive rates and unlimited free kilometers, but don't for 1 minute think you'll escape attention. **Spaceships** (© 0800/ 772-237 in NZ; www.spaceships.tv), has great little cars that convert to mini campervans. They're much easier to drive and they have depots in Auckland, Wellington, and Christchurch.

By Motorcycle

If you enjoy the thrill of speed and the wind in your hair, you can rent motorcycles or purchase tour packages with or without guides. Just bring your full motorcycle license or international driving permit and call **New Zealand Motorcycle Rentals and Tours,** 25 Selwyn Rd., Onehunga, Auckland (© 09/634-9118; www. nzbike.com), which has a wide range of BMW, Honda, Harley-Davidson, and Yamaha bikes. They're official New Zealand Tourism Award winners, and all their gear is in top condition.

Adventure New Zealand Motorcycle Tours & Rentals, 29 Bolt Rd., Nelson (© 03/548-5787; www.gotournz.com), offers a range of deluxe tours with topclass bikes and upmarket accommodations for the 35-to-65 age bracket. **Towanda Women,** Christchurch (© 03/314-9097; www.towanda.org), specializes in guided New Zealand–wide motorcycle tours for women only.

By Bicycle

New Zealand's mild summer climate and varied landscape make it an ideal cycling destination. Many companies run tours or rent bicycles. Start with **Bicycle Rentals,** 130B Montreal St., Christchurch (© 0800/444-144 in NZ, or 03/982-2966; www.bicyclerentals.co.nz), which offers a range of cycles for rental, plus a buyback option that allows you to sell your bike for 50% of its cost at the end of your tour. **City Cycle Hire,** 73 Wrights Rd., Christchurch (© 03/377-5952; www.cyclehire-tours.co.nz), has a 5-day adventure on the Central Otago Rail Trail. **Adventure South,** P.O. Box 33–153, Christchurch (© 03/942-1222; www. advsouth.co.nz or www.remarkable adventuresnz.co.nz), has a wide range of guided cycle tours in the South Island.

By Taxi

Taxi stands are located at all airport and transport terminals and on major shopping streets of cities and towns. You cannot hail a taxi on the street within a quarter-mile of a stand. Taxis are on call 24 hours a day, although there's an additional charge if you call for one. Drivers don't expect a tip just to transport you, but if they handle a lot of luggage or perform other special services, it's perfectly acceptable to add a little extra. Be aware that many taxi drivers in Auckland, Wellington, and Christchurch are new immigrants and don't always have a comprehensive grasp of English. See regional chapters for specific taxi companies throughout New Zealand.

By Interisland Ferry

Crossing Cook Strait on one of the ferry services will give you a chance to see both islands from the water, as well as the serene Marlborough Sounds. There are two ferry companies operating on the Strait, which can be boarded in either Wellington or Picton.

The **Interislander** ferry system (© 0800/802-802 in NZ; www.inter islander.co.nz) operates every day yearround with three vessels—*Arahura, Kaitaki,* and *Aratere*—that offer a tourism experience in their own right, not just a practical means of getting across the water. You can choose from six daily departure times; the crossing takes 3 hours. The ferries have licensed bar and cafe areas, TV lounges, shops, and play areas, and the new *Kaitaki*, the biggest ferry in New Zealand, has two movie theaters and room for 1,600 passengers. These three ferries have three fare types: Easy Change, Saver Change, and Ultra Saver. **Easy Change** fares are the most flexible and can be canceled right up to check-in without cancellation fees. **Saver Change** fares are the midrange fares that incur a 50% fee if canceled. **Web Saver** fares are the cheapest way to travel, but once booked they're nonrefundable. They are available all year but numbers are limited, so book early. **Overseas bookings** can be made by international customers online, or by calling ℂ 64/4-498-3302, but from outside of New Zealand you can book only Easy Change fares. Web Saver and Saver Change fares can be booked only within New Zealand, and they sell out quickly during peak season.

If you're traveling by train or InterCity Coach, ask about the cost-effective through-fares, which are subject to availability.

Bicycles and sports gear can be taken on the ferry for a small additional cost, as well as campervans or motor homes—though these travel at a premium fare. *Note:* If you plan to transport a vehicle by ferry, you need a confirmed reservation.

Bluebridge Cook Strait Ferry (ℂ **0800/844-844** in NZ; www.blue bridge.co.nz) sails twice daily between Wellington and Picton. The vessel features lounges, cafe and bar facilities, outdoor decks, free big-screen movies, and a shop. Fare bookings are transferable until 24 hours before travel subject to availability, but they're nonrefundable.

Regardless of which ferry you select, keep in mind that Cook Strait is a notoriously changeable stretch of water, and

high swells can affect those prone to seasickness. Bad weather may also affect scheduled departures.

By Coach (Bus)

Coaches offer a cost-effective way of getting around New Zealand; as a bonus, you don't have to worry about driving on the left and studying maps. Most give excellent commentaries and stop frequently for refreshments en route, but smoking is not permitted. There are three major services in New Zealand (all owned by the same company). **InterCity** operates three-star coaches on New Zealand's most comprehensive coach network, visiting 600 towns and cities, with over 170 services daily; **Newmans** is a standard route option throughout the country, except on the South Island's West Coast, where it operates as a tourist service and a code-share with Great Sights; and **Great Sights,** New Zealand's premier daily sightseeing operator, provides the most extensive sightseeing network nationwide. *Reminder:* Book coach journeys in advance during peak travel periods (summer and holidays).

INTERCITY InterCity (ℂ **09/623-1503** in Auckland and 03/377-0951 in Christchurch; www.intercity.co.nz) offers discounts to students, seniors 60 and over, and YHA members and VIP (Backpackers) cardholders. Check out their **Flexi-Pass,** which allows travelers to buy blocks of travel time, up to 40% cheaper than standard fares on all InterCity and Newmans journeys. The Flexi-Pass gives you total freedom to explore the country with an hours-based pass that can be topped up like a prepaid phone card. Set your own itinerary and travel when and where you like. You can lock in discounts on every seat, every service, nationwide, every day; and the more hours you buy, the cheaper it becomes. The pass is valid for a year and can be used on the Interislander and on selected tours and dolphin-watching cruises in the Bay of Islands. As an example, 5 hours of travel will cost you NZ$57;

10 hours costs NZ$115 (both coach only); and 60 hours of travel costs NZ$605. For more information, check out www.flexi pass.co.nz.

InterCity and **Newmans** (© **09/623-1504;** www.newmanscoach.co.nz), coaches are also included in the **Travelpass New Zealand** deal, which brings together 17 "hop on and off" fixed itinerary passes based on the most popular touring routes throughout New Zealand. It allows you to travel with New Zealand's largest coach, train, air, and ferry network. There are a number of different Travelpass deals. For instance, the Aotearoa Adventurer gives you 14 days travel (minimum) throughout New Zealand for NZ$1,283; a Kiwi Explorer gives you 9 days travel (minimum) for NZ$623. Among the North Island Passes on offer, the Discovery package gives 4 days travel (minimum) for NZ$243 and includes visits to Auckland, Rotorua, Napier, Taupo, and Wellington. In the South, the **West Coast Pass** costs from NZ$135 to NZ$180 depending on departure point and is good for 3 months on the route from Nelson to Queenstown. For information, contact **Travelpass New Zealand** (© **0800/339-966** in NZ, or 09/638-5780; fax 09/638-5774; www. travelpass.co.nz).

Great Sights, 102 Hobson St., Auckland (© **0800/744-487** in NZ, or 09/583-5790; www.greatsights.co.nz), offers a wide range of day, overnight, and multiday tours throughout New Zealand, utilizing a modern fleet of luxury coaches with complimentary hotel pickups. Experienced drivers offer informative commentaries, and modern, low-emission luxury vehicles are equipped with air-conditioning, reclining seats, and onboard restrooms. They offer over 30 daily sightseeing trips across the country, including the Bay of Islands, Auckland Sights, Waitomo Caves, Rotorua, Mount Cook, Christchurch Sights, Milford Sound, and the West Coast Glaciers.

Alternative Buses & Shuttles

For the young and/or adventurous, **Kiwi Experience,** 195–197 Parnell Rd., Parnell, Auckland (© **09/366-9830;** www.kiwi experience.com), and the **Magic Travellers Network,** 120 Albert St., Auckland (© **09/358-5600;** www.magicbus.co.nz), provide something that's between a standard coach and a tour.

Popular with backpackers, they travel over a half-dozen preestablished routes, and passengers can get off whenever they like and pick up the next coach days or weeks later. The coaches make stops at scenic points along the way for bush walking, swimming, and sometimes even a barbecue. Prices vary according to the route, but typically are from around NZ$790 to cover both islands in 14 days. Passes are valid for 12 months with Magic Travelers and 12 months with Kiwi Experience.

Flying Kiwi Expeditions, 4B Forests Rd., Stoke, Nelson (© **03/547-0171;** www.flyingkiwi.com), is another fun-packed flexible alternative to the well-beaten tourist trail. They have 10 offers that combine travel and outdoor activities, priced according to the number of activities included. For other zany southern alternatives try **Bottom Bus,** P.O. Box 434, Dunedin (© **03/442-9708;** www. bottombus.co.nz), which offers fully guided bus tours exploring the very south of New Zealand.

Shuttle transport is another alternative. Numerous companies on both islands run minibus shuttles between cities. Some of them are listed in the regional chapters, and you can also get details from area information centers. **Atomic Shuttles** (© **03/322-8883;** www.atomictravel.co. nz) in Christchurch offers service between 30 South Island destinations.

By Train

Tranz Scenic (© **0800/872-467** in NZ; www.tranzscenic.co.nz) now operates three long-distance train routes through rugged landscapes—the Overlander, which runs Auckland to Wellington; the TranzCoastal, Christchurch to Picton; and the TranzAlpine, Christchurch to Greymouth. The trains are modern and comfortable, heated or air-conditioned, carpeted, and ventilated. Service has greatly improved under new management, and views of spectacular landscapes are assured. Tranz Scenic offers discounts for students, YHA members, Backpackers cardholders, and those 55 and over. It also has a limited number of Saver Fares and Super Saver Fares during off-peak times. Also inquire about the **Scenic Rail Pass** (© **0800/872-467** in NZ; www.tranz scenic.co.nz), which enables you to discover New Zealand by train at your own pace and includes one ferry crossing. A 7-day Tranz Scenic Rail Pass includes an Interislander ferry crossing and costs NZ$379; a 14-day pass costs $479 and also includes one ferry trip.

The train routes and their fares are as follows:

- **Auckland-Wellington:** The Overlander has reclining seats and a licensed buffet car that serves drinks and food. A Super Saver fare costs NZ$99; if you miss out on one of those, check online for other good specials. You get informative commentary as you pass through many scenic highlights. Hostesses and stewards supply newspapers, magazines, and drinks service.

- **Christchurch-Picton:** The TranzCoastal passes through dramatic landscapes for 5½ hours; the economy one-way fare is NZ$76 and you can choose to stop off in Kaikoura for a spot of whale-watching. There is also an excellent value standard through-fare available for NZ$125, which takes you from Wellington to Christchurch (or vice versa) and includes an Interislander fare.

- **Christchurch-Greymouth:** The TranzAlpine is the best of the lot. It goes through the unforgettable landscape of Arthur's Pass National Park, depositing you 4½ hours later in Greymouth. The standard return fare is NZ$199, but look out for specials online. Day excursions are also available on these routes.

4 MONEY & COSTS

CURRENCY

It's always advisable to bring money in a variety of forms on your New Zealand vacation: a mix of cash, credit cards, and traveler's checks. You should also exchange enough petty cash to cover airport incidentals, tipping, and transportation to your hotel before you leave home, or withdraw money upon arrival at an airport ATM.

Most travelers find New Zealand to be very reasonably priced in most things—ludicrously so in some cases, I'm sure. Certainly anyone converting from British pounds or American or Canadian dollars is going to get incredible value across-the-board.

The Value of the New Zealand Dollar vs. Other Popular Currencies

NZ$	US$	UK£	Aus$	Can$	Euro €
NZ$1.00	$0.68	£0.42	A$0.82	C$0.74	0.48 €

What Things Cost in New Zealand

A cup of coffee is usually NZ$3.50 to NZ$4 for a flat white (coffee with milk) or a latte.

Inner city bus fares vary from city to city and zone to zone, but are usually NZ$2 to NZ$4 for a short trip.

A moderate hotel room is between NZ$150 and NZ$250.

A three-course meal at a good restaurant will set you back around NZ$70 to NZ$80 per person, without wine.

A taxi from the airport varies greatly depending on the city you're in, from around NZ$90 in Auckland to NZ$50 in Christchurch.

A muffin or a small cake is usually around NZ$3.50.

A 2-liter bottle of milk is NZ$3.90.

The **New Zealand dollar** (NZ$) is based on the decimal system, and there are 100 cents in the dollar. There are coin denominations of 10, 20, and 50 cents and $1 and $2, as well as bank notes in $5, $10, $20, $50, and $100 amounts.

At this writing, US$1 equals approximately NZ$1.41 and 1 British pound was approximately equal to NZ$2.77, and these were the rates of exchange used to calculate the values given above.

International exchange rates fluctuate depending on economic and political factors. Thus, the rates given in the table above may not be the same when you travel to New Zealand. Before departing consult a currency exchange website such as **www.oanda.com/convert/classic** to check up-to-the-minute rates.

ATMS

ATMs are common throughout New Zealand. You'll find them inside and outside all banks, in major shopping centers, in supermarkets and gas stations. Some smaller towns in remote locations—on Stewart Island or Great Barrier Island for instance, or in some parts of the South Island's West Coast—don't have ATMs at all, but you'll find that noted in each appropriate chapter.

Most likely, your **ATM card** is compatible with New Zealand systems. The machines generally accept four-digit PINs, but it always pays to check with your bank beforehand. The Bank of New Zealand accepts ATM cards in the **Cirrus** system (© **800/424-7787**; www.mastercard.com); other banks accept cards in the **PLUS** system (© **800/843-7587**; www.visa.com).

CREDIT CARDS

Most New Zealand businesses take MasterCard and Visa. American Express, Diners Club, Bankcard, and Japan Credit Bank are also widely accepted in major tourist centers, but less so in smaller towns.

You can withdraw cash advances from your credit cards at banks or ATMs, but high fees make credit card cash advances a pricey way to get cash. Keep in mind that you'll pay interest from the moment of your withdrawal, even if you pay your monthly bills on time. Also, note that many banks now assess a 1% to 3% "foreign transaction fee" on **all** charges you incur abroad (whether you're using the local currency or your native currency).

STAYING HEALTHY
Before You Go

Vaccinations are not required to enter New Zealand. **Health insurance** is strongly advised because New Zealand's public and private medical/hospital facilities are not free to visitors, except as a result of accident. Make sure your health insurance covers you when you're out of the country; if it doesn't, get temporary medical coverage for the duration of your trip. Be sure to carry your identification card in your wallet.

Contact the **International Association for Medical Assistance to Travelers (IAMAT)** (© **716/754-4883** or, in Canada, 416/652-0137; www.iamat.org) for tips on travel and health concerns in the countries you're visiting, and for lists of local, English-speaking doctors. The United States **Centers for Disease Control and Prevention** (© **800/311-3435;** www.cdc.gov) provides up-to-date information on health hazards by region or country and offers tips on food safety. **Travel Health Online** (www.tripprep.com), sponsored by a consortium of travel medicine practitioners, may also offer helpful advice on traveling abroad. You can find listings of reliable medical clinics overseas at the **International Society of Travel Medicine** (www.istm.org).

As mentioned in "Medical Requirements" under "Entry Requirements," earlier in this chapter, it is advisable to bring any of your current prescription drug requirements with you. That way you can relax, knowing you have everything you need to stay well and enjoy your journey. It is not necessary to pack anti-diarrheal and/or anti-emetic products as these are available over-the-counter in New Zealand pharmacies—as are most generic prescription drugs for common problems like headaches, coughs, fevers, and influenza.

For more details, see below in "What to Do if You Get Sick Away From Home."

COMMON AILMENTS

Bugs, Bites & Other Wildlife Concerns You've heard that New Zealand is a relatively safe place? Believe it! We have no snakes, no alligators or crocodiles, no wild animals of note, no scorpions. The worst we can offer you is our poisonous **katipo spider,** but because you're about as likely to see one of those, much less be bitten, as you are encountering a bison in the main street of Auckland, I wouldn't start panicking just yet.

But knowledge is power, so here are the spidery details. The New Zealand katipo— *Latrodectus katipo* and *L.atritus* (yes, there are two species)—favors sparsely vegetated sand dunes and driftwood above the high-tide mark on sandy beaches. *L. katipo* is distinguished by the coloration of the adult female: black with a red stripe on the abdomen. The mature male is about one-sixth the size of the female and is predominantly white with a series of orange-red triangles and black lines on the abdomen. *L.atritus* is completely black.

Both species are poisonous, but they are rarely seen. And given that New Zealand is a nation of beach-lovers, it is comforting to know that there have only been two recorded fatalities, both in the 1800s—largely unconvincing evidence of toxic spiders. If, in the unlikely event that you are bitten by something black while on the beach, try to have the presence of mind to capture the offender and then take yourself off to the nearest hospital.

Heading inland, especially in the deep south around Fiordland, Te Anau, and up the South Island's West Coast, the biggest irritation will be **sand flies.** They may be tiny, but they have the power to drive you absolutely crazy. Take gallons of strong insect repellent, and keep dousing yourself in it. If you still get bitten, try not to scratch and ladle on plenty of antihistamine to prevent swelling. The good news is that not everybody suffers. I'm one of the lucky ones—sand flies don't seem to like my blood. You'll just have to hope you're as unattractive to them as I am.

ENVIRONMENTAL HAZARDS The ocean holds its fair share of dangers. Most popular New Zealand beaches are patrolled by lifeguards, and you should always swim between the flags. Ask if you're unsure, because many beaches have **dangerous currents and holes.** In more remote areas, beaches are not patrolled, and you should exercise common sense before entering the waves. This particularly applies to the hazardous west coast beaches of the whole country. You'll notice most New Zealanders swim on the much safer east coast beaches and seldom on any west coast beaches. I would strongly advise against swimming on any west coast beaches unless they have lifesaving patrols on duty. Never swim alone anywhere.

On the subject of beaches, it's important to point out the danger of **sharks.** *Always* check with the locals as to the possibility of sharks in the ocean. As we all know, the threat of being attacked can never be underestimated.

As with beaches, **mountain and bush safety** *should* be a matter of common sense, but you would be amazed at how many people think they know better than the locals, setting off on a bush walk with no warm clothing (just because the sun is shining at the beginning is no guarantee that it will be farther on), no extra water, and no precautionary measures taken whatsoever. Hypothermia, exposure, and excessive sunburn are very real dangers in New Zealand, and you take your life in your hands if you ignore warnings. Every year we read the news reports of some international visitors who have ignored the warning and ventured into the mountains

ill-prepared, and have never returned. Some have never been found.

Pay very particular note of rain warnings if you're going into the mountains. Most New Zealand rivers rise very quickly, especially in the South Island, and many people have drowned trying to cross swiftly flowing, flooded rivers.

DIETARY DISTRESS The only thing to look out for in the bush is the possibility of *Giardia,* a waterborne parasite that causes diarrhea. Always boil water when you're hiking. Closer to civilization, do take particular care in summer that all food is kept cool, especially chicken, eggs, and meat products. I'm sad to report that studies have shown that New Zealand has the highest incidence of *Campylobacter* in the developed world. Over 75,000 New Zealanders get stomach upsets as a result of these bacteria every year, so take care. Like *Salmonella* (also relatively common here), it is usually associated with poor hygiene and contaminated food products. Always eat fresh food, make sure all chicken is thoroughly cooked, and always wash your hands before eating. Food poisoning is usually indicated by symptoms like diarrhea, abdominal cramps, fever, nausea, vomiting, headaches, and muscle aches. Most people recover without treatment in a few days, but if symptoms persist, you should see a doctor.

WHAT TO DO IF YOU GET SICK AWAY FROM HOME

For travel abroad, you may have to pay all medical costs upfront and be reimbursed later. Medicare and Medicaid do not provide coverage for medical costs outside the U.S. Before leaving home, find out what medical services your health insurance covers. To protect yourself, consider buying medical travel insurance (see "Before You Go," under "Staying Healthy," above).

Very few health insurance plans pay for medical evacuation back to the U.S. (which can cost $10,000 and up). A number of companies offer medical evacuation services anywhere in the world. If you're ever hospitalized more than 150 miles from home, **MedjetAssist** (𝒞 **800/527-7478;** www.medjetassistance.com) will pick you up and fly you to the hospital of your choice virtually anywhere in the world in a medically equipped and staffed aircraft 24 hours day, 7 days a week. Annual memberships are $225 individual, $350 family; you can also purchase short-term memberships.

U.K. nationals will need a **European Health Insurance Card (EHIC)** to receive free or reduced-costs health benefits during a visit to a European Economic Area (EEA) country (European Union countries plus Iceland, Liechtenstein, and Norway) or Switzerland. The European Health Insurance Card replaces the E111 form, which is no longer valid. For advice, ask at your local post office or see www.dh.gov.uk/travellers.

Almost all New Zealand cities and many smaller towns have a general hospi-

tal or emergency medical facilities, and the standard of medical care in New Zealand is excellent. Obviously, the bigger the city, the better the facilities, with Auckland, Hamilton, Wellington, Christchurch, and Dunedin having the most, the biggest, and the best hospital facilities. As a visitor to New Zealand you will pay for any hospital or medical care, unless you are admitted via an accident situation. Most cities also have a 24-hour doctor and pharmacy facility for filling urgent prescriptions. I list **emergency numbers** under "Fast Facts" in each chapter and in chapter 18.

If you suffer from a chronic illness, consult your doctor before your departure. Pack **prescription medications** in your carry-on luggage, and carry them in their original containers, with pharmacy labels—otherwise they won't make it through airport security. Carry the generic name of prescription medicines, in case a local pharmacist is unfamiliar with the brand name.

6 SAFETY

New Zealand is generally a very safe destination, one of the safest in the world. Still, exercise the same care that you would in any major city. People-oriented dangers—theft, assault, murder—should be mentioned, but it's important to remember that violent crimes in most countries, especially in New Zealand, occur between acquaintances. As a traveler, it's unlikely you'll be a victim. If you're hitchhiking, however, that may be another matter; women should never hitchhike alone or at night.

On the subject of theft, it should be noted that many travelers are lulled into a false sense of security, leaving cars unlocked and valuables clearly visible. Always park your car in a well-populated area whenever possible; lock it and cover your luggage

with a blanket or a coat. *Never* leave handbags or cameras in cars. The simple rule should be, if you can't do without it, don't leave it in the car, locked or otherwise.

The downtown areas of New Zealand's major cities, especially Auckland, Wellington, and Christchurch, are now well covered by closed-circuit cameras, which are monitored by police. This has significantly helped to reduce crime. It is still advisable to exercise caution, especially on Thursday, Friday, and Saturday nights, when social drinking sometimes gets out of hand.

There is a significant youth drinking problem in New Zealand, and this tends to manifest itself in areas with a large concentration of bars—Wellington's Courtenay Place and Christchurch's Oxford Strip are two good examples. That doesn't necessarily make these areas dangerous—far from it—but it is a good idea to be more vigilant and to stay away from any fights that might break out. Leave it to the security guards and doormen to sort out.

When it comes to traveling in the countryside, you should always be as cautious as you would be anywhere else. New Zealanders are generally friendly and welcoming, but if you're going to encounter any gender or racial bigotry, it is more likely to be in smaller rural communities. The risk is small, though. New Zealand is a bicultural country with increasing numbers of immigrants residing here. We are more often than not a very tolerant bunch.

7 SPECIALIZED TRAVEL RESOURCES

In addition to the destination-specific resources listed below, visit Frommers.com for additional specialized travel resources.

GAY & LESBIAN TRAVELERS

Gay and lesbian travelers will feel at ease in New Zealand, especially in Auckland and Wellington. For information, go to the **New Zealand Gay and Lesbian Tourism Association** website at www.iglta.org, or write to them at P.O. Box 24-558, Wellington 6015, NZ (© **04/917-9184;** fax 04/917-9176). Other New Zealand gay and lesbian websites include www.gaynz.com, **Pink Pages New Zealand** (www.pinkpagesnewzealand.com), **Queer Resources Aotearoa** (www.qrd.org. nz), and **Gay Queenstown** (www.gayqueenstown.com).

The **International Gay and Lesbian Travel Association (IGLTA)** (© **800/448-8550** or 954/776-2626; www.iglta. org) is the trade association for the gay and lesbian travel industry, and offers an online directory of gay- and lesbian-friendly travel businesses and tour operators.

TRAVELERS WITH DISABILITIES

New Zealand is a relatively good destination for visitors with disabilities. Since 1975, every public building and major renovated structure in the country has been required by law to provide reasonable and adequate access for those with disabilities. In addition, accommodations with five or more units are required to provide at least one room for guests with disabilities. For general information, contact the **New Zealand Disability Resource Centre,** 14 Erson Ave., Royal Oak, Auckland (© **09/625-8069;** www.disability resource.org.nz).

If you're traveling by air in New Zealand, you'll be relieved to hear our airline staff is very considerate. You will always be taken onto the aircraft ahead of other passengers and you'll be last off.

If you have a disabled parking pass, bring it with you. You can contact the New Zealand Disability Resource Centre (above) well ahead of your travel time to organize a New Zealand pass, but bringing your own is a good backstop. Every town center and shopping mall has designated disabled parking spaces, so you're unlikely to encounter parking problems, even in peak tourist season.

FAMILY TRAVELERS

New Zealand offers some of the most exciting vacation opportunities for families with kids. Hiking, swimming, sailing, and whale-watching are only a few of the activities children of all ages can enjoy. A day at the beach may well end up being one of their best memories, and you won't have to pay a cent for the pleasure. All cities and towns also have free parks, walkways, and children's playgrounds; and if you're here in summer, swimming pool complexes in most towns make for a fun, inexpensive day out for all the family.

Make sure you ask at all visitor centers for advice on the best kids' attractions, although I have marked most in each chapter. Also ask about specific summer holiday festivals and kids' activities. Many of these are short-term, one-off events that could be the very thing to ease the family stresses that come with traveling with children.

Older, more adventurous kids will no doubt love caving, rafting, kayaking, and bungy jumping. Most sightseeing attractions admit children at half-price, and family prices are usually available.

Although many of the better B&Bs and upmarket lodges do not accommodate children, motels and farmstays are ideal for families. Both are usually cheaper, motel rooms are regularly equipped with cooking facilities, and children will enjoy roaming the fields and helping out on a working farm.

To locate accommodations, restaurants, and attractions that are particularly kid friendly, refer to the "Kids" icon throughout this guide.

SENIOR TRAVELERS

Discounts for those 60 and over are increasingly available in New Zealand, so be sure to inquire when making reservations for accommodations and attractions. Don't forget to carry photo identification. Those 60 and over are entitled to a 20% discount on InterCity coaches and Tranz Scenic trains. Newmans Coaches offers a 20% discount to anyone 60 and over.

STUDENT TRAVELERS

The **International Student Travel Confederation (ISTC)** (www.istc.org) was formed in 1949 to make travel around the world more affordable for students. Check out its website for comprehensive travel services information and details on how to get an **International Student Identity Card (ISIC),** which qualifies students for substantial savings on rail passes, plane tickets, entrance fees, and more. It also provides students with basic health and life insurance and a 24-hour help line. The card is valid for a maximum of 18 months. You can apply for the card online or in person at **STA Travel** (© **800/781-4040** in North America; www.statravel.com), the biggest student travel agency in the world; check out the website to locate STA Travel offices worldwide. The New Zealand headquarters is at 10 High St., Auckland (© **09/309-0458**). The ISIC card is also accepted by many New Zealand tourism operators including hotels, bars, transport providers, theaters, major attractions, and tour companies. The ISIC website provides a list of New Zealand operators offering discounts.

If you're no longer a student but are still 25 and under, you can get an **International Youth Travel Card (IYTC)** from the same people, which entitles you to some discounts. **Travel CUTS** (© **800/592-2887;** www.travelcuts.com) offers similar services for both Canadians and U.S. residents. Irish students may prefer to turn to **USIT** (© **01/602-1904;** www.usit.ie), an Ireland-based specialist in student, youth, and independent travel.

SINGLE TRAVELERS

New Zealand is a perfectly safe place for traveling solo, although I assume that everyone will act with common sense in terms of personal safety and late-night wanderings. (And of course, you won't want to take off on a long trek into the mountains on your own.)

You'll find that people here are friendly and often go out of their way to make solo travelers feel welcome. It's likely that you'll go home with a book filled with the addresses of new friends. Some accommodations charge significantly less for one person than for two. All rates listed in this book are for doubles, so be sure to ask about single rates if you intend to travel alone.

On package vacations, single travelers are often hit with a "single supplement" to the base price. To avoid it, you can agree to room with other single travelers or find a compatible roommate before you go, from one of the many roommate-locator agencies.

Many reputable tour companies offer singles-only trips. **Singles Travel International** (© 877/765-6874; www.singles travelintl.com) offers singles-only escorted tours to New Zealand.

New Zealand operators like **Kiwi Experience** (www.kiwiexperience.com) and the **Magic Travellers** network (www.magic bus.co.nz) have changed the face of singles travel in New Zealand. Their hop-on-and-hop-off bus tours of New Zealand are

geared specifically toward backpacker culture, loads of fun, spontaneity, and great deals. Mostly filled with travelers in their 20s and 30s, they're a terrific way to meet people and make new friends as you travel—and isn't that half the fun of travel?

There are also a good number of operators catering to single and independent travelers with small group and singles tours. **Let's Trek Australia** (www.lets trekaustralia.com) is a partnership of small group and singles adventure specialists working together throughout Australia and New Zealand. **Relaxing Journeys** (www.relaxingjourneys.co.nz) specializes in small, escorted tours for independent travelers. They can help you into self-drive tours, day tours, cruises, or coach trips. You'll also find a lot of useful tips and information at www.independenttraveler. com and www.solotravel.org.

8 SUSTAINABLE TOURISM

New Zealand has a long-established, international reputation for being "clean and green," and Tourism New Zealand's 100% Pure New Zealand brand campaign has reinforced that. It goes without saying that tourism in this country is largely shaped by the uniqueness of our environment and culture, and as the major contributor to the nation's economy, it is vital that all New Zealanders have a genuine desire to ensure its future.

No surprise, then, that ecotourism is now the fastest growing sector of New Zealand's tourism industry. Everyone is jumping on the sustainable tourism bandwagon, and while most are driven by genuine altruistic motives, the cynic in me suspects many are becoming "green-rated" as a marketing ploy, without backing up their claims of being ecofriendly with anything beyond tokenism.

In light of the worldwide focus on sustainability issues, it is apt that New Zealand takes a second look at itself. Despite all those "clean and green" claims, the country has

long been a poor performer in industrial and agricultural waste management and recycling. That is changing fast. Farmers are developing cutting-edge technology to improve dairy farm effluent management; industries are being forced to comply with new waste management regulations aimed to help clean up our waterways; and businesses across-the-board are taking a lively approach to pest and weed control, reforestation, and the restoration of prime ecological environments. Tourism operators and organizations are also working much more closely with central and local governments to address concerns about waste disposal associated with campers and motor homes, and tourists' accessibility to local recycling programs. In short, there has been a groundswell of interest in sustainability measures, and there is now an expectation that business operators will put their best foot forward—especially in the tourism arena.

Leading the charge is Tourism New Zealand, with its unique approach to sustainability based on the traditional Maori principles of *manaakitanga* (hospitality) and *kaitiakitanga* (guardianship)—welcoming visitors while protecting and managing our culture and environment. Its Tourism Strategy 2015 is based on a whole of New Zealand approach that will see increasing numbers of sustainability initiatives put into action over the coming 5 years. This includes initiatives like the New Zealand Emissions Trading Scheme, which aims to encourage all sectors of the economy, including tourism, to find smart, efficient ways to cut back their emissions. A transport strategy will focus on creating a sustainable transport network throughout the country.

Already in place is the Qualmark Responsible Tourism Operations program, a partnership between Tourism New Zealand and the New Zealand Automobile Association. While the system does have its detractors (with negativity focused on the nature of its rating system), it has gone some way toward tidying up New Zealand's accommodations sector. In terms of sustainability and ecotourism, it must be said that some rating system is better than no rating system. You'll now find many tourism providers boasting about having a Qualmark Enviro Bronze, Silver, or Gold rating—so many, in fact, that it's hard not to suspect some of the motives behind this huge rush to sign on. Businesses performing at the top level of this rating system, though, will be energy efficient and will have active waste management and water conservation practices, and will be taking part in conservation initiatives and community activities. It is largely thanks to this integrated quality and environmental tourism performance assurance system—the first of its kind in the world—that New Zealand was voted Overall Winner and Best Destination in the Virgin Holidays Responsible Tourism Awards in London in 2008. The judges recognized Qualmark Green as one of New Zealand's most important achievements in responsible tourism.

New Zealand's Environmentally Sustainable Tourism Project is another worthy of attention. Jointly run by the Ministry for the Environment and the Ministry of Tourism, it established six regional sustainable tourism charters committed to the sustainable practices as laid down in Tourism New Zealand's sustainable strategy. Enterprise Northland, Destination Rotorua, Tourism Bay of Plenty, Latitude Nelson, Lake Wanaka Tourism, and Venture Southland/Destination Fiordland all work toward improving the environmental performance of participating tourism operators. You can find all members signed up to these charters by asking at the appropriate regional visitor centers.

Increasing numbers of New Zealand businesses are also becoming Green Globe Benchmarked or Green Globe Certified. Green Globe is based on Agenda 21, a comprehensive plan of action regarding sustainable development endorsed at the United Nations Earth Summit in 1992. There are currently Green Globe participants in more than 50 countries around the world. A tourism operation can only use a Green Globe logo once it has been measured to be above the benchmarking base-line performance level. The Green Globe website (www.greenglobeint.com) lists New Zealand operations affiliated to the program.

Recycling generally has taken on a new impetus in New Zealand in the last 2 years. Every major city's rubbish collection program now has separate bins for paper and recyclable goods, organic waste and nonrecyclable matter; and national parks and public areas are well equipped with rubbish bins. Recycling within hotels (for guests) is much less common. Many hotels have instituted sustainable practices but that doesn't usually extend to providing recycling bins within guest rooms. I suspect that will change as pressure on the environment continues. I've provided a separate box listing a number of

Sustainable Properties in New Zealand

Following is a selection of properties that have either attained Green Globe benchmarking, a Qualmark Enviro rating, or both. Throughout the book I have also noted the properties and tourism operators who have a commitment to sustainable practices.

Auckland
Langham Hotel Auckland (p. 126)
SKYCITY Grand Hotel (p. 126)
Braemar on Parliament Street (p. 128)
The Great Ponsonby Arthotel (p. 130)
Bethells Beach Cottages (p. 133)

Northland & Coromandel
The Summer House (p. 185)
Carrington Resort (p. 185)
Base Pipi Patch (p. 182)
Colleith Lodge (p. 198)
Villa Toscana (p. 198)

Waikato & Bay of Plenty
Novotel Tainui (p. 207)
Kamahi Cottage (p. 208)
Ridge Country Retreat (p. 213)

Rotorua & Tongariro National Park
Treetops Lodge & Estate (p. 230)
Peppers on the Point (p. 229)
Maruata Rotorua (p. 231)
Bayview Chateau Tongariro (p. 249)

Gisborne & Hawke's Bay
Knapdale Eco Lodge (p. 258)
The County Hotel (p. 269)

Wanagnui
The Flying Fox (p. 284)

Wellington
Ohtel (p. 300)
InterContinental Wellington (p. 297)
Bolton Hotel (p. 297)
James Cook Hotel Grand Chancellor (p. 298)
Mount Victoria Homestay (p. 300)

Nelson
Shelbourne Villa (p. 346)
39 Russell (p. 345)
Awaroa Lodge (p. 353)
Abel Tasman Marahau Lodge (p. 353)
Abel Tasman Ocean View Chalets (p. 352)

Christchurch & Canterbury
Crowne Plaza Christchurch (p. 363)
The George Christchurch (p. 365)
Hotel SO (p. 364)
Hadleigh (p. 367)
Wilderness Lodge (p. 398)

West Coast
Rough and Tumble Bush Lodge (p. 407)
Chelsea Gateway Motor Lodge (p. 407)
Breakers Boutique Accommodation (p. 411)
Te Waonui Forest Retreat (p. 424)
Wilderness Lodge Lake Moeraki (p. 426)

Wanaka
Whare Kea Lodge (p. 434)
Wanaka Springs (p. 437)
Maple Lodge (p. 436)
Edgewater Resort (p. 435)
Lime Tree Lodge (p. 434)

Mount Cook
Hermitage Hotel (p. 440)

Queenstown
The Heritage (p. 459)
Queenstown Top 10 Holiday Park Creeksyde (p. 460)
Remarkables Lodge (p. 460)
The Rees Hotel & Luxury Apartments (p. 459)

Fiordland & Southland
Fiordland Lodge (p. 473)
The Lodge at Tikana (p. 503)

Stewart Island
Stewart Island Lodge (p. 511)

Dunedin
Nisbet Cottage (p. 493)

General Resources for Green Travel

In addition to the resources for New Zealand listed above, the following websites provide valuable wide-ranging information on sustainable travel. For a list of even more sustainable resources, as well as tips and explanations on how to travel greener, visit www.frommers.com/planning.

- **Responsible Travel** (www.responsibletravel.com) is a great resource of sustainable travel ideas; the site is run by the spokesperson for ethical tourism in the travel industry. **Sustainable Travel International** (www.sustainabletravelinternational.org) promotes ethical tourism practices, and manages an extensive directory of sustainable properties and tour operators around the world.

- **Carbonfund** (www.carbonfund.org), TerraPass (www.terrapass.org), and Carbon Neutral (www.carbonneutral.org), provide info on "carbon offsetting," or offsetting the greenhouse gas emitted during flights.

- **Greenhotels** (www.greenhotels.com) recommends green-rated member hotels around the world that fulfill the company's stringent environmental requirements. **Environmentally Friendly Hotels** (www.environmentallyfriendlyhotels.com) offers more green accommodations ratings.

- For information on animal-friendly issues throughout the world, visit **Tread Lightly** (www.treadlightly.org). For information about the ethics of swimming with dolphins, visit the **Whale and Dolphin Conservation Society** (www.wdcs.org).

- Volunteer International (www.volunteerinternational.org) has a list of questions to help you determine the intentions and the nature of a volunteer program. For general information on volunteer travel, visit **www.volunteerabroad.org** and **www.idealist.org**. I have also listed volunteer travel programs in "The Active Vacation Planner," chapter 5, on p. 109.

accommodations and tourism providers that I think are approaching the matter of sustainability with commitment and integrity.

While sustainable tourism operations and community initiatives are increasingly common in New Zealand, there are very few restaurants totally committed to organic menus. That said, increasing numbers of chefs are sourcing some organic meats and ingredients to include in their menus. Organic produce is much more widely available in New Zealand now, but it is still more highly priced—sometimes ridiculously so. Even the huge groundswell of farmers' markets throughout the country has done little to lower the price of

genuine organic produce. So if you order organic, expect to pay more.

One of the most exciting aspects of sustainability in New Zealand has been the huge growth in volunteer projects with a sustainability focus. I have detailed several of those in "Volunteering & Working in New Zealand" in chapter 5, "The Active Vacation Planner," on p. 109. In short, there are numerous opportunities to sign on for replanting programs, track and walkway building projects, native bird breeding programs, pest trapping in national parks, working on organic farms, and more. This is an excellent way to give your holiday a meaningful edge that will be rewarding for both yourself and New Zealand's unique environment.

You can help even more by flying here with our national airline, **Air New Zealand**. Not only did they carry out the world's first commercial aviation test flight using a sustainable second-generation biofuel derived from the plant *Jatropha curcas,* they also have an active carbon offset program, which allows customers to make a donation to the Air New Zealand Environment Trust. The Trust's first project is the native reforestation of more than 40 hectares (100 acres) on Mangarara Station in the Hawke's Bay. More than 85,000 trees will be planted there over the next 3 years to create a public conservation reserve.

9 SPECIAL INTEREST TRIPS & ESCORTED TOURS

Package tours are simply a way to buy the airfare, accommodations, and other elements of your trip (such as car rentals, airport transfers, and sometimes even activities) at the same time and often at discounted prices. One good source of package deals to New Zealand is the airlines themselves. Most major airlines offer air/land packages, including **American Airlines Vacations** (© 800/321-2121; www.aavacations.com), **Delta Vacations** (© 800/654-6559; www.deltavacations.com), **Continental Airlines Vacations** (© 800/301-3800; www.covacations.com), and **United Vacations** (© 888/854-3899; www.unitedvacations.com). Several big **online travel agencies**—Expedia, Travelocity, Orbitz, Site59, and Lastminute.com—also do a brisk business in packages. **Qantas Vacations USA** (© 800/641-8772 in the U.S., or 310/322-6359; fax 310/535-1057) and **Qantas Vacations Canada** (© 800/268-7525 in Canada; fax 416/234-8569) offer good deals as well.

In the United States, **Artisans of Leisure,** 18 E. 16th St., Ste. 301, New York, NY 10003 (© **800/214-8144** in the U.S.; www.artisansofleisure.com), offers exclusive, highly personalized luxury tours for individuals, groups of friends, or families, and New Zealand is one of their most popular destinations. Their tours run 7 to 19 days and combine top rooms in premium lodges with activities that range from tasting wine and food to arts and cultural events and outdoor activities. You choose, they organize. **Active Downunder,** 1220 Rosecrans St., #911, San Diego, CA 92106 (© **800/425-9036** in the U.S.; www.activedownunder.com), is owned and operated by New Zealanders; their specialty is highly customized active, leisure, and luxury vacations in New Zealand. They are experts with insider knowledge, and their personalized itineraries include boutique and luxury accommodations, along with cultural and adventure activities. **Nature Expeditions International,** 7860 Peters Rd., Ste. F-103, Plantation, FL, 33324 (© **800/869-0639** in the U.S.; www.naturexp.com), offers 1 to 15 day guided, cultural, wildlife, and "soft" adventure tours to New Zealand. They cater specifically to small "pre-formed" groups.

In New Zealand, there are many companies offering escorted tour options. Some of the reputable tour companies include:

- **Contiki Holidays,** P.O. Box 68640, Newton, Auckland (© **0800/266-8454** in NZ; www.contiki.com), offering 3- to 15-day coach tours for 18- to 35-year-olds throughout New Zealand.
- **Thrifty Tours,** P.O. Box 31257, Milford, Auckland (© **0800/803-550** in NZ, or 09/359-8380; www.thriftytours.co.nz), with well-planned 2- to 16-day tours.
- **Discover New Zealand,** 120 Albert St., Auckland (© **0800/330-188** in NZ, or 09/356-2190; www.discovernew

zealand.com), which offers a range of 3- to 8-day tours designed for travelers who want the value and security of prebooked arrangements combined with the freedom and independence of doing their own thing.

- **Scenic Pacific Tours,** P.O. Box 14037, Christchurch (✆ **0800/500-388** in NZ, or 03/359-3999; www.scenic

pacific.co.nz), which offers a large range of day excursions, short tours, and independent holidays.

- **Navigator Tours,** 553 Richmond Rd., Grey Lynn, Auckland (✆ **09/817-1191;** www.navigatortours.co.nz), offers a diverse range of unique, personalized, guided tours throughout New Zealand, staying at high-end accommodations.

10 STAYING CONNECTED

TELEPHONES

To call New Zealand from another country:

1. Dial the international access code: 011 from the U.S.; 00 from the U.K. or Ireland; or 0011 from Australia.
2. Dial the country code, **64.**
3. Dial the area code (for example, 03, 09, or 06, but without the zero) known as **STD (subscriber toll dialing),** and then the number.

To call long distance within New Zealand: First dial the STD—**09** for Auckland and Northland, **07** for the Thames Valley, **06** for the east coast and Wanganui, **04** for Wellington, or **03** for the South Island—and then the local number. (If you're calling from outside New Zealand, omit the zero.) There are three main kinds of public telephones in New Zealand: card phones, credit card phones, and coin phones. Magnetic strip **phone cards** for public phones can be purchased from supermarkets, post offices, dairies, and service stations.

To make international calls: To make international calls from New Zealand, first dial ✆ 00 and then the country code (U.S. or Canada 1, U.K. 44, Ireland 353, Australia 61). Next dial the area code and number.

The most economical way to make international phone calls from New Zealand is to charge them to an international calling card (available free from your long-distance company at home). All calls, even international ones, can be made from public phone booths. (Long-distance calls made from your hotel or motel often have hefty surcharges added.) You can also call home using **Country Direct** numbers. They are **000-911** for the U.S.; **000-944** for British Telecom (operator); **000-912** for British Telecom (automatic); **000-940** for UK Mercury; **000-919** for Canada; **000-996** for Australia-Optus; and **000-961** for Australia-Telstra.

For directory assistance within New Zealand: Dial ✆ **018.** For operator assistance within New Zealand, dial ✆ **010.**

For international operator assistance: If you need operator assistance in making a call, dial ✆ **0170;** for directory assistance for an international call, dial ✆ **0172.**

Remember that calling a 1-800 or toll-free number in your country from New Zealand is not toll-free. In fact, it costs the same as an overseas call.

CELLPHONES

The three letters that define much of the world's **wireless capabilities** are GSM (Global System for Mobiles), a big, seamless network that makes for easy cross-border cellphone use throughout Europe and dozens of other countries worldwide. In the U.S., T-Mobile, AT&T Wireless, and Cingular use this quasi-universal system; in Canada, Microcell and some Rogers customers are GSM; and all Europeans and most Australians and New Zealanders use GSM.

If your cellphone is on a GSM system, and you have a world-capable phone such as many (but not all) Sony Ericsson, Motorola, or Samsung models, you can make and receive calls across civilized areas on much of the globe, from Andorra to Uganda. Unfortunately, per-minute charges can be high. New Zealanders, it should be noted, currently pay some of the highest cellphone usage charges in the world.

Phone rental isn't cheap. You'll usually pay $40 to $50 per week, plus airtime fees of at least a dollar a minute. The bottom line: Shop around.

Two good wireless rental companies outside of New Zealand are **InTouch USA** (© **800/872-7626;** www.intouchglobal. com) and **RoadPost** (© **888/290-1606** or 905/272-5665; www.roadpost.com). Give them your itinerary, and they'll tell you what wireless products you need. InTouch will also, for free, advise you on whether your existing phone will work overseas; simply call © **703/222-7161** between 9am and 4pm EST, or go to http://intouchglobal.com/travel.htm.

Cellphone rental is not always cheap, and there is only one cellphone rental provider within New Zealand—Vodafone—so you can't shop around. If you wish to rent a cellphone for the duration of your visit in New Zealand, you need to call at the Vodafone Rental shop at either Auckland International Airport or Christchurch International Airport. The base rental rate for less than 1 week is NZ$6 per day. For more than 1 week it's NZ$3.60 per day, or NZ$25 per week. On top of that you pay a call rate of NZ90¢ per minute anytime, anywhere within New Zealand. International calls will cost more. You can check details at www.vodarent.co.nz.

It is important to note that that in New Zealand, the two main telecommunications providers are Telecom, which operates on an 800 megahertz frequency, and Vodafone, which operates on a 900 megahertz frequency. If your own cellphone is able to operate within either of those frequencies, your best-value option is to bring it with you and purchase a local SIM card when you get here.

You'll get good cellphone coverage in most urban areas in New Zealand, but be prepared for "black holes" where there is no coverage at all. These areas are usually off the beaten track and are too numerous to list. Thankfully, you seldom have to travel far before coverage resumes. The West Coast, Arthur's Pass, parts of Eastland, and parts of the far south are notorious for weaker coverage.

True wilderness adventurers should consider renting a **satellite phone.** Per-minute call charges can be even cheaper than roaming charges with a regular cellphone, but the phone itself is more expensive (up to $150 a week), and depending on the service you choose, people calling you may incur high long-distance charges.

INTERNET/E-MAIL
Without Your Own Computer

To find cybercafes in New Zealand, check **www.cybercaptive.com** and **www.cyber cafe.com**.

Aside from formal cybercafes, most **youth hostels** nowadays have at least one computer you can get to the Internet on. And most **public libraries** across the world offer Internet access free or for a small charge. Avoid **hotel business centers,** unless access to them is included in your rates; otherwise, you'll find yourself paying an additional charge to use it. Most major airports now have **Internet kiosks** scattered throughout their gates. Most public libraries in New Zealand offer Internet access free, or for a small charge, as do many i-SITE visitor centers. All cities and most larger towns have retail Internet providers, and these can be easily found by asking at the visitor center.

With Your Own Computer
More and more hotels, resorts, airports, cafes, and retailers are going **Wi-Fi** (wireless fidelity) and becoming "hot spots" that offer free high-speed Wi-Fi access or charge a fee for usage. In New Zealand hotels, that fee varies greatly and in many cases is far more expensive than justifiable. From my own experience, check hotel Internet fees before signing on. If you only want to check your e-mail, you're better off paying a mere NZ$5 to NZ$6 for an hour's computer use at a retail Internet provider. Most towns on the main tourist beat have at least two or three, and infor-

mation centers will point you in the right direction. Many hotels, by comparison, charge as much as NZ$35 for a 24-hour period and guests are often only in the hotel for an overnight stay. This is a steep rate if you're only checking and sending a few e-mails.

Most laptops sold today have built-in wireless capability. To find public Wi-Fi hot spots at your destination, go to **www.jiwire.com**; its Hotspot Finder holds the world's largest directory of public wireless hot spots. The New Zealand Yellow Pages telephone directories also list wireless and Internet hot spots under "Internet Service." Most upscale accommodations and many B&Bs in New Zealand offer a free high-speed or Wi-Fi service.

Wherever you go, bring a **connection kit** of the right power and phone adapters (the voltage is 230 volts in New Zealand, and plugs are the three-prong type), a spare phone cord, and a spare Ethernet network cable.

11 TIPS ON ACCOMMODATIONS

Unfortunately, there's nothing standard about accommodations rates here, and what you get for NZ$150 can be much better than something for two or three times the price. My words of advice: Ask around, visit websites for photographs, and don't just assume that all places in the same price range offer the same standard of accommodations. (They probably do in the Expensive range, but certainly not in the Moderate and Inexpensive categories.)

New Zealand tourism's official mark of quality, **Qualmark** (www.qualmark.co.nz), has now been applied to all accommodations types and tourism businesses. This means they have been independently assessed as professional and trustworthy and graded one star (acceptable), two stars (good), three stars (very good), four stars (excellent), and five stars (exceptional,

among the best in New Zealand). Each business has undergone a rigorous assessment and licensing process to become part of the Qualmark licensing system.

However, you should realize that—according to this Qualmark system—a three-star hotel is not the same as a three-star B&B or a three-star lodge, and that a five-star B&B is not the same as a five-star hotel. Each category of accommodations is assessed on different criteria.

It is also worth noting that many accommodations operators have little faith in this rating system because it's voluntary and not all properties have been assessed. There is particular discontent at the top end of the market, where operators are disillusioned that star ratings are being applied to businesses that are already self-regulated.

If you would like more information when you arrive in New Zealand, pick up the free **Qualmark Accommodation Guide** from information centers (or order it at **www.qualmark.co.nz**); it lists all participating hotels, motels, B&Bs, backpackers, campgrounds, and tourism businesses.

Note that New Zealand now has an across-the-board legal ban on smoking in public buildings. That includes hotels and restaurants. Therefore, you should assume that accommodations listed in the individual regional chapters throughout this guide have adopted a nonsmoking policy. It is also a legal requirement that all public buildings have access for travelers with disabilities. You should therefore assume that properties reviewed in this guide offer rooms with access for travelers with disabilities, although in the case of B&Bs it will pay to double-check before booking.

There is a multitude of lodging options available in New Zealand—here's a rundown on what you'll find.

HOTELS A hotel generally provides a licensed bar and restaurant, and guest rooms do not usually have cooking facilities. In New Zealand, "hotel" refers to modern tourist hotels, including the big international chains and older public-licensed hotels generally found in provincial areas. The latter are completely different from the former.

The country hotel, or pub, offers inexpensive to moderate accommodations of a modest nature. It's often noisy and old-fashioned with shared bathrooms down the hall. There are definitely exceptions, with upgrading a big trend in popular tourist areas. One way or another, they're usually rich in character.

Modern hotels come in all price levels. Several big international chains have two or three grades of hotels, and you can get exceptionally good deals if you book with the same chain throughout the country. In major tourist centers such as Queenstown,

competition is fierce and good prices can be found. In major corporate destinations such as Auckland and Wellington, rates will be considerably higher during the week, with weekends bringing superb specials.

APARTMENTS In the last 5 years, apartment-style accommodations have sprouted up in New Zealand like mushrooms on a damp day. Some have been added to existing hotels but most are free-standing complexes. If you'd like to stay in a modern apartment I suggest you contact one of the two following first-class operators. **Touch of Spice,** Queenstown (✆ 03/442-8672; www.touchofspice.co.nz), has been rated by *Conde Nast Traveler* as one of only 49 villa rental agents worldwide, best qualified to match its readers with suitable holiday properties. This meticulous concierge and luxury lifestyle specialist offers a range of 30 luxury properties from inner city apartments to country hideaways and private island retreats—all featuring modern furnishings and five-star quality, and full staff if required. **New Zealand Apartments** (✆ 0800/692-727; www.nzapartments.co.nz) has a catalog of 48 stylish apartments in 33 locations nationwide. Most are under 10 years old and go for unbelievably good prices. They're serviced on demand and all have on-site managers to welcome you.

MOTELS & MOTOR INNS A motel unit is self-contained and usually has cooking facilities, a bathroom, and one or two bedrooms. A motor inn often has a restaurant on the premises.

Don't assume that New Zealand motels are the same as those you find in, say, the United States. There has been a major shake-up of standards in the motel industry, and many motels and motor inns are superior to some hotels. Look for the Qualmark sign of quality, which is prominently displayed on signs and promotional material. If you aim for four- and five-star properties I'm sure you'll be happy. **New**

> ### (Tips) En Suites
>
> In New Zealand, the term *en-suite bathroom* refers to a bathroom incorporated within the bedroom. A private bathroom refers to a bathroom outside the bedroom, which is used exclusively by the guests of one room. A shared bathroom is a communal bathroom used by all guests in the establishment. Many accommodations within New Zealand have en-suite bathrooms, but it still pays to request them in B&Bs and backpacker establishments, many of which still have shared or private bathrooms.

Zealand Luxury Motels (© 0800/692-727; www.nzluxurymotels.co.nz) can save you a lot of time. They have 23 top-end motels nationwide on their books—15 of them built in the last 3 years to the highest specifications.

BED & BREAKFASTS As the name suggests, B&B rates include bed and breakfast, but it's often difficult to tell the difference between a bed-and-breakfast, a homestay, a farmstay, a guesthouse, a lodge, and a boutique hotel. B&B operators seem to be using a plethora of terms to describe much the same thing. Suffice it to say, in all of the above, that the key advantage is interaction with New Zealanders.

Homestays and bed-and-breakfasts are pretty much the same thing, but the variation in quality within both can be disconcerting—you'll find both the ludicrously cheap and the ludicrously expensive, and price is not necessarily an indicator of what you'll get. **Homestays** tend to be more family oriented and modest, especially in rural areas and provincial towns. Be prepared to simply get a bed in a family home. **B&Bs,** on the other hand, can be as down-market or as upmarket as you're prepared to pay; some rival the best hotels for quality.

I strongly advise you to check websites, or wait until you're in New Zealand to purchase one of the numerous B&B guides. Look for *The New Zealand Bed & Breakfast Book,* which illustrates every property in full color. Another reliable source is *Heritage & Character Inns of New Zealand* (www.heritageinns.co.nz), which details about 90 of the country's best B&B lodgings in heritage homes. Ask for brochures at visitor centers.

You can safely assume that **farmstays** are located on farms. They present an ideal opportunity to get a feel for New Zealand's rural life. There are several organizations that will put you in touch with a reliable farmstay: **Accommodation New Zealand** (© 09/444-4895 or 03/487-8420; www.accommodation-new-zealand.co.nz), and **Hospitality Plus,** the New Zealand Home & Farmstay Company (© 03/693-7463; fax 03/693-7462; www.hospitalityplus.co.nz).

Guesthouses generally offer good value: modest rooms at modest prices. You can check out a selection of them with **New Zealand's Federation of Bed & Breakfast Hotels, Inc.,** 52 Armagh St., Christchurch (© 03/358-6928; fax 03/355-0291; www.nzbnbhotels.com).

COUNTRY LODGES There are many establishments calling themselves "lodges" when, strictly speaking, they don't meet lodge criteria as defined by the New Zealand Lodge Association. In the truest sense, country lodges in New Zealand are small and highly individual, with 4 to 20 bedrooms. They're fully licensed and have an all-inclusive tariff. They generally offer the very best of everything, including fine dining (three- to five-course dinners). The unspoken factors are the degree of exclusivity that exceeds B&Bs and the degree of personalized service and pampering that exceeds most hotels. For information, go to **www.lodgesofnz.co.nz.** A new luxury accommodations category was also added to the Qualmark program in 2003.

HOLIDAY HOMES When they're not being used by their owners, holiday homes can be rented by the night or for longer periods. Known as **baches** in the North Island and **cribs** in the South Island, they are a good value for independent travelers. You can buy *Baches & Holiday Homes to Rent,* which details over 500 properties, from bookstores or the **Automobile Association,** 99 Albert St., Auckland (✆ **09/966-8800**); 343 Lambton Quay, Wellington (✆ **04/931-9999**); or 210 Hereford St., Christchurch (✆ **03/964-3650**). For a wider variety—from cozy cottages to super-luxury homes—contact **New Zealand Vacation Homes** (www.nzvacationhomes.co.nz), which lists self-catering properties throughout the country.

HOSTELS Hostels are generally frequented by backpackers, but most welcome people of all ages and have single and double rooms as well as dorms. They have shared facilities (some have en-suite bathrooms) and communal lounges and kitchens; some have cafes and/or bars.

Further information can be found by contacting the following: **YHA New Zealand National Reservations Centre** (✆ **03/379-9808;** fax 03/379-4415; www.yha.co.nz) has hostels open 24 hours a day that do not impose curfews or duties. **Budget Backpacker Hostels New Zealand** (✆ **03/379-3014;** www.bbh.co.nz) lists over 300 hostels around the country; and **VIP Backpacker Resorts of New Zealand** (✆ **09/827-6016;** fax 09/827-6013; www.vip.co.nz) is supported by over 60 hostels. **Nomads** (✆ **0800/666-237;** www.nomadsworld.com) offers hostel accommodations at 16 sites.

MOTOR CAMPS & HOLIDAY PARKS These properties have communal kitchens, toilets, showers, and laundries, and a variety of accommodations from campsites and cabins to flats and backpacker-style lodges. They are very popular with New Zealand holidaymakers during the summer months, so make sure you book ahead. They make an ideal base if you are traveling by motor home. Two contacts for holiday parks are **Top 10 Holiday Parks** (✆ **0800/867-836** in NZ; fax 03/377-9950; www.top10.co.nz) and **Holiday Accommodation Parks New Zealand** (✆ **04/298-3283;** www.holidayparks.co.nz).

Suggested New Zealand Itineraries

Making your way around New Zealand is simple, and many tourists find renting a car the cheapest and most flexible option. But if you're short on time, fly between major destinations and pick up a rental car for short journeys.

Many of you will find the roads "virtually empty" compared to those in your own countries. That said, don't be misled by the seemingly short distances between places. Most roads are only two lanes—except near bigger cities, where they become four-lane highways—and in some places they're steep, winding, and narrow as they negotiate river gorges and mountain tracts. Allow much more time than you would for a similar length journey at home.

1 THE REGIONS IN BRIEF

THE NORTH ISLAND

AUCKLAND ★★★   Far too often overlooked as little more than a landing port, Auckland has first-rate attractions, quality accommodations, and diverse leisure opportunities. It is without doubt the most cosmopolitan of the cities, and its balmy climate has a special appeal. Waitemata Harbour and Hauraki Gulf offer some of the world's finest sailing, boating, and fishing, and in the aftermath of the 2002–03 America's Cup yachting challenge, many quality hotels, bars, and restaurants are thriving. Cultural offerings abound in museums, galleries, and performing arts centers; and shopping is the most diverse in the country. There are more than 1,000 restaurants and a wild nightlife scene, and if you're into a beach lifestyle, there are numerous choices within easy reach. You may think it's just another big city, but Auckland has a Polynesian backbone that makes it quite unique. If you're touring only the North Island, Auckland is a perfect base.

NORTHLAND ★ & COROMANDEL   Both are within easy reach of Auckland and can be tackled as a day trip if you're short on time. However, each warrants at least a couple of days' exploration; if you have to choose between the two, I'd definitely swing up to the far north.

Northland is served by a far better infrastructure in terms of transportation, hotels, and restaurants, and its beach attractions (on the east coast) are too numerous to itemize. That said, you'll find far more tourists here, too, at least in the Bay of Islands area. Head north, though, and a whole world of unpopulated beaches awaits. Fishing, diving, boating, and camping are all big draws. The area's rich Maori culture is also an excellent introduction to New Zealand's history.

The Coromandel Peninsula is a slightly more rugged version of Northland, to the south of Auckland. It has a craggier coastline, a more remote landscape, and sections with very poor roads. Accommodations are middling to say the least (with a few exceptions). Still, there's color and character here, and it's long been a favorite with New Zealand campers and beach bunnies—especially the eastern side of the peninsula, where you'll find some top surf beaches.

WAIKATO & BAY OF PLENTY ★ I spent my childhood in the Waikato region, but I find little to recommend for the visitor. Hamilton is trying its hardest, and it would be fair to say that it suffers from being in Auckland's shadow. The Waitomo Caves have traditionally been the area's biggest attraction, and although their natural splendor is undeniable, I find Waitomo a rather depressing place—a strange hive of tourist buses, darting in and out of otherwise undisturbed farmland.

The Bay of Plenty, on the other hand, has come of age. Tauranga and Mount Maunganui have always been hot spots. Again, the emphasis is on a beach lifestyle—boating, fishing, surfing, sunbathing, and golf are the main attractions—and some stunning accommodations are available. If you've been to Australia's Gold Coast, you'll sense a hint of that style here.

ROTORUA ★★★, **TAUPO** ★ **& TONGARIRO NATIONAL PARK** ★★ Rotorua is on almost every visitor's hit list. Some would say that makes the area objectionably touristy. I don't agree. Rotorua has spent millions refining its attractions and accommodations, of which there are many, and it offers a unique geographic and Maori cultural slice of New Zealand life. In terms of adventure tourism, it is biting at the heels of Queenstown.

Taupo and Tongariro National Park, in combination with Rotorua, make the whole central region an unbeatable value in terms of volcanic landscape and adventure variety. And the area is plenty big enough to avoid being bothered by others. (It's away from key attractions.) Come here for volcanic and Maori attractions, the world's best trout fishing, mountaineering, skiing (water and snow), mountain biking, and tramping.

This is one of the most underrated areas of the country. East Cape and Gisborne offer a rare insight into Maori culture, free of tourist hype. The area has amazing beaches and world-class surfing conditions, and, in combination with Hawke's Bay, is probably the country's most important wine-producing region. In terms of accommodations, Gisborne is definitely lacking, and its laid-back rural approach doesn't always find favor with visitors. Hawke's Bay, on the other hand, has the best range of boutique B&Bs and cottages in the country. Napier's Art Deco charms are legendary and definitely worthy of inspection.

TARANAKI & WANGANUI Let's put it this way—if you want the best of small-town, provincial New Zealand, this is it. I'm most drawn to Taranaki. New Plymouth is surprisingly vibrant in its own right, and you can't help but feel that, stuck out here on its own western limb, it couldn't care less about the rest of the country. Mount Egmont and the sea are big attractions for trampers and surfers, and the region's gardens are stunning. And Tom Cruise seemed to like the area when he was filming *The Last Samurai*. Wanganui has a major asset in its river, but it needs to spruce up accommodations.

WELLINGTON ★★★ The capital has come alive in almost every aspect. The Museum of New Zealand—Te Papa Tongarewa is, of course, a major attraction and has been built with style and flair. Once you have explored it, you will understand more clearly much of what you have seen, or are about to see, throughout the country. Wellington is also home to several national cultural companies, so you'll find a rich performing arts program. In addition, its restaurant, nightlife, and shopping opportunities are many and varied.

And don't overlook the vineyard and craft delights of the **Wairarapa** ★, where you'll find the biggest selection of stunning rural cottages in New Zealand.

THE SOUTH ISLAND

NELSON ★★ & MARLBOROUGH ★
The best year-round climate in New Zealand can be found here. Characterized by three stunning national parks and gorgeous beaches, Nelson is often talked about with a mix of derision and envy for its alternative, slightly hippie/artsy communities, but this is a top region to visit if you're into arts and crafts and outdoor pursuits. And for oenophiles, there's a growing pocket of wineries that, in combination with the Marlborough wine region, make it a must-see destination. Both areas have some superb B&Bs, homestays, and backpacker accommodations.

CHRISTCHURCH & CANTERBURY ★★★
After Auckland, Christchurch is the second major destination for overseas tourists. Quite apart from the fact that it's the primary starting point for South Island exploration, Christchurch is loved for its fine Victorian-Gothic architecture, its hints of old England, and its increasingly vibrant city lifestyle. It has several ski fields within a 2-hour drive, good surfing beaches, and over 40 wineries. Day trips to Hanmer, Kaikoura, Akaroa, and Methven are all popular, but each of them warrants a longer stay.

WEST COAST ★ & THE GLACIERS ★★
The top of the West Coast, from Westport north to Karamea, and the south, from Haast to the glaciers, are quite remarkable. It's just a pity about the middle bit. Apart from greenstone shopping and the crazy Hokitika Wildfoods Festival, I can never find much to recommend in the central part of the West Coast. But I will concede that it has played a vigorous and important role in shaping New Zealand's history and economy, and you certainly won't find anything quite like it elsewhere.

QUEENSTOWN & ENVIRONS ★★★
For sheer physical impact, this southwestern portion of New Zealand is utterly unbeatable. It's easy to understand why everyone flocks here at least once. Don't be put off by this nonsense about Queenstown being "too touristy." It's a recognized international tourist resort, for goodness sake, so of course there will be lots of tourists! It has a long-standing reputation for being a work-hard, play-hard, party-hard sort of a place, and as far as I'm concerned, the more the merrier.

Milford Sound ★★★ is another matter entirely. It is simply stunning, but the excessive number of buses (over 50 a day) is quite disgusting and should be reduced to make it a better experience for everyone. It is a remote wilderness area, but it's hard to sense that with 3,000 other people standing around looking at the same mountain peak!

Wanaka ★ has a much more low-key personality than Queenstown. It makes a beautiful stopover between Queenstown and the West Coast. You'll find some stunning lodges and B&Bs here.

DUNEDIN ★, SOUTHLAND & STEWART ISLAND ★★
Invercargill and Southland are sleepy, slow, incredibly friendly, and very, very green, but not that well prepared for the visitor. Dunedin is simply gorgeous, very Gothic, and in winter, very grim. But as a summer destination, it's lovely and has lots to offer the wildlife lover. Get out onto Otago Peninsula and be prepared to have your breath taken away. It also has some handsome B&B and lodge-style accommodations in the most amazing old houses.

Farther south, the Catlins Coast and Stewart Island are remarkably unspoiled by anything—especially tourism. I'm almost loath to mention either for fear of instigating a mass influx of visitors, but good old Kiwi pride gets in the way, and I can't help boasting about these two truly magical destinations.

2 NEW ZEALAND IN 1 WEEK

I hear it all the time: "This is such a small country, but we never realized there would be so much to see; we wish we'd allowed more time." Seeing New Zealand in 1 week is possible, but it will require early starts and long days. Personally, I'd ditch the car idea and fly between four major stops—Auckland, Wellington, Christchurch, and Queenstown— to save time. There are regular internal flights between all major towns and cities, and if you shop around some of the smaller airlines, you can get good deals. Otherwise, you'll spend 90% of your time in a vehicle suffering from jet lag, with little left over for the sights.

Day ❶: Arrive in Auckland ★★★

Try to arrive early and focus your attention on **Viaduct Basin** (p. 143), a great introduction to New Zealand's passion for boats. Go for a sail on *NZL 40* (p. 144), which is moored here. The **New Zealand National Maritime Museum** (p. 144) is also here and gives a great overview of our maritime history and short cruises on the historic scow *Ted Ashby*. In between, join the crowds lazing about over good coffee and fine food. There are at least a dozen restaurants to choose from. Stay at **Hilton Auckland** (p. 123), perched on the end of the wharf.

Day ❷: Waiheke Island ★★★

Catch a ferry across to Waiheke Island for a day of laid-back wine tasting and beach walking. Factor in lunch at **Te Whau Vineyard** (p. 164), where you can gaze over staggering views and one of the best wine cellars in the country. Visit **Connells Bay Sculpture Park** (p. 163) with work by leading New Zealand artists, and swim in the clear warm waters of **Onetangi Bay** (p. 162). Return to Auckland in the late afternoon, visit **Auckland Museum** (p. 140), and eat at the **French Café** (p. 135).

Day ❸: Wellington ★★★

Get up early and fly to Wellington. For the definitive overview of New Zealand, go straight to **Te Papa** (p. 306). Don't miss the Passports and Manu Whenua displays. Walk along the waterfront, down the Lambton Quay shopping precinct, and catch the **cable car** (p. 307) up to the **Botanic Garden** (p. 308). Go down the other side to Tinakori Village for lunch. Walk back down Bowen Street, past the **Beehive and Parliament** (p. 308). After unwinding at **Caffe Astoria** (p. 302), enjoy dinner at **Logan Brown** (p. 301).

Day ❹: Christchurch ★★★

Take an early flight to Christchurch, hire a car at the airport, skip the city, and drive 1 hour to pretty Akaroa, admiring rural landscapes along the way. For interesting art and great coffee, stop at **Little River Gallery** (p. 392). Take another break at the hilltop for great camera shots. Over the hills, try tasty **Barrys Bay Cheese** (p. 393). In Akaroa, take a nature cruise with dolphin-watching, or saunter along the promenade, taking in quaint architecture and dinky shops. When you return to Christchurch, stay at **Clearwater Resort** (p. 369), which is close to the airport.

Day ❺: Arrive in Queenstown ★★★

Sleep in and wake up to ducks floating on the lake outside your window. Ease yourself into a late breakfast before flying to Queenstown. Once there, at the airport, take a memorable helicopter ride with **Over The Top** (p. 451) and land high on a mountain peak for lunch in total solitude. You'll remember this forever. Back on the ground, spoil yourself at the **Sofitel** (p. 457).

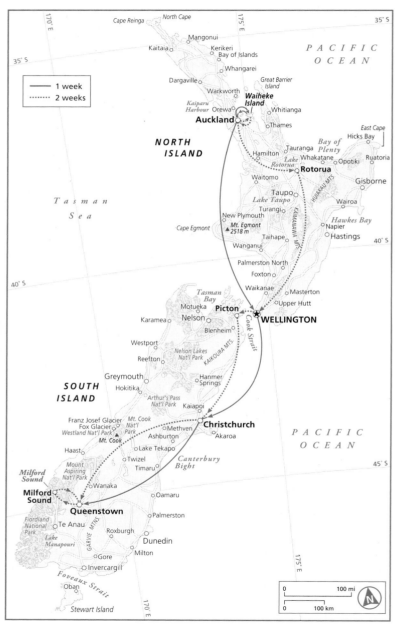

Day ❻: Queenstown Adventures

Rise early, meet the locals for breakfast at **Joe's Garage** (p. 465), and then have the quintessential adventure experience on **Shotover Jet** (p. 453). Move on to Arrowtown, explore the quaint old Chinese gold mining area, and have lunch at **Saffron** (p. 466). If you're ready for more action, do the **Kawarau Bungy** (p. 448), or watch others, and then visit **GVW Winery** (p. 450). Alternatively, use this day to enjoy **a scenic flight to Milford Sound,** a cruise, and return flight (p. 451).

Day ❼: Back to Christchurch

Fly back to Christchurch to connect with your international flight. If you have time between flights, visit the nearby **International Antarctic Centre** (p. 376), **Orana Park** (p. 378), or **Willowbank Wildlife Reserve** (p. 378)—where you're sure to see a kiwi. Alternatively, unwind with a round of golf at **Clearwater Resort** (p. 369). If you decide you were silly to try and cram it all into a week, see the next itinerary.

3 NEW ZEALAND IN 2 WEEKS

Two weeks in New Zealand gives you more opportunities to drive between destinations and take in the color of the provinces. Still, don't underestimate the time your journey will take. New Zealand has good roads, but 20km (12 miles) in some parts of the country could be narrow, steep, and winding—which means it might take you twice as long to negotiate them as it would back home. In general, roads are well maintained and all major roads are paved. Drive with care on narrow, unpaved roads if you venture in to more remote areas. What I've suggested here gives you a taste of both main islands, sticking to main centers with the greatest concentration of activities.

Day ❶: Arrive in Auckland ★★★

Arrive in Auckland and rest for a whole day, doing nothing more taxing than eating and drinking at **Viaduct Basin** (p. 143). At night, go to the top of **Sky Tower** (p. 141) for the big daddy of views and a meal in the revolving restaurant.

Day ❷: Auckland's Major Sights

Prepare to sightsee until you drop. Get on the **Explorer Bus** (p. 120)—the cheapest and easiest way to see as much as possible in 1 day. You'll set eyes on Mission Bay's pretty beach promenade, visit **Kelly Tarlton's Underwater World** (p. 142), and get a taste of Maori culture at **Auckland Museum** (p. 140). The bus drives through the leafy **Botanic Gardens** (p. 148) and through Parnell village. It stops at the **SKYCITY** complex (p. 126), the **Victoria Park Market** (p. 156), and much more.

Day ❸: Waiheke Island ★★★

Rise early and catch a ferry to **Waiheke Island** (p. 160). Hire a car and drive around the island, visiting wineries, olive groves, artists' studios, and unspoiled beaches. Some of the best surprises are in the little bays away from Oneroa township. Following visits to **Whittaker's Musical Museum** (p. 162) and **Te Whau Garden** (p. 163), have lunch at **Mudbrick Vineyard** (p. 164). Later in the day, sit in Onetangi Beach and watch the sunset. Stay at the **Boatshed** (p. 165).

Day ❹: Rotorua ★★★

Arrive back in Auckland by midday and fly to Rotorua. Hire a car. If you want a day of complete rest and solitude in unabashed luxury, head for **Treetops Lodge** (p. 230). If you want to see the sights, go straight to **Rotorua Museum** (p. 218) for an excellent overview of geothermal and volcanic history. Spend the rest of the afternoon at **Te Puia** (p. 221) to see bubbling mud and Maori cultural performances. Watch the sun set over the lake and relax in a hot rock pool at **Polynesian Spa** (p. 220).

Day ❺: The Thermal Attractions ★★

Drive 30 minutes south to see the wonders of **Waimangu** and **Waiotapu** (p. 218). Waimangu has shorter walks but fewer spectacular sights; I prefer Waiotapu. If you're back in town by early afternoon you could take a guided tour of **Ohinemutu** (p. 223), the original Maori village on the lakefront, followed by a walk among the **Whakarewarewa Forest** redwoods (p. 228). Finish the night with a tour and cultural performance at **Tamaki Maori Village** (p. 226).

Day ❻: Drive to Wellington

Rise early for a day of driving, but *be careful,* as roads in the Rotorua region are busy with huge logging trucks. A 5-hour journey will take you around **Lake Taupo** (p. 245), where there are plenty of lake-edge stops for photographs, through the stark beauty of **Tongariro National Park** (p. 245), and through heartland farming provinces. You could stop off for a night in the **Wairarapa** (p. 319)—or at least stop to eat in one of **Greytown's cute cafes** (p. 324)—or drive the last taxing, winding, uphill leg over the Rimutaka Hills to Wellington. Alternatively, go the coastal route along the Kapiti Coast.

Day ❼: Wellington ★★★

Te Papa (p. 306) is a must-visit. Spend 2 to 3 hours there and don't miss the gift shop for top-quality crafts. And you can't visit the capital without a ride up the **cable car** (p. 307), a wander through the **Botanic Garden** (p. 308) at the top, and a sit-in at a session of **Parliament** (p. 308). Art lovers should see **City Gallery Wellington** (p. 310) and if you like the funky side of life, wander up **Cuba Street**

(p. 304). Late afternoon, amble around the waterfront to **Oriental Parade** (p. 305). Have dinner at **Logan Brown** (p. 301) or **Matterhorn** (p. 317).

Day ❽: A Ferry Crossing

Rise early and catch one of the first ferries to **Picton** (p. 325) on the **Interislander** (p. 327). The 3-hour trip is an experience in its own right and if the weather's good you'll have a picturesque passage through **Queen Charlotte Sound** (p. 328). Catch the 1:40pm **TranzCoastal** (p. 326). This rail journey is a scenic feast through vineyards and along a rugged coastline hugged by steep mountains. You might want to get out at **Kaikoura** (p. 399) and go **whale-watching** (p. 400), or continue on to Christchurch, arriving around 7pm.

Day ❾: Christchurch ★★★

Get up early and head up Dyers Pass Road (in a hired car) to the top of the **Port Hills** (p. 381). My favorite drive is along the top, heading east, stopping for the fabulous views down into **Lyttelton Harbour** (p. 378) on your right. Drop down into the trendy seaside village of **Sumner** (p. 360, have coffee at **Coffee Culture** (p. 374), and walk along the white sands of Sumner Beach. Back in town, the swanky new architectural wonder that is **Christchurch Art Gallery** (p. 376) is bound to impress—don't leave without visiting their shop and Form Gallery. Wander down the boulevard to **Canterbury Museum** (p. 375), the **Arts Centre** (p. 375), and the **Botanic Gardens** (p. 376).

Day ❿: Drive to Queenstown

Prepare to be impressed by the landscapes on this 5- to 6-hour journey. You'll pass by the unbelievably turquoise Lake Tekapo—look out for the stop at the south end of the lake, which affords picture-perfect views of Mount Cook—and through the grand beauty of Lindis Pass. The lupines will be flowering along the summer roadsides of the Mackenzie Country and you won't be able to resist pulling out your camera. Stop on the Queenstown side of Cromwell at the **Big Picture** (p. 441) for refreshments, wine tastings, and an overview of the region's vineyards and wineries. Don't miss stops at the fresh summer fruit stalls along the way. Apricots are near perfect here.

Day ⓫: Queenstown ★★★
Sleep in and breakfast late at **Joe's Garage** (p. 465) before taking an early cruise across Lake Wakatipu on the vintage steamship **TSS *Earnslaw*** (p. 449). You'll be back in plenty of time to take the **gondola** (p. 445) up to **Bob's Peak** for breathtaking views over Queenstown. Leap off the **bungy** (p. 452) if you dare, or descend on the gondola and wander into the **Kiwi & Birdlife Park** (p. 446). Dine on seafood at **Boardwalk** (p. 462).

Day ⓬: The Wineries
Hire a car (or take a guided tour) and drive yourself around the best of Central Otago's wineries. The top four closest to Queenstown are **GVW Winery** (p. 450), **Peregrine** (p. 450), **Amisfield** (p. 450), and **Chard Farm** (p. 450). Don't miss Gibbston's wine cave, its cheesery, and its excellent lunches under a canopy of vines. Alternatively, wander around central Queenstown stores for excellent duty-free

shopping and have lunch at **Eichardt's** (p. 463), or take in a round of golf at **Millbrook Resort** (p. 453) and eat in one of its restaurants, finishing off with a soothing massage in the splendid spa. Have dinner at the **Bunker** (p. 464).

Day ⓭: Fly to Milford Sound ★★★
Be up early for a memorable scenic flight or helicopter ride to **Milford Sound** (p. 474). Take a **boat cruise** (p. 476) and make sure you include the **Underwater Observatory** (p. 476). Flying is by far the best option if you're short on time, although it is weather dependent. Bus trips can take around 12 hours—including the return. When you're back in Queenstown at the end of the day, dine at **Saffron** (p. 466) in **Arrowtown** (p. 447).

Day ⓮: Back to Christchurch
Enjoy a lazy morning in Queenstown before flying to Christchurch to connect with your international flight. If you have time between the two flights, go to the **International Antarctic Centre** (p. 376) near the airport, or, if you've yet to see a live kiwi, check out the nearby **Willowbank Wildlife Reserve** (p. 378). If you fancy big cats, visit the cheetahs at **Orana Park** (p. 378).

4 NEW ZEALAND FOR FAMILIES

Kids will love New Zealand. There are enough weird, wonderful, curious, funny, and interesting things on these islands to amuse the most inquiring child's mind. I'd recommend 3 weeks if you're traveling with a family (you can stretch out the 2-week itinerary below), so it's less taxing on everyone. And I'd either go "bush and beach" with a tent at a northern beach camping ground so the kids can run wild and free; or I'd stick to three major centers—Auckland, Rotorua, and Nelson—for the best concentration of kid-related activities. Much of the gut-busting excitement of Queenstown has age limits, but if your kids are old enough and you want a longer trip, tack on the "Ten Action-Packed Days in the South Island" tour, below.

Day ❶: Arrive in Auckland ★★★
Start slowly with an easy day, checking out combo deals and family passes at the visitor center at **Viaduct Basin** (p. 143),

where the kids can watch the boats and visit the **New Zealand Maritime Museum** (p. 144). Boys, especially, seem to get a real kick out of a ride on the historic scow,

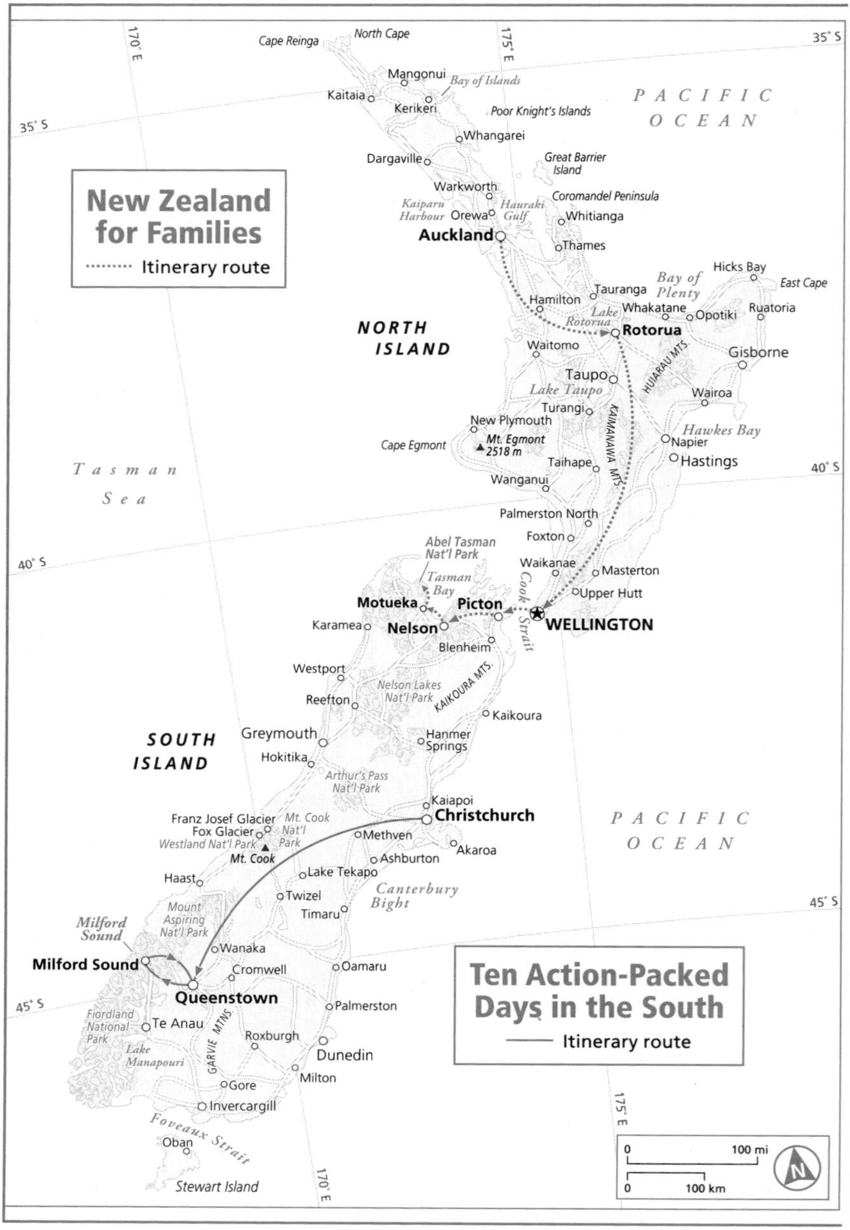
New Zealand for Families
Itinerary route
Ten Action-Packed Days in the South
Itinerary route
PACIFIC OCEAN
PACIFIC OCEAN
Tasman Sea
NORTH ISLAND
SOUTH ISLAND
Cape Reinga
North Cape
Mangonui
Bay of Islands
Kaitaia
Kerikeri
Poor Knight's Islands
Whangarei
Dargaville
Great Barrier Island
Warkworth
Kaiparu Harbour
Orewa
Hauraki Gulf
Coromandel Peninsula
Whitianga
Auckland
Thames
Hicks Bay
East Cape
Tauranga
Bay of Plenty
Hamilton
Whakatane
Opotiki
Ruatoria
Lake Rotorua
Rotorua
Waitomo
Gisborne
HUIARAU MTS.
Taupo
Lake Taupo
Wairoa
Turangi
New Plymouth
KAIMANAWA MTS.
Hawkes Bay
Napier
Cape Egmont
Mt. Egmont 2518 m
Hastings
Taihape
Wanganui
Palmerston North
Foxton
Abel Tasman Nat'l Park
Waikanae
Masterton
Tasman Bay
Upper Hutt
Cook Strait
Motueka
Picton
WELLINGTON
Karamea
Nelson
Blenheim
Westport
Nelson Lakes Nat'l Park
KAIKOURA MTS.
Reefton
Kaikoura
Greymouth
Hanmer Springs
Hokitika
Arthur's Pass Nat'l Park
Kaiapoi
Christchurch
Franz Josef Glacier
Mt. Cook Nat'l Park
Fox Glacier
Methven
Westland Nat'l Park
Mt. Cook
Akaroa
Ashburton
Lake Tekapo
Haast
Canterbury Bight
Twizel
Mount Aspiring Nat'l Park
Timaru
Milford Sound
Wanaka
Milford Sound
Oamaru
Cromwell
Queenstown
Palmerston
Fiordland National Park
Te Anau
GARVIE MTNS
Roxburgh
Dunedin
Lake Manapouri
Milton
Gore
Invercargill
Foveaux Strait
Oban
Stewart Island
0
100 mi
0
100 km
N

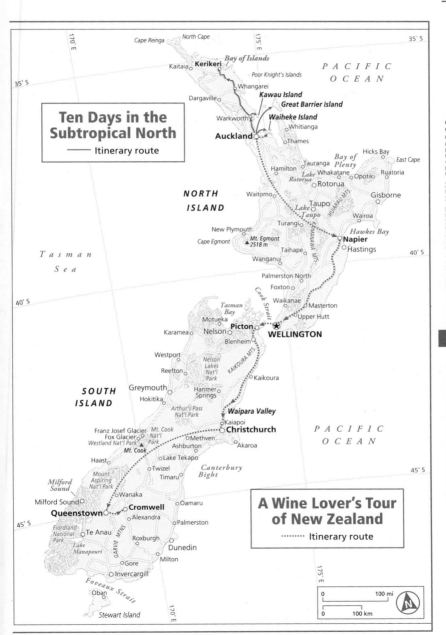

Ten Days in the Subtropical North
—— Itinerary route

A Wine Lover's Tour of New Zealand
········· Itinerary route

Ted Ashby. Give them a bird's-eye view of the city from the **Sky Tower** (p. 141), taking them up in the exterior glass lift and letting them walk over the glass floor. Dine in the revolving restaurant at the top.

Day ❷: Auckland Sights

Impress the kids right from the start with **Kelly Tarlton's Antarctic Encounter & Underwater World** (p. 142)—where else can they see an underground colony of penguins? Drive around to **Mission Bay** (p. 119), rent roller blades, swim at the beach, have a picnic lunch, and feed the sea gulls. Spend the afternoon at **Auckland Museum** (p. 140) and make sure you let them loose in the superb Discovery Centre, where they can open drawers and touch exhibits. The Wild Child display and the Maori Treasures are also good value.

Day ❸: More of Auckland

Get off to an early start at **Auckland Zoo** (p. 145), which has heaps of great stuff for kids. Check out the daily animal encounters and view sea lions through underwater viewing windows. Or consider their Safari Night Sleepovers and guided night walks instead of a day outing. Drive to **Butterfly Creek** (p. 145), flirt with winged beauties, ride on the Red Admiral Express, and see animals at Buttermilk Farm. Drive north to **Snowplanet** (p. 145), where you have the unlikely pleasure of a midwinter snow experience in the midst of a subtropical summer.

Day ❹: Drive to Rotorua

Hire a car and start the 3-hour drive to Rotorua early. Stop at **Hamilton** (p. 202) along the way and feed the ducks at **Hamilton Lake** (p. 204). In the afternoon, visit **Rotorua Museum** (p. 218) and "experience" a volcanic eruption in the theater there. Follow this with a leisurely drive around the Blue and Green Lakes to the **Buried Village** (p. 222), to see the remains of Te Wairoa village, which was buried by the eruption of Mount Tarawera in 1886.

Day ❺: Rotorua ★★★

The kids will be screwing their noses up at the smell of sulfur in the air, so get out there and show them what it's all about. Drive down to **Waimangu** and **Waiotapu** (p. 224). Allow half a day for both, or, if you have to choose, 2 hours for Waiotapu. Back in town, feed the kids from one of the takeaway stands at the lakefront and then let them loose at **Skyline Skyrides** (p. 221), where they can plummet downhill on a luge, or better still, have an adventure in the **Zorb** (p. 229). The **Agrodome** (p. 221) is a hive of kids' activities—I'd plan to spend the afternoon here. Finish with a relaxing dip at **Polynesian Spa** (p. 220).

Day ❻: Maori Experiences

Spend the morning investigating the wonders of **Te Puia** (p. 221), which includes the Whakarewarewa Thermal Reserve and the New Zealand Maori Arts & Crafts Institute. Stay and watch Pohutu Geyser blow its top. In the afternoon, take a guided tour of **Ohinemutu Maori Village** (p. 223) on the lakefront. Set the evening aside for a hangi meal and a Maori experience at **Tamaki Maori Village** (p. 226).

Day ❼: Drive to Wellington

The drive south normally takes about 5 hours, but allow a day. Stop at **Lake Taupo** (p. 234) for a go at the **Hole-in-One Challenge** (p. 240). And visit **Huka Falls** (p. 237), just off the main highway north of Taupo. Have a picnic at one of the little beaches around the lake and then head into **Tongariro National Park** (p. 245) for beautiful mountain landscapes. The kids will be ready for another stop at **Pukaha Mount Bruce National Wildlife Centre** (p. 319)—keep your eyes open to spot a kiwi; and maybe there'll be time to squeeze in a snack stop at **Greytown** (p. 319) before you wind your way across the Rimutaka Ranges and down into Wellington by late afternoon.

Day ❽: Wellington ★★★

Spend your first 3 hours exploring the **Museum of New Zealand—Te Papa Tongarewa** (p. 306) and allow extra time for the kids to experience the interactive displays on the ground floor. Let them run free along the waterfront after that—there'll be boats and people aplenty for them to watch. Head up the **cable car** (p. 307) next to the **Botanic Garden** (p. 308), where you should take them to the **Carter Observatory** (p. 308) for a bit of stargazing. If you never got to the zoo in Auckland, don't miss the **Wellington Zoo** (p. 308) and its interactive animal experiences. Wander down **Cuba Mall** (p. 293) late afternoon and let the kids get wet in the **Bucket Fountain** (p. 309).

Day ❾: Ferry Ride to Picton

Catch the early **Interislander** (p. 327) across to Picton. The ferry has movie theaters and play areas for kids. Hire a car and drive to Nelson. Stop 10 minutes short of Nelson at **Happy Valley Adventures** (p. 343) for 4WD bike adventures and the sky swing. In Nelson, hunt out **Penguino** (p. 348) for a well-deserved specialty ice cream.

Day ❿: Nelson ★★★

Start at the **World of Wearable Art & Classic Cars Museum** (p. 338) where everyone's eyes will pop out on stalks. Let the kids loose next at **Nelson Fun Park** and **Natureland Zoo** (p. 341). Enjoy a picnic at nearby **Tahunanui Beach** (p. 341) and then spend the afternoon swimming, making sand castles, and generally relaxing on one of the most popular beaches in the area. You'll probably want to visit Penguino again after that.

Day ⓫: Exploring the Area

Watch glass blowing at **Höglund Art Glass International Glass Centre** (p. 341), then drive to **Mapua** (p. 347), visiting pottery studios along the way.

Stop at orchard stalls for a crisp apple snack. Dabble fingers in open displays at **Touch the Sea Aquarium** (p. 342) and have a yummy late lunch at the **Naked Bun Patisserie** (p. 350). Drive on through **Motueka** (p. 336) and turn right to **Kaiteriteri** (p. 342), one of the prettiest golden-sand beaches you'll ever see. Spend the afternoon playing and swimming, or take a water taxi around the gorgeous coast of **Abel Tasman National Park** (p. 351). Stay at Kaiteriteri or Motueka for the night.

Day ⓬: Abel Tasman National Park ★★★

Drive through Kaiteriteri and around to **Marahau** (p. 350) to get yourselves aboard one of the Abel Tasman kayaks (p. 351). This unbeatable experience amid clear waters will amaze you. Watch for seals and penguins and don't forget to take your swimming togs. Alternatively, take a guided day walk on the **Abel Tasman Coastal Track** (p. 93). Get back to Nelson in time for dinner—perhaps fish and chips on the beach as the sun sets.

Day ⓭: Outdoor Adventures

Get a feel for Nelson's big open spaces on a 4-hour outing with **Stonehurst Farm Horse Treks** (p. 343). They'll take you over hill-country farming land, down valleys, along rivers, and over plains. Don't forget to take your camera and a picnic to have in the country afterward. In the afternoon hire **bikes** (p. 343), go swimming at the beach, or fish off the end of the Nelson wharves. Visit **Founder's Heritage Park** (p. 338).

Day ⓮: Return to Wellington

Rise early for the 2-hour drive to Picton. Allow time to wander along the shore, watching boats coming and going before getting back on the ferry to Wellington. Connect with your international flight home in the afternoon or early evening.

5 A WINE LOVER'S TOUR OF NEW ZEALAND

New Zealand has come of age as a producer of internationally acclaimed wines, and the great thing about the country's six major grape-growing regions is that they're packed into some of the most stunning landscapes. They're often close to gourmet food producers, many have terrific restaurants, some offer boutique lodgings, and impressive architecture is to the fore. In an ideal world, you could easily spend 2 to 3 weeks "soaking" in a New Zealand wine tour because it offers so much more than just wine and vineyards, but the following itinerary outlines a more realistic (for most travelers) 10-day tour of highlights.

Day ❶: Arrive in Auckland ★★★

The greater Auckland region (including Waiheke Island) has over 100 vineyards and wineries. In the interests of early research, head for the **NZ Winemakers Centre** (p. 149) in Central City to sample your first New Zealand wines and to pick up information on New Zealand wine tourism. Have dinner at **Vinnies Restaurant** (p. 137).

Day ❷: Henderson Valley

Drive 30 minutes from the city to New Zealand's oldest grape-growing region, where there are a bundle of wineries along Henderson Valley Road and Lincoln Road. Seek out **Soljans Estate's winery and cafe** (p. 149) for lunch and then drive on to **Nobilo Wine Group** (p. 149). If you don't want to drive yourself, contact Phil Parker's **Fine Wine Tours** (p. 151) to get a comprehensive overview in a short time. Stay at **Bethells Beach Cottages** (p. 133), which are set among sculptured gardens with views of the Tasman Sea. If you return to the city, dine at the **French Café** (p. 135).

Day ❸: Waiheke Island ★★★

Catch the ferry to **Waiheke Island** (p. 160). Pick up a rental and visit some of the 45 vineyards on the island. **Fullers** (p. 160) and **Ananda Tours** (p. 162) both offer wine tours. If you'd rather be independent, make sure you visit **Te Whau Vineyard** (p. 164), which has more than 500 cellared wines. It's highly rated by

Wine Spectator and has an impressive menu. You can't really get lost on this little paradise, and if you did, would you care? Splurge on a stay at **Te Whau Lodge** (p. 165), where you'll wine and dine in style overlooking vineyards.

Day ❹: Fly to Hawke's Bay ★★★

Head back to the mainland (reluctantly, I'd guess) and fly to **Napier** (p. 261)—a twin heaven of endless grapes and oh-so-pretty **Art Deco architecture** (p. 266), not to mention gorgeous boutique vineyard accommodations, a dazzling array of restaurants, and some of the best wines in the country. Spend the afternoon at the **National Aquarium of New Zealand** (p. 262) for a change of pace and drink afternoon champagne at the **County Hotel's bar** (p. 272).

Day ❺: The Wine Trail

Do a fun bicycle tour of a handful of vineyards with **On Yer Bike Winery Tours** (p. 265), passing olive groves, orchards, wineries, and ostrich farms. Take your camera, as well as bottled water, a hat, sunscreen, and sunglasses to protect against the hot sun. Switch back to your car in the evening and splash out on dinner at the unforgettable **Terroir** (p. 272) at **Craggy Range Winery** (p. 264) in the Havelock North area. Get there in daylight so you can look through the fabulous winery and tasting gallery. Try their classy vineyard stay, or plant yourself at nearby **Millar Road** (p. 270).

Day 6: More Tasting at Maraekakaho Road

If you haven't been there yet, head for the vineyards in the Maraekakaho Road area, finishing up at **Sileni Estates Winery & Epicurean Centre** (p. 265) in time for a drawn-out lunch at their classy restaurant. Head back into Napier for a 2-hour, self-guided afternoon **Art Deco Walk** (© 06/ 835-0022; www.artdeconapier.com; p. 266). Make sure you stop at **Ujazi** (p. 270) for coffee and cake, and right next door, loosen your purse strings on fabulous New Zealand arts and crafts at **Statements Gallery** (p. 262).

Day 7: The Marlborough Wine Region ★★★

Rise early and drive the 4 hours to Wellington, where you'll catch the **Interislander** (p. 289) to Picton. You'll find world-class vineyards here as far as the eye can see. Take plenty of film and stamina, along with a wine map from the **visitor center** (p. 292), which lists all the wineries open for meals and tastings, plus the wines they produce. There are over 50 cellar doors open to you, so make a day of it. Splurge on dinner at **Herzog** (p. 334), an epicurean and wine lovers' heaven with top European chefs, and stay in the heart of the Renwick wine area at **Vintners Retreat** (p. 330).

Day 8: Waipara Valley ★★★

Hire a car and drive the 4 hours south to Waipara Valley. Look out for Omihi School on your left, just north of Waipara (about 1 hr. south of Kaikoura) and turn there for **Daniel Schuster Wines** (p. 381). Danny is an internationally recognized wine consultant with boundless knowledge and one of the prettiest vineyards and tasting rooms around. Call in at **Waipara Springs Winery** (p. 382) for coffee and save yourself for lunch at award-winning **Pegasus Bay** (p. 382) just down the road. Visit other local wineries and stop by **Athena Olive Groves** (p. 381) for a different taste sensation. Drive 45 minutes south to Christchurch and catch a flight to Queenstown.

Day 9: Queenstown ★★★

Hire a car, pick up a wine map from the visitor center, and head out to **Amisfield Winery** (p. 450) overlooking Lake Hayes. Be impressed by **Peregrine** (p. 450) unique architecture and make an extended stop at **GVW Winery** (p. 450). Explore their wine tunnel, the great gift shop, and the cheesery. When you get back, hunt down the **Bunker** (p. 464) for perfectly matched wine and gourmet food.

Day 10: Cromwell & Bannockburn

Take a scenic drive through Kawarau Gorge. Near Cromwell stop at fruit stalls and the **Big Picture** (p. 441) for an excellent film, a tasting auditorium, a selection of wines and gourmet foods, and a cafe. Set your sights on **Felton Road,** the **Mt. Difficulty Wines cafe,** and **Olssen's Garden Vineyard.** If you'd rather take a tour of this area, contact **Queenstown Wine Trail** or **Appellation Central Wine Tours** (p. 450). Try the degustation menu at the **Rees True South** (p. 463) for dinner if you have time, or catch a late flight to Christchurch to meet your international connection.

6 TEN ACTION-PACKED DAYS IN THE SOUTH ISLAND

The title of this itinerary assumes you're a fun-loving, adventure-seeking, fear-proof adrenalin addict with tons of stamina. If that's the case, you might want to head straight for Queenstown and stay there. It has more crazy, pulse-quickening activities per square inch than anywhere else, and most are easily accessed without a vehicle. There's also an active hotel pickup plan at work. Make sure you check out the many money-saving combo deals available. I haven't listed late-night fun here because that's a whole other story; chapter 16 gives you the pointers you'll need to ensure your nights are as vigorous as your days.

Day ❶: Arrive in Queenstown ★★★

Spend the day regaining preflight energy with a leisurely amble around the town's adventure suppliers. Get social at **Joe's Garage** (p. 465), the preferred hangout of local adventure types, and soak up the energetic hum of hundreds of fellow international adventure seekers. Do some research at the **i-SITE Visitor Centre** (p. 444) and have a few drinks at **Tatler** (p. 464), where local bar staff will fill you in on all the best nightspots.

Day ❷: Up & About

Start with a gobsmackingly daring burst of speed through high rock canyons on the **Shotover Jet** (p. 453). Pick up your stomach and head back into town and take the **gondola** (p. 445) to the top of Bob's Peak. Pick up speed with a few **luge rides** (p. 453), scare yourself with a **bungy** (p. 452) overlooking the town, and float back down to Queenstown park via a **tandem parapente** (p. 453).

Day ❸: The Ultimate Jump

Be the ultimate daredevil and tackle the full bungy package—yes, that means all four of them! Start with 43m (140 ft.) at the "original" **Kawarau Suspension Bridge** and work your way up (and down) from there. If you've already done the **Ledge** at the top of Bob's Peak, do the **Ledge Swing** instead—or try the bungy here again at night. Forget being squeamish, and take your camera because all four bungys are located in stunning landscapes. Make sure you get the T-shirt that attests to your courage!

Day ❹: The Dart River ★★★

Imagine rivers wild and calm overhung with lush green ferns, the sound of native birdcall, and nothing else—except the excited squeals of your fellow adventurers. The Dart River deserves all the superlatives. Start with a 5-hour jet boat and a walk through unspoiled native bush with **Dart River Safaris** (p. 455). If you're short on daredevil confidence after all the bungy jumps, float the river with **Funyaks** (p. 455). A day to remember!

Day ❺: Taking to the Air

Push your budget to the limits with a helicopter ride into the mountains and have the highest altitude picnic you're ever likely to enjoy. Choppy Paterson of **Over The Top** (p. 451) knows how to impress with remote mountaintop lake settings. Calm down after that adventure by taking a leisurely afternoon cruise on the *Earnslaw* (p. 449).

Day ❻: Watersports

Fast-paced watersports are on today's agenda. Start with **Canyoning NZ** (p. 452), and find yourself slipping down river canyons in a wet suit and a helmet. **Serious Fun River Surfing** (p. 453) brings a new twist to an old sport—it's all washing-machine rapids and rapid slithering down rocky river gorges. In the afternoon, go **white-water rafting** (p. 454). There are several operators to choose from and river grades to suit your nerves, physical prowess, and stamina. The Shotover River is generally viewed as more challenging than the Kawarau.

Day ⑦: Milford Sound ★★★

Your toughest choice will be "fixed wing" or helicopter. Whichever you choose, be prepared to be impressed by jagged mountain peaks, lush green bush, unbelievably blue lakes, golden tussock, and azure blue skies. If a **Milford boat cruise** (p. 476) is not energetic enough for you, team up with **Rosco's Milford Sound Sea Kayaks** (p. 476) for a surreal paddling adventure. Take your camera and stay overnight at **Milford Sound Lodge** (p. 477).

Day ⑧: Milford Track ★★★

Join a 1-day guided walk on **Milford Track** (p. 472) with **Trips 'n' Tramps** (p. 476)—just 12 people getting a taste of this world-famous mountain route. Enjoy total silence, majestic mountain landscapes, remote passes, a wilderness tea break, photography stops, waterfalls, and rainforest glades. This may be the quietest

of your adventures, but it may be the *pièce de résistance.*

Day ⑨: Back to Queenstown

Before you fly out of Milford, visit the **Underwater Observatory** (p. 476) for a unique glimpse of rare underwater life forms. Return to Queenstown by helicopter or plane (the 5- to 6-hr. bus trip is dead time) and spend the afternoon doing a mountain bike tour with **Gravity Action** (p. 452), which will give you an up-close and personal look at the landscapes you've just flown over.

Day ⑩: Back to Christchurch

Rise before dawn and join **Sunrise Balloons** (p. 453) for a last magical overview of this splendid place where mountains and lakes rise out of the early morning mists. It's the perfect memory to take away before you fly home.

7 TEN DAYS IN THE SUBTROPICAL NORTH

It always astounds me that so many overseas visitors arrive in Auckland and immediately drive or fly south—or that they avoid the North Island altogether in favor of the south. Sure, the South Island landscapes are more dramatic, but the top of the North, especially in summer, is a quintessential Kiwi experience: white-sand beaches, warm oceans, endless days of swimming and sunbathing, barbecues at the beach, campfires, parties, boats, surf, and sun. I've mapped out 10 days that include three of Auckland's nearby islands to give you a feel for the more laid-back side of New Zealand life. Waiheke Island is the most populated and the most popular and heaven for wine drinkers, while the much less-visited Great Barrier Island (many New Zealanders have never even been there) is an unspoiled treasure that operates on its own clock.

Day ❶: Arrive in Auckland ★★★

Rest for a while before heading off to **Viaduct Basin** (p. 143), which will give you an instant appreciation of New Zealanders' obsessions with boats. Sit in one of the stylish cafes and restaurants, and watch the boats come and go. Visit the **New Zealand National Maritime Museum** (p. 144) for an insight into what the ocean really

means to northerners. In the afternoon, take the **Explorer Bus** (p. 120) to **Auckland Museum** (p. 140), where you can admire the views and the grassy green swathe of the **Botanic Gardens** (p. 148). Drive around to **Mission Bay's seaside promenade** (p. 119) and have a picnic dinner as you watch people swim at sunset.

Day ❷: Taking to the Water

Have a rare sailing experience on America's Cup yacht, *NZL 40* (p. 144), or join **Fullers Auckland** (p. 151) for an invigorating cruise of Waitemata Harbour. It's all sea spray, sunshine, and flapping sails out there, plus you'll have great views of the city skyline. Enjoy lunch wharf-side and then go up the **Sky Tower** (p. 141) for the best views in New Zealand.

Day ❸: Waiheke Island ★★★

Rise early and take the ferry to **Waiheke Island** (p. 160). Save time and go straight into a guided tour of the island, or hire a car and drive around the beaches, wineries, and pretty, unpopulated bays. There's something intangible at work here and you'll quickly be seduced into the relaxed pace of island life. Have lunch at **Te Whau Vineyard** (p. 164) and dinner at **Mudbrick Vineyard** (p. 164), or eat fish and chips on **Onetangi Bay** (p. 162) after a late-afternoon swim.

Day ❹: Matakana & Kawau Island

Head back to Auckland and then drive north to Warkworth and the **Matakana/Sandspit** (p. 166) area. Catch a water taxi across to **Kawau Island** (p. 166) for a fun day out. New Zealand's early governor, Sir George Grey, built the historic Mansion House on the island; you'll find unexpected Australian "natives" here—eucalyptus trees, wallabies, kookaburras, and rosella parrots.

Day ❺: The Bay of Islands ★★★

Back on the mainland, drive north to **Paihia** (p. 175). Base yourself here if you want to try all the attractions, or go to **Russell** (p. 177) if you're after a peaceful retreat. Visit **Waitangi Treaty Grounds** (p. 176) for a dose of Maori culture and some lovely boardwalks through native bush and mangrove swamps. Wander through the cool, green leafy grounds to find **Waikokopu Café** (p. 187) and the

massive Maori *waka* (canoe) on display by the beach. Sit on the beach and enjoy the sun.

Day ❻: Kerikeri

This is our northern fruit capital. Enjoy citrus, persimmons, kiwifruit, and macadamia nuts. Stop at **Makana Confections** (p. 178) for mouthwatering chocolates and at **Kerikeri Bakehouse** (p. 187) for picture-perfect picnic food. Take your bounty down to the **Kerikeri Basin** and eat by the river before exploring the local sights. Spend the afternoon at **Marsden Estate Winery** (p. 187) or drive to a local beach and swim until the sun goes down.

Day ❼: Drive to Auckland

Drive back to Auckland Airport and catch a plane to **Great Barrier Island** (p. 168). It's a 35-minute flight in a small plane, so don't go taking everything but the kitchen sink. Your fellow passengers are likely to be dogs, surfers with their boards, and other eccentric sorts who have made this charming island home. The flight is a worthwhile experience in its own right. Fly in over the beach and drop down onto the grass runway. Grab a hire car and make your way to **Earthsong Lodge** (p. 170) on the sandhills of Medlands Beach.

Day ❽: The North of the Island

Drive north to **Glenfern Sanctuary** (p. 169) and take Tony Bouzaid's guided walk through native bush. Watch for dolphins leaping about in the deep green waters of Fitzroy Harbour. Drive farther north along unpaved roads to **Whangapoua Beach** (p. 170) and don't be surprised if you're the only person there. It's a surreal experience to feel like the last person left on earth as you stand on this perfect horseshoe of pristine white sand. Walk along the beach to the **S.S.** *Wairarapa* (p. 170) shipwreck graves.

Day ❾: Tryphena & Okupu

Spend the morning at **Tryphena** (p. 169). Take a kayak trip and watch for the friendly dolphins that swim here. Drive back to **Claris** (p. 169) for lunch at **Claris Texas Café** (p. 170) and ask about the historic pigeon post at the postal agency next door. Follow the road over to Okupu, calling at **Christine Young's unique little museum** (p. 170). Drop down to the beach, park your car, and walk to the south end of Okupu Beach to meet with the little track that takes you around the headland and into Blind Bay.

Day ❿: Fly Back to Auckland

You'll have fallen in love with "the Barrier" by now, so have a lazy morning on the beach, go for a swim, watch the surfers, or take a boat ride with Richard Lintott to see the **gannet colony** (p. 266). Fly back to **Auckland** in the late afternoon to connect with your flight.

The Active Vacation Planner

From the northernmost tip to the last speck of land in the south, New Zealanders have found ways to tackle the great outdoors, and their enthusiasm for the whole adventure game has drawn millions of curious people to see just what it's all about.

Regardless of your fitness level, you'll find something to suit you. You can do almost anything in New Zealand—rock climbing, caving, horse trekking, paragliding, and much more. Following are details on the major activities, such as tramping, skiing, and biking; look to the regional chapters for additional information.

The **Tourism New Zealand** website (www.newzealand.com) will key you into wilderness and big thrills. Ask for the excellent *Naturally New Zealand Holidays* guide at an New Zealand Tourism Board office near you or from **Naturally New Zealand Holidays** (© 03/318-7540; fax 03/318-7590; www.nzholidays.co.nz).

1 TRAMPING

Tramping (also known as hiking) is one of the best ways to explore the pristine forests, clear blue lakes, sparkling rivers, fern-filled valleys, and snowcapped peaks of New Zealand. The **Department of Conservation (DOC),** P.O. Box 10-420, Wellington (© 04/471-0726; fax 04/471-1082; www.doc.govt.nz), maintains more than 12,500km (about 7,700 miles) of tracks (trails) and 1,000 backcountry huts throughout New Zealand's 13 national parks and numerous scenic reserves.

A series of short walks or one big multiday hike? Both are available, but much will depend on your fitness level and the amount of time you have. Consider whether you want to be a **freedom walker** (independent) or a **guided walker.** Independent walkers can sleep in huts with bunk beds, cooking facilities, and toilets, but they must carry their own food, bedding, and cooking utensils. These overnight huts are sometimes staffed, should you need any assistance or advice along the way.

Tramping in New Zealand is best tackled from late November to April, when temperatures are the most moderate. From May to October, alpine tracks can be difficult and often dangerous once snow falls. (See the weather and temperature information in chapter 3 before planning a hiking vacation.) Don't forget to bring broken-in boots, a day pack, water bottles, sunglasses, sunscreen, a flashlight (known as a "torch" in New Zealand), and a hat. *Remember:* You should never attempt any multiday hikes without first checking in, paying your fees, and giving DOC staff an idea of your plans; and always be aware of changeable weather conditions and the very real potential for hypothermia—even in summer. **The importance of this cannot be underestimated.** Every tourist season dozens of people ignore this sound advice and a good number end up being rescued by emergency services. Be warned that in some circumstances you will now have pay for the rescue services and that is never a cheap exercise. For more information see "Safety in the Great Outdoors," on p. 90.

SHORT WALKS   There are literally hundreds of fabulous short walks through all sorts of landscapes. From a leisurely stroll along a city promenade to deserted beaches, fern-lined bush walks, forest trails, volcanic wanders—you name it, and you can probably have it. Every region has its hidden treats. Look in the regional chapters that follow for some of the most popular choices and seek advice from any visitor center or Department of Conservation office, most of which have an extensive array of walking brochures.

Short walks tend to range from 45 minutes to a full day. Depending on your interests, don't forget to bring along binoculars, a camera, and a sketch pad or journal. If you're in doubt about the difficulty of a trail, always ask the visitor center staff, or be prepared to turn back if the going gets too tough. Hiking trails in New Zealand are generally very well maintained.

HIKING SAFARIS   Many companies offer combinations of hiking, kayaking, and other adventures in one or more areas. The **New Zealand Guided Walks Network** (www.walknewzealand.com) was set up in conjunction with Tourism New Zealand to raise the profile of high-quality guided walking experiences available in New Zealand. The Walks Network is a group of independent companies that operate guided walks in our national parks, wilderness areas, and special reserves, providing the best available accommodations with meals, comfortable bedding, and bathroom facilities. Qualified guides provide comprehensive interpretation of natural and cultural history; walkers need only carry personal items—not including food or bedding.

Hiking New Zealand ★★, in Christchurch (✆ **03/384-3706;** fax 03/376-6483; www.hikingnewzealand.com) offers small group hiking/camping tours of 3 to 10 days throughout the national parks. **Bush and Beyond** (✆/fax **03/528-9054;** www.bushandbeyond.co.nz) offers guided 1- to 8-day tramps in Kahurangi National Park; you can also add in photography and wildlife excursions. **Kahurangi Guided Walks** (✆ **03/525-7177;** www.kahurangiwalks.co.nz), also operates in this area, offering year-round small-group guided walks in the Abel Tasman and Kahurangi national parks. **New Zealand Wild Walks** (✆ **03/443-9422;** www.wildwalks.co.nz) offers remote treks for fit, adventurous travelers in the backcountry of Mount Aspiring National Park. Small guided groups of five people maximum tackle everything from picturesque beech forests and isolated valleys to alpine meadows and glacier trekking. **Canterbury Trails,** in Christchurch (✆ **03/337-1185;** fax 03/337-5085; www.canterburytrails.co.nz), offers easy to moderate 9-day Wilderness South Expeditions via minivan, which include guided walks and heritage and ecology experiences. It also offers 14-day Natural North'South New Zealand tours in conjunction with Kiwi Dundee Adventures in the Coromandel (see chapter 7). And in the far south, **Kiwi Wilderness Walks** (✆ **021/359-592;** fax 03/442-8342; www.nzwalk.com) offers 3- to 5-day tramping, kayaking, and wildlife experiences in remote areas of Stewart Island, the Waitutu Track, and Dusky Sound. **Tuatara Tours** ★★ (✆ **0800/377-378** in NZ, or 03/962-3280; www.tuataratours.co.nz), specializes in fully guided outdoor walking adventures aimed at people with an average-to-excellent level of fitness. They offer 4- to 14-day guided walks (and cycling tours) throughout the South Island, with well-informed guides and a very comfortable level of accommodations. More excellent "moderate" hikes in the North Island are offered by **Walking Legends** (✆ **07/345-7363;** www.walkinglegends.com), which has 3- to 6-day packages around Lake Waikaremoana and in the remote regions of Te Urewera National Park.

Safety in the Great Outdoors

You won't find snakes and predatory animals here (at least not the four-legged kind), but anyone venturing out into wilderness areas ought to be prepared with a few common-sense safety hints.

- **Emergencies:** For emergencies anywhere in the country, dial ☎ **111.**
- **Getting lost:** Trampers must register their intended route and estimated time and date of return with the Department of Conservation (DOC) office closest to where they plan to trek. This is vitally important because, if no one knows you're out there, they're not going to start looking for you if you get lost or injured. Likewise, let DOC know as soon as you're finished so search parties are not set into action—and be aware that you can now be billed hundreds of thousands of dollars for an unnecessary search brought about by your actions and lack of consideration. Be very careful—if you hike alone and get lost or injure yourself, you are much more likely to become a statistic.
- **Weather:** Although New Zealand has a mild climate, the weather can change rapidly at any time of year, especially in the high country. *Always* tell people where you are going and when you are due back, and always go prepared with the right all-weather gear (at all times of the year), a sensible survival kit, and a good topographical map *that you can read!*
- **Hypothermia:** Hypothermia can kill—even in summer, and its signs and symptoms should never be ignored. Watch for early warning signs: feeling cold, shivering, tiredness or exhaustion, anxiety, lethargy, lack of interest, clumsiness, slurred speech, difficulty seeing, a sense of unreality, and irrational behavior. The later signs indicating a serious medical emergency are obvious distress, the cessation of shivering despite the cold, collapse and unconsciousness, and coma. The progress of hypothermia can be very fast, with as little as 30 minutes from the first symptoms to unconsciousness. It is imperative that you stop and find shelter, prevent further heat loss, assist

MULTIDAY WALKS   New Zealand has some of the best multiday walks in the world. The trails are well maintained and take you through unforgettable scenery. Several can also be done as guided walks, which makes them accessible to people of all fitness levels.

Not everyone can agree on which one is the *best* walk, but the Department of Conservation has identified these tramping tracks as the "Great Walks" in New Zealand: the **Waikaremoana,** the **Tongariro Crossing,** and the **Ruapehu Circuit** on the North Island; the **Abel Tasman Coastal Track** and the **Heaphy, Routeburn, Milford,** and **Kepler tracks** on the South Island; and the **Rakiura Track** on Stewart Island.

If you'd like to strike out on your own, contact the **Department of Conservation,** P.O. Box 10-420, Wellington (☎ **04/471-0726;** fax 04/471-1082; www.doc.govt.nz). It maintains visitor centers throughout the country. Freedom walkers (independent hikers) need to get hut passes or tickets and register their hiking plans (known as "intentions") before setting out. The Milford and the Routeburn are generally the only two tracks

in rewarming, get the victim into dry clothes, and seek help as quickly as possible.

Hypothermia is caused by cold, wind, wet clothing, lack of food, fatigue, injury and anxiety, and recent illness, especially the flu. Everyone is at risk, even the fit and healthy. It is always best to have four or more people in your party so one can stay with the victim and two can go for help.

- **Avalanches:** Skiers and snowboarders often start the avalanche that catches them. Most avalanches occur during and immediately after storms, and they are common on slopes steeper than 20 degrees.
- **Sun:** New Zealand's clear, unpolluted atmosphere produces strong sunlight and high ultraviolet levels. Wear brimmed hats, sunglasses, and lots of SPF 15+ sunscreen if you plan to be outdoors for longer than 15 minutes.
- **River levels:** Plan your trip around the use of bridges. Avoid river crossings and be aware of rising water levels during heavy rain.
- *Giardia:* In the bush, you should boil, filter, or chemically treat all water from lakes and rivers to avoid contracting this waterborne parasite, which causes diarrhea.
- **Sand flies:** Small in size, but big in nuisance value, sand flies are found in wet bush areas around rivers, lakes, and streams. They can be effectively controlled with regular use of strong insect repellents. If you get bitten, topical application of hydrocortisone ointment or tea-tree lotion should ease itching.
- **Safety brochures:** All of the above issues are dealt with in detail in a range of excellent free brochures produced by the **New Zealand Mountain Safety Council,** P.O. Box 6027, Te Aro, Wellington (*© **04/385-7162;** fax 04/385-7366; www.mountainsafety.org.nz), and are available at visitor information and DOC centers.

where freedom walkers need to make advance reservations. Facilities along other trails are on a first-come, first-served basis. The DOC advises against children 9 and under attempting any of the serious multiday hikes.

See the individual walks below for information on **guided walks.** Outfitters will arrange a guide, accommodations, meals, and the carrying of all gear except day packs, which individual walkers carry themselves.

NEW ZEALAND'S BEST TRAMPS
Marlborough, Nelson & Beyond
See the map "Marlborough, Nelson & Beyond," on p. 326, for the tramps in this area.

QUEEN CHARLOTTE WALKWAY This 71km (44-mile) track passes through lush coastal forest, around coves and inlets, and along ridges offering spectacular views of the Queen Charlotte and Kenepuru sounds. (Boating is also popular here.) Stretching from historic Ship Cove to Anakiwa, the track can be walked in 3 to 5 days, and if you want a richer experience, you can add kayaking, mountain biking, diving, fishing, and bird-watching along the way. If you take a guided walk, you'll stay in cabins, rustic lodges, and homestays, and your pack will be carried by boat, meeting you at each overnight stop. If you'd rather not complete the whole 5-day venture, you can take a guided 1-day walk. Access to Ship Cove is by boat or floatplane, and you can start or finish the walk at any point.

Duration/Distance: 5 days/71km (44 miles)

Start: Ship Cove, Marlborough Sounds

End: Anakiwa, Marlborough Sounds

Open: Year-round; guided walks conducted November through May only

Contact Information: For an independent walk, contact the **Department of Conservation,** Picton Field Centre, Picton (✆ **03/575-7582;** fax 03/573-8262; www.qctrack.co.nz). Camping costs NZ$10 per night; lodging is available at various price levels. All adult unguided track visitors will also be asked to contribute NZ$5 to the Queen Charlotte Track Tribute Fund, a trust fund established to maintain the track as a place of rare beauty. QCT Tribute tickets can be purchased from the dedicated machine located at Picton Town Wharf prior to your departure, or paid to the water transport operator you use. *Note:* there are no rubbish facilities on the walk, so you must take out everything you take in. Transfers are available with the **Cougar Line** (✆ **0800/504-090** in NZ; fax 03/573-7926; www.queencharlottetrack.co.nz), which will drop you off, transfer your pack, and pick you up. Similar services are offered by **Endeavour Express** (✆ **03/573-5456;** fax 03/573-5434; www.boatrides.co.nz).

You can arrange a guided walk with the **Marlborough Sounds Adventure Company** (✆ **0800/283-283** in NZ, or 03/573-6078; fax 03/573-8827; www.marlboroughsounds.co.nz). Its 3- to 5-day walks include boat transfers, a guide, meals, hot showers, and accommodations in three lodges for around NZ$1,500. The Ultimate Sounds Adventure (3 days/2 nights) starts at NZ$525 with bunkroom accommodations, or NZ$765 twin-share en suite. It features 1 day of walking, 1 day sea kayaking, and 1 day of mountain biking. **Wilderness Guides Marlborough Sounds** (✆ **0800/266-266** in NZ, or 03/520-3095; fax 03/520-3096; www.wildernessguidesnz.com) organizes 1- to 5-day guided or independent walks including luggage transfers and hotel-style accommodations.

ABEL TASMAN COASTAL TRACK   Because of the enormous popularity of this stunning walkway through coastal forest and gorgeous beaches, the Department of Conservation has introduced a booking system for overnight huts that is in effect from October through April each year. The four huts have bunks, heat, and water, but no cooking facilities. Access to Marahau, where you begin, is by road or boat. Water taxis make it convenient to do just 1 day of the walk if your time is short. Buses pick you up at the end of the trail.

Duration/Distance: 3 to 5 days/52km (32 miles)

Start: Marahau, Abel Tasman National Park

End: Wainui Bay, Abel Tasman National Park

Open: Year-round; guided walks available year-round

Contact Information: Independent walkers can contact the **Department of Conservation,** King Edward and High streets, P.O. Box 97, Motueka (✆ **03/528-1810;** fax 03/528-1811). Hut fees are NZ$30 to NZ$35 per night; camp fees are NZ$12 to NZ$15 per person per night; transport is extra.

For guided walks, contact **Abel Tasman Wilson's Experiences** (☎ **03/528-2027;** fax 03/528-2029; www.abeltasman.co.nz). Its 5-day kayak-and-walk package costs NZ$1,820 for adults only. They also have a 3-day guided walk for NZ$1,200 for adults and NZ$985 for children ages 8 to 14. **Kahurangi Guided Walks** (☎ **03/525-7177;** www.kahurangiwalks.co.nz), has 1-, 2-, and 3-day walks in the Abel Tasman and customizes trips to meet customer needs.

HEAPHY TRACK   This track is known for its beauty and diversity. It crosses a range of landscapes, from the junction of the Brown and Aorere rivers over expansive tussock downs to the lush forests and roaring sea of the West Coast. The seven huts on the track have bunks, heat, water, and cooking facilities (except at two huts), and although you need a hut and camp pass, this does not guarantee a bunk. There are accommodations and transport at each end of the track, but be sure to arrange this before setting out. For transport to the beginning of Heaphy Track, contact **KBus Services** (☎ **0508/458-835** in NZ, or 03/358-8355; fax 03/358-8585; www.kbus.co.nz). They offer scheduled service between Nelson, Abel Tasman National Park, Golden Bay, and Heaphy Track for approximately NZ$30. If you're planning to travel to Westport or return to Nelson at the end of the track, make your transport reservations before you leave through the **Golden Bay Visitor Information Centre,** Willow Street, Takaka (☎ **03/525-9136;** gb.vin@ nelsonnz.com).

Duration/Distance: 4 to 6 days/77km (48 miles)
Start: Brown Hut, Kahurangi National Park
End: Kohaihai River Mouth, north of Karamea, Kahurangi National Park
Open: Year-round; guided walks available year-round
Contact Information: For an independent walk, contact the **Department of Conservation,** 1 Commercial St., P.O. Box 53, Takaka (☎ **03/525-8026**). Hut fees are NZ$25 per night; camping fees are NZ$15 per night; transport is extra.

For guided walks, call **Kahurangi Guided Walks** (☎/fax **03/525-7177;** www. kahurangiwalks.co.nz); **Bush and Beyond** (☎/fax **03/528-9054;** www.naturetreks.co. nz); or **Southern Wilderness NZ** (☎ **03/520-3095;** fax 03/520-3096; www.southern wilderness.com).

Canterbury

KAIKOURA COAST TRACK   This popular, dramatic coastal walk takes you through the best of New Zealand's high-country farming territory, with cottage accommodations at three farms along the way. You'll need a reasonable degree of fitness, as the track climbs from the sea to a height of 600m (1,970 ft.), with wonderful views over the Kaikoura Mountains. The track is also suitable for mountain biking. It's located a 1½-hour drive north of Christchurch and 45 minutes south of Kaikoura.

Duration/Distance: 3 days/43km (27 miles)
Start & End: "Hawkswood" historic sheep station, Kaikoura
Open: October through April
Contact Information: Contact Sally and David Handyside (☎ **03/319-2715;** fax 03/319-2724; www.kaikouratrack.co.nz). The track costs NZ$185 per person; groups are limited to 10 people. A 2-day mountain-bike option is available for NZ$85 per person. Public transport is available in the form of shuttle buses and the InterCity coach service, both of which run between Christchurch, Kaikoura, and Blenheim. Shuttles leave from the Christchurch visitor center, which can provide details on the service. The cost of a shuttle to the track beginning at the Staging Post (on St. Hwy. 1) is NZ$45.

BANKS PENINSULA TRACK This private Canterbury track crosses farmland, Hinewai Reserve, and volcanic coastline. You'll experience sandy beaches, safe swimming, waterfalls, cliff faces, beech forest, penguins, seals, dolphins, and rich bird life. The track twice rises to over 600m (1,970 ft.) and features rugged exposed headlands, requiring a reasonable level of fitness. Children must be accompanied at all times. Accommodations are supplied in four farm cottages, two of which have a small shop for purchasing basics.
Duration/Distance: 4 days/35km (22 miles)
Start & End: Akaroa Village, 80km (50 miles) from Christchurch
Open: October 1 to April 30
Contact Information: Call **Banks Peninsula Track Ltd.** (© **03/304-7612;** fax 03/304-7738; www.bankstrack.co.nz). The 4-day tramp costs NZ$230 per person; the 2-day tramps costs NZ$150.

Queenstown & Fiordland

Independent walkers must have a reservation for walking the Milford and Routeburn tracks discussed below. Contact the **Department of Conservation,** Great Walks Booking Desk, Fiordland National Park Visitor Centre, P.O. Box 29, Te Anau (© **03/249-8514** or fax 03/249-8515 outside NZ; 03/249-7924 or fax 03/249-7613 inside NZ; www.doc. govt.nz). The number of people allowed on the tracks is limited and the demand great, especially from mid-December through January, so reserve as early as possible—6 months ahead is sometimes necessary. Remember those safety rules and warnings about hypothermia (see "Safety in the Great Outdoors," above)—they hold particularly true here. In this region, unpredictable weather can occur at any time, in any season, and you should always carry appropriate clothing for the worst weather conditions.

ROUTEBURN TRACK ★ The Routeburn is a moderate track that links Mount Aspiring and Fiordland national parks via the Harris Saddle. In summer, it is one of the most popular tracks, but in winter, it's extremely hazardous and impassable with high avalanche danger. It takes you into the heart of unspoiled forests, along river valleys, and across mountain passes, and requires a good level of fitness. Bus transfers are available to the start of the track and from the finish for about NZ$105 one-way from Queenstown; the DOC can furnish you with a list of all transport options. Remember that the Routeburn is not a circuit track and there are over 350km (220 miles) of road transport required between both ends of the track. Transport may cost you up to NZ$200 if you need to return to your starting point.
Duration/Distance: 2 to 3 days/39km (24 miles)
Start & End: The Routeburn Shelter, 75km (47 miles) from Queenstown via Glenorchy, or the Divide Shelter, 80km (50 miles) from Te Anau on the Milford Road. The Routeburn can be walked in either direction.
Open: Late October to mid-April
Contact Information: For independent walks, contact the **Department of Conservation,** Great Walks Booking Desk, Fiordland National Park Visitor Centre, P.O. Box 29, Te Anau (© **03/249-8514;** fax 03/249-8515; greatwalksbooking@doc.govt.nz). Hut fees are NZ$45 per night, camping fees NZ$15 per night. Transport costs are extra; advance track reservations are required.

For guided walks, call **Ultimate Hikes** (© **0800/659-255** in NZ, or 03/450-1940; www.ultimatehikes.co.nz). It offers the 3-day guided Routeburn Walk package that begins in Queenstown. A coach will take you to "The Divide" (on Milford Rd.); you'll walk to Lake McKenzie, across the Harris Saddle, and past the Routeburn Falls. A coach will return you to Queenstown. Comfortable lodges are provided. The cost is from NZ$1,100 for adults and NZ$900 for children ages 10 to 15. Rates include transport, meals, and accommodations. Tours depart regularly from November through April, but you should reserve as far in advance as possible. Richard Bryant of **Guided Walks New Zealand** (✆ **03/442-7126;** fax 03/442-7128; www.nzwalks.com) also offers a 1-day option on the Routeburn.

For a 6-day excursion, called the **Grand Traverse,** combine the Routeburn and Greenstone Valley (see below) tracks. With Ultimate Hikes, this will cost from NZ$1,625 for adults, NZ$1,425 for children ages 10 to 15 (no children 9 and under permitted), and includes transport, meals, and accommodations.

GREENSTONE VALLEY TRACK   This walk follows an ancient Maori trail used by tribes to access the rich greenstone lodes near Lake Wakatipu. The trail you'll walk, however, was cut in the late 1800s by Europeans, who created a route between Lake Wakatipu and Martins Bay on the Fiordland coast. You'll pass Lake Howden and Lake McKellar, and follow the Greenstone River through deep gorges and open valley to Lake Wakatipu. Boat transfers are available to and from Elfin Bay. The Greenstone track can be walked in either direction, or can be linked to the Routeburn or Caples tracks for a 4- to 5-day round-trip (see "The Grand Traverse," below).
Duration/Distance: 2 days/40km (25 miles)
Start & End: Elfin Bay, Lake Wakatipu, 86km (53 miles) from Queenstown via Glenorchy
Alternative Start & End: Lake Howden near the Divide Shelter, 80km (50 miles) from Te Anau on the Milford Road
Open: November through April
Contact Information: For independent walks, contact the **Department of Conservation,** Fiordland National Park Visitor Centre, Lakefront Drive, P.O. Box 29, Te Anau (✆ **03/249-7924;** fax 03/249-7613). The hut fee is NZ$30 per night, plus transport.

For guided walks, call **Ultimate Hikes** (✆ **0800/659-255** in NZ, or 03/450-1940; www.ultimatehikes.co.nz), which provides accommodations and knowledgeable guides.

THE GRAND TRAVERSE   This is a 6-day excursion that follows the Routeburn Track northbound for 3 days and then crosses into the Greenstone Valley Track for 3 days; available between November and April. The guided walk costs NZ$1,625 for adults and NZ$1,425 for children ages 10 to 15. Make arrangements through **Ultimate Hikes** (✆ **0800/659-255** in NZ, or 03/450-1940; fax 03/450-1941; www.ultimatehikes.co.nz).

HOLLYFORD TRACK   This relatively flat track follows the Hollyford River out to the coast at Martins Bay. You can walk it as a round-trip or as a one-way with a fly-out from Martins Bay. You can also jet-boat the Demon Trail section of the track. Because there are no alpine crossings, this is one of the few Fiordland tracks that can be done year-round.
Duration/Distance: 4 days/56km (35 miles) one-way
Start: Hollyford Camp, 9km (5½ miles) off Milford Road
End: Martins Bay (walk back or fly out)
Open: Year-round; guided walks available October through April only
Contact Information: For independent walks, contact the **Department of Conservation,** Fiordland National Park Visitor Centre, P.O. Box 29, Te Anau (✆ **03/249-7924;** fax 03/249-7613). There is a hut fee of NZ$25 per night. The jet-boat, flight out, and bus transportation are extra.

For guided walks, contact **Hollyford Valley Guided Walk** (𝒞 **0800/832-226** in NZ, or 03/442-7789; fax 03/442-7781; www.hollyfordtrack.co.nz). It offers stays in a comfortable lodge with hot showers. The 3- to 4-day package costs from NZ$1,655 including pretour accommodations in Te Anau.

KEPLER TRACK This 4-day tramp starts and ends at the Lake Te Anau outlet control gates. You'll pass through beech forests and a U-shaped glacial valley, and walk along the edges of Lakes Te Anau and Manapouri. This is a challenging hike with a lot of altitude variations. The track zigzags up 800m (2,600 ft.) and drops 1,000m (3,300 ft.)—the single most useful thing you can take is a walking pole. Access is provided by shuttle bus and boat transfer.

Duration/Distance: 3 to 4 days/67km (42 miles)
Start & End: Te Anau Control Gates
Open: Late October to mid-April
Contact Information: For independent walks, contact the **Department of Conservation,** Fiordland National Park Visitor Centre, P.O. Box 29, Te Anau (𝒞 **03/249-7924;** fax 03/249-7613). Hut fees are NZ$45 per night; the night camping fee is NZ$15. Transport is extra. Early bookings are essential.

MILFORD TRACK ★ Many consider the famous Milford Track the finest anywhere in the world. Known for its glacially carved valleys, alpine flowers, and waterfalls, the 4-day walk is closely regulated by DOC staff, both for the safety of hikers and for the preservation of the wilderness region. You'll walk from Glade Jetty at Lake Te Anau's northern end to Sandfly Point on the western bank of Milford Sound. The track follows the Clinton and Arthur valleys and crosses MacKinnon Pass, the one steep and more difficult stretch that takes about 2 hours to ascend. From here, at 1,073m (3,519 ft.), it's all downhill to Sandfly Point, where you'll be ferried across Milford Sound. You can spend the night at Milford or return to Te Anau, but reservations must be made for either option.

Duration/Distance: 4 days/54km (33 miles)
Start: Lake Te Anau (Te Anau Downs)
End: Sandfly Point near Milford Sound
Open: Late October to mid-April
Contact Information: For independent walks, contact the **Department of Conservation,** Great Walks Booking Desk, Fiordland National Park Visitor Centre, P.O. Box 29, Te Anau (𝒞 **03/249-8514;** fax 03/249-8515; greatwalksbooking@doc.govt.nz). Reservations are accepted from early November to mid-April for the following tramping season, which runs from mid-October to mid-April. No more than 24 people can start the walk on any given day. The cost is NZ$250, which includes huts and transportation. The peak season hut fee alone is NZ$135 adults and NZ$75 for children 10 and over.

Milford Track Guided Walk (𝒞 **0800/659-255** in NZ, or 03/450-1940; fax 03/450-1941; www.milfordtrack.co.nz) provides coach transport to Te Anau via Queenstown and allows walkers greater flexibility in making international flight connections. Prices include guides, meals at overnight lodges, and accommodations at each end of the trek. Walkers carry their own day packs. From December to March 13, fees for a 6-day package (beginning and ending in Te Anau) run from NZ$1,900 for adults and NZ$1,700 for children ages 10 to 15. In November and from March 14 to April 4 (dates vary slightly each year), the package costs slightly less.

The highly rated **Trips 'n' Tramps** (© **03/249-7081;** fax 03/249-7089; www.milford tourswalks.co.nz) offers a 1-day option, with one guide for a maximum of 12 people. The package includes a scenic Lake Te Anau cruise, up to 5 hours on the Milford Track, easy walking (no hills), and a lunch stop (bring your own) at Clinton Hut. The cost is NZ$165; it's available November through March.

Stewart Island

This is New Zealand's third-biggest island and a veritable nature paradise overlooked by most of the world—including the rest of New Zealand. But it is a spot for some astounding multiday treks and hundreds of delightful short walks. For information on the island, see chapter 17.

RAKIURA TRACK This is one of New Zealand's Great Walks and is suitable for anyone of moderate fitness. It takes trampers through bush and along beaches and open coast, and much of it is boardwalked. There are two huts and three designated campsites.
Duration/Distance: 3 days/36km (22 miles)
Start & End: Half Moon Bay, Oban
Open: Year-round
Contact Information: For independent walks, contact the **Department of Conservation,** P.O. Box 3, Stewart Island (© **03/219-0002;** fax 03/219-0003; stewartislandfc@ doc.govt.nz). You must purchase a date-stamped Great Walks Pass or campsite pass (NZ$15 per-night hut fee) before taking this walk. Conservation staff may be on the track, and they will impose a surcharge on trampers using accommodations facilities without a pass, which must be displayed on packs at all times. Nightly campsite fees are NZ$15 per adult, NZ$5 per student.

NORTH WEST CIRCUIT ★ This track is designed for well-equipped, experienced trampers who will take 10 to 12 days working their way around the island's northwest arm. Nature is at its best in clean beaches, birds, and bush, but mud is widespread and often knee-deep on the track. You'll get great views and complete solitude.
Duration/Distance: 8 to 12 days/125km (78 miles)
Start & End: Half Moon Bay, Oban
Open: Year-round
Contact Information: For independent walks, contact the **Department of Conservation,** P.O. Box 3, Stewart Island (© **03/219-0002;** fax 03/219-0003; stewartislandfc@ doc.govt.nz). The North West Circuit Pass costs NZ$50. A Great Walks Pass (NZ$15 per night) is required for Port William and North Arm huts, which are part of the Rakiura Track. This also applies to campgrounds at Port William, Maori Beach, and Sawdust Bay. All other huts require hut tickets. A NZ$99 Backcountry Pass may be used on the North West Circuit or Southern Circuit tracks. Huts are equipped with running water, mattresses, toilets, and wood-fired stoves. Before undertaking this walk, it might be a good idea to watch the excellent video of the track at the Department of Conservation office in Oban village, Half Moon Bay.

Kiwi Wilderness Walks, 90 Fitzpatrick Rd., Queenstown (© **0800/733-549** in NZ, or 021/359-592; fax 03/442-8342; www.nzwalk.com), offers a 5-day tour in Stewart Island National Park, which includes kiwi spotting at Mason Bay, a visit to Ulva Island, and sea kayaking in Paterson Inlet for NZ$1,695 adults. This walk is not recommended for children 9 and under.

2 FISHING

Any prospective fisherman in New Zealand should get a copy of *Sports Fishing Guide,* a free booklet produced by the **New Zealand Fish and Game Council** (© **04/499-4767;** fax 04/499-4768; www.fishandgame.org.nz). This guide supplies you with the myriad rules and regulations you need to know. It also gives details on major freshwater fishing spots. The **New Zealand Professional Fishing Guides Association** (© **06/867-7874;** fax 06/867-1563; www.nzpfga.com) may also be helpful. Go to www.newzealand fishing.com for *New Zealand Fishing Magazine* online. For assistance in planning a New Zealand fishing holiday from North America, contact the **Best of New Zealand Adventure Travel,** 2817 Wilshire Blvd., Santa Monica, CA 90403 (© **800/528-6129** in the U.S., or 310/998-5880; fax 310/829-9221). This agency specializes in angler activities and has a 48-page brochure called *The Best of New Zealand Fly Fishing* (which also includes information on saltwater fishing). More information can also be found at www. bestofnzflyfishing.com.

FRESHWATER FISHING

New Zealand's reputation as a trout fisherman's paradise is well established internationally. It is the world's best place to fish for wild **brown trout** during the season, which lasts from the first Saturday in October to the end of April. During this time, all rivers and streams are open for brown and **rainbow trout,** but local restrictions may apply. There are several areas where you can fish year-round: the **Rotorua District** and **Lake Taupo** on the North Island, and **Lake Te Anau, Lake Brunner,** and **Lake Wakatipu** on the South Island.

The **Tongariro River,** near Turangi, is one of the prime trout-fishing rivers in the world. May through October are the best months to snag rainbow and brown trout, which average nearly 2 kilograms (over 4 lb.)! This period is also good for fishing in Lakes Taupo and Rotorua. Lake Rotorua is not stocked, but it has one of the highest catch rates in the district.

Keeping New Zealand Waterways Clean

Sadly, Many New Zealand waterways now carry the unwanted organism *Didymosphenia geminate (Didymo),* also known as "rock snot," which is a freshwater diatom (type of alga) that was first reported on the Lower Waiau River in the South Island in 2004. Biosecurity New Zealand (www.biosecurity.govt.nz) has since declared the whole of the South Island a controlled area for *Didymo.* This means that fishermen, boat owners, and others using waterways for pleasure activities are legally required to do everything they can to prevent its spread. Unfortunately, *Didymo* is a microscopic pest that can be spread in a single drop of water. You therefore need to ensure that all watersport equipment, including boots, waders, fishing lines, boats, skis, and anything else used in the water is thoroughly clean and dry before moving from one waterway to another. As the name suggests, when *Didymo* takes over a waterway, it forms a slimy brown mass that attaches itself to everything. Please help us contain this pest by taking extreme care not to aid in its spread.

The Eastern Fish and Game region is also an angler's land of opportunity, with a huge range of fishing opportunities and diversity in both lake and river fishing. The bush-clad **lakes Waikaremoana** and **Waikareiti** provide spectacular boat and shoreline fishing for both brown and rainbow trout in untouched Te Urewera National Park.

Fishing is good in almost all areas of the South Island. In **Nelson,** you'll get rainbow trout and also quinnat salmon in many places, but it's the brown trout that's king of these mixed waters. **Canterbury** is best known for its prolific salmon runs that enter the large braided rivers such as the **Rakaia** and **Waimakariri,** and high-country rivers are known for small numbers of big fish.

In the West Coast region, **Lake Brunner** has brown trout averaging 1.1 kilograms (2½ lb.) and is the most popular angling water in the region. Farther south, the **Waitaki** and **Rangitata rivers** have been known to land trophy chinook salmon of 15 kilograms (33 lb.).

Fish and Game Otago has an excellent book, *Guide to Trout Fishing in Otago,* which covers 140 waters and gives information on access and methods. In **Southland,** dozens of rivers, streams, and lakes hold brown and rainbow trout, plus quinnat salmon. The waters of this region are widely known throughout New Zealand, but you have to be a competent fisherman and know your way around to be successful. **Southland Fish and Game,** P.O. Box 159, Invercargill (© **03/214-4501;** fishgame@southnet.co.nz), will be happy to supply maps, advice, information, and guides.

FISHING GUIDES   If fishing is your passion, consider investing some cash in a good guide. Be warned, however, that freshwater fishing guides in New Zealand are not cheap; some run as high as NZ$1,200 to NZ$1,800 per day for one or two people. If you shop around, cheaper deals can be found. I've listed a few outfitters in the regional chapters where fishing is popular.

If you'd like to organize a fishing holiday, contact **South Island Fishing Tours** (©/fax **03/755-8032;** www.flyfishingnewzealand.co.nz). Tony and Marj Allan of Kawhaka Lodge in Hokitika offer 2- to 14-day fishing tours for one to two people, starting and finishing in Christchurch. **Chris Jolly Outdoors** (© **07/378-0623;** fax 07/378-9458; www.chrisjolly.co.nz) specializes in trout fishing on Lake Taupo (among other things) and can take you to the best trout rivers that flow into the lake. In Wanaka, **Gerald Telford** (©/fax **03/443-9257;** www.flyfishhunt.co.nz) offers a number of multiday fishing excursions that start at NZ$650 per person.

SALTWATER & BIG-GAME FISHING

Deep-sea fishing is at its best along the magnificent 500km (310 miles) of Northland's coastline, slipping down into the Bay of Plenty. Waters less than an hour out from shore can yield **marlin, shark** (mako, thresher, hammerhead, tiger), five species of **tuna, broadbill,** and **yellowtail.** The season runs from mid-January to April, and you'll find well-equipped bases at the Bay of Islands in Northland, Whitianga on the Coromandel, and Tauranga and Whakatane in the Bay of Plenty. You can also fish for **kahawai, snapper,** and more anywhere along the New Zealand coast. Licenses are not required.

3 BOATING & OTHER WATERSPORTS

BOATING

Whether it's cruising a secluded bay or inlet, exploring uninhabited islands, or sailing in harbors and on lakes, New Zealanders have got boating down to a fine art. Of course,

Auckland is famous for its excessive boat tally, but you'll find this passion reflected everywhere (except perhaps on the South Island's West Coast). The Marlborough Sounds are another big boating haven, as are the Bay of Plenty and Northland. Anytime between December and April, you'll find Kiwis taking to the water in some kind of seaworthy vehicle.

CANOEING & KAYAKING   The prime kayaking spot is Abel Tasman National Park, where boats appear to float in midair because the water is so clear. Sea kayaking is also popular in the Bay of Islands, in Hauraki Gulf, around Coromandel Peninsula, in Marlborough Sounds, in Milford Sound, and around Banks Peninsula and Otago Peninsula.

Try to book your adventures with members of **SKOANZ**, the **Sea Kayak Operators Association of New Zealand** (✆ **021/735-536**; www.skoanz.org.nz), who must adhere to a code of practice covering safety, service, guides, and environment.

In Northland, you'll find reliable operators at **Coastal Kayakers,** Paihia (✆ **09/402-8105;** fax 09/403-8550; www.coastalkayakers.co.nz), which explores the outer islands with lagoons, rock caves, and sandy beaches. You can have canoe adventures with **Canoe Safaris,** Ohakune (✆ **06/385-9237;** fax 06/385-8758; www.canoesafaris.co.nz). It has 5-day expeditions in rugged Whanganui National Park from late October to mid-April.

In Abel Tasman National Park, **Ocean River Adventure Company** (✆ **0800/447-352** in NZ, or 03/527-8330; www.oceanriver.co.nz) offers guided tours of 1 to 3 days, and **Abel Tasman Kayaks** (✆ **0800/732-529** in NZ; fax 03/527-8032; www.abel tasmankayaks.co.nz) has 13 years of experience with guided trips.

JET-BOATING   For an adrenaline rush, try jet-boating—which is possible along most major rivers throughout the country. See regional chapters for more information.

SAILING   Given the running of the 1999–2000 and the 2002–03 America's Cup Challenge in Auckland, it's a bit of an understatement to say that sailing is popular. For the warmest, balmiest, most subtropical experiences, head for Northland, Auckland, and the Bay of Plenty; there's plenty of excellent sailing farther south, too.

For bareboat and skippered charters, contact **Moorings Rainbow Yacht Charters,** Bay of Islands (✆ **09/377-4840;** fax 09/377-4820; moorings@onenz.co.nz), or **Royal Akarana Yacht Club,** Auckland (✆ **09/524-9945;** fax 09/520-1380; www.rayc.org.nz), which charges from NZ$95 per hour, from NZ$450 for an 8-hour sailing day with hands-on experience for everyone. In Marlborough Sounds, try **Compass Charters,** 20 Beach Rd., Waikawa (✆ **03/573-8332;** fax 03/573-8587; www.compass-charters.co.nz), offering budget to luxury yacht and launch charters.

Pride of Auckland (✆ **09/359-5987;** www.prideofauckland.com) has four 15m (50-ft.) yachts available for daily scheduled and charter cruises for all ages and abilities (see chapter 6); and **tall ship** *Soren Larsen* (✆ **09/817-8799;** www.sorenlarsen.co.nz) is the tall ship that starred in the BBC's *The Onedin Line* television series in the late 1970s. It has a rich history and is available for day sailings and holiday cruises in New Zealand and the South Pacific (see chapter 6).

For general information on sailing, contact **Yachting New Zealand** (✆ **09/367-1471;** fax 09/360-2246; www.yachtingnz.org.nz).

WHITE-WATER RAFTING   The challenging Wairoa, Mohaka, and Kaituna rivers are popular on the North Island; in the south, you'll find action on the Shotover, Kawarau, and Rangitata rivers. You can do this year-round—wet suits and warm clothing are required in winter, though. Operators give instruction, supply equipment, and arrange transfers to and from launch points.

Rapid Sensations, Taupo (✆ **0800/353-435** in NZ; fax 07/378-7904; www.rapids. co.nz), takes 3-day trips on the upper Mohaka River. If you want an all-out 9 days of crazy fun, contact **Ultimate Descents,** Motueka (✆ **0800/748-377** in NZ; fax 03/523-9811; www.rivers.co.nz), which exposes you to the serious thrills of the Buller, Karamea, and Clarence rivers on the top of the South Island.

OTHER WATERSPORTS: SCUBA DIVING & SURFING

SCUBA DIVING   With over 32,000km (20,000 miles) of coastline, New Zealand has no shortage of diving opportunities. The best diving seas in the land are around the **Poor Knights Islands** in Northland. This is where you'll find the wreck of the *Rainbow Warrior,* which is now covered quite nicely with reef formations. Visibility ranges from 20 to 69m (66–226 ft.) in the best months (Feb–June). Another excellent dive spot, renowned for its crystal-clear waters, is the much chillier **Stewart Island.** Brave divers can also immerse themselves in the murky, tannin-stained waters of **Milford Sound** for a truly unique experience.

No matter where you take the plunge, you must have evidence of your diving certification with you. For details, contact the **Dive Industry of New Zealand** (✆ 09/849-5896; fax 09/849-3526). Good resources include *Dive New Zealand* magazine online (www.divenewzealand.com); the internationally renowned **Waikato Dive Centre** (✆ **07/849-1922;** fax 07/849-1942), which offers courses and dive trips; and Napier-based **Adventure Dive** (✆ **06/843-5148;** fax 06/843-5149) for courses and dive tours.

SURFING & WINDSURFING   "Surf" is an interesting four-letter word that brings to mind a whole culture—not to mention big waves, big breaks, and big parties. When asked, every surfer will, of course, tell you his or her favorite beach is best, although it does seem unanimous that **Eastland** and **Gisborne** reliably turn out some of the best waves in the country. **Raglan,** west of Hamilton, is also popular; **Whangamata** and **Mount Maunganui,** in Bay of Plenty, and **Taylor's Mistake,** near Christchurch, are others to consider. For surfing tours contact **New Zealand Surf Tours** (✆/fax **09/832-9622;** www.newzealandsurftours.com), offering 1- to 5-day tours of the Auckland-Northland region.

Windsurfing is popular in many areas around Auckland: at Ferrymead in Christchurch; on Lyttelton Harbour, Christchurch; on Otago Peninsula; at Oakura near New Plymouth; and on Wellington Harbour.

4   GOLF

New Zealand is a nation of golfers. There are approximately 400 private and public courses that offer myriad opportunities. And we're lucky to have some of the best, yet cheapest, golfing facilities you'll find anywhere. Greens fees are well below the world's average—you'll pay anything from NZ$10 to NZ$125 for 18 holes on a good course, and up to NZ$150 to NZ$450 for the country's top links. Clubs, equipment, and a motorized cart (trundler) can be rented.

Die-hards hit the courses year-round, but the best time to golf is from October to April, when temperatures range from 60°F to 70°F (16°C–21°C). Courses tend to be crowded on weekends, less so during the week.

There are 40 golf courses in the Auckland area alone. The **Gulf Harbour** and **Formosa Country Clubs** are the newest on the scene, and the former hosted the 1998

World Cup of Golf. In Rotorua, the **Arikikapakapa** course is dotted with geothermal activity, which makes the course tricky to play; near Taupo, you'll find one of the country's finest, the **Wairakei International Golf Course.** Wellington's **Paraparaumu Beach Golf Club** was rated one of the world's top 50 courses by *Golf Digest.* In Christchurch, both **Russley** and **Shirley** are well rated, along with **Balmacewan** and **St. Clair** in Dunedin.

For more information, contact the **New Zealand Golf Association** (✆ **09/485-3230;** fax 09/486-6745; www.nzga.co.nz).

For golf packages, contact **New Zealand Golf Excursions USA, Inc.,** 2141 Rosecrans Ave., no. 1199, El Segundo, CA 90245 (✆ **800/622-6606** in the U.S.; fax 310/322-4972), or **Kiwi Golf Tours** (✆ **800/873-6360**).

In New Zealand, try **Golf NZ** (✆ **06/870-8740;** fax 06/870-8749; www.golfnew zealand.co.nz), which offers multiday tours for 12 to 36 golfers and partners from NZ$1,600 per person including accommodations, travel, and golf; or **Big Boys Golf Tours** (✆ **025/512-020;** fax 07/843-9677; www.bigboysgolf.co.nz), which offers tours of top golf courses in the Auckland region. Also check www.bestofgolfnewzealand.com for golf holiday planning.

---

5 SKIING & SNOWBOARDING

When the sun warms up in the Northern Hemisphere, skiers and snowboarders come down to the Southern Hemisphere. The ski season generally runs from late June to September. The country has 13 conventional ski areas; as an added bonus at Mount Cook, you can fly by ski plane or helicopter to the 2,400m (7,900-ft.) head of the Tasman Glacier and ski down the 14km (8¾-mile) run. For up-to-the-minute South Island ski details, check out www.nzski.com.

SKIING

The two major ski fields on the North Island are Whakapapa and Turoa, on the slopes of **Mount Ruapehu** in Tongariro National Park, now both owned by a single company, Ruapehu Alpine Lifts. Ruapehu, with a simmering crater lake, is an active volcano and extends up some 2,760m (9,050 ft.), making it the North Island's highest peak. It erupted in 1995 and again in 1996, effectively ending all skiing activity for about 2 years. **Whakapapa** (✆ 07/892-3738; fax 07/892-3732; www.mtruapehu.com) offers challenges for intermediate skiers and snowboarders and has good beginners' packages. **Turoa** (✆ **06/385-8456;** fax 06/385-8992; info.turoa@mtruapehu.com) has great terrain for all levels of skiing, with good half-pipes for snowboarders. It also has good "Learn to Ski" and "Learn to Snowboard" packages.

On the South Island, **Mount Hutt Ski Field** (✆ **03/302-8811;** fax 03/302-8697; www.nzski.com) is 1¾ hours from Christchurch, with a good shuttle service operating from the city. There are numerous club fields close to Christchurch, especially in the Porters Pass region. You'll find information on some of these fields at www.snow.co.nz, www.dobson.co.nz, www.skiporters.co.nz, www.mtlyford.co.nz, www.mtcheeseman. com, www.brokenriver.co.nz, www.craigieburn.co.nz, www.templebasin.co.nz, www. mtolympus.co.nz, www.foxpeak.co.nz, and www.skihanmer.co.nz.

Coronet Peak (✆ **03/442-4620;** www.nzski.com) is 18km (11 miles) from Queenstown with moderate to challenging fields. It's the oldest commercial field in the South

(Tips) Sloping Off to Ski School

The **Mount Hutt Ski School** ((C) **03/308-5074;** www.mthutt.co.nz) was the 1997 winner of the New Zealand Tourism Board Awards Training & Education Programme. It has an extensive training program that caters to everyone from rank beginners all the way through to Advanced Level 6 skiers. It also offers extensive snowboarding instruction. **Whakapapa Ski & Snowboard School** ((C) **07/892-3410**) makes it easy for everyone, with special learning packages and beginners-only slopes. Intermediate or advanced skiers can also improve their skills with group or private lessons. **Cardrona Development Centre** ((C) **03/443-7411;** fax 03/443-8818; www.cardrona.com) has an extensive program of beginners' lessons, private and group lessons, specialist improvement workshops, ski board instruction, plus an instructor-training program. **Treble Cone Ski School** ((C) **03/443-7443;** fax 03/443-8401; www.treblecone.com) has everything from the TC Cat Club Junior Ski School, for kids 3 to 12, to middle-range instruction and workshops to women's workshops, carving clinics, snowboard holiday camps, and a masters program for competitive skiers 30 and over.

Island and has several chairlifts including a new six-seater high-speed lift, beginners' facilities, and good variety for experienced skiers. The **Remarkables** ((C) **03/442-4615**), 23km (14 miles) from Queenstown, has more diversity for experienced skiers. It's a smaller field with three chairlifts, one magic carpet, and a beginner handle tow and is good for middle-ability skiers. It gets the afternoon sun, so it's slightly warmer in winter. There's a lot of heli-skiing on virgin snow in this area and an incredibly steep access road. **Cardrona Alpine Resort** ((C) **03/443-7411;** fax 03/443-8818; www.cardrona.com) is a middle-range field with good family facilities, including brand-new social facilities, but it's a bit tame for experienced skiers. It lies 57km (35 miles) from Queenstown and 33km (20 miles) from Wanaka. **Treble Cone** ((C) **03/443-7443;** fax 03/443-8401; www.treble cone.co.nz) has the newest and biggest express chairlift in the country, which has improved the flow of skiers on the field. It's one of the more challenging fields and has a lot of variety, with very steep areas and narrow valleys. It also has a good base lodge and the best food facilities of all the southern ski areas. There's also heli-skiing in the Harris Mountains.

Lift ticket prices in New Zealand range from NZ$99 to NZ$120; ski, boot, and pole rentals run from NZ$40 to NZ$60; and lessons are from NZ$110 for a half-day group class. Costs are lower for children and all ski fields offer a range of day and multiday passes, plus online specials.

For cross-country skiing, head for **Snow Farm,** located in the Pisa Range, near Wanaka ((C) **03/443-0300;** fax 03/443-9717; www.snowfarmnz.com), which is the only Nordic ski field of its kind in New Zealand. The area has ideal terrain for first-time cross-country skiers as well as good conditions for advanced skiers.

SKI PACKAGES & OUTFITTERS In winter, you'll always find good ski deals from the three major cities—Auckland, Wellington, and Christchurch—that usually include cheap transport, accommodations, and a specified number of ski days. Check with the visitor centers in each city for the latest ski-package brochures.

Check out the highly recommended **Snowco** (www.snowco.co.nz), which features online ski and snowboarding packages, and **Ski New Zealand Online** (www.ski-new zealand.co.nz), which offers numerous ski package holidays starting at around NZ$175 per person. The **NZ Super Pass** can be used at any time on any of the following South Island ski fields: Treble Cone, Mount Dobson, Mount Lyford, Ohau, Broken River, Mount Olympus, Craigieburn, and Temple Basin, or you can choose a day's skiing or snowboarding at Coronet Peak, the Remarkables, or Mount Hutt. You can also swap a day on the mountains with one of a huge range of other activities, including heli-skiing, ballooning, jet-boating, and many more. Coupons for the NZ Super Pass start from NZ$275 for a 3-day pass. For information, contact **Coronet Peak** (✆ **03/450-1970**; www.nzski.com or www.nzsuperpass.com).

For heli-skiing in the Queenstown area, contact **HeliSki** (✆ **03/442-7733**; fax 03/442-3299; www.flynz.co.nz). Members of the Gardner family are all expert skiers, with one or two pilots among them, too. They have access to some of the most fantastic heli-ski terrain in New Zealand. Another contact is **Harris Mountain Heli-Skiing** (✆ **03/442-6722**; fax 03/442-2983; www.heliski.co.nz).

For more information on New Zealand skiing, check out the **New Zealand Snows-ports Council** (✆ **04/499-8135**; fax 04/499-8136; www.snow.co.nz), or the websites www.goski.com and www.onthesnow.com.

SNOWBOARDING

Treble Cone is "home to some of the best gully runs in New Zealand, which form into awesome quarter pipes, hips, and spines." So says one of the experts on www.board theworld.com, who rates Treble Cone eighth in the world for freeriding. Treble Cone is rated the top freeriding resort in Australasia and is best for experienced boarders. It has an active training program.

Cardona is better for beginner and intermediate boarders. It has undulating terrain, lots of gullies, and four half-pipes, and it offers a whole heap of support for snowboard-ers in general. It also has half-pipe camps throughout the season for all levels. **Coronet Peak** has lots of long groomed runs to tabletops, with quarter-pipes, kickers, and rollers. It's essentially a tourist field and is more expensive. The **Remarkables** offers pretty ho-hum snowboarding on the field itself, but the out-of-bounds territory offers extreme boarding for the daring. There's good stuff up in the backcountry if you're prepared to hike. Generally, though, the Remarkables is not a destination of choice for boarders.

Farther north, there's good snowboarding at **Temple Basin Ski Area,** in Arthur's Pass (✆ **03/377-7788**), and at **Turoa Ski Resort,** in Tongariro National Park (✆ **06/385-8456**).

SNOWBOARDING DEALS & TOURS New Zealand Surf'n'Snow Tours (✆ 09/828-0426; www.newzealandsnowtours.co.nz) has a wide range of North and South Island snowboard packages. **Gravity Action,** 19 Shotover St., Queenstown (✆ **03/442-5277**; www.gravityaction.com), has its finger on the pulse when it comes to all things snow-board related, including good hire rates.

Mount Aspiring Guides, in Wanaka (✆ **03/443-9422**; fax 03/443-9540; www.aspiringguides.com), offers a 5-day snowboarding tour in alpine wilderness areas, but snowboarders must be set up for backcountry travel. This is boarding in untracked areas, and you'll need an adventurous spirit and the proper gear. Accommodations are in high mountain huts. (You get flown in.) This little venture will cost you in the vicinity of NZ$1,600 per person.

6 BICYCLING

Bicycle touring is a breathtakingly fresh way of seeing New Zealand, and it's an increasingly popular choice, especially on the South Island, where traffic densities are lower and the scenery is spectacular. There are numerous companies offering guided cycle tours—everything from short day tours through vineyards to more serious challenges like a month-long tour of the whole country.

The best news for many cyclists and tourism operators in May 2009 was Prime Minister John Key's announcement that the government, through the Ministry of Tourism, would spend NZ$50-million over the next 3 years to build a new National Cycleway, running the length of New Zealand. Rather than being one direct north-south route, though, it is being designed as a network comprised of existing cycleways with new sections to create a linked Great Rides passage through provincial New Zealand—similar in concept to the already-established Great Walks network. This means riders will get a much more comprehensive overview of New Zealand than they would by riding State Highway 1 from Kaitaia in the north to Bluff in the south.

Nine million dollars has been earmarked to kick-start the first stage of the development, which has identified seven key routes—five in the North Island and two in the South Island. These will build on existing cycleways, facilities, and tourism attractions. Track One will be in the Far North, linking the Hokianga on the West Coast to Opua and Russell on the east coast. Track Two will focus on the Hauraki Plains, linking Paeroa to Waihi and Thames. Track Three will be created around two Waikato River Trails near Hamilton and Lake Karapiro. Track Four will see the creation of the Central North Island Rail Trail linking Puerora to Taumaranui. Track Five, Mountains to Sea, will also be set in unique central North Island landscapes; and Track Six, the St James Great Trail, will focus on the very pretty Hanmer area in the South Island. Last but not least, Track Seven, in the Southland-Queenstown Lakes area, will take cyclists around the Mountain Rail Trail, through Walter Peak and Mount Nicholas Stations, along the Von Valley, and from Mosstown along the old railway line to Lumsden.

The new cycleways are expected to create many new jobs, both during the construction phase and in the resulting tourism operations that spring up in their wake. Those riding the trails will gain access to many remote landscapes and small towns and villages that would normally be bypassed on traditional tourist schedules; and for those who have always been nervous about cycling New Zealand on the main highways, the development of the Great Rides tracks will be welcome news. The tracks will also appeal to those who may only want to ride through one or two scenic sections. Several of the tracks in the first stage of the overall development are expected to be open for use in 2010.

SAFETY TIPS   Regardless of where you bike, always wear your helmet—they are mandatory in New Zealand, and you will be fined for not wearing one. Also, remember the following: Cyclists are not permitted on motorways (freeways); they must always ride on the left side of the road; and all traffic turning left gives way to everything on the right. At night, make sure you have a working white front light and a red rear light and reflector. It doesn't hurt to have pedal and jacket reflectors. A few cities—Christchurch is the standout in this regard—have designated cycle lanes within city limits, which makes pedaling safer.

THE ACTIVE VACATION PLANNER

5

BICYCLING

RENTALS   If you're not interested in an organized tour and want to rent a bike when you get here, **Adventure Cycles,** in Auckland (© **09/309-2453;** www.adventure-auckland.co.nz), offers rentals throughout New Zealand and sales with a guaranteed buyback plan. It is also part of an association of 24 operators that can arrange organized activities. **Nelson Bike Rentals** (© **03/548-1666;** www.nelsonbikerentals.co.nz) has a huge range of road and mountain bikes available for short or long-term rental. They also have a buyback scheme for long-term rentals, which is much more economical than bringing your own bike to New Zealand. **City Cycle Hire** in Christchurch (© **0800/ 343-848;** www.cyclehire-tours.co.nz) offers short- and long-term cycle hire, along with mountain biking riding adventures.

TOURS   There's an increasing number of organized bike-tour companies in New Zealand and I've listed many in "Outdoor Pursuits" in individual regional chapters. **New Zealand Pedaltours** ★★★, in Parnell, Auckland (© **09/585-1338;** fax 09/585-1339; www.pedaltours.co.nz), offers both North and South Island trips on 12 routes lasting from 2 to 37 days, on- and off-road. It creates customized tours of moderate exertion level, and a support van is always around to take the load off your pedals. **Adventure South** (© **03/942-1222;** fax 03/942-4030; www.advsouth.co.nz) offers a range of 6- to 21-day cycle tours, mainly in the South Island, that may also include some walking excursions. They are geared to all fitness levels and are backed up by support vehicles. **Tuatara Tours** ★★, in Christchurch (© **0800/377-378** in NZ, or 03/962-3280; www. tuataratours.co.nz), has two excellent cycle tours for people who want to focus on fun and comfort. Their 4-day Hanmer Cycle Trail covers 170km (105 miles), taking you through the Waipara vineyard region to the alpine village of Hanmer, where you can end your journey in hot pools; and their Tekapo Canal Trail (140km/87 miles) introduces you to the South Island's dramatic landscapes. The Hanmer trail does have some small hills to cover; and you may have to battle against strong winds on both trails if you strike an infamous "Nor'wester."

7 OTHER SPORTS

ROCK CLIMBING

Rock climbing and bouldering are alive and well in New Zealand, and the best place to start to get the lowdown on this activity is to go to www.climb.co.nz, which gives a regional overview of the country's best outdoor climbing locations, plus listings of the best rock climbing guidebooks and adventure operators. The Canterbury region is known to provide the most quality rock climbing locations in the country. If you want to join a rock climbing course, **Wanaka Rock Climbing** (© **03/443-6411;** www. wanakarock.co.nz) offers 1-, 3-, and 5-day courses in the beautiful Matukituki Valley on the edge of Mount Aspiring National Park, near Wanaka. Auckland-based **Cliffhanger Training & Tours** (© **09/818-5451;** www.cliffhanger.co.nz) caters to all skill levels with its 2-hour to full-day rock climbing coaching adventures, which are overseen by qualified instructors. I have detailed indoor rock climbing facilities in the "Outdoor Pursuits" section of regional chapters.

HORSEBACK RIDING

Like cycling, horse riding is a beautiful way to see the details of the country. It is the perfect way to get an up-close-and-personal view, rather than flashing through in a fast-moving vehicle. Unlike most cycling tours, though, horse riding operators will take you off the beaten track, into landscapes you would otherwise never see. I have detailed a number of horse riding operations in "Outdoor Pursuits" in regional chapters. Most horse riding operations in New Zealand only offer short-term outings; that is, between 1- and 4-hour treks. Most operators cater to a wide range of riding abilities, with horses of varying sizes and temperaments. One of the best providers of longer horse riding treks is North Canterbury-based **Alpine Horse Safaris** ★★★ (✆ **03/314-4293;** www.alpine horse.co.nz), which offers 3- to 12-day treks covering up to 400km (more than 200 miles) of some of the most beautiful landscapes in the South Island. Laurie and Jenny O'Carroll are very experienced riders and trekkers, and you'll be in safe hands as they guide you across mountain passes and scree slopes, across rivers and through beech forests. Plan to spend around 6 hours a day in the saddle. Accommodations are provided in mountain camps and musterers' huts. (Musterers are farm workers who gather livestock; their huts provide them with shelter when they're working in the high country.) **Cape Farewell Horse Treks,** 23 McGowan St., Puponga, Collingwood, Nelson (✆ **03/524-8031;** www.horsetreksnz.com), have 1-hour to 7-day horse treks across the farmlands and beaches of the Abel Tasman region, near Nelson.

8 FOOD, COOKING & WINE TRIPS

A bounty of fresh ingredients, limitless supplies of fine wine, and a growing appreciation of both have meant a proliferation of small, boutique cooking schools in New Zealand. Daylong or weekend classes are the main focus. One of the best is **Ruth Pretty Cooking School** ★★, 41 School Rd., Te Horo, north of Wellington (✆ **06/364-3161;** www. ruthpretty.co.nz). Ruth is well known in New Zealand food circles and she stages classes for a maximum of 34 people most weekends from February through December. Lessons from Ruth and invited top chefs culminate in long, outdoor lunches. She also teaches private "hands-on" classes for small groups.

    Auckland Seafood School, First Floor, Auckland Fish Market, 22 Jellicoe St., Freemans Bay, Auckland (✆ **09/379-1497;** www.afm.co.nz), holds regular short courses in its state-of-the-art facility that includes a 66-seat auditorium and a hands-on kitchen with eight self-contained cooking stations. From barbecue to traditional French, Vietnamese, or classical recipes, it's all about fish. Also in Auckland, **Main Course,** 20 Beaumont St., Auckland (✆ **09/302-1460;** www.maincourse.co.nz), offers courses in everything from seafood and vegetarian to gluten-free and Italian cooking. Located in the Historic Gas Buildings in Victoria Park, its high-tech kitchens are just the place to roll up your sleeves and learn at a friendly, relaxed pace with a meal at the end.

    In Christchurch, Celia Hay's **New Zealand School of Food & Wine** ★★, 63 Victoria St., Christchurch (✆ **03/379-7501;** www.foodandwine.co.nz), has a well-earned reputation for turning out accomplished hospitality graduates. The school runs full-time 16-week courses in cookery, restaurant and cafe management, and professional wine knowledge. It has an associated award-winning restaurant, a professional kitchen, and a demonstration kitchen.

    In Queenstown, **Kia Toa Cuisine,** at Punatapu Lodge (✆ **03/442-6985;** www.cuisine queenstown.com or www.punatapu.com), offers specialized, short-term classes in a luxury lodge environment. From short demonstration classes to hands-on residential weekend courses for individuals or small groups (8–16 people), the focus is always on New

Zealand produce. The courses may include foraging for wild foods or visits to farmers' markets, wineries, orchards, local restaurants, and high country sheep stations.

You'll find details of local wine tours in each regional chapter. In addition, you should arm yourself with both the *Classic New Zealand Wine Trail Guide* and the *Jasons Taste Traveller* guide, which are free from all i-SITE visitor centers around the country.

9 HOTEL SPAS & YOGA RETREATS

RETREATS

If you're looking to come to New Zealand to take time out and rejuvenate yourself, you'll find plenty of opportunities to do so. For a full list of spiritual and/or meditation retreats, check www.nzspiritualdirectory.net.nz. It details a wide variety of spiritual, healing, and meditation retreats and workshops throughout New Zealand. The website www.retreats online.com/newzealand also refers you on to a number of North and South Island retreats. The **Mahamudra Centre,** Main Road, Colville, Coromandel (© **07/866-6851;** www.mahamudra.org.nz), is a Tibetan Buddhist meditation center on 3.2 hectares (8 acres) in the peaceful Colville Valley in the Coromandel region. It hosts group or solo courses and retreats with visiting lamas and teachers. Accommodations are in camping grounds, dormitories, or self-contained cabins.

The **Auckland Buddhist Centre,** 381 Richmond Rd., Grey Lynn, Auckland (© **09/ 378-1120;** www.aucklandbuddhistcentre.org), is part of the worldwide movement Friends of the Western Buddhist Order, which is dedicated to the teaching and practice of Buddhism in a modern world. The center invites visitors for meditation, or to attend courses and retreats, which are updated regularly on their website.

The **Om Centre Retreat,** in Mount Maunganui in Bay of Plenty (© **07/575-8239**), offers private, confidential, personally tailored retreats for detox, cancer, depression, anxiety, and stress relief from 3 to 28 days, one guest at a time.

Yoga enthusiasts will find great value at **Stillpoint,** 109 Kelling Rd., Upper Moutere, Nelson (© **03/543-2218;** www.stillpointyoga.co.nz), which is home to world-renowned Ashtanga Yoga teachers John and Lucy Scott. They offer morning classes, practice holidays, and teacher training for beginners through advanced practitioners. The retreat is set in 1.2 hectares (30 acres) of rural grounds, and accommodations are provided. Courses are 1 week to 1 month in duration.

HOTEL & DAY SPAS

Most major hotels in New Zealand now feature their own day spa, and there has been a proliferation of privately owned day spas opening throughout the country. I have detailed many of these in the body of the guide. Most offer an assortment of massage and body treatments; some also offer manicures, pedicures, facials, and makeup and hairdressing services.

In my view, the most luscious of the Auckland hotel spas are as follows: **Chuan Spa,** the Langham Auckland, 83 Symonds St. (© **09/300-2960;** www.chuanspa.co.nz), which opened in 2008 and offers an extensive range of treatment packages (p. 126); **East Day Spa,** SKYCITY Grand Hotel, 123 Albert St., Auckland (© **09/363-7050;** www. eastdayspa.com), which is another beautifully appointed den of indulgence offering the full array of restorative beauty and body treatments (p. 126); and the **Spa at Hyatt Regency Auckland,** corner of Princes Street and Waterloo Quadrant (© **09/355-1234;**

www.auckland.regency.hyatt.com), an oasis of calm adjacent to the best hotel gymnasium facility in the country, with a swimming pool, steam rooms, Jacuzzis, saunas, and a high-rise sun deck. See p. 128.

In the Bay of Islands, **Paihia Beach Resort & Spa,** 116 Marsden Rd., Paihia ((C) **0800/870-111** in NZ, or 09/402-0111; www.paihiabeach.co.nz), has a splendid new spa facility, **La Spa Naturale,** which has already been voted one of the top 10 spas in Australasia and the South Pacific by *Condé Nast Traveller (UK)*. In addition to the full range of massage and body treatments, they have a very extensive hair and makeup facility. See p. 183.

In the far south, the new day spa at **Sofitel Queenstown,** 8 Duke St. ((C) **03/450-0045;** www.sofitel.com), also deserves a mention for its luxurious appointments and its delicious body treatments. See p. 457.

Beyond hotels, you'll find a good number of other day spa facilities. Perhaps two of the largest and the best are Rotorua's multi-award-winning **Polynesian Spa,** Government Gardens ((C) **07/348-1328;** www.polynesianspa.co.nz), which is world renowned for its therapeutic hot mineral pools and its lakeside spa therapy rooms (p. 220); and the **Spa at Hanmer Springs,** 42 Amuri Ave., Hanmer Springs ((C) **03/315-0029;** www.hanmer spa.co.nz), which was judged Best Natural Bathing Spa in the inaugural Australasian Spa Association's Spa of Excellence Awards. It offers a full range of body and massage treatments and sits adjacent to the large hot water pool complex. See p. 396.

10 VOLUNTEERING & WORKING IN NEW ZEALAND

If you wish to work in New Zealand during your trip, you need to acquire a working holiday permit. You can research the details of visa and work permits required by checking into the New Zealand Immigration website www.immigration.govt.nz. There are usually plenty of short-term working opportunities here, especially in the summer when orchards, market gardens, and vineyards often need casual workers. The New Zealand hospitality industry usually employs large numbers of working tourists as well. That said, the current global recession has impacted the availability of jobs, so make sure you do your research before landing here. For wider job information check www.seek.co. nz, www.nzrecruitme.co.nz, www.anyworkanywhere.com, www.jobstuff.co.nz, or www. jobzone.co.nz. The New Zealand immigration website lists many more links to specialized agricultural, horticultural, ski, hospitality, or general jobs.

Personally, I think there are far more interesting jobs available in the volunteer arena. Admittedly, you don't earn money while you're working, but you will take home the intense satisfaction of knowing you have helped others while enjoying a rewarding, personal experience. There are many organizations offering volunteer positions within New Zealand. The **Global Volunteer Network** operates in many countries, including New Zealand. Their comprehensive website, www.volunteer.org.nz, details their programs, offering assistance to conservation groups and conservation projects within New Zealand. Volunteers are involved in habitat restoration, predator control projects, tree planting, invasive weed removal, monitoring revegetation growth rates, and more. Working within a kiwi sanctuary to help preserve our national icon must be rated as a rare and privileged experience. This program is based in Wellington, and you need to be moderately fit, proficient in English, and 18 and over to participate.

Volunteering New Zealand (© 0800/865-268; www.volunteernow.org.nz) focuses on putting the age, wisdom, and acquired experience of those from age 55 to 65 to good use. Their website features an Opportunities Page that lists volunteer positions for these "young seniors" who may have retired from the workforce but still have much to give to community welfare. **Volunteer Abroad,** www.volunteerabroad.com, lists numerous opportunities to take part in interesting community projects, from conservation work to educational and outdoor leadership courses. Other good websites to check are www. conservationvolunteers.org.nz, www.transitionsabroad.com, www.unitedplanet.org, www.geovisions.org, www.wwoof.co.nz, www.greenhearttravel.org, and www.partnership volunteers.org.

11 OTHER GUIDED TOURS, OUTFITTERS & PACKAGE DEALS

In addition to all of the above, you can trust New Zealanders to come up with a tour for just about every specialty. Here are a few of them—if you still haven't found what you're looking for after this, well, I just don't know what to do with you!

- **Agritour,** Palmerston North (© 06/354-9063; fax 06/354-9064; www.agritour. co.nz), arranges technical study tours visiting agribusinesses, research stations, orchards, and forests to suit your needs.
- **American Wilderness Experience,** a member of the **GORPtravel** family, 10055 Westmoor Dr., Ste. 215, Westminster, CO 80021 (© 800/444-0099 in the U.S., or 720/887-8500; www.gorptravel.com), arranges trips to the national parks and the World Heritage Area; they include walking, rafting, and wildlife observation.
- **Backcountry Concepts,** Christchurch (© 021/644-507; fax 03/302-8701; www. backcountry-nz.com), offers a wide range of fishing tours with stays in luxury accommodations, several raft-based options, and custom tours that include time with local artists, wine-tasting tours, shopping tours, and garden tours.
- **Clean Green Photo Tours,** Wanaka (www.cleangreen.co.nz), can arrange anything from a 2-hour instructional course to multiday excursions to Stewart Island, Fiordland, and even the unforgettable Sub-Antarctic Islands on board the 18m (59-ft.) ketch *Talisker*. Photographer Gilbery van Reenan shares his most beautiful, off-the-beaten-track locations.
- **Fiordland Ecology Holidays,** Manapouri (©/fax 03/249-6600; www.fiordland.gen. nz), will take you away on its oceangoing yacht for 3 to 7 days of low-impact natural-history adventure in the remote areas of Fiordland. A maximum of 12 people can swim with seals and dolphins, go snorkeling and diving, and set out on bush walks. There are also berths available on scientific research trips.
- **Mid-Life Adventures,** Mount Roskill, Auckland (© 09/627-9683; fax 09/626-3607; midlifeadventures@xtra.co.nz), has 13-day North or South Island adventures ready and waiting for those 35 and over.
- **Nimbus Paragliding Adventure Tours,** Christchurch (© 0800/111-611 in NZ; www.nimbusparagliding.co.nz), is just the ticket for you addicts who want to stay airborne. Grey Hamilton and his crew have three campervans, all the paragliding equipment, and the local knowledge. They'll personalize an itinerary that will take you to as many of the country's best paragliding sites as you can afford to visit.

- **Red Carpet Tours,** Auckland (© **09/410-6561;** fax 09/410-6591; www.redcarpet-tours.com), takes *The Lord of the Rings* fans to Middle Earth and the sites of Peter Jackson's famous film trilogy.
- **Southern Discovery Holidays,** Greymouth (© **03/768-6649;** fax 03/768-9149; www.nzholidayheaven.com), offers a 12-day Millionaires Tour, visiting the South Island's gold fields in search of gold; 14-day School Geography Study Tours on the South Island, which include adventure activities; Golden Age Holidays, which offer small groups of retired people a new approach to vacationing; plus a wide range of special-interest holidays, including photography, painting, gardens, farms, ornithology—you name it, the staff will prepare it for you.
- **Unimog 4WD Adventure Tours,** Greymouth (offered by Southern Discovery Holidays; for contact information, see above), has serious 17-seat, 4WD vehicles that go places most people only dream about (or dread). It has great 5- and 14-day tours that take you into back areas around the South Island, throwing in other delights, such as guided walks, seal colonies, and mountain biking.
- **Untapped Potential,** P.O. Box 128-231, Remuera, Auckland (fax **09/524-0567;** www.utp.co.nz), which is especially geared toward visiting sporting teams, takes you into the heart of New Zealand sporting culture by introducing you to grass-roots rugby.
- **Wai–natur,** Wairau Valley, Marlborough (© **03/572-2681;** www.naturist.co.nz), is not so much a tour as a chance to get your clothes off and paddle a canoe, or swim in a spring-fed creek amid stunning scenery. Kay Hannam and Brian Williams have a clothes-free homestay and camping facility where you can relax completely.
- **Navigator Tours,** Auckland (© **09/817-1191;** www.navigatortours.co.nz), is a specialist in organizing high-end indigenous Maori experiences that focus on real people, living real lives in fresh, innovative ways. Whether it be learning to make a *hangi* (earth oven), meeting a Maori professor for coffee, taking a ride in a *waka* (war canoe), or enjoying a forest walk or a visit to a marae, a Navigator experience is one you will never forget.

Auckland

Auckland, known as the City of Sails, is as big, as cosmopolitan, as hedonistic, as subtropical, and as congested as any New Zealand city gets. If you're starting here, you're starting at the top. And if you haven't visited Auckland in the last 5 years, you're in for a major surprise—it has slipped into a new stylish skin that is leaving the rest of New Zealand in its wake. And now—at the time of writing—it's been designated a Super City, and by 2010 a new single council will be elected to govern a huge geographical area currently covered by five individual city councils. This won't make any difference to visitors, but it marks a huge turning point in Auckland's future urban growth and governance.

Along with its much-touted 48 dead volcanoes, Auckland is home to more than 1.3 million people. It has the largest Polynesian population in the world; more boats per capita than any other city; 22 regional parks covering 37,038 hectares (91,484 acres); 50 islands; and more than 500km (310 miles) of walking and hiking tracks. It also has the tallest tower in the Southern Hemisphere, which attracts the most lightning, and if a daily shower is no longer enough, Auckland, surrounded on all sides by water, offers more ways of getting wet than just about anywhere.

This is our baby Sydney, and most of us are proud of it. It's a luscious, leafy city, and there's a contagious energy about this sprawling, showoff place. The injection of billions of dollars into the 1999–2000 and the 2002–03 America's Cup preparations and other international events polished Auckland's public face to gleaming. And now, to coincide with the staging of World Cup Rugby in Auckland in 2011, a NZ$30-million development is planned on Queens Wharf, near Viaduct Harbour. This will become "party central" during the games, but all the restaurants and bars built for the occasion will remain and will become a lively part of the city's future.

Europeans arrived in Auckland in 1839, and the thriving area served as the nation's first capital until 1864, when the seat of government was transferred to Wellington because of its central location. Auckland, though, is still a capital place to visit. It isn't typical of New Zealand any more than New York and Los Angeles are typical of the United States, or Sydney is typical of Australia, but it does have a huge amount to offer.

1 ORIENTATION

ARRIVING
By Plane
The **Auckland International Airport** (© **0800/247-767** in NZ; www.aucklandairport.co.nz) is 21km (13 miles) south of the city, behind Manukau Harbour; a motorway makes it a swift 30- to 35-minute car trip into town. More than 25 international airlines serve the airport. The **Jean Batten International Terminal** opened in 1998 and fresh from a NZ$100-million upgrade, it has doubled its retail space. The first thing to

greet you is "A World of Shopping," almost 100 retail outlets *before* you even hit Customs and Immigration. Auckland is the only airport in the world with two competing duty-free agencies (DFS and Regency), so you'll get great deals on fashion, souvenirs, accessories, and New Zealand art and crafts.

From the terminal, proceed down the escalator to Customs and Immigration. If you're connecting to a domestic flight, before entering the arrivals hall, turn left into the Independent Travelers' Area, where you'll find Air New Zealand transfer desks. This area also contains the **Auckland i-SITE Visitor Centre** (✆ **0800/282-552** in NZ, or 09/367-6009; www.aucklandnz.com), rental-car companies, and currency exchange. For luggage storage, ask at the information center. A children's play area is on the second floor. If you want to rest between flights, take an airport day room, which includes a bed, shower, and desk and may be rented "airside" (after you pass through Immigration) between 5am and 11pm for around NZ$45 to NZ$65; for information, visit the **Collection Point** (✆ **09/256-8845**). If you feel like pampering yourself after a long flight, call in to the **Traveller's Oasis** (✆ **09/256-6167;** www.auckland-airport.co.nz), between Oceanic and Art Port near the departure gates. It offers specialized treatments to prevent deep-vein thrombosis, plus therapeutic massage for face, body, and feet.

The **Domestic Terminal** is a 15-minute walk from the International Terminal. Simply follow the blue-and-white lines painted on the pavement. Alternatively, catch the free interterminal bus, which departs every 20 minutes between 6am and 10:30pm. It has been significantly improved after a NZ$42-million makeover, which enlarged retail and check-in areas and expanded security screening points. Another **i-SITE Visitor Centre** is in the Air New Zealand Terminal (✆ **09/367-6009**). It's open daily 7am to 5pm.

The **Airbus** (✆ **0800/103-080** in NZ; www.airbus.co.nz) is the best value for transport between the airport and the city. It runs every 20 minutes between 5:50am and 6pm, and every 30 minutes between 6 and 10pm, calling at most major hotels and backpackers in the city. The fare is NZ$15 one-way, NZ$25 round-trip. If you're staying in a city hotel on the direct route, the driver will drop you off.

Taxis wait outside the airport terminal; the fare between the airport and city center is NZ$55 to NZ$65 on weekdays, more on weekends and at night. **Auckland Co-op Taxi** (✆ **09/300-3000**) is a reliable company.

Numerous shuttle companies will take you from the airport to your inner city lodging for around NZ$25. **Super Shuttle** (✆ **0800/748-885** in NZ, or 09/306-3960; www.supershuttle.co.nz) and **Auckland Airport Shuttle** (✆ **09/576-8904**) both offer reliable service.

By Train & Coach (Bus)

The big news on the Auckland city transport scene is the opening of the **Britomart Transport Exchange** (✆ **09/366-6400;** www.maxx.co.nz or www.veoliatransport.co.nz for local rail). Near the central business district, ferry terminals, and Central City bus stops, it has streamlined all transport services. It features a new underground transport center where intercity and commuter rail, buses, taxis, light rail, and ferry services all connect. The train system has undergone major changes, with the old railway at Beach Street closing and services relocating to Britomart. There are five train platforms within Britomart, and trains depart from the same platform each day.

Most city buses have relocated to Britomart Bus Precinct, with a few exceptions. The Maxx website remains the best source of current information about these changes, and information centers also provide up-to-the-minute information. Most airport shuttles

AUCKLAND

6

ORIENTATION

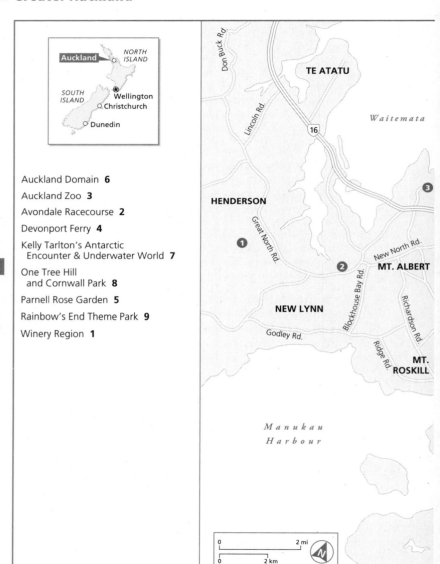

NORTH
ISLAND

Auckland

SOUTH
ISLAND

Wellington

Christchurch

Dunedin

Don Buck Rd.

TE ATATU

Lincoln Rd.

Waitemata

16

HENDERSON

Great North Rd.

New North Rd.

MT. ALBERT

Blockhouse Bay Rd.

NEW LYNN

Richardson Rd.

Godley Rd.

Ridge Rd.

MT.
ROSKILL

Manukau
Harbour

0   2 mi

0   2 km

N

✈ Airport
---- Ferry

Auckland
International
Airport ✈

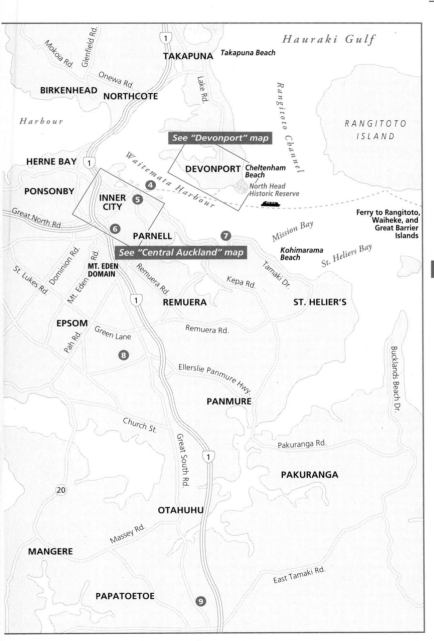

Maori Auckland

In Maori, Auckland is known as **Tamaki-Makau-Rau**—"the city of 100 lovers."
The name is appropriate, for the area was desired by all and conquered by many.
More than 18 Maori tribes have had claims to Auckland at one time or another.
The first Maori settlers arrived in Hauraki Gulf about 1,000 years ago; the earliest
Maori settlement, a site at Motutapu Island dating to the 1100s, was apparently
buried under volcanic dust from the Rangitoto eruption. Of the 48 volcanic cones
dotting Auckland's landscape, almost all wear the distinctive horizontal terracing
that denotes a Maori *pa* site. A *pa* is essentially a fort built in a high place to
defend the Maori people.

AUCKLAND

6

ORIENTATION

include Britomart in their circuits, and inner city bus services like The Link and the free
City Circuit (see below) also travel via Britomart. For more detailed information about
current fares, see "Getting Around," below.

The new center is open daily. It has storage lockers; electronic visual displays of departure and arrival times; camera security; a cafe, sushi bar, florist, and convenience store;
tour operators; toilets; currency exchange; and ATMs.

For information on the Tranz Scenic trains that serve Auckland, contact **TranzRail**
(© **0800/802-802** in NZ, or 09/366-6400). **InterCity Coachlines** (© **09/623-1503**)
and **Newmans** (© **09/623-1504;** www.newmanscoach.co.nz) buses arrive and depart
from the SKYCITY Travel Centre Coach Terminal, 102 Hobson St. (© **09/913-6100**).

By Car

If you're driving, you will enter Auckland on **State Highway 1** from the south, on the
major motorway system. I advise you to call ahead to your hotel and ask which motorway
exit to take. Traffic congestion is an issue in Auckland, especially during morning and
evening rush hours. If you don't have to drive in the city, avoid it. Parking is also increasingly expensive.

VISITOR INFORMATION

There are two centrally located Auckland visitor centers: **i-SITE Visitor Centre–Viaduct
Basin,** Princes Wharf, Quay and Hobson streets, downtown; and **i-SITE Visitor Centre**
at the Atrium, SKYCITY Auckland, Victoria and Federal streets. Both are open daily
from 8am to 8pm. They share a phone number and website (© **09/367-6009;** www.
i-site.org.nz).

The **Takapuna i-SITE Visitor Centre,** 49 Hurstmere Rd., Takapuna (© **09/486-
8670;** www.northshorenz.com), is open Monday through Friday from 8:30am to 5pm;
and Saturday, Sunday, and public holidays 10am to 3pm. The **Devonport I-SITE Visitor Centre,** 3 Victoria Rd., Devonport (© **09/446-0677;** www.northshorenz.com), is
open daily from 8:30am to 5pm. All are closed December 25. Other useful resources
include the **Department of Conservation Centre** (© **09/379-6476;** www.doc.govt.nz),
which has information on walks, campgrounds, the gulf islands, and the national parks.

Online, you'll find endless amounts of information on Auckland at the following
websites:

- **www.aucklandnz.com**: The home page of Tourism Auckland. Comprehensive listings of events in the Auckland region and helpful information for parents and families.
- **www.maxx.co.nz**: Auckland bus, ferry, and train information.
- **www.aucklandcitylibraries.com**: Information for parents and families.
- **www.akcity.govt.nz/whatson**: The Auckland City Council's guide to events in the city.
- **www.northshorenz.com**: Information on the North Shore.
- **www.destination-waitakere.com**: A source of information about the primary wine region of Auckland.
- **www.manukau.govt.nz**: Information on Manukau City.
- **www.greatbarriernz.com**: Information on Great Barrier Island.
- **www.doc.govt.nz**: The Department of Conservation's information on the national parks and marine reserves.
- **www.waihekenz.com**: Information on Waiheke Island.

SPECIAL EVENTS

The annual **Auckland Anniversary Day Regatta** (✆ 09/534-8186) attracts local and international entrants on the last Monday in January. Held in Windsor Reserve in late February, the **Devonport Food & Wine Festival** ★ (✆ 09/446-0688 or 445-3011; www.devonportwinefestival.co.nz) offers nonstop entertainment, samples from 20 wineries, and food galore. Jazz, classical music, and opera play a part. The **Auckland Festival** (✆ 09/309-0101; www.aucklandfestival.co.nz), a premier arts-and-cultural event held in the last week of September, celebrates Auckland's distinct characteristics—especially its Pacific style. The next festival will be staged in 2011. **Air New Zealand Fashion Week** ★★, held in October, presents over 60 New Zealand designers to the world. International buyers and media arrive to check out fashion that is rapidly becoming a "must-see" on the global fashion map; visit www.nzfashionweek.com for details.

The fun **Round the Bays Run** ★★ (✆ 09/525-2166), held in late March, attracts runners from around the South Pacific who participate in the 8km (5-mile) run around the central bays. It ends with a barbecue in one of the city's parks. The **Royal Easter Show** ★★ (✆ 09/638-9969; www.royaleastershow.co.nz), held at the Epsom Showgrounds, focuses on excellence in agriculture and animal husbandry, with fresh produce stalls and the biggest carnival in New Zealand.

CITY LAYOUT

Greater Auckland is actually a fusion of four cities—Auckland, Manukau, North Shore, and Waitakere. Each is on a motorway network, which crosses the harbor, rivers, creeks, and bays and carries the thousands who commute into the inner city to work. You can pick up a city map at the visitor center, but the **Automobile Association** (✆ 0800/500-213 in NZ) has a better one.

 Tips   **Staying Safe**

Personal safety is always a matter of common sense. Police cameras have been installed in several city areas to reduce crime, but it still pays to be vigilant. Much like public parks anywhere, the Auckland Domain is a place to avoid after dark. And it pays to take care at night in Albert Park and the Aotea Square area.

The main street is **Queen Street,** which ends in Queen Elizabeth Square at **Customs Street. Quay Street** runs along the Waitemata Harbour. At the top end of Queen Street is **Karangahape Road** (usually called "K'Road"), a mere 2km (1¼ miles) from Quay Street. Within that area you'll find most of the city's shops, restaurants, nightspots, major hotels, and bus, rail, and air terminals. The most popular inner city suburbs with the best restaurants are **Parnell** and **Ponsonby. Newmarket** is favored for clothes and shoe shopping.

THE NEIGHBORHOODS IN BRIEF

First, let's get a feel for the four cities. **North Shore City** is contemporary, casual, and cool with, I'm told, a hint of California; **Central City** and East Auckland are much more cosmopolitan, with a growing Asian community in the wealthy eastern areas. To the west, **Waitakere City** is the principal winegrowing region; it retains strong evidence of early Eastern European settlement from the 1900s. To the south, **Manukau City** is a melting pot of Polynesian, Maori, and European lifestyles. Now on to the main areas:

Inner City It's hard to decide where the inner city begins and ends, but let's say it's the central business district. This is where you'll find the major hotels and many attractions, including the boisterous and exciting Viaduct Basin, home of the former America's Cup Village. It's also where you'll see the clearest evidence of New Zealand's increasingly multicultural society. The High Street/Vulcan Lane area is an "edgy" part of town if you're looking for a good time. Most water-based tours leave from the downtown Quay Street area. This is a great place to base yourself if you don't want to bother with a vehicle; everything is in walking distance.

Ponsonby/Herne Bay This is quintessential Auckland—bold, brazen, bohemian. It's where most of the best restaurants, bars, and cafes are; it's where the nouveau riche and the almost famous hang out; and you'll find some exquisite specialty shops and lots of divine old wooden houses. Some lovely B&Bs are here, and you won't need a car to have fun. Just off Ponsonby Road is **Karangahape Road,** famous for everything from off-the-wall nightclubs and sassy restaurants to ethnic stores and the whole gamut of sex shops, mas-

sage parlors, tattoo and body-piercing studios, and strip joints.

Mount Eden/Epsom These leafy, green hillside suburbs reek of old money. You'll find stunning mansions and villas aplenty—not all peopled by resident blue bloods, though, because the area has a good number of student flats. Both Mount Eden and Epsom have trendy little villages, where old shops and restaurants have been tarted up so the resident folk can feel they're living on the edge. There are some lovely B&Bs in the area, and it's a very pretty place to base yourself, close to One Tree Hill, Cornwall Park, and the inner city.

Parnell/Newmarket If you want plush, trendy, and sophisticated with an undercurrent of hedonism and excess, this is the suburb for you. Parnell Village is perfectly charming, with lots of super (and expensive) shops and restaurants (with nighttime bar action). It's close to the inner city, the Auckland Museum, and the beauteous Auckland Domain park. There are a few good B&Bs in this area, and in Newmarket, the fashion shopper's Saturday-morning paradise, you'll find heaps of good motels.

Remuera Known locally as "Remmers," this is Auckland's most affluent suburb. Stunning mansions, new high-rise apartments, some great upmarket B&Bs, and an easily accessed village full of specialty shops make it a good base. It's also close to the inner city.

Mission Bay/St. Heliers Wealthy seaside suburbs with big real estate price tags—if you have a Porsche or Ferrari, this is where you bring it to show off on a sunny weekend. Not such a good place to stay if you want to be within walking distance of the city, but it makes a delightful half-day outing. There are lots of excellent restaurants and cafes, and the place really buzzes on weekends, with people walking, running, and in-line skating along the waterfront.

Devonport/Takapuna These two lie over the Harbour Bridge, which can be a nightmarish drive in rush-hour traffic, but if you stay in Devonport you won't need a car at all. Simply lock it up, wander the cute village, and catch a ferry to the inner city when you want a faster pace. There are lots of excellent B&Bs here. Takapuna is the main shopping area of the North Shore, but it doesn't have as much character as Devonport.

The Eastern Suburbs Pretty to visit, all very well kept, but too far from inner city action—if that's what you're after. **Pakuranga, Howick,** and **Panmure** do, however, have a quiet beachside charm and are popular with boaties. To the south is **Otara,** home to Auckland's ever-growing Polynesian community.

2 GETTING AROUND

BY BUS

The Link bus service runs both ways in a circuit around the attractions of the inner city rim. These distinctive, environmentally friendly green buses charge a NZ$1.60 fare. The whole circuit takes an hour and includes Quay Park, Downtown, the Britomart Transport Exchange, Parnell, Newmarket, Karangahape Road, Ponsonby, SKYCITY, Queen Street, the University, Domain, Museum, and more. It operates every 10 minutes from 6am to 7pm Monday through Friday, and 7am to 6pm on Saturday; every 15 minutes from 6 to 11:30pm Monday through Saturday, and 7am to 10pm on Sunday. Stagecoach Day and Group Passes (see below) are good on The Link. For more information, call **Stagecoach** (see below).

Stagecoach Auckland (✆ **09/366-6400;** www.stagecoach.co.nz), the intracity bus system, offers good service to most city highlights. You can pick up timetables from the **Bus Place,** Victoria Street West; at Britomart; and at the visitor centers listed above. For schedules, fares, and routes, call the company or pick up the free brochure *Auckland's Top Spots by Public Transport* from a visitor center. Fares depend on zones, running from NZ$1.60 to NZ$10. Children 5 to 15 pay half-price; those 4 and under ride free. Exact change is not required. If you intend to ride the bus frequently, spend NZ$11 and get a 1-day **Auckland Day Pass** for unlimited travel. The pass is good on The Link and on the ferry services to Devonport, Bayswater, and Birkenhead. There's also a NZ$22 Group Pass for up to four people traveling together. Buy passes from the driver or at the terminals.

Warning: Auckland buses stop running around 11:30pm (earlier on some routes) Monday through Saturday, and 10pm on Sunday. If you're planning a night of revelry,

> ## ⓘ Tips   Are You Lost?
>
> If you need help finding your way around the city, keep an eye out for the **Auckland City Ambassadors** (✆ **09/379-2020**; www.aucklandcity.govt.nz). They're decked out in bright yellow jackets and are on the streets in the downtown area daily from 9am to 6pm.

count on taking a taxi home; or look out for Stagecoach's **NiteRider Bus** ★★ (✆ **09/366-6400**; www.maxx.co.nz), which runs from 1 to 3am on Friday and Saturday. Fares are NZ$4.50 to NZ$6.50.

The double-decker **Auckland Explorer Bus** ★★ (✆ **0800/439-756** in NZ, or 09/524-7929; www.explorerbus.co.nz) departs from the Ferry Building on Quay Street every half-hour from 9am to 5pm daily in summer and 10am to 5pm in winter. It visits 14 major Auckland attractions; for NZ$35 adults, NZ$15 children 4 to 16, and NZ$80 family, you can hop on and off as many times as you want in a day.

Look out for the **City Circuit** (✆ **09/366-6400**), a free inner city bus loop operated by Stagecoach Auckland. It runs daily every 10 minutes between 8am and 6pm, connecting the waterfront and Viaduct Basin to Queen Street, the central universities, Civic Theatre, the Edge, and Sky Tower.

BY TAXI

Typical rates start at NZ$5 and go up NZ$2 per kilometer. Cabs can be flagged down, ordered by phone, or picked up at taxi stands. Stands are at all terminals and on the corner of Customs Street West at Queen Street. Call **Auckland Taxi Co-Op** (✆ **09/300-3000**; www.cooptaxi.co.nz) or **Corporate Cabs** (✆ **09/377-0773**; www.corporatecabs.co.nz).

BY TRAIN

Veolia Transport runs between Auckland, Newmarket, Waitakere, Papakura, and Orakei, stopping at Remuera, Mount Eden, Mount Albert, and many other suburbs along the way. Fares range from NZ$1.40 to NZ$10. You can buy 10-trip passes, a **Day Rover Pass** (NZ$10 for adults, NZ$7 for children ages 5–15), or a Family Pass (NZ$20). Contact Maxx (✆ **09/366-6400**; www.maxx.co.nz) for details and schedules.

BY FERRY

The **Devonport Ferry** departs every half-hour daily from Queen's Wharf, Quay Street (✆ **09/367-9111**; www.fullers.co.nz). The fare is NZ$10 round-trip. Fullers and SeaLink ferries serve Waiheke Island; for details, see "A Side Trip to Waiheke Island" (p. 160).

BY CAR

Driving in downtown Auckland can be problematic, and finding parking is difficult. Given the efficiency of the Explorer, The Link, and the City Circuit buses, it's a much better idea to explore the town without a car. However, if you insist, there are parking buildings operated by the City Council on Beresford Street just off Karangahape Road; near the waterfront on Albert Street, west of Queen Street; on Victoria Street, slightly east of Queen Street; at Britomart off Customs Street, east of Queen Street; downtown

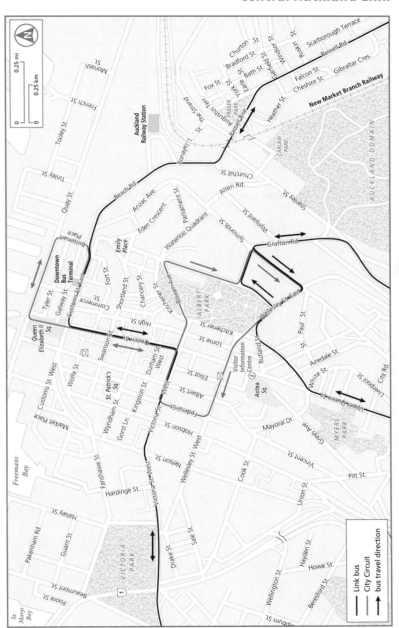

to the east of Queen Street; downtown to the west of Queen Street, with an entrance from Customs Street West; Civic Underground on Mayoral Drive; and Victoria Street East. They're all open 24 hours daily; rates can be expensive.

BY BICYCLE

You can rent a bike from **Adventure Cycles,** 9 Premier Ave., Western Springs (© **09/ 940-2453;** www.adventure-auckland.co.nz). It's open Thursday through Monday from 7:30am to 7pm, Wednesday and weekends by appointment only. Rates start at NZ$15 for a half-day and include the mandatory helmet.

(Fast Facts   Auckland

American Express Offices are at 105 Queen St. (© **09/379-8286**) and 67–69 Symonds St. (© **09/367-4422**). For credit card queries, call © 0800/656-660; for traveler's check queries, © 0508/555-358; www.americanexpress.co.nz.

Area Code Auckland's area code (STD) is **09.**

Babysitters Most major hotels can furnish babysitters.

Currency Exchange Go to city center banks and most neighborhood branches for your banking needs. Banks are open Monday through Friday from 9am to 4:30pm. Hotels and restaurants usually convert traveler's checks, but you'll get a much better rate at banks. There is a dedicated currency exchange outlet at **TravelEx NZ,** 32 Queen St. (© **09/358-9173;** www.travelex.co.nz; open normal business hours), and at SKYCITY and Auckland International Airport (both open daily during normal business hours).

Dentists For emergency and after-hours dental service, call **Emergency Dental Service,** on the corner of Greenlane East Road and Peach Parade, Remuera (© **09/523-3030**). It's open Monday through Saturday from 8am to 11pm, Sunday until 10pm.

Doctors For emergency ambulance service, dial © **111.** For emergency medical services, call the **CityMed Medical Centre,** on the corner of Mills Lane and Albert Street, inner city (© **09/377-5525;** www.citymed.co.nz).

Embassies & Consulates Embassies are in Wellington (see "Fast Facts: Wellington," in chapter 12). For additional information on embassies in New Zealand, contact the **Ministry of Foreign Affairs & Trade** in Wellington (© **04/494-8500;** www. mft.govt.nz; enquiries@mft.govt.nz).

Auckland has consulates of the **United States,** Level 3, 23 Customs St. E. (© **09/303-2724;** fax 09/366-0870); **Canada,** 318 Shortland St. (© **09/309-3690**); **Ireland,** Level 7, 23 Customs St. E. (© **09/977-2252**); and the **United Kingdom,** IAG House, 151 Queen St. (© **09/303-2973**).

Emergencies Dial © **111** to call the police, report a fire, or request an ambulance.

Hospitals Area hospitals include **Auckland City Hospital,** 2 Park Rd., Grafton (© **09/367-7000**), which incorporates the National Women's Hospital and the Starship Children's Hospital; and **Greenlane Clinical Centre,** 214 Greenlane West Rd., Epsom (© **09/367-0000**).

Internet Access Give either of these a go: **Cyber Max,** 291 Queen St. ((C) **09/979-2468**); **Net Central Cyber Café,** 5 Lorne St. ((C) **09/373-5408**).

Laundromat There is a 24-hour laundromat at 511 Great North Rd., Grey Lynn ((C) **09/376-6062**).

Lost Property Call the Central Police Station ((C) **09/379-4240**) or any local police station.

Luggage Storage & Lockers "Left luggage" facilities are at the Visitor Information Centre in the International Airport. The fee for 24 hours is about NZ$8 for hand luggage, NZ$15 for large items, and NZ$12 per suitcase. For more information, call (C) **09/256-8845.**

Newspapers & Magazines The *New Zealand Herald* is the daily paper. The *Sunday Star Times* and *Sunday News* are Sunday-morning publications.

Police For emergencies, dial (C) **111.** For other matters, call the Central Police Station ((C) **09/379-4240**).

Post Office Most post offices are open Monday through Friday from 9am to 5pm. The central city Post Shop is at 23 Customs St. E. ((C) **09/302-1059**); it's open Monday through Friday from 9am to 5pm, and Saturday from 9am to noon. For poste restante pickup, go to the Post Shop in the Bledisloe Building on Wellesley Street ((C) **09/379-6714**). There is also a Post Shop on the ground floor of Courier Post House, 151 Victoria St. W. ((C) **09/367-9617**); and others in suburban locations. For post office questions, call (C) **0800/501-501;** www.nzpost.co.nz.

Services for Travelers with Disabilities For information on ramps, toilets, parking lots, telephones, and an equipment showroom, contact the **Disability Resource Centre,** 14 Erson Ave., Royal Oak ((C) **09/625-8069;** www.disabilityresource.org.nz). Both The Link and City Circuit bus routes have wheelchair-accessible buses.

3 WHERE TO STAY

If your idea of a holiday is the best views, the best beds, the best food, and the last word in service, Auckland's luxury hotels won't disappoint. For long stays, you might opt for a fully serviced apartment. Among the best options is **CityLife Auckland A Heritage Hotel** ★, 171 Queen St. ((C) **0800/368-888** in NZ, or 09/379-9222; www.heritagehotels.co.nz), with 216 one- to three-bedroom suites and hotel rooms from NZ$275 to NZ$689. Or treat yourself to their penthouse suite for NZ$1,630.

If you want home comforts, bed-and-breakfasts abound, many in homes of fine character. Pick up the free booklet *Auckland Home, Farmstay and Bed & Breakfast Accommodation* from the visitor center.

Rates include 12.5% GST (goods and services tax) and parking, unless stated otherwise.

IN THE INNER CITY
Very Expensive
Hilton Auckland ★★★ There's no other Hilton in the world like the boutique-style Hilton Auckland, which opened in 2001. It's almost surrounded by water, perched on

AUCKLAND

6

WHERE TO STAY

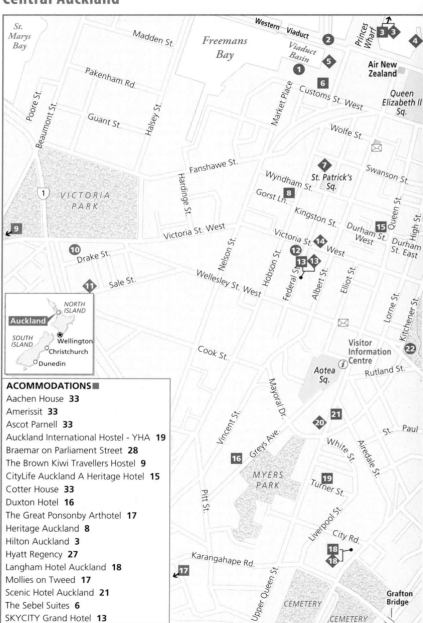

St. Marys Bay

Madden St.

Freemans Bay

Western Viaduct

Viaduct Basin

Princes Wharf

3 **3**

4

2

1

5

Air New Zealand

Pakenham Rd.

Customs St. West

6

Queen Elizabeth II Sq.

Poore St.

Beaumont St.

Guant St.

Halsey St.

Market Place

Wolfe St.

Fanshawe St.

Swanson St.

St. Patrick's Sq.

7

Wyndham St.

Gorst Ln.

8

Kingston St.

Durham St. West

15

Queen St.

High St.

Durham St. East

1

VICTORIA PARK

Hardinge St.

Victoria St. West

Victoria St. West

14

12

13

13

Federal St.

Albert St.

Elliot St.

Lorne St.

Kitchener St.

9

Drake St.

10

Nelson St.

Hobson St.

Sale St.

Wellesley St. West

11

NORTH ISLAND

Auckland

SOUTH ISLAND

Wellington

Christchurch

Dunedin

Cook St.

Mayoral Dr.

Visitor Information ⓘ **Centre**

Aotea Sq.

Rutland St.

22

ACOMMODATIONS■

Aachen House **33**
Amerissit **33**
Ascot Parnell **33**
Auckland International Hostel - YHA **19**
Braemar on Parliament Street **28**
The Brown Kiwi Travellers Hostel **9**
CityLife Auckland A Heritage Hotel **15**
Cotter House **33**
Duxton Hotel **16**
The Great Ponsonby Arthotel **17**
Heritage Auckland **8**
Hilton Auckland **3**
Hyatt Regency **27**
Langham Hotel Auckland **18**
Mollies on Tweed **17**
Scenic Hotel Auckland **21**
The Sebel Suites **6**
SKYCITY Grand Hotel **13**

Vincent St.

Greys Ave.

White St.

Airedale St.

St. Paul

21

20

16

MYERS PARK

Turner St.

19

Pitt St.

Liverpool St.

City Rd.

18

18

Karangahape Rd.

17

Upper Queen St.

CEMETERY

CEMETERY

Grafton Bridge

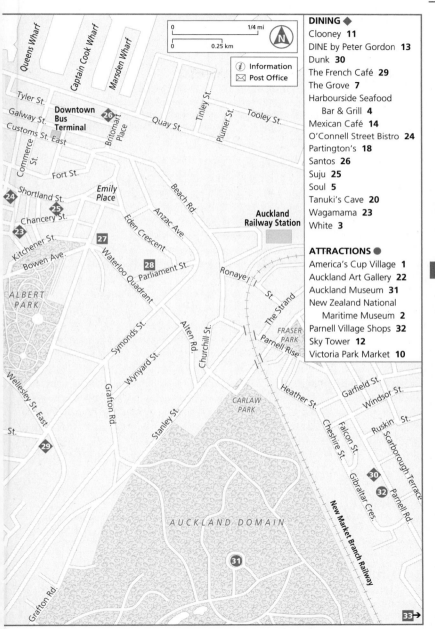

DINING ◆
Clooney **11**
DINE by Peter Gordon **13**
Dunk **30**
The French Café **29**
The Grove **7**
Harbourside Seafood
    Bar & Grill **4**
Mexican Café **14**
O'Connell Street Bistro **24**
Partington's **18**
Santos **26**
Suju **25**
Soul **5**
Tanuki's Cave **20**
Wagamama **23**
White **3**

ATTRACTIONS ●
America's Cup Village **1**
Auckland Art Gallery **22**
Auckland Museum **31**
New Zealand National
    Maritime Museum **2**
Parnell Village Shops **32**
Sky Tower **12**
Victoria Park Market **10**

the end of Princes Wharf like the giant ship that inspired it and like those that tie up alongside it. Rooms are modern, sophisticated, stylish—not overly large in some cases, but always exquisitely furnished, with fabulous bathrooms and amazing sea views. If you want super views, take one of the 12 deluxe corner rooms that feature two whole walls of glass. The suites are shaped like the bow of a ship and boast vast decks. Ask about the new presidential suite for ultimate luxury. The hotel is right in the heart of Viaduct Basin, amid the best restaurants and bars in Auckland.

Princes Wharf, 137–147 Quay St. ℂ **0800/448-002** in NZ, or 09/978-2000. Fax 09/978-2001. www.hilton. com. 165 units. NZ$645 guest room; NZ$720 deluxe; NZ$815 deluxe plus; NZ$1,294 bow suite; NZ$1,645 relaxation suite; NZ$2,145 presidential suite. Off-season and special rates. AE, DC, MC, V. Valet parking NZ$35. **Amenities:** Restaurant; bar; babysitting; concierge; gym w/trainer; glass-fronted heated outdoor pool suspended from 4th-floor bridge; room service; day spa at adjacent Spa de Seville. *In room:* A/C, TV, fridge, hair dryer, minibar, Wi-Fi.

Langham Hotel Auckland ★★★ Fresh from a sumptuous multimillion-dollar makeover, this business favorite is now Auckland's plushest hotel. I love it. They have service down to a fine art and staff are the friendliest in the city. All rooms are opulent but the four floors of Club Rooms offer that little bit extra: king-size beds and lovely marble bathrooms, plus Club Lounge access and business facilities. The hotel has Green Globe Certification and was awarded Qualmark Enviro-Gold status in 2008. Treat yourself to dinner in the award-winning Partington's Restaurant—it's a feast for the eye and the stomach. Overall, the Langham is more traditional than the Hilton and it's my favorite.

83 Symonds St. ℂ **0800/616-261** in NZ, or 09/379-5132. Fax 09/377-9367. www.langhamhotels.com. 410 units. NZ$321 superior; NZ$377 executive; NZ$501 club; NZ$614 park suite; NZ$782 executive suite; NZ$2,121 governor suite; NZ$2,796 royal suite. Leisure packages and long-stay rates. AE, DC, MC, V. Valet parking NZ$30. **Amenities:** 3 restaurants (Partington's [fine dining], SBF [brasserie], SPE [bar food]); 2 bars; airport transfers; babysitting; concierge; concierge-level rooms; health club w/fully equipped gym and trainer; Jacuzzi; heated rooftop lap pool; room service; 2 saunas; Chuan day spa; Wi-Fi in lobby. *In room:* A/C, TV/DVD, fridge, hair dryer, Internet, kitchenette in studio suites, minibar.

SKYCITY Grand Hotel ★★★ This is the five-star baby in the SKYCITY stable. Linked to the SKYCITY hotel and casino complex by a bridge, it offers the best of everything: smart rooms with good bathrooms, one of the best restaurants in Auckland, and a gorgeous lap pool and spa facility. It's a centrally located oasis of luxury offering very good deals and a wow-factor New Zealand contemporary art collection. I like the fact that it's close to the heart of SKYCITY activity, which is always a busy, happening hub. It's much bigger than the Hilton and less formal than the Langham. The hotel has a Qualmark Enviro-Gold rating.

90 Federal St. ℂ **0800/759-2489** in NZ, or 09/363-7000. Fax 09/363-7010. www.skycitygrand.co.nz. 316 units. NZ$619 luxury king or twin room. Long-stay, off-peak, and special rates. AE, DC, MC, V. Valet parking NZ$30. **Amenities:** 2 restaurants (DINE by Peter Gordon [fusion cuisine] and the Terrace Bar & Restaurant); 2 bars; Mercedes airport transfers NZ$95 one-way; babysitting; concierge; gym; Jacuzzi; heated indoor lap pool; room service; sauna; East West Day Spa, specializing in Eastern-style holistic treatments; Wi-Fi and business center in lobby. *In room:* A/C, TV/DVD, fridge, hair dryer, Internet, minibar.

Expensive

Heritage Auckland ★ With two distinct parts—the Hotel wing in a restored, landmark Art Deco building; and the purpose-built contemporary Tower wing—completed in 1998 and 1999, respectively, this property offers a choice of two of everything. All rooms are generous suite-style units with good-size bathrooms. A slight premium applies on the self-contained Tower suites, many of which boast great harbor views.

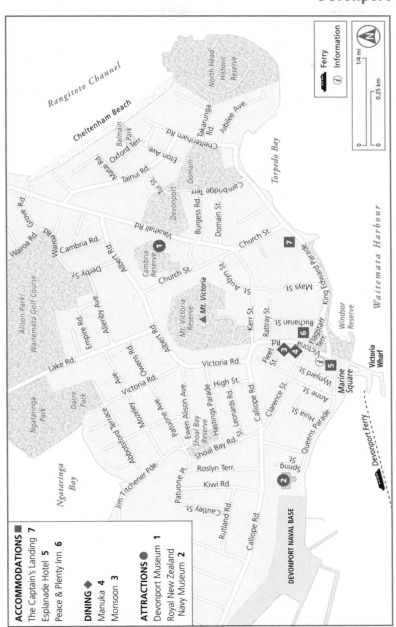

AUCKLAND

6

WHERE TO STAY

Rangitoto Channel

Cheltenham Beach

North Head Historic Reserve

Torpedo Bay

Waitemata Harbour

Ferry
Information

1/4 mi
0.25 km

Takarunga Rd.
Jubilee Ave.
Balmain
Oxford Terr.
Eton Ave.
Matai Rd.
Tainui Rd.
Tui St.
Cheltenham Rd.
Domain
Cambridge Terr.
Devonport
Burgess Rd.
Domain St.
Vauxhall Rd.
Church St.
Wairoa Rd. Grove Rd.
Wairoa Rd.
Cambria Rd.
Cambria Reserve
Derby St.
Church St.
St. Aubyn St.
Alison Park
Waitemata Golf Course
Albert Rd.
Mt. Victoria Reserve
Mt. Victoria
Kerr St.
Mays St.
King Edward Parade
Windsor Reserve
Empire Rd.
Allenby Ave.
Albert Rd.
Rattray St.
Buchanan St.
Flagstaff Terr.
Lake Rd.
Victoria Owens Rd.
Victoria Rd.
Victoria Rd.
Fleet St.
Victoria Terr.
Victoria Wharf
Ngataringa Park
Dacre Park
Moselev
Patuone Ave.
High St.
Anne St.
Wynard St.
Marine Square
Abbotsford Terrace
Ewen Alison Ave.
Shoal Bay Reserve
Hastings Parade
St. Leonards Rd.
Calliope Rd.
Clarence St.
Huia St.
Queens Parade
Jim Titchener Pde.
Patuone Pl.
Shoal Bay Rd.
Roslyn Terr.
Kiwi Rd.
Spring St.
Ngataringa Bay
Cautley St.
Rutland Rd.
Calliope Rd.
Devonport Ferry
DEVONPORT NAVAL BASE

ACCOMMODATIONS ■
The Captain's Landing **7**
Esplanade Hotel **5**
Peace & Plenty Inn **6**

DINING ◆
Manuka **4**
Monsoon **3**

ATTRACTIONS ●
Devonport Museum **1**
Royal New Zealand Navy Museum **2**

Hotel Wing, 35 Hobson St.; Tower Wing, 22 Nelson St. ☎ **0800/368-888** in NZ, or 09/379-8553. Fax 09/379-8554. www.heritagehotels.co.nz. 327 units. NZ$249–NZ$279 standard rooms; NZ$274–NZ$589 suites. Long-stay, off-peak, and special rates. AE, DC, MC, V. Valet parking NZ$30. **Amenities:** 2 restaurants (Hectors in Hotel wing; Azure in Tower wing); 2 bars; babysitting; concierge; 2 gyms; 2 Jacuzzis; rooftop heated outdoor pool; heated indoor lap pool; room service; sauna; all-weather outdoor lit tennis court; Wi-Fi throughout. *In room:* A/C, TV, fridge, hair dryer, kitchenette and full kitchen, minibar.

Hyatt Regency ★★   The Hyatt Regency's smart new apartment suites and a gymnasium and health spa facility to die for should make you sit up and take notice. The suites contain kitchenettes, balconies, and swanky bathrooms; the 20 roomy corner suites with wraparound balconies are the pick of the bunch. Connecting rooms make them perfect for families or couples traveling together. Residence suites have kitchens. It has more of a boutiquey, personalized style than some of the other inner city biggies—an unassuming elegance that's very easy to feel comfortable in. Like most of its competitors, it offers enticing extras in club-level rooms, but even standard rooms are a rich reward after a hard day of sightseeing. Come here for the best health spa, pool, and gymnasium of any New Zealand hotel.

Waterloo Quadrant and Princes St. ☎ **0800/441-234** in NZ, or 09/355-1234. Fax 09/303-2932. www.auckland.regency.hyatt.com. 363 units. NZ$430 regency deluxe king; NZ$465 residence king and regency king suite; NZ$500 club king; NZ$495–NZ$555 residence suite; NZ$635 residence 2-bedroom suite. Long-stay and special rates. AE, DC, MC, V. Valet parking NZ$25. **Amenities:** Restaurant; bar; babysitting; concierge; gym; Jacuzzi; heated indoor pool; room service; sauna; day spa. *In room:* A/C, TV/DVD, fridge, hair dryer, kitchens in residence rooms, minibar, Wi-Fi.

Moderate

Braemar on Parliament Street   I fell in love with the history and character of this three-story Edwardian gentleman's town house (ca. 1901) the minute I walked in the door. Four rooms here—two with en-suite bathrooms, two with shared bathroom—are riddled with charm. The Batten Suite (once home to legendary pilot Jean Batten's father) is the best and biggest. John and Susan Sweetman have an astonishing collection of historic Auckland photographs, and the numerous Persian rugs and colonial antiques make this place a feast for the eye and a home away from home. It's the only upmarket B&B in the central business district and it's just a short walk from trendy High Street, downtown activities, restaurants, and transport systems. Braemar has a Qualmark Enviro-Gold rating for its ecofriendly approach to hosting, energy conservation, and recycling.

7 Parliament St. ☎ **0800/155-463** in NZ, or 09/377-5463. Fax 09/377-3056. www.aucklandbedand breakfast.com. 4 units. NZ$225–NZ$350. Long-stay rates. AE, DC, MC, V. Free parking. **Amenities:** Babysitting; free bikes; nearby golf course, pool, and tennis courts. *In room:* TV, hair dryer, Wi-Fi.

Duxton Hotel ★   There is something intangibly serene about the Duxton. Maybe it's the leafy, tree-lined street it sits on, or the green park it overlooks. Either way, it's quieter and more intimate than some of the bigger hotels. Treat yourself to a special executive suite Jacuzzi package that includes breakfast and Internet access. Apartments with full laundry facilities and kitchens are also a big plus. Just 10 years old, this little oasis of calm demands your attention.

100 Greys Ave. ☎ **0800/655-555** in NZ, or 09/375-1800. Fax 09/375-1801. www.duxton.com.au. 149 units. NZ$185–NZ$225 deluxe; NZ$285–NZ$325 executive suite; NZ$385 penthouse suite. Long-stay, off-peak, and special rates. AE, DC, MC, V. Valet parking NZ$20 per day; self-parking NZ$10 per day. **Amenities:** Restaurant (The Grill [contemporary New Zealand]); bar; airport transfers NZ$60 one-way; babysitting; concierge; guest access to small gym across road; NZ$10 day pass; Jacuzzi; outdoor heated pool; room service; Wi-Fi in lobby. *In room:* A/C, TV/DVD, fridge, hair dryer, Internet, kitchenette, minibar.

The Sebel Suites   If you're a fan of all things nautical, you'll feel right at home at the popular Sebel Suites, where big views take in the comings and goings of the Viaduct Basin. Right in the middle of the action, with classy restaurants and bars right on the doorstep, these all-suite accommodations were built for the America's Cup. Suites are fresh and crisp, and all marina suites have separate living rooms and balconies overlooking the water. If you like being within easy reach of a good time, the Sebel is for you— and given its prime location, you'll find the rates extremely reasonable. It wouldn't hurt to pack your ear plugs as social capers can get boisterous around here.

85–89 Customs St. W. (☎ **0800/937-373** in NZ, or 09/978-4000. Fax 09/978-4099. www.mirvachotels. com.au. 123 units. NZ$197–NZ$300 studio suite; NZ$225–NZ$331 city 1-bedroom suite; NZ$287–NZ$408 marina suite; NZ$328–NZ$452 executive suite. Long-stay, off-peak, and special deals. AE, DC, MC, V. Valet parking NZ$25. Closed Dec 31. **Amenities:** Nearby restaurants and bars, many w/charge-back facility for guests; babysitting; concierge; gym across the road (NZ$8 for guest use); heated pool, Jacuzzi, saunas across road; room service; Wi-Fi in reception. *In room:* A/C, TV/DVD, fridge, hair dryer, Internet, fully equipped kitchen, minibar.

Inexpensive

For a sensibly priced stay in a landmark building right in the heart of the city, **Scenic Hotel Auckland,** 380 Queen St. (☎ **09/374-1741;** www.scenicgroup.co.nz), has 100 very comfortable rooms priced from NZ$225 to NZ$518. Ask for one of the eight rooms on the northwest face that have incredible views straight down Queen Street. It's a modest but perfectly placed option with a very nice cafe and bar at street level.

Auckland International Hostel-YHA   This hostel opened in mid-1999 in a large converted office block, so everything is clean, modern, and comfortable. It's one of the best hostels in the country, with over 50,000 guests a year. Security is tight. It's just a 5-minute walk to Central City. This is the flagship YHA hostel; its sister establishment, Auckland City YHA, is only 100m (330 ft.) away. This facility has a communal lounge, a smokers' room, bike and luggage storage, and large kitchens.

1–35 Turner St. (P.O. Box 68-149). (☎ **0800/278-299** in NZ, or 09/302-8200. Fax 09/302-8205. www.yha. co.nz. 170 beds. NZ$20–NZ$30 multishare; NZ$55–NZ$119 private room. NZ$3 extra per person per night for non-YHA members. AE, MC, V. Limited off-street parking NZ$5; reservation required. *In room:* No phone.

IN PONSONBY
Very Expensive

Mollies on Tweed ★★★   This grand old 1870s home has been extensively renovated and expanded to provide 13 stylish suites and apartments. If you take the upstairs level, you'll have a balcony; downstairs rooms open onto the garden. Nothing has been spared to create upmarket interiors filled with antiques and smart furniture. The location is handy to Ponsonby Road restaurants, bars, and boutique shopping. Mollies combines the comforts of home with the privacy of apartment living. A member of Small Luxury Hotels of the World, it has accumulated plenty of international accolades. The hotel's award-winning gourmet restaurant, the Dining Room, complete with dining terrace, is definitely a must-have experience.

6 Tweed St., St. Mary's Bay. (☎ **09/376-3489.** Fax 09/378-6592. www.mollies.co.nz. 13 units. NZ$613 junior suite; NZ$855 villa suite; NZ$979 premier villa suite. Off-season, long-stay, and weekend rates. AE, DC, MC, V. Free off-street parking. Closed July. Children 11 and under on request only. **Amenities:** Restaurant (The Dining Room; Pacific Rim); bar; airport transfer NZ$120 one-way; babysitting; concierge; gym; Jacuzzi; room service. *In room:* A/C (apts only), TV/DVD, hair dryer, fully equipped kitchen, minibar, Wi-Fi.

Moments One Tree Hill

A stroll in **Cornwall Park** in Epsom is a must. You'll find fields with grazing sheep, charming walks, and One Tree Hill, which is famous for its lone tree. Stop first at the **Cornwall Park Visitor Centre** (☎ **09/630-8485;** www.cornwallpark.co.nz) for maps and information on self-guided walks.

Moderate

The Great Ponsonby Arthotel ★   This restored villa owned by hosts Sally James and Gerard Hill will delight you. It's quiet, yet within walking distance of the best of Ponsonby, and the comfortable rooms reflect a colorful Pacific mood. Three suites have both bathtubs and showers. The lovely Dunedin Room has its own deck, while the upstairs penthouse has a sitting room and balcony. Don't overlook the Palm Garden studios if you want extra space and privacy; some of these come with kitchenette, mini-bar, and VCR. There's a sunlit lounge bulging with books, lots of New Zealand art and magazines, verandas to unwind on, and breakfasts to linger over. The property has a Qualmark Enviro-Gold rating and participates in recycling and energy conservation programs.

30 Ponsonby Terrace. ☎ **0800/766-792** in NZ, or 09/376-5989. Fax 09/376-6527. www.greatpons.co.nz. 11 units. NZ$235 villa rooms; NZ$250 courtyard studios; NZ$300 palm garden suite; NZ$400 penthouse. Long-stay and off-peak rates. Rates include breakfast. AE, DC, MC, V. Free off-street parking. Children 11 and under in some rooms. **Amenities:** Fixed-price taxi airport transfers; free bikes; nearby golf course and pool. *In room:* LCD TV/DVD, fridge (in some), hair dryer, kitchenette (in some), minibar (in some), MP3 docking station, free Wi-Fi.

Inexpensive

The Brown Kiwi Travellers Hostel   This 100-year-old house is on a quiet street just a block from the main Ponsonby action. The best deals here are the two rooms in the lovely little garden house, a purpose-built corrugated-iron dwelling tucked among banana palms and ponds. It serves as a double or triple facility and is less sardinelike than the in-house rooms. Overall, this place offers a good atmosphere and a terrific garden courtyard in which to while away summer days and nights.

7 Prosford St. ☎/fax **09/378-0191.** www.brownkiwi.co.nz. 32 beds, all with shared bathroom. NZ$24 dorm per person; NZ$56 twin/double. MC, V. **Amenities:** Bar. *In room:* Hair dryer.

IN MOUNT EDEN/EPSOM

Inexpensive

Bavaria Bed & Breakfast Hotel Ⓥ**Value**   It says FREE STATE OF BAVARIA on the gate and, as you can imagine, Rudi and Ulricke Stephan get a lot of German guests. But it's a cosmopolitan establishment in a quiet, leafy neighborhood, equally enjoyed by large numbers of Americans and Canadians. The three upstairs rooms are the sunniest, and all have doors leading out onto the balcony. All units have en-suite bathrooms. The big, old villa is close to Mount Eden village, where there are several restaurants and cafes, and you can catch buses on nearby Dominion Road heading into the city, which is 10 minutes away. You can feel good about your stay here, because Bavaria uses solar energy and environmentally friendly cleaning products.

83 Valley Rd., Mount Eden. ☎ **09/638-9641.** Fax 09/638-9665. www.bavariabandbhotel.co.nz. 11 units. **131**
NZ$149; NZ$50 each extra adult; NZ$25 children 2–12; free for children 1 and under. Off-season and
long-stay rates. Rates include breakfast. AE, MC, V. Free off-street parking. **Amenities:** Nearby golf course;
nearby tennis courts. *In room:* Hair dryer on request, free Wi-Fi throughout.

IN PARNELL/NEWMARKET

To get to Parnell if you don't have a car, take The Link bus from Queen Street, which
travels down Customs Street and along Beach Road to Parnell Rise. Sadly, most of the
best B&Bs in this area have closed or are not what they used to be. One new option is
Ascot Parnell, St. Stephens Ave., Parnell (☎ **09/309-9012;** www.ascotparnell.com),
owned by experienced hosts Bart and Therese Blommaert. They'll meet you in person at
the airport and take you back to one of their three beautiful, ecofriendly suites, which are
priced at NZ$225 to NZ$385. There's even an elevator for guests and luggage and free
Wi-Fi throughout.

IN REMUERA
Expensive

Aachen House ★★   If you're looking to sloth it out in total elegance, surrounded by
stunning antiques and top service, Joan McKirdy's Edwardian villa is for you. Suites are
furnished with the busy executive in mind, with two direct-dial phones, a fax hookup,
and a classic writing desk, plus a modern en-suite bathroom and big super-king-size beds.
The Victoria, with its own lounge and balcony, is particularly enticing. The house is 4km
(2½ miles) from downtown; bus service is a block away. I don't like to use the word
"perfect" too much, but this little boutique hotel fits the description.

39 Market Rd., Remuera. ☎ **0800/222-436** in NZ, or 09/520-2329. Fax 09/524-2898. www.aachenhouse.
co.nz. 8 units. NZ$439–NZ$665. Rates include breakfast and predinner drinks. Long-stay and off-peak
rates. AE, DC, MC, V. Free off-street parking. Children 11 and under by arrangement. **Amenities:** Concierge; nearby golf course; room service on request. *In room:* Hair dryer, Wi-Fi.

Cotter House ★★   Gloria Poupard-Walbridge has taken this exquisite 1847 British
Regency–style mansion and turned it into a stunning B&B. You'll gasp at the splendor
when you walk through the door. Cotter House is a heritage building overflowing with
antiques, fine international art, dramatic window treatments, and luxurious marble
bathrooms—a lavish haven for the discerning traveler. The two-room suite is my pick,
but you can take the whole house if you like, or have exclusive use of the 1892 ballroom
for formal gatherings, cocktail parties, or weddings. The property has a Qualmark
Enviro-Silver rating and a carbon offset policy. And Gloria's cooking will knock your
socks off. Her fabulous French breakfasts are the *pièce de résistance.*

4 St. Vincent Ave., Remuera. ☎ **09/529-5156.** Fax 09/529-5186. www.cotterhouse.com. 4 units. NZ$485
Blue Provencal, Oriental, and Burgundy suites; NZ$640 2-bedroom Bronze suite; NZ$2,700 entire property per day. Extra person NZ$110. Long-stay and special packages. Rates include 4-course breakfast.
Dinner on request. AE, DC, MC, V. Free off-street valet parking. **Amenities:** Bar; babysitting; free bikes;
concierge; nearby golf course; exercise pavilion; heated outdoor pool. *In room:* TV/DVD, hair dryer, shared
minibar, free Wi-Fi.

Moderate

Amerissit ★ (Value)   Barbara McKain's quiet cul-de-sac address in an affluent suburb
will quickly lull you into a state of bliss. She's one of those special hosts who go out of
their way to ensure guests' needs are well and truly met over and above expectations. Her
modern rooms are exceptionally well priced and the atmosphere here is much more

AUCKLAND 6 WHERE TO STAY

relaxed than at either Cotter or Aachen House. The Mount Hobson room has a huge Jacuzzi and shower, and the second upstairs room has its own lounge. The large downstairs room looks out on a leafy garden.

20 Buttle St., Remuera. (C) **09/522-9297.** Fax 09/522-9298. www.amerissit.co.nz. 3 units. NZ$240–NZ$295. Rates include breakfast and charged airport transport. Long-stay and off-peak rates. AE, DC, MC, V. Free off-street parking. **Amenities:** Airport transfers; bikes; nearby golf course and tennis courts. *In room:* TV/DVD, fridge (in 1 room), hair dryer, minibar, Wi-Fi.

IN DEVONPORT/BIRKENHEAD
Expensive
Stafford Villa ★★ (Finds) Guests lavish praise upon the Stafford Villa's upmarket B&B experience. Once home to a missionary family, the old two-story home, set in a quaint and tranquil Victorian suburb, was transformed by the industrious Mark and Chris Windram. Chris spent many years marketing small luxury hotels and resorts around the world, so she has a pretty keen idea of what makes a good holiday experience. The two rooms are lush and indulgent—"just a little over the top," says Chris, who believes guests like something different. You can breakfast in the conservatory, tucking into local produce and homemade preserves from the garden; and then take a 5-minute walk to the ferry and end up in downtown Auckland just 10 minutes later. Stafford Villa has a Qualmark Enviro rating.

2 Awanui St., Birkenhead Point. (C) **09/418-3022.** Fax 09/419-8197. www.staffordvilla.co.nz. 2 units. NZ$445. Rates include full breakfast, predinner aperitif, and canapés. Long-stay and special rates, and weekend packages. AE, DC, MC, V. Free off-street parking. **Amenities:** Airport transfers NZ$105–NZ$115 one-way; nearby golf course; Wi-Fi in library. *In room:* LCD TV/DVD/CD, hair dryer.

Moderate
Devonport has numerous excellent B&Bs in this price range. If you'd like a roomy retreat all to yourself, then opt for the **Captain's Landing,** 22 King Edward Parade, Devonport ((C) **09/445-4188;** www.thecaptainslanding.co.nz), where you can enjoy two bedrooms, a bathroom, and a sitting room for the excellent price of NZ$275, and NZ$100 for each extra person. It's right on the waterfront and wireless Internet is available in your suite. If you like to be in the center of the village, you can unwind at the **Esplanade Hotel,** 1 Victoria Rd. ((C) **09/445-1291;** fax 09/445-1999; www.esplanadehotel.co.nz), which has 15 character-filled rooms with en-suite bathrooms, plus a suite and a two-bedroom penthouse apartment. Rates range from NZ$275 to NZ$750.

Peace & Plenty Inn ★ (Moments) Romantics will love this gorgeous old home, which Judy Machin has transformed into the ultimate sumptuous, floral-themed haven. Every room has an en-suite bathroom—two with tub and shower, the rest shower only. The downstairs Albert is the smallest unit but has the best bathroom; the Windsor is the

> (Finds) **Scented Heaven**
>
> You don't have to be a rose lover to appreciate the intoxicating perfumes that rise from Parnell's beautiful rose gardens at **Dove-Myer Robinson Park.** The 5,000 rosebushes in formal beds make the park the perfect picnic spot. And look out for the gorgeous and historic little **St. Stephen's Chapel,** one of the city's first churches. Access to both is off Gladstone Road and Judges Bay Road.

> ## ⓂMoments   Sunset Views
>
> Take a picnic basket and go up the easy 10-minute bush walk to the top of Mount Hobson in Remuera. Watch the sun go down over wonderful 360-degree views of the harbor and city. Access to Mount Hobson Reserve is signposted on Remuera Road, just before you reach the village.

biggest. Three upstairs rooms are sunny, with views and balconies. The whole place oozes character and ambience. The garden suite overlooks the lush subtropical garden, and the property has a Qualmark Silver Shield for Responsible Tourism.

6 Flagstaff Terrace, Devonport. ☎ **09/445-2925.** Fax 09/445-2901. www.peaceandplenty.co.nz. 7 units. NZ$350. Long-stay and off-peak rates. Rates include breakfast. MC, V. **Amenities:** Airport transfers NZ$100; babysitting; bike rentals; nearby golf course and tennis courts. *In room:* TV, fridge (in some), hair dryer, Wi-Fi.

IN THE WESTERN SUBURBS

Beach lovers should consider **Bethells Beach Cottages,** 267 Bethells Rd. (☎ **09/810-9581;** www.bethellsbeach.com). They have two sunny, self-contained holiday cottages and a self-contained apartment set in lush, private gardens—the ultimate Kiwi getaway—for NZ$285 to NZ$395. They're very ecofriendly and have Green Globe 21 status aligned with Waitakere City Eco Plan. In addition, owners John and Trude Bethell-Paice have extensive knowledge of the Auckland region and are happy to help their guests find the best places to visit. And let's not forget the free Scandinavian hot tub!

IN THE EASTERN SUBURBS

The **Point View Lodge,** 316 Point View Dr., Howick (☎ **09/537-5678;** www.point view.co.nz), has three beautiful rooms that go for NZ$350 to NZ$450.

NEAR THE AIRPORT

If you have an early-morning flight or you're checking into Auckland at night and want a quick bed, call **Centra Auckland Airport,** Kirkbridge and Ascot roads, Airport Oaks (☎ **0800/080-236** in NZ, or 09/275-1059; www.centra.co.nz), which is set in 4 hectares (10 acres) of gardens and has 250 recently refurbished rooms for NZ$168 to NZ$250.

4 WHERE TO DINE

You get no points for finding a brilliant restaurant in Auckland; there are too many of them for that to be considered a feat. And a good number of them are offering world-class cuisine at very affordable prices. The predominant cuisines are ethnic and Pacific Rim, the latter being that variable trend of combining the freshest, high-quality ingredients with whatever cultural element (theoretically Pacific-based) grabs the chef's fancy. As you can imagine, the interpretations are endless.

Although there are restaurants scattered all over the city, you'll find they rub shoulders with each other in the Viaduct Basin area and along Ponsonby Road—still the trendiest areas and favorites with big spenders. There is also a good haul along the downtown waterfront, at Mission Bay, and in Devonport and Takapuna on the North Shore. You can take your pick from innumerable Italian/Mediterranean-style eateries with starched white tablecloths and timber floors, and fashionable California/New York–style brasseries and elegant bistros. If you're looking for cheap eats, they abound throughout the city. There are literally thousands of places to choose from and you're seldom far from any of them—Asian restaurants and sushi bars in particular.

If you've singled out a popular favorite, it's a good idea to make reservations, especially on weekends, but in many cases you can simply stroll and choose. Tipping is perfectly in order but is not a custom anywhere in New Zealand.

A word on wine: New Zealand restaurants are generally classified as **licensed** (to sell beer, wine, and spirits) or **BYO** (bring your own). Some stipulate wine only or are unlicensed.

IN THE INNER CITY
Expensive

Harbourside Seafood Bar & Grill ★ , first floor, Ferry Building, Quay Street (✆ **09/307/0556;** www.harboursiderestaurant.co.nz), is a chic place with great views and seriously good seafood. Two others not to be missed are the **Grove** ★★ , St. Patrick's Square, 55 Albert St. (✆ **09/368-4129**), a new, groovy favorite with terrific food and an excellent degustation menu; and **O'Connell Street Bistro** ★★ , O'Connell and Shortland streets (✆ **09/377-1884**), a tiny but perfect 28-seat restaurant that's big on international style and flavors—definitely a place for special moments. **Soul** ★★ , Hobson and Customs Street West (✆ **09/356-7249**), is now an institution in a prime Viaduct Basin location with fabulous people-watching potential. Top chefs, an open-air style, and the best New Zealand fish make it a winner with international travelers, the business crowd, and high-flyers in general.

For something entirely different, head for award-winning **Partington's** ★★★ , in Langham Hotel (✆ **0800/616-261** in NZ), where a team of European chefs, Christofle silverware, Rosenthal plateware, handmade German crystal glasses, and an opulent decor combine to create an evening you'll never forget. Take a fat wallet.

Clooney ★★ INTERNATIONAL   Once an industrial warehouse and now one of Auckland's top dining experiences, this highly ranked dining space is a complete night out. From its elegant main dining area to its private dining rooms and basement lounge, it's all about style and delicious tastes. It's inclined to be a little pretentious and is certainly favored by the who's who, but expect top flavors in fire-grilled and rotisserie meat and seafood dishes.

33 Sale St. ✆ **09/358-1702.** www.clooney.co.nz. Reservations required. Main courses NZ$30–NZ$40. AE, DC, MC, V. Daily 11am–late.

ⓕ **Finds** **Quick & Easy**

For a quick snack try **Suju,** 37 Chancery St. (✆ **09/309-3006**), a terrific little soup-and-fresh-juice bar. Nearby, the London chain **Wagamama,** Level 2, Metropolis Building, 1 Courthouse Lane (✆ **09/359-9266**), is a snazzy noodle bar offering fresh and tasty Japanese food served on long communal tables.

Finds   Do the Hokey Pokey

A blend of vanilla ice cream with pieces of toffee, Hokey Pokey ice cream is unique to New Zealand and was first manufactured by the Meadowgold Ice Cream Company of Papatoetoe, Auckland, in the 1940s.

DINE By Peter Gordon ★★★ INTERNATIONAL FUSION   Founder of London's legendary Sugar Club restaurant, top New Zealand chef Peter Gordon is in charge of the menu at this chic upmarket eatery. Floating circles of dimmed light, artwork, and an inventive menu make it worth seeking out. Kick off with Japanese-inspired starters or panfried scallops, leaving space for duck breast on smoked polenta with cumin-roasted baby carrots and rainbow chard with a truffle, olive, radicchio, and chestnut salad. They have a great New Zealand wine list.

In the SKYCITY Grand Hotel, 90 Federal St. *©* **09/363-7030.** www.skycityauckland.co.nz. Reservations required. Main courses NZ$33–NZ$45. AE, DC, MC, V. Daily 5:30pm–late. Also open for dessert 10–11pm.

The French Café ★★★ CONTEMPORARY EUROPEAN   I've never heard a bad word about this perpetual award winner. Come here to savor sensational, finely crafted dishes in a sophisticated interior that you will remember forever. From the foie gras to the roast duckling, you'll be sighing with pleasure. Better yet, you don't have to take out a bank loan to dine in this elegant little gem, which sits proudly in one of the seedier parts of town.

210 Symonds St. *©* **09/377-1911.** www.thefrenchcafe.co.nz. Reservations required. Main courses NZ$28–NZ$40. AE, DC, MC, V. Tues–Sat 6pm–late.

White ★★★ NEW ZEALAND/EUROPEAN   As the name suggests, this sleek, award-winning culinary haven—consistently rated as one of Auckland's top restaurants—is a fully glazed, all-white foodies' paradise, where they celebrate the best New Zealand produce. The words "glamour, sophistication, and exceptional" fall readily from the tongue. From a delicious seafood risotto to steamed red snapper in a coriander, lemon grass, and tomato broth with bok choy and white radish, it's all about exquisite tastes and outstanding service, with sea views to match. If you can't decide what to have, eat your way slowly through the degustation menu. They also cater to vegetarians with a separate menu.

In the Hilton Auckland, Princes Wharf, 147 Quay St. *©* **09/978-2000.** Reservations required. Main courses NZ$30–NZ$40. AE, DC, MC, V. Daily 6pm–late.

Moderate

Mexican Café ★★ MEXICAN   Now an institution, this restaurant has served reliable, reasonably priced meals in a lively, colorful atmosphere for more than 2 decades. The menu is huge, the servings generous, and the enchiladas divine. For the best fun, go on a Tuesday, Wednesday, or Thursday night when the cafe schedules live Latin music. And don't overlook the rare tequila supply.

Upstairs, 67 Victoria St. W. *©* **09/373-2311.** www.mexicancafe.co.nz. Reservations recommended. Main courses NZ$15–NZ$25. MC, V. Mon–Fri noon–late; Sat–Sun 5pm–late.

AUCKLAND

6

WHERE TO DINE

Tanuki's Cave ★ (**Value**) JAPANESE YAKITORI   I fell in love with this place the minute I descended underground. This hugely popular dark den pulses most nights of the week and you have to get in early (like 6pm) to get a spot. People line up all the way back up the stairs to the street, but don't let their hungry looks make you rush through the delicious and incredibly well-priced menu. Choose a selection of skewers (chargrilled yakitori and deep-fried, breaded kushiage) or the delicious tofu salad. If you can't get a spot here, Tanuki's Sake & Sushi Bar is next door at ground level and is also well worth trying.

319B Upper Queen St. ✆ **09/379-5151.** Reservations recommended. Main courses NZ$6–NZ$12. MC, V. Wed–Sat 6pm–late.

Santos CAFE   You'll find this excellent cafe down in the exciting Britomart area, where a huge amount of boutique development is due for completion by the end of 2010. I got my best Auckland cup of coffee here and their big Caesar salad was perfect. The large menu roams through pastas, big tasting platters, salads, homemade breads, and a wide range of all-day breakfast options. They also have a great fresh juice menu. It's a relaxed spot that attracts a mixed business crowd.

130 Quay St., Britomart. ✆ **09/337-0088.** www.santoscoffee.co.nz. No reservations. Main courses NZ$15–NZ$24. MC, V. Mon–Fri 6:30am–5pm; Sat 8am–4pm.

IN PONSONBY/HERNE BAY
Expensive
Also try the upmarket Italian cafe **Prego** ★★ , 226 Ponsonby Rd. (✆ **09/376-3095**).

SPQR Café & Bar ★★ INTERNATIONAL   If you want to see trendy Ponsonby at its strutting best and most colorfully diverse, come to SPQR. The menu is just a few

---

(Value) A Cheap Feed at the Food Halls

If you're after a dollar-stretching fill-up, the city has plenty of food courts, where even NZ$5 to NZ$15 will satisfy the hunger pangs. One of the most popular is in **Downtown Shopping Centre,** QEII Square on Quay Street. It's open Monday through Thursday from 7am to 6pm, Friday from 7am to 8pm, and Saturday and Sunday from 7am to 4pm. There is an international food boulevard at **SKYCITY Metro,** 291–297 Queen St., open daily from 9am until late.

At the **Atrium Food Gallery,** Atrium Shopping Centre, on Elliot Street between Victoria and Wellesley streets, you'll find everything from McDonald's to pasta, kabobs, Chinese, sushi, and a bakery. It's open Monday through Thursday from 7am to 6pm, Friday from 7am to 9pm, Saturday from 7am to 6pm, and Sunday from 7:30am to 6pm. Also in this area and a few notches higher in style is **Elliott Stables,** 39–41 Elliott St. (✆ **09/308-9331;** www.elliottstables.co.nz), which is a little epicurean lane filled with over a dozen specialty food stores and restaurants. There are artisan wine suppliers, cheesemakers, sushi joints, a chocolate cake company, and French and Italian cafes.

(Finds)   The Healthy Stuff

Rocket Kitchen, 234A Ponsonby Rd. (📞 **09/360-8834;** www.rocketkitchen.co.nz), is a yummy little urban food store selling great deli and takeout food items. **Greys Ave Deli,** 108 Greys Ave. (📞 **09/373-2908;** greysavedelic@ahc.org.nz), provides all things kosher; and **Ripe Delicatessen** ★, 172 Richmond Rd., Grey Lynn (📞 **09/360-6159;** www.ripedeli.co.nz), is my favorite spot for a wide range of takeout meals, salads, and goodies in general. It's very easy to find—just turn into Richmond Road off Ponsonby Road and drive for about 3 minutes. It will be on a corner on your left. They make terrific treat-filled baskets and for a minimal cost they will courier them anywhere in central Auckland, so you don't ever have to leave your hotel.

strides above average, but it's the atmosphere and the people-watching that make it such a winner. In what was once a tire-retread shop, now stylishly spartan with stainless steel and concrete, the film and media crowd, the gay community, and your average run-of-the-mill Joe Bloggs all lean about looking supercool and hungry. SPQR serves up tasty morsels such as paper-thin Roman pizza with unusual toppings until well after midnight. (See "The Club & Bar Scene" under "Auckland After Dark," later in this chapter.)

150 Ponsonby Rd. 📞 **09/360-1710.** Reservations recommended. Main courses NZ$25–NZ$35. AE, DC, MC, V. Mon–Fri noon–2am; Sat–Sun 10am–2am.

Vinnies Restaurant ★★★ **(Moments** MODERN NEW ZEALAND   Vinnies invariably appears on any top-five list of Auckland restaurants. Its wall full of awards draws attention to the chefs' superior level of culinary artistry and innovation. It's acknowledged as the place to go to if you aspire to (or claim) sophisticated urban tastes. There's plenty of game on the menu—try the farm-raised duck or the wild rabbit tart; or graze (elegantly) from the degustation menu. The interior is romantic, the service tops. Hire out the private dining room if you feel like spoiling yourself and pause to admire the contemporary art.

166 Jervois Rd., Herne Bay. 📞 **09/376-5597.** www.vinnies.co.nz. Reservations recommended. Main courses NZ$37–NZ$42. AE, DC, MC, V. Tues–Sun 5pm–late.

Moderate
Bambina **(Value** CAFE   This is a lively, popular spot with delicious counter food presented under glass domes. There's a big blackboard menu for all-day breakfasts with all the conventional favorites—eggs any way you want them, ricotta hot cakes, muesli, and fruit. Lunch fare runs to Turkish sandwiches, bruschetta, and rare-grilled tuna with coriander and lime.

268 Ponsonby Rd. 📞 **09/360-4000.** Reservations not required. Main courses NZ$12–NZ$22. AE, MC, V. Daily 8am–5pm.

Chapel ★★ BISTRO   This is favored by locals, who rave about its crazy, over-the-top wallpaper, its delicious thin-crust pizzas, and its generally hip vibe. The Chapel Platter is also worth trying and an a la carte menu deals out big rib-eye steaks. They have an excellent wine list and cocktails that will make you appreciate the eclectic design even more.

147 Ponsonby Rd. 📞 **09/360-4528.** www.chapel.co.nz. Reservations recommended. Main courses NZ$25–NZ$32. AE, MC, V. Daily noon–late.

> **(Moments** Dining with a Difference
>
> If you're looking for something different, then **Finale,** 350 Karangahape Rd.
> (℃ **09/377-4820;** www.350finale.co.nz), is for you. Help yourself to a delicious
> buffet and sit back for outrageous cabaret entertainment provided by the glam-
> orous drag queen extravaganza. **Caluzzi Restaurant & Bar,** 461 Karangahape Rd.
> (℃ **09/357-0778;** www.caluzzi.co.nz), also features a drag cabaret.

Dizengoff ★ CAFE   When Dizengoff opened several years ago, everyone wanted to
be here—or, more precisely, to be seen here. The place is invariably filled with stylish
types who like to pick delicately at their healthy bagels and sip strange health drinks
without mussing up their lip gloss. All that aside, the food is just as tasty as it is healthy,
and if you can squeeze into this swirling den of style, you'll certainly relish the big
brunchy breakfasts.

256 Ponsonby Rd. ℃ **09/360-0108.** Reservations recommended. Main courses NZ$16–NZ$25. AE, DC,
MC, V. Daily 7am–5pm.

GPK ★ NEW ZEALAND/EUROPEAN   This Ponsonby haunt has been around for a
long time. It's what we call a stayer. I blame its reliably good pizzas, its lively mood, its
fresh a la carte menu, and its good prices. I come here often, knowing I'll walk out happy
and well fed. It's one of the more consistent options on Ponsonby Road.

262 Ponsonby Rd. ℃ **09/360-1113.** Reservations recommended. Main courses NZ$18–NZ$28. AE, MC,
V. Mon–Fri 11:30am–late; Sat–Sun 9am–late.

Inexpensive

Café Cezanne CAFE   Everyone seems to love this old favorite, especially on weekends. The food is good and the atmosphere terrific. There's a worn-but-loved quality to
it that I really enjoy. They do very good breakfasts—the mushroom and smoked chicken
omelet is one of the best I've ever had—and the big, fattening cakes will tempt if you're
just in for coffee. There's nothing "designery" about the place; it's slightly frayed at the
edges, in fact, but it has genuine warmth that is very appealing.

296 Ponsonby Rd. ℃ **09/376-3338.** NZ$15–NZ$25. MC, V. Mon–Fri 7:30am–late; Sat–Sun 8:30am–late.

IN MOUNT EDEN/EPSOM/GREY LYNN

Try **One Tree Grill** ★, 9 Pah Rd., Greenwoods Corner, Epsom (℃ **09/625-6407**), a
smart little restaurant with a cute-as-a-button bar upstairs. It's hugely popular with locals
and has excellent service. Another highly recommended option is **Bowmans** ★★, 597
Mount Eden Rd., Mount Eden (℃ **09/638-9676**), which puts many inner city establishments to shame with its top service and consistently good food. **Molten** ★★, 42
Mount Eden Rd., Mount Eden (℃ **09/638-7236**), is another suburban treasure producing great meals bound to impress.

   Circus, Circus, 447 Mount Eden Rd., Mount Eden (℃ **09/623-3833**), is a little cafe
gem filled with circus memorabilia and show posters, along with food and staff that make
it worth visiting. My new favorite, though, is **Delicious** ★★, 472 Richmond Rd., Grey
Lynn (℃ **09/360-7590;** www.delicious.co.nz), a divine little Italian restaurant that's big
on melt-in-the-mouth handmade pastas. My eggplant, walnut, and ricotta tortelloni with
taleggio cream was to die for. The tables are a bit close together for my liking but I put

up with it just to savor the meal. Make sure you reserve a table—and save room for their **139**
delicious tiramisu dessert.

IN PARNELL/MISSION BAY/NEWMARKET
Expensive
In contrast to Ponsonby's artsiness, Parnell attracts a trendy corporate crowd—the work-hard, play-hard crew. The result is icons such as **Veranda Bar & Grill** ★★, or **VBG,** 279 Parnell Rd. (✆ **09/309-6289**), where expensive Pacific Rim cuisine and a party atmosphere reign supreme. For an elegant fine-dining experience, head for **Antoines** ★★★, 333 Parnell Rd. (✆ **09/379-8756**), which attracts a well-heeled clientele with rich French cuisine and impeccable service.

Cibo ★★ MODERN NEW ZEALAND   Almost 19 years old, Cibo has proven that a restaurant with all the right ingredients will endure. Elegant, favored by the business crowd, and popular for special occasions, it serves up the likes of pepper-crusted lamb with mint potato cakes and venison loin with cauliflower couscous, with an assurance that guarantees return visits. You might need a map or a friendly local to point you in the direction, but it's worth the hunt.

Axis Building, 91 St. Georges Bay Rd., Parnell. ✆ **03/303-9660.** www.cibo.co.nz. Reservations recommended. Main courses NZ$36–NZ$40. AE, MC, V. Mon–Fri noon–late.

Mikano ★ INTERNATIONAL   Mikano is all about fabulous architecture, vibrant color, sensational sea views, good jazz, fine wine, and innovative food. It has won numerous awards for its eclectic, often themed menu, and it's an excellent place to opt for fish. Try the tuna roasted with harissa and served with orange fennel and black olive salad; or panfried salmon with crushed peas. The wine list is vast, and the sofas in the bar are just the place to sample it.

1 Solent St. (off Tamaki Dr.), Mechanics Bay. ✆ **09/309-9514.** www.mikano.co.nz. Reservations recommended. Main courses NZ$37–NZ$45. AE, DC, MC, V. Mon–Fri noon–late; Sat 5:30pm–late; Sun 10am–late.

Moderate
In Newmarket, the **Turkish Café,** 80 Broadway (✆ **09/520-2794**), has tasty Turkish and Middle Eastern dishes, plus Italian wood-fired pizzas served up in a contemporary interior, *plus* belly dancers on Wednesday, Friday, and Saturday nights. If you love Spanish food, try **Tasca Newmarket** ★, 8/25 Nuffield St. (✆ **09/522-4443**). **Caffe Massimo** ★, 23–27 Nuffield St. (✆ **09/522-6700**), has excellent counter food, a lively atmosphere, and big windows open to the street.

Iguacu Restaurant & Bar ★ PACIFIC RIM   Iguacu (pronounced Ig-wa-*soo*) deserves full marks for its fabulous interior. Giant silver-framed mirrors lend a grandiose atmosphere to an environment made light and airy by a glazed ceiling; earthy colors and big windows to the street keep you in touch with reality. Food here is generally very good. It's a favorite spot for the lunching business crowd. See also "The Club & Bar Scene" under "Auckland After Dark," later in this chapter.

269 Parnell Rd., Parnell. ✆ **09/358-4804.** www.iguacu.co.nz. Reservations recommended. Main courses NZ$25–NZ$36. AE, DC, MC, V. Mon–Fri 11am–late; Sat–Sun 10am–late. Closed Dec 25.

Portofino ★★ (Finds) NORTHERN ITALIAN   When you're exhausted and just want to eat quickly and well, Portofino will oblige with delicious pastas, pizzas, and chicken and veal dishes. It's small, dark, cozy, and terribly popular, so get in early if you want a guaranteed spot. Watch the chefs cooking, enjoy the friendly staff, and leave without spending a fortune. Portofino has several other city locations—the best is on Viaduct Basin—but the Parnell eatery still scores more for atmosphere.

156 Parnell Rd., Parnell. ℭ **09/373-3740**. www.portofino.co.nz. Reservations recommended. Main courses NZ$20–NZ$25. AE, MC, V. Daily 11am–late.

Inexpensive

Dunk Cafe   If all you want is breakfast or a light lunch, Dunk will deliver. They have a very tasty range of pies, flans, soups, and salads, plus yummy sweet things to go with coffee. It's a no-fuss sort of place and service can be patchy, but their central location makes them easy to find.

297 Parnell Rd., Parnell. ℭ **09/377-2414.** No reservations. Main courses NZ$10–NZ$15. MC, V. Mon–Fri 7:30am–5:30pm; Sat 8:30am–4pm.

IN REMUERA

New on the scene in Remuera is the **Maple Room** ★, 93–95 Upland Rd., Benson Road Village (ℭ **09/522-1672**), which is scoring big points for its tapas-style dishes and main courses like duck risotto and mint-and-chili lamb rump. It's open Monday through Friday from 11:30am until late, Sunday from 11am to late. **Sierra Café,** Clonbern and Remuera roads (ℭ **09/523-1527**), is definitely the best cafe in the area, with amazingly good counter food. Pick up freshly baked pies, quiches, frittatas, and extravagant cakes for an over-the-top picnic. Tucked behind the Remuera shops, the **Thai Village** ★★, 415 Remuera Rd. (ℭ **09/523-3005**), has a nice ambience and can always be trusted to deliver an excellent dining experience. **Café Jazz** ★, 563 Remuera Rd., Upland Village (ℭ **09/524-0356**), is another nice, moderately priced spot for lunch or a light evening meal. It offers standard New Zealand cafe fare, such as sandwiches, salads, and pizza.

IN DEVONPORT/BIRKENHEAD

Another Devonport standout is **Monsoon** ★, 71 Victoria Rd. (ℭ **09/445-4263**), a snappy little Thai/Malaysian place. Because it's so popular, either go early or reserve. Birkenhead Point has a surprising array of eating choices. **Hayashi** ★★, 261 Hinemoa St. (ℭ **09/418-3011**), is a standout Japanese restaurant that successfully mixes the traditional with contemporary flair. **Manuka,** 49 Victoria Rd. (ℭ **09/445-7732;** www.manukarestaurant.co.nz), consistently delivers good light meals, terrific wood-fired pizzas, and home-smoked salmon and chicken. They have a special children's menu.

5 EXPLORING AUCKLAND

If you're short on time, the best thing to do is leap aboard the **Aukland Explorer Bus** ★★★ (see "Getting Around," earlier in this chapter) and see as much as you can.

THE TOP FOUR ATTRACTIONS

Auckland Museum ★★★ (Kids)   Auckland's imposing museum building stands in the Auckland Domain on the rim of an ancient volcano surrounded by parks and gardens. Major refurbishment of the museum is complete, and it now has two entrances—the original harbor entrance has the stunning views, the new rear dome entrance in the Atrium shows off contemporary New Zealand architecture. Get a shaky start at Volcanoes, a gallery that introduces you to Auckland's turbulent natural history. It's the only city in the world built on a volcano field, and the interactive movie room, simulating the birth of a new volcano, will set you to thinking we're slightly crazy for living here at all.

The museum has the largest collection of Maori and Polynesian artifacts in the world, and for this reason alone is worth a visit. The extensive **Maori Treasures Gallery** is a must-see. Key attractions in this area are the impressive 25m (80-ft.) war canoe chiseled from one enormous totara trunk and covered with intricate carvings. That same artistry is reflected in the 26m (85-ft.) meetinghouse, with its carved and painted walls and rafters. Also on display are magnificent greenstone weapons, tools, and feather cloaks. Three times a day—at 11am, noon, and 1:30pm—concerts by the Manaia Maori Performance Group bring the culture to life.

The museum is easy to negotiate. Just remember the first floor is about the people, the second is about the land, and the third is our war memorial.

Pacific Pathways is a moody area housing a world-renowned collection of Pacific artifacts; *New Zealand at War: Scars on the Heart* tells an emotional story of New Zealand in conflict, from the Land Wars of the 1840s to its present-day peacekeeping operations. The first-floor **Natural History Galleries** showcase everything from dinosaur skeletons to live seaside rock pools. It's a fascinating area well supported by the superb **Discovery Centre.**

This first-rate museum experience gives a marvelous introduction to New Zealand history and culture. To get the most from it, allow 2 to 3 hours minimum. An on-site cafe is open during museum hours, although the service can be patchy and the coffee isn't always the best. There are two very good shops worth a visit, and don't forget to ask about the free Family Trails tours and the Night at Auckland Museum—a school holiday treat that the kids will love. Booking ahead is essential or check the website for holiday activity timetables. Be sure to take a stroll around the magnificent sculpture walk featuring eight works by New Zealand artists. The museum supplies a map and has the models on display.

Auckland Domain. ✆ **09/309-0443** or 306-7067 for recorded Infoline. www.aucklandmuseum.com. Admission to permanent collection NZ$5 donation is suggested; charges for special exhibitions may apply. Maori cultural performance NZ$25 adults, NZ$13 children 6 and over. Daily 10am–5pm. Closed Dec 25 and Apr 25 (ANZAC morning). Wheelchair access throughout. Explorer Bus every 30 min. The Link bus from and to downtown every 10 min.

Sky Tower ★★★ (**Kids**)   In the first 18 months after it opened in August 1997, Sky Tower drew over a million visitors, making it New Zealand's most popular paid attraction. At 328m (1,076 ft.), it is one of the tallest buildings in the Southern Hemisphere, affording unforgettable views over the sprawling mass of Auckland. It has three observation decks, including an outdoor area, a glass lift and glass floor panels, multilingual

AUCKLAND

6

EXPLORING AUCKLAND

(Fun Facts   Afraid of Heights?

Sky Tower has been designed to provide a high level of performance in the event of earthquakes, severe winds, storms, or fire. It is built to withstand winds gusting to 200kmph (124 mph); it has protected fire refuges; and analysis shows it would stay standing in an earthquake of 8.0 magnitude on the Richter scale occurring within 20km (12 miles) of the tower. So put aside your fears (if I can, anyone can), and have a breathtaking experience.

Moments Sky Jump

When we talk about special moments, this may not be what you had in mind, but one thing's for sure: You won't forget this experience in a hurry. **Sky Jump** is one of New Zealand's wackiest adrenaline rushes—perhaps the ultimate! For details on this 192m (630-ft.) controlled free fall from the Southern Hemisphere's tallest tower, call ☎ **0800/759-586** in NZ, or 09/368-1835, or check www.skyjump.co.nz. It costs NZ$195 for adults and NZ$145 for children and operates daily from 10am to 5:30pm, weather permitting (closed Dec 25). Minimum age is 10 years with parental consent. Maximum weight is 120 kilograms (265 lb.). And if that isn't thrill enough on its own, brace yourself for **Sky Walk** (☎ **0800/759-925** in NZ, or 09/368-1835; www.skywalk.co.nz), operated by the same company, at the same location. Sign up for this daredevil adventure and you'll be attached to a harness and asked to walk around the pergola ring of Sky Tower, 192m (630 ft.) above the streets below. It requires far more courage than I could muster and costs NZ$135 adults and NZ$100 for children.

audio guides, and a revolving restaurant. Access to the observation decks is on three glass-fronted elevators, which can whiz up the building in a speedy 40 seconds. I'm petrified of heights but even I got a thrill out of going to the top. I just closed my eyes in the glass lift!

The Lower Observation level is accessible by stairs (for the very fit) and has two restaurants, Orbit (a revolving restaurant) and Observatory (buffet-style), for a meal with a difference (reservations are suggested). The Main Observation level features the latest technology, with live weather feeds and touch computer screens giving geographical information. The Outdoor Observation area holds high-powered binoculars and is open to the elements. The Sky Deck is the highest public viewing area, with 360-degree views through seamless glass.

SKYCITY, Victoria and Federal sts. ☎ **0800/759-2489** in NZ, or 09/363-6355. Fax 09/363-6378. www.skytower.co.nz. Admission to observation decks NZ$28 adults, NZ$11 children 5–14, NZ$61 families. Admission to Sky Deck NZ$5 extra. Daily 8:30am–late. Underground parking for small fee.

Kelly Tarlton's Antarctic Encounter & Underwater World ★★ **Kids** In your wildest dreams, you might have imagined a live underground penguin colony; at Kelly Tarlton's **Penguin Encounter,** it's an amazing reality. For full insight into this unique self-sustaining population of king and gentoo penguins, make sure you pick up the free brochure, which details the establishment of a full simulated Antarctic environment, complete with saltwater pools, in the heart of subtropical Auckland. You'll be able to board heated, soundproof Snow Cats and enter the frozen landscape.

Just as awe-inspiring is **Underwater World,** the dream and final project of the late Kelly Tarlton, a famous New Zealand diver. At Underworld World, visitors travel on a moving walkway through an acrylic tunnel under the ocean. Surrounded by giant stingrays, eels, sharks, and over 1,500 fish, you're treated to a diver's view without having to wear the wet suit. **Stingray Bay** shows off the remarkable creatures at close quarters. This area also includes the adjacent NIWA Interactive Room for kids, a refreshment kiosk, and large educational touch screens. This is a special attraction for all ages; allow 45 minutes to 2 hours. Ring ahead for daily feeding times.

23 Tamaki Dr., Orakei. (ℓ) **0800/805-050** in NZ, or 09/531-5065. Fax 09/528-5175. www.kellytarltons. co.nz. Admission NZ$33 adults, NZ$17 children 5–14, free for children 4 and under. Special rates for families and seniors. AE, DC, MC, V. Daily 9am–5:30pm (last entry 5pm). Take Mission Bay city bus, Explorer Bus, or Fullers Harbour Explorer. Free Kelly Tarlton's shuttle calls at several inner city hotels 4 times daily 9:30am–5:30pm. Free parking.

Auckland Art Gallery ★   Recognized as the leading New Zealand art gallery, Auckland Art Gallery holds more than 10,000 New Zealand and European works. Expect the Main Gallery to be closed for a NZ$90-million upgrade during 2010. It is expected to reopen in 2011 with 50% more exhibition space. In the meantime, all exhibitions will be staged at the New Gallery, which opened across the street in 1995. It houses a magnificent contemporary collection of new ideas, new works, and new artists. This is where you'll find the McCahon Room, which displays works by the late Colin McCahon, New Zealand's most respected modernist artist. The gallery has an ongoing program of family days, tours, lectures, and holiday programs.

Main Gallery: Wellesley and Kitchener sts. (ℓ) **09/307-7700,** or 309-0831 for recorded information. Fax 09/302-1096. www.aucklandartgallery.govt.nz. Free admission; fees for some touring shows. New Gallery: Wellesley and Lorne sts. (ℓ) **09/307-4540.** Free admission to downstairs galleries; NZ$12–NZ$20 for temporary and touring exhibitions. Both galleries: Daily 10am–5pm. Closed Good Friday and Dec 25.

THE VIADUCT BASIN

For the first time in the 152-year history of the America's Cup, a village was created to support syndicates, corporations, superyachts, and the public together in one venue. This is Auckland's Viaduct Basin, a glistening creation that includes new apartment blocks, hotels, restaurants, cafes, bars, shops, markets, and every facility an earnest yachtie could ever want.

Between October 1999 and March 2000, and again from October 2002 to March 2003, the village was the place to soak up the excitement of the America's Cup challenge. Millions of visitors crammed in over the two periods, along with more than 2,000 competitors and team personnel, plus 200 international media representatives during each challenge. In addition to the America's Cup action, the village played host to up to 80 **superyachts** on each occasion, the largest gatherings in the Southern Hemisphere, turning Auckland into a Pacific Monte Carlo. Superyachts are luxury motor and sailing vessels in excess of 30m (98 ft.) long, ranging in value from NZ$4 million to over NZ$40 million. Viaduct Harbour can accommodate 88 superyachts of up to 50m (165 ft.).

(Value) Auckland MultiPass

Get four of Auckland's leading attractions for one unbelievable price—a discount of over 25%. **Sky Tower, Kelly Tarlton's, Fullers Auckland,** and **Rainbow's End** have combined for this great offer, which can be used over a 2-week period and includes a pass to revisit whichever attraction you liked the best. Purchase the pass from any one of the included attractions, from an i-SITE Visitor Centre, or online at www.aucklandmultipass.com. It costs NZ$99 for adults and NZ$59 for children ages 5 to 15. Also pick up Tourism Auckland's **Hot Deals Auckland** brochure, which details a wide range of special packages. It's available from Auckland i-SITE Visitor Centres ((ℓ) **0800/282-552** in NZ; www.aucklandnz.com).

Visitors can experience grand-prix sailing on an authentic America's Cup yacht, *NZL 40* or *NZL 41,* built for the 1995 San Diego Challenge. You can be as involved as you want in the crewing action, no sailing experience required. For information on the daily sailings from Viaduct Harbour, call **Explore NZ** (© **0800/397-567** in NZ, or 09/359-5987; www.explorenz.co.nz). The price per person is NZ$150 for 2 hours of sailing, NZ$195 for a 3-hour match race. Lower rates available for children ages 10 to 15; children 9 and under are not permitted. Sailing usually begins at 2pm depending on tides.

The Viaduct Basin development has changed the face of Auckland forever, providing a fistful of fabulous restaurants, clubs, and bars that have endured—despite the fact that Team New Zealand relinquished the America's Cup in the 2002–03 challenge. It is a marvelous place to explore, and given that some of Auckland's best eateries are here, you'd be silly to miss it.

Viaduct Harbour has also been a stopover point in the epic Volvo Ocean Race (formerly the Whitbread Round-the-World Race).

WALKING OVER WATER

Bring on the nerves of steel for **Auckland Bungy & Bridge Climb** ★★★ (© **09/361-2000;** www.aucklandbridgeclimb.co.nz; www.bungy.co.nz). Based on a concept similar to the successful Sydney activity, walkers are guided underneath and over the top of Auckland Harbour Bridge. The 1½-hour adventure begins with a full briefing by a professional guide at the base complex. Guests are then fitted with overgarments, radio headsets, and safety harnesses. It's achievable for people of almost all ages and all fitness levels, but you must be age 8 and over and preferably not have a fear of heights. The walk costs NZ$120 for adults and NZ$65 for children 7 to 15. Discounts for seniors are available. A bungy jump is NZ$120 and jumpers must be 10 and over. See "Outdoor Activities & Spectator Sports," later in this chapter. You can take a bus or a short walk from city hotels; pickup service is available on request. There's limited parking at the site.

OTHER MUSEUMS, MONKEYS & MORE

Museum of Transport & Technology ★ **Kids** This is the largest museum of transport and technology in the country, covering 16 hectares (40 acres) in Western Springs, 5km (3 miles) from the city center. You'll find trams, trains, steam engines, aircraft, and more. The museum houses major collections of road transport, historical buildings, and medical and dental equipment displays. You can take a tram ride (every 20 min.) from the Great North Road entrance past the zoo to the **Sir Keith Park Memorial** (there's a small charge). Displays here include interesting military exhibits, rail memorabilia, and one of the most impressive collections of historical aircraft in Australasia, including the only Solent Mark IV flying boat in the world. There are some great hands-on exhibits to keep you amused. Allow 2 hours.

805 Great North Rd., Western Springs. © **0800/668-286** in NZ, or 09/815-5800. www.motat.org.nz. Admission NZ$14 adults, NZ$7 children 5–16 and seniors, NZ$30 families. Daily 10am–5pm. Closed Dec 25. Explorer Bus.

New Zealand National Maritime Museum ★ **Kids** The National Maritime Museum is perfectly placed—right in the heart of the America's Cup action. Inside are intricate working displays and fascinating exhibitions documenting 1,000 years of New Zealand maritime history. Watch traditional craftsmen restoring historical vessels, wood turning, and working on sails. Of course there's an exhibit on America's Cup history.

Plus, you get the chance to hit the high seas yourself: The historic scow *Ted Ashby* gives 45- to 60-minute rides Tuesday, Thursday, Saturday, and Sunday at noon and 2pm. It's definitely the cheapest cruise you'll find. I particularly like the 1950s beach shop and bach (holiday house) display, which sums up much of the quintessential Kiwi seaside holiday experience. The 14 galleries and interactive displays in this acclaimed museum will keep you busy for at least 2 hours.

Hobson Wharf, Viaduct Basin. ✆ **0800/725-897** in NZ, or 09/373-0800. Fax 09/377-6000. www.maritimemuseum.co.nz. Admission NZ$16 adults, NZ$8 children 5–15, free for children 4 and under, NZ$40 families. Museum Combo (museum entry plus Ted Ashby harbor cruise) NZ$24 adults, NZ$12 children 5–15, NZ$48 families. AE, DC, MC, V. Summer daily 9am–6pm; winter daily 9am–5pm. Closed Dec 25.

Auckland Zoo ★★ (Kids) Within 5 minutes of city high-rises, you can watch and hear Sumatran tigers snarl, lions roar, and monkeys chatter. Over 1,000 birds and animals from every continent make their home in this outstanding parkland, recognized as one of Australasia's leading zoos. It is home to New Zealand's largest collection of native and exotic species. You can meet kiwi, tuatara, and other locals at the Daily Native Fauna Encounter. Or you can visit the beach and see shorebirds and little blue penguins. You can also watch sea lions through a spectacular underwater viewing window. At the McDonald's South American Rainforest, troops of spider monkeys, bonnet macaques, squirrel monkeys, and siamangs swing from branch to branch. Check out Pridelands for giraffes, zebras, lions, and rhinos. And visit the zoo's two most famous residents, Kashin and Burma, in their state-of-the-art elephant house. Ask about the special ZOOM tours, which take you behind the scenes, or treat the kids to a Safari Night sleepover and barbecue.

Motions Rd., Western Springs. ✆ **09/360-3800,** or 360-3819 for recorded information. Fax 09/360-3818. www.aucklandzoo.co.nz. Admission NZ$19 adults, NZ$14 students and seniors, NZ$9 children 4–15, family passes NZ$35–NZ$67. AE, DC, MC, V. Daily 9:30am–5:30pm (last admission 4:15pm). Closed Dec 25. Explorer Bus or Pt. Chevalier 045, which departs from Downtown Centre, inner city. Free parking.

Butterfly Creek ★★ (Kids) Just minutes from Auckland International Airport and built over a large wetland, Butterfly Creek shows off more than 800 free-flying tropical butterflies. The big butterfly house is a delight. Complete with waterfalls, ponds, lush foliage, turtles, fish, and exotic birds, it allows you to get up close to stunningly colorful butterflies. If you're lucky, you'll see the world's largest moth, which has a wingspan of up to 280 millimeters (11 in.); and look out for tarantula, lizards, and giant weta.

Tom Pearce Dr. ✆ **09/275-8880.** Fax 09/275-1110. www.butterflycreek.co.nz. Butterfly House NZ$14 adults, NZ$8 children 3–15. Red Admiral Express NZ$5. Buttermilk Farm NZ$8 adults, NZ$6 children. Combo Butterfly House, Bugs About, Pirates Below & Buttermilk Farm NZ$18 adults, NZ$9 children. Family rates available. Daily 9am–5pm.

Snowplanet ★★ (Kids) If you want to polish up your ski or snowboard skills before heading south, take a trip over the Harbour Bridge and let loose in one of the largest indoor snow resorts in the world and the first snowdome in Australasia. You can guarantee snow here 365 days of the year, and young and old can have a ball. It features three lifts, a terrain park, and a separate learners' area.

91 Small Rd., Silverdale. ✆ **09/427-0044.** www.snowplanet.co.nz. Day Pass NZ$54 adults, NZ$42 children 11 and under, family NZ$148; Night Pass 7–10pm, NZ$39 adults, NZ$29 children. Rental equipment and clothing available for extra cost. Mon–Fri 10am–10pm; Sat–Sun 8am–10pm.

BeesOnline Honey Centre ★ It would be silly to call this a honey of an excursion, but I'm going to anyway. You'll love this beautifully designed attraction, which reveals the inner workings of a beehive. Set in picturesque countryside beside two small lakes, the modern, ecofriendly center showcases production, honey tastings, and bee-related products and gifts. It is a 2007 Sustainable Business award winner and produces a large range of certified organic honeys. After a visit, you can dine at the award-winning cafe. On weekends there is a free honey tasting and honey and bee talk.

791 St. Hwy. 16, RD3, Waimauku. © **09/411-7953.** Fax 09/411-5216. www.beesonline.co.nz. Free admission. NZ$12 factory tour and tasting. Daily 9am–5pm.

HISTORIC HOUSES

Alberton ★★, 100 Mount Albert Rd. (© **09/846-7367;** fax 09/846-1919; www.alberton. co.nz), is perhaps the finest of all Auckland's historic homes that are open to the public. The once-simple farmhouse, built in 1863, grew into the fairy-tale mansion that stands today. Owned by the New Zealand Historic Places Trust, it provides an intimate glimpse into Victorian life. It's open Wednesday through Sunday, 10am to 4pm, closed Good Friday and December 25. Admission is NZ$8 adults, free for children. **Ewelme Cottage,** 14 Ayr St., Parnell (©/fax **09/379-0202;** www.historic.org.nz), was built for the Rev. Vicesimus Lush from 1863 to 1864 and named for Ewelme Village in England. The roomy kauri cottage is authentically preserved, right down to its 19th-century wallpaper. It contains an important collection of more than 800 books. Admission is NZ$7.50 adults, free for accompanied children. It's open Friday through Sunday, 10:30am to noon and 1 to 4:30pm, closed Good Friday and December 25. **Highwic,** 40 Gillies Ave., Epsom (© **09/524-5729;** www.highwic.co.nz), is one of New Zealand's finest Gothic Revival houses. Built in 1862, it gained additions modeled from an American pattern book in 1873. Its distinctive architecture and gardens offer insight into the lives of the wealthy Victorian family who retained possession of it until 1978. Admission is NZ$7.50 adults, free for accompanied children. It's open Wednesday through Sunday 10:30am to 4:30pm (closed Good Friday and Dec 25).

ESPECIALLY FOR KIDS

Most of Auckland's major attractions—Kelly Tarlton's, the Discovery Centre at Auckland Museum, the Auckland Zoo, Sky Tower, Snowplanet, Butterfly Creek, and the Museum of Transport & Technology (all described above)—will give the kids hours of fun.

Rainbow's End Theme Park ★★ (Kids Value) This is New Zealand's premier adventure playground, with 9 hectares (22 acres) devoted to crazy rides and attractions for children. For those under 10, there's a Dream Castle with its own miniature roller coaster, carousel, and Ferris wheel. Older kids will scream their lungs out on New Zealand's only double-loop roller coaster, and there's more fun to be had on the log flume, on the pirate

(Tips) **The Gallery Guide**

The bimonthly booklet, *The Auckland Gallery Guide,* which includes information about leading galleries and their exhibitions, is available free from information centers and art galleries. Its user-friendly maps are a great help. For galleries and exhibitions, call © **09/378-4070,** or fax 09/378-4063.

Tips Photo Ops

Of course you can't beat the 360-degree view from **Sky Tower** (p. 141), and once you've seen that, all others seem to pale by comparison—with the exception perhaps of shots taken on your **Auckland Bridge Climb.** An old favorite is **One Tree Hill,** accessible through the very pretty **Cornwall Park.** The obelisk is visible from everywhere in the city. Like Mount Eden, it was once a Maori *pa* (fort) dating from the 14th century. The one tree that dominated its profile was, sadly, damaged by a Maori activist in 1996. It has been replaced by a grove of small trees that have yet to reach a significant height. **Mount Eden** is an extinct volcano and Auckland's highest natural point. It boasts terrific views of the city, the harbor, and Hauraki Gulf. **North Head Maritime Park** in Devonport offers a different perspective—looking back at the city from North Shore. You'll get great photos of the cityscape from here.

ship, in the Enchanted Forest, and in an abandoned mine. Add bumper boats, cars, and virtual theater, and the whole family will be glad you came.

Great South and Wiri Station roads, Manukau City. ✆ **0800/438-672** in NZ, or 09/262-2030. Fax 09/262-1958. www.rainbowsend.co.nz. All-day Super Pass (includes unlimited rides) from NZ$44 adults, NZ$34 children 4–13, free for children 3 and under. Family passes and combo deals available. AE, V. Feb–Dec daily 10am–5pm; Jan daily 10am–10pm. Closed Dec 25. Take the Manukau motorway exit 15 min. south of Auckland and drive 400m (1,300 ft.) to the end of the Rainbow. Free parking.

PARKS & GARDENS

The Auckland area has 22 regional parks, covering 37,038 hectares (91,484 acres) and more than 500km (310 miles) of walking tracks. The **Auckland Domain** ★, the city's oldest park, is an imposing crown of green just minutes from the city center. Within it, the **Wintergarden,** the steamy **Tropical House,** and **Fernz Fernery** are botanical showcases for indigenous and exotic plant specimens. Admission is free. The Wintergarden is open daily from 10am to 4pm. There are also extensive formal gardens, sweeping lawns, statuary, duck ponds, sports grounds, and dozens of picnic spots. Summer Sundays bring free jazz and rock concerts in the band rotunda, chamber music in the Wintergarden, and megaconcerts on the sports fields. Call ✆ **09/379-2020** or fax 09/571-3757 for details. There are several well-signposted entrances to the Auckland Domain. Two of the busiest are on Stanley Street and Parnell Road. There are also entrances on Grafton Road and Park Road.

Cornwall Park is a true urban oasis; with **One Tree Hill Domain,** it forms the largest park in Auckland. The two parks fan out from the hill and are grazed by sheep and cattle. Stone walls, beautiful avenues of oak trees, and dozens of pretty walkways wind their way through this haven. Access is off Manukau Road at Royal Oak and Greenland West and Campbell roads. **Cornwall Park Visitor Centre** (✆ **09/630-8485;** www.cornwallpark.co.nz) has information on walks in the park.

The **Parnell Rose Garden** and **Dove-Myer Robinson Park** (named after a popular former city mayor) are off Gladstone and Judges Bay roads in Parnell. One of the city's first churches, little St. Stephen's Chapel, is also here.

(Moments **Day Spa Delights**

Day spas are sprouting all over Auckland. The most luxurious is **Spa de Servilles** ★★★, Level 1, Shed 20, Princes Wharf (© **09/309-9086;** www. servilles.co.nz), which will lull you into luxury and sloth at the touch of a finger. It's the nearest you'll get in New Zealand to sophisticated European spas. Half-and full-day treatments range from NZ$260 to NZ$895. And boys—don't forget, you can enjoy these indulgences, too! Also worth checking out is **Spa at the Hyatt** ★★, Hyatt Regency hotel (© **09/355-1234**), a stunning facility that has six exquisite treatment rooms, a 25m (80-ft.) lap pool, saunas, Jacuzzi, steam room, juice bar, and fully equipped gym. **East Day Spa** ★★, SKYCITY Grand Hotel, 123 Albert St. (© **09/363-7050;** www.eastdayspa.com), focuses on East-ern-style holistic skin-care, massage, and beauty treatments. **Bliss,** Crowne Plaza Hotel, 128 Albert St. (© **09/368-4698;** www.blissreflexology.com), offers tradi-tional Chinese reflexology in a stylish, relaxing inner city haven.

The **Auckland Botanic Gardens,** 102 Hill Rd., Manuwera (© **09/267-1457;** www. aucklandbotanicgardens.co.nz), cover 64 hectares (158 acres). It's home to more than 10,000 plants. The gardens are open daily from 8am to 8pm in summer and 8am to 6pm in winter; the visitor center is open Monday through Friday from 9am to 4pm, Saturday and Sunday from 9am to 4pm; the cafe is open daily from 8:30am to 4:30pm. Guides for organized groups are available Monday through Friday. Call © **09/266-3698,** e-mail botanicgardens@arc.govt.nz, or ask at the visitor center. To get here from the city, travel south and take the Manuwera motorway exit, turn left onto Hill Road, and drive to the entrance.

Also worth a look are **Eden Gardens,** 24 Omana Ave., Mount Eden (© **09/638-8395;** www.edengarden.co.nz). They're open daily 9am to 4:30pm; the on-site cafe is open from 9am to 4pm. Admission is NZ$6 adults, NZ$4 seniors and students, free for children. Once a quarry, it is now a showplace for an amazing collection of rhododen-dron, vireya, hibiscus, bromeliads, palms, and many other subtropical species.

WINE OUT WEST

Greater Auckland is home to more than 110 vineyards. Henderson Valley is the country's oldest grape-growing area, dating to the arrival of Croatian and other Northern Hemi-sphere immigrants in the early 1900s. Today, the western suburbs and areas north to Kumeu are a major grape-growing region. Cabernet sauvignon is the most commonly planted grape; merlot and pinot noir are also important. Chardonnay and sauvignon blanc are the main white varieties. Most West Auckland wineries also draw fruit from other regions, mostly Gisborne, Marlborough, and Hawke's Bay. The Henderson and Kumeu areas are the most accessible for a day's outing. They're about 30 minutes from Central City. Waiheke Island is about 30 to 40 minutes away by ferry; it's by far the prettiest region and worth the time.

You'll find a good cluster of wineries along Lincoln and Henderson Valley roads, and nestled in the surrounding hills. The small townships of Kumeu, Huapai, and Waimauku also have good selections. For information on wine tours, see "Organized Tours & Cruises," below. For further details on the area, pick up the free brochure *Winemakers of West Auckland* from the visitor center. Following are the notables.

Babich Wines, 10 Babich Rd., Henderson (© **09/833-7859;** www.babichwines. co.nz), is only 20 minutes from Central City and is open for tastings Monday through Friday from 9am to 5pm, Saturday from 9am to 6pm, and Sunday from 11am to 5pm. One of the most picturesque wineries, it has a pleasant picnic area near its shop. It often has vintages going back to 1990. **Soljans Estate,** 366 St. Hwy. 16, Kumeu (© **09/412-5858;** www.soljans.co.nz), produces internationally competitive wines. It has cellar sales and tastings and a cafe and winery complex. Daily winery tours (11:30am–2:30pm) followed by a tasting cost NZ$12 per person. The winery is open daily 9am to 5:30pm; the cafe, Monday through Friday 10am to 4pm, weekends 9am to 4pm. **Nobilo Wine Group,** 45 Station Rd., Huapai (© **09/412-6666;** www.nobilowinegroup.com), is the country's second-largest winemaker. Tours cost NZ$12 per person and begin at set times Saturday through Monday. The winery is open daily from 10am to 5pm. **Matua Valley Wines,** Waikoukou Road, Waimauku (© **09/411-8301;** www.matua.co.nz), produced the first New Zealand sauvignon blanc over 25 years ago. The winery is open Monday through Saturday, 10am to 5pm, and Sunday from 11am to 4:30pm. The Hunting Lodge, an excellent fine-dining restaurant on-site, is run separately. There is also a lovely picnic area.

For information on Waiheke Island wineries, see "A Side Trip to Waiheke Island," later in this chapter.

If you're short on time, call at **NZ Winemakers Centre** ★★, Victoria and Elliot streets (© **09/379-5858;** www.nzwc.co.nz), where you'll find an extensive range of varietals from most New Zealand regions. It offers tax-free wine sales, wine tastings, worldwide home delivery, and wine-tour information. In summer it's open Monday through Saturday 9am to 9pm, Sunday 11am to 7pm; in winter Monday through Saturday 9am to 8pm, Sunday 10am to 6pm.

DOING DEVONPORT

TAKING THE FERRY   Catching the **Fullers Ferry** ★ to Devonport is one of the nicest day's outings you can have in Auckland. Make your way to the Ferry Building on Quay Street (© **09/367-9111;** www.fullers.co.nz) and take to the water. You'll get great views of the city, Viaduct Basin, and the America's Cup Village as you head out aboard the catamaran *Kea.* The ferry operates daily every half-hour from 7:15am to 8pm and every hour from 8 to 11pm, and the trip takes 12 minutes. The round-trip fare is NZ$10 adults, NZ$5 children ages 5 to 15. If you're planning to base yourself in Devonport, buy a 10-trip or weekly ferry pass.

DEVONPORT VILLAGE ATTRACTIONS   The village of Devonport is all about atmosphere, charm, historic buildings, the arts, and cafes. It has a summer holiday feel, even in the middle of winter, and especially on weekends. Stop at the **Devonport i-SITE Visitor Information Centre,** 3 Victoria Rd. (© **09/446-0677;** www.northshorenz. com), where you can find out about things to see and do. It's open daily from 8:30am to 5pm.

The two historic backbones of the village are Victoria and Church streets, now the main business area. Many of the buildings here date to the first European settlement; a brochure called *The Old Devonport Walk* gives you all the details as you wander.

There are three excellent white-sand beaches in close range—**Devonport,** a good swimming spot with a playground; **Cheltenham,** a safe tidal beach; and **Narrow Neck Beach,** with safe swimming and a playground. **Mount Victoria** sits near the business center and allows great harbor views, and **North Head** was a significant defense spot for both Maori and the Europeans. The volcanic hill was further developed during World

War II, and it's honeycombed with underground tunnels, chambers, and gun emplacements. **Devonport Explorer Tours** (☎ **09/357-6366;** www.devonporttours.co.nz) can take you here on a 1-hour minibus tour (allow 2 hr. with ferry ride) for NZ$30 per adult (including ferry ride); booking ahead is essential. Tours run daily 10am to 3pm all year.

At the colorful **Art by the Sea,** King Edward Parade and Church Street (☎ **09/445-6665**), you'll find top-quality work by New Zealand artists. It's right next door to cafes and across the road from the sea; hours are Sunday through Friday from 10am to 5pm, Saturday from 10am to 5:30pm. **Peter Raos Glass Gallery** ★ , Shop 5, 2 Queens Parade (☎ **09/445-4278;** www.raos.co.nz), is also worth checking out for handmade art glass by a local resident and master glass artist. It's open Monday through Friday from 10am to 4pm and Saturday 10am to 1pm.

Two museums to visit are the **Devonport Museum,** 31A Vauxhall Rd. (☎ **09/445-2661**), open Saturday and Sunday from 2 to 4pm; and the **Royal New Zealand Navy Museum,** Spring Street (☎ **09/445-5186**), open daily from 10am to 4:30pm. If you decide to stay for dinner, there are numerous restaurants and cafes (see "Where to Dine," earlier in this chapter). For something completely different, check out **Devonport Chocolates** ★ , 17 Wynyard St. (☎ **09/445-6001;** www.devonportchocolates.co.nz), where you can see chocolate being made. The shop is open Monday through Friday 9:30am to 5:30pm, and weekends 10am to 4pm. (If you don't get to Devonport, visit their second store at 177B Ponsonby Rd., Ponsonby.)

ORGANIZED TOURS & CRUISES

You can book several half- and full-day tours of the city and its environs at the visitor center. The half-day tours cover sightseeing highlights, while all-day tours usually include something of the east or west suburbs, the zoo, and the vineyards.

Mike's Garden Tours (☎ **09/846-5350;** www.mikesgardentours.co.nz) are the only ones that combine sightseeing with private garden visits. There are several options, ranging in price from NZ$85 to NZ$175 for adults, half-price for children ages 5 to 15.

Tamaki Hikoi ★★ (☎ **0800/282-552** in NZ; www.aucklandnz.com) is a 3-hour Maori walking tour through Auckland. A guide from the Ngati Whatua tribe retells legends, beginning at the dormant volcano of Mount Eden. After a picnic lunch, you continue past local landmarks, finishing at the downtown waterfront. The tour costs NZ$80 per person. There is also a 1-hour tour of Mount Eden for NZ$30. It's an easy to moderate walk, mainly on road surfaces, but wear sensible walking shoes.

Bush & Beach ★★ (☎ **09/837-4130;** www.bushandbeach.co.nz) will take you out to the wild west coast to experience the elemental side of Auckland. Half- or full-day tours can include a gannet colony, winery visits, and virgin rainforest. They cost NZ$130 to NZ$195 per person. They also offer an all-day tour to Great Barrier Island for NZ$545 per person. Children 11 and under pay half-price. Make sure you wear sensible walking shoes. Their Best of Both Worlds tour takes in the city in the morning and the bush and beaches of West Auckland in the afternoon. It's a good overview of Auckland's diversity.

For a range of tours with a Maori flavor, contact **Potiki Adventures** ★★ (☎ **0800/692-3836** in NZ; www.potikiadventures.com). From an urban marae visit to gathering shellfish to learning about flax weaving and Maori plant medicine, the company can organize personalized itineraries or take you on a full-day tour for NZ$195 adults, or NZ$75 children 14 and under. They're the only company taking people to Otara Markets—probably the largest Polynesian market you will ever get to see.

Moments Island Escape

If you feel like spoiling yourself, join **Island Escape Cruises** ★★★ ((℃ **09/358-1717;** www.islandescape.co.nz) for a 6-day luxury cruise of Hauraki Gulf islands. Make your home in one of the boat's 10 big cabins and enjoy fishing trips, picnics ashore, bush walks, and expeditions from the ship by helicopter or boat. The 42m (138-ft.) *Island Passage* is stylish from start to finish, and this adventure guarantees memories to write home about. The 5-day cruise is NZ$1,950 to NZ$3,250 for double or twin occupancy, which includes all meals, snorkel equipment, fishing gear, and boat tours. This is a particularly indulgent way to get to Great Barrier Island.

One of the best wine tours is with **Auckland Scenic Wine Trail Tours** ★ ((℃ **09/630-1540;** www.winetrailtours.co.nz). It specializes in taking small groups to leading growers. Half- and full-day tours cost NZ$110 to NZ$225 per person. The full-day Matakana tour, which costs NZ$225 per person, introduces you to the wines of one of the loveliest rural areas near the city. **Auckland Fine Wine Tours** ★★ ((℃/fax **09/849-4519;** www.finewinetours.co.nz) has a great choice of half- and full-day food and wine tours for NZ$149 to NZ$249. The Food & Wine Lovers Tour (Mon–Sat) is especially good. It introduces you to cheesemaking, ice cream, a busy fish market, delis, a chocolate boutique, a distillery, and a winery. The NZ$200 price per person includes a cafe lunch.

On the Water

With 96 boat charter companies, Auckland won't deprive you of an opportunity to get out on the waves. **Fullers Auckland,** Ferry Building, Quay Street ((℃ **09/367-9111;** www.fullers.co.nz), is one company that makes it easy. One of its best-value deals if you're on a tight itinerary is the **Harbour Cruise,** a 1½-hour sightseeing excursion that shows off Viaduct Harbour, Devonport Naval Base, and the Harbour Bridge, with coffee and commentary. Fares are NZ$33 for adults, NZ$17 for children ages 5 to 15. The cruise includes a round-trip ticket to Devonport so passengers can visit the seaside village at their leisure, or on any scheduled Fullers sailing. Tours depart from Pier 2, Ferry Terminal, 99 Quay St., at 10:30am and 1:30pm. Fullers also has a Volcanic Explorer option that visits Rangitoto Island at a cost of NZ$55 for adults, NZ$28 for children ages 5 to 15, and several Waiheke Island Explorer options, including a **Taste of Waiheke Tour** ★, which visits three award-winning wineries and a top olive oil producer. It costs NZ$105 and includes a light lunch at Stonyridge.

After winning the America's Cup twice, New Zealand is big on yachting. **Explore NZ** ★★★ ((℃ **0800/397-567** in NZ; www.explorenz.co.nz) has some very exciting ways to experience Auckland from the water. Its **Pride of Auckland** operates a fleet of purpose-built sailboats, which offer lunch, dinner, coffee, and half-day cruises. And their **Sail New Zealand** operation offers a variety of tours in both Auckland and the Bay of Islands. *NZL 40, NZL41,* and *Lion New Zealand* are all available for sailing or match-race tours (see "The Viaduct Basin," earlier in this chapter).

The Maritime Museum's own cruises on heritage vessels are a little cheaper, but the luncheon cruise has a boxed lunch as opposed to a sit-down meal; it's also shorter and on an entirely different type of vessel. All are excellent experiences.

AUCKLAND

6

EXPLORING AUCKLAND

If you want tall ship sailing, the **Soren Larsen** (© 0800/767-365 in NZ, or 09/817-8799; www.sorenlarsen.co.nz), star of *The Onedin Line* television series, is your vessel. You can book day sails, coffee cruises, or holiday voyages, which include a 5-night sailing cruise between Auckland and the Bay of Islands. Auckland day trips start at NZ$150 per person, longer voyages at NZ$1,500, which includes all meals. The New Zealand season is December through February.

6 OUTDOOR ACTIVITIES & SPECTATOR SPORTS

OUTDOOR PURSUITS

AIR BUNGY   The **Sky Screamer,** Albert and Victoria streets, just down from Sky Tower (© 09/377-1328), will send you skyward with a maximum adrenaline rush at 200kmph (124 mph). Prices start at NZ$50 per person. Open 11am to late.

BUNGY JUMPING   **A.J. Hackett Bungy Auckland,** Westhaven Reserve (bottom of Curran St.), Herne Bay (© 0800/462-8649 in NZ, or 09/361-2000; www.bungy.co.nz), is the world's first harbor bridge bungy. For NZ$120, you leap out over Waitemata Harbour—but you must be 10 and over.

CANYONING   **Canyonz** (© 0800/422-696 in NZ, or 09/832-3244; www.canyonz.co.nz), offers a range of energetic rappelling adventures on Auckland's west coast and in the Coromandel Peninsula (see chapter 7). Costs range from NZ$175 for the Blue Canyon adventure to NZ$255 per person for a Coromandel excursion to Sleeping God Canyon, where you can slither down a 300m (1,000-ft.) waterfall way off the beaten track.

FOUR-WHEEL-DRIVE BIKING   If "real" adventure in the country is your thing, call **4 Track Adventures,** Restall Road, Woodhill Forest (© 0800/487-225 in NZ, or 09/420-8104; www.4trackadventures.co.nz). Its quad bikes are easy to ride, and you don't need previous experience. Expect to pay NZ$155 per person for a 1-hour safari. Two- and 3-hour safaris are also available. Van pickup from central hotels and backpackers is available for NZ$40.

GOLF   You'll find more than 40 golf courses in the Auckland region. For details, call the **Auckland Visitor Golf Association** (©/fax 09/522-0491), Monday through Thursday between 9am and 5pm, and ask for the course nearest you and current greens fees.

HORSEBACK RIDING   The Auckland region is home to about 20 riding operations. Visitor centers can give you advice about the outfitter nearest you. One of the closest to the inner city is **Valley View Riding** (© 09/837-0525), in Henderson.

KAYAKING   Ian Ferguson was one of New Zealand's top athletes; he competed in five Olympic games, won four gold medals and one silver, and in 1996 was named New Zealand Olympian of the century. He is also the man behind **Fergs Kayaks** ★★. Located at **Ian Ferguson Marine Sports Centre,** 12 Tamaki Dr., Okahu Bay (© 09/529-2230; www.fergskayaks.co.nz), it offers several kayaking options; the most fun, perhaps, is the Rangitoto Night Trip, which involves a 75-minute paddle out to the island and a 45-minute walk to the top of Rangitoto for a spectacular night view of Auckland. The trip leaves at 6pm, returns by 11pm, and costs NZ$120.

MOUNTAIN BIKING   Downhill mountain biking—my kind of stuff—is what you get with **Auckland Adventures** (✆ 09/379-4545; www.aucklandadventures.co.nz). It offers a number of mountain bike tours for groups of five people or more, taking in the best of West Auckland. Costs start at NZ$85 per person; biking time varies from 1 to 3 hours, depending on your level of fitness.

SAILING   You'll find numerous brochures about sailing charters at the visitor center, and the staff there can help you decide. See also "Organized Tours & Cruises," above. If you'd like to learn the basics, contact **Sailing Away School of Sailing** ★★ (✆ 09/521-2387; www.sailingaway.co.nz), and sailing master Suzanne Bourke will take you out on *French Connection.*

SKY DIVING   You'll forget all the other views once you get airborne with Auckland's only 7-day parachute center, **Skydive Auckland,** Mercer Skydiving Centre (✆ 0800/865-867 in NZ, or 09/373-5778; www.skydiveauckland.com). It offers free pickup service.

SURFING   **New Zealand Surf 'n' Snow Tours** (✆ 0800/787-386 in NZ, or 09/828-0426; www.newzealandsurftours.com) offers 1-day surf tours for NZ$99, 1- and 2-day surf schools for NZ$120 to NZ$150, and a 5-day surf tour at NZ$799 in the Auckland and Northland regions.

SWIMMING   Accessible from Tamaki Drive (where there's frequent bus service from Britomart), the beaches at Judges Bay, Okahu Bay, Mission Bay, Kohimarama, and St. Heliers Bay are popular inner-harbor swimming spots. If you want pool swimming, the visitor center has an excellent brochure that details 10 major complexes.

WALKING   An easy, enjoyable walk is along the promenade of **Tamaki Drive** ★★, which takes you from the inner city around to the pleasant seaside suburbs of Mission Bay and Kohimarama. **One Tree Hill, Cornwall Park,** and **Mount Eden** all offer a bit of physical exertion. If you really want to explore, contact **Waitakere Wilderness Walks** (✆/fax **09/838-9007;** www.wildwalks.co.nz). It offers 1- and 2-day walks and photographic excursions in the unspoiled west coast. An excellent self-guided trek is the **Coast to Coast Walk** ★★★, a 4- to 6-hour walk through the inner city and suburbs. A comprehensive map available from the visitor center shows the 15km (10-mile) route.

SPECTATOR SPORTS

For information on current events, contact the **Auckland i-SITE Visitor Centre** (✆ 09/367-6009; reservations@aucklandnz.com), or check out the events listings at www.aucklandnz.com.

HORSE RACING   **Auckland Cup Week** (✆ 09/524-4069; www.aucklandcupweek.co.nz) usually takes place over 3 party-filled days in late February to early March at Ellerslie Race Course. It's the biggest day in New Zealand thoroughbred racing, with over 30,000 spectators.

Alexandra Park Raceway, Greenlane West Road, Epsom (✆ **09/630-5660;** www.alexpark.co.nz), mounts the **Lion Red Auckland Trotting Cup Carnival,** an extravaganza that includes the NZ$100,000 Great Northern Derby for 3-year-olds and the NZ$250,000 Lion Red Trotting Cup. Regular **Night Trotting** meets are on Friday and Saturday nights.

For more information on horse racing, call the **Recorded Racing Information Service** (✆ **09/520-7507**).

MARATHON   The **Round the Bays Run** (✆ 09/525-2166) is held around Tamaki Drive each March.

RUGBY   Check with the visitor center for current schedules of **All Blacks** and fiercely fought provincial rugby games nationwide. The rugby season runs from April to September. For rugby and league match information, contact **New Zealand Rugby Football Union** (✆ 04/499-4995) or **New Zealand Rugby Football League, Inc.** (✆ 09/524-4013).

TENNIS   The **ASB Bank Classic,** in January, attracts women tennis players from around the world; the **Heineken Open,** the men's event, generally follows the women's event, also in January. Call ✆ **09/373-3623** or fax 09/373-3625 for details.

7   SHOPPING

Most shops are open Monday through Friday from 9am to 5:30pm, with many staying open late on Thursday and Friday. Saturday hours are normally 10am to 4pm, although some shops stay open all day. Many are also open on Sunday. Several free shopping guides are available at visitor centers.

Tip: If you have the store mail your purchases back home, you won't have to pay the 12.5% GST—and you won't have to lug them all around the country.

Duty-Free Delights   **DFS Galleria Custom House,** Customs and Albert streets (✆ **0800/388-937** in NZ, or 09/308-0700; www.dfsgalleria.com), is New Zealand's most luxurious duty- and tax-free department store. It offers complimentary shuttle service, free delivery of purchases to the airport, and currency exchange. It's open daily from 10am to 10pm. For a list of all New Zealand duty-free stores, pick up the free *Duty Free & GST Free Shopping Guide* at the airport or visitor centers. If you shop at an off-airport duty-free store, be sure you have your airline ticket with you.

INNER CITY

Shoppers seeking the latest in cutting-edge fashion and design can pick up the pocket-size **Auckland Fashion Guide** from visitor information centers and then head for the **High Street–Vulcan Lane–O'Connell Street areas** ★★★ (www.hotcity.co.nz). This is

---

⌐ Tips   **Antiques Hunting**

The most popular concentrations of antiques stores are around the Epsom area and in Parnell, Remuera, Ponsonby, and the inner city. **Lord Ponsonby Antiques,** 86 Ponsonby Rd. (✆ 09/376-6463), is as good a place as any to start. **Piper Antiques,** 31A Sale St. (✆ 09/376-9000), is another good hunting ground.

Look for **John Stephens Antiques,** 15 Shore Rd. (✆ 09/529-1660); in Epsom, you'll find **Auckland Antique Shop,** 465 Manukau Rd. (✆ 09/630-4048), and **Country Antiques,** 489 Manukau Rd. (✆ 09/630-5252). In Remuera, look for **Antiquities,** 89 Great South Rd. (✆ 09/520-0353), **Abbey Antiques,** 87 Great South Rd. (✆ 09/520-2045), and several others on the same stretch of Great South Road. And if you like old china you'll adore **Babushka,** 156 Garnet Rd. (✆ 09/378-9226).

(Finds) **Great Tastes**

To satisfy your gourmet tastes or pick out tasty morsels for a picnic, head for **Kapiti Shop,** 136–142 Fanshawe St. (© **09/377-2473**), which has a huge selection of premium New Zealand cheeses—and make sure you try Kapiti's ice cream. It's divine! **Zarbo,** 24 Morrow St., Newmarket (© **09/520-2721;** www.zarbo.co.nz), carries an excellent range of delicious items. **Pandoro,** 427 Parnell Rd., Parnell (© **09/358-1962**), and 290 Dominion Rd., Mount Eden (© **09/631-7416**), is an authentic Italian bakery offering organic, non-genetically modified, and additive-free products. And enjoy the sights and sounds of an authentic working fish market at **Auckland Fish Market,** Sanfords, Jellicoe Street, near Viaduct Harbour (© **09/379-1490;** www.aucklandfishmarket.co.nz). It has a daily early-morning auction and a seafood school.

the place to go for leading New Zealand fashion houses, accessories, art, coffee, and interesting food. It's where you'll find international fashion hotshots **Karen Walker, Zambesi,** and **World.** Also here are excellent bookstores such as **Unity** (© 09/307-0731) and **Touchwood** (© 09/379-2733). The lovely and innovative **Pauanesia ★★**, 35 High St. (© 09/366-7282), sells the very best in contemporary New Zealand and Pacific homeware. The **Vault,** 13 High St. (© 09/377-7665), is the perfect place for reasonably priced New Zealand and international design items—everything from jewelry to stationery to small gifts. The new **Chancery shopping area** (© 09/368-1863) is also here. It's packed with international brand stores and exclusive fashion names. If you're a *Lord of the Rings* fan, check out the big range of movie collectibles and jewelry at **DMC,** 61 High St. (© 09/303-4757; www.lotrshop.co.nz).

All manner of middle-of-the-road stores line **Queen Street** from top to bottom, but I think you find much better shops down the little side streets running off it; here you'll often find excellent specialty shops, such as **Compendium,** 5 Lorne St. (© 09/300-3212), which has an impressive collection of quality New Zealand craft work. It schedules regular exhibitions of glass, jewelry, pottery, wood, sculpture, clothes, and furniture. **Fingers ★★**, 2 Kitchener St. (© 09/373-3974), is Auckland's most established New Zealand jewelry collective. **Kura Gallery,** 188 Quay St. (© 09/302-1151; www.kuragallery.co.nz), has a great range of original New Zealand art and crafts. There are also a wide range of retail outlets and eateries under construction as part of the Britomart extensions behind the Britomart Transport Centre. These should begin to open in 2010.

PONSONBY/HERNE BAY/K'ROAD

Although better known for its wealth of eateries, Ponsonby also has some terrific specialty design stores and boutiques, with an emphasis on housewares, fashion, and furniture. Karangahape Road is worth browsing for its diversity and cultural mix, but don't expect high-quality goods here; it's better known for art galleries, featuring both the quirky and the bizarre. Check out **www.ponsonbyroad.co.nz** and www.kroad.com for details.

PARNELL/NEWMARKET

Shopping Parnell is a special experience, albeit an expensive one, with everything from Timberland to Cartier. You'll find all sorts of exclusive gifts in a rabbit's warren of little historic buildings, restored to picturesque splendor, that stretch along a mile of Parnell

The Markets

Everyone makes a big deal about **Victoria Park Market,** 210 Victoria St. W. (✆ **09/309-6911;** www.victoria-park-market.co.nz), but I find it a tedious shuffle between jaded retail outlets. It's different, I'll grant it that, but different doesn't necessarily mean better. More than 100 outlets purvey everything from the ridiculous to the bizarre. There are some interesting things, but you have to look carefully; a lot of it is junk but I'm told a revamp is on the way—it's long overdue. The market is open daily 9am to 6pm.

For an excellent Pacific experience, definitely visit the **Otara Market** ★★★, Newbury Street, Otara (✆ **09/274-0830**), held Saturday from 6am to noon. It's the largest Polynesian market in the world, with larger-than-life personalities, exotic foods and smells, wonderful *tapa* cloth, flax mats and baskets, and bone carvings.

Avondale Market, Avondale Racecourse, Ash Street (✆ **09/818-4931**), on Sunday from 6am to noon, has a strong Polynesian and Asian influence. It features a mass of fruit, vegetables, new and used clothes, and bric-a-brac. The **Aotea Square Markets,** the Edge, Queen Street (✆ **09/309-2677**), take place Friday and Saturday from 10am to 6pm; they feature New Zealand fashion labels, retro gear, foods, fabric, jewelry, and furniture. There is an excellent **City Farmers' Market** held every Saturday morning from 8am to noon in the large courtyards behind the Britomart Transport Centre. The **French Style Market** is held every Saturday and Sunday from 8am to 1pm at La Cigale, 69 St. Georges Bay Rd., Parnell.

Road. Be sure to investigate **Höglund Art Glass,** 285 Parnell Rd. (✆ **09/300-6238;** www.hoglund.co.nz), a beautiful store with original work by leading glass blowers Ola and Marie Höglund. Click on to **www.parnell.net.nz** for more information about this area. And head for Newmarket's latest hot spots, Nuffield and Teed streets ★★★ for the high-end stores of iconic international and Kiwi fashion brands like Karen Walker, Trellise Cooper, Kate Sylvester, and Zambesi. There are a number of excellent cafes and restaurants here too—the ideal place to pause between parcels. I like to go here just to look at the beautifully designed stores and to watch "the pretty people." Newmarket as a whole (www.newmarket.co.nz), has over 40 designer fashion stores and New Zealand's largest concentration of shoe stores—24 in fact. In this area also look out for the Poi Room, 17 Osborne St., Newmarket (✆ 09/520-0399; www.thepoiroom.co.nz), for high-quality New Zealand art, design, jewelry, prints, glass, and textiles.

8 AUCKLAND AFTER DARK

Auckland has something for everyone—the adventurous, the sophisticated, the young, and the young at heart. From 24-hour casinos and live theater to cinema, clubs, pubs, bars, and dance spots, you can party all the way to breakfast time.

For information about current cultural and entertainment events in the city, contact **Ticketek,** Aotea Centre (© **09/307-5000;** www.ticketek.co.nz), which provides easy credit card booking with next-day courier delivery. It also makes bookings around the country—a good way to save time and avoid disappointment. The free newspaper *Tourist Times* also lists current happenings.

THE PERFORMING ARTS

The **Edge,** 50 Mayoral Dr. (© **09/309-2677;** www.the-edge.co.nz), is the cultural core of Auckland. Located in the central area bordered by Mayoral Drive and Albert, Wellesley, and Queen streets, it includes the modern Aotea Centre, the impressive Auckland Town Hall, and the refurbished Civic Theatre. The **Aotea Centre** (© **09/307-5060**), opened in 1990 by Dame Kiri Te Kanawa, features theater, ballet, dance, opera, major stage productions, art exhibitions, and lots of local drama. The **Auckland Town Hall** is the city's best-known building. The Great Hall seats over 1,600 and is modeled after the Gewandhaus Concert Hall in Leipzig, Germany, which was bombed during World War II. It is regarded as one of the finest acoustically tuned concert halls in the world, and it schedules regular performances by the Auckland Philharmonia and the New Zealand Symphony Orchestra. For listings of events at the Edge, call © **09/307-5060** or go to www.akcity.govt.nz.

The **SKYCITY Theatre** is the newest addition to the city's performance venues. The 700-seat theater features state-of-the-art technology and major local and international performers in dance, theater, rock, pop, jazz, and cabaret. For details on events, call © **0800/759-2489** or visit www.skycity.co.nz.

The **Maidment Theatre** at Auckland University (© **09/308-2383**) is well known for New Zealand drama and theater sports; the **Bruce Mason Centre,** in Takapuna (© **0800/005-959** in NZ, or 09/488-2940), offers a little of everything.

THE LIVE MUSIC SCENE

Pick up the free *Auckland What's On* guide from the visitor center for the latest on the music scene. You'll find jazz and rhythm-and-blues gigs at places such as **London Bar,** Wellesley and Queen streets (© **09/373-3864**); and **Deschlers,** High Street (© **09/379-958**), which is popular with the 20- to 30-something after-work crowd. The **Alto Casino & Bar** at SKYCITY (© **09/363-6368**) also has live jazz performances.

The **Devonport Folk Music Club** meets in the Bunker, Mount Victoria, Devonport (© **09/445-2227**), Monday evenings at 8pm; new faces are welcome.

If Irish music is your thing, you'll find it at **Danny Doolan's,** Viaduct Basin (© **09/358-2554**), where there's live entertainment on Thursday, Friday, and Saturday nights; the **Dogs Bollix,** Karangahape and Newton roads (© **09/376-4600**), which schedules piano nights and jam sessions; and the **Bog,** 196 Parnell Rd., Parnell (© **09/377-1510**).

The **Mexican Café,** 67 Victoria St. W. (© **09/373-2311**), has live Latin music every Wednesday and Thursday.

THE CLUB & BAR SCENE

No matter how many nightspots I list here, I'll always overlook somebody's favorite. If you want a night with the work-hard, play-hard business crowd, head for Parnell; older, richer, devil-may-care types flock to Viaduct Harbour and its many nighttime haunts. The younger, funky, black-clothed set hangs out in High Street/Vulcan Lane in the inner city; most of the all-night clubs, drag clubs, and gay bars are along Karangahape Road;

Placing Your Bets: A Night at the Casino

Auckland's **SKYCITY Casino,** Victoria and Federal streets (© **0800/759-2489** in NZ, or 09/363-6000; www.skycity.co.nz), receives over 12,000 visitors per day! The **SKYCITY Casino** is the largest in New Zealand. This vast expanse of gaming tables (blackjack, roulette, craps, Caribbean stud poker, baccarat, tai sai, pai gow, and money wheel), an 80-seat keno lounge, and more than 1,200 slot machines is not the most stimulating of environments—unless you're keen to try your luck. Everyone is earnest and intent, as well they might be, given the amount of money changing hands. Still, it's worth a look, if nothing else. The upmarket **Alto Casino & Bar** ★, on the third level, is much more stylish and intimate, and **Bar 3** is popular with locals. It has live music and a strict dress code (jackets for men; jeans, shorts, active sportswear, and sports shoes not permitted). It opens at 4pm and continues through the night. The **SKYCITY Members Club** is a more exclusive, invitation-only gaming room.

You may not be interested in gambling, but I think a visit to SKYCITY is essential at some point in your visit to Auckland. The casinos are not the only aspect of this multifaceted complex. It holds several excellent restaurants (17 overall) the Sky Tower, the SKYCITY Theatre complex, and one of the best contemporary New Zealand art collections in the country. The casinos are open 24 hours a day, every day.

and Ponsonby is a favored upmarket place for drinks, dinner, and a general wind-up before hitting the club scene.

Inner City   If you want to check out the yachting scene, head for the **Loaded Hog,** Viaduct Harbour, Hobson and Quay streets (© 09/366-6491), where the pace is fairly frisky after a day on the water. **Spy Bar,** 204 Quay St., Viaduct Harbour (© 09/377-7811), is Auckland's top after-hours bar for a sophisticated older crowd. The very chic **Chic,** 201 Quay St., Viaduct Harbour (© 09/377-5360), has exotic fabrics, lavish "beds," and plush pillows, which set the mood for a seductive night out with the glam crowd. **Northern Steamship Company,** 122 Quay St., Britomart (© 09/374-3952), is a very cool Macs Brewbar, located in a historic building with dozens of small table lamps glued upside down to the ceiling. They serve nine of their own beers on tap and have live music Thursday through Saturday nights.

Minus 5, Princes Wharf (© 09/377-9865), is the "coolest" experience in town. Everything from the walls to the glasses is made of ice, and the temperature is a constant –5°F (–21°C), so make the essential booking and don your warmest coat. **Crow Bar,** 26 Wyndham St. (© 09/366-0398), is a classy little rich joint that's trendy in the wee small hours. **Honey,** 5 O'Connell St. (© 09/369-5639), is a sophisticated spot offering over 30 varieties of champagne and New Zealand's very own vodka label, 42-Below—the cocktails are winners. **Opium,** 291–297 Queen St. (© 09/378-0888), is a very sexy, dimly lit restaurant and bar frequented by Auckland's aspiring cognoscenti. The all-blue Ming Bar is quite the place to be seen. It's located within the Sky Metro Building on Aotea Square. **Galatos,** 17 Galatos St. (© 09/303-1928), is a plush bar that veers toward the alternative international gig scene with live funk, soul, hip-hop, and jazz.

Coco Club, 3 Fort Lane, inner city (© **09/309-3848**), an upmarket alley bar—a
hidden gem—for sophisticates, offers vintage champagne by the glass and live jazz every
night; and **Match Lounge Bar,** Hopetoun and Pitt streets, City (© **09/379-0110**), is a
slick little joint designed to accommodate an intimate crowd with plenty of quieter spots
for conversations. Don your glad rags for this one and arrive late if you want to appear
cool. **Khuja Lounge,** 536 Queen St. (© **09/377-3711**), is an institution. Its Latin/hip-
hop/funk DJ scene is ever-popular with the 20s and 30s crowd. And don't miss chef Peter
Gordon's latest inspiration, **Bellota,** 91 Federal St., opposite SKYCITY Grand Hotel. It's
a supercool, dark, sensuously modern take on a Spanish tapas bar. **La Zeppa,** 33 Drake
St., Freemans Bay (© **09/379-8167**), is another popular tapas bar in the Victoria market
area. It's popular with the corporate crowd.

Karangahape Road/Ponsonby   **Suede,** 213 Symonds St. (© **09/366-3906**), is a
favorite with a mixed crowd of locals; **Club 4:20,** 373 Karangahape Rd. (no phone), is
the place to find out all about New Zealand's growing hip-hop scene.

SPQR, 150 Ponsonby Rd. (© **09/360-1710**), is the staple of Ponsonby Road. It has
a great bar scene late Friday and Saturday nights; you'll see all sorts, both gay and straight,
indulging in cocktails with fanciful names such as Horny Monkey and the Slapper. **Lime,**
167 Ponsonby Rd. (© **09/360-7167**), is the smallest bar of all, and everyone, just everyone, is determined to be first or second here—after that, there's always a queue to get in.

Sponge, 198 Ponsonby Rd. (© **09/360-0098**), attracts a younger dance crowd; and
Whiskey, 210 Ponsonby Rd. (© **09/361-2666**), is the best late-night scene on Friday
and Saturday. The very popular **Malt,** 442 Richmond Rd., Grey Lynn (© **09/360-
9537**), has the feel of a local corner pub with a bit more warmth and style.

Parnell/Newmarket   **Iguacu,** 269 Parnell Rd., Parnell (© **09/358-4804**), has established a reputation for hedonism. A business crowd tends to let loose here on Friday and
Saturday nights, and it's pretty much a case of anything goes—certainly lively, and certainly a pickup joint of the first degree. A younger hip crowd looking for good house
music favors **Denim,** 207 Parnell Rd., Parnell (© **09/337-0227**). The **Paddington,** 117
St. Georges Bay Rd., Parnell (© **09/309-3586**), might seem cast adrift in industrial land
between Parnell and the city, but it's a big hit with the advertising crowd and designers
after work. Don't be put off by the big-screen televisions; it gets more glamorous later in
the evening. In Newmarket, there's the slightly unruly, "boys' night out" atmosphere of
the **Penny Black** (© **09/529-0050**), Khyber Pass and Broadway.

THE GAY SCENE

It's hard to keep up with Auckland's ever-changing gay scene—especially when you're not
gay. But I have it on good authority that **Urge,** 490 Karangahape Rd. (© **09/307-2155**),
is a good bar for the "more masculine" crowd. Just be sure to wear leather! **Kamo,** 382
Karangahape Rd. (© **09/377-2313**), is a gay-friendly scene. The suggestively named
Flesh Nightclub & Lounge Bar, 15–17 O'Connell St., City (© **09/336-1616**), is
popular; and **Family Bar,** 270 Karangahape Rd. (© **09/309-0213**; www.familybar.
co.nz), attracts a colorful gay crowd. The **Den,** 348 Karangahape Rd. (© **09/307-9191**),
is a men's safe-sex cruise club; and you'll find a gay (male) sauna at **Centurian Sauna,** 18
Beresford Sq. (© **09/377-5571**; www.centuriansauna.co.nz). **Flirt,** on the corner of Pitt
Street and K'Road (© **09/373-3410**; www.wannaflirt.co.nz), is a popular lesbian nightclub.

9 A SIDE TRIP TO WAIHEKE ISLAND ★★★

This divine little paradise is just 35 minutes from downtown Auckland by ferry; of its permanent population of about 8,000, nearly 1,500 commute to the city each day to work. In summer, the island's population swells to over 40,000 as visitors come to languish in the enchanting mix of white-sand beaches, lush native bush, green farmland, top wineries and vineyards, and swish little cafes and restaurants. I strongly recommend that you stay at least 1 or 2 nights.

ESSENTIALS

GETTING THERE   By Ferry   Fullers Ferries (© **09/367-9111;** www.fullers.co.nz) offers an hourly service (20 sailings daily) from downtown Auckland to Waiheke Island. Ferries depart from Pier 2, Quay Street, in Central City. Most sailings are met by buses, shuttles, and taxis at Matiatia, near the main township of Oneroa. The Fullers trip takes 35 minutes and costs NZ$32 round-trip for adults, NZ$16 for children ages 5 to 15.

The **SeaLink Travel Group** (© **0800/732-546** in NZ, or 09/300-5900; www.sealink.co.nz) passenger and vehicular ferry leaves from Half Moon Bay, Pakuranga, and arrives at the Kennedy Point Wharf farther east across the Surfdale Causeway. Ferries run every hour daily between 6am and 6pm. The fare is NZ$130 round-trip for a car and driver. Passengers without cars pay NZ$30 adults, NZ$17 children ages 5 to 15. Reservations are essential.

Pine Harbour Ferry, Jack Lachlan Drive, Pine Harbour, Auckland (© **09/536-4725;** www.pineharbour.co.nz), operates regular service to Waiheke, between 8:30am and 5:40pm, with extended hours between December 27 and January 31. The round-trip fare is NZ$25 adults, NZ$15 children. It's a shorter, cheaper ferry trip, but you have to drive farther on the Auckland side if you're staying in the city.

By Tour   Fullers Waiheke Explorer Tour ★★ (© **09/367-9111**) gives you the option of being met on the island by a bus and taken on one of four tours, which last from 1½ hours to all day. It's an excellent option if you're short on time and it includes unlimited bus travel on the island for the rest of the day. It departs daily at 10am and noon and costs NZ$48 for adults, NZ$24 for children 5 to 15 years old.

ORIENTATION   The island is approximately 19km (12 miles) long and has 90km (56 miles) of coastline, 40km (25 miles) of which is white-sand beaches. **Oneroa,** the largest shopping village on Waiheke, is a 15- to 20-minute uphill walk from Matiatia Wharf, where the passenger ferries dock. It's a 10-minute drive from the Kennedy Point Wharf, where the vehicular ferry docks. This western end of the island has the most settlement around **Sandy** and **Enclosure Bays** and **Palm Beach. Ostend** and **Surfdale** also have shops and cafes. The best supermarket is at Surfdale.

GETTING AROUND   By Car   If you don't want to take a car to the island, pick up a rental when you arrive. **Waiheke Auto Rentals,** Matiatia Wharf (© **09/372-8998;** www.waihekerentals.co.nz), has good hourly rates and offers pickup and key drop-off service. Four-wheel-drive vehicles, scooters, motorbikes, and mountain bikes are also available. For bicycle rental, contact **Waiheke Bike Hire** (© **09/372-7937;** www.waihekebikehire.co.nz), open daily from 8:30am. Rates begin at NZ$30 per day and subsequent days are NZ$15 each. They also offer a free rescue service.

By Bus   For information on Waiheke Island bus services visit **Maxx** (© **09/366-6400;** www.maxx.co.nz). Buses serve most bays and beaches at the west end of the island. Pick

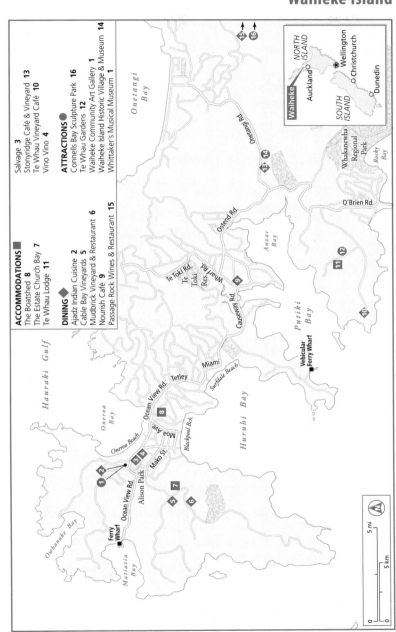

ACCOMMODATIONS
The Boatshed **8**
The Estate Church Bay **7**
Te Whau Lodge **11**

DINING
Ajadz Indian Cuisine **2**
Cable Bay Vineyards **5**
Mudbrick Vineyard & Restaurant **6**
Nourish Café **9**
Passage Rock Wines & Restaurant **15**

Salvage **3**
Stonyridge Café & Vineyard **13**
Te Whau Vineyard Café **10**
Vino Vino **4**

ATTRACTIONS
Connells Bay Sculpture Park **16**
Te Whau Gardens **12**
Waiheke Community Art Gallery **1**
Waiheke Island Historic Village & Museum **14**
Whittaker's Musical Museum **1**

AUCKLAND

6

A SIDE TRIP TO WAIHEKE ISLAND

up a schedule from bus drivers. Inquire about the **All-Day Bus Pass,** which costs NZ$8 adults, NZ$5 children ages 5 to 15, and NZ$20 family.

By Tour An excellent way to get a feel for Waiheke is to go with **Ananda Tours** ★★ (✆ **09/372-7530** or 027/233-4565; www.ananda.co.nz). It offers art studio, gourmet food and wine, and eco walking tours with knowledgeable guides; prices begin at NZ$105 per person. A good way to see the less-populated east end of the island is to join the **Rural Mail Run** for NZ$25. It leaves Monday through Friday at 8:30am; for details and bookings, call ✆ **09/372-9166.**

VISITOR INFORMATION The best place to get information is at **Waiheke i-SITE,** Oneroa (✆ **09/372-1234;** www.waihekenz.com). Their staff has extensive knowledge of available accommodations on the island. There is also an information kiosk at Matiatia Wharf.

For more information on Waiheke Island, check out www.waihekeonline.com and www.gotowaiheke.co.nz.

SPECIAL EVENTS Book accommodations months ahead for the hugely popular **Easter Jazz Festival** (www.waihekejazz.co.nz), because Aucklanders flock to the island for the event. The **Waiheke Island Wine Festival** (✆ **09/372-7676;** www.aucklandnz.com), in February, is a great chance to taste the island's terrific, award-winning wines. Tickets go on sale in October. **Headland Sculpture on the Gulf** (✆ **09/372-9907;** www.sculptureonthegulf.co.nz) is a must-see in late January and early February. It's held every 2 years (2011 dates on website soon) and is an unforgettable outdoor exhibition of large scale contemporary sculpture along Waiheke Island's coastal walkway.

EXPLORING THE ISLAND

In Oneroa, visit the upgraded **Waiheke Community Art Gallery,** 2 Kororoa Rd. (✆ **09/372-9907;** www.waihekeartgallery.org.nz), where you'll find a wide range of works from the many resident artists and craftspeople on the island. It's open daily from 10am to 4pm. You can pick up a copy of the Waiheke Art Guide there (or at the Visitor Centre). It lists around 20 local artists, many of whom open their studios to visitors. The guide also marks the location of six large public sculptures acquired from previous Headland Sculpture on the Gulf events. Nearby is the fascinating **Whittaker's Musical Museum,** 2 Korora Rd. ★ (✆ **09/372-9627;** www.musical-museum.org), where Lloyd and Joan Whittaker will hold you spellbound with their live performances for about NZ$12 on a range of antique musical instruments, including organs, concertinas, pianolas, and mouth organs. It's open daily, 1 to 4pm.

The **Waiheke Island Historic Village & Museum,** 165 Onetangi Rd. (✆ **09/372-2970**), is overlooked by a fortified Maori settlement site first inhabited 700 years ago. There are old cottages with collections of furniture, books, documents, and photographs. It's open Wednesday, and weekends year-round, and daily during school holidays and in summer, from noon to 4pm. Catch the Onetangi Bus no. 1 to get there.

Be up early to experience a bit of local culture at the **Ostend Market** ★, Ostend Hall, on the corner of Ostend Road and Belgium Street (✆ **09/372-4475;** www.ostendmarket.co.nz). A parade of local pottery, island-made goods, fruit and vegetables, herbal remedies, massage, plants, herbs, and more, it's held every Saturday from 8am to 1pm. On Sunday between 10am and 2pm, visit the **Oneroa Market,** Artworks Courtyard, Ocean View Road, where you'll find musicians and other performers, crafts, and food.

Another "must" activity is a drive to the glorious **Onetangi Bay** ★★—in my mind, one of the best beaches in New Zealand. Here you can swim and surf in crystal-clear

> **Moments Sailing Away**
>
> Bernard Rhodes, owner/skipper of *Flying Carpet* ★★★ ((C) 09/372-5621; www.
> flyingcarpet.co.nz), is a man with a thousand sea stories, and a day out on his
> 12m (38-ft.) yacht—which he built himself from recycled timber—will leave a
> lasting impression. His son Andrew is the qualified onboard chef. A day sail with
> three-course lunch starts at NZ$180 for adults and NZ$100 for children.

water with views as far as the eye can see. If you want to feel the true spirit of freedom, take it all off at the western end of **Palm Beach,** a small bay used for nude swimming.

If you'd like a peek into a fabulous private garden, check out Lance and Kay Peterson's **Te Whau Garden,** 31 Vintage Lane ((C) 09/372-6748; www.tewhaugarden.co.nz), which features a stunning combination of art and native bush. Even better is **Connells Bay Sculpture Park** ★★★, Cowes Bay Road ((C) 09/372-8957; www.connellsbay. co.nz), where you'll find a superb display of work by top New Zealand sculptors set into the magnificent native bush landscape. Admission is NZ$30 adults and NZ$15 children 14 and under. This outstanding guided experience is by appointment only from late October through April. If you're a real art fan you might consider their accommodations for one or two couples. See the website for details.

Speaking of walking, pick up the excellent *Waiheke Island Walkways* ★ brochure from the visitor center. It outlines and maps out eight wonderful island walks, which have been upgraded.

Another fabulous way to see the island is to **Drive the Loop** ★★, a 1-day self-drive tour that starts and finishes at Waiheke Auto Rentals on Matiatia Wharf (see "Getting Around," above). The company provides the rental vehicle and loop tour package, which includes maps with all the most interesting people and places highlighted. It takes 4 to 8 hours (65km/40 miles), depending on how often you stop, and costs NZ$120 to NZ$160, depending on the vehicle category. For information, call (C) 09/372-8998 or fax 09/372-9822.

VISITING VINEYARDS

To the surprise of many, more than 40 vineyards operate on Waiheke Island, where the Mediterranean-style climate is perfect for growing grapes (and olives). Some of the country's best red wines come from the island. Before you start exploring, pick up the free *Waiheke Winegrowers' Map,* or check out the Waiheke Winegrowers' Association website, www.waihekewine.co.nz. Plan your visits around eating time, because several growers have excellent restaurants.

The leader among the Waiheke vineyards is undoubtedly **Stonyridge** ★★, 80 Onetangi Rd. ((C) 09/372-8822; www.stonyridge.com). In 1987, Stonyridge produced the first Larose vintage, which was immediately judged one of the world's top red wines by the London World Guide to Cabernet. It has the dreamiest vineyard, with an incredibly picturesque view from its restaurant, which is one of the nicest places on the island to dine (lunch only; see "Where to Dine," later in this chapter). Tours of their cellar, vineyard, and olive grove (with two wine tastings) begin at 11:30am on Saturday and Sunday; admission is NZ$10 per person.

(Finds) **The Good Oil**

Waiheke is fast becoming known for its premium extra-virgin olive oils. Around 20,000 trees grow on the island; harvest season is April through May or June. There is no better place to start sampling than **Rangihoua Estate** ★, 1 Gordons Rd. (© **09/372-6214;** www.rangihoua.co.nz). The Frantoio Room is open Monday through Saturday during January and February; otherwise, tours and tastings are held every Saturday from 11am until 4pm, or by appointment.

Mudbrick Vineyard & Restaurant ★★, 126 Church Bay Rd., Oneroa (© **09/372-9050;** www.mudbrick.co.nz), is another magical setting for a meal. **Goldwater Estate,** 18 Causeway Rd., Ostend (© **09/372-7493;** www.goldwaterwine.com), is a small premium winegrower producing top cabernet/merlots. It's open daily noon to 4pm from December through February with reduced hours for the rest of the year. It offers tasting sessions and tours by arrangement.

Kennedy Point Wines & Olive Oil ★, 44 Donald Bruce Rd., Kennedy Point (© **09/372-5600;** www.kennedypointvineyard.com), has a winery and tasting room in a beautiful setting. **Te Whau Vineyard & Cafe** ★★★, 218 Te Whau Dr. (© **09/372-7191;** www.tewhau.com), has a smart cafe that serves lunch daily in summer and dinner Thursday through Saturday, with reduced winter hours. Tours are NZ$10 per person. With more than 500 cellared wines, Te Whau houses the most diverse collection of New Zealand wine in the world. **Passage Rock Wines & Restaurant,** 438 Orapiu Rd. (© **09/372-7257;** www.passagerockwines.co.nz), is in a tranquil bay. Its award-winning wines have grabbed international attention—as have its wood-fired pizzas. In addition to all of the above, my new favorite is **Cable Bay Vineyards** ★★★, 12 Nick Johnstone Dr., Oneroa (© **09/372-5889;** www.cablebayvineyards.co.nz), which features a beautiful architecturally designed winery, tasting room, restaurant, and bar complex with dramatic views over Motukaha Island. They are open for lunch daily from 11am, and offer dinner Thursday through Saturday from 6pm.

If you want to take a wine tour, contact **Jaguar Tours** (© 09/372-7312; www.waihekejaguartours.co.nz). Fullers and Ananda Tours also offer vineyard tours; see "Getting There," above, for more information.

WHERE TO STAY

Big news for luxury lovers was to be the 2010 opening of the five-star NZ$50-million **Langham Place Vineyard Resort & Spa,** Isola Estate (http://waiheke.langhamplace hotels.co.nz or www.isolaestate.com); but the economic recession took its toll. Although construction was frozen in early 2009, it will begin if the developer successfully sells the 78 condominium-style rooms and suites. This Tuscan-style resort will feature one-, two-, and three-bedroom luxury apartments, a Chuan Spa, an interactive wine theater, sophisticated restaurants and bars, and just about every other luxury amenity we've come to expect of the internationally regarded Langham Hotel brand. Check the websites for progress and opening dates. At the other end of the scale, the island has plenty of good backpacker and hostel options, priced from NZ$22 to NZ$80 per night; or call © 021/709-302 (www.visitwaiheke.co.nz) for a range of excellent self-contained holiday houses to rent.

You'll find plenty to be pleased about at the **Estate Church Bay**★★, 56 Church Bay Rd. (🕿 **09/372-2637**; www.theestatechurchbay.com). Four beautiful rooms overlook vineyards and country views.

The Boatshed ★★★   There's a real feel of New Zealand about this gorgeous spot above the beach, overlooking little Oneroa. To call it "relaxed luxury" is a little undefined, but I think you'll love the clean-cut elegance of the marine-themed suites. The Boatshed offers terrific sea views from private balconies and every comfort, right down to heated bathroom floors. For something special, go for the three-story Lighthouse suite, which has a private top-floor lounge and a first-floor bedroom with commanding views and a balcony. Ground-floor rooms are more spacious. You may never want to leave.

Tawa and Huia sts. 🕿 **09/372-3242.** Fax 09/372-3262. www.boatshed.co.nz. 7 units. NZ$745–NZ$910. Rates include breakfast, and airport and ferry transport. Off-season rates. AE, DC, MC, V. Children 11 and under not accepted. **Amenities:** All-day dining; bar; bike rentals; concierge; nearby golf course; outdoor Jacuzzi; room service; sauna; watersports equipment rentals. In room: TV/DVD, fridge, hair dryer, minibar, Wi-Fi.

Te Whau Lodge ★★ (Value   Gene O'Neill and Liz Eglinton have an unbeatable combination: awesome views, dynamite culinary skills, and relaxed, friendly personalities. Built to blend with the landscape, the lodge utilizes timber finishes and that intrinsic New Zealand building material, corrugated iron. Every spacious room has its own theme, its own bathroom, and its own fabulous balcony. Gene and Liz will take care of all your activity bookings. And just when you think it can't get any better, Gene will present you with one of his delectable two-course *table d'hôte* dinners, using vegetables fresh from the lodge garden. The lodge has its own sewage disposal and gray water treatment plant, too. Te Whau doesn't have some of the extras of the Boatshed, but in my view it's a more intimate, friendly experience.

36 Vintage Lane, Te Whau Point, Waiheke. 🕿 **09/372-2288.** Fax 09/372-2218. www.tewhaulodge.co.nz. 4 units. NZ$585. Rates include breakfast, predinner canapés, and airport and ferry transport. Dinner NZ$50–NZ$100. AE, DC, MC, V. Children 11 and under not accepted. **Amenities:** Bar; bike rentals; concierge; nearby golf course; outdoor Jacuzzi; room service; watersports equipment rentals; Wi-Fi in main reception areas. In room: TV/DVD on request, hair dryer.

WHERE TO DINE

One of the best Waiheke restaurants is **Te Whau Vineyard Café**★★★, 218 Te Whau Dr. (🕿 **09/372-7191**). *Wine Spectator* rated it one of the top New Zealand restaurants for wine lovers, and it has an amazing collection of over 500 New Zealand wines. It offers daily lunch from 11am to 5pm, dinner Thursday, Friday, Saturday in summer, and Friday, Saturday, Sunday in winter from 6:30 to 11pm. Main courses average NZ$38.

At **Mudbrick Vineyard & Restaurant**★★, Church Bay Road, Oneroa (🕿 **09/372-9050**), diners gaze out over rolling farmland to the waters of Hauraki Gulf while enjoying French rural cuisine; main courses are NZ$28 to NZ$38. **Stonyridge Café & Vineyard**★★, 80 Onetangi Rd. (🕿 **09/372-8822**), serves excellent Pacific Rim cuisine in a glorious romantic setting. It serves lunch only—daily in summer, and on Saturday and Sunday in winter. Main courses cost around NZ$30; reservations are required.

In Oneroa village, you'll find residents amassed for coffee, snacks, lunch, and dinner at **Salvage,** Ocean View Road (🕿 **09/372-2273**). The food is reasonable, but I think you'll be far more impressed by my favorite—**Nourish Café**★, 3 Belgium St., Ostend (🕿 **09/372-3557**; www.nourish.co.nz). It has a fresh seasonal menu with main courses around NZ$26, as well as a great range of cakes and baked goods. It's open daily 8am to

Meandering in Matakana ★★

Approximately 1 hour north of Auckland is the village of **Warkworth,** at the heart of the Kowhai Coast. It gives access to the very pretty **Sandspit/Matakana/Leigh area,** where you can catch a ferry to Kawau Island or visit a range of excellent swimming beaches. It's not exactly off the beaten track, but the whole area offers some fine accommodations, wineries, and boutique food operations, and the chance to mellow out away from fellow tourists. In recent years, the area has become increasingly popular and you'll now find a number of enjoyable low-key attractions here.

The **Warkworth i-SITE Centre,** 1 Baxter St., Warkworth (*C* **09/425-9081;** fax 09/425-7584; www.warkworth-information.co.nz), is open daily from 9am to 5:15pm year-round (closed Dec 25). For Matakana information, check www.matakanacoast.com or www.matakanavillage.co.nz.

You'll find a nice little cluster of activities in the Sandspit and Matakana areas just a few minutes out of Warkworth. There are several crafts outlets, among them **Morris & James Country Pottery & Café,** 48 Tongue Farm Rd., Matakana (*C* **09/422-7116;** www.morrisandjames.co.nz), makers of quality terra-cotta and glazed pots, tiles, and platters. It's open daily with free guided pottery tours Monday through Friday at 11:30am.

Don't miss **Zealandia Sculpture Garden** ★★★, 138 Mahurangi West Rd. (*C* **09/422-0099;** www.zealandiasculpturegarden.co.nz). Created by leading New Zealand sculptor Terry Stringer, it features a sculpture park surrounded by farmland. It's open every weekend November through March and every day during January from 10am to 4pm, with guided tours at 11am and 2pm. Admission is NZ$10. **Brick Bay Wines & Sculpture Trail** ★★, Arabella Lane, Snells Beach (*C* **09/425-4690;** www.brickbaysculpture.co.nz), is another fine choice for art lovers. The **Matakana Village Farmers' Market** ★★, 2 Matakana Valley Rd. (*C* **09/422-7503;** www.matakanavillage.co.nz), is staged every Saturday from 8am to 1pm. Look out for the artistic cooking workshops that are held at the market on the last weekend of every month; or explore the trendy new Matakana shopping complex adjacent to the market. Refresh yourself afterward at **Brookview Tea House** ★, 1335 Leigh Rd., Matakana (*C* **09/423-0390;** www.brookviewteahouse.co.nz); or pick up perfect bread and picnic foods from **Matakana Patisserie** ★★, 70 Matakana Valley Rd. (*C* **09/422-9896;** www.matakanapatisserie.co.nz), which is open daily from 7am.

No trip to this area is complete without a cruise or ferry ride from Sandspit Wharf to **Kawau Island** ★★ (www.kawauisland.org.nz). Sir George Grey, an early governor of New Zealand, built the Mansion House 150 years ago. It's now restored and open for visits, and on the grounds you'll find the descendants of his "Australian imports": wallabies, kookaburras, and rosellas. **Reubens Water Taxis** (*C* **0800/111-616** in NZ, or 09/425-8006; www.reubens.co.nz), will take you to the island for NZ$50 round-trip for adults and NZ$26 for children.

If you'd like to stay on Kawau Island, David and Helen Jeffery of **Kawau Lodge** ★, North Cove (✆ **09/422-8831;** www.kawaulodge.co.nz), offer an ecofriendly stay with three rooms at NZ$695, which includes 2 nights' accommodations, all meals, and transfers from Sandspit to the island. It's a good base for exploring the famous **Goat Island Marine Reserve** ★★★, 4km (2¹/₂ miles) northeast of Leigh and about 40 minutes from Warkworth, which was established in 1975 as New Zealand's first marine reserve and is a mecca for divers. If you'd like to explore the marine life here, the **Glass Bottom Boat** at Leigh (✆ **09/422-6334;** www.glassbottomboat.co.nz) offers a 45-minute trip on *Aquador,* or an excellent, 30-minute "round the islands" trip.

If you decide to spend a night here—and I strongly advise you do—you will be spoiled for choice. **Tera del Mar** ★, 140 Rodney Rd., Leigh (✆ **09/422-6090;** www.teradelmar.co.nz), is about 25km (16 miles) from Warkworth but well worth the drive through pretty countryside. It offers four lovely, big bedrooms (three with en-suite bathrooms, one with private bathroom) for NZ$295 to NZ$325. The **Saltings Estate** ★★, 1210 Sandspit Rd., Warkworth (✆ **09/425-9670;** www.saltings.co.nz), is a double-barreled delight. Terry and Maureen Baines have three gorgeous en-suite rooms in their own home, and just a stroll away is a separate self-contained apartment that can accommodate seven adults. The added bonus is that it overlooks a small biodynamic vineyard and winery. Allow for the fact that you may never want to leave and stay at least 2 nights. It's idyllic, and B&B rooms will cost you NZ$265 to NZ$395, NZ$295 to NZ$495 for the apartment. At **Takatu Lodge & Vineyard** ★★★, 518 Whitmore Rd., Matakana (✆ **09/423-0299;** www.takatulodge.co.nz), Heather and John Forsman offer four gorgeous suites in a stunning new, contemporary property set amid a working vineyard. They've attended to every detail to ensure guest comfort, adding candles, essential oils, and complimentary local goodies as a final touch. Their own Takatu wine is also available and you'll get a free vineyard wine-tasting session with antipasti. Rooms cost NZ$695, which includes a three-course breakfast.

In Warkworth, stop by the visitor center for the good brochure listing restaurants as well as attractions and accommodations. About 10 minutes out of town is **Heron's Flight Vineyard & Café** ★, 49 Sharp's Rd., Matakana (✆ **09/422-7915;** www.heronsflight.co.nz), where you'll find fine wines, good coffee, and food; you can stroll among grapes, figs, roses, and olives. It's open daily from 10am to 6pm for delicious light lunches. Main courses cost NZ$25 to NZ$35 and its romantic vineyard environment makes it a winner. **Mariposa Palm Café,** 253 Point Wells Rd., Matakana (✆ **09/422-7597**), is another delightful cafe destination, this one set amid a subtropical garden and nursery. It's open daily 9am to 4pm. Matakana Village also has several cafes and restaurants in addition to the two listed earlier in this section.

4pm, with late nights on Friday and Saturday. The expert hosts at **Ajadz Indian Cuisine** ★, Artworks, Oneroa (𝒞 **09/372-2588**), offer authentic tandoori and curry dishes from northern and southern India. It's open daily in summer and Wednesday to Monday in winter for lunch and dinner. **Vino Vino** ★, behind Green Hills Wines & Spirits, Oneroa (𝒞 **09/372-9888;** www.vinovino.co.nz), is another local favorite for its big Mediterranean platters and full a la carte dining on a huge deck with stunning views.

10 A SIDE TRIP TO GREAT BARRIER ISLAND ★★

Imagine pristine white-sand beaches empty of people, lush mountains, and a vast network of walking tracks. Add rare birds and plant life, a permanent population of less than 1,000, and a seductive, laid-back lifestyle, and you have New Zealand's fourth-largest landmass, Great Barrier Island. The Department of Conservation administers over 70% of the island, and locals like to say that there are more conservationists per square inch than anywhere else in New Zealand.

This seductive paradise is *the* place if you're looking for a unique New Zealand wilderness experience. It's New Zealand as it used to be—all 285 sq. km (111 sq. miles) of it. It's isolated, yet it's only a 35-minute plane ride from our biggest city. It's a place the locals call "the Barrier" and I call "heaven." Get yourself there and you'll remember it forever.

ESSENTIALS

GETTING THERE   By Plane   Great Barrier Airlines (𝒞 **0800/900-600** in NZ, or 09/275-9120; www.greatbarrierairlines.co.nz) runs daily flights to the island from Auckland International Airport and North Shore Aerodrome. **Mountain Air Great Barrier Xpress,** Domestic Terminal, Auckland International Airport (𝒞 **0800/222-123** in NZ, or 09/256-7025; www.mountainair.co.nz), also has daily flights to the island. Most flights land at Claris airfield in the center of the island; some land at Okiwi airfield, 8km (5 miles) from Port Fitzroy. The 35-minute trip costs NZ$90 to NZ$110 one-way.

By Ferry   Ferries land at Tryphena, at the southern end of the island. **SeaLink,** 45 Jellicoe St., Auckland Viaduct (𝒞 **0800/732-546** in NZ, or 09/300-5900; www.sealink. co.nz), runs 4½- to 5-hour trips to the island daily in summer and 3 days a week in winter (timetables vary). The *Eco Islander* has two theaters with plasma screens showing movies and documentaries, a cafe, and a reading room on board. The long trip can be grueling when the sea is rough. Round-trip fares are NZ$120 adults, NZ$96 seniors and students, NZ$80 children ages 5 to 15, and NZ$350 for a car. I think it's far better to pay a little more for the short flight. And don't worry about taking a car—it's easy to pick up a cheap rental at the Claris airfield. **Fullers Ferry** (𝒞 **09/367-9111;** www.fullers. co.nz) is a much faster (2½-hr.) trip, but its timetable service operates only in high season (roughly, Dec–Jan).

ORIENTATION

Great Barrier Island is approximately 15km (9⅓ miles) wide and 30km (19 miles) long, with Mount Hobson (621m/2,037 ft.) rising in the center. The island landscape is rugged, and much of it is inaccessible by road. The west coast is characterized by steep, forested ranges that run down to the sea; the east coast offers sweeping, white-sand beaches and rolling hills. The main areas of settlement are **Port Fitzroy** in the north;

Claris, **Whangaparapara,** and **Okupu** in the center; and **Tryphena** in the south. Good roads connect them all. Claris and Tryphena are the main villages, though neither is much more than a few shops, cafes, a pub, and a post office. Port Fitzroy boasts one store, a dive station, and a boat club. There are no banks or ATMs on the island (although many businesses accept credit cards). Be prepared to pay more for basic supplies than you would on the mainland.

GETTING AROUND

By Car   Reasonably priced rental options include **GBI Rent-A-Car,** 67 Hector Sanderson Rd., Claris (© **09/429-0062;** www.gbirentacar.co.nz), which has a wide range of vehicles and offers free delivery to Claris airfield and Tryphena Wharf. Prices start at around NZ$50 per day. **Aotea Rentals** (© **0800/426-832** in NZ; www.greatbarrier travel.co.nz), offers a similar service and prices from around NZ$95 per day. It is important to remember that the island is far from a suburban destination. Roads are often narrow and unsealed, there are no streetlights, and cellphone coverage is limited.

By Bus and Shuttle   There is no scheduled public transport on the island, but regular bus services meet boats and planes. **Great Barrier Buses** (© **09/429-0474;** www.great barrierbuses.co.nz) has daily service to walking tracks, beaches, and Port Fitzroy. A 1-day pass costs around NZ$50. There are also several shuttle companies.

By Bike   Rental mountain bikes are available from **GBI Rent A Car** (© **09/429-0062;** www.gbirentacar.co.nz) for NZ$45 to NZ$60 per day. **Paradise Cycles,** Tryphena (© **09/429-0474**), has multiday special deals.

VISITOR INFORMATION

The **Great Barrier Island Information Centre,** Main Road outside Claris Airport (© **09/429-0767;** www.greatbarrierisland.co.nz), is open daily from 7am to 8pm in the summer and 8am to 7pm in the winter. Auckland i-SITE Visitor Centres also supply some Great Barrier Island information at www.greatbarriernz.com.

SPECIAL EVENTS

In January, the **Port Fitzroy Mussel Fest** (© **09/429-0072**) provides stalls, entertainment, and as many succulent mussels as you can eat. The annual **Santa Parade,** in December at the Claris Sports Club, has a legendary reputation for fun.

EXPLORING THE ISLAND

Great Barrier has a rich history. Maori have inhabited the island for over 1,000 years, and Europeans created a thriving timber industry, milling the huge stands of native kauri trees for the shipbuilding industry. The island was a whaling station until the 1960s, and the relics of old stamping batteries attest to a rich gold- and silver-mining history. The remains of the **Oreville Stamping Battery** are beside the road on the way to Whangaparapara. Also in this area you'll find the very popular **Kaitoke Hot Springs Track,** which leads to natural hot springs in a creek. Use the toilet by the roadside—it's the last one you'll see for a while. The springs are 45 minutes in. Don't forget insect repellent.

Farther north, at Port Fitzroy, you must visit Tony Bouzaid's **Glenfern Sanctuary** ★★★, Glenfern Road (© **09/429-0091;** www.glenfern.org.nz). Take his guided walk and be witness to one of the most wonderful native wildlife sanctuaries anywhere. Over 8,000 trees have been planted as part of an ongoing reforestation project, and timber boardwalks make the walk easy. Tony also offers multiday tramp-sail packages that might include a visit to the otherwise inaccessible Sven Stellin of **Barrier Gold,** a backyard enterprise making a range of kanuka oil products on the shore of Wairahi Bay.

Even farther north, you'll find the **S.S. *Wairarapa* Walkway** at the very beautiful (and deserted) **Whangapoua Beach.** The steamer *Wairarapa* wrecked on cliffs near Miners Head on October 29, 1894, with the loss of around 130 lives. A little gravesite at the northern end of the beach serves as a reminder of one of New Zealand's worst shipping disasters.

A range of tracks crisscross **Mount Hobson,** a focal point for keen trampers. There are stunning views from the top on a clear day, and the summit is the main nesting ground for the rare black petrel. It's at least a 2-hour round-trip walk. A signposted side track will take you to **Kaiaraara Kauri Dam,** one of the tallest kauri dams, built over 70 years ago to transport logs out of the forests. If you feel like a steep climb, you'll find the remains of two more dams farther upstream.

In Okupu is a delightful surprise: **Young's Museum** ★, 212 Blind Bay Rd. (✆ 09/429-0388). Christine Young, spurred on by the memory of her father, has put together the cutest little museum you'll find anywhere. It's a real Kiwi experience, with Christine showing you through her father's astounding collection of old photographs that depict early life on the island. Phone ahead for an appointment.

A good number of **artists and sculptors** live on the island; the visitor center can furnish a brochure detailing their whereabouts.

Aotea Sea Kayaks, Mulberry Grove, Tryphena (✆ 09/429-0664; aoteakayak@hotmail.com), offers night kayak trips, sunset paddles, and harbor kayak cruises. Prices range from NZ$45 to NZ$75. **Bush and Beach** ★ (✆ 0800/042-3224 in NZ, or 09/837-4130; www.bushandbeach.co.nz) offers a range of excellent ecowalks and tours on the island.

WHERE TO STAY

If you plan on traveling to Great Barrier Island during the summer months, book your accommodations well in advance. In Port Fitzroy, **Fitzroy House,** Glenfern Road (✆ 09/429-0091; www.fitzroyhouse.co.nz), has a three-bedroom, self-contained cottage; rates start at NZ$200 but expect that to double during peak season from December 24 to January 15. On a hill above Okupu Beach, you'll find a real ecofriendly gem in self-contained **Bay Lodge Cottage** ★, Moana View Road, Okupu (✆ 07/843-2000 or 09/429-0927; www.gamesail.co.nz), for NZ$275. You'll be treated to chilled wine, fruit, cheese, and flowers.

At the top end of the market, you won't regret a hilltop stay at **Earthsong Lodge** ★★, 38 Medland Rd., Tryphena (✆ 09/429-0030; www.earthsong.co.nz), where Trevor and Carole Rendle cook amazing meals as part of the NZ$975 room rate. The property is completely self-sustaining for energy and water and it has a strong recycling policy.

WHERE TO DINE

Don't get too excited about dining possibilities on the island—they're few and far between, and relatively expensive compared to the city. **Claris Texas Café,** Claris (✆ 09/429-0811), is one of the best choices. It serves hearty breakfast fare, tasty lunches, and good coffee daily. You can eat out in the courtyard overlooking fields and idly wonder what might have become of the rest of the world. **Earthsong Lodge** (see "Where to Stay," above), is open to casual diners. Bookings are essential. The menu at Earthsong specializes in French and nouveau cuisine. Things are more modest at **Tipi and Bobs Waterfront Restaurant** in Tryphena. You can expect good-value meals, especially if you like fresh fish and chips. **Currach Irish Pub,** Pa Beach, Tryphena ((C) **09/429-0211**), offers excellent seafood.

---

11 OUT FROM AUCKLAND

For information about Northland and the Coromandel Peninsula, see chapter 7.

EN ROUTE TO NORTHLAND: THE HIBISCUS COAST

Located 48km (30 miles) north of Auckland, the Hibiscus Coast comprises the communities of Silverdale, Whangaparoa, Orewa, Waiwera, and Puhoi. The area is a 45-minute drive from Auckland, and InterCity coaches offer service that makes a day's outing a reasonable option.

The **Hibiscus Coast Information Centre,** 214A Hibiscus Coast Hwy. (next to KFC), Orewa ((C) **09/426-0076;** hbcvic@rodney.govt.nz), is open Monday through Friday from 10am to 5pm, Saturday and Sunday from 10am to 4pm.

On the drive north, stop at **Waiwera Thermal Resort** ★★, State Highway 1 ((C) **0800/924-937** in NZ, or 09/427-8800; www.waiwera.co.nz), open daily from 9am to 9pm. Nineteen indoor and outdoor pools are kept at 82°F to 113°F (28°C–45°C); there are both private and communal pools. They also have a new Inifinity Day Spa, which offers many excellent treatment packages online. Admission to the pools is NZ$25 for adults, NZ$15 for children 5 to 14, NZ$20 for students, and NZ$10 for seniors.

EN ROUTE TO THE COROMANDEL PENINSULA: THE PACIFIC COAST HIGHWAY

The Pacific Coast Highway is not exactly a highway, certainly not in the American sense of the word. Rather, it is a combination of roads that make up one of the best scenic routes in the country, following the coastline from Auckland all the way to Hawke's Bay. Along the way, it delivers you to Coromandel Peninsula via the very pretty **Seabird Coast** ★.

It's worth stopping here for the **Kaiaua Fisheries Licensed Seafood Restaurant & Takeaways** ((C) **09/232-2776**), open daily from 9am to 9pm, which serves some of the best fish and chips in the country. And once you've filled your empty stomach, check out the **Miranda Shorebird Centre** ★, East Coast Road ((C)/fax **09/232-2781;** www.miranda-shorebird.org.nz), where you'll find information about the millions of migratory birds that swing by here on their way north. The 8,500 hectares (21,000 acres) of tidal flats are a big attraction for wading birds and bird-watchers alike.

You can also relax in one of the largest hot mineral pools in the Southern Hemisphere or unwind in a private Jacuzzi at **Miranda Hot Springs Thermal Pools** ((C) **07/867-3055**). It's open Monday through Thursday from 8am to 9pm, Friday and Saturday from 8am to 10:30pm.

Northland & Coromandel

Northland—Te Tai Tokerau, or "Birthplace of a Nation"—is one of nature's best playgrounds, but surprisingly, visitors often overlook it. The Bay of Islands is what most people know of Northland. This is home to the fabulous Waitangi National Reserve, where the Treaty of Waitangi was signed between Maori and European settlers in 1840; this is also where visitors are best catered to in Northland. Beyond that, the region offers an idyllic summer lifestyle that seems to last year-round.

Northland's peninsular shape offers two contrasting coastlines: white scenic beaches that curve around sheltered coves and harbors to the east, and long stretches of wild, dune-backed beaches and kauri forests pounded by the Tasman Sea to the west.

Northland is made up of five main areas: Whangarei and the east coast; the Bay of Islands; the Far North; Hokianga; and the Kauri Coast. The population is sparse—just 148,000 for the whole region and in the Far North area alone, there are 7,250 sq. km (2,800 sq. miles) of farmland and forest occupied by just 56,000 people. Only three towns—Kaitaia, Kaikohe, and Kerikeri—have more than 4,000 residents. Clearly, you'll have large patches all to yourself, so start exploring.

The Coromandel region, like Northland, has long been a haven for New Zealand holidaymakers. It's closer to Auckland than most of Northland, but it has less to offer in terms of accommodations and organized tourism. Certainly the scenery is just as dramatic, and you'll get that same surfeit of remote beaches and laid-back lifestyle. Leaving Auckland and following the Pacific Coast Highway will take you into Coromandel's quaint, sometimes tatty seaside townships, around endless beaches and bays, and over rugged hill country into the heart of an area made famous by logging, gold mining, gum digging, alternative lifestyles, and artists. There's a raw quality to the Coromandel Peninsula that even the fledging tourist industry hasn't yet tamed.

Northland was the first region to participate in New Zealand's Environmentally Sustainable Tourism pilot project in 2002. It continues to actively promote and facilitate regional sustainability through its Sustainable Tourism Charter. Check www.enterprisenorthland.co.nz for a list of participating tourism operators.

1 BAY OF ISLANDS & THE FAR NORTH ★★★

Bay of Islands: 233km (144 miles) N of Auckland; Cape Reinga: 440km (273 miles) N of Auckland

The essential personal items for this area are swimsuit, sunglasses, and suntan lotion—perhaps a fishing rod or a wet suit if you're so inclined. With endless beaches, over 144 islands, and warm, clear blue waters to play in, you'll need little else. Recreation is king up here. There's great fishing, excellent diving, and a climate with average winter temperatures ranging from 45°F to 61°F (7°C–16°C) and summer days of 57°F to 77°F (14°C–25°C).

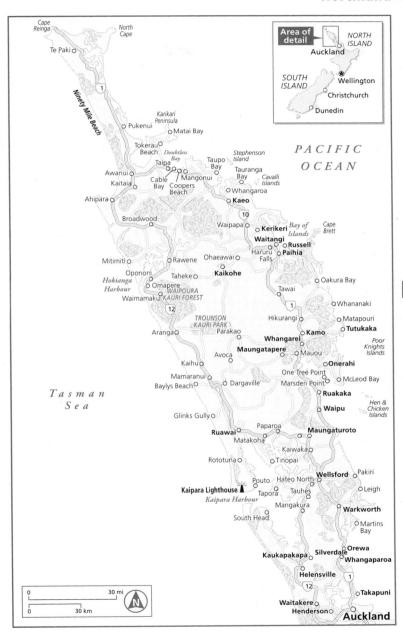

> **Tips** **Don't Miss the Best!**
>
> Don't be like the majority of visitors who go only as far as the Bay of Islands. Some of the best beaches, natural landscapes, and tranquil retreats lie much farther north. It makes sense to travel up an extra day or two, rather than staying in the Bay of Islands and, at best, taking a long 12-hour bus trip to Cape Reinga and back. Go the extra mile: You won't regret it.

The Bay of Islands features three little townships: **Paihia/Waitangi, Russell,** and **Kerikeri.** In the Far North, the hot spots are **Doubtless Bay; Kaitaia,** the largest town; and up that last thin finger of land to **Cape Reinga,** believed to be the departing point for the spirits of the Maori dead.

ESSENTIALS

GETTING THERE & GETTING AROUND   **By Plane**   There are three Northland airports: Whangarei, Kerikeri, and Kaitaia. **Air New Zealand Link** (✆ **0800/737-000** in NZ, or 09/357-3000) has daily service from Auckland to Kerikeri, with a shuttle bus to Paihia, and daily service from Auckland to Kaitaia. Charter flights are available with **Salt Air Bay of Islands** (✆ **09/402-8338;** www.saltair.co.nz) or **Skylink Air Charter** (✆ **09/422-7018;** www.skylink.co.nz).

By Coach (Bus)   Both **InterCity** (✆ **09/623-1503;** www.intercity.co.nz) and **Northliner Express** (✆ **09/583-5780;** www.northliner.co.nz) have daily service between Auckland and Paihia, Kerikeri, and Kaitaia. Both offer discounts to VIP backpackers and seniors. There's no local bus service in the Bay of Islands, Doubtless Bay, or Kaitaia.

By Car   If you plan to spend a few days in this area, pick up the free *Twin Coast Discovery Highway* map from any visitor center. It's an easy drive however you do it, with beautiful coastal views and rolling farmland all the way and usually very little traffic. Rather than going straight to the Bay of Islands (about a 3-hr. drive), you might want to explore the Whangarei area, which is described later in this chapter in "Whangarei." The drive from Auckland direct to Kaitaia via the east coast takes about 5 hours. Northland's west coast is also worth a visit if you have the time. The best plan is to go up the east side and drive back to Auckland via the west coast.

If you arrive via plane or bus, rental cars are available through **Pegasus Rental Cars** (✆ **0800/354-512** in NZ, or 09/402-8491; www.carrentalsbayofislands.co.nz). Help keep Northland roads clean by getting the official Northland visitor guide from information centers. It maps all recycling drop-off locations, and prepaid recycling bags are sold throughout Northland at service stations, supermarkets, camping grounds, and information centers for NZ$1.50 each.

By Ferry   If you stay in Russell but want to eat in Paihia, you'll need to take the passenger ferry that connects the two. It's the only inexpensive means of getting from one shore to another, and it runs hourly beginning at 7am and ending at 7:30pm. In summer, crossings are extended to 10:30pm. Fares are NZ$7 each way or NZ$11 round-trip for adults, NZ$3.50 or NZ$5.50 round-trip for children 5 to 15. If you miss the last boat, you can take the slightly more expensive water taxi. *Note:* The ferry from Paihia carries pedestrians only. If you're driving to Russell, take the car ferry at Opua. No reservations are needed; the ferry shuttles back and forth every 10 minutes, daily from 7am to 10pm, and costs NZ$12 one-way for a car and driver and NZ$1 per extra passenger. Campervans cost NZ$15 and motorcycles NZ$5 one-way. The car ferry lands at Okiato, which is about 10 minutes' drive from Russell township.

By Water Taxi   The **Island Water Taxi** (book at the visitor center) offers 24-hour service; fares depend on the time of day and the number of passengers.

By Tour   Several companies in Auckland offer 1-, 2-, and 3-day tours to the Bay of Islands and beyond. For good value and personal service, contact **Great Sights** (© **0800/653-339** in NZ; www.greatsights.co.nz). **Northliner Express** (© **09/307-5873;** www.northliner.co.nz) also has a range of packages and good-value **backpacker passes. Kiwi Experience** (© **09/366-9830;** www.kiwiexperience.com) offers well-priced 1-, 2-, and 3-day tours to the Bay of Islands and Cape Reinga. Tours to Cape Reinga operate from Bay of Islands, Doubtless Bay, and Kaitaia (see "To Cape Reinga," below).

ORIENTATION   **Paihia** and **Waitangi** basically form one settlement, which is the hub of the region's commercial and visitor action. All tours and cruises for the Bay of Islands start here. It's a short (1.5km/1-mile) walk to Waitangi, where the historic Treaty House is located. The main street is Marsden Road, which runs along the waterfront. Williams Road is a one-way street perpendicular to the coast; many of the shops are here.

Russell is a tiny community across the water. The Strand runs along the waterfront. Most of the charter boats in the area are anchored here; access is by ferry.

Kerikeri is a 20-minute drive north from Paihia. Once you turn off State Highway 10 onto Kerikeri Road, you'll find most of the main attractions and eateries.

In **Doubtless Bay,** the little fishing village of **Mangonui** (82km/51 miles from Paihia) is the core settlement. **Coopers Beach, Cable Bay, Taipa,** and **Tokerau Beach** are all within a few minutes of Mangonui. From Cable Bay, the coast swings in a huge arc of fabulous remote beaches all the way up to **Karikari Peninsula.**

Kaitaia is the major town of the Far North, 116km (72 miles) south of Cape Reinga. To the southwest lies the small town of **Ahipara** at the base of **Ninety Mile Beach,** which runs all the way up to the Cape.

VISITOR INFORMATION   You'll find the **Bay of Islands i-SITE Information Centre** at The Wharf, Marsden Road, Paihia (© **0800/363-463** in NZ, or 09/402-7345; fax 09/402-7314; www.visitnorthland.co.nz). Hours are 8am to 5pm in winter, 8am to 8pm in summer. Get your Kerikeri information here, too. Online, go to www.northlandnz.com, www.paihia.co.nz, or www.kerikeri.co.nz.

The **Far North i-SITE Visitor Centre** is at Jaycee Park, South Road, Kaitaia (© **09/408-0879;** fax 09/408-2546; www.fndc.govt.nz). It's open daily from 8:30am to 5pm, closed only December 25. For information on Ahipara, Ninety Mile Beach, and Far North activities, see www.ahipara.co.nz or www.topofnz.co.nz.

SPECIAL EVENTS   **Waitangi Day** on February 6 is a national holiday and cultural day and Paihia is the center of events. Over 45 *waka* (war canoes) from New Zealand and the Pacific Islands have been confirmed to take part in a Year of the Waka event as part of the February 6, 2010, celebrations—guaranteed to be a spectacular sight. In late January the **Bay of Islands Sailing Week Regatta** is staged. The **Russell Spring Festival** is held in early September; and the **Bay of Islands Jazz and Blues Festival** (© **09/402-7345**) runs day and night from early to mid-August at various venues around Paihia and Russell.

In Paihia/Waitangi

Waitangi Treaty Grounds ★★★   Even if you're not interested in history, I guarantee you'll love it here. This 506-hectare (1,250-acre) reserve has had a massive face-lift, and quite apart from its historical importance, there are fabulous boardwalks through beautiful parklike grounds and mangrove swamps. It's somewhere you can comfortably spend 2 hours.

It was on the grounds of the small Georgian house that the Confederation of Chiefs signed the first treaty with the British government. The treaty granted to the Maori the rights of British subjects in exchange for recognition of British sovereignty. The home of James Busby from 1832 to 1880, its broad lawn was the scene of colorful meetings between Maori and Pakeha during the treaty negotiations on February 6, 1840. Inside, you'll see a facsimile of the treaty written in Maori, an exhibition of James Busby's family mementos, and rooms with period furnishings.

The reserve is also home to one of the most magnificent whare runanga (meeting-houses) in the country, complete with an inspiring sound-and-light show. The house contains elaborately carved panels from all the Maori tribes in New Zealand and it is one of the few meetinghouses in the country that allows you to take photographs inside. Just below the sweeping lawn, on Hobson's Beach, is an impressive 35m-long (115-ft.) Maori *waka* (war canoe) made for the treaty centennial celebrations from three giant kauri trees. Both this and the carved meetinghouse are highlights in my view.

You'll get far more from your visit if you take one of the tours. I recommend Embrace Waitangi for a comprehensive overview; or Talk the Walk, which focuses on the natural environment and its relationship to Maori. (The more you see the more you save on entry). If your visit coincides with the February 6 celebration of **Waitangi Day,** you'll find the center of activity is the Waitangi National Trust Estate. There's lots of Maori song and dance, plus Pakeha officials in abundance, dressed to the nines in uniforms of then and now. Reserve way ahead, as it's a huge family day with crowds of vacationing Kiwis in attendance.

Waitangi Treaty Grounds, Waitangi. (℃ **09/402-7437.** Fax 09/402-8303. www.waitangi.net.nz. Admission NZ$20 adults, NZ$5 children 14 and under. There are several packages that include tours and activities. May–Sept daily 9am–5pm; Oct–Apr daily 8:30am–7:30pm. Closed Dec 25.

Culture North ★★   Located in the Waitangi Estate grounds, this addition to the cultural program has been a finalist in the New Zealand Tourism Awards. It tells the 1,000-year story of the Maori people from the discovery of New Zealand through to the

---

ⓘTips   Heritage Journeys

For a truly unique, award-winning cultural experience, climb into a traditional *waka* (canoe) with **Waka Taiamai Heritage Journeys ★★** (℃ **09/405-9990;** www.taiamaitours.co.nz). You'll be invited to paddle a canoe alongside members of the Ngapuhi tribe. They offer three options based on a traditional experiences, which can include a marae welcome, a traditional hangi (meal), traditional prayers, speechmaking, and a soak in mineral hot springs with Ngapuhi elders. Tours depart from Horotutu Beach at Paihia at 10am, 1, and 3pm (weather permitting) and cost from NZ$120 adults, NZ$75 children 6 to 12.

(Tips) Fine Food

Pick up the **Northland Food and Wine Trail** brochure from the Bay of Islands Visitor Centre (see above) and discover the wealth of boutique food producers and wineries throughout the whole Northland region. You can tailor-make your own food trail, from their detailed descriptions and maps, to suit your own timetable.

present day. Combining drama with a stunning light-and-dance show, it's sure to please. It's a 2-hour program, and they provide hotel pickup service. They also provide guided tours of the treaty grounds, a marae visit, and other Maori cultural experiences.

Waitangi, RD2, Okaihau. (C)/fax **09/402-5990** or 401-9301. www.culturenorth.co.nz. Admission NZ$60 adults, NZ$30 children 3–15. Oct–Apr Mon, Wed–Thurs, and Sat 7:30–9:30pm. Closed Dec 24, 25, 26, 31; Jan 1, 2; and Feb 6. Open May–Sept by arrangement; call for information.

In Russell

Russell is a veritable minefield of historic sites. This is where the great Maori chief Hone Heke burned everything except the mission property, and chopped down the flagstaff (four times) in defiance of British rule.

If you plan to wander the historic sites, first visit the **Russell Museum,** 2 York St. ((C)/fax **09/403-7701;** www.russellmuseum.org.nz), open daily from 10am to 4pm (till 5pm in summer), closed December 25. Admission is NZ$7.50 for adults and NZ$2 for children. You can learn all about Maori-European contact and pick up heritage brochures pointing out other sites in the village. Behind the museum, check out the **Bay of Islands Maritime Park Headquarters and Visitors Centre,** The Strand ((C) **09/403-7685;** fax 09/403-7649). Its free 15-minute audiovisual *The Land is Enduring* gives an overview of Maori-European history in the area. It's open from 8:30am to 4:30pm (till 5pm in summer).

Farther down The Strand, you'll find **Pompallier Mission** ★ ((C) **09/403-9015;** www.pompallier.co.nz). Built in 1841, this is New Zealand's oldest surviving Roman Catholic building. It housed a printing press used from 1842 to 1849 to print religious documents in the Maori language. Today, along with the press, there's a working tannery and bookbindery. Admission is NZ$7.50 for adults and free for children. Prebooked tours cost NZ$5 per person. It's open from 10am to 4pm (till 5pm in summer).

For a look at the oldest wooden church in New Zealand, go to **Christ Church,** Church Street and Robertson Road. You can't miss the dear little building surrounded by colorful flowering hibiscus bushes. It's open from 9am to 5pm.

In Kerikeri

The pretty town of Kerikeri has the most to offer in the Bay of Islands in the way of land-based attractions. Visiting the **Kerikeri Mission Station** ★, 246 Kerikeri Rd. ((C) **0800/802-010** in NZ, or 09/407-9236; www.historic.org.nz; www.stonestore. co.nz), is essential if you want to continue the historic theme. It's home to New Zealand's oldest stone building, the **1835 Stone Store,** which has been open for business since 1836. Next door you'll see **Kemp House,** the first mission house and the oldest wooden house in the country. Entry to the ground floor of the store is free and you can shop for authentic heritage goods reminiscent of the store's golden era. The full Mission Experience, which includes an overview of the area's important early history, costs NZ$9, and a visit to the upper levels of the store costs NZ$5. **Northern Steamship Company** (℃ **0800/944-785** in NZ, or ℃/fax 09/407-9229; www.steamship.co.nz) offers 1-hour cruises of Kerikeri Inlet aboard SS *Eliza Hobson,* departing from the Stone Store Sunday through Friday at 2pm. The cost is NZ$30 for adults, NZ$15 for children ages 5 to 15, and NZ$85 for families.

Above the Basin is the well-preserved **Kororipo Pa,** a fort occupied by the fearsome chief Hongi Hika; across the river from the *pa* site is **Rewa Village** (℃ **09/407-6454**), a full-scale reconstruction of a *kainga* (fortified pre-European Maori fishing village). It's open daily 9am to 5pm; admission is NZ$5 for adults and NZ$1 for children.

Garden enthusiasts should also enjoy **Wharepuke Subtropical Garden,** 190 Kerikeri Rd., Stone Store Hill (℃ **09/407-8933;** www.subtropicalgarden.co.nz), which is a growing "art gallery" of subtropical plants. It's open daily 8:30am to 6pm. Entry to the gardens and art gallery is free, but you need to make an appointment for the interactive subtropical garden tours and art courses. There is also a very good cafe here, which is open daily at 10am for lunch and from 6 to 10pm for dinner.

Kerikeri is also home to a thriving arts community. Pick up the excellent free brochure *The Kerikeri Art & Craft Trail,* which details 17 excellent outlets within a few kilometers of Kerikeri. **Keriblue Ceramics** ★, 560 Kerikeri Rd. (℃ **09/407-1111;** fax 09/407-5588; www.keriblue.co.nz), is especially fine. It's open 9am to 5pm daily. Directly opposite is the **Kauri Workshop** ★ (℃ **09/407-9196;** kauriw@xtra.co.nz), where you can watch Brian Cliffin making swamp kauri bowls.

You haven't lived until you've savored the unspeakably indulgent pleasures of **Makana Confections** ★★★ (℃ **09/407-6800;** www.makana.co.nz), right beside the Kauri Workshop. The hand-dipped chocolates are indescribable—try them yourself at the tasting bar and watch the whole process through glass windows; it's open daily 9am to 5:30pm. A much wider variety of top-quality Northland produce is showcased at the **Bay of Islands Farmers' Market** ★★, beside Take Note Bookshop, Hobson Avenue, Kerikeri (www.boifm.org.nz), which is held rain or shine every Sunday from 8:30am to noon.

To sample Northland wines, head for **Cottle Hill Winery,** 28 Cottle Hill Dr. (℃ **09/ 407-5203;** www.cottlehill.co.nz), open daily 10am to 5:30pm with tastings for NZ$5; **Marsden Estate Winery,** 56 Wiroa Rd. (℃ **09/407-9398;** www.marsdenestate.co.nz), open daily 10am to 5pm, closed Good Friday, December 25 and 26; or **Bishops Wood Estate,** 1329 St. Hwy. 10 (℃ **09/407-9628;** bishopswood@value.net.nz), open daily 10am until late.

For fine New Zealand–made skin-care products, free of all synthetic preservatives or synthetic parabens, check out the highly successful **Living Nature** ★★★, State Highway 10 (℃ **0508/548-464** in NZ, or 09/407-7895; www.livingnature.com).

In the Far North

The **Wagener-Subritzky Homestead,** Houhora Heads Road, RD4, Kaitaia (℃ **09/409-8564;** www.northlandholiday.co.nz), was the area's first, built in 1860, and its original inhabitants owned or leased almost all the land between Awanui and Cape Reinga—about 12,600 hectares (31,122 acres). The homestead is currently closed for major restoration and is expected to reopen in mid-2010. It's open daily between 10am and 3pm for the summer season only. It's a 40km (25-mile) drive north of Kaitaia, signposted off the Main Road to Cape Reinga. The scenery is stunning, and there is also a cafe, a souvenir shop, dinghies for hire, bullock rides, fabulous beach swimming, a backpackers lodge, and a campground.

The other must-see is the **Ancient Kauri Kingdom** ★★, State Highway 1, Awanui (℃/fax **09/406-7172;** www.ancientkauri.co.nz), 7km (4⅓ miles) north of Kaitaia. You can view massive 30,000- to 50,000-year-old kauri logs that have been hauled from the Northland swamps, then see the fine furniture and crafts that are made from them. It's open daily, and admission is free. You can also see the remnants of ancient buried kauri forests, over 42,000 years old, at **Gumdiggers Park,** Heath Road, Waiharara (℃ **09/406-7166;** www.gumdiggerspark.co.nz). It's 25km (16 miles) north of Kaitaia and is open daily. It will also give you an insight into the tough lives of the early gum-digging pioneers.

In the Taipa area, **Matthews Vintage Collection,** State Highway 10, 5km (3 miles) north of Taipa (℃ **09/406-0203;** www.matthewsvintage.com), has an extensive array of restored vintage cars, tractors, and farm and domestic equipment. Admission is NZ$8 adults, NZ$4 children. **Butler Point Whaling Museum,** Butler Point, Hihi Road, Mangonui (℃ **09/406-0006;** www.butlerpoint.co.nz), features Capt. William Butler's residence (1847) and whaling memorabilia along with extensive gardens and a macadamia nut orchard. Admission is NZ$12 adults, NZ$2 children.

ORGANIZED TOURS & CRUISES

There's no need to prebook before arriving in town, as there are plenty of operators; by shopping around, you'll get better deals. The only exception is between December 23 and January 15—if you're planning to visit then, you'll need to reserve ahead.

Fullers Bay of Islands, Maritime Building, Waterfront, Paihia (℃ **0800/653-339** in NZ, or 09/402-7421; www.fboi.co.nz; www.awesomenz.com), has several tours. The most popular is the **Cream Trip—Day in the Bay** ★, which includes swimming with dolphins, a trip to the Hole in the Rock (a large natural rock formation that rises up from the ocean with a hole in it, forming a tunnel that boats can pass through), and boom netting off the back of the boat. It costs NZ$99 adults, NZ$50 children ages 5 to 15, and NZ$30 per person extra to swim with dolphins. The tour runs daily from 9:30am to 4pm, and includes an island stopover for lunch (bring your own). Their **Dolphin Eco Encounter** ★★, puts you in some of New Zealand's warmest waters. The purpose-built vessel *Orca II* has a large boom net so less confident swimmers also have the chance to enter the water to see these beautiful marine mammals. This trip costs NZ$89 for adults and NZ$45 for children. It's NZ$30 per person extra to swim with the dolphins.

Explore NZ ★★, Paihia (℃ **0800/397-567** in NZ, or 09/359-5987; www.explorenz.co.nz), will get your adrenalin pumping with an exhilarating sailing adventure on New Zealand's largest and fastest catamaran. Its **On the Edge** day-sail in the bay has daily departures from Paihia and Russell from October through April and costs NZ$125 adults, and NZ$89 children 5 to 15. It includes lunch on one of the gorgeous islands in the bay. And if you'd like to try an overnight cruise, step on board **Great Sights Bay of Islands** ★★, Paihia Waterfront (℃ **0800/653-339;** www.greatsights.co.nz). Their brand-new NZ$12-million luxury vessel, *Ipipiri,* a 46m (151-ft.) catamaran, was launched in late 2009. Rates for the overnight cruise will range from NZ$366 to NZ$409 per person.

To Cape Reinga

You'll be hard-pressed to find more dazzling seascapes than those on your way to **Cape Reinga** ★★★. The cape is situated at the top of Aupouri Peninsula, which features famous **Ninety Mile Beach** and three magnificent harbors: **Parengarenga,** with silica

Tips **Sailing Away**

You won't find any shortage of charter yachts and yacht tours. The Kiwi Experience (backpacker) crowd tends to favor **"She's a Lady" Island Sailing Adventures** (℡ **0800/724-584** in NZ, or 09/402-8119; www.bay-of-islands.com), which include knee boarding, fishing, and two island stops in the full-day outing for NZ$99. For the best value, consider **Gungha's Super Cruise** ★ (℡ **0800/478-900** in NZ, or 09/407-7930; www.bayofislandssailing.co.nz), which has both the 14m (46-ft.) *Gungha* and a 20m (64-ft.) maxi yacht, *Gungha II*. It gets lots of repeat business for the full-day sailings, which include a scenic tour of the Bay of Islands with at least one island stopover and a yummy lunch for NZ$90. It has departures from Kerikeri, Paihia, and Russell. For a 3-day sailing adventure, join the friendly crew of **Ecocruz,** The Wharf, Paihia (℡ **0800/432-627** in NZ, or 027/459-2154; www.ecocruz.co.nz), for NZ$595 to NZ$675. For a tall-ship adventure, step back in time with a voyage on the *R. Tucker Thompson,* Maritime Building, Paihia (℡ **0800/882-537** in NZ, or 09/402-8430; www.tucker.co.nz). It sails from October to the end of April and costs NZ$120 adults, NZ$60 children ages 5 to 15. If you want to try New Zealand's fastest commercial sailing catamaran, contact **Sail on the Edge,** Paihia (℡ **0800/724-569** in NZ, or 09/402-7900; www.explorenz. co.nz). Its 22m-long (72-ft.), 12m-wide (40-ft.) vessel is capable of speeds in excess of 30 knots. A day's outing costs NZ$135 adults, NZ$65 children ages 5 to 15.

sand so white you need dark glasses; **Houhora;** and **Pukenui.** The **Cape Reinga Lighthouse** stands above the battling currents of the Tasman Sea and the Pacific Ocean.

Private cars are not allowed on Ninety Mile Beach, which can be hazardous because of tidal sweeps, quicksand, runoff channels, sand holes, and plankton buildup. Leave the driving to the experts: Take one of the numerous coach tours to the cape, and you'll be able to make the return trip down the hard-packed sands, stopping first at the mountainous **Te Paki sand dunes** ★★★ and **quicksand stream.**

Note: The round-trip from the Bay of Islands to Cape Reinga by private car takes about 7 hours—and that's not allowing for decent stops en route. A day tour from Kaitaia is a more reasonable alternative. I'd strongly advise you to spend an extra night and stay at Doubtless Bay or Kaitaia so you can do the area justice without feeling rushed.

FROM PAIHIA   You can take the 11-hour Cape Reinga tour with **Great Sights** (℡ **0800/653-339;** www.greatsights.co.nz) for NZ$115 adults and NZ$58 children ages 5 to 15. A barbecue lunch costs NZ$25 per person. It's a more family-oriented trip. **Awesome Adventures,** Maritime Building, Paihia (℡ **09/402-6985;** www.awesomenz. com), is less formal, attracts a younger crowd, and stops at a fish-and-chips shop to eat. It costs NZ$118 for a full day and is less likely to have children on board. See "Organized Tours & Cruises," above, for more information.

FROM KAITAIA   Go with a full-day excursion from **Sand Safaris Cape Reinga Tours,** 221 Commerce St., Kaitaia (℡ **0800/869-090** in NZ, or 09/408-1778; www.sand safaris.co.nz), or **Harrisons Cape Runner Tours,** 123 North Rd., Kaitaia (℡ **0800/227-373** in NZ, or 09/408-1033; www.ahipara.co.nz/caperunner). The cost is NZ$55 for adults and NZ$25 for children 14 and under.

FROM MANGONUI (DOUBTLESS BAY)   You can do a 4×4 day tour with **Paradise Connexion Tours** (✆ **0800/494-392** in NZ, or 09/406-0460; www.paradisenz.co.nz). They offer a range of activities within their tailor-made tours, including winery visits.

OUTDOOR PURSUITS

BEACHES   The farther north you go, the better and more deserted the beaches get. Those on **Karikari Peninsula ★★★** have always been my favorites, but good swimming beaches dominate the whole northeast coast, from Auckland up.

FAST BOATING   **Excitor,** Maritime Building, Paihia (✆ **09/402-6985;** www.awesomenz.co.nz), can take you out to the Hole in the Rock in *Excitor* for NZ$89 for adults, NZ$45 for children 14 and under. *Mack Attack* (✆ **09/402-8180;** www.mackattack.co.nz), charges NZ$85 for adults and NZ$45 for children.

FISHING   Light-line fishing is affordable; the visitor center in Paihia can furnish you with a list of fishing charters. Most supply rods and bait, and run 3- to 5-hour trips. Snapper fishing is especially popular; it ranges from NZ$60 to NZ$150 for a 4-hour boat trip. For game fishing contact **Wild Bill Sports Fishing Charters,** Opua Marina, Paihia (✆ **09/402-7085;** www.wildbill.co.nz), or **Earl Grey Fishing Charters,** Paihia and Russell Wharf (✆ **09/407-7165;** www.earlgreyfishing.co.nz). Both will arrange trips to suit individual preferences.

GOLF   You can arrange to play at the beautiful 18-hole waterfront **Waitangi Golf Club** (✆/fax **09/402-7713;** www.waitangigolf.co.nz). Greens fees are NZ$50 per person. Club, shoes, and cart hire are available.

KAYAKING   **Coastal Kayakers,** Paihia (✆ **09/402-8105;** www.coastalkayakers.co.nz), can take you to explore waterfalls, mangrove swamps, and a deserted island. No experience is necessary. A 4-hour trip costs NZ$55; a full-day trip is NZ$85. Farther north in the Tauranga Bay area, **Northland Sea Kayaking,** Tauranga Bay Road, Northland (✆ **09/405-0381;** www.northlandseakayaking.co.nz), is more of a wilderness experience, with accommodations provided on private beaches. Full- and half-day tours start at around NZ$85.

PARASAILING   For a bird's-eye view of the islands, soar with **Flying Kiwi Parasail** (✆ **09/402-6078;** www.parasail-nz.co.nz) for NZ$89.

WALKING   Around the Bay of Islands, you can't go past the boardwalks and walkways in the **Waitangi National Trust Estate ★★★**. The visitor center in Paihia can furnish details of all the trails, as well as the very good booklet *Walking in the Bay of Islands Maritime and Historic Park* (NZ$4). The **Park Visitor Centre** in Russell, P.O. Box 134 (✆ **09/403-7685;** fax 09/403-7649), or the **Ranger Station** in Kerikeri (✆ **09/407-8474**) can help with trail maps and details. There are also some beautiful campsites, some on uninhabited islands in the bay, with nominal per-night fees. You must reserve with the park rangers in Russell. Try the **Kerikeri River Walk**—it's an easy 1-hour hike to **Rainbow Falls.**

WHERE TO STAY

Remember one important fact if you want to stay in the Bay of Islands: From December to January, the population swells from a mere 2,000 to over 30,000. Reserve well in advance.

Paihia has the biggest concentration of motels and hotels, while Russell and Kerikeri offer more bed-and-breakfast options. Paihia is definitely the most convenient place to

ⓘ Tips Backpacker Paradise

Backpackers will think they've arrived in paradise: Paihia is the best-serviced backpacker town in the country. There are around 10 top-quality backpacker lodges, most of them cheek-by-jowl on Kings Road. **Base Pipi Patch,** 18 Kings Rd. (ℂ **0800/227-369** in NZ, or 09/402-7111), attracts a lot of the Kiwi Experience buses and it has a Qualmark Enviro-Bronze rating for its efforts toward sustainability. It's just 50m (165 ft.) from the beach and has a pool set in a sunny courtyard; every room has its own bathroom. **Lodge Eleven Backpackers-YHA** ★, MacMurray and Kings roads (ℂ/fax **09/402-7487;** www.yha.co.nz), is highly rated; every room has its own shower and toilet. Located 100m (330 ft.) from the beach, the place is immaculate and has personalized service.

Peppertree Lodge ★★, 15 Kings Rd. (ℂ **09/402-6122;** www.peppertree. co.nz), was built for backpacker comfort and is seen by many as the best of the best. The **Pickled Parrot Backpackers Lodge,** 9 Grey's Lane (ℂ **09/402-6222;** www.pickledparrot.co.nz), is the smallest backpacker lodge and offers free breakfast. The **Mousetrap Backpackers,** 11 Kings Rd. (ℂ **09/402-8182;** www. mousetrap.co.nz), is another small one (25 people only) in a big, old house with sunny balconies.

Saltwater Lodge ★★, 14 Kings Rd. (ℂ **0800/002-266** in NZ, or 09/402-7075; www.saltwaterlodge.co.nz), has top facilities and private bathrooms in every unit; and it is a member of the Northland Sustainable Tourism Charter. And the well-equipped **Bay Adventurer Apartments & Backpacker Resort,** 28 Kings Rd. (ℂ **0800/112-127** in NZ, or 09/402-5162; www.bayadventurer. co.nz); has its own swimming pool and Jacuzzi, which are big draws.

stay if you intend to take lots of tours and participate in organized activities. It also has the better food outlets, and you won't have to worry about missing the last ferry to Russell. Russell is the place to be if you want a quiet spot—for most of the time, there are far fewer people here, but I wouldn't go so far as to say that it's less touristy. Rates below include 12.5% GST and free parking.

If you want information about Department of Conservation campsites in Northland, contact the **Department of Conservation Visitor Centre,** 92 Otaika Rd., Whangarei (ℂ **09/430-2007;** www.doc.govt.nz).

In Paihia/Opua

In addition to the options listed below, you might try the good-value contemporary comforts of **Scenic Hotel Bay of Islands** ★, on the corner of Seaview and MacMurray Road, Paihia (ℂ **09/402-7826;** www.scenicgroup.co.nz), where you'll find 114 recently renovated rooms. The new deluxe rooms (NZ$338) are best. They open onto private subtropical gardens. There's a solar-heated pool, and it's all within walking distance of the township.

Bay of Islands Lodge ★★ ⓕ Finds Just 6 years old, this sophisticated custom-built gem is tucked into a bush-clad hillside with just native birds for company. Simply put, it's divine. From the French oak floors and the large, stylish living rooms to the big bedrooms with decks and state-of-the-art fittings, you'll want for nothing. It's beautifully done—a fabulous value and perfect for those wanting total privacy.

St. Hwy. 11, Paihia Rd., Opua. ℂ/fax **09/402-6075.** www.bayofislandslodge.co.nz. 4 units. NZ$580; NZ$50 each extra person; NZ$2,100 for whole house. Rates include breakfast and open bar. Dinner by arrangement. Off-peak rates. AE, MC, V. 5 min. by car from Paihia. Well signposted on Paihia Rd., just after Opua Hill, before you enter the township. **Amenities:** Chef for in-house dining; airport transfers NZ$50; nearby golf course; heated outdoor pool; nearby tennis courts. *In room:* TV/DVD, hair dryer, Wi-Fi.

Copthorne Hotel & Resort (Value This is a standard hotel in a unique and stunning location, right beside Waitangi National Trust, the sea, and a wealth of walking opportunities. Its peacefulness, sensible pricing, and one of the best outdoor swimming pool complexes in the country make up for any lack of glamour. Eighty-five percent of the modest rooms are king/splits with either sea views (premium) or garden views (standard). The one-level Hibiscus wing overlooks the pool and in the Seaspray wing every room has a deck or balcony. Don't be put off by tour groups; there's room for everyone. I prefer Scenic Circle Bay of Islands Hotel for its smarter rooms, but Copthorne has a better pool and location.

Tau Henare Dr., Paihia. ℂ **0800/808-228** in NZ, or 09/402-7411. Fax 09/402-8200. www.copthornebay ofislands.co.nz. 180 units. NZ$150–NZ$300. Long-stay and off-peak rates and special packages. AE, DC, MC, V. Located around the bay from Paihia township—5 min. by car. **Amenities:** Restaurant; bar; babysitting; bike rentals; nearby golf course; Internet; Jacuzzi; outdoor heated pool; room service; outdoor tennis courts. *In room:* TV, fridge, hair dryer, minibar.

Paihia Beach Resort & Spa ★★ This waterfront resort has undergone a NZ$6-million revamp, and spacious apartments here are sure to please. They have everything you're ever likely to need and are ideal for longer stays and for two couples or families traveling together. Modern, spacious, elegant, and well-sited between the township and Waitangi, the resort also has the best and biggest day spa in Northland, where you can be pampered in every conceivable way.

116 Marsden Rd., Paihia. ℂ **09/402-0111.** Fax 09/402-6026. www.paihiabeach.co.nz. 21 units. NZ$543 spa and poolside studio; NZ$650 superior; NZ$816 2-bedroom apartment; NZ$62 each extra person. Long-stay rates. Rates include breakfast. AE, DC, MC, V. Located just around the corner from township on way to Waitangi. **Amenities:** Restaurant [Pure Tastes; Pacific Rim]; bar; babysitting; nearby golf course; Internet; 4 Jacuzzis; heated outdoor pool; room service; sauna rooms; large state-of-the-art La Spa Naturale day spa; watersports equipment. *In room:* TV/DVD, CD, hair dryer, Internet, kitchen.

Sanctuary Palms ★ (Value Three gorgeous, modern, self-contained apartments, each with their own character, sit high over Paihia township (which is a 5-min. walk away); they offer style, luxury, and privacy at an incredibly reasonable price. The ground-floor room, Moulin Rouge, has a stunning bathroom and, like all the apartments here, truly feels like your home away from home. The upstairs Pasifika has a bigger lounge and a huge balcony with bush views; and the cool Waterfall room opens onto the garden waterfall.

31 Bayview Rd., Paihia. ℂ **09/402-5428.** Fax 09/402-5427. www.sanctuarypalms.co.nz. 3 units. From NZ$350–NZ$450. Special packages and off-peak rates. MC, V. No children 17 and under. **Amenities:** Airport transport; nearby golf course. *In room:* TV/DVD, hair dryer, free Internet, full kitchen, minibar.

In Russell

A lot of the lodgings on this side of the water are high priced for what you get, so shop around. Personally, I think you get better value for your money in the Paihia-Opua area.

For a budget-conscious stay, head for the **Top 10 Holiday Park,** Longbeach Road (✆ **09/403-7826;** fax 09/403-7221; russelltop10@xtra.co.nz). **Te Maiki Villas,** Flagstaff Road (✆ **0800/156-777** in NZ, or 09/403-7046; www.temaikivillas.co.nz), has nine smart three-bedroom villas with spectacular views from NZ$200 to NZ$375.

Russell Cottages ★, 16 Chapel St. (✆ **09/403-7737;** fax 09/403-8002; www.russell cottages.co.nz), are my pick for the independent traveler who likes a modern, self-contained stay. Sixteen one- to four-bedroom, two-level cottages sit in parklike gardens with a heated pool and Jacuzzi.

Eagles Nest ★★★ (Finds) It's hard to find the words to adequately describe this sublime ecofriendly retreat that is committed equally to luxury and environmental protection. Daniel and Sandie Biskind found the perfect place for their world-class sanctuary and spared no expense in creating something you'll remember forever. Sacred Space is the main house, which contains three luxury suites—the living room converts to an in-house theater at the flick of a switch. Across the gorgeous pool is the two-story honeymoon love nest known as First Light Villa, and on a far hill, the three-bedroom Eyrie, Eagle Spirit, and Tikitiki Ora offer a more low-key version of this sumptuous style. Rahimoana (the Presidential Villa), which comes with the use of a Porsche Cayenne Turbo and a personal concierge, is the ultimate in international luxury—and is priced accordingly. The core philosophy at Eagles Nest is relax, regenerate, rejuvenate. It's an experience you'll relish and want to relive, over and over again—as long as you have a bottomless wallet.

60 Tapeka Rd., Russell. ✆ **09/403-8333.** Fax 09/403-8880. www.eaglesnest.co.nz. 19 rooms in 6 self-contained units. From NZ$2,025–NZ$5,062 per villa; NZ$17,990 for Rahimoana. Rates include breakfast and airport transport. Long-stay, off-peak, and special deals. AE, DC, MC, V. Drive up and over Flagstaff Hill in Russell township; Tapeka Rd. is the 2nd left after the brow of the hill. **Amenities:** Exclusive dining room (spa cuisine) w/10,000-bottle wine cellar; airport transport; babysitting; free bikes; concierge; helicopter access to Kauri Cliffs luxury golf club; gym equipment in each villa; Jacuzzi in all villas; 5 villas have heated outdoor pool; room service; sauna in Sacred Space; Wi-Fi in all villas. *In room:* A/C (in 4), TV/DVD, CD, hair dryer, full kitchen in all, minibar, MP3 docking station.

Orongo Bay Homestead ★★ This is a simple, tranquil haven in what was New Zealand's first American Consulate in the 1860s. It's a charming old home set amid acres of big trees and organically certified gardens. The Consul's Room is the best in the house, with wonderful garden views; but my favorite is the Retreat, which is built out over a stream, with doors opening onto a balcony where you can sit and watch the ducks in complete silence. If you want even more privacy, go for the two Barn Rooms that sit across the stream in a lovely meadow. Delicious dinners are derived from the garden's organic produce; in summer, these are enjoyed on the veranda.

Aucks Rd., RD1, Russell. ✆ **0800/242-627** in NZ, or 09/403-7527. Fax 09/403-7675. www.thehomestead. co.nz. 4 units. NZ$650. Rates include breakfast; 4-course organic dinner by arrangement. Long-stay, off-peak rates, and special deals. AE, DC, MC, V. Closed May–Oct. **Amenities:** Bar; nearby golf course; sauna. *In room:* DVD, CD, fridge, hair dryer.

In Kerikeri
Kauri Cliffs ★★★ (Moments) Set on 2,630 hectares (6,500 acres) of rolling coastal farmland, this golf club and lodge offers world-class facilities with an unforgettable view—not to mention the par-72 David Harman–designed golf course that sweeps along the cliff tops (voted 49th best in the world by *Golf* magazine). If you want premium pampering in a breathtaking setting, this is the place—luxury and comfort are a given, and every whim can be indulged. Rooms are spacious, bathrooms luxurious, and style greets you at every turn. It's much bigger and more extensively appointed than Eagle's

Nest in Russell, but it has that same distinctive mark of quality that discerning international travelers expect. A world-class health spa completed in 2006 is just another reason to linger in "paradise."

Matauri Bay, 25 min. northeast of Kerikeri. © **09/407-0010.** Fax 09/407-0061. www.kauricliffs.com. 22 units, 1 2-bedroom cottage. NZ$1,305–NZ$2,138 suite; NZ$1,530–NZ$2,678 deluxe suite; NZ$6,188–NZ$9,844 cottage. Rates include full breakfast, predinner drinks, a la carte dinner, use of all facilities except golf, and airport transport. Off-season rates and special deals. AE, DC, MC, V. 20 min. from Kerikeri Airport. **Amenities:** Restaurant (jacket required); bar; airport transport; babysitting; mountain bikes; concierge; world-class golf course; large gym; Internet; 2 outdoor Jacuzzis; outdoor heated pool, indoor heated lap pool; room service; sauna; full-service spa; 2 tennis courts. *In room:* TV/DVD, fridge, hair dryer, minibar, Wi-Fi.

Stone Store Lodge ★   This elegant little stay is nestled into native bush just minutes from Kerikeri Inlet and a short drive from Kerikeri township. Each of the three well-appointed suites has its own bathroom (complete with heated floors and solar-heated water) and a balcony with pretty views across the Basin. It's a contemporary spot and host Richard Millar has a deft hand at preparing tasty wood-fired pizzas, should you wish to dine in. He also cares about his environment and has a Kiwi Green rating for his sustainable tourism efforts.

210 Kerikeri Rd. © **09/407-6693.** Fax 09/407-6693. www.stonestorelodge.co.nz. 3 units. NZ$210–NZ$260; NZ$50 each extra person. Long-stay and off-peak rates. Rates include breakfast. MC, V. No children 11 and under. **Amenities:** Airport transport; nearby golf course; outdoor tub set in bush (NZ$22). *In room:* A/C, TV/DVD/CD, fridge, hair dryer, minibar, Wi-Fi.

The Summer House ★   If you're garden lovers, you'll be right at home here among citrus orchards and subtropical gardens. Hosts Christine and Rod Brown are passionate about plants and their peaceful retreat will seduce you into a long stay. The two upstairs bedrooms both have showers and views over the pond. But my preference is for the self-contained, downstairs semidetached suite, which has a Pacific theme and a much bigger bathroom. The house was purpose-built on energy-efficient principles and was the world's first B&B to be benchmarked by Green Globe in 2002. It currently has a Qualmark Enviro-Gold rating for its outstanding approach to environmentalism.

424 Kerikeri Rd. © **09/407-4294.** Fax 09/407-4297. www.thesummerhouse.co.nz. 3 units. NZ$265–NZ$340. Rates include breakfast. Long-stay and off-season rates. MC, V. No children 11 and under. **Amenities:** Free airport transport to Kerikeri; 3 nearby golf courses. *In room:* TV/DVD in suite, fridge, hair dryer, kitchenette (self-contained suite only), minibar, Wi-Fi.

In the Far North

For a special treat, take yourself to the Karikari Peninsula, where you'll find some of the best beaches in New Zealand. You'll also find the superlative **Carrington Resort** ★★★, Maitai Bay Road, Karikari Peninsula (© **09/408-7222;** www.heritagehotels.co.nz/Carrington-Resort), set amid 3,000 hectares (7,410 acres) of rolling coastal land. It offers 10 spacious, modern lodge suites that open onto wide verandas with beach views. Fourteen separate villas set away from the main lodge provide three-bedroom comforts with golf-course views. A resort par excellence, it's well worth going the extra mile. Lodge rooms with breakfast start at NZ$395, or NZ$750 for breakfast and dinner. The villas cost NZ$495. The lodge has a strong conservation and environmental policy in action and is responsible for the restoration of a large expanse of nearby wetlands. In Doubtless Bay, one of the best spots is **Beach Lodge,** 121 St. Hwy. 10, Coopers Beach (©/fax **09/406-0068;** www.beachlodge.co.nz). Its five delightful, two-bedroom, self-contained units are just a few paces from the white-sand beach; rates are NZ$375 to

NZ$450. **Coopers Beachfront Suites,** 18 Bayside Dr., Coopers Beach (✆ **09/406-1018;** www.coopersbeach.net), has two suites for NZ$325 with lower rates off peak. **Taipa Bay Resort** ★★, 22 Taipa Point Rd. (✆ **09/406-0656;** www.taipabay.co.nz), is 7km (4⅓ miles) north of Mangonui village. Their 32 suites and apartments allow you to enjoy sand and surf at your doorstep for NZ$175 to NZ$335.

In Kaitaia are several motel options and in nearby Ahipara you can enjoy very nice self-contained, two-bedroom apartments at **Shippies** ★, Reef View Road, Shipwreck Bay (✆ **09/409-4729;** www.shippies.co.nz). Farther north at Houhora Heads, you'll find great waterfront camping at **Wagener Holiday Park & Backpacker Cabins** (✆ **09/409-8564;** www.northlandholiday.co.nz). Nonpowered sites cost NZ$12 per adult; powered sites are NZ$14 per person per night. Backpacker beds range from NZ$22 to NZ$24 per person. Farther south, near Dargaville and Waipoua Forest, check out **Waipoua Lodge** ★★, State Highway 12, Katui, Northland (✆ **09/439-0422;** www.waipoualodge.co.nz). This very welcome addition to Northland's west coast is a must. It features four stylish apartments set in gardens separate from the 120-year-old main villa and dining room. I recommend you stay 2 or 3 days and take the guided night walk to see rare wild kiwi (an extra charge) and during the day, check out the remarkable kauri forests, or laze about on deserted golden sand beaches. The bed-and-breakfast rate is NZ$570 to NZ$590; if you include dinner it starts at NZ$830. A less expensive option is **Copthorne Hotel & Resort Hokianga,** SH12, Omapere South (✆ **09/405-8737;** fax 09/405-8801; www.copthornehokianga.co.nz), which has 33 guest rooms right on the water's edge of Hokianga Harbour, with regular rate packages available.

WHERE TO DINE

The biggest and best concentration of restaurants and cafes is in Paihia, but there are some close rivals in nearby Kerikeri. As always in the provinces, service tends to wax and wane. The **Sugar Boat Restaurant,** Waitangi Bridge, Paihia (✆ **09/402-7018;** www.sugarboat.co.nz), offers excellent meals in a unique ship setting. It's open daily in summer from 5pm to late with main courses around NZ$33. They also have a cocktail and tapas bar. A very nice new addition on the Paihia waterfront is **Salt Brasserie** ★★, Marsden Road (✆ **09/402-6199;** www.saltpaihia.co.nz). Its a la carte menu presents a little of everything—Pacific Rim, Asian, Classic European; and the Deli serves lovely breakfasts and lunches. You can also order wonderful picnic hampers here, or take-home evening meals. It's open daily 8am until late.

In Paihia

Only Seafood ★★ SEAFOOD   The name says it all—seafood takes center stage here in a smart, white-walled, timber-floored interior. Start with delicious sushi and raw fish salads, then tuck into mains like a salmon filet filled with oysters, oven baked and served with sauce Provençal, or marinated, chargrilled, and served with teriyaki sauce. If you're a seafood lover, you'll be in seventh heaven.

40 Marsden Rd. (upstairs), Paihia. ✆ **09/402-7085.** Main courses NZ$28–NZ$30. AE, DC, MC, V. Daily 5pm–late. Closed Dec 25.

Pure Tastes ★★ ASIAN/INTERNATIONAL   Whatever else you do, don't miss this culinary gem. Chef Paul Jobin and his team have combined a cooking school, cafe, and restaurant in a winning format. The menu emphasizes seafood with strong Asian overtones—Penang fish curry, Asian wok toss, and Thai crispy beef are cases in point. It's bright and delicious, and the homemade ice creams are real winners. You can also choose a four- or five-course set menu, with or without wine matches.

Paihia Beach Resort & Spa, 116 Marsden Rd., Paihia. (℃ **09/402-0003.** www.puretastes.co.nz. Main courses NZ$32–NZ$34. 4-course set menu NZ$70, with wine NZ$110; 5-course set menu NZ$80, with wine NZ$120. MC, V. Daily 7am–late.

Waikokopu Café ★ (Finds) CAFE/LIGHT MEALS   Waikokopu wins with its dreamy lakeside, bush-enclosed location and its well-priced light meals. The menu changes regularly, but generally features delicious lunch goodies like Cajun chicken salad and corn and coriander fritters. If your wallet is feeling thin, pig out on the pancake pileup—a stack of wild-berry pancakes topped with Greek yogurt, drizzled with honey, or served with bacon, banana, and maple syrup. Vegetarians and children are attended to, and you can't beat sipping a good espresso while sitting out on the timber deck overlooking the water.

Treaty Grounds, Waitangi. (℃ **09/402-6275.** Reservations required for dinner in summer. Main courses NZ$16–NZ$20. MC, V. Daily 9am–5pm (until 6pm in summer).

In Russell

The **Gables,** The Strand ((℃ **09/403-7618**), has previously won widespread praise, but it seems to have lost its gloss and is overpriced compared to some of the competition. The **Duke of Marlborough,** The Strand ((℃ **09/403-7829;** www.theduke.co.nz), gets good comments for sound pub-style food but variable service, and **Gannets** ★, on York Street ((℃ **09/403-7990**), scores the most points for tasty, good-value meals in a simple interior. The broadbill fish steaks are excellent. **Omata Estate** ★★, Aucks Road ((℃ **09/403-8007**), is part of a luxury lodge and winery on the water's edge, nearer the Opua Ferry Landing than Russell itself, but it gets good reviews for its six-course degustation menu and dishes like confit of salmon and scallops with lime risotto. Make sure you make a reservation. **Kamakura** ★★★, 29 The Strand ((℃ **09/403-7771;** www.kamakura.co.nz), is my pick for the best on this side of the water. It's a sophisticated upmarket restaurant where "Pacific Rim cuisine meets Mediterranean with a touch of Japanese." You'll get the finest local produce and seafood, including fresh New Zealand crayfish blended into first-class meals with a high level of creativity. It's open daily, 11am until late with main courses around NZ$28 to NZ$35.

In Kerikeri

Good cafes and restaurants come and go in Kerikeri, but worthy of mention are **Café Zest,** 73 Kerikeri Rd. ((℃ **09/407-7164**), which is a great spot for vegetarians; and **Marsden Estate Winery** ★, Wiroa Road ((℃ **09/407-9398**), which serves fabulous antipasto platters with estate-grown wine on a grape-covered courtyard overlooking lakes and vineyards. **Ake Ake Vineyard** ★★, 165 Waimate North Rd., Kerikeri ((℃ **09/407-8230;** www.akeakevineyard.co.nz), presents a delicious lunch Tuesday through Sunday in summer (Fri–Sun in winter) and dinner Thursday through Sunday all year-round. **Curry King,** Cobblestone Mall, Kerikeri Road, Kerikeri ((℃ **09/401-6172**), is a popular choice for dinner from 5pm Tuesday through Sunday. If you're looking for the best picnic food in town, don't drive past **Kerikeri Bakehouse Café** ★★, 324 Kerikeri Rd. ((℃ **09/407-7266**), open daily from 7am to 5pm, supplying the most astounding range of edibles you'll find for hundreds of miles.

2 WHANGAREI ★★

169km (105 miles) NE of Auckland; 62km (38 miles) S of Paihia; 58km (36 miles) E of Dargaville

On my previous visit to Whangarei (pop. 48,000), the place seemed dreary and dull—but not any longer. Like so many provincial New Zealand towns, it's got its act together, and the development of the Town Basin has given it a fresh sparkle. With international yachts moored quay-side and a sprouting of cafes, galleries, and gift stores, it's a pleasant place to wander.

If you're a keen scuba diver, you'll certainly want to base yourself here—nearby **Tutukaka** and the **Poor Knights Islands** are the supreme diving spots. They're part of a fascinating marine reserve and one of the world's top dive locations. Big-game fishing is the other star attraction.

ESSENTIALS

GETTING THERE & GETTING AROUND   **By Plane**   Whangarei is a 40-minute flight from Auckland with **Air New Zealand Link** (✆ **0800/737-000** in NZ), which provides service several times a day. **Great Barrier Airlines** (✆ **0800/900-600**) flies to Whangarei from Auckland on Friday and Sunday. The **Airport Shuttle** (✆ **09/437-0666**) offers passenger service to Whangarei.

By Coach (Bus)   Both **InterCity** (✆ **09/623-1503**) and **Northliner Express** (✆ **09/307-5873**) pass through Warkworth and Whangarei several times a day.

By Car   Warkworth is about 1 hour north of Auckland; Whangarei is 2 hours away. The highway between Auckland and Whangarei has a high incidence of accidents, so drive carefully. If you need a rental car, the major companies have offices at the airport.

VISITOR INFORMATION   The **Whangarei i-SITE Visitor Centre,** 92 Otaika Rd., Whangarei (✆ **09/438-1079;** fax 09/438-2943; www.whangareinz.com), is open daily from 8:30am to 5pm weekdays and 9:30am to 4:30pm on weekends and public holidays, with extended hours over summer.

EXPLORING THE TOWN
In Whangarei

I'd begin with a browse around the **Town Basin ★★**. This is where you'll find, among other things, the world's largest sundial and **Clapham's Clocks, The National Clock Museum** (✆ **09/438-3993;** www.claphamsclocks.com), a rather zany collection of timepieces, clocks, and music boxes; an in-house Austrian clockmaker; and a gift store. It's open daily 9am to 5pm (closed Dec 25) and costs NZ$8 adults, NZ$4 children ages 5 to 15, and NZ$20 families.

Whangarei Museum ★, including the Kiwi House, Heritage Park, and Clarke Homestead, is on State Highway 14 (the road to Dargaville), 3 minutes from downtown (✆ **09/438-9630;** www.whangareimuseum.co.nz). It's open daily from 10am to 4pm and costs NZ$10 for all attractions. The **Native Bird Recovery Centre** (beside the museum; ✆ **09/438-1457**) is open Monday through Friday 10am to 4pm.

The **Whangarei Art Museum,** Cafler Park Rose Gardens, Water Street (✆ **09/430-4240**), features local and national exhibitions and is open from 10am to 4pm Tuesday through Friday and noon to 4pm on weekends. If you've ever wondered how paper is made, check out the **Paper Mill ★**, 300 Otaiki Rd. (✆ **09/438-2652**), which offers

Into the Deep Blue Sea

Why stay on land when there's so much to see underwater? I've never fancied myself in a wet suit, but I can see the advantages if you plan to explore the magnificent marine environment off the Tutukaka Coast and the Poor Knights Islands (1 hr. offshore by boat). **Tutukaka,** 30 minutes from Whangarei, is the gateway to the **Poor Knights Island Marine Reserve** ★★★, where crystal-clear waters near the edge of the continental shelf are bathed in subtropical currents. Sheer cliff faces, sea caves, tunnels, and archways are teeming with a range of sea life, including subtropical fish not usually found in New Zealand waters.

The reserve was rated as one of the top 10 diving spots in the world by Jacques Yves Cousteau and is strictly controlled by the Department of Conservation with regard to fishing zones and restricted areas; make sure you go fishing or diving with a licensed operator. The main operator is **Dive! Tutukaka,** the Poor Knights Dive Centre, Marina Road, Tutukaka, Whangarei (© **0800/288-882** in NZ, or 09/434-3867; www.diving.co.nz), which offers a full range of snorkeling and diving options. Its staff members know all the best places—there are over 100 to choose from. Some of the team are also award-winning underwater photographers, so if that's what gets your heart ticking, you're in the right place. They have the largest dedicated dive charter fleet in New Zealand, accompanied by fully qualified dive guides and dive masters. They also offer a Twin Wrecks dive adventure on the scuttled ex-naval ships *Tui* and *Waikato,* which were prepared for adventure diving before being sunk to diver-friendly depths.

40-minute papermaking tours (9:30am–2:30pm). The mill is open Monday through Friday, 10am to 3pm.

Gardeners will get a special joy out of the **Quarry Gardens** ★, Russell Road (© **09/437-7210;** www.whangareiquarrygardens.org.nz), which have changed an old quarry site into a lush subtropical display with numerous tracks linking to the Coronation Scenic Reserve. The **Quarry Arts Centre** ★, 21 Selwyn Rd. (© **09/438-1215;** www.quarryarts. org), is also near here and is well worth a visit. It shows a diverse range of artwork by members of the Northland Craft Trust, some of whom open their studios to the public.

If you're a keen photographer, you might want to join the thousands who have been captivated by **Whangarei Falls,** 5km (about 3 miles) from the town center on the road to Tutukaka Coast. They're easily accessed and make for some stunning images. Keen walkers, meanwhile, should consider **Bream Head Coast Walks** ★★★ (© **09/434-0571;** www.coastwalks.co.nz), which is a beautiful 3-day unguided wander along the Whangarei Heads on private farmland, beaches, rural roads, and recreational reserves. It costs NZ$435 per person, which covers 3 nights' lodging, all food, and daily transfers. A reasonable fitness level is required but you only carry a day pack. It's open from October 1 to May 31.

Get a glimpse of local life at the **Whangarei Growers' Market** ★★, held every Saturday morning in the carpark beside the Shell Service Station on Water Street, 6am until 10:30am.

WHERE TO STAY
In Whangarei

Whangarei has a good selection of motels; you can find out about them at the visitor center. Backpackers will find top-line comforts at **Bunkdown Lodge,** 23 Otaika Rd. (© 09/438-8886; www.bunkdownlodge.co.nz), from NZ$24 per person. If you prefer a boutique hotel atmosphere, check in to the 15-room **Lodge Bordeaux** ★, 361 Western Hills Dr., SH1 (© 09/438-0404; www.lodgebordeaux.co.nz), where you can ease your travel stresses in a big double Jacuzzi for NZ$195 to NZ$300. There are two excellent new options just out of Whangarei. **Tahi Beach** ★★, 1980 Pataua Nth Rd., Pataua North (© 09/436-5495; www.tahinz.com), offers two lovely self-contained, environmentally aware cottages (one two-bedroom, one four-bedroom), sitting in 296 hectares (740 acres) of beach, forest, and wetlands 30 minutes northeast of Whangarei. Rates are NZ$560 to NZ$620. **Breakaway Retreat** ★, 1856 Whangarei Heads Rd., McLeod Bay, Whangarei Heads (© 09/434-0711; www.breakawayretreat.co.nz), is 30km (about 18 miles) east of Whangarei and its purpose-built, two-bedroom, self-contained, beachfront guesthouse is an idyllic hide-out for just NZ$290 (NZ$45 each extra person). It accommodates four people comfortably and is ideal for two couples or a family.

WHERE TO DINE

Numerous new cafes and restaurants have sprung up in Whangarei, and you'll get a good overview by picking up the free brochure *Eating Out in Whangarei.* Making an impression is award-winning **A'Deco** ★★★, 70 Kamo Rd. (© 09/459-4957), which is highly praised for its modern, fine dining in an elegant Art Deco residence. It's open Tuesday through Saturday for dinner and Wednesday through Friday for lunch. Award-winning **Tonic** ★★, 239 Kamo Rd. (© 09/437-5558), is less formal and offers modern French-style cuisine in a cozy 30-seat restaurant; it's open daily from 6pm. Both charge city prices—in the realm of NZ$25 to NZ$32 for main courses. **Killer Prawn** ★, 26–28 Bank St. (© 09/430-333; www.killerprawn.co.nz), remains one of Whangarei's most popular dining establishments with its ultimate seafood, big steaks, chicken, and sizzling lamb dishes. I find it a little lacking in charm, without the class of Tonic and A'Deco, but perfectly fine for a reasonable meal. It's open Monday through Saturday from 11am. Three cafes are worth noting: **Nectar Café,** 88 Bank St. (© 09/438-8084; www.nectarcafe.co.nz), which is a new spot well liked for its coffee and lively atmosphere; **Fresh** ★★★, 12 James St. (© 09/438-2921), which has an excellent all-day menu and is open Monday through Friday 8am to 5pm, and Saturday 8am to 2pm; and **Caffeine Espresso** ★★, 4 Water St. (© 09/438-6925), which has a lively, older, funkier atmosphere and is open Monday through Friday 7am to 3pm and weekends 7am to 2pm.

EN ROUTE BACK TO AUCKLAND, VIA THE WEST COAST

If you came up to the Far North from Auckland on Highway 1, you may want to return on a longer, less direct route that takes in the **Waipoua Kauri Forest** ★★★ and the **Trounson Kauri Park.** If you do this, be sure to also enjoy the scenic beauty of **Hokianga Harbour.**

ⓘ Moments   Meeting the Giants

Take home unforgettable memories by stepping into the spiritual environment of Waipoua Forest with **Footprints Waipoua** ★★★, 29 St. Hwy. 12, Opononi (ⓒ **0800/687-836** in NZ, or 09/405-8207; www.footprintswaipoua.com). Local Maori guides will take you to meet *Tane Mahuta* (Lord of the Forest), the largest kauri tree in New Zealand. The night tour will make your spine tingle. **Crossings Hokianga** ★★★, 29 SH 12, Opononi (ⓒ **0800/687-836** in NZ; www.crossings hokianga.co.nz), puts you in the hands of quality Maori guides who will take you on an afternoon boat cruise, introducing you to local Maori legends and communities in historic Hokianga Harbour.

The **Kauri Museum,** Church Road, Matakohe (ⓒ **09/431-7417;** www.kauri museum.com), is south of Dargaville and worth visiting. It's open daily 8:30am to 5:30pm from November to April and 9am to 5pm in winter. Admission is NZ$12 adults, NZ$3 children, NZ$30 family.

The kauri is the giant of the New Zealand native forest, and at Waipoua the largest trees are over 1,000 years old. Look for **Tane Mahuta (God of the Forest)** ★★, the largest known kauri in New Zealand, and **Te Matua Ngahere (Father of the Forest),** by volume the second-biggest known tree in the country. These and other special trees are signposted on the tourist drive through the forest. You'll find the **Kauri Coast i-SITE Information Centre** at 65 Normanby St., Dargaville (ⓒ **09/439-8360;** www.kauricoast. co.nz).

3 THE COROMANDEL PENINSULA ★★

119km (74 miles) E of Auckland

At the height of the gold rush in the late 1800s, the towns of the Coromandel Peninsula were heavily populated and thriving. Thames, now seen as the gateway to the peninsula, had a population of nearly 20,000 and between 80 and 90 pubs. Today, there are around 7,000 permanent residents and just four pubs, and it's still the biggest town on the peninsula. There's a sense of that more-colorful history all along the west coast, but as in Northland, most of the action is on the picturesque east coast.

This scenic finger of land, reaching into the sea between Auckland and the Bay of Plenty, is famous for its jagged western coastline and its balmy eastern beach recesses that provide endless opportunity for swimming, diving, boating, fishing, and general lazing about. Thousands of New Zealanders have been doing just that for decades. Big, bush-covered ranges divide the two coasts and offer the ultimate challenge for fit trampers, and there are quaint attractions scattered throughout.

You can comfortably reach the base of the Coromandel Peninsula from Auckland in just 1½ hours, and from Rotorua in 2¾ hours. While it's feasible to do most of the peninsula in a day trip, try to spend a couple of extra days in the area and explore more of what it has to offer. Keep in mind that it is a favorite summer holiday destination for New Zealanders, so book well ahead or you'll miss out on accommodations.

GETTING THERE & GETTING AROUND **By Plane** **Air Coromandel/Great Barrier Airlines** (© 0800/900-600 in NZ, or 09/275-9120; www.greatbarrierairlines. co.nz) runs daily services and scheduled scenic flights between Whitianga and Auckland, Great Barrier Island, the Bay of Islands, Waiheke Island, Rotorua, and Tauranga.

By Ferry Operating between Auckland and Coromandel town is **360 Discovery Cruises** (© 0800/360-3472 in NZ; www.360discovery.co.nz). The trip takes 2 hours and costs NZ$89 round-trip for adults and NZ$49 children ages 5 to 15, which includes a transfer into town. They can also arrange for a rental car for you.

By Coach (Bus) **InterCity** (© 09/623-1503) runs regular services between Auckland, Whitianga, and Coromandel.

By Car If you're coming from Auckland: Drive south on State Highway 1 for about 50km (30 miles), then turn east on State Highway 2. About 34km (21 miles) later, you'll pick up State Highway 25 to Thames. If you want to head straight to the east coast beaches of Whitianga, Tairua, and Pauanui: Take the direct route, signposted EASTERN BEACHES, turning right at Kopu (St. Hwy. 26) away from Thames. Approximately 1km (½ mile) from this point, turn left onto State Highway 25a, which is the direct route. If you follow the Pacific Coast Highway through Thames and Coromandel town: Turn left at Kopu and follow the PCH "Hook" signs. This is a terrific trip, but if your destination is the east coast beaches, it will add at least 1 to 1½ hours to your journey. If you're traveling up the west side of the peninsula, through Whitianga to Pauanui, pass through Tairua township and continue south until you reach the service station on the left. This is where you turn off to Pauanui (there's a small sign) and travel north again.

The road from Colville village, north of Coromandel town, to the top of the peninsula is unpaved all the way and takes around 1½ hours. It's a stunning trip, but not recommended for the fainthearted. It is dirt only, very steep, narrow, and often a one-way lane with no room for passing—plus steep drops to the ocean. If you want to explore this area, I strongly advise you to join **Coromandel Discovery,** 316 Tiki Rd. (© 07/866-8175; www.coromandeldiscovery.co.nz).

By Taxi Contact **Mercury Bay Taxi,** in Whitianga, at © 07/866-5643.

Tips **A Word on Driving**

Remember that getting to places on the peninsula often takes longer than you think. Many of the roads are narrow and winding and, off State Highway 25, generally unsealed (unpaved). Thames to Coromandel village takes almost 2 hours driving through numerous little coastal settlements. There are pretty beaches aplenty to stop at along the way, but *drive carefully!* North of Coromandel township, the roads become significantly worse. Rental-car companies previously forbade vehicles from traveling here, but if you stick to the Pacific Coast Highway path (St. Hwy. 25), you're generally okay. The route from Coromandel to Whitianga takes about 1 hour by State Highway 25 (recommended for rentals), and a similar length of time on the "infamous" 309 route, which has 24km (15 miles) of unpaved road and is narrow and winding. It may be scenic with some interesting stops along the way, but State Highway 25 is far less harrowing.

VISITOR INFORMATION The **Thames i-SITE Visitor Centre,** 206 Pollen St., Thames (© **07/868-7284;** fax 07/868-7584; www.thamesinfo.co.nz), is open Monday through Friday from 8:30am to 5pm; Saturday, Sunday, and public holidays 9am to 4pm. The **Coromandel i-SITE Visitor Centre,** 355 Kapanga Rd., Coromandel (© **07/ 866-8598;** fax 07/866-8527; www.coromandeltown.co.nz), is open in summer daily from 9am to 5pm; and in winter Monday through Saturday from 9am to 5pm, Sunday 10am to 2pm. The **Whitianga i-SITE Visitor Centre,** 66 Albert St., Whitianga (© **07/ 866-5555;** fax 07/866-2205; www.whitianga.co.nz), is open Monday through Friday from 9am to 5pm, Saturday and Sunday from 9am to 4pm, and December 26 to January 31 from 8am to 6pm. Pick up the free 72-page *Coromandel Visitor's Guide* at any one of the above locations.

The Thames office of the **Department of Conservation** is on Kauaeranga Valley Road (© **07/867-9080;** www.doc.govt.nz).

Coromandel Peninsula is well served with websites. You can find information on the region at any of the following: www.thecoromandel.com, www.mercurybay.co.nz, www. thepeninsula.co.nz, www.whitianga.co.nz, www.pacificcoast.co.nz, and www.waihi. org.nz.

SPECIAL EVENTS For details of the colorful 2-week annual **Pohutukawa Festival,** held every November to celebrate the red-flowering native pohutukawa trees that line the coast, call © **07/867-9077,** or check www.pohutukawafestival.co.nz. In late summer, Coromandel town celebrates with the **Coromandel Flavours Festival.** Contact the visitor center for details or check www.coromandelflavours.co.nz.

EXPLORING THE PENINSULA

Personally, I prefer Northland, but Coromandel has an intangible, rustic quality that makes it rather alluring. Certainly, from a purely physical point of view, there's nothing quite like the sight of New Zealand's famous pohutukawa in full scarlet bloom (Dec–Jan), against black rock and white beach, for mile after endless mile.

There are good walks around Paeroa (near the Karangahake Gorge), Waihi, Whangamata, Tairua, Whitianga, Colville, Coromandel, and Thames. Information on the **Coromandel Forest Park** is available at the Department of Conservation office in Thames (see "Visitor Information," above). There's also a DOC office in Coromandel township at the i-SITE Visitor Centre.

In Thames, you'll find historic mining areas well signposted. For gold-mining tours in the Thames area, try **Goldmine Experience,** Main Road, State Highway 25 (©/fax **07/ 868-8514;** www.goldmine-experience.co.nz), which offers a guided tour through an operational, 19th-century Stamper Battery and into one of the richest gold mines of the time. They're open daily from 10am to 4pm in summer.

ⓘ **Tips To Market, To Market**

There's nothing like a local market to give you an insight into a community, so visit the **Thames Market,** Pollen Street North, Grahamstown (© **07/868-7213**), which is open 8am to noon every Saturday. It's a mixed bag—everything from local produce to crafts and collectibles—but it has lots of local characters and a "down-home" charm that might appeal.

(Finds) **Waterfall Walk**

The **Waiau Falls** are 11km (7 miles) east of Coromandel. A 5-minute walk from the 309 Road ends at the foot of the falls. The **309 Kauris,** 1km ($\frac{1}{2}$ mile) farther east, are the finest, easily accessible stand of kauri trees on the peninsula. It's a delightful 10-minute bush walk to see them.

From 1885 over 30 schools of mining provided practical training for gold miners; the largest of those, the **Thames School of Mines Museum** ★★, Brown and Cochrane streets (© **07/868-6227**), is open daily from 11am to 3pm in summer (reduced winter hours). In complete contrast, you can escape into the Tropics with over 400 butterflies at the **Butterfly and Orchid Garden,** Dickson Holiday Park, Victoria Street (© **07/868-8080;** www.butterfly.co.nz). They're 3km (1¾ miles) north of the town and are open daily 10am to 4pm. Admission is NZ$10. If you feel like a wander, pick up the *Historic Grahamstown* brochure and check out the town's past. Add in a visit to **Thames Historical Museum,** corner of Pollen and Cochrane streets, Grahamstown (© **07/868-8509**), which is open daily 1 to 4pm. Admission is NZ$5 adults and NZ$3 for children.

As you head north, just beyond Tapu, turn east off State Highway 25 and go 6.5km (4 miles) to the spectacular **Rapaura Watergardens** ★★, 586 Tapu-Coroglen Rd., Tapu, Thames Coast (© **07/868-4821;** www.rapaura.com). Numerous paths meander through the 26 hectares (64 acres) of gardens and 14 waterlily ponds, which are open daily from 9am to 5pm. Admission is NZ$12 for adults and NZ$5 for children ages 5 to 15. They also have a cafe if you feel like refreshments. About 2.5km (1½ miles) past Rapaura Gardens, stop at Tapu and ask directions to one of nature's oddities, the **"square kauri,"** a 2,500-year-old kauri whose trunk is a perfect square. **Te Mata Beach** ★, also at Tapu, is a good hunting ground for specimens of carnelian-agate gemstones.

In Coromandel is the **Driving Creek Railway and Potteries** ★★★, 410 Driving Creek Rd. (© **07/866-8703;** www.drivingcreekrailway.co.nz). Barry Brickell, an accomplished potter, owns the country's only narrow-gauge mountain railway, which passes through replanted native forest. There are usually at least two departures daily (10:15am and 2pm), costing from NZ$20 adults and NZ$50 families. The station is 2.5km (1½ miles) from Coromandel town, and the 1-hour trip covers 3km (2 miles) of track, which took 27 years to build. A new glass-blowing studio operates over summer and you can view working potteries and kilns.

Pick up the *Coromandel Craft Trail* brochure, which details over 30 of the peninsula's craftspeople, or visit **Weta Design** ★★, 46 Kapanga Rd., Coromandel Town (© **07/866-8823;** www.wetadesign.co.nz), which shows work by New Zealand's top artists and craftspeople. It's open 10am to 5pm and organizes tax-free purchase and overseas mailing. **Waitati Gardens** ★, 485 Buffalo Rd., Coromandel Town (© **07/866-8659;** www.waitatigardens.co.nz), are a pleasant horticultural diversion (admission is NZ$7); and make sure you visit the weird and whimsical at **Waiau Waterworks** ★★★, 309 Road, Coromandel (© **07/866-7191;** www.waiauwaterworks.co.nz). This haven of strange, water-based sculptures and gadgets is a great place for kids—as long as they're well supervised. It's open daily from 9am to 5pm; admission is NZ$10 for adults and NZ$5 for children ages 5 to 15.

On the east coast, Whitianga has the excellent **Mercury Bay Museum,** opposite the wharf ((C) **07/866-0730**), open daily from 10am to 4pm (closed December 25), featuring exhibits dating from A.D. 800 to 950. For something entirely different, visit **Mill Creek Lavender** ★★, 445 Mill Creek Rd. ((C) **07/866-0088;** www.millcreeklavender. co.nz), a sweet-smelling haven open to visitors October to Easter on weekends from 10:30am to 5pm, or by appointment. At **Bay Carving** ★★, The Esplanade, Whitianga ((C) **07/866-4021;** www.baycarving.com), you can carve your own bone souvenir in 2 to 3 hours. They're open 10am to 4pm, daily in summer and closed winter Sundays. Carving costs from NZ$45 per person, per piece, depending on the design chosen.

A fun activity is taking the **Whitianga Water Transport** ((C) **07/866-5472;** www. whitiangaferry.co.nz) passenger ferry to the Ferry Landing. It operates daily from 7:30am to 10:30pm (extended hours from Christmas Day to the end of Jan). Once at the Ferry Landing, you can link up with **Hot Water Beach ConXtions** ((C) **07/866-2478**) and go to Hahei, Hot Water Beach, Cathedral Cove, and other area attractions. The bus costs NZ$25 per person for the day's outing. And if you want to unwind at the end of the day, visit the **Lost Spring** ★★★, 121A Cook Dr., Whitianga ((C) **07/866-0456;** www.the-lostspring.co.nz), which is one man's passion come to reality. Alan Hopping began drilling for hot water in 1989. Twenty years and two failed attempts later, he finally hit the spring, and the luscious hot pools and day spa opened in 2008. They've been beautifully landscaped and are well worth a visit. They're open 11am to 9:30pm daily and you pay NZ$20 per hour, or NZ$45 for a day pass. Children must be 14 and over.

ORGANIZED TOURS

The best tour companies are located at Pauanui, but their tours cover the whole peninsula. **Johansen & Wincorp Adventures** ★★, 430 Settlement Rd., Pauanui Beach ((C)/fax **07/864-8731;** www.coromandel.co.nz; www.remotenzjourneys.co.nz), offers a wide range of hikes, nature treks, and guided and personalized tours. Their Night Glow Worm Experience is a lot of fun, and all tours include some history of the region, as well as information on Maori medicines and foods of the forest. Tours range in price, but start at NZ$90 per person. **Aotearoa Lodge & Tours,** 70 Racecourse Rd., Whitianga ((C) **07/ 866-2807;** www.tournz.co.nz), specializes in multiday tours of Coromandel Peninsula, Rotorua, and East Cape, departing Auckland daily. Its 3-day A Touch of Coromandel tour is NZ$850 per person.

Kiwi Dundee Adventures ★★★, Bond and Harbourview Road, Whangamata ((C)/fax **07/865-8809;** www.kiwidundee.co.nz), is the brainchild of passionate outdoors enthusiast Doug Johansen and his partner, Jan Poole. Doug is one of New Zealand's foremost nature guides, and he and Jan offer a range of full-day tours. Day tours are priced from NZ$230 per person, including lunch. They also have several upmarket 3-day

---

> **Tips** **Hot Bath at the Beach**
>
> At **Hot Water Beach** ★★★, inquire about the time of the next low tide—thermal water heats parts of this beach for 2 hours on either side of low tide. That's when you can dig a hole in the sand, settle in, and soak in the hot salt water that comes up from underground springs. The underground volcanic fissures issue water as hot as 147°F (64°C) at a rate of 15 liters per minute.

tours running between Auckland, Coromandel, and Rotorua, offering top-level accommodations for two to six people. These are priced on application and according to the accommodations used.

Take to the water in the **Glass Bottom Boat** ★★ (© **07/867-1962;** www.glass bottomboatwhitianga.co.nz) to see a little of the area's amazing marine life. They have an excellent ecotour to Cathedral Cove (snorkeling included) for NZ$85 adults, NZ$50 children ages 5 to 15. Or join **Whitianga Adventures** ★★ (© **0800/806-060** in NZ; www.whitianga-adventures.co.nz) to explore sea caves and islands for about 2 hours, for NZ$65 adults and NZ$40 children ages 5 to 12.

OUTDOOR PURSUITS

BEACHES   **Whangamata** is a top surfing and swimming beach. **Cooks Beach** has safe swimming and lovely picnic areas, while **Buffalo Beach** is good for swimming and shellfish collecting—both are in the Mercury Bay area.

FISHING   There are numerous boat charter operations based in Whitianga, Whangamata, and Waihi, and the visitor centers have masses of brochures. Tairua Beach offers excellent surf-casting. Coromandel's northern islands provide excellent snapper fishing. For an organized fishing experience, try **Infinity Charters** (© **07/866-5936;** infinitycharters@clear.net.nz), which offers competitively priced half- and full-day excursions.

GOLF   The **Mercury Bay Golf & Country Club,** Golf Road, Whitianga (© **07/866-5479**), is an 18-hole course; greens fees are NZ$25 to NZ$40. The **Dunes Golf Resort,** Matarangi Drive, Whitianga (© **07/866-5394;** www.thedunesmatarangi.co.nz), is one of New Zealand's top 10 courses; fees are NZ$70 for 18 holes of casual play, or NZ$35 for 9 holes. **Coromandel Golf Club,** Hauraki Road, Coromandel (© **07/866-8539**), is a scenic 9-hole course; fees are NZ$30 for nonmembers. And **Thames Golf Club,** State Highway 26, Kirikiri, Thames (© **07/868-9062**), is a par-70, 18-hole course; greens fees are NZ$25 per person.

HORSE TREKKING   Riders with a sense of adventure might like to try the guided horse treks into the rugged Coromandel Ranges offered by **Rangihau Ranch,** Rangihau Road, Coroglen (© **07/866-3875;** www.rangihauranch.co.nz). They're halfway between Whitianga and Tairua. Or experience an outback sheep station with **Twin Oaks Riding Ranch,** State Highway 25, Kuaotunu Road, Whitianga (© **07/866-5388;** www.twin oaksridingranch.co.nz), which charges NZ$50 for a 2-hour trek.

KAYAKING   **Cathedral Cove Kayaks** ★★★ (© **07/866-3877;** www.seakayaktours. co.nz) operates from Hahei and offers daily tours from October to May. It's a fabulous way to see beaches, islands, caves, and coves—no experience is necessary. They have a range of tours priced from NZ$85 to NZ$145.

MOUNTAIN BIKING   North of Coromandel, you'll find a testing track between Stony Bay and Fletcher Bay, which takes about 2 hours each way. There are also good tracks in the Carter Holt Harvey (CHH) forests south of Tairua and at Whangamata. To get into

---

(Finds)   **Cathedral Cove**

This gorgeous sheltered cove is part of the Hahei Marine Reserve and famous for its large sea cave. The beach and cave are accessible by walkway from Hahei.

these areas, you need to register at the CHH office, just north of Whangamata (☏ 07/ 865-8473), or at one of the visitor centers in the area.

SCUBA DIVING The waters around Whitianga are ideal for diving. **Cathedral Cove Dive & Snorkel,** 48 Hahei Beach Rd., Hahei (☏ **09/866-3955;** www.hahei.co.nz/ diving), has dive trips for certified divers, plus PADI dive courses for all levels, in the marine reserve or in the waters beyond. Snorkeling trips in divine locations are offered as well.

WHERE TO STAY

North Islanders flock to Coromandel Peninsula during December and January, when you'll need to book well ahead. In the off season, you'll get motel beds at laughably good rates. Lodgings on the east coast are generally nicer than those on the Thames side.

Van and caravan sites in **Conservation Lands** are available on a first-come, first-served basis; camping fees are from NZ$6 per adult and NZ$3 per school-age child. For details, contact the **Department of Conservation,** P.O. Box 78, Thames (☏ **07/868-6381**), or the **Kauaeranga Visitor Centre** (☏ **07/867-9080;** www.doc.govt.nz).

The rates given below include the 12.5% GST.

In or Near Thames

Tuscany on Thames ★★, Jellicoe Street, Thames (☏ **07/868-5099;** www.tuscanyon thames.co.nz), is a smart, new motel complex with a swimming pool and 14 units with lovely bathrooms with big tubs.

Coastal Motor Lodge ★ Tararu is a great place for migratory seabirds and brilliant sunsets, and a chalet at Coastal Motor Lodge is just the place to enjoy them. The spacious A-frame chalets sleep two and have cute kitchens and balconies. The front unit near the road is particularly cozy, with bathtub, shower, and queen-size and single beds. The complex is set in parklike grounds just across the road from the water (not a swimming beach, unfortunately). There are newer properties about but this one has a good location just out of town, it's always clean and tidy, and they also have bach-style, self-contained cottages.

608 Tararu Rd. (Coromandel Coast Rd.), Thames. ☏ **07/868-6843.** Fax 07/868-6520. www.stayatcoastal. co.nz. 15 units. NZ$110–NZ$140 cottages; NZ$115–NZ$170 motel units. Long-stay and off-peak rates. AE, MC, V. Located 1.5km (1 mile) north of Thames. **Amenities:** Nearby golf course; Jacuzzi. *In room:* TV, fridge, hair dryer, kitchenette, free Wi-Fi.

In or Near Coromandel

Driving Creek Villas ★★ Finds Three boutique villas are located in a private bush setting and fitted out with all the modern goodies. Each villa has two bedrooms, one bathroom, a big lounge, and a private garden. Listen to native birds singing outside your window as you unwind in these cute self-contained havens.

21a Colville Rd., Coromandel Town. ☏ **07/866-7755.** Fax 07/866-7753. www.drivingcreekvillas.com. NZ$295. Extra person NZ$40. Long-stay rates. MC, V. **Amenities:** Free bikes; nearby golf course; 2 villas have Japanese hot tub; nearby tennis courts. *In room:* A/C, TV/DVD/CD, hair dryer, full kitchen, Wi-Fi.

Flax Bach ★ If a delightful 1960s Kiwi holiday cottage set in a small citrus orchard sounds tempting, head for this two-bedroom hideaway (sleeps five) just across the road from a safe swimming beach, backed by Department of Conservation native forest and right next door to the coastal walkway.

Long Bay Rd., Coromandel Town. ✆ **09/419-5005** or 021/855-645. www.flaxbach.co.nz. NZ$130 for 4 people. Extra person NZ$25; NZ$15 linen hire per stay. 2-night minimum stay (1-week minimum stay during Christmas). No credit cards.

In or Near Whitianga

I like the convenience and uncluttered modern style of **Marina Park Apartments** ★★, 84 Albert St., Whitianga (✆ **07/866-0599;** www.marinapark.co.nz), which overlook the marina in the heart of the village. The bright, roomy one-, two-, and three-bedroom apartments are perfect for families and couples traveling together. There is the added bonus of two heated Jacuzzis, swimming pool, and gym; and prices range from NZ$195 for one bedroom to NZ$350 for a three-bedroom apartment. **Within the Bays,** 49 Tarapatiki Dr., Whitianga (✆ **07/866-2848;** www.withinthebays.co.nz), has two very nice, modern guest rooms with great beach views for NZ$275 to NZ$360. They are very ecofriendly and operate a single-party booking system.

Mercury Bay Beachfront Resort ★ Friendly hosts Kate and Paul Dimock have a terrific establishment here. In a matter of seconds, you can walk from your comfortable room to the sparkling sands of Buffalo Beach. Upstairs units have balconies; downstairs, a private patio opens onto the garden and beach. All rooms are cool, clean, and comfortable.

113 Buffalo Beach Rd., Whitianga. ✆ **07/866-5637.** Fax 07/866-4524. www.beachfrontresort.co.nz. 8 units. NZ$150–NZ$350. Extra person NZ$25. Long-stay and off-peak rates. AE, DC, MC, V. **Amenities:** Babysitting; free bikes; children's play equipment; nearby golf course; Jacuzzi; free watersports equipment, fishing rods, and golf clubs. *In room:* TV, hair dryer, kitchen, Wi-Fi NZ$10 per day.

Villa Toscana ★★★ (**Moments**) Giorgio and Margherita Allemano have replicated a Tuscan villa high on a hill overlooking native bush and the ocean, where they take great pleasure in welcoming guests from all over the world. Their Kiwi Green certified, fully self-contained two-bedroom guest suite has its own entrance, deck, garden, barbecue, and outdoor Jacuzzi. You'll find no fault with the spacious, airy bedrooms. The decor is simple—lots of traditional Italian tiles and marble—plus a large bathroom with Italian fixtures, a granite kitchen, and a wide lounge for relaxing at the end of a busy touring day. Giorgio is happy to show you his underground wine cellar and, as a marine biologist and keen fisherman, he has plenty to talk about. Don't miss the genuine Italian gourmet dinners. It's not cheap but it's a fully Italian experience that you'll remember long after leaving.

Ohuka Park, Whitianga. ✆ **07/866-2293.** Fax 07/866-2269. www.villatoscana.co.nz. 1 2-bedroom suite. NZ$850; NZ$150 each extra person. Rates include breakfast and Whitianga Airport transport. NZ$180 per person for Italian gourmet dinner. Off-season rates. MC, V. Located 4km (2½ miles) north of Whitianga. **Amenities:** Dinner on request; bar; free airport transport; babysitting; free mountain bikes; nearby golf courses; Jacuzzi; 2 nearby outdoor tennis courts; 11m (35-ft.) Bertram game fishing launch for hire (NZ$1,100 per day); kayaks. *In room:* TV/DVD, hair dryer, kitchen, minibar, Wi-Fi.

In Pauanui/Tairua

Colleith Lodge ★★, 8 Rewarewa Valley Rd., Tairua (✆ **07/864-7970;** www.colleith lodge.co.nz), has three very nice, modern B&B rooms with en-suite bathrooms overlooking a lap pool and Jacuzzi for NZ$495. They have a Qualmark Enviro-Silver rating and Wi-Fi throughout the property. **Harbourview Lodge** ★, 179 Main Rd., Tairua (✆ **07/ 864-7040;** www.harbourviewlodge.co.nz), also has three en-suite rooms and a swimming pool and is more reasonably priced at NZ$200 to NZ$220 with an extra-person rate of NZ$25. Both make an ideal base for exploring the peninsula.

Grand Mercure Puka Park Resort ★★★ There's been a major upgrade at this **199** idyllic hideaway and if you're a discerning traveler who expects nothing but the best, you'll love being spoiled—it has the premier upmarket accommodations on the peninsula. Built 20 years ago, this series of exquisite "treehouses" climbs uphill, away from the main lodge, and is completely enclosed by native bush. But you won't have to walk or carry a thing; service is tops here and every scrap of luggage is attended to by the smiling (and incredibly fit) staff. Standard chalets contain a shower-only bathroom; superiors are larger with both tub and shower. Executive chalets have separate lounge/dining areas, while the luxurious Royal Puka Suite is a free-standing two-story, three-bedroom chalet with everything you're ever likely to need on an indulgent holiday.

Mount Ave., Pauanui Beach. © **07/864-8088.** Fax 07/864-8112. www.pukapark.co.nz. 48 units. From NZ$350 standard room; NZ$1,600 suite. Long-stay and off-peak rates. AE, DC, MC, V. Drive into Pauanui with the Waterways Development on your left, go through the roundabout and onto a 2nd roundabout where Puka Park Resort is signposted. Make a hard right onto Pauanui Beach Rd.; turn right at the 2nd street onto Mount Ave. and follow this as far as you can. Turn left and go uphill to the resort. **Amenities:** Restaurant; bar; babysitting; free bikes; concierge; nearby golf course; gym; outdoor Jacuzzi; heated outdoor pool; room service; sauna; day spa beauty treatments; tennis court; watersports equipment rentals. *In room:* TV/DVD, fridge, hair dryer, minibar, Wi-Fi.

In Whangamata

Brenton Lodge ★ (Finds) This lodge's super location overlooks the whole of Whangamata town and beaches. Even better, it's now the home of House of Hamilton handmade chocolates and you can organize tastings. Lovely gardens surround the delicious private suites, each fitted out with crisp cotton sheets, bathrobes, beach towels, and fresh flowers. Lavender Cottage is the farthest from the main house and has the best view; Rose Cottage is all fresh and white with sloping ceilings; and the Garden Room above the main house is a blue-and-white haven overlooking the pool. To top it all off, a gourmet breakfast is served in your room or alfresco on your private balcony.

2 Brenton Place, Whangamata. ©/fax **07/865-8400.** www.brentonlodge.co.nz. 4 suites. NZ$390. Rates include breakfast. 3-course dinner NZ$55 per person. AE, MC, V. **Amenities:** Nearby golf course; Jacuzzi; outdoor pool. *In room:* TV/DVD, CD, hair dryer, kitchenette.

WHERE TO DINE
In Thames

You won't find a lot of slick dining choices in Thames, but **Sealey Café,** 109 Sealey St. (© **07/868-8641**), in an old villa, offers light lunches and coffee, although **Waiomu Beach Café,** 622 Thames Coast Rd., Waiomu Bay (© **07/868-2554**), comes with higher recommendations. They're just across the road from the beach and have a good range of light food to enjoy with coffee. **Sola Café** ★★, 720B Pollen St. (© **07/868-8781**), is probably your best good-coffee choice in Thames itself. They have a small vegetarian menu and are open daily 9am to 4pm and for dinner on Friday nights.

In Coromandel

Driving Creek Café ★★, 180 Driving Creek Rd. (© **07/866-7066**), just north of town in an old villa, serves delicious meals using local and organic produce. It's open Wednesday through Sunday from 9:30am to 4pm and is *the* place to get a feel for local culture—it's a laid-back venue set in the bush, with a piano planted in its center. The **Success Café,** 104 Kapanga Rd. (© **07/866-7100**), is a nice place for a light lunch or a quiet evening

NORTHLAND & COROMANDEL

7

THE COROMANDEL PENINSULA

meal. It serves local seafood in a relaxed environment; open summer daily from 9am to 6pm, with reduced hours in winter.

Peppertree Restaurant & Bar ★, 31 Kapanga Rd. (© **07/866-8211**), is probably the best eatery in town, and its dinners present seafood, sushi, mussel fritters, local beef, and fresh vegetables in interesting combinations. It's open daily from 10:30am until late in summer, 11am to 9pm in winter. If you'd like a snack of fresh-smoked fish, mussels, scallops, salmon, or roe, then head for the **Coromandel Smoking Company** ★★★, 70 Tiki Rd. (© **07/866-8793;** www.corosmoke.co.nz). It's open daily from 8am until 6pm with reduced winter hours. **Coromandel Oyster Company** ★, 1611 SH25, Tiki Rd., Coromandel (© **07/866-8028;** corooysterco@xtra.co.nz), is another good spot to get fresh premium oysters, local mussels, prawns, scallops, chowders, sauces, and smoked seafood at wholesale prices—just the thing if you're considering a beach barbecue.

In Whitianga

Whitianga has quite a range of fair-to-middling restaurants and cafes, so you won't go short of a meal. As in most provincial centers, service can be patchy and changes of ownership after printing can sometimes mean things aren't quite what they used to be. One of my favorite and most consistent Whitianga spots is **Café Nina** ★, 20 Victoria St. (© **07/866-5440**), open daily in summer from 8am to 10:30pm and winter from 9am to 5:30pm. You'll get the best coffee and counter food in town at this 100-year-old miner's cottage tucked away in a small back street. It's hugely popular and always has a mixed, slightly alternative crowd.

The **Fireplace,** 9 The Esplanade (© **07/866-4828**), is a great waterfront spot with a courtyard, good seafood, and wood-fired pizzas. They're open daily from 11am to late; be sure to make a reservation. The **Eggsentric Café** ★★, 1047 Purangi Rd., Flaxmill Bay (© **07/866-0307**), is near Cooks Beach and just a ferry ride from Whitianga itself. It has a great atmosphere and a chef who does inspiring and delicious things with fresh seafood. They're open Tuesday through Friday 10:30am till late, and weekends 9am until late. They'll even pick you up from the ferry if you wish. That's what I call service! **Salt Bar and Restaurant** ★★, 1 Blacksmith Lane (© **07/866-5818;** www.whitiangahotel. co.nz), has been revamped under new management and it's one of the best spots for fine dining. It's open daily from 11am until late. For good seafood and tapas, try **Tuatua** ★, 45 Albert St. (© **07/866-0952**). They serve tapas all day and switch to an a la carte menu that focuses on seafood at night. Make sure you book ahead at night.

In Pauanui/Tairua

The one thing lacking in Pauanui is good eateries. You can go upmarket and have no regrets at **Grand Mercure Puka Park Resort** ★★★ (see above), or you can take the passenger ferry (NZ$5; hourly until 1am in summer) across to Tairua and dine at **Manaia** ★, 228 Main Rd. (© **07/864-9050**), or at the **Old Mill** ★, 1 The Esplanade (© **07/864-7884**), which is the more formal of the two.

In Whangamata

Café Onemana, Onemana Drive, Onemana (© **07/865-7200**), is open for lunch and dinner. They've got great ocean views and a friendly atmosphere. Bookings are recommended for evening dining.

EN ROUTE TO TAURANGA

Katikati, known locally as "The Mural Town," is south of Waihi on State Highway 2. In 1996, a festival was held to celebrate the painting of its 20th outdoor mural since 1991 and to reinforce its image as the mural town of New Zealand. For information on the town and surrounding Bay of Plenty area, call into the **Mural Town Visitor Centre,** 34 Main Rd. (© **07/549-1658;** katikatiinfo@wbopdc.govt.nz).

EN ROUTE TO HAMILTON

From Waihi, take State Highway 2 through the Karangahake Gorge and at Paeroa, turn onto State Highway 26. Follow this 76km (47 miles) to Hamilton.

Waikato & Bay of Plenty

Forty percent of New Zealand's total population—that's nearly 1.5 million people—lives within a 242km (150-mile) radius of the Waikato district. First settled by the Maori, who recognized its agricultural potential and appreciated its temperate climate, the Waikato is rich in natural resources and is a leading food producer. Its biggest natural asset is the Waikato River, the longest river in New Zealand.

The seaside townships of Tauranga, Te Puke, the mural town of Katikati, and Mount Maunganui (one of the country's most popular beach resorts) are the main components of the Bay of Plenty. Forget woolly sheep and start thinking fuzzy kiwifruit, because that's what this area is famous for. The area grows 80% of the country's export kiwifruit crop. It's also a place of mellow summers; great surf and beaches; big game fishing; long, lazy holidays; and the biggest retired population in the country. It literally is a bay of plenty. It is also one of the six pilot participants in the Environmentally Sustainable Tourism Project, dedicated to improving the environmental performance of local tourism operators.

1 HAMILTON & THE WAIKATO ★

127km (79 miles) S of Auckland; 107km (66 miles) NE of Rotorua; 107km (66 miles) E of Tauranga

Unfortunately for Hamilton, its proximity to Auckland (just a 1-hr. drive) means it's often overlooked as a sightseeing destination. Many travelers pass through the city heading south, usually to the famed Waitomo Caves in south Waikato or to Rotorua and Taupo.

If you want to linger awhile, though, you'll discover the hot springs and horse-racing world of Matamata township; the rich Maori culture of Ngaruawahia and more hot springs at Waingaro; the surf and beaches of Raglan; and the antiques and Kentucky-like thoroughbred world of Cambridge.

Hamilton—the country's largest inland city (pop. 131,000)—is a commercial and industrial center. There's something bland about the place despite its pretty face, but there's always a hint of change in the air.

ESSENTIALS

GETTING THERE & GETTING AROUND   **By Plane**   **Air New Zealand National & Link** (☎ 0800/767-767 in NZ) provides daily service to Hamilton Airport (www.hamiltonairport.co.nz). The airport is about 15 minutes south of the city. A shuttle service is provided by **Roadcat Transport** (☎ 07/823-2559) or **Airport Shuttle** (☎ 07/843-7778).

By Coach (Bus)   Both **InterCity** (☎ 09/623-1503) and **Newmans** (☎ 09/623-1504) link Hamilton to other major centers. Within Hamilton, **Busit** (☎ 0800/428-754; www.busit.co.nz), runs the free **CBD Shuttle,** which loops around the inner city; while the **Orbiter** connects the city's suburbs and main shopping areas. You'll find details of

their departure times at the Transport Centre on the Corner of Bryce and Anglesea streets, where the visitor center is (see below).

By Train The **Tranz Scenic Overlander** route passes through Hamilton on the route between Auckland and Wellington. Call ℂ **0800/872-467** or visit www.tranzscenic. co.nz for timetables and reservations.

By Car Hamilton is on State Highway 1, so you'll pass through it heading north or south. It's usually slightly over an hour's drive from Auckland, but the stretch of road between the two cities is notorious for bad accidents that result in fatalities. Please take particular notice of all yellow-line road markings, which designate no-passing sections of a highway. It's 1 to 1½ hours to Rotorua, Tauranga, or Taupo.

For rental cars call **Waikato Car Rentals,** Brooklyn Road, Hamilton (ℂ **0800/154-444** in NZ, or 07/855-0094; www.waikatocarrentals.co.nz).

By Taxi **Hamilton Taxi Society** (ℂ **0800/477-477** or 07/847-7477; www.hamilton taxis.co.nz) operates a 24-hour service.

ORIENTATION Both State Highway 1 and the Waikato River run through the heart of Hamilton, although there is now a rather convoluted bypass through the suburbs if you want to avoid the inner city area altogether—just follow the signs as you approach either the north or south ends of the city. Victoria Street is the main street, and the main shopping area fills a compact area around it. The central area is easily negotiated on foot or by car.

VISITOR INFORMATION The **Hamilton i-SITE Visitor Centre** (℅ 07/839-3580; www.visithamilton.co.nz) is in the new Transport Centre on the corner of Anglesea and Bryce streets. It's open Monday through Thursday from 7:15am to 5:30pm, Friday to 7pm, Saturday 9am to 5:45pm, Sunday 9:30am to 4:45pm; closed December 25. The **Waitomo i-SITE Visitor Information Centre,** 21 Waitomo Caves Rd., Waitomo (℅ 0800/474-839 in NZ, or 07/878-6184; www.waitomoinfo.co.nz), is open daily 8:45am to 7:30pm in summer, 8:45am to 5pm in winter. **Cambridge i-SITE Information Centre,** corner of Queen and Victoria streets, Cambridge (℅ 07/823-3456; fax 07/823-3457; www.cambridge.co.nz), is open Monday through Friday from 9am to 5pm and weekends 10am to 4pm in summer; and in winter, Monday through Friday from 9am until 5pm, weekends 10am to 4pm. **Information Raglan** is at 4 Wallis St., Raglan (℅ 07/825-0556; fax 07/825-0557; www.raglan.org.nz), and is open Monday through Friday from 10am to 5pm, and Saturday, Sunday, and holidays from 9am to 4pm.

SPECIAL EVENTS The **Hamilton Gardens Summer Festival** (℅ 07/856-3200) is held in mid-February each year. **Balloons Over Waikato** (℅ 07/839-3580) is a spectacular event featuring over 30 hot-air balloons in mid-April. The **NZ National Agricultural Fieldays** (℅ 07/843-4499; www.fieldays.co.nz) is a huge event staged at Mystery Creek in mid-June. It attracts nearly 150,000 national and international visitors. For further information on Waikato events, contact **Events Hamilton** (℅ 07/838-6679; www.whatsonhamilton.co.nz or www.visithamilton.co.nz).

EXPLORING THE AREA

To learn about activities in the smaller rural towns of Morrinsville, Matamata, Ngaruawahia, Te Aroha, and Te Awamutu, pick up brochures from the Hamilton visitor center.

In Hamilton

Hamilton Gardens ★★, Cobham Drive (℅ 07/838-6782; www.hamiltongardens.co.nz), is the region's most popular visitor destination. It consists of 58 hectares (143 acres) of specialty gardens along the banks of the Waikato River. You don't have to be a gardener to appreciate the serenity of the Japanese Garden or the beauty of the herb garden. The Gardens Terrace restaurant and the Gardens Café are both open daily from 10am to 5pm in summer and until 4pm in winter. The gardens themselves are open 6am to 7pm in summer, and to 6pm in winter. **Hamilton Lake** and its 56-hectare (138-acre) reserve is also a pleasant place for a quiet wander. It's just outside the central business district.

The **Waikato Museum** ★★★, Victoria and Grantham streets (℅ 07/838-6606; www.waikatomuseum.co.nz), and **Exscite** ★★★ (℅ 07/838-6553; fax 07/838-6571) are especially good value and fun experiences for children. The museum has a fine display of Maori art and carving from the area's Tainui people. Exscite is a madhouse of colorful fun designed as a learning environment for children. Museum admission is by donation (some exhibitions are charged); Exscite costs NZ$5 for adults, NZ$3 for children, and NZ$15 for a family. Both are open daily from 10am to 4:30pm (closed Dec 25).

> ### (Kids) The Sweet Stuff
>
> At **Chocolate Expo,** Donovans Chocolates, 137 Maui St. (✆ **07/847-5771;** www. donovanschocolates.co.nz), you can buy from the factory store or linger in the cafe. On the other side of town, **Candyland,** 75 Henry Rd., Taupiri (✆ **07/824-6818;** www.candyland.co.nz), is New Zealand's largest candy shop. Visit the Candy Museum, watch chocolates being made, or create your own lollipop at the candy-making show. The show costs NZ$10 for adults and NZ$5 for children 11 and under. Candy demonstrations are at 10:30am and 1pm on weekends and holidays.

Hamilton Zoo and the FreeFlight Sanctuary ★, Brymer Road (✆ **07/838-6720;** www.hamiltonzoo.co.nz), is a 21-hectare (52-acre) retreat for birds and animals; it's 5 minutes off State Highway 1, west of Hamilton. It's open daily from 9am to 5pm. They also have late night openings (until 8pm) on Wednesdays and Saturdays in January and on Saturdays in February. And if you're at this end of town, you might consider going a bit farther to **Waingaro Hot Springs** ★ (✆/fax **07/825-4761;** waingaro.hot.springs@ clear.net.nz); it's 23km (14 miles) west of Ngaruawahia (about 30 min. from Hamilton). Big waterslides, thermal mineral pools, bumper boats, and barbecues make this a terrific family outing. It's open daily from 9am to 10pm.

When it turns dark, you might like to try your luck in Hamilton's new casino complex, **SKYCITY Hamilton,** 346 Victoria St. (✆ **07/834-4900;** www.skycityhamilton. co.nz), which has 20 gaming tables, 300 gaming machines, plus bar and restaurant facilities. It's open daily 9am to 3am.

In Cambridge

This pretty oak-filled town of 11,000 is the bright star of the Australasian bloodstock industry—sort of a miniature Kentucky, if you like. Its old homes and rolling green fields make it a delightful spot for a day visit from Hamilton, or a stopover on your journey south. In the last 2 years it has become more lively, and it deserves at least a 1-night stopover.

The **Cambridge Thoroughbred Lodge,** on State Highway 1, 6km (3¾ miles) south of Cambridge (✆ **07/827-8118;** www.cambridgethoroughbredlodge.co.nz), is home to the **NZ Horse Magic Show.** The 1-hour shows are given Tuesday through Sunday at 10:30am; reservations are essential. The cost of NZ$12 for adults, NZ$5 for children ages 3 to 14 includes a tour and horse ride. If you fancy **"A Night at the Trots,"** head to the **Cambridge Raceway,** Taylor Street (✆ **07/827-5506;** www.cambridgeraceway.co. nz), for the thrill and excitement of live harness and greyhound racing.

The **Cambridge Country Store** ★, 92 Victoria St. (✆ **07/827-8715;** www. cambridgecountrystore.co.nz), is a wonderful place to loosen your purse strings. You'll find a wide range of top New Zealand arts and crafts in this old converted church. It's open Monday through Saturday from 8:30am to 5pm, and Sunday 9am to 5pm. **All Saints Café** (✆ **07/827-7100**), upstairs, is the perfect place to contemplate your purchases. It's open Monday through Saturday 8:30am to 4:30pm, and Sunday 9am to 5pm.

The town is also a treasure-trove of antiques. Antiques fairs are in September and April and the Cambridge Information Centre has a good brochure that lists the best antiques dealers in Hamilton and Cambridge. If you're in the mood for a stroll, pick up the *Heritage Trail* brochure, which details heritage sites in town.

Nearby **Lake Karapiro**—8km (5 miles) from town—is also a pleasant outing for boating, sailing, water-skiing, swimming, and rowing. If you're lucky, you might even spy one of New Zealand's Olympic rowing champions in training. Cambridge is home to the gold medal–winning Evers-Swindell twins, Georgina and Caroline.

In Waitomo: Experiencing the Caves

The busy little pocket of tourist activity that is Waitomo is the exception in the otherwise quiet, cow-filled south Waikato pasture. The tiny village owes its existence to the remarkable limestone caves 70km (43 miles) south of Hamilton.

You can get to the area via the **Waitomo Shuttle** (☎ **0800/808-279** in NZ, or 07/873-8214), which connects to InterCity and Newmans coach services and Tranz Scenic trains in nearby Otorohanga. **Waitomo Wanderer Scenic Shuttle** (☎ **0508/926-337** in NZ, or 07/873-6108; www.waitomotours.co.nz) offers daily service between the caves and Rotorua. Kiwi Experience and Magic Travellers also run to the area. If you're driving from the north, take State Highway 1 south to State Highway 3, just south of Otorohanga, and turn west at the signpost for Waitomo Caves.

The **Museum of Caves & i-SITE Visitor Information Centre,** 21 Waitomo Caves Rd., Waitomo (☎ **07/878-7640;** www.waitomo-museum.co.nz), is open daily (see hours above). Admission to the museum is NZ$5 for adults and free for children.

The caves *are* what make Waitomo a visitor destination, and the best among them are the **Waitomo Glowworm Caves** ★★★, 39 Waitomo Caves Rd. (☎ **0800/456-922** in NZ, or 07/878-8227; www.waitomo.com), which opens daily at 9am. The caves' most impressive feature is **"The Cathedral"** ★★★, which rises 14m (46 ft.) and is an acoustically perfect auditorium that has been the site of performances by the Vienna Boys' Choir and Dame Kiri Te Kanawa. Your tour takes you through 250m (820 ft.) of stunning underground scenery, culminating in the glowworm caves. A cafe and shop complex are also on-site.

If you have time, include **Aranui Cave** ★★—15 minutes down the road—which doesn't have glowworms, but does have the most spectacular natural formations; you're allowed to take photographs here. Tickets for both are sold at the Waitomo Glowworm Cave ticket office.

Tours in the Glowworm Cave include a magical boat ride through the **Glowworm Grotto.** These leave daily every half-hour from 9am to 5pm, and hourly in the Aranui Cave from 10am to 3pm. A two-cave combination ticket costs NZ$59 adults, NZ$25 children ages 4 to 14, and NZ$149 for a family. The best time to visit the Glowworm Grotto is mid- to late afternoon, when the crowds are smaller. Bring a sweater because it's cooler underground, and wear strong footwear for walking. The caves are easily accessible to those with reasonable mobility and there are good handrails and pathways.

After being closed to the public for 15 years, **Ruakuri** reopened in June 2005. Laced with myth and legend, Ruakuri ("den of dogs") was first discovered by Maori almost 500 years ago. It takes its name from the pack of wild dogs that lived in the cave entrance. Tours of the cave now depart from the **Ruakuri Information Centre,** at the Legendary Black Water Rafting Company, 585 Waitomo Caves Rd. (☎ **0800/782-5874;** www. ruakuri.co.nz), daily (except Dec 25) at 9am, 10:30am, 11:30am, 12:30pm, 1:30pm, 2:30pm, and 3:30pm. Admission is NZ$58 adults, NZ$22 children ages 5 to 14. You can get a two-cave combo pass for Waitomo and Ruakuri Caves for NZ$78 for adults and NZ$29 for children.

If you'd rather stay aboveground, consider tackling the new **Dundle Hill Walk** (✆ **0800/924-866** in NZ, or 07/878-7788; fax 07/878-6266; www.waitomowalk.com). During this 2-day, clearly marked, self-guided walk through native bush, forest, and farmland, you'll walk about 12km (7½ miles) a day and stay at Dundle Hill hut. It requires moderate fitness and costs around NZ$75 adults, NZ$35 children 15 and under.

WHERE TO STAY
In Hamilton

If you want rural charm 20 minutes from Hamilton, ring Peter and Daphne Searle at **Uliveto Country Stay & Olive Grove** ★★, 164 Finlayson Rd., Ngahinapouri (✆ **07/825-2116;** www.uliveto.co.nz), which has two lovely rooms for NZ$150. Near the airport, **Hamilton Airport Motor Inn** ★★, Airport Road (✆ **0800/106-679** in NZ, or 07/843-8412; www.airportinn.co.nz), has rooms from NZ$105 to NZ$165. You'll also get good standard, well-equipped motel rooms and a three-bedroom town house at **Anglesea Motel** ★, 36 Liverpool St. (✆ **0800/426-453** in NZ, or 07/834-0010; fax 07/834-3310; www.angleseamotel.com). Some units have big Jacuzzis, and there's an outdoor pool and free high-speed Internet access. It's ideal for families and couples traveling together. All rates include 12.5% GST and free parking.

Novotel Tainui ★★ (Value) This is still one of my favorite hotels—there's just something open and welcoming about the place, and for the price, you get great amenities. New in 1999, its large rooms have contemporary decor and overlook either the city or the river. All have desks and nice bathrooms; there are two slightly larger standard rooms on each floor. If you want reliable service and immaculate rooms, Novotel offers great value—and all rooms were given a complete soft-furnishings refurbishment in 2005. The hotel is Qualmark Enviro-Gold certified and Green Globe benchmarked.

7 Alma St., Hamilton. ✆ **0800/450-050** in NZ, or 07/838-1366. Fax 07/838-1367. www.novotel.co.nz/hamilton. 177 units. NZ$160–NZ$340. Rates include airport transport. Long-stay and special rates. AE, DC, MC, V. Valet parking NZ$15. **Amenities:** Restaurant (Cafe Alma); bar; babysitting; children's programs; concierge; nearby golf course; small gym; indoor Jacuzzi; room service; sauna; Wi-Fi in reception and lobby. *In room:* A/C, TV w/pay movies, fridge, hair dryer, minibar.

In Cambridge

There's lots of old-world charm at **Emanuels Lake Karapiro Lodge** ★★, Karapiro Heights, State Highway 1, 20km (12 miles) south of Cambridge (✆ **07/823-7414;** fax 07/823-7219; www.karapirolodge.co.nz), where Ed and Ann Rompelberg have created a country retreat overlooking Lake Karapiro. The six rooms are beautifully appointed and have private patios and en-suite bathrooms, and there's a gym, sauna, and Jacuzzi to unwind in. Deluxe rooms cost NZ$400 to NZ$500 and the suite costs NZ$700 to NZ$900.

Huntington Stables Retreat ★★★ (Finds) This luxury retreat in the middle of lush Waikato farmland is a real find. They've done everything right, and their two stable suites skimp on nothing. One has a king-size bed, the other a super-king-size/twin setup. The smartly furnished rooms are generous in size, plus there is a beautiful pool, Jacuzzi, and sauna right outside the back door. The luxurious bathrooms feature a shower and tub, and Egyptian cotton towels; and French doors open out from your private lounge to a deck overlooking farmland. From the wine cellar to the well-stocked pantry and fridge, you'll be exceedingly well looked after with every comfort at your fingertips. I was reluctant to leave.

106 Maungakawa Rd., RD4, Cambridge. (🕿/fax **07/823-4136.** www.huntingtonstables.co.nz. 2 units. From NZ$390–NZ$475. Rates include breakfast provisions. Long-stay and weekend packages. AE, MC, V. **Amenities:** Airport transport; nearby golf course; Jacuzzi; outdoor pool; sauna. *In room:* TV/VCR, hair dryer, kitchen, minibar, Wi-Fi.

The Mews ★ (**Value**) Every comfort has been accounted for in this smart motel complex. All units have fabulous double Jacuzzis—after a day on the road, I can think of nothing better than filling it with bubbles and soaking. Don't drive past this picturesque stone-and-shingle complex—it's even better on the inside.

20 Hamilton Rd., Cambridge. (🕿 **07/827-7166.** Fax 07/827-7163. www.cambridgemews.co.nz. 12 units. NZ$150–NZ$275. Extra person NZ$25. Rates include airport transport. Long-stay, off-peak, and special rates. AE, DC, MC, V. **Amenities:** Nearby golf course. *In room:* TV, hair dryer, kitchen.

Thornton House ★★ Christine Manson and David Cowley have opened the doors of their gorgeous 1902 villa, providing two rooms that are bound to please. The Blue Room is smaller, cozy, and moody, with a shower-only en suite. The bigger Garden Room has a tub, an extra single bed, and a door to the veranda. Both are beautifully decorated with stereos and CD selections. The town center is just a 5-minute walk away, but because this is so much a family home, you may just want to stay indoors.

2 Thornton St., Cambridge. (🕿 **07/827-7567.** Fax 07/827-7568. www.thorntonhouse.co.nz. 2 units. From NZ$240–NZ$270. Rates include breakfast. Long-stay rates. AE, DC, MC, V. **Amenities:** Nearby golf course and tennis courts. *In room:* TV/DVD, fridge, hair dryer, Wi-Fi.

In Waitomo

Given the nature of this place, I'm surprised no one has thought to build an underground hotel. Perhaps it would be better than some of the aboveground choices: The pickings are slim here. **Juno Hall Backpackers** ★★, Main Road (🕿/fax **07/878-7649;** www.junowaitomo.co.nz), a new farmhouse-style hostel, has dorm rooms for NZ$24, and doubles for NZ$65. A nice B&B in Waitomo, **Abseil Inn,** Waitomo Caves Village (🕿 **07/878-7815;** www.abseilinn.co.nz), has four rooms from NZ$125 to NZ$175.

Kamahi Cottage ★★, 229 Barber Rd., RD5, Otorohanga (🕿/fax **07/873-0849;** www.kamahi.co.nz), is 30 minutes from Waitomo Caves and is the nicest B&B in the area. They have a charming self-contained, one-bedroom cottage for NZ$335 to NZ$450. They have an active recycling and conservation program operating on the family farm, with 200 hectares (500 acres) of native forest protected under legal covenant. Free Wi-Fi is available in the nearby homestead and dinners are available on request. As an alternative, you can try the **Waitomo Caves Hotel,** Lemon Point Road (🕿 **07/878-8204;** www.waitomocaveshotel.co.nz), but I consider it highly overrated. It's a shame that this fabulous old building with its rich history and terrific location doesn't live up to its potential. Rooms run from NZ$120.

WHERE TO DINE
In Hamilton

The visitor center has a helpful free *Dine Out* guide. You'll find the bulk of the best restaurants, cafes, bars, and nightspots in a tight cluster in and around the south end of Victoria Street.

The favorite trendy restaurant is **Domaine** ★★★, 575 Victoria St. (🕿 **07/839-2100**), which attracts a mixed business crowd during the day and has just enough flair to keep you coming back. **Hydro Majestic** ★★, 33 Jellicoe Dr., Hamilton East (📞 07/ 859-0020), is favored for its funky kitsch atmosphere and great food. **Tables on the River** ★, 12 Alma St. (📞 07/839-6555), which overlooks the river, still gets top marks from many, but I think there's a better over-the-river setting at the Novotel's **Cafe Alma** (see "Where to Stay," above). Also popular is the **Balcony Restaurant and Bar,** next door to Tables (📞 07/838-3133), and yes, it also has river-view dining. For the best breakfasts and lunches, I go to **Scott Epicurean Café** ★★, 181 Victoria St. (📞 07/839-6680); it's open daily.

Another good choice is **Escaba** ★, 237 Victoria St. (📞 07/834-3131), which, despite its stark interior, has friendly staff and well-priced food. Just down the road, **Metropolis Caffé** ★, 211 Victoria St. (📞 07/834-2081), has excellent coffee, vegetarian meals, and a slightly crazy interior popular with a crowd in their 20s and 30s. Next door is **Iguana** (📞 07/834-2280), which deserves a mention for its sushi, gourmet pizzas, comfy booths, and fast-paced night scene. **Barzurks,** on Victoria Street, opposite Rydges Le Grand Hotel, is sought out for its superb pizzas and laid-back atmosphere. **Museum Café** ★★, 1 Grantham St. (📞 07/839-7209), offers dinner Tuesday through Saturday and over-the-river cafe service throughout the day.

In Cambridge

At last! The Cambridge dining scene has something to boast about. **Onyx** ★★, 70 Alpha St. (📞 07/827-7740), should be your first port of call. Here you'll find fabulous wood-fired pizzas, great salads, and tasty seafood platters. **Instone Café** ★, 85 Victoria St. (📞 07/827-8590), is open for great coffee and snacks daily 7am to 7pm; and there's a hidden rural gem called the **Boatshed Café** ★★, RD2, Amber Lane (📞 07/827-8286), which overlooks Lake Karapiro and also runs a rental kayak operation that takes you through a canyon sparkling with glowworms.

In Waitomo

About the best you'll find in these parts is Blackwater Rafting's **Long Black Café,** Main Road (📞 07/878-7361), where the counter food includes good vegetarian fare. They have all-day breakfasts and excellent coffee. That said, a new addition, **Huhu Café** ★, 10 Waitomo Caves Rd., Waitomo (📞 07/878-6674), is winning lots of fans for its tasty all-day breakfasts and delicious evening meals (reservations recommended), that feature dishes like braised lamb medallions. They're open daily from 8:30am to 8:30pm.

2 TAURANGA & BAY OF PLENTY ★★★

208km (129 miles) SE of Auckland; 86km (53 miles) NW of Rotorua

Tauranga is no longer the sleepy place of my childhood holidays. Somewhere along the way it has transformed itself into a sort of miniature version of Australia's Gold Coast. Today it is New Zealand's second-fastest-growing area after Queenstown, and it has one of the largest natural harbors in the country, with over 1,000 yachts and launches moored in two marinas. The Port of Tauranga is also a popular stop for cruise ships. It has a population of about 104,000 and boasts 2,400 hours of sunshine per year. Tauranga and its nearby beachfront neighbor, Mount Maunganui, are confident, thriving urban centers, and no matter what time of year you visit, you'll be spoiled with choices for anything related to outdoor beach-driven activity.

GETTING THERE   By Plane   Air New Zealand (© 0800/767-767 in NZ), operates daily flights from Tauranga and Whakatane to Auckland, Wellington, and Christchurch. The airport is located in Mount Maunganui, 5km (about 3 miles) from Tauranga city.

By Coach (Bus)   InterCity (© 09/623-1503) and **Newmans** (© 09/623-1504) both operate daily services between Tauranga and Auckland, Napier, Rotorua, Taupo, Thames, and Wellington. The **Magic Travellers** (© 09/358-5600) buses also stop in Tauranga en route to Rotorua.

By Car   Drive south from Auckland on State Highway 1, then go east on State Highway 2; the trip takes around 3 hours. From the Coromandel Peninsula, take Highway 25 or 26 to Waihi and pick up Highway 2; this route takes about 1½ hours. If you're coming from Hamilton, the trip takes 1½ hours, and from Rotorua, around 1 hour.

ORIENTATION   Once you get used to the frequent roundabouts, you'll find this an easy city to navigate. **Edgewater** is the beautifully paved product of multimillion-dollar inner city redevelopment. It's one of the prettiest downtown areas in the country. **Cameron Road** is the main arterial route. The toll bridge offers a shortcut to **Mount Maunganui,** where you'll find that Project Phoenix has converted the downtown shopping area into a palm-filled promenade that's hard to beat. **Ocean Beach** features great stretches of sand and a growing number of high-rise apartments and holiday homes. More than 60km (37 miles) of continuous white-sand beach runs from Mount Maunganui to Whakatane.

GETTING AROUND   Some distance out from Tauranga, expect to share the road with a scary number of huge trucks, all bound for the port. The traffic flow is fast and often congested. Public transport is limited within Tauranga itself. Walk if you can.

VISITOR INFORMATION   The **Tauranga i-SITE Visitor Centre,** Civic Centre, 95 Willow St. (© 07/578-8103; fax 07/578-7020), is open Monday to Friday 8:30am to 5:30pm, and Saturday and Sunday 9am to 5pm. Pick up a free copy of the excellent *Bay of Plenty Visitor Guide.* The **Mount Maunganui i-SITE Visitor Centre** is on Salisbury Avenue (© 07/578-8103; fax 07/578-7020). The **Katikati Information Centre** is at 36 Main Rd. (© 07/549-1658; fax 07/549-1798). For more information on the area, check out www.bayofplentynz.com, www.cityoftauranga.co.nz, and www.tauranga.co.nz.

SPECIAL EVENTS   Tauranga and Mount Maunganui offer a profusion of summer events that cover everything from ironman competitions and yachting regattas to beauty pageants and jazz festivals. Pick up the free *Oceanfest* guide to summer events at the visitor center, call © 07/577-7209, or visit www.bayofplentynz.com/events for more information.

EXPLORING THE AREA
In & Near Tauranga

Sun, sea, and surf rule here. But before you take to the water, take a look at **Kiwi360** (© 07/573-6340; www.kiwi360.com), on the main Rotorua/Tauranga highway 5km (3 miles) south of Te Puke. It's definitely different, and if you want insight into this multimillion-dollar industry, this is the place—and it's great for kids, too. There are daily tours every hour through orchards and theme parks (NZ$22 adults; NZ$10 children ages 5–15), a kiwifruit souvenir shop, and a restaurant. It's open daily 9am to 5pm, except December 25.

The mural town of **Katikati** is worth a brief stopover. Ask at the visitor center for the location of some of the town's many professionally painted street murals—there are over 40. And take a dip in the thermal **Sapphire Springs,** 274 Hot Springs Rd. (© **07/549-0768;** www.sapphiresprings.net.nz), set on 31 hectares (78 acres) of native bush. They're open daily 8am to 7pm.

In Tauranga, the **Elms Mission House,** Mission and Chapel streets (© **07/577-9772;** www.theelms.org.nz), is one of the finest examples of colonial architecture of its time (1847). The house is open Wednesday, Saturday, Sunday, and public holidays from 2 to 4pm and costs NZ$5. If you're interested in more of the town's history, pick up the excellent brochure *Historic Tauranga* from the information center.

Garden enthusiasts can pick up the *Garden Trail* brochure at the visitor center. **McLaren Falls Park ★★**, McLaren Falls Road, Tauranga (© **07/577-7000**), is another lovely stop. It consists of 170 hectares (420 acres) of lake-land park set amid pastoral farming and horticulture, containing one of the best botanical tree collections in the North Island. If you have a license you can fish for trout, or simply enjoy the arboretum and numerous walking tracks.

If wine is your passion, go to **Mills Reef Winery & Restaurant,** Moffat Road, Bethlehem, Tauranga (© **0800/645-577** in NZ, or 07/576-8800; www.millsreef.co.nz); and while you're in the area, call in to **Prenzel of Tauranga,** 171 Moffat Rd. (© **07/579-2668;** www.prenzel.com), distillers of delicious liqueurs, schnapps, flavored olive oils, and cooking products. They're open daily and offer free tastings.

Just south of Tauranga, two more stops are creating a buzz. **Mossop's Honey ★**, State Highway 29 (© **07/543-0971;** www.mossopshoney.co.nz), has an interesting live bee display and myriad honey-based products and gifts. It's open daily from 9am to 5:30pm in summer and 9am to 5pm in winter. At the **Comvita Visitor Centre ★★**, Wilson Road South, Paengaroa (© **0800/493-782** in NZ, or 07/533-1987; www.comvita.com), 9km (5½ miles) south of Te Puke, you'll find a multi-award-winning heart of natural health and bee products, with over 100 honeys to sample. It's open from 8:30am to 5pm daily, except December 25 and 26, December 31, January 1 and 2. The manuka honey-flavored ice cream is my personal highlight.

The most spectacular of Tauranga's attractions is nearby **White Island ★★★**, New Zealand's only active marine volcano. Known as Whakaari to Maori, this active volcano sits 48km (29 miles) off the Bay of Plenty coast. It is privately owned and was declared a scenic reserve in 1953. Visitors cannot land on the island without permission and its spectacular sights are best seen via a guided tour.

Given its easy accessibility, White Island is something of a mecca for the world's volcanologists and scientists, who come to study its lava flows and explosive ash eruptions. Attempts to mine sulfur on the island in 1914 ended when a lahar killed 10 workers; and a major eruption here in 1981 to 1983 completely altered the island's landscape and destroyed an entire pohutukawa forest. Another eruption in 2000 covered the island in mud and scoria.

Despite its fiery reputation, though, White Island remains a highlight for many visitors. If you're considering a visit, rest assured that the island's volcanic activity is constantly monitored by surveillance cameras, seismographic equipment, and sensors within the crater walls. You won't be allowed on the island if there is even the slightest risk of increased activity. Fishermen might like to know that the waters around White Island are home to an abundance of fish—everything from marlin to tuna. Fishing excursions operate out of both Whakatane and Tauranga.

Among the operators offering aerial excursions are **Vulcan Helicopters** (℗ **0800/804-354** in NZ, or 07/308-4188; www.vulcanheli.co.nz) and **East Bay Flight Centre** (℗ **07/308-8446;** fax 07/308-8042). Both operate out of Whakatane and cost around NZ$400 per person. **White Island Tours with PeeJay** ★★★, 15 Strand St. E., Whakatane (℗ **0800/733-529** in NZ, or 07/308-9588; www.whiteisland.co.nz), will put you on a luxury launch and give you a 6-hour guided tour with lunch and safety gear included. This is an award-winning eco experience that you won't forget in a hurry. It costs NZ$180 per person and you need to be reasonably agile to negotiate the inflatable boat that takes you ashore from the main launch. There are no significant hills to climb on the island, but tracks can be uneven and you'll be on your feet for around 2 hours. No open-toed footwear or sandals are permitted, and it is not recommended for children 7 and under. Don't despair if you don't make it to White Island from here, as there are several Rotorua operators, which also offer great flights.

In Mount Maunganui

The town is named after the small mountain known to Maori as **Mauao,** which is a place of cultural and legendary significance to the local Maori tribes. The biggest attraction here has always been **Ocean Beach** ★★★, famed for its surf and great swimming. The **Mount** ★★ itself has a network of lovely walkways. The full 3.5km (2-mile) walk around the Mount takes about an hour. You can also climb to its 252m (827-ft.) summit, which takes about 2 hours. Pick up the free *Walker's Guide to Mauao* from the visitor center. The Mount is also home to New Zealand's first artificial surf reef, which is located just offshore on Marine Parade.

At the base of the Mount, on Adams Avenue, the **Mount Hot Pools** ★★★ (℗ **07/575-0868;** www.mounthotpools.co.nz), is a modern complex where you can soak away all your aches and pains in water warmed to 102°F (39°C); the active and children's pools are 90°F (32°C). Private pools and massage services are available. Hours are Monday through Saturday 6am to 10pm, and Sunday 8am to 10pm. Admission is NZ$14 for adults and NZ$8 for children ages 5 to 15. My advice is to wallow in a private pool (from NZ$12 per person for 30 min.) and then take a massage.

OUTDOOR PURSUITS

DOLPHIN SWIMMING   Several companies offer the opportunity to get in the water with the common dolphins that live in the bay. Try **Butler's Swim With Dolphins,** Pier C, Berth C60, Tauranga Bridge Marina (℗ **0508/288-537** in NZ, or 07/578-0821; www.swimwithdolphins.co.nz). Expeditions depart Tauranga daily at 8:45am and the Mount at 9:15am for a full-day outing; and cost NZ$125 for adults and NZ$100 for children. For information on the ethics of swimming with dolphins, see p. 62 in chapter 3.

FISHING   **Blue Ocean Charters,** Tauranga Bridge Marina, Tauranga (℗ **0800/224-278;** www.blueocean.co.nz), offers half- and full-day reef fishing, day and overnight hapuka fishing, and ecotrips to Mayor Island. Prices range NZ$70 to NZ$120 per person depending on trip type.

FOUR-WHEEL-DRIVE ADVENTURES   **Longridge Fun Park** (℗ **0800/867-386** in NZ, or 07/533-1515; www.longridgefunpark.co.nz) is at Paengaroa on State Highway 33, a half-hour south of Tauranga. Open daily from 9am (closed Dec 25), they have self-drive 4WD cars from NZ$100 for adults and NZ$45 for children ages 14 and under for 3km (2 miles) of fun.

JET-BOATING There are reliable thrills to be had with **Longridge Jet** (© **0800/867-286** in NZ, or 07/533-1515; www.longridgepark.co.nz). Prices start at NZ$110 per adult, NZ$45 for children 15 and over; children 14 and under are not allowed.

SKY DIVING **Tauranga Tandem Skydiving** at Tauranga Airport (© **07/576-7990;** www.tandemskydive.co.nz) is your best bet. A basic jump will cost NZ$245 to NZ$325.

SURFING **Hibiscus Surf School,** Mount Maunganui (© **07/575-3792;** www.surf school.co.nz), offers exclusive personal tuition with surf instructor Rebecca Taylor, who will quickly bring you up to speed on local surf and ocean conditions.

WHITE-WATER RAFTING There's no shortage of rafting operators. **Wet 'n' Wild Rafting** ★, 2 White St., Rotorua (© **0800/462-723** in NZ; www.wetnwildrafting. co.nz), operates on five rivers in this region, offering a wide range of adventures depending on your level of experience. You can add more fun by combining rafting with jet-boating, a helicopter ride, and mountain biking. Prices start at NZ$95 per person.

WHERE TO STAY

Every summer, more than 60,000 New Zealanders make their annual holiday pilgrimage to Tauranga and Mount Maunganui. If you plan to come here between December and February, book well in advance. All rates below include 12.5% GST and free parking.

In & Near Tauranga

You'll find most motels on Waihi Road and 15th Avenue. The **Tauranga YHA** is at 171 Elizabeth St. (© **0800/278-299** in NZ, or 07/578-5064; www.yha.co.nz). The new and classy **Hotel on Devonport** ★★★, 72 Devonport Rd. (© **0800/322-856** in NZ, or 07/578-2668; www.hotelondevonport.net.nz), is a boutique establishment right in the center of the city and my pick for the most stylish, contemporary stay in this region. Rooms are big and modern and very reasonably priced at NZ$180 to NZ$350.

Ridge Country Retreat ★★★ (Finds) This gorgeous boutique lodge and spa provides just about anything you could wish for in a smart, contemporary environment on 14 hectares (35 acres) of sloping hills and native bush just out of the city. It has fabulous facilities, including a whole range of beauty therapies and massages, and rooms are big and sumptuous. Bathrooms are also large and very well appointed. It's all about understated luxury and a chance to recharge, revitalize, and replenish. Best of all, they've just added six new villas to the complex, each one featuring a private deck and its own outdoor geothermal tub.

300 Rocky Cutting Rd., Welcome Bay, Tauranga. © **07/542-1301.** Fax 07/542-2116. www.rcr.co.nz. 11 units. NZ$750–NZ$980 suite; NZ$1,150 villa. Rates include full breakfast, predinner drinks, canapés, and 4-course dinner. Long-stay and off-peak rates. AE, MC, V. **Amenities:** Free airport transport by arrangement; bar; babysitting; nearby golf course; Jacuzzi; geothermally heated outdoor lap pool. In room: A/C, TV/DVD, fridge, hair dryer, minibar, Wi-Fi.

In Mount Maunganui

Pacific Coast Backpackers, 432 Maunganui Rd. (© **0800/666-622** in NZ, or 07/574-9601; www.pacificcoastlodge.co.nz), is just a few hundred meters from the beach and downtown. Dorm beds start at NZ$24. At the top end, you'll be well looked after with 40 gorgeous seaside apartments at **Oceanside Resort & Twin Towers** ★★, 1 Maunganui Rd., Mount Maunganui (© **07/575-5371;** www.oceanside.co.nz). The high-rise complex also features a heated lap pool, gym and sauna, and secure underground parking. Rates range from NZ$180 for a studio to NZ$300 for a two-bedroom suite. A selection of restaurants and cafes are available inside the complex and within walking distance.

WHERE TO DINE
In Tauranga

The dining scene in this area has taken off, and you'll probably miss restaurants and cafes every time you blink. There's a cluster of very good ones on The Strand, in the Wharf Street area, and on Devonport Road between Spring and Elizabeth streets. Pick up the free *Dine Out* guide from the visitor center.

Try **Spinnakers Restaurant & Bar,** Tauranga Bridge Marina (✆ **07/574-4147**), on the water's edge, for fabulous seafood and a wide range of breakfast, lunch, and dinner offerings; or **Bravo** ★★, Red Square, Tauranga (✆ **07/578-4700**), a consistent award winner serving up delicious meals, gourmet pizzas, and good coffee. It's open daily from 9am until late.

Tucked away in the Old Yacht Club Building, at the south end of The Strand, **Harbourside Brasserie & Bar** ★★★ (✆ **07/571-0520**) is eternally popular. It's open daily from 10:30am until late; there's a strong seafood slant to its excellent menu and the views are unmatched. For something a bit different, head for **Kestrels @ The Landing** ★★★, The Strand, water's edge (✆ **07/928-1123**), where you can dine on board the historic vessel *Kestrel* (or on the landing). It's open daily until late. **Amphora Café & Bar** ★★, 43 The Strand (✆ **07/578-1616**), is a stylish place for coffee overlooking the waterfront. **Collar & Thai** ★★, Goddards Centre, 21 Devonport Rd. (✆ **07/577-6655**), is a popular local haunt serving the best Thai curries. It's open for lunch Tuesday to Friday from 11:30am, and for dinner daily from 5:30pm until late.

In Mount Maunganui

The favorite here is **Thai-phoon Restaurant** ★★, 14a Pacific Ave. (✆ **07/572-3545**). **Astrolabe Café & Bar** ★★, 82 Maunganui Rd. (✆ **07/574-8155**), is big on space and style. **Zambezi Bar & Café,** 108 Maunganui Rd. (✆ **07/575-4202**), does a good job catering to vegetarians, with superb platters and fresh salads, plus monthly live shows. The cafe gets a younger crowd.

EN ROUTE TO ROTORUA

As you head south to Rotorua on State Highway 2, you'll pass through **Te Puke,** the "Kiwifruit Capital of the World." Here's where you'll find **Kiwi360** (see "Exploring the Area," above). The road is good for the hour-long journey, but it gets crowded with lots of heavy logging trucks headed for the port in Tauranga—drive with extreme care!

Rotorua, Taupo & Tongariro National Park

Rotorua sits on the edge of one of the most awesome and concentrated volcanic areas in the world. In every direction is tangible evidence of a riotous geological past extending back millions of years. The Te Arawa people settled the area in the mid–14th century, and their descendants began tourism in the area in the 19th century, guiding visitors to the famous Pink and White terraces. The 1886 eruption of Mount Tarawera destroyed the terraces, but the legendary Maori hospitality lives on. Coupled with enough daredevil activities to rival Queenstown's reputation as New Zealand's adventure capital, the famous welcome continues to draw international visitors at a rate of 1.6 million a year.

Volcanic activity was also responsible for the formation of Lake Taupo. In A.D. 186, an enormous eruption—estimated to have been 100 times greater than that of Mount St. Helens in 1980—tore a savage hole 30km (20 miles) wide, 40km (25 miles) across, and 180m (600 ft.) deep. Today, we're thankful for that. Where would New Zealand holidaymakers be without the cool blue waters that provide ideal conditions for fishing, water-skiing, and boating?

South of Taupo lies Tongariro National Park, home to three volcanoes. Tongariro was New Zealand's first national park (the world's second after Yellowstone), and today it is a winter playground for skiers and a perfect place for summer tramping.

1 ROTORUA ★★★

221km (137 miles) SE of Auckland; 86km (53 miles) S of Tauranga

You'll smell Rotorua long before you see it. The sulfuric aroma in the air is an unmistakable prelude to geothermal things to come. This natural wonderland and the 11 major lakes in the area are the draw for visitors. In fact, Rotorua has long had a reputation for being too touristy, but recent city beautification and heaps of new adventures, accommodations, and attractions have given it a whole new lease on life. And if you're interested in Maori culture, this is the most accessible place to find it. A third of the population of 68,000 is Maori; that's the highest percentage of any city in the country. I love the place. It may attract a lot of visitors (2.9 million annually), but unlike Queenstown, its attractions are spread wide and you seldom have to jostle with others. There's plenty of room for everyone. And if you're keen to support sustainable initiatives, the Rotorua Sustainable Tourism Charter (www.sustainableNZ.com), has identified a group of tourism operators committed to protecting and enhancing the natural environment. Members are assessed and their operations carry the charter logo. You can find out who they are and what role they are playing at the Rorotua i-SITE Visitor Centre & Travel Office.

GETTING THERE **By Plane** **Air New Zealand National and Link** (✆ 0800/767-767 in NZ; www.airnewzealand.com) provides daily service to all other major centers. **Super Shuttle** (✆ 07/349-3444) provides daily transport to and from the airport, 15 minutes out of town, for around NZ$25.

By Coach (Bus) **InterCity, Newmans, Magic Travellers,** and **Kiwi Experience** all provide service to Rotorua. Contact the **Bus Stop,** 67 Fenton St. (✆ 07/348-179; fax 07/348-6044), for coach and ferry bookings throughout New Zealand.

By Car Centrally located Rotorua is only a 1-hour drive from the cities of Taupo, Hamilton, and Tauranga; a 3-hour drive from Auckland; and a 5-hour drive from Wellington. Roads in the area are excellent, but Rotorua is in the heart of the forestry industry, which means a heavy volume of large, fast-traveling logging trucks. Take care at all times.

ORIENTATION Rotorua sits in the curve of Lake Rotorua's southwestern shore, spreading inland in a neat pattern. **Fenton Street** is the main drag and the home of the area's souvenir shops. It runs from the lake for 3.5km (2 miles) south to **Whakarewarewa Village** (just call it "Whaka," as the locals do), the area's most accessible thermal reserve. The center of town is not large. **Tutanekai Street** is the main shopping street; **City Focus,** under the sail-like structure, is in the middle of it all.

Note: Don't wander in Kuirau Park after dark. Make sure to remove all valuables from cars, and lock those cars, too.

GETTING AROUND City and suburban buses run approximately every hour on weekdays, less frequently on weekends. You'll find taxis at the visitor center and on Fenton Street, or you can call ✆ 07/348-5079. If you need a car, call the **Rental Car Centre,** 14 Ti St. (✆ 07/349-3993).

VISITOR INFORMATION **Rotorua i-SITE Visitor Centre & Travel Office,** 1167 Fenton St. (✆ 0800/768-678 in NZ, or 07/348-5179; fax 07/348-6044; www.rotorua nz.com), is open daily from 8am to 6pm in summer, 8am to 5:30pm in winter. It provides travel and sightseeing reservations, currency exchange, luggage storage, a cafe and restaurant, an excellent souvenir shop, and showers and toilets. The visitor center's guide booklets are an excellent value.

Travel information is also available at **AA Travel Centre,** 1121 Eruera St. (✆ 07/348-3069; fax 07/346-2034). The **Redwoods Visitor Centre, Whakarewarewa Forest,** Long Mile Road (✆ 07/350-0110; fax 07/350-0111; www.redwoods.co.nz), provides information on the extensive walking tracks in Whakarewarewa Forest and Redwood Grove. It's open weekdays 8:30am to 5:30pm (until 4:30pm in winter), and weekends 10am to 4pm. For more information on the area, check www.rotoruanz.com and www.rdc.govt. nz. The Redwoods is located 5km (about 3 miles) southeast of the city and you can be there in 5 minutes by car.

(Tips) **Sore Feet?**

A sheltered seat and a free, hot, thermal footbath are right outside the main entrance to the visitor center and bus stop. Go ahead and take your shoes off and soak your weary feet for a few minutes.

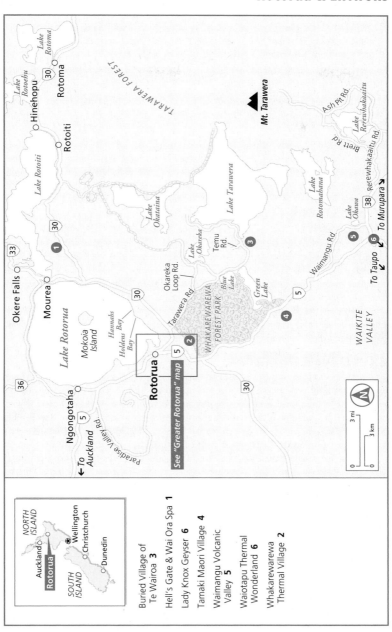

ROTORUA, TAUPO & TONGARIRO NATIONAL PARK

9 ROTORUA

Buried Village of
Te Wairoa **3**

Hell's Gate & Wai Ora Spa **1**

Lady Knox Geyser **6**

Tamaki Maori Village **4**

Waimangu Volcanic
Valley **5**

Waiotapu Thermal
Wonderland **6**

Whakarewarewa
Thermal Village **2**

> **(Fun Facts** Sacred Lake
>
> Of the 11 major lakes in the area, most are ideal for swimming and watersports—
> except Lake Rotokakahi, the Green Lake. This lake is *tapu* (sacred) to the Maori
> and, therefore, off-limits for swimming, boating, and fishing.

Pick up a free copy of *Thermal Air,* an excellent little publication listing activities, attractions, eateries, and events. The local newspaper, the *Daily Post,* also has event listings.

FAST FACTS The **post office,** Hinemoa Street (✆ **07/347-7851**), is open Monday through Friday from 7:30am to 5pm, Saturday 8am to 4pm, and Sunday 10am to 3pm. **Thomas Cook,** Fenton and Hinemoa streets (✆ **07/348-0640**), is open Monday through Friday from 9am to 5pm, Saturday 9:30am to 12:30pm. For Internet access, try the **Cyber World,** 1174 Haupapa St. (✆ **07/348-0088**), or **Cybershed,** 1176 Pukuatua St. (✆ **07/349-4965**).

SPECIAL EVENTS The route of the **Rotorua Marathon** (✆/fax **07/348-8448;** www. rotoruamarathon.co.nz) goes around Lake Rotorua. This very serious competition takes place in late April or early May. In April, fishermen compete in the **Tagged Trout Tournament** (✆ **07/348-5179;** www.taggedtrout.co.nz), which presents 2 days of fishing with great prizes. The **Rotorua Festival of Arts Te Ihi Te Wehi** (✆ **07/348-9134;** www. rotoruaartsfestival.co.nz), presents 16 days of creative events in early March. In late January, **Opera in the Pa** (✆ **07/348-9047**) presents New Zealand's best young Maori, European, and Polynesian opera voices in Ohinemutu on the Lakefront. It's held every second year. Check www.rotoruaNZ.com/events closer to time for the 2011 venue.

EXPLORING ROTORUA

Although the major thermal areas and Maori culture remain very popular, **Mount Tarawera** ★★★ now plays a big part in Rotorua tourism. It has a strong mystical history for the Maori, and I keep hearing rave reports about four-wheel-drive and fly-over crater tours. If your time is short, the four must-see/must-do attractions are the **Te Puia; Rotorua Museum;** either of the geothermal reserves, **Waiotapu** or **Waimangu;** and a scenic flight over **Mount Tarawera.** This is easy to manage in 2 days. Visit the museum first or last for a comprehensive overview of Mount Tarawera's role. And pick up the *Passport to Rotorua's Finest Attractions* brochure from the visitor center—it details the bus service that frequents 18 leading attractions.

The Major Sights & Attractions
In the City Area
Rotorua Museum of Art & History ★★★   Set in the world-famous Bath House, the Rotorua Museum has a new lease on life. After a NZ$22-million refurbishment and the addition of a fabulous state-of-the-art cinema experience, it's well worth a visit, especially if you want insight into the Mount Tarawera eruption of 1886. The restored section of the Great South Seas Spa is equally fascinating. People came from all over the world to visit the spa and were encouraged to take "electric baths," a rather bizarre practice that saw electric currents fed into the bath water. There is also an excellent exhibition

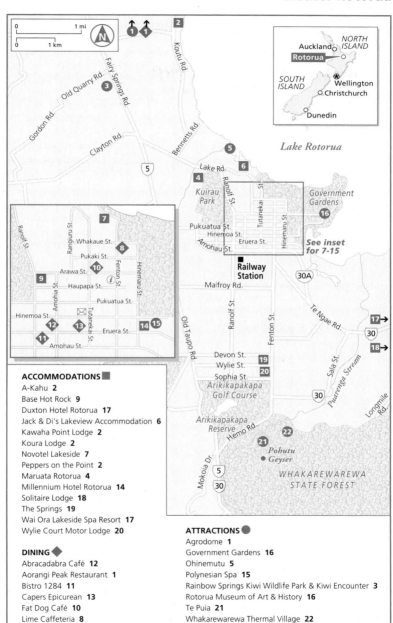

ACCOMMODATIONS
A-Kahu **2**
Base Hot Rock **9**
Duxton Hotel Rotorua **17**
Jack & Di's Lakeview Accommodation **6**
Kawaha Point Lodge **2**
Koura Lodge **2**
Novotel Lakeside **7**
Peppers on the Point **2**
Maruata Rotorua **4**
Millennium Hotel Rotorua **14**
Solitaire Lodge **18**
The Springs **19**
Wai Ora Lakeside Spa Resort **17**
Wylie Court Motor Lodge **20**

DINING
Abracadabra Café **12**
Aorangi Peak Restaurant **1**
Bistro 1284 **11**
Capers Epicurean **13**
Fat Dog Café **10**
Lime Caffeteria **8**

ATTRACTIONS
Agrodome **1**
Government Gardens **16**
Ohinemutu **5**
Polynesian Spa **15**
Rainbow Springs Kiwi Wildlife Park & Kiwi Encounter **3**
Rotorua Museum of Art & History **16**
Te Puia **21**
Whakarewarewa Thermal Village **22**

(Value) **Saving on the Sights**

A number of offers represent significant savings on the leading attractions. Check at the visitor center or its website (www.rotoruanz.com) for the latest **Rotorua Hot Deals** (www.rotoruahotdeals.com). New packages and deals are added regularly throughout the year; they typically include Tamaki Tours, Polynesian Spa, Agrodome, Skyline Skyrides, and many other star attractions and activities. **Rotorua Adventure Combos** ((C) **0800/338-786** in NZ, or 07/357-2236; www.rotoruacombos.com), also combines many of the city's leading attractions in well-priced packages; and **Rotorua 5 Star Super Pass** ((C) **07/343-1732;** www.rotorua5star.co.nz), gives you good deals on access to Polynesian Spa, Skyline Skyrides, and Te Puia.

of the *taonga* (treasures) of the Te Arawa people. And changes continue. The new wing has been built and the refurbishment of the South Wing is due for completion by September 2011, with bigger and better viewing for the Arawa and Tarawera displays. Until then, they will be shown in other parts of the museum. And don't forget to go down into the basement and up onto the roof. This will give you a unique insight into the makeup of this stunning building, not to mention great lake and city views.

Government Gardens. (C) **07/349-4350.** Fax 07/349-2819. www.rotoruamuseum.co.nz. Admission NZ$12 adults, NZ$5.50 children, NZ$16–NZ$28 family. Summer daily 9am–8pm; winter daily 9am–5pm. Free tours daily on the hour from 10am. Rotorua Stories Cinema every 20 min. from 9am; Maori Battalion Cinema every 30 min. from 9:30am. Closed Dec 25.

Polynesian Spa ★★★ (Moments) Don't leave town without indulging in this divinely soothing experience—voted by U.K. *Condé Nast* readers as being among the top 10 thermal spas in the world in 2009. The jewel in this watery crown is the **Lake Spa** complex, with four Japanese Rotem Buro pools at different temperatures, set among rocks and waterfalls beside the lake. Add to that the **Lake Spa Retreat,** where you can lie back and have delicious things done to your body in the name of stress release and relaxation. (Try the mud body wrap, and you'll be happier than a pig in mud.) This is the upmarket area of the complex: You get extra service, a private bar, and a lounge—it's well worth the cost. The **Family Spa** is another top addition. It has a warm freshwater pool with a toddlers' pool and a mini water slide; adults can enjoy two adjacent hot mineral pools while they supervise the brood. The complex has 27 bathing pools in total, including 13 beautiful new private pools, refurbished in 2007. Ask for one of the four private lake-view pools and lie back and savor the magic.

Adults have the use of a large hot mineral pool, plus the three adjacent Priest Spa acidic pools, famous for their curative effects on ailments such as arthritis and rheumatism. The water in these pools comes from acidic springs, and the temperature varies from 102°F to 108°F (39°C–42°C). The water in all other pools is quite different. It's soft alkaline water, which flows from a boiling spring 100m (330 ft.) from the complex and is cooled by the addition of the town's water. The Polynesian Spa is incredibly popular, so you'll seldom be alone unless you opt for a private pool or Luxury Spa experience, but it's worth it nonetheless—especially if you have aching muscles.

Government Gardens, lakefront end of Hinemoa St. © **0508/765-977** in NZ, or 07/348-1328. Fax 07/348-9486. www.polynesianspa.co.nz. Admission adults-only pool and Priest Spa NZ$20; Lake Spa NZ$40 adults, NZ$15 children 5–14; Family Spa bathing NZ$13 adults, NZ$6 children, NZ$32 family; private pools NZ$20 adults, NZ$6 children 5–14, NZ$25 deluxe lake view. Spa therapies NZ$80 for 30 min., NZ$140 for 1 hr. AE, MC, V. Daily 8am–11pm.

Te Puia ★★★   Te Puia encompasses the Geothermal Valley, the Maori Cultural Experience, and the New Zealand Maori Arts & Crafts Institute; and after a NZ$20-million revamp, it is now Rotorua's top attraction in my opinion. It boasts two excellent interactive galleries (no photographs allowed) and both the weaving and carvings schools have swanky new premises where you can watch artworks evolve. The highlight of the thermal reserve is definitely the effusive **Pohutu Geyser.** It usually erupts 10 to 25 times a day to a height of 16 to 20m (53–66 ft.). This steamy little valley is also known for its mud pools, which average 194°F to 203°F (90°C–95°C). The 1½-hour guided tour is a good option, allowing you a chance to learn about the culture and the thermal activity. It includes a look through a replica of a Maori village (as opposed to the real living Maori village of nearby Whakarewarewa), and the New Zealand Maori Arts & Crafts Institute, established in 1963 to foster traditional Maori carving and weaving skills. If this is your first experience with Maori culture, I'd spend about 2 to 3 hours here minimum—if only to get value from the rather exorbitant entry fee—and see one of the live performances as well—either the midday concert or the evening Te Po performance, which includes a full *hangi* (earth oven) meal. And make sure you allow time to look through the excellent gift shop.

Hemo Rd. © **0800/837-842** in NZ, or 07/348-9047. Fax 07/348-9045. www.tepuia.com. Admission NZ$42 adults, NZ$21 children 5–15. Cultural performance NZ$11; Te Po performance NZ$99 adults, NZ$50 children 5–15. AE, MC, V. Daily 8am–6pm (winter until 5pm). Guided tours hourly 9am–5pm. 3 Maori concerts daily at 10:15am, 12:15pm, and 3:15pm.

In & Around Nearby Ngongotaha

Skyline Skyrides ★ (Kids)   Skyline Skyrides is one of the most popular Rotorua attractions, and for the panoramic views from Mount Ngongotaha alone, the ride up is definitely worth it. Entertain the whole family with crazy ways to descend—the regular scenic luge, intermediate and advanced luge tracks, or the chairlift. The scenic track has viewing bays so you can stop and take photographs of the terrific views. The Sky Swing is also based here. It hoists three passengers to over 36m (120 ft.) before swinging them out over Mount Ngongotaha at speeds up to 140kmph (90 mph). A restaurant (with an excellent buffet) and cafe provide for the peckish.

Fairy Springs Rd. © **07/347-0027.** Fax 07/348-2163. www.skylineskyrides.co.nz. Gondola NZ$24 adults, NZ$12 children 5–14; luge ride NZ$9. Packages available for gondola plus multiple luge rides. Daily 9am–late. 4.5km (3 miles) north of town on St. Hwy. 5.

Agrodome ★ (Kids)   Not everyone wants to come face-to-face with 19 different sheep breeds in one place at one time, but if you do, this is your chance. You can also see a shearing display and a working sheepdog demonstration, tour the 160-hectare (395-acre) farm, or find yourself something satisfyingly woolly in the souvenir shop. There's a range of adventure activities here, too—helicopters, jet-boating, bungy jumping, Swoop, Zorb, and Freefall Xtreme (see "Outdoor Pursuits," later in this chapter, for details)—plus a cafe, restaurant, and a woolen mill. You pay individually for these. All in all, it's a great one-stop show that should keep the kids happy. And don't forget to ask about the wide range of adventure packages, which provide multiple activities at a reduced rate.

Western Rd. ⓒ **0800/339-400** in NZ, or 07/357-1050. Fax 07/357-5307. www.agrodome.co.nz. Admission to Agrodome show NZ$25 adults, NZ$13 children 5–15; Agrodome show and farm tour combo NZ$48 adults, NZ$24 children 5–15, NZ$105 families. AE, MC, V. Daily 8:30am–5pm. Shows daily 9:30am, 11am, and 2:30pm.

Paradise Valley Springs ★ (Kids) From sheep to trout in a few easy minutes, and an unexpected bonus: lions! This very pretty place has delightful bush walks through a wildlife sanctuary, trout-filled streams, and a wetlands area. There is also an underwater viewing cave and a spawning stream where you can hand-feed the trout. When there are suitably sized lion cubs in-house, you can pet them—something the kids will love. Even the farmyard animals here have a look of happy contentment that probably comes from living in such idyllic surrounds. The bush walk is bigger and better than that at Rainbow Springs (below) and you have a lovely country drive on the way out.

467 Paradise Valley Rd. ⓒ **07/348-9667.** Fax 07/349-3359. www.paradisevalleysprings.co.nz. Admission NZ$27 adults, NZ$14 children 5–15, family pass NZ$70. AE, MC, V. Daily 8am–dark (last ticket sales 5pm). Lion feeding daily 2:30pm; cub petting 10:30am–5pm.

Rainbow Springs Kiwi Wildlife Park & Kiwi Encounter ★★ (Kids) As at Paradise Valley Springs (above), you'll find water teeming with trout. But instead of lions, you'll get kiwi and tuatara. Both the springs and the farm across the road have shops filled to brimming with sheepskin products and souvenirs. Kiwi Encounter is unique in that it presents "conservation in action"—the raising of kiwi chicks from eggs for release into the wild. It's the only purpose-built Operation Nest Egg Project open to the public. The excellent tour will give you a terrific insight into these rare birds and how they are being saved from extinction. Watching a kiwi hatch on video is a special experience.

Fairy Springs Rd. ⓒ **0800/724-626** in NZ, or 07/350-0440. Fax 07/350-0441. www.rainbowsprings.co.nz and www.kiwiencounter.co.nz. Admission NZ$26 adults, NZ$15 children 5–15; Kiwi Encounter tour NZ$29 adults, NZ$19 children 5–15; combo NZ$46 adults, NZ$26 children 5–15. AE, MC, V. Daily 8am–10pm (9pm in winter). Shows daily 10:30am, 11:45am, 1pm, 2:30pm, and 4pm. Guided springs tours 11:45am and 1pm. Ask about their night tours.

Just Outside Rotorua

Buried Village of Te Wairoa ★ (Overrated) The Buried Village has an excellent little museum that details the eruption of Mount Tarawera and its aftermath. It displays many of the objects unearthed after the Mount Tarawera eruption buried the small village of Te Wairoa in 1886. A meandering pathway set among trees and meadows by the Te Wairoa Stream connects the Buried Village's excavated dwellings. You'll see remains of a flour mill, Maori whare (house), stores, the Rotomahana Hotel, and more. Thirty-minute guided tours (included in the admission price) begin at various times. If you're fit and agile, make sure you include the steep path to view the pretty waterfall—to my mind it's the best thing about the place. It's certainly a pretty spot with an interesting story, but I can't help feeling it's a little overpriced for what you get.

Tarawera Rd., RD5. ⓒ/fax **07/362-8287.** www.buriedvillage.co.nz. Admission from NZ$30 adults, NZ$8 children 6–15, NZ$68 families. AE, MC, V. Daily 9am–5pm (winter until 4:30pm). Closed Dec 25. 15 min. from the city on a scenic drive past the Blue and Green lakes.

Maori Cultural Experiences

It's easy to be completely confused by the number of Maori cultural experiences available in Rotorua. Basically, they all offer a *hangi* (earth oven feast) and a song-and-dance performance, and they're all similarly priced. The hangi is the traditional Maori method of cooking. A large pit is filled by a wood fire topped by stones; when the stones are heated through, baskets of food are placed on top and covered with damp cloths. Earth is then shoveled over to create a natural oven. After about 3 hours, dinner is unveiled, with intermingling flavors of various foods lightly touched by wood smoke. Not all hangi are this authentic—many hotel hangi are now steamed for health and safety requirements.

The prize for the best concert and hangi is a tossup between three leading players, **Tamaki Maori Village** (see below), **Te Puia** (see above), or at **Mitai Village** ★★★, 196 Fairy Springs Rd., Rotorua (℃ **07/343-9132;** www.mitai.co.nz), which is open daily with a concert and hangi performance from 6:30 to 9:45pm (NZ$99 per person). The Tamaki evening has become more commercial and has lost a little of its shine, but it gives a good rundown of Maori history and is in a re-created village out of town. Mitai scores big with its stunning arrival by *waka* (war canoe) and guests get taken into the bush to see glowworms afterward. It's a more authentic performance and the food is better. Both will get you home around 10:30 or 11pm. A singalong in the homeward bound Tamaki bus may better suit a younger crowd.

Te Po ★★★ at Te Puia is also a terrific performance with smaller numbers and it will have you home by around 8:30pm. If you choose to do their combo, you are picked up at 4:30pm and do the last guided walk of the Whakarewarewa Thermal Valley before the cultural event and hangi. Their hangi food—which includes mussels, shrimps, and their famous steam pudding—wins hands down.

All the major hotels have nightly hangi and concerts. Of these, the **Royal Lakeside Novotel,** Tutanekai Street (℃ **0508/446-244** or 07/346-3888; www.novotel.co.nz), is one of the best and cheapest. The show presents a good balance between old and new. The steamed hangi (not as smoky or tasty as the earth-cooked version) is beautifully presented and has lots of extras. While you eat, a contemporary Maori guitarist performs and traces the development of Maori tourism. Although you don't get the feel of a marae here, a strong and consistently good performance group sings in several languages. It runs from 6:30 to 9pm. Most of the hotel hangi and performance experiences are priced from NZ$75 to NZ$100 per person.

A visit to **Whakarewarewa Thermal Village** ★★, 17 Tyron St., Rotorua (℃ **07/349-3463;** www.whakarewarewa.com), will give you insight into the workings of a modern, real-life Maori village set among geothermal activity. It may be a little overrated in terms of actual geothermal activity, but this is the only place in New Zealand—perhaps in the world—where people continue the 300-year-old tradition of using natural geothermal energy as part of their everyday cooking and washing practices. You can also see Pohutu Geyser from here for half the price you pay to see it at Te Puia; and in the summer it's fun to watch the kids diving for coins in the river below the bridge. It's open daily from 8:30am to 5pm, with guided tours between 9am and 4pm and cultural performances with hangi (NZ$60) daily at 11:15am and 2pm. Admission is NZ$28 adults, NZ$13 children, NZ$69 family.

Keep in mind that Maori land claims currently under negotiation may see the adjacent government-owned Te Puia land returned to the Ngati Wahiao people of Whakarewarewa in coming years. This is unlikely to impact on your visitor experience, but we'll keep you posted.

You can make your own way to **Ohinemutu Maori Village** ★, on Rotorua's lakefront. Follow the lake road past the Royal Lakeside Novotel, and just by the first little group of shops, turn onto Houkotuku Street. Turn right onto Ariariterangi Street and drive to the historic Tamatekapua meetinghouse, cemetery, and the very beautiful St. Faith's Church.

Bubble, Bubble, Toil & Trouble: The Geothermal Attractions

When you enter this region, you quickly realize there's something hard at work under your feet. Steam rises out of gutters and along roadsides, and you can never be entirely sure where the next hiss and roar will come from. Volcanic and geothermal activity has always played a major role in the landscape here, so be sure to experience it for yourself. The visitor center has information on shuttle services to the main geothermal areas. These usually cost NZ$25 to NZ$45; in some cases, prices include admission to the chosen area.

Twenty minutes south of Rotorua, you'll find **Waimangu Volcanic Valley** ★★ (② 07/366-6137; www.waimangu.com). Created on June 10, 1886, by Mount Tarawera's impressive blowout, Waimangu is the only hydro-thermal system in the world wholly formed in historic times as a result of a volcanic eruption. Today, you can walk through the valley and look at the many features, the best of which fall during the first 45 minutes of the 1¹/₂-hour walk. These include **Frying Pan Lake,** the world's largest hot-water spring, and the impossibly turquoise **Inferno Crater** ★★—a mysterious lake where the level rises and falls on a regular 38-day cycle. The valley is open daily from 8:30am to 5pm. The walk costs NZ$35 for adults, NZ$13 for children ages 6 to 16, and NZ$83 for a family. You can get a package that includes a boat cruise, a total of 3 hours. If you include the 2-hour hiking trail you'll see more craters, but make sure you're fit as the trail takes you up and over a mountain.

Personally, I'd do just the first 45 minutes of the above walk, skip the boat cruise altogether, and head 10 minutes farther south to **Waiotapu Thermal Wonderland** ★★★ (② 07/366-6333; www.waiotapu.co.nz). Waiotapu is a much more intensive and colorful geothermal exhibition. It's open daily from 8:30am to 5pm (last admission 3:45pm), and you'll want to allow 1 to 1¹/₂ hours. You can go it alone or with a guided tour, and once again, the bulk of the best attractions are within the shorter (30- to 40-min.) walk. The best features here are the reliable **Lady Knox Geyser** ★★, which performs around 10:15am daily. It's in a separate park nearby, but you get in on the same ticket price. If you want to see the geyser, I strongly advise you to acquire tickets no later than 9:45am in peak season. My favorite highlights are the spectacular **Champagne Pool** ★★★; New Zealand's largest bubbling **mud pool;** and the vivid green **Devil's Bath.** Admission is NZ$30 for adults, NZ$10 for children 5 to 15, and NZ$75 for families. Just prior to arriving at Waiotapu, look out for the signpost to the mud pool—it's big and it's free.

(Always ask permission before entering, and please respect the fact that photographs are not allowed inside the church.) You'll see tons of natural thermal activity in the area, much of it steaming up in people's gardens. Be warned that the streets are extremely narrow—drive slowly because kids often play in the streets here. Also look out for **Ohine-mutu Maori Handcrafts,** just past the church on Mataiawhea Street (② 07/350-3378). It's open daily 8am to 6:30pm in summer and from 9am to 5pm in winter. If you'd like

Forty-five minutes south of Rotorua, you'll find the **Orakei Korako Cave & Thermal Park** ★★ (② 07/378-3131; www.orakeikorako.co.nz), a pocket wonderland of geysers, hot springs, boiling mud, and the majestic Aladdin's Cave on the shores of Lake Ohakuri. This little valley of incredible beauty is preserved by its isolation and inaccessibility—it can be reached only by boat (no extra charge). Boats don't run on a timetable; you can cross at any time. You might want to save this for the journey south—Taupo is just 25 minutes away. Allow at least an hour for a good look around. As in any geothermal area, stay on the formed pathways to avoid danger. The resort is open daily from 8am to 4:30pm. Admission is NZ$34 for adults, NZ$14 for children under 16, and NZ$86 for families. To get there, turn off on State Highway 5, just after Golden Springs at Mihi Bridge.

Hell's Gate & Wai Ora Spa ★★ (② 07/345-3151; www.hellsgate.co.nz) is 15km (9¹/₃ miles) northeast of Rotorua on State Highway 30 to Whakatane. This Maori-owned reserve is steeped in culture, and its 8 hectares (20 acres) of thermal activity are different every day—and magnificent in the rain. Reputedly the fiercest of the thermal valleys, it features hot-water lakes, sulfur formations, Rotorua's only mud volcano, and the largest boiling whirlpool in New Zealand. It also offers a range of spa experiences, including massage and semi-private outdoor mud baths. Don't forget to ask about cheaper combo packages. The thermal walk is pretty but not as spectacular as Waiotapu's, and while the soak in thermal mud is sensual, it's a little uninspired and the mud is hard to wash out of your swimsuit. It's open daily from 8:30am to 8:30pm (closed Dec 25). Admission is NZ$35 for adults, NZ$20 for children under 16, and NZ$80 for families—you pay extra for the spa experiences. Personally, I think you get a better mud experience at the Mud Room at **Spa at QE** ★, Whakaue Street, Rotorua (② 07/348-0189; www.qehealth.co.nz), which is open Monday to Friday 8am to 10pm and weekends from 9am to 10pm. It costs NZ$50 to NZ$75 and you'll sleep well after it.

If you want to get a glimpse of geothermal action in the city free of charge, head for **Kuirau Park,** off Pukuatua and Ranolf streets. This is the site of the huge eruption in 2000, and you can still see the dead trees and white ash in the cordoned-off area. There are steaming vents everywhere, and it is vital that you stay on formed pathways. Stay out of the park at night.

a deeper insight into the village, take a 1½-hour tour with **Mitere** (② **0508/648-373;** miteretours@gmail.com). They host tours every 2 hours from 9am to 3pm, and bookings are essential.

If learning the traditional Maori *haka* (war dance) appeals, visit **Haka World,** Kiwi Paka, 60 Tarewa Rd. (② **07/347-1717;** www.hakaworld.com), and let Tiki Edwards put you through the paces for NZ$30. He runs two sessions—9 to 11am and 1 to 3pm.

Tamaki Maori Village & The Chronicles of Uitara—Journey of Ages ★★

This family company has taken numerous honors in the New Zealand Tourism Awards. The re-created, presettlement Maori village, 20 minutes from the city, presents tribal life as it used to be. Carving, weaving, *moko* (tattooing), singing, dancing, chanting, and cooking are all part of the living-village experience. At night, you can enjoy one of the best Maori performances and genuine hangi meals in Rotorua. The Chronicles of Uitara, in Rotorua itself, is a blend of guided tour, character theater, and storytelling on a series of indoor sets. You get to experience the lifestyle and warrior traditions of pre-European times, as well as the story of Uitara IV's campaign for a place within a rebel warrior cult, destined to change Aotearoa forever. It is an ideal scene setter or follow-up to the village experience, and this is where the evening tours begin. The Tamaki operation is now very large and commercial, which may not appeal to some, but they're still very professional; and if you miss them in Rotorua, you can visit Tamaki Heritage Village in Christchurch, which opened in 2007 and features a different part of the early Maori story.

1220 Hinemaru St. © **0508/826-254** in NZ, or 07/349-2999. Fax 07/347-2913. www.globalstorytellers. com. Hangi and concert NZ$105 adults, NZ$60 children 5–15; NZ$300 family pass. Prices include evening pickup from your hotel. Combo deals. V. Daily 5:30pm. Closed Dec 25. The village is on St. Hwy. 5, 20 min. north of Taupo.

ORGANIZED TOURS

You'll find heaps of brochures for half- and full-day tours at the visitor center. Most of the tours take in the main geothermal attractions and are similarly priced.

One of the best tours is **Destination Tarawera** ★★★, which begins with a pickup from your lodging by **Mt. Tarawera New Zealand Ltd.** (© **07/349-3714;** www. mt-tarawera.co.nz). You'll either be driven or helicoptered up Mount Tarawera via Kaingaroa Forest and take a guided walk through and around the craters. If you choose the helicopter option, you'll be whisked off the mountaintop to fly over nine craters and follow the 15km (9⅓-mile) path of the 1886 eruption to Waimangu Volcanic Valley. You return to Rotorua (landing at Te Puia) via the volcanic crater lakes. It's about 4 amazing hours altogether, and costs NZ$455 per person for the helicopter option for a minimum of two passengers.

Walking Legends Guided Walks (© **07/308-0292;** www.walkinglegends.co.nz) operates fully guided 4-day treks from Rotorua, in the **Lake Waikaremoana Track** ★★ in Te Urewera National Park, 150km (93 miles) southeast of Rotorua. It has its own launch to transport passengers and luggage to and from the start and finish of the track. You'll get into real outback country with this one; the 4-day experience costs NZ$1,190 adults and NZ$990 children 12 and under. Moderate fitness is required.

OUTDOOR PURSUITS

Rotorua is teeming with fast-paced opportunity, and everything is within easy reach. Ten minutes in one direction and you get jet-boating, Zorbing (see below), luging, bungy jumping, four-wheel-drive safaris, off-roading, and horseback riding; just 20 minutes from Rotorua on the Tauranga Highway, you can raft the highest Grade V waterfall in the Southern Hemisphere, leap in a jet boat, or go mountain biking, walking, or off-roading.

BUNGY JUMPING At **Rotorua Bungy and Swoop,** Agrodome (© **07/357-4747;** www.rotoruabungy.co.nz), you can leap from a 43m (141-ft.) tower; and just when you thought things couldn't get any more insane, they go and invent New Zealand's first **Swoop.** You'll be strapped into a hang-gliding harness with two others and lifted 40m

(Tips) **Get Out on the Water**

The *Lakeland Queen,* Lakefront ((**C** **07/348-0265;** www.lakelandqueen.com), underwent a major makeover in 2006 and emerged 10m (33 ft.) longer and able to carry 300 guests. You can take a breakfast, lunch, or dinner cruise, or a 1-hour afternoon tea cruise (2:30pm). Breakfast cruises (NZ$38 for adults, NZ$19 for children ages 5–12) depart at 7 and 8am; the 1-hour luncheon buffet cruise (NZ$46 for adults, NZ$24 for children ages 5–12) departs at 12:30pm. The 3-hour dinner cruise, departing 7pm, includes a four-course menu and costs NZ$70 for adults, NZ$36 for children ages 5 to 12. *Note:* The *Lakeland Queen* does not land on Mokoia Island, the lake's sanctuary for endangered native birds. If you'd like to explore Mokoia Island, contact **Mokoia Island WaiOra Experiences** ★★, Rotorua Lakefront ((**C** **07/345-7456;** www.mokoiaisland.co.nz). They offer a number of excellent tours from a Maori perspective, including their Ultimate Island Experience—a 3-hour guided tour that includes a fast catamaran ride, a traditional Maori welcome, an exploration of the island's flora and fauna, a soak in a hot pool, plus tastes of indigenous foods. This costs NZ$120 for adults and NZ$60 for children. This is a great place to go if you're interested in conservation and bird life.

(131 ft.) in the air. Pull the rip cord and experience the feeling of flying at 130kmph (81 mph) with a G-force factor of 3. For NZ$120 you can do the bungy plus either the Swoop, the Agrojet (jet-boating), or the Freefall Extreme (sky diving). The bungy alone is NZ$90.

FISHING   Within minutes of the city, you can be in the thick of some of the best wild trout fishing in the country. Lakes Tarawera, Okataina, and Rotoiti offer the best chance of catching a trophy fish. They're open for fishing from October to the end of June and hold both wild and stocked trout. The greatest trout population per acre is in Lake Rotorua, where wild fighting rainbow trout average 2 to 4 pounds and brown trout 5 to 7 pounds. Make sure you get your Rotorua fishing license before you start.

Bryan Colman Trout Fishing ★★, 32 Kiwi St., Rotorua ((**C** **07/348-7766;** www. troutfishingrotorua.com), is run by a top guide—the longest-serving in Rotorua—who offers light tackle trolling and fly- and spin fishing for rainbow trout for NZ$120 per hour, minimum 2 hours (this can be shared by four people). A fishing license is NZ$25 per person.

FLIGHTSEEING   **Volcanic Air Safaris,** Memorial Drive ((**C** **0800/800-848** in NZ, or 07/348-9984; www.volcanicair.co.nz), has a range of helicopter and floatplane tours, from an 8-minute floatplane or helicopter spin over the city (NZ$75) to 3-hour volcanic tours all the way out to **White Island** ★★ in the Bay of Plenty (NZ$745 per person by helicopter, NZ$495 by floatplane). A tour of Orakei Korako Hidden Valley with a landing, by helicopter or floatplane, is a popular choice for NZ$415.

FOUR-WHEEL-DRIVE ADVENTURES   Test your nerve at **Off Road NZ** ★★, 193 Amoore Rd. ((**C** **07/332-5748;** www.offroadnz.co.nz), 20 minutes north of the city off State Highway 5. The four-wheel-drive bush safari departs daily, every hour from 9am to 5pm, and costs NZ$90 for adults and NZ$15 for children up to 16. You'll find yourself in tunnels, waterfalls, mud, and more mud. Otherwise, try out the Monster 4×4 Thrill Ride designed to test the best at NZ$40 per driver.

GOLF The Arikikapakapa course at the **Rotorua Golf Club,** 399 Fenton St. (© 07/ 348-4051; www.rotoruagolfclub.co.nz), is a gently undulating, all-weather course with an international reputation. Greens fees are NZ$70 for international visitors, and club hire is NZ$30. **Government Gardens Golf,** Government Gardens (© 07/348-9126; www.governmentgardensgolf.co.nz), has a 21-bay driving range, is open daily from 7am to 8:30pm, and costs NZ$30 for 18 holes.

HORSEBACK RIDING The **Farmhouse,** 55 Sunnex Rd. (© 07/332-3771; www. thefarmhouse.co.nz), is the largest horse-trekking facility in New Zealand, with over 100 horses for all ages and abilities. It's a working farm and homestay as well, and all gear is provided. It's open daily 9am to 7pm in summer (4pm in winter), and riding starts at NZ$40 per person.

JET-BOATING You can spin out on the **Agrojet** at Agrodome (© 07/357-2929; www.agrojet.co.nz) on a special man-made watercourse that will see you reach speeds of 100kmph (62 mph) in 4.5 seconds. Or leap aboard **Longridge Jet,** which is based much farther out, south of Te Puke on State Highway 3 (© 0800/867-386 in NZ, or 07/533-1515; www.funpark.co.nz). If you opt for the Agrojet experience, don't forget to check out the Agrodome combo packages. A single Agrojet ride is very good value at NZ$45.

KAYAKING Take it easy on Rotorua's lovely lakes with **Adventure Kayaking** (© 07/ 348-9451; www.adventurekayaking.co.nz). Half-day paddles with a thermal pool swim cost NZ$80; full-day tours are NZ$110; and individual kayak hire goes for NZ$45 per seat per day.

LUGING See the "Exploring Rotorua" section, earlier in this chapter, for information about the endlessly popular **Skyline Skyrides luge** ★★ (© 07/347-0027; fax 07/348-2163).

MOUNTAIN BIKING Rotorua is a mecca for mountain bikers. You'll find out everything you need to know at www.riderotorua.com, which details all the latest trail updates, maps, and activities. Go it alone on rented bikes from **Kiwi Bikes,** 1128 Hinemoa St. (© 07/348-2929; www.kiwibikes.co.nz), and head for the trails at Redwoods Forest, Whakarewarewa. You'll pay NZ$45 for a half-day, NZ$60 for a full day. Or team up with the crew at **Planet Bike** ★★, Whakarewarewa Forest (© 07/346-1717; www.planetbike.co.nz), which caters to all levels. Prices start at NZ$35 per person for 2 hours. Half-day tours and full-day adventure combos are available.

SKY DIVING Leap out over Rotorua at around 2,850m (9,348 ft.) with **NZONE–The Ultimate Jump** (© 0800/376-796; www.nzone.biz). Be prepared to drop around NZ$299. Courtesy transport from the city is provided.

WALKING Apart from numerous strolls around the various lakes, the **Whakarewarewa Forest** ★★★ has six well-marked walking tracks for all ages and levels of fitness. You can spend half an hour or a whole day making your way through the forest. The beautiful **Redwood Memorial Grove Track** ★★★ is the most popular. It meanders through giant 60m (200-ft.) California coastal redwoods and takes 30 minutes from the forest visitor center on Long Mile Road. Also popular is the **Motutara Walkway** ★★, which wanders around the lakefront to Sulphur Bay. The 1½-hour walk passes through unusual "moonscape" outcrops of sulfur along the way. **Lake Okareka Walkway** ★★, located 12km (7 miles) southeast of Rotorua, is a pretty walk that takes you 2.5km (about 1½ miles) around the lake shore. The return walk takes around 1½ hours and **229** you'll see plenty of bird life. The walkway and composting toilets (at Silver Beach) are stroller and wheelchair accessible.

Whirinaki Rainforest Guided Walks ★★★, Whirinaki Forest (✆ **0800/869-255** in NZ, or 07/377-2363; www.rainforest-treks.co.nz), offers 1- to 3-day fully catered treks led by professional Maori guides, starting at Rotorua or Taupo. You'll pay NZ$165 for a 1-day ecocultural walk; NZ$355 for a 1-day privately guided walk; or NZ$755 for the 3-day Rainforest Trek.

WHITE-WATER RAFTING If you want world-rated championship rafting guides, head for **Kaituna Cascades Raft & Kayak Expeditions,** Trout Pool Road, Okere Falls, Rotorua (✆ **07/345-4199;** www.kaitunacascades.co.nz). It'll give you the best time you've ever had, including a 7m (23-ft.) drop over the Southern Hemisphere's highest commercially rafted waterfall. The company operates on the Kaituna, Rangitaiki, and Wairoa rivers. Prices range from NZ$82, depending on the river. **River Rats Raft & Kayak** (✆ **0800/333-900** in NZ, or 07/345-6543; www.riverrats.co.nz) is another excellent company. It operates on the above rivers, plus the Tongariro, with trips priced from NZ$90.

ZORBING Where else can you find yourself inside a giant plastic bubble, with the option of being wet or dry as you roll 250m (820 ft.) down a steep, slippery slope? It's like nothing you've ever done before. A wet or dry ride costs from NZ$49. Ask about combo deals. The **Zorb™** is at Agrodome, Western Road, Ngongotaha (✆ **0800/227-474** in NZ, or 07/357-5100; www.zorb.co.nz), and it's great fun to watch even if you don't want to participate.

WHERE TO STAY

There are at least 14,000 visitor beds in Rotorua, so you shouldn't have any trouble finding one to suit you. Hotels and motels abound—Fenton Street is a veritable motel mile—and many motels in Rotorua provide private heated Jacuzzis in each unit. Be warned, though: These are not all thermal pools. New motel complexes are not allowed to draw off the city's geothermal reserves, so check first if you want a thermal pool. If you're interested in a personalized hospitality experience, pick up the *Rotorua Farm and Homestay* brochure at the visitor center.

Rates below include 12.5% GST and parking.

Very Expensive

Kawaha Point Lodge ★, 171 Kawaha Point Rd. (✆ **07/346-3602;** fax 07/346-3671; www.kawahalodge.co.nz), has eight serene lakeside rooms that have become increasingly pricey (NZ$1,212–NZ$1,430). They are lovely, but even their B&B price (NZ$880–NZ$1,210) seems a little exorbitant. I think you get better value at **Solitaire Lodge** ★★, Lake Tarawera (✆ **07/362-8208;** fax 07/362-8445; www.solitairelodge.com), which has nine rooms in an unbeatable tranquil location 20 minutes out of the city. They're priced from NZ$1,650 to NZ$1,870, but you get bigger rooms and more facilities than at Kawaha Point.

Peppers on the Point ★★ (Finds) Opened in 2004, this grand 1930s home has been remodeled into a stylish nine-suite lodge with fabulous lake views plus a modern four-bedroom villa. Set on 2 hectares (5 acres), it has retained a character-filled charm and elegance that surpasses others in the Kawaha Point area. The main suite is one of the best bedrooms in Rotorua, complete with huge deck and large bathroom. All suites here are

ROTORUA, TAUPO & TONGARIRO NATIONAL PARK

9

ROTORUA

large and unlike many, the lodge is family friendly. The cottages are my favorite hideouts. Like the villa, they are for single-party bookings only. They even have a small chapel on-site, and the property is a member of the Rotorua Sustainable Charter.

214 Kawaha Point Rd., Rotorua. © **07/348-4868.** Fax 07/348-1868. www.peppers.co.nz. 9 units (including 2 cottages), 1 4-bedroom villa. NZ$1,643 premier suite; NZ$1,406 lodge and cottage suite; NZ$2,813 villa. Long-stay, off-peak, and special deals. Rates include breakfast, predinner drinks and canapés, and dinner. AE, DC, MC, V. Take St. Hwy. 5 from Central City; after 5 min., turn right onto Kawaha Point Rd., just before Skyline Skyrides. Turn left at shops, then take 1st right. **Amenities:** In-house chef, bar, and wine cellar; babysitting; concierge; 3 nearby golf courses; small gym; 3 Jacuzzis in lake cottages and villa; room service; sauna; outdoor tennis court; Wi-Fi in main lodge building. *In room:* A/C, TV/DVD, fridge, hair dryer, Internet.

Treetops Lodge & Estate ★★★   The sublime Treetops Lodge is unique among New Zealand's first-rate lodges. It's Rotorua's top stay and one of my favorites. It's perfect for nature lovers and those who appreciate the finer things in life, and the lodge has a proactive stance when it comes to conservation and sustainability. Set on 1,000 hectares (2,470 acres) of wilderness game reserve, which includes an 800-year-old forest, and surrounded by 24,300 hectares (60,000 acres) of Department of Conservation land, Treetops opened in January 2000, a half-hour outside Rotorua. It is a true sanctuary that specializes in big-game hunting, as well as a peaceful retreat, but you don't have to do either. It's all about world-class luxury. Once nestled into your big, stylish suite, savoring the valley or lake vistas, you'll think you're in paradise. Every suite is appointed with top-quality furnishings in the best of taste. Rooms and huge bathrooms are exquisite in every detail. Guests in lodge suites have exclusive use of a kitchen; villas have kitchenettes.

351 Kearoa Rd., RD1, Horohoro. © **07/333-2066.** Fax 07/333-2065. www.treetops.co.nz. 12 units. NZ$1,666 lodge suite; NZ$2,454 villa. NZ$6,664 exclusive use of owner's retreat for up to 8 guests. Extra person NZ$478. Rates include breakfast, predinner cocktails, dinner, selected lodge activities, and airport transport. Long-stay rates and special deals. AE, DC, MC, V. 30 min. from Central City. **Amenities:** Bar; babysitting; bike rentals; concierge; nearby golf course; room service; watersports equipment rentals. *In room:* TV/DVD/VCR, fridge, hair dryer, kitchenette (villas), minibar, Wi-Fi.

Expensive

Novotel Lakeside ★★, lake end of Tutanekai St. (© **0800/776-677** in NZ, or 07/346-3888; fax 07/347-1888; www.accorhotels.com), is definitely one of the better Rotorua hotels, and the closest to Central City and the main restaurant beat. The lake-view superior rooms are the most popular, but parkside units are generally quieter. The eight king suites have Jacuzzis in the bathrooms, and two executive suites are split-level, with mezzanine bedrooms. Prices range from NZ$165 to NZ$575; more for the royal suite. Another good choice is **Millennium Hotel Rotorua** ★★, corner of Eruera and Hinemaru streets (© **0800/654-685** in NZ, or 07/347-1234; fax 07/348-1234; www.millennium rotorua.co.nz), which is similarly priced and perfectly located across the road from the internationally acclaimed Polynesian Spa.

Moderate

For a range of very smart lodgings, check out **Jack & Di's Lakeview Accommodation** ★, 5 Arnold St. (© **0800/522-526** in NZ, or 07/357-4294; www.jackanddis. co.nz). The four excellent options include a charming waterfront cottage, a city penthouse apartment, a friendly lodge, and a lakefront resort. Prices range from NZ$150 to NZ$450. Another great value B&B choice is **Koura Lodge** ★★, 209 Kawaha Point Rd. (© **07/348-5868;** www.kouralodge.co.nz), which has 11 lakefront rooms (including

(Moments) Manaakitanga—Maori Hospitality

Treat yourself to a firsthand experience of contemporary Maori hospitality at two drop-dead gorgeous B&Bs run by young professional Maori couples and their families. The very classy **A-Kahu** ★★, 155 Kawaha Point Rd. (✆ **07/347-4148;** www.akahu.com), has four sumptuous en-suite bedrooms set apart from main living areas. Kiri Atkinson-Crean and her husband, Nigel, share their strong tribal links, and their modern home is filled with contemporary Maori art. It's a big-hearted, family-oriented experience that I loved. Rooms are great value at NZ$350. Across town, Oscar and Renee Nathan have established a very chic, self-contained experience at **Maruata Rotorua** ★★, 2 Kuirau St. (✆ **021/801-559;** www.explore.maori.nz), where you'll be able to connect with Maori culture at all levels—through art, music, videos, books, wine, and food. It features changing displays of contemporary Maori art (for sale), and I love the central locality (close to mud pools) and the serenity of the little cottage. It costs from NZ$325 per couple and gets cheaper the more nights you stay. They are members of the Rotorua Sustainable Charter and there is free Wi-Fi throughout.

family suites) and a classy self-contained apartment. Prices range from NZ$295 to NZ$595, and you can enjoy a lakeside Finnish sauna and open-air Jacuzzi. There's another just-out-of-town choice worth considering for its quiet, lakeside location and its terrific new day spa. **Wai Ora Lakeside Spa Resort,** 77 Robinson Ave., Holdens Bay, Rotorua (✆ **0800/345-318** in NZ, or 07/343-5100; www.waioraresort.co.nz), is 10 minutes out of the city but you get silence, a good restaurant, a lovely pool, free Internet, gorgeous day spa treatments, and the choice of 30 rooms priced from NZ$325 to NZ$495. It's a little overpriced compared to the Duxton (below), but it does have the spa facility on its side.

Duxton Hotel Rotorua ★★ (Value) If you favor the peace and quiet of an out-of-town lakeside location, then the relatively small Duxton is for you. Rooms look out to lake and garden views. Some have Jacuzzis with shutters that fold open to the bedroom, and all are roomy and nicely furnished. Just 15 minutes out of town, the Duxton is also a destination in its own right and incredibly good value for money.

366 St. Hwy. 33, Okawa Bay, Rotorua. ✆ **0800/655-555** in NZ, or 07/362-4599. Fax 07/362-4594. www. duxton.com. 44 units. NZ$199 garden room; NZ$229 lake-view room; NZ$299–NZ$399 lake-view suite. Long-stay and off-peak rates. Rates include airport transport and transport to nearby thermal springs. AE, DC, MC, V. **Amenities:** Restaurant (Grill; Contemporary NZ); bar; bike rentals; concierge; nearby golf course; gym; outdoor heated pool; room service; 2 tennis courts; kayaks, pedal boats, pontoon boat for trips to private hot pools. *In room:* TV, fridge, hair dryer, minibar, Wi-Fi.

The Springs ★★ Guests have a choice of four sumptuous rooms with king-size beds, fine linens, walk-in wardrobes, lovely en-suite bathrooms, and doors to a private terrace. Murray and Colleen Ward treat you well, and the tall hedges give this central residential property a sense of privacy. This stay is hospitality-plus.

16 Devon St., Rotorua. ✆ **07/348-9922.** Fax 07/348-9964. www.thesprings.co.nz. 4 units. NZ$385. Rate includes breakfast. Long-stay rates. DC, MC, V. Closed July–Aug. Children 14 and under not accepted. **Amenities:** Nearby golf course. *In room:* TV, hair dryer, Wi-Fi.

Wylie Court Motor Lodge, 345 Fenton St. (✆ **07/347-7879;** fax 07/346-1494; www. wyliecourt.co.nz), is my pick for a sensibly priced, fun option, especially for families. Rooms at the 20-year-old property are nothing flashy, but they're comfortable and every unit has its own thermally heated outdoor Jacuzzi; and the whole place is set amid beautiful gardens with two playgrounds. Rooms cost NZ$140 to NZ$180. Backpackers, meanwhile, have many choices in Rotorua. Two of the best are **Base Hot Rock,** 1286 Arawa St. (✆ **0800/223-363** in NZ, or 07/348-8636; fax 07/348-8616; www.hot-rock. co.nz); and **Kiwi Paka YHA,** 60 Tarewa Rd. (✆ **07/347-0931;** fax 07/346-3167; www. yha.co.nz). Kiwi Paka is much bigger than Hot Rock and it's not quite as central, but both are similarly priced with dorm beds at NZ$28 and doubles at NZ$70.

WHERE TO DINE

Not so long ago, finding even a decent cup of coffee here was a struggle. Things have improved a little, but the selection is still limited and there is a fairly flexible interpretation of the word "service." There's a growing cafe scene, much of it concentrated at the lake end of Tutanekai Street, known as "The Streat," although I've always found most of the eateries in this area overrated. Rotorua also has around 50 restaurants—everything from Turkish to Korean, Indonesian to Italian, so you'll certainly never want for inexpensive fare. For a family dining experience with great views, feast 600m (2,000 ft.) up at **Aorangi Peak Restaurant** ★, Mountain Road, Ngongotaha (✆ **07/347-0046;** www. aorangipeak.co.nz). It pays to reserve a table. And don't forget to try the traditional **Maori hangi** while you're in Rotorua (see "Maori Cultural Experiences" under "Exploring Rotorua," earlier in this chapter). Pick up the free dining guide and *The Streat* cafe brochure at the visitor center.

Expensive

Bistro 1284 ★★★ **(Finds** NEW ZEALAND/INTERNATIONAL There's a very good reason why this place has been judged Rotorua's best restaurant multiple times. A cynic might say it's because this is the best of a middling bunch, but I've always eaten very well here. My lasting memory is of the incredibly friendly and personal service, and the good reports keep coming back. It's as popular as ever as Rotorua's top choice. The food is excellent; the atmosphere simply stylish. It's definitely the most "citified" of Rotorua's restaurants, and with menu items such as smoked duck breast on porcini risotto with Kumara salad, or grilled beef filet with field mushrooms, you can be sure your taste buds will be tickled.

1284 Eruera St. ✆ **07/346-1284.** www.bistro1284.co.nz. Reservations required. Main courses NZ$33–NZ$36. AE, DC, MC, V. Tues–Sat 6pm–late.

Moderate

Abracadabra Café ★ **(Value** CAFE/LIGHT MEALS I love the mood in this colorful joint. Moroccan-themed rooms give it a pizazz other places lack, and big verandas and a beer garden are great summer options. The owners have spent time in Morocco, which is obvious in the menu choices—North African chicken kabobs, couscous salad, and star anise vegetable tangine. In addition, they have excellent baked goods and counter choices to enjoy with fair trade coffee. Or opt for late afternoon tapas with wine.

1263 Amohia St. ✆ **07/348-3883.** www.abracadabracafe.com. Main courses NZ$16–NZ$25. V. Tues–Sat 8:30am–11pm; Sun–Mon 9am–3pm.

Capers Epicurean ★★ (Value) CAFE/DELI   This modest little place has almost no   **233**
street appeal, but once you're inside it's a culinary heaven. Their cabinets bulge with a
huge array of eat-in or takeout delicacies, and an all-day menu has another good range
of choices—everything from soups, omelets, pancakes, and pastas to salads and fresh fish
and chicken dishes. It's also a terrific place for picnic goodies and gift boxes of New
Zealand food products. Good news: they're now open for dinner each night, offering
dishes like prime sirloin steak, roasted tuna loin, and lemon risotto with smoked salmon.

1181 Eruera St. ✆ **07/348-8818.** www.capers.co.nz. Dinner reservations recommended. Main courses
NZ$15–NZ$26. AE, MC, V. Daily from 7:30am; dinner 6–9pm.

Lime Caffeteria ★★★ CAFE/LIGHT MEALS   This is my favorite Rotorua haunt.
It's light, bright, and as fresh as a squeezed lime. The food is divine. You haven't lived
until you've sampled the amazing blueberry and custard brioche! But there's more to
Lime than small, tasty snacks and good coffee. It also turns out a delectable range of
lunch options, like chicken and chorizo salad; and blue brie, fig, and pine nut phyllo
parcels with green-grape salad, or Thai green curry risotto. Don't forget to buy a few
picnic treats to munch while you're out walking.

1096 Whakaue St. ✆ **07/350-2033.** Reservations recommended. Main courses NZ$18–NZ$25. MC, V.
Daily 7:30am–4:30pm.

Relish ★★ CAFE/PIZZERIA   Drop in for coffee or a light lunch, linger over one of
the delicious pizzas turned out on the wood-fired oven, or choose from the a la carte
menu. You'll be glad you indulged. Chicken teriyaki pizza gets my vote, but you might
prefer an evening meal of Middle Eastern spiced duck breast. It's a casual dining environment, ideal after a busy day of sightseeing, and possibly the best option in The Streat
zone.

1149 Tutanekai St. ✆ **07/343-9195.** Reservations required for dinner. Main courses NZ$20–NZ$30. MC,
V. Mon–Tues 7am–4pm; Wed–Sat 7am–9pm; Sun 8am–4pm.

Inexpensive

Fat Dog Café ★★ (Value) CAFE/LIGHT MEALS   This place is tops for atmosphere,
a fact that people of all ages seem to have discovered. You'll find them here draped over
old chairs and sofas—everyone from a whole herd of mountain bikers to someone who
could be your granny. Food is not only cheap, it's also incredibly tasty and, dare I say it,
healthy! There's a fabulous selection of counter food and a simple blackboard menu that
lists the old adolescent favorites such as nachos and pies. Vegetable bakes, lasagnas,
bagels, and salads can all be followed by something sweet and delicious, washed down
with the best espresso in Rotorua. A funky little dive that's all color and charming chaos.

1161 Arawa St. ✆ **07/347-7586.** Main courses NZ$12–NZ$25. AE, DC, MC, V. Daily 8am–late.

SHOPPING

Pick up the excellent *Rotorua Arts Trail* brochure from the visitor center. It gives names
and contact details of many of the city's best artists, jewelers, and craftspeople.

The best places to shop for Maori arts and crafts are **Tamaki Maori Village,** State
Highway 5 (✆ **07/346-2823**), which has one of the best displays of indigenous work in
the country; **Te Puia,** at Whakarewarewa Thermal Reserve (✆ **07/348-9047**), where
you'll find superb carvings; and the **Best of Maori Tourism,** Haupapa Street (✆ **07/347-
4226**), which has contemporary and traditional crafts and especially good weaving and
carved gourds.

Simply New Zealand, Tourism Rotorua Centre, 1161 Fenton St. (℃ **07/348-8273;** www.simplynewzealand.com), has an excellent range of New Zealand–made merino wool knitwear, delightful toiletries, and a host of souvenirs. **Rainbow Springs** and **Agrodome** (see "The Major Sights & Attractions," earlier in this chapter) have good shops for wool products. At the **Jade Factory,** 1288 Fenton St. (℃ **07/349-3968;** www. jadefactory.com), you can watch the creative process of carving jade as it happens. For contemporary New Zealand art, visit **Madhouse Store & Gallery,** 1093 Tutanekai St., across from the Royal Lakeside Novotel (℃ **07/347-6066;** www.madhousedesign.co.nz).

ROTORUA AFTER DARK

Rest assured, there is more to Rotorua's nightlife than Maori hangi and concert performances. For a start, pick up a free copy of *Thermal Air,* which will point you in the direction of some of the best places to go.

There's an Irish pub in every town, and in Rotorua that's **O'Malley's Irish Bar,** 1287 Eruera St. (℃ **07/347-6410**), which schedules live music most Friday and Saturday nights. Another good hotel nightspot is the **Mezz Bar ★,** in Rydges on Fenton Street.

Backpackers will invariably have a good night at **Base Hot Rock Lava Bar,** 1286 Arawa St. The **Pig & Whistle City Bar,** 1182 Tutanekai St. (℃ **07/347-3025**), has a boutique brewery and hearty pub-style meals, with live music on Friday and Saturday. **Fuze City Bar ★★,** Lake End, Tutanekai Street (℃ **07/349-6306**), is open from 3pm until late Tuesday through Saturday and offers a smart environment for evening drinks, tapas, and gourmet pizza.

EN ROUTE TO TAUPO

It's a short drive to Taupo, just 84km (52 miles) over excellent roads. Throughout this area, watch out for logging trucks. If you haven't already done so, this could be a good time to call at one of the three main geothermal reserves, especially the Hidden Valley Orakei Korako Geyserland Resort, which is closer to Taupo than to Rotorua. Eight kilometers (5 miles) before you reach Taupo, look for the steamy **Wairakei Geothermal Power Station,** which harnesses all that underground energy to furnish electric power.

2 TAUPO ★

287km (178 miles) SE of Auckland; 84km (52 miles) S of Rotorua; 155km (96 miles) NW of Napier

I've always found Taupo somewhat disappointing, but many New Zealanders practically worship this little lakeside town. Certainly, from a visitor's point of view, it makes a perfect central base from which to take in the area attractions. It's within half a day's drive of the Hawke's Bay wine region, the mountains and ski fields of Tongariro National Park, the thermal wonderland of Rotorua, the white-sand surf beaches of Bay of Plenty, and the glowworms of Waitomo.

Taupo itself also has its merits—the vast sparkling waters of Lake Taupo are perfect for boating, water-skiing, and fishing; there are thermal pools, plenty of accommodations, some good, fast-paced outdoor activities, and a small permanent population of 30,000, which more than doubles in summer. There are also a number of new attractions and accommodations that make it a worthy stop. Make sure you take warm clothes because if it's not midsummer you're likely to freeze.

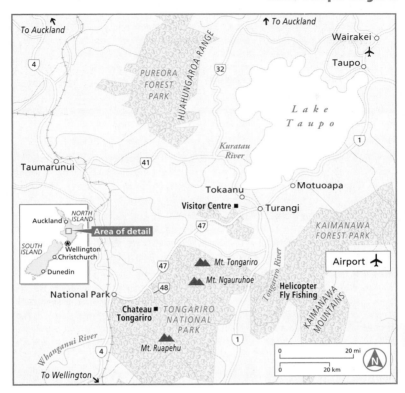

ESSENTIALS

GETTING THERE & GETTING AROUND **By Plane Air New Zealand Link** (☏ **0800/737-000**; www.airnewzealand.com) flies to Taupo from Auckland and Wellington five times a day, with connections to other destinations. In winter, **Mountain Air** (☏ **0800/922-812**; www.mountainair.co.nz) has daily flights between Auckland and Turangi airports. For a taxi or airport shuttle, call ☏ **07/378-5100.**

By Coach (Bus) **InterCity** and **Newmans** buses arrive and depart from the Taupo Travel Centre on Gasgoine Street (☏ **07/378-9032**). **Magic Travellers** and **Kiwi Experience** also serve Taupo. **Guthreys Express** (☏ **0800/759-999** in NZ, or 07/376-0027) has daily services from Taupo to Auckland, Rotorua, and National Park village, which is in Tongariro National Park. There is no local bus service but look out for the **Tongariro Taupo Hot Bus** (☏ **0508/468-287** in NZ; www.hotbus.co.nz), which provides return transport to most attractions. It departs from the i-SITE Visitor Centre on the hour every hour from 10am to 3pm daily. One attraction costs NZ$15 and you pay NZ$5 for each subsequent attraction visited. You can spend as much time as you like at each attraction.

Tips **A Word on Parking Security**

The carparks at Huka Falls Lookout, Craters of the Moon, and Spa Park are very prone to theft. Volunteers do patrol some carparks but make sure you remove all valuables from your vehicle and lock all doors. Lock other possessions in the trunk where they cannot be seen, and report anyone acting suspiciously in carparks to Taupo Police (☎ **07/378-6060**). The good news about parking in Taupo township is that it is generally free.

By Taxi   For service in and around Taupo, call **Taupo Taxis** (☎ **07/378-5100**).

By Car   State highways 1 and 5 pass through Taupo. All roads in the area are excellent, but drive with care in winter (when they're icy) and when there's a heavy flow of logging trucks. The drive to Rotorua is 1 hour; to Waitomo or Napier, 2 hours; to Hamilton or Tauranga, 2 hours; to Auckland, 4 hours; and to Wellington, 5½ hours.

By Bicycle   To rent a bike, contact **Cycle World,** 30 Spa Rd. (☎ **07/378-6117**), or **Rent-A-Bike Taupo,** 106–108 Rifle Range Rd. (☎ **07/378-7947** or 027/432-2729). Taupo is particularly geared for cyclists, with dedicated lanes, shared paths, and numerous recreational off-road rides. For more information check www.biketaupo.org.nz.

ORIENTATION   Taupo spreads along the northeastern tip of the lake, where the Waikato River, New Zealand's longest, flows out of Lake Taupo's Tapuaeharuru Bay. The main road is **Tongariro Street.** Perpendicular to that are **Heu Heu** and **Horomatangi streets,** two of several that form the main shopping area. Tongariro Street runs into **Lake Terrace,** the continuation of State Highway 1 that runs around the lake and takes you to most of the motels. The settlements of **Acacia Bay** and **Jerusalem Bay** are just across on the western shore of the lake.

VISITOR INFORMATION   The **Taupo i-SITE Visitor Centre** (☎ **07/376-0027;** www.laketauponz.com) is easy to find—it's on Tongariro Street, the main road through Taupo. It has a wide selection of brochures and can arrange fishing guides and licenses, tours, and activities. It also sells stamps, phone cards, and souvenirs. Hours are 8:30am to 5pm daily. **Experience Taupo,** 57 Tongariro St. (☎ **0800/368-775** in NZ, or 07/377-0704; www.experiencetaupo.co.nz), is another good source of information. They stay open later than the visitor center (till 7pm in summer, 6pm winter), and they can organize all your adventures in the region with no booking fees.

FAST FACTS   The **post office** is at the corner of Ruapehu and Horomatangi streets; it's open Monday through Friday from 8:30am to 5pm. Internet access is available at **CyberGate Internet Cafe,** 12 Gasgoine St. (opposite the bus station; ☎ **07/377-8118**). It's open daily 9:30am to 11pm. The first 3 minutes are free.

SPECIAL EVENTS   The last Saturday in November is the **Lake Taupo Cycle Challenge** (☎ **07/378-1546;** www.cyclechallenge.com). In October, more than 3,000 cyclists gather for the **Powerade Day-Night Thriller** (☎ **07/378-0455;** www.eventpromotions.co.nz), the largest mountain-bike event of its kind in the world. The annual **Levene Half Marathon** (☎ **07/378-1546;** www.taupohalfmarathon.org.nz) takes place in August. Check www.laketauponz.com or www.eventscapital.co.nz for a full events calendar.

Most of Taupo's interesting attractions are just north of the town in a cluster around the Wairakei Tourist Park. The visitor center has a good brochure on this area. At the top of the hill as you leave town heading north, turn right onto Huka Falls Road and stop first at the **Huka Falls Lookout** ★★★. The falls themselves aren't huge, but they are impressive for the speed at which the blue-green water of the Waikato River moves over the 24m (79-ft.) drop. You can walk alongside the gorge on a path and across the rushing water on a footbridge, which provides a safe but thrilling way to enjoy the falls. You can also walk to the falls from Taupo (see "Outdoor Pursuits," below).

After you visit the other attractions in this area, divert down Aratiatia Road on your way back into town to see the **Aratiatia Rapids.** The gates of the dam above the rapids open every day at 10am, noon, 2pm, and 4pm from October to March. In less than 10 minutes, the dry riverbed goes from an empty basin of boulders to a raging river. After about half an hour, the gates close, the released water flows downstream, and the dry bed reappears. It's fascinating to watch. The best view is about 5 minutes' walk downstream, but you can also observe from the lookout.

The **Taupo Museum,** Story Place (✆ **07/376-0414;** www.taupomuseum.co.nz), is open daily from 10:30am to 4:30pm (closed Good Friday and Dec 25). Galleries display Maori art and culture, and a wide selection of exhibits related to fishing, the timber industry, geology, and the lake. Check out the unique New Zealand garden that was a gold medal winner at England's Chelsea Flower Show in 2004. Admission is NZ$5 for adults, free for children 17 and under. They offer a free guided heritage walk on Sundays at 2pm.

Honey Hive ★ (**Kids**)   After your stop at the Huka Falls Lookout, get back on the Huka Falls Road Tourist Loop and continue to the Honey Hive. Dare I say it? The place is buzzing with activity, and you don't need to be a bee enthusiast to appreciate the astounding array of bee-related products inside. You'll see an excellent range of gifts, from cosmetics and fruit wines to chocolate bees and woolly bees. Suffice to say that this makes a pleasant change from sheep. Also on-site is the Bees Knees Café, but don't go getting too excited about that—it definitely needs a revamp. The delicious honey ice cream is worth the stop.

Huka Falls Loop Rd. ✆ **07/374-8553.** www.honeyhivetaupo.com. Free admission. Daily 9am–5pm. Closed Good Friday and Dec 25–26.

Volcanic Activity Centre ★★★ (**Value**)   The Taupo volcanic region is one of the world's largest, spanning 282km (175 miles), and this is the best place in the country to get an understanding of what's bubbling underfoot. Along with 3-D maps of the area, there are touch-screen computers, a working model of a geyser, a tornado machine, an

---

| (**Finds**)   **Hot Dip**

If you're walking the very pleasant Huka Falls Track, test out the hot stream that runs into the Waikato River at the Spa Park end of the track—but as in all geothermal pools, *don't* put your head under! Just after the start of the track, you'll cross a bridge over the stream. Access to the pool is below that. It's popular with Magic Traveller and Kiwi Experience types, so don't expect to always be alone.

(Kids) Just for Kids

Lilliput Farm, 136 Link Rd. (℃ **07/378-2114;** www.lilliput-farm-park.co.nz), is a 4-hectare (10-acre) treat for kids who like animals. They can hand-feed 20 different species and enjoy pony and donkey rides. The farm is open Monday to Friday 10am to 2pm, weekends 10am to 4pm. Admission is NZ$8 adults, NZ$5 children, NZ$22 families. Follow SH1 to Hamilton. Link Road is the first left, 4.5km (2 miles) from the Wairakei turnoff. Watch for signs.

earthquake simulator, interactive volcanoes, and fabulous short films on all aspects of volcanic and geothermal activity. Allow at least an hour for a worthwhile visit.

Huka Falls Rd. ℃ **07/374-8375.** Fax 07/374-8370. www.volcanoes.co.nz. Admission NZ$10 adults, NZ$6 children, NZ$26 families. Mon–Fri 9am–5pm; Sat–Sun 10am–4pm. Closed Good Friday, Dec 25, and till noon Apr 25.

Huka Prawn Park ★★ (Kids) This is the place to see Malaysian river prawns happily getting fat in Wairakei's geothermally heated prawn farm. Interesting 30-minute tours operate hourly between 11am and 4pm. You can feed the prawns by hand, then end your visit at the Prawn Works Bar 'n' Grill, where you can eat the ones that grew the fattest. It's a lovely setting overlooking the Waikato River. You can also jet-boat from here (see "Outdoor Pursuits," below). The restaurant has a special kids' menu and play areas; for an extra charge, you can play Killer Prawn Golf after eating.

Huka Falls Rd. ℃ **07/374-8474.** Fax 07/374-8063. www.hukaprawnpark.co.nz. Admission NZ$15 adults, NZ$8 children 14 and under, NZ$42 families. Hole-in-One Golf Challenge NZ$10 for 20 golf balls. Daily 9am–4pm. Closed Dec 25.

Wairakei Natural Thermal Valley ★★ This attraction is worth visiting if you enjoy geysers, mud pools, and other strange geothermal phenomena. Call first at the Wairakei Geothermal Visitor Centre for guided steam-field and historical tours that will give you insight into geothermal power generation. And check out **Wairakei Terraces** ★★, next to Wairakei Steamfield (℃ **07/378-0913;** www.wairakeiterraces. co.nz), where, in a mysterious steamy setting, you'll learn about Maori legends and history. They've done a good job of replicating the original Wairakei silica terraces that disappeared with the development of the geothermal power plant in the 1950s. There is also an evening concert, hangi, and a Maori village tour.

Just off St. Hwy. 1. ℃ **07/374-8004.** Fax 07/374-8656. Geothermal tours NZ$18 adults, NZ$9 children; the Terraces NZ$18 adults, NZ$9 children, NZ$55 family. Maori cultural experience NZ$85 adults, NZ$43 children. Daily 8:30am–5pm. Closed Jan 1, Good Friday, and Dec 25–26.

Soaking in Taupo Hot Springs

Set in the unique natural Onekeneke Thermal Valley, **Taupo Hot Springs Spa** ★★, behind the De Brett Thermal Resort and the Outrigger Terraces Resort, State Highway 5 (℃ **07/377-6502;** www.taupohotsprings.com), has been a favorite bathing spot for over 120 years. The water here is said to be the ultimate in providing therapeutic relief for muscular, bone, and skin ailments. Pools are filtered, drained, and cleaned every night. The pool complex is not as big, as modern, or as attractive as Rotorua's **Polynesian Spa** (p. 220), but it's definitely cheaper and feels just as good, and there is no sulfur in the water here. Facilities include 12 private pools, a children's pool, two Jacuzzis, a

> **Tips** **Fun Savings**
>
> If you plan on making the rounds of adventure activities, check out the savings that package deals represent. The visitor center and Experience Taupo (above) will point you in the direction of seasonal savings.

hydroslide, a volleyball court, *pétanque,* and a barbecue area. Admission to the public pools costs NZ$15 for adults, NZ$4 for children ages 3 to 12; NZ$5 for the giant dragon slide; barbecue hire from NZ$10. Private pools cost from NZ$18 for adults, and spa treatments range from NZ$60 to NZ$160. The complex is open daily from 7:30am to 9:30pm.

If you don't have time for a soak in Taupo, you can stop at the **Tokaanu Thermal Pools,** at the south end of Lake Taupo (see "En Route to Tongariro National Park," later in this chapter).

Cruising the Lake

Taupo is New Zealand's biggest lake, with three excellent options for heading out on the water: the replica steamboat *Ernest Kemp,* the motor launch *Cruise Cat,* and the old yacht *Barbary.* The first two follow a similar path and pass the **Maori rock carvings** ★★, which are accessible only by boat. **Ernest Kemp Cruises** (✆ 07/378-9222; adiwalker@ reap.org.nz) operates 2-hour cruises daily for NZ$40 adults, NZ$10 children ages 5 to 15. It is essential to book through the visitor center or the Taupo Boat Harbour office. Cruises run three times daily at 10:30am, 2pm, and 5pm. The **Cruise Cat Experience** (✆ 07/378-0623; www.chrisjolly.co.nz) covers a longer distance than the *Ernest Kemp* in a shorter time. The tour operates daily from 11:30am to 1pm and costs NZ$40 for adults, NZ$16 for school-age children. The *Barbary* **Carvings Cruise** (✆ 07/378-3444; www.barbary.co.nz) departs at 10:30am, 2pm, and 5pm and costs NZ$45 for adults, NZ$12 for children ages 5 to 15.

ORGANIZED TOURS

The fun way to start your visit to Taupo is by leaping aboard the double-decker bus for the **Discover Taupo Town Tour** (✆ 07/377-0774; www.taupotours.com). The 1951 vintage bus will take you on a 15-minute spin around town for NZ$4 adults, NZ$2 children 2 to 15. Tours depart on the hour and half-hour between 10am and 3pm (4pm in summer), stopping on the corner of Ferry Road and Tongariro Street, next to the playground behind the Superloo.

Paradise Tours (✆ 07/378-9955; www.paradisetours.co.nz) has a range of half-day excursions to local attractions from NZ$99 adults, NZ$40 for children 5 to 12, free for children 4 and under, plus full-day tours to Rotorua, Napier, and Waitomo. Their popular Taupo Sights tour includes a visit to the thermal wonders of Orakei Korako, Huka Falls, Honey Hive, Aratiatia Rapids, the marina, and the geothermal borefield. It's a good way to see the best of Taupo if you're short on time.

One of the best new tour options in the Taupo area is **pureORAwalks** ★★★ (✆ 021/715-947; www.pureorawalks.com), which has a range of excellent walks from 3 hours to 3 days duration in Tongariro National Park, Pureora Forest Park, and Whirinaki Forest Park. They also take guided walks over the magnificent Tongariro Alpine Crossing, and all their walks are led by local Maori guides. If you're short on time, their

Nature-Culture Walk (3–6 hr.) is a good choice. It costs NZ$84 for adults and NZ$62 for children. Their 8-hour guided hike over the Tongariro Alpine Crossing costs NZ$275 for adults and NZ$190 for children, but you need to be very fit for this excursion and *always* take lots of warm clothing, even in midsummer.

OUTDOOR PURSUITS

BIKING   Bike tours and rentals can be arranged through **Rapid Sensations,** 413 Huka Falls Rd. (🕿 **0800/353-435** in NZ, or 07/374-8117; www.rapids.co.nz). Its tours go to the Craters of the Moon thermal area, a 2½-hour ride that costs NZ$75 per person. Rentals are NZ$55 per day. In Taupo, you can also rent bikes from **Cycle World,** 30 Spa Rd. (🕿 **07/378-6117**). For more information, including tours, suppliers, and recommended cycle tracks, pick up the excellent brochure *Cycling Around Lake Taupo.*

BUNGY JUMPING   You don't even have to jump to be impressed by the scenery that surrounds the 47m (154-ft.) bungy platform cantilevered out over the Waikato River. Call **Taupo Bungy,** 202 Spa Rd. (🕿 **0800/888-408** in NZ, or 07/377-1135; www. taupobungy.com). You'll pay from NZ$109 for a solo jump or NZ$218 to go tandem. The company offers free pickup from accommodations for jumpers. The bungy operates 9am until 7pm in summer (closed Dec 25).

CLIMBING   Try something a bit different at **Rock 'n' Ropes,** State Highway 5, Wairakei (🕿 **0800/244-508** in NZ, or 07/374-8111; www.rocknropes.co.nz). If you've ever dreamed of being part of a circus act, this is your chance to polish up on rope walking, trapezing, rock climbing, and assorted other airborne fun. Courtesy transport to the site is available. Adventures here are reasonably priced from NZ$20 to NZ$65. It's open daily 10am until 5pm.

FISHING   More than 100 years have passed since the first trout fry were released into the Lake Taupo region. Today, their plump descendants are one of the main draws. It's the best of New Zealand's trout fishing. You'll need a special Taupo-issued fishing license, which can be good for a day to a full season. Remember that the minimum legal size is 45 centimeters (18 in.) and the daily limit is three. The best river fishing is during the winter spawning runs (June–Sept) but lake fishing is good all year. The visitor center can give you a list of the dozens of fishing guides in the area. Two I recommend are **Chris**

(**Moments**)   **Lakeside Hole-in-One** ★★

If it feels like your lucky day, or perhaps you've given up on Lotto, try Taupo's crazy **"Great Lake Hole-in-One" Challenge** (🕿 **07/378-8117**). It's addictive, it's fun, and, to my mind, it's impossible. The truth is, it's not. Apparently, more than 200 people have managed to make it, winning fabulous prizes, including trips to Europe, bungy jumps, and dinners. The object is to stand on the shoreline and whack a golf ball 115m (378 ft.) over the water in the hope that it will fall directly into the tiny hole in the middle of a floating pontoon. Balls cost NZ$1 each, NZ$15 for 18, and NZ$20 for 25. A red hole-in-one wins NZ$5,000; an ace-in-one of the 12-inch-wide blue-and-white holes will earn you local lodgings, attractions, products, adventure packages, or dinners. And can you believe it? There's about one winner per week! You can take a shot daily from 9am to 9pm, depending on weather conditions, with reduced hours in winter.

Jolly Outdoors (✆ **07/378-0623;** www.chrisjolly.co.nz), which is great for large groups; and **Go Fish Taupo** (✆ **07/378-9395;** www.gofishtaupo.co.nz), which offers guides for beginners and experienced fishermen alike.

FLIGHTSEEING   Scenic rides in **Taupo's Floatplane** ★★ (✆ **07/378-7500;** www. tauposfloatplane.co.nz) leave from the lakefront near Taupo Boat Harbour; they range from a 10-minute flight to a 2-hour White Island excursion for NZ$550. Ask about the 10-minute backpacker special for four people, at NZ$75 per person. **Mountain Air** ★★★ (✆ **0800/922-812** in NZ, or 07/892-2812; www.mountainair.co.nz) offers breathtaking flights over the Volcanic Plateau. Helicopter fans will love a spin with **Clark & Jolly Helicopters** ★★, Taupo Airport (✆ **0800/424-677** in NZ, or 07/377-8805; www.helinz.com), which can put a package together to suit your whims and budget, starting at a quick 10-minute buzz over Taupo for NZ$95 per adult.

FOUR-BY-FOUR BIKING   Quad bikes are all the rage, and **Taupo Quad Adventures,** 24km (15 miles) north of Taupo on State Highway 1 (✆ **07/377-6404;** www.taupo quads.co.nz), offers rides through native bush, farms, and forest trails that cost from NZ$95 to NZ$300.

GOLF   Wairakei International Golf Course ★★★, State Highway 1 (✆ **07/374-8152;** www.wairakeigolf.co.nz), is rated among the top 20 golf courses in the world outside the United States. Book well ahead; greens fees are NZ$150 for affiliated and NZ$200 for nonaffiliated members. The **Taupo Golf Club,** 32 Centennial Dr. (✆ **07/ 378-6933;** www.taupogolf.co.nz), is one of only two New Zealand clubs to have two 18-hole courses. You have the choice of the Centennial Championship Course or the Tauraha Course. Greens fees are NZ$40 for affiliated and NZ$60 for nonaffiliated members.

JET-BOATING   Two operators work two completely different areas of the Waikato River. **Hukafalls Jet** ★★★, Wairakei Tourist Park (✆ **0800/485-253** in NZ, or 07/374-8572; www.hukafallsjet.com), specializes in impressive 360-degree spins and close-ups of Huka Falls. It charges NZ$99 for adults, NZ$59 for children 15 and under for a 30-minute adventure. **Rapids Jet,** Rapids Road, Aratiatia (✆ **0800/727-437** in NZ, or 07/378-5828; www.rapidsjet.com), runs farther upstream in the fast waters of the Aratiatia Rapids; prices are NZ$95 adults, NZ$55 children 5 to 15. Riders must be 5 and older, and taller than 1m (3 ft., 4 in.).

KAYAKING   Paddle over the turquoise-blue waters of the Waikato River with **Canoe & Kayak** (✆ **0800/529-256** in NZ; www.canoeandkayak.co.nz). A 2-hour guided trip includes a soak in hot springs and costs NZ$55. For lake kayaking, call **Kayaking Kiwi** (✆ **0800/353-435** in NZ, or 07/374-8117; www.kayakingkiwi.com); it offers rock drawing and volcanic kayaking trips (around 4–5 hr.) priced from NZ$95.

SWIMMING   The completely revamped and extended **AC Baths,** top end of Spa Road (✆ **07/376-0350;** www.taupovenues.co.nz), opened in 2003. New indoor and outdoor pools, nine private pools, two hydroslides, a Jacuzzi, a sauna, and a cafe make it well worth a visit in summer, when Taupo gets fiercely hot. A rock climbing wall is a fun addition for all ages.

WALKING   The visitor center's excellent *Taupo Walkways* brochure outlines the area's 10 most popular tracks. They range from 15 minutes to 1½ hours in length. One option is the 3km (2-mile) walk from Spa Park, in Taupo, along the riverbank to Huka Falls (2 hr. round-trip). You can carry on to Aratiatia Rapids, which takes another 2 hours.

(Finds Local Treasure

For lovely forest walks and mountain-bike tracks, head for **Craters of the Moon Park,** on Poihipi Road. Head north from Taupo, cross the bridge, and at the top of the long hill turn onto the road to Kinloch (Poihipi Rd.). The park is about 5km (3 miles) farther on. Make sure you lock your car in this area.

WHITE-WATER RAFTING   The guides with **Kiwi River Safaris** (② **0800/723-8577** in NZ, or 07/377-6597; www.krs.co.nz) know their stuff. They've had a minimum of 5 years' full-time experience and are qualified swift-water rescue technicians, with first aid and CPR certification updated annually. Options include daily Grade III to IV trips on Rangitaiki River and float trips on the Waikato River. The Grade IV to V trips on Wairoa River are for serious thrill seekers and happen only 26 days a year, when the hydro waters are released. Prices start at NZ$110 per person.

WHERE TO STAY

All rates below include 12.5% GST and parking.

Very Expensive

Huka Lodge ★★★   When an upmarket lodge has been around as long and won as many awards as Huka, you might be inclined to approach it with reverence and trepidation. That would be a mistake. They're all human here, and the key to enjoying Huka is to cast aside preconceptions and simply wallow. It's hard to find fault with the 17-acre setting, the facilities, or the rooms. Guest rooms want for nothing, and the public spaces, especially the wine cellar and the Trophy Room, are divine. Once all alone in this price bracket in New Zealand, Huka faces increasing competition from new players in the field and can't afford to be complacent; yet it still has a certain something that few others can match. If you have a fat budget, opt for the sublime four-suite Owner's Cottage—it's been so popular they've added the gorgeous two-suite Alan Pye Cottage. Both provide an added level of privacy and service and have their own infinity swimming pools and Jacuzzis.

Huka Falls Rd., Taupo. ② **07/378-5791.** Fax 07/378-0427. www.hukalodge.co.nz. 19 units, 2 cottages. NZ$1,643–NZ$3,094 lodge room; NZ$2,858–NZ$5,738 lodge suite; NZ$3,443–NZ$9,450 1 double room in cottages. NZ$450 per person Christmas Day/New Year's Eve surcharge. Minimum 3-night stay Dec 22–Jan 5. Rates include breakfast, cocktails, 5-course dinner, Taupo airport transport, and use of lodge facilities. Off-peak rates. AE, DC, MC, V. From St. Hwy. 1, turn onto Huka Falls Rd. and follow signs; lodge is 300m (1,000 ft.) upstream from Huka Falls. **Amenities:** Dining room; bar and wine cellar w/biggest private collection in New Zealand (more than 30,000 bottles); babysitting; free bikes; concierge; nearby golf course; 2 Jacuzzis in cottages; outdoor heated pool; room service; all-weather tennis court. *In room:* A/C, TV/DVD, fridge, hair dryer, kitchen in 2 cottages, minibar, Wi-Fi.

Moderate

There are over 70 motels in Taupo alone, but they fill up fast on weekends and during summer holidays, so book ahead. In addition to the listings below, **Bayview Wairakei Resort** ★★, State Highway 1, Wairakei (② **07/374-8021;** www.wairakei.co.nz), is a good base; it's just 7km (4⅓ miles) out of town and in the heart of most of the attractions. The bulk of its 187 rooms go for NZ$150 to NZ$350, with some of the larger suites up to NZ$700. There are swimming pools, two restaurants, two bars, a gym, a 9-hole golf course, six Jacuzzis, and saunas at your disposal. It's a terrific spot for families (with children's programs), and an excellent value for longer stays.

Baycrest Lodge ★★ Built in 1997, Baycrest is one of Taupo's best motels. It's a first-class establishment just minutes from the town center. Upstairs units all have spacious bathrooms with Jacuzzis, plus balconies overlooking the lake; downstairs units have their own individual courtyard, each with a private thermal tub. All rooms have European fittings and lovely furnishings. The two- to three-bedroom apartment is great value for families or friends traveling together. It has two large bathrooms. Everything was refurbished in 2004.

79 Mere Rd., Taupo. © **0800/229-273** in NZ, or 07/378-3838. Fax 07/378-4007. www.baycrest.co.nz. 16 units. NZ$175 studio; NZ$225 family suite; NZ$240–NZ$400 executive suite. Long-stay rates. AE, DC, MC, V. **Amenities:** Bar; babysitting; several nearby golf courses and golf practice net; hot thermal tubs in ground-floor patios; thermally heated outdoor pool; room service. *In room:* TV, fridge, hair dryer, kitchenette, free Wi-Fi.

Quest Taupo ★★ (Value) This is a combination of a revamped 1960s motel complex (where rooms are cheaper and smaller) and a much newer group of two-story apartments that I didn't want to leave. Expect all the mod-cons and plenty of space. Either two or three bedrooms, the newer apartments are much nicer and they're ideal for families or couples traveling together. It's a 10-minute walk to town and rates are much cheaper Monday through Friday.

9 Tui St., Taupo. © **0800/350-005** in NZ or 07/378-7487. www.questtaupo.co.nz. 32 units. NZ$250–NZ$550; NZ$30 each extra person. Long-stay and off-peak rates. AE, DC, MC, V. **Amenities:** Babysitting; nearby golf course; outdoor heated pool. *In room:* A/C, TV/DVD, fridge, hair dryer, high-speed Internet, minibar.

Inexpensive
For something more modest, go for backpacker accommodations at the **Rainbow Lodge,** 99 Titiraupenga St. (© **07/378-5754;** www.rainbowlodge.co.nz), where beds go for NZ$25 to NZ$75. Backpackers will find useful information on www.backpacklake taupo.com.

WHERE TO DINE
I'm told there are around 60 restaurants in Taupo, and I'd like to know where they're all hiding. Although there's no shortage of places to eat, "shining stars of cuisine" are a bit thin on the ground. As is the case anywhere in New Zealand, restaurants and cafes keep reinventing themselves and changing their names, styles, and menus. The good news is, there are plenty of reasonably priced ethnic restaurants to choose from. A delicious lunch or summer evening meal at **Huka Prawn Park** ★★ (p. 238), Huka Falls Road (© **07/374-8474**), is worth your attention. It's the world's only geothermally heated prawn farm, and the prawn platter need not make you feel guilty. **Huka Vineyard Restaurant** ★★, Wishart Estate Vineyard, 56 Huka Falls Rd. (© **07/377-2326**), is open for lunch daily (from 10am). It's in a 100-year-old barn and specializes in wine and food matches.

Flax ★, 5 Horomatangi St. (© **07/377-8052**), is a great little cafe with local color. Sporty types should head for **Hub Café** ★★, 415 Huka Falls Rd. (© **07/374-8409**). It's where the mountain bikers hang out and they don't mind you turning up in your cycling gear. Bike racks are available. **L'Arte Mosaic Café & Sculpture Garden** ★, 255 Mapara Rd., Acacia Bay, Taupo (© **07/378-2962;** www.larte.co.nz), is where you'll find resident ceramic artist, Judi Brennan, who has created this crazy, creative place. The food,

> **Finds Say Cheese**
>
> The **Merchant of Taupo** ★, 111 Spa Rd. (📞 **07/378-4626;** www.themerchant. co.nz), stocks a wide variety of imported and New Zealand cheeses, salamis, oils, sauces, wines, and other specialty items that you might like to take home as gifts—or personal treats! **Scenic Cellars** ★★, 32 Roberts St. (📞 **07/378-5704;** www.sceniccellars.co.nz), stocks over 3,000 wine labels—32 available for tasting in the store every day—in New Zealand's largest underground wine cellar.

the colorful environment, and the good service make it a little winner. For the best ice cream in town head straight for **Kaffe Eis** ★★, 10 Tongariro St. (📞 **07/378-8535**).

The Brantry Restaurant ★★ CONTEMPORARY NEW ZEALAND If you managed to find Zest (below), the Brantry is just a few doors away. Tucked into a two-story 1950s house, it gets rave reviews from the locals for its moody interior and good food. It's one of the pricier options in town, but dishes like stuffed lamb rump will leave you pleased to have made the effort.

45 Rifle Range Rd. 📞 **07/378-0484.** Reservations recommended. Main courses NZ$25–NZ$35. AE, MC, V. Tues–Sat 6pm–late.

Replete Café ★ DELI/CAFE Trying to get lunch at Replete is like queuing for tickets to a sold-out show; everyone wants a piece of the action. The service can be flustered, but the food does tend to be good—great salads and pies. Replete appears to be Taupo's favorite daytime haunt for all ages, especially 30- to 40-something business types.

45 Heu Heu St. 📞 **07/377-3011.** www.replete.co.nz. Lunch main courses NZ$15–NZ$25. AE, DC, MC, V. Mon–Fri 7:45am–5pm; Sat–Sun 8:30am–late afternoon.

Zest ★★ CAFE Wedged between a fruit shop and a suburban butchery, this little gem is well worth hunting out. It's immensely popular with in-the-know locals—especially the ladies—who appear to delight in its reliable coffee and tasty soups and salads. There is always a freshly baked array of sweet temptations to end with.

65 Rifle Range Rd. 📞 **07/378-5397.** Main courses NZ$10–NZ$22. AE, MC, V. Mon–Fri 9am–4pm; Sat–Sun 9am–2pm. Shorter hours in winter.

TAUPO AFTER DARK

The core of Taupo's nightlife is geared toward backpackers. If you want to make a quiet start to the evening, head for **19th Hole,** at Wairakei International Golf Course, State Highway 1 (📞 **07/374-8152**), where you can enjoy a drink and chat. **Holy Cow,** upstairs at Tongariro and Tuwharetoa streets (📞 **07/378-0040**), is definitely the happening place for the young crowd. Anything goes, especially dancing on the tables. If you feel like a good beer followed by a quieter dining experience, head for **Plateau** ★★, 64 Tuwharetoa St. (📞 **07/377-2425**), which celebrates Kiwi music and a range of Monteith's craft beers. For a touch of the Irish, head to **Finn MacCuhal's Irish Pub,** Tongariro and Tuwharetoa streets (📞 **07/378-6165**), where you can enjoy a Guinness and rowdy music. **Bond Lounge Bar** ★★, 40 Tuwharetoa St. (📞 **07/377-2434**), is a good place for a quiet, early evening cocktail.

The 94km (58-mile) drive from Taupo to Tongariro National Park is an easy one along the eastern shore of Lake Taupo. At the southern end of the lake, stop at **Turangi** if trout fishing is your passion. The **Tongariro River** is one of the best-known trout-fishing sites in the world (see chapter 5). If you have time, also detour to **Tokaanu Thermal Pools.** Even if you don't swim, there's a nice nature walk. Or call in at the **National Trout Centre** ★★, south of Turangi (✆ **07/386-9243;** www.doc.govt.nz), which features interactive displays and an award-winning underwater viewing chamber that allows you to observe trout in their natural habitat.

If you didn't fancy stopping in Taupo, let me introduce you to a hidden gem—**River Birches Lodge** ★★★, 19 Koura St., Turangi (✆ **0800/102-025;** www.riverbirches. co.nz), which is a serene hideaway on the banks of the Tongariro River, with three beautiful suites. Cedar tubs, big decks, lovely gardens, fine cuisine and, should you be a fisherman, a webcam that monitors the river's best fishing spots, make this an almost perfect stay. It's an incredible value at NZ$385 to NZ$515, or NZ$1,100 for the whole house. Meals are NZ$75 per person for three courses.

State Highway 47 cuts off from State Highway 1 to lead you through plateau tussock land to State Highway 48 and the entrance to park headquarters. It's clearly signposted. As you leave Lake Taupo behind, you enter a world dominated by the grand volcanic landscape. Drive with great care on the Desert Road in winter, when ice and snow cause major traffic hazards.

---

3 TONGARIRO NATIONAL PARK ★★

99km (61 miles) SW of Taupo; 141km (87 miles) NE of Wanganui

Tongariro National Park is New Zealand's oldest national park and, as of 1990, a World Heritage Area in recognition of its outstanding natural and cultural features. It is a place of extremes and surprises that will make you ponder your own diminutive reality.

The park can be explored from one of two main areas—**National Park** and **Whaka-papa villages** on the western side of the mountains, or **Turoa Ski Resort** and **Ohakune township** to the south.

The core of the park consists of the sacred peaks Tongariro, Ngauruhoe, and Ruapehu, which were presented to the people of New Zealand in 1887 by Te Heuheu Tukino IV, Paramount Chief of the Tuwharetoa tribe. At 2,797m (9,174 ft.), **Mount Ruapehu** is the highest mountain on the North Island and is the principal skiing spot in the region. Its **Crater Lake,** filled with acidic tepid water, has a bottom layer of 6m (20 ft.) of sulfur mud, which acts as a barrier between the water and the molten rock below. In June 1996, this active volcano erupted, surprising scientists monitoring its activity. A few days earlier, they had downgraded its danger rating after 8 months of relative inactivity following the spectacular eruptions of September and October 1995. Before that, Ruapehu had been quiet for 8 years. There was a major lahar in 2007 when the crater-lake overflowed. Up-to-date information on Ruapehu is at www.geonet.org.nz or call Eastern Ruapehu Lahar and Warning System (✆ **0508/452-427** in NZ; www.horizons.govt.nz).

Mount Ngauruhoe rises 2,290m (7,513 ft.), smolders constantly, and from time to time (the last in 1975) sends showers of ash and lava from its crater.

> **(Fun Facts** Movie Mountain**
>
> A digitally altered representation of Mount Ngauruhoe appears as Mount Doom in *The Lord of the Rings* trilogy.

Mount Tongariro is the lowest and northernmost of the three, measuring 1,968m (6,455 ft.). It is also the focus of Maori legends. The peaks are at the end of a volcanic chain that extends all the way to the islands of Tonga, 1,610km (1,000 miles) away. Their origin is fairly recent in geological terms, dating back only about 2 million years.

The weather in Tongariro National Park is always changeable and can be savage regardless of the season. Trampers and skiers should always seek the latest track and weather details before venturing into the park.

ESSENTIALS

GETTING THERE & GETTING AROUND   By Plane   Mountain Air (© 0800/922-812 in NZ; www.mountainair.co.nz) has daily service linking Auckland with Mount Ruapehu. It also has a range of ski-flight packages.

By Train   The **TranzRail** (© 0800/802-802; www.tranzscenic.co.nz) *Overlander* trains stop at National Park and Ohakune.

By Coach (Bus)   InterCity (© 07/378-9032) provides service to the national park. **Whakapapa Express** (© 0800/828-763 in NZ, or 07/377-0435) offers daily ski and mountain transport between Taupo, Ohakune, and Whakapapa. **Ruapehu Ski Shuttle** (© 0800/331-995 in NZ, or 09/379-8886; fax 09/379-8151) serves National Park village, Whakapapa, and Ohakune from Auckland Sunday through Wednesday and on Friday.

By Car   Highway 1 runs along the eastern side of the park; Highway 4 goes through National Park Village on the western side; highways 47 and 48 bring travelers from the south shore of Lake Taupo into the heart of the park; and Highway 49 turns off State Highway 1 at Waiouru at the south end of the park and travels to Ohakune. Mount Ruapehu is a 4-hour drive from either Auckland or Wellington.

VISITOR INFORMATION   The **Whakapapa Visitor Centre** is in the village of Whakapapa at the end of State Highway 48 (© 07/892-3729; fax 07/892-3814; www. doc.govt.nz). It's open daily from 8am to 6pm in summer, 8am to 5pm in winter (closed Dec 25). It provides current volcanic, weather, and track information, as well as hut and camping passes, maps and brochures, hunting permits, and other items. The center has exhibits on the natural and human history of the park along with two excellent audiovisual displays, *The Sacred Gift of Tongariro* and *The Ring of Fire.* Information about the Whakapapa Ski Field, 7km (4⅓ miles) above the village, is also available.

The **Ruapehu Visitor Centre,** 54 Clyde St., Ohakune (© 0800/782-734 in NZ, or 06/385-8427; fax 06/385-8527; www.visitruapehu.com), is open weekdays from 9am to 5pm, weekends from 9am to 3:30pm. You can reach the Ohakune **Department of Conservation** office at © 06/385-0010. The **Turangi i-SITE Visitor Centre,** Ngawaka Place, Turangi (© 0800/288-726 in NZ, or 07/386-8999; fax 07/386-0074; www. laketauponz.com), is another useful stop. It's open daily from 8:30am to 5pm. For information on National Park Village, go to www.nationalpark.co.nz.

On the Slopes
Skiing is *the* activity in season (June–Oct), when the weather and Mount Ruapehu permit. The 1996 eruption closed the two main fields—Whakapapa and Turoa—for 2 years, and a mild winter in 1999 didn't improve things, but the situation appears to have recovered. Combined, these two fields offer over 700 hectares (1,730 acres) of patrolled, skiable terrain (and almost the same amount off-trail), with facilities and geographical variety to satisfy any skier. Whakapapa and Turoa will always be the names of the two ski areas, but since 2001, they've been united under one brand, Mount Ruapehu—New Zealand's largest ski area. You can get seamless lift passes to ski on either field; the company operates bus service between the two.

The **Whakapapa Ski Area** (☎ 07/892-3738; www.mtruapehu.com), above the Grand Chateau, is heavily populated compared to South Island fields, which is its biggest disadvantage. There's something for everyone in terms of skiing, but be careful that you don't sail over bluffs. A lot of skiers stay in the club huts on the field. Whakapapa's sister resort is Copper Mountain, in Colorado, with which it shares some reciprocal privileges. Ski lifts operate daily from 8:30am to 3:45pm and cost NZ$83 for adults, NZ$48 for children ages 5 to 18; for the lower mountain (beginners' area), they cost NZ$63 adults, NZ$36 for children. Packages including lift passes, rental, and lessons start at NZ$85 for adults, NZ$60 for children.

The Whakapapa summer operation (Dec–Apr, daily 9am–4pm) includes guided Crater Lake walks from NZ$85 adults, NZ$55 children ages 5 to 15; and scenic chairlift rides for NZ$25 adults, NZ$15 children.

Whakapapa Shuttle (☎ 07/892-3716) offers the best transport to the mountain, which costs NZ$25 round-trip from National Park Village.

Many prefer **Turoa Ski Resort** (☎ 06/385-8456; www.mtruapehu.com), above Ohakune, because it draws fewer people. It boasts the longest vertical drop of any ski area in Australasia, plus an abundance of gullies for snowboarders. Ski lifts operate daily from 9am to 3:45pm and cost the same as at Whakapapa (above). Turoa is open only in winter (late June to early Nov). **Snow Express** (☎ 06/385-9280) offers the best transport, which departs from Ohakune's Junction Ski Shop every half-hour and costs NZ$20 round-trip.

Skiers and snowboarders can find more information on these ski fields and others in chapter 5. For the latest snow conditions and ski information, call **Snowphone** (☎ 083/222-180 in Turoa, or **083-222-182** in Whakapapa).

On the Tracks: A Tramper's Paradise
Walking in Tongariro National Park is spectacular, to say the least, and there are plenty of possible routes. Pick up the Department of Conservation's brochure *Whakapapa Walks* for an introduction to some of the best. **Taranaki Falls** ★ is a 2-hour, 6km (4-mile) circular track that starts above Whakapapa Village and takes in both native bush and stark tussock vegetation. Taranaki Falls plunges 20m (66 ft.) over the edge of a large lava flow, which erupted from Ruapehu 15,000 years ago. **Silica Rapids Walk** is a 2- to 3-hour loop track that also starts above Whakapapa Village. It takes you through a beech forest, past streams and rapids, and through subalpine plants and swamp as it returns to Bruce Road, 2km (1 mile) above the starting point.

The best walk of all is also the toughest—the famous **Tongariro Crossing** ★★★. Regarded as New Zealand's greatest 1-day walk, it takes you between Tongariro and

Ngauruhoe, over the most stunning volcanic landscapes in the country. It involves an 800m (2,600-ft.) altitude gain and a couple of very sharp but short stretches. People of all fitness levels can generally cope, but many underestimate the climate at altitude and almost every year visitors, who think they know better than the local experts, have to be rescued. Forget the fact that it is summer and take plenty of warm woolen clothing (cotton is useless), as conditions change fast and furiously. The walking season is usually November to May. If you plan a winter walk take a guide, crampons, and an ice axe. It is important to organize transport at both ends of the walk. Contact the **Tongariro Track Transport** (📞 **07/892-3716;** www.tongarirotrack.co.nz), or **Howard's Lodge Transport,** Carroll Street, National Park Village (📞 **07/892-2827;** www.howardslodge.co.nz). For more details on the Tongariro Crossing, see the "Tramping" section in chapter 5.

On Your Bike

An essential information source for mountain bikers in this area is the pocket-size publication *Volcanic Plateau Mountain Bike Rides,* written and published by Kennett Brothers in association with the Department of Conservation and printed on waterproof paper. It details a host of rides in the area, including the highly regarded 42nd Traverse. The booklet is for sale at visitor centers and bike stores in the area.

The **42nd Traverse** ★★★ is one of the most popular bike rides on the North Island. It covers old logging tracks through remote native bush and has an overall descent of 570m (1,870 ft.) through spectacular scenery. Depending on your enthusiasm for the task, it takes anywhere from 3 to 7 hours to complete. You'll need to organize transport to and from your vehicle; **Howard's Lodge,** Carroll Street, National Park Village (📞/fax **07/892-2827;** www.howardslodge.co.nz), or **Ski Haus,** Carroll Street, National Park Village (📞 **07/892-2854;** www.skihaus.co.nz), can arrange that for you. Howard's Lodge also offers guided rides, but the best mountain bike company in this area is **Tongariro Mountain Bikes** ★★, the Rafting Centre, Atirau Road, Turangi (📞 **0800/101-024** in NZ or 07/386-6445; www.trr.co.nz). They have exclusive access to 3,800 hectares (9,400 acres) of backcountry trails and they offer a shuttle and hire service.

WHERE TO STAY

Ohakune and National Park villages offer a good range of winter accommodations, but Whakapapa Village has fewer choices. You'll need to book well ahead to beat New Zealand skiers to the best beds—and even the best are fairly mediocre. In summer, the area is popular with trampers and mountain bikers, and because some accommodations close after the ski season, it's still wise to reserve ahead. Rates given below include 12.5% GST.

In Ohakune

This is where you'll find the greatest variety of accommodations, and it's only about an hour to Whakapapa, making it a good base. **Powderhorn Chateau** ★★, bottom of Mountain Road (📞 **06/385-8888;** www.powderhorn.co.nz), has the closest accommodations to the mountain on the Turoa side. It's definitely the best the town has to offer. It was built in 1995 and has 30 well-appointed rooms with private bathrooms for NZ$98 to NZ$230. Luxury apartments that sleep six go for NZ$750 to NZ$850 per night, with significantly lower off-peak rates. **Ossie's SkiChalets & Apartments,** 59 Tainui St. (📞 **06/385-8088;** www.ossies-ohakune.co.nz), offers 14 two-story chalets with lovely Scandinavian-style timber interiors. Prices start at NZ$160, a good value for the money and cheaper again in summer.

In National Park Village

Centrally located just west of Whakapapa Ski Area, National Park Village has a nice selection of good-value, low-cost accommodations. It's also the only place that offers a view of all three mountains. **Howard's Lodge** ★, Carroll Street (✆/fax **07/892-2827;** www.howardslodge.co.nz), is a friendly budget spot with backpacker dorm beds and simple twins, doubles, and quads with shared facilities, plus deluxe rooms with en-suite bathrooms. Their prices range from NZ$85 to NZ$180. **National Park Backpackers** ★, Finlay Street (✆/fax **07/892-2870;** www.npbp.co.nz), is a new complex that's drawing a big crowd to its indoor climbing wall. Dorm beds are around NZ$25; doubles with en-suite bathrooms are NZ$70 to NZ$80.

In Whakapapa Village

This small alpine village has limited accommodations, unless you take a Whakapapa On-Snow package deal and stay in one of the on-field ski clubs. **Whakapapa Holiday Park** (✆ **07/892-3897;** www.whakapapa.net.nz) has cabins, a self-contained lodge that sleeps 32, caravan and tent sites, and a fully stocked store. Prices start at NZ$65 for the lodge, NZ$18 per person for caravan and tent sites, and NZ$75 for cabins. It's pretty basic but sometimes it may be the only option left. **Skotel Alpine Resort** (✆ **0800/756-835** in NZ, or 07/892-3719; www.skotel.co.nz), has everything from backpacker rooms to smart deluxe units and self-contained chalets. There's a restaurant, a good sauna and Jacuzzis, and a fun-filled bar during ski season. Superior rooms and chalets are priced from NZ$175 to NZ$225. Backpackers pay NZ$30 to NZ$45.

The **Bayview Chateau Tongariro** ★★ (✆ **0800/242-832** in NZ, or 07/892-3809; www.chateau.co.nz), is the grande dame of the area. Built in 1929, the glorious old building has a New Zealand Historic Places Trust category I classification. Most guest rooms have been refurbished, and 40 new rooms are now available. This is where you'll find the nicest rooms. The junior suites are especially good value; if you feel like splashing out, go for the gorgeous, big Te Heu Heu suite and enjoy your own fireplace, Jacuzzi, and telescope. You pay top dollar in winter—NZ$190 to NZ$475—and get a much better rate in summer. Guests enjoy access to a heated indoor pool, sauna, gym, bars, restaurants, and New Zealand's highest 9-hole golf course.

WHERE TO DINE

In Ohakune

Don't hold your breath for fine dining in Ohakune, National Park, or the Whakapapa villages. I can only assume that skiers and trekkers get so hungry they'll eat anything. Most of the time the offerings are fair to middling; but if it's any comfort, you won't starve. Ohakune has the best range of eateries, but be aware that some of them close in summer. **Powderkeg Restaurant and Bar** ★★, at Powderhorn Chateau (✆ **06/385-8888**), is a good winter bet for hearty meals and heaps of partying. It offers brasserie-style food. A more subdued, semi-fine-dining atmosphere characterizes Powderhorn's other year-round restaurant, the **Matterhorn.** There's always good food at the **Fat Pigeon Cafe** ★★, bottom of Mountain Road (✆ **06/385-9423**), where you can relax in a charming garden setting. The **Mountain Rocks Café & Bar,** Clyde and Goldfinch streets (✆ **06/385-8295**), is the newest eatery where you can enjoy everything from big breakfasts to hearty dinners. It has a nice courtyard for outdoor summer dining.

The dining scene is finally improving here, although it is still rather limited, and open hours are unpredictable at best. **Ski Haus Restaurant & Bar,** Carroll Street (© 07/892-2854), is open year-round for breakfast and dinner, serving filling fare such as steaks, chicken dishes, and a few vegetarian offerings. **Eivins Café Bar,** State Highway 4 (© 07/892-2844), is now in a new building, and the breakfasts, lunches, and dinners are guaranteed to fill a gap—if the place is open! **Basekamp Gourmet Burger Bar,** Carroll Street (© 07/892-2872), is good for pizzas and chunky burgers—try the venison and lamb burgers. The newest eatery, **Station Café,** National Park Railway Station, Station Road (© 07/892-2881), is proving popular, but it, too, is often closed during the day.

In Whakapapa Village

Your best meals here will be at the **Ruapehu Restaurant** ★★ (© 07/892-3809) at the Bayview Chateau Tongariro (see "Where to Stay," above). The Chateau's **Pihanga Cafe** is open daily from 11:30am until late, and although it's long overdue for a decor revamp, the reasonably priced meals, all under NZ$25, will fend off hunger pangs. That's the best I can say about it. Across the road, **Fergussons Café** has counter food, light meals, and good coffee daily from 8:30am to 5pm, but it won't be winning prizes anytime soon, either. **Skotel** (© 07/892-3719; see "Where to Stay," above) has a restaurant open to casual diners for breakfast and dinner. Once again, food is of the no-fuss, filling variety, but you'll find a great party atmosphere here in winter.

EN ROUTE TO GISBORNE

There are two ways of getting to Gisborne from Rotorua. You can either drive along the Bay of Plenty route past Whakatane to Opotiki, and then cut through the Waioweka Gorge (St. Hwy. 2), or you can allow much more time and follow the East Cape Road (St. Hwy. 35), which takes in stunning scenery on the easternmost point of New Zealand.

The Cape drive will take 7 to 8 hours minimum—more if you stop to take photographs. This is probably the least-visited part of the country. Take great care on this road; there is often wandering stock, and locals don't always obey the road rules. For information on the East Cape Road and its attractions, see chapter 10.

The short route from Opotiki to Gisborne on State Highway 2 will take just 3 hours, but much of it is steep and winding through the Waioweka Gorge. It's faster, but it's boring compared to the East Cape Road.

EN ROUTE TO HAWKE'S BAY

Head back to Taupo, where you'll turn onto the Napier-Taupo Highway, State Highway 5. The journey follows excellent roads and takes around 1½ hours. That said, take care, as this stretch of road is notorious for fatal accidents.

Gisborne & Hawke's Bay

Gisborne and the East Cape epitomize all that's special about New Zealand—stunning unspoiled scenery, rich culture and history, white-sand beaches, fabulous wines, and friendly, hospitable people. Gisborne, the most isolated city in the country, lies just south of the sparsely populated East Cape in Poverty Bay and is separated by mountain ranges from both Bay of Plenty and Hawke's Bay.

Nearby Mount Hikurangi, the tallest nonvolcanic mountain on the North Island at 1,839m (6,032 ft.), is the first point on mainland New Zealand the sun touches each day, and Gisborne the first city in the world to see the light.

It is the place where both Maori and European voyagers first set foot on land.

The *waka* (canoe) *Horouta* brought the first Maori settlers of the Great Migration from Hawaiiki over 1,000 years ago, and Captain James Cook stepped ashore at Kaiti Beach in Gisborne in 1769.

The Hawke's Bay region, 215km (134 miles) to the southwest, shares many of the same alluring natural features and has more than 30% of the country's finest vineyards. The adjacent cities of Napier and Hastings and the smaller community of Havelock North curve along the coast.

Both Gisborne and Hawke's Bay are blessed with mild climates, long hours of sunshine, and fertile soil—the perfect combination for horticulture. The landscape is a patchwork of orchards, market gardens, pasture, and vineyards.

1 GISBORNE & THE EAST CAPE ★★

293km (182 miles) NE of Rotorua; 298km (185 miles) SE of Tauranga; 504km (312 miles) SE of Auckland

Gisborne (pop. 44,500) had its big moment when it welcomed in the first light of the new century. There were hopes that the NZ$9.5-million revamp of the city would signal a bright, rich future for the area, but I think things have pretty much reverted to the same old quiet, provincial atmosphere that always prevailed. Mind you, the beautification was much needed, and it's good to see the place looking tidier and slightly more alive.

However, the small-town atmosphere is part of Gisborne's charm, and we shouldn't overlook the fact that it is a prosperous river port city and commercial center. It moves at a relaxed pace (and some days that's an understatement) and enjoys 2,200 hours of sunshine annually with summer temperatures consistently above 77°F (25°C), often rising above 95°F (35°C).

Apart from being the country's second-largest grape-growing district and the self-appointed Chardonnay Capital, this area is also the last genuine bastion of bicultural society largely unaffected by tourism. That bicultural heritage is evident everywhere, in the use of the Maori language in everyday life and in the fact that 45% of the population is Maori—the highest proportion of people of Maori descent anywhere in New Zealand.

If you'd like to experience an isolated part of the country that is more like New Zealand "used to be," then come to Gisborne and the East Cape.

GETTING THERE & GETTING AROUND **By Plane** **Air New Zealand Link** (☎ **06/867-1608;** www.airnewzealand.com) operates daily flights from major New Zealand cities. Don't be shocked by the fact that aircraft share the runway with a railway line. Planes give way to the freight trains, and there are no problems. For airport transport, call **Link Shuttles** (☎ **06/867-4765**).

By Coach (Bus) **InterCity** (☎ **09/623-1503**) offers daily bus service to Gisborne from Auckland, Wellington, and Rotorua. **Coachrite** (☎ **06/868-9969**) travels to Hastings Monday through Friday. City buses operate Monday through Friday only, but Gisborne is better explored by car or taxi.

By Shuttle Shuttle buses provide transportation around East Cape between Opotiki and Gisborne. They leave daily from the visitor centers in both towns, which can provide information on schedules and fares.

By Taxi Call the **Gisborne Taxi Society** (☎ **06/867-2222**).

By Car No matter which route you take to Gisborne—via East Cape, via Waioweka Gorge, or via Napier—you're in for a long and winding drive. The most interesting way, via East Cape, is also by far the longest. To make the most of the rich culture and stunning scenery in this area, you really need to stop overnight halfway (at Te Kaha or Hicks Bay, perhaps). Otherwise, be prepared to be on the road for 8 to 10 hours once you leave Opotiki. Also be very alert to stray animals and horsemen on these roads; and make sure you pick up the very informative *Pacific Coast Highway* guide from visitor centers. It's free, and it gives a good introduction to all the settlements you pass through.

ORIENTATION Gisborne is on the northern shore of Poverty Bay, where the Waimata and Taruheru come together to form the Turanganui River, the country's shortest river at just 1,200m (3,900 ft.). The city center is compact. **Gladstone Road** is the main thoroughfare. **Centennial Marine Drive** runs from the bustling port area around the bay to the mouth of the Waipaoa River. Most of the best restaurants are around the port area at the north end of Gladstone Road.

Opotiki lies at the eastern end of Bay of Plenty. It is the gateway to the **East Cape Road,** which is the final leg of the Pacific Coast Highway (St. Hwy. 35).

Wairoa, 99km (61 miles) south of Gisborne at the mouth of the Wairoa River, is the gateway to the wilderness areas of Urewera National Park and Lake Waikaremoana. The 3-day tramp around the lake is one of the Department of Conservation's Great Walks of New Zealand (see chapter 5).

VISITOR INFORMATION The **Gisborne i-SITE Visitor Centre,** 209 Grey St., across from Pizza Hut (☎ **06/868-6139;** fax 06/868-6138; www.gisbornenz.com), is open daily from 8:30am to 5pm (closed Dec 25). You can also find information on the area at www.eastlandnz.com, www.destinationgisborne.co.nz, and www.pacificcoast.co.nz.

The **Wairoa i-SITE Visitor Centre** is at the corner of State Highway 2 and Queen Street, Wairoa (☎ **06/838-7440;** fax 06/838-3901; www.wairoanz.com). It is open weekdays 8:30am to 5pm, weekends 10am to 4pm. The **Opotiki i-SITE Visitor Centre** is at the corner of Elliot and St. John streets, Opotiki (☎ **07/315-3031;** fax 07/315-3032; www.opotikinz.com).

FAST FACTS The Gisborne **post office** is at 74 Grey St. It's open Monday through Friday from 9am to 5pm. For **Internet access,** inquire at visitor centers (see above), though keep in mind that the Gisborne Library (www.gpl.govt.nz) in Peel Street has free wireless Internet.

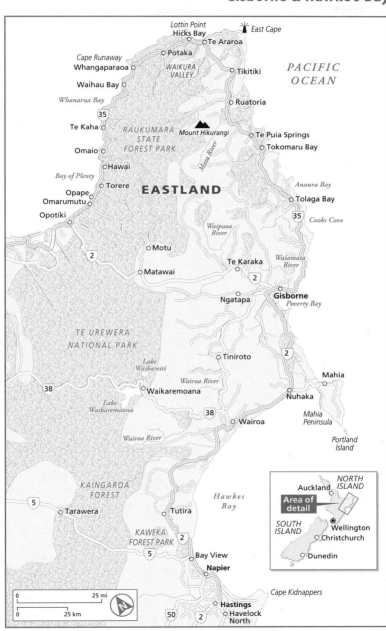

Lottin Point
Hicks Bay
East Cape
Te Araroa
Potaka
Cape Runaway
Whangaparaoa
WAIKURA
VALLEY
Tikitiki
PACIFIC
OCEAN
Waihau Bay
Whanarua Bay
Ruatoria
35
Te Kaha
RAUKUMARA
STATE
FOREST PARK
Mount Hikurangi
Te Puia Springs
Omaio
Tokomaru Bay
Hawai
Bay of Plenty
Torere
EASTLAND
Anaura Bay
Opape
Omarumutu
Tolaga Bay
Opotiki
35
Cooks Cove
Motu
Waipaoa
River
Matawai
Te Karaka
Waimata
River
2
Ngatapa
Gisborne
Poverty Bay
TE UREWERA
NATIONAL PARK
2
Tiniroto
Mahia
Lake
Waikareiti
Wairoa River
38
Waikaremoana
Nuhaka
Lake
Waikaremoana
38
Wairoa
Mahia
Peninsula
Wairoa River
Portland
Island
KAINGAROA
FOREST
Hawkes
Bay
NORTH
ISLAND
Auckland
Area of
detail
5
Tarawera
Tutira
SOUTH
ISLAND
Wellington
KAWEKA
FOREST PARK
2
Christchurch
5
Bay View
Dunedin
Napier
25 mi
Cape Kidnappers
25 km
Hastings
50
2
Havelock
North

SPECIAL EVENTS The **Gisborne Wine & Food Festival** ★ is on Labour Weekend in October. For information, call ℂ **0800/447-667** in New Zealand. For details on all Eastland area events, contact local visitor centers.

EXPLORING GISBORNE

To get a panoramic view of Poverty Bay, the city, and the harbor and rivers, head for **Kaiti Hill Lookout.** It's signposted at the northern end of Gladstone Bridge, and you can drive all the way to the brick semicircular lookout point. A statue of Captain Cook looks out to Young Nick's Head, at the opposite end of the bay. At the foot of Kaiti Hill is one of New Zealand's largest carved Maori meetinghouses, **Te Poho-o-Rawiri Marae** ★★ (ℂ **06/868-5364**). Visits can be arranged by appointment, providing an opportunity to see a living gallery of Maori art in the exceptionally detailed *tukutuku* (woven wall panels) and *kowhaiwhai* (painted scroll ornamentation) on the rafters.

The **Tairawhiti Museum** ★★, 18–22 Stout St. (ℂ **06/867-3832;** www.tairawhiti museum.org.nz), is one of the best small provincial museums in the country. It has displays on the Maori and European history of the area as well as geological and natural history, decorative arts, and maritime history. Admission is NZ$5 for adults and NZ$2 for children. It's open Monday through Saturday from 10am to 4pm and Sunday from 1:30 to 4pm (closed Good Friday and Dec 25). The **East Coast Museum of Technology,** Main Road, Makaraka (ℂ **06/868-8254;** www.ecmot.8m.com), is 6km (4 miles) from the city. Its huge collection of vintage farm machinery, fire engines, and general equipment from a bygone era is open daily from 9:30am to 4:30pm. Admission is NZ$5 for adults, NZ$2 for children.

The internationally renowned **Eastwoodhill Arboretum** ★★★, 2392 Wharekopae Rd., Ngatapa (ℂ **06/863-9003;** www.eastwoodhill.org.nz), lies 35km (22 miles) and 20 minutes west of Gisborne. It is an extraordinary testament to one man's passion for trees. This magnificent 70-hectare (173-acre) woodland park was the life's work of William Douglas Cook, who began planting the bare site in 1910. Today, it holds more than 3,500 species of 750 tree genera, making it the largest arboretum in New Zealand. The arboretum is a haven for scientists, photographers, and garden enthusiasts alike—especially in autumn when the colors are lush and extravagant. It features over 25km of marked walking tracks, so allow at least 1½ hours and plan to have a picnic under the maples. It's open year-round daily from 9am to 5pm (closed Good Friday and Dec 25); admission is NZ$10 for adults and NZ$8 for seniors. Children 14 and under are free. The 1-hour **Curator's Botanical Tour** costs NZ$15 (in addition to general admission). **Hackfalls Arboretum,** Tiniroto Road, 1 hour from Gisborne (ℂ **06/863-2655**), has one of the biggest collections of maples and oaks in New Zealand. It's open daily; admission is NZ$5 per person. **Gisborne Botanical Gardens,** Aberdeen Road, are a pleasant distraction on the banks of the Taurheru River in the heart of town. Admission is free. Pick up the *Gardens to Visit* brochure from the Gisborne visitor center if you're interested in even more greenery.

A Drop of Wine

Gisborne is New Zealand's second-largest producer of chardonnay grapes (after Marlborough), growing over a third of the national crop. The area also produces significant quantities of award-winning Riesling and a wide range of other varieties. Pick up the *Winery Guide* at the visitor center, fix yourself a picnic, and head out to explore. *Note:* Not all wineries are open to the public all the time, so it pays to phone ahead for hours. You'll find additional information at www.gisbornewine.co.nz.

The **Millton Vineyard** ★★, 119 Papatu Rd., Manutuke (© **06/862-8680;** www. millton.co.nz), was established in 1984 as New Zealand's first commercial, fully certified organic winery. It's known for its Riesling, chenin blanc, and late-harvest dessert wines. It's set in a superb garden with a picnic area and is open daily from 10am to 5pm in summer, or by appointment year-round. **Montana Wines** ★★, Lytton Road, Gisborne (© **06/867-9819;** www.montana.co.nz), was established in 1934 and is New Zealand's leading winemaker and wine exporter. The company has wineries in Auckland, Marlborough, Hawke's Bay, and Gisborne. The Gisborne winery produces the Ormond Estate, Patutahi Estate, Saints, and Montana labels—some of the country's best chardonnay. And check out the newest addition, the **Lindauer Cellars,** Solander Street (© **06/868-2757;** www.montana.co.nz), which is open daily December through February, and Tuesday through Saturday from March to November.

The **Works & Longbush Wines** ★★, the Works, Esplanade, Inner Harbour, Gisborne (© **06/863-1285;** www.longbush.com), is where the Thorpe family has worked its vineyards for more than 35 years and now produces three ranges of Gisborne-made wines under the Woodlands, Longbush, and Nick's Head labels. It focuses on chardonnay and merlot. You can taste the production at the Works, a restaurant and wine bar, from 10am to 6pm daily.

In addition to the above, you can also visit **Waiohika Estate,** 75 Waimata Valley Rd. (© **06/867-4670**), for wine tastings and garden visits; **Amor-Bendall,** 24 Moana Rd., Wainui Beach (© **021/859-435;** www.amor-bendall.co.nz), for chardonnay and pinot gris; and **TW Chardonnay** ★★, Back Ormond Road (© **021/864-818;** call for an appointment; www.twwines.co.nz) for very good vineyard tours and tastings. If you'd like to learn the secrets of cider making, visit the **Cidery,** 91 Customhouse St. (© **06/868-8300**), home to New Zealand's leading cider producer, Bulmer Harvest. It's open weekdays 9am to 5pm, weekends 10am until 3pm.

A Spot of Culture

Rotorua may have the most accessible concentration of Maori culture in the country, but Eastland is one of the few places in New Zealand where strong cultural and tribal affiliations are obviously evident in day-to-day activities. The Maori language is part of everyday life here.

The area is home to more than 100 working marae (village commons), which still form a focal point for most Maori communities. They are used regularly for meetings, celebrations, funerals, and family and tribal functions. Many can be viewed by arrangement, but there are two important rules to remember: You must not take photographs inside marae anywhere in New Zealand, and you must not smoke or take food inside. In many, you will also have to remove your shoes.

The remnants of ancient *pa* sites (Maori fortresses) abound throughout the region. Among the most notable are the one at Ngatapa near Gisborne and another in the hills to the north of Waikohu. The district also has a large number of *kohanga reo* (early-childhood education centers) and *kura kaupapa* (primary schools) where only Maori is spoken. Most other schools in the region have bilingual units.

You can see Maori culture at work and play in the many small communities around the East Cape Road. Just remember that these are ordinary New Zealanders, not museum exhibits, so be respectful of their privacy.

Two very good Maori-owned-and-operated tour companies will offer you a unique insight into Maori culture. **Tipuna Tours,** P.O. Box 19, Tolaga Bay (© **06/862-6118;**

www.tipunatours.com), can take you to the *Whale Rider* film location at very pretty Whangara, just north of Gisborne (NZ$70 per person); or they will customize half- and full-day tours that include marae visits, ancient *pa* sites, beautiful bays, and possibly a marine reserve. **Waka Toa,** P.O. Box 51, Gisborne (✆ **06/868-5425;** www.wakatoa. com), will take you high above the city at dusk to an old *pa* site, where you'll be treated to several hours of cross-cultural sharing through music, drama, conversation, and humor. It costs NZ$250 for adults and NZ$175 for children. A Family Experience (two adults, three children), costs NZ$360.

EXPLORING THE EAST CAPE ★★★

State Highway 35 between Opotiki and Gisborne is a memorable 334km (207-mile) journey. The road is etched into the coastline, rewarding the traveler with an ever-changing vista of the South Pacific. In summer, scarlet pohutukawa trees border the bright blue bays, and all along the way you'll see deserted white-sand beaches that afford innumerable opportunities for walking and fishing.

Make sure you get a copy of **Jason's Pacific Coast Highway Touring Guide** (www. jasons.com), free from visitor centers throughout the North Island. As well as providing a detailed, very readable map, it illustrates highlights along the way.

The route is also a genuine cultural experience. Many of the larger bays are centers of Maori settlements, usually surrounding their home marae. At **Te Kaha,** the Tukaki meeting-house in the marae has an elaborately carved lintel, which you can view by asking permission. **Whangaparaoa** is where the great migration canoe *Tainui* landed, and Potaka is the northern boundary of the Ngati Porou tribe. Hicks Bay, not quite midway, has marvelous views and the **Tuwhakairiora meetinghouse ★★,** one of the finest examples of carving on the cape. The carving was carried out in 1872 and is dedicated to local members of Ngati Porou who died in overseas wars. Turn left at the general store to reach the meetinghouse.

Not far from Hicks Bay, the road descends to sea level and follows a narrow bay to **Te Araroa.** Here you'll find the country's oldest (600 years) and largest pohutukawa tree and a wealth of Maori history. A 20-minute side trip from here will bring you to the picture-book vista of the historic **East Cape Lighthouse ★★.** The track to the 1906 lighthouse must be covered on foot; it leads up 700 steps.

The next settlement is Tikitiki, where the historic **St. Mary's Church ★★★,** stands like a sentinel above the road. Built as a memorial to Ngati Porou soldiers who died in

---

ⓘ **Moments**   **Sunrise at Mount Hikurangi**

At 1,839m (6,032 ft.), Mount Hikurangi is the first point on mainland New Zealand to see the sunrise each day. At the summit are nine carved sculptures. A walking track to the top crosses private property, but because it is sacred to the Maori, you must gain permission from **Te Runanga o Ngati Porou,** who have offices in Ruatoria (✆ **06/864-8660;** www.ngatiporou.com). An excellent alpine hut on the higher reaches allows early-morning climbs to see the sunrise. Hut fees are NZ$5 per person; bookings are essential. It's best to take the Ngati Porou 4WD tour with tourism coordinator, Paora Brooking, to see the magnificent carvings on top of the mountain. He will give you a unique perspective into this mystical place.

missed—the interior craftsmanship is breathtaking.

Next stop, just a short diversion off the main road, is **Ruatoria,** the center of Ngati Porou. Although scattered around the country, they compose New Zealand's second-largest Maori tribe. For more information on the local Ngati Porou tribe, check out the website www.ngatiporou.com. It lists a network of indigenous tour operators on the east coast, from Gisborne north to Potaka, who are committed to providing authentic, culturally appropriate experiences, which can include stays at a marae.

There are four marae at **Tokomaru Bay** ★★, plus a glorious sweep of beach and a selection of interesting old unused buildings. Take care when swimming in the ocean here.

The road then leads to **Tolaga Bay** ★, which has one of the longest free-standing jetties in New Zealand, plus, rather unexpectedly, the **Tolaga Bay Cashmere Company** ★★, 31 Solander St. (✆ **06/862-6746;** www.cashmere.co.nz), which produces fine merino, cashmere, and silk knitwear. The company's high-fashion garments are renowned throughout Australasia. This shop, which specializes in wholesale prices and seconds, is open in summer Monday through Friday from 9am to 4pm, and Saturday from 10am to 3pm. It is closed on winter weekends. Tolaga Bay is 54km (33 miles) north of Gisborne.

The **Ernest Reeve Walkway** ★, at the northern end of Tolaga Bay, leads to a lookout on the cliffs, overlooking the bay. The stunning views are worth capturing on film. Allow an hour for the return walk.

OUTDOOR PURSUITS

BEACHES   Gisborne has three major swimming beaches, **Midway, Waikanae,** and **Wainui.** Lifeguards patrol all three in season. **Kaiaua Beach,** 60km (37 miles) north of Gisborne and 6km (3¾ miles) off State Highway 35, is good for fishing, swimming, and picnics. **Anaura Bay,** 77km (48 miles) north of Gisborne and 6km (3¾ miles) off State Highway 35, was Captain Cook's second landing spot in New Zealand. It has a beautiful beach of unspoiled golden sand, offering safe swimming and good fishing. A 3.5km (2-mile) bush walk gives wonderful scenic views; allow 2½ hours. You can make marae visits here; there is a motor camp as well.

FISHING   In this area, you can do anything from freshwater fly-fishing for brown trout to game fishing for marlin in the Pacific. For the independent angler, the Pacific Coast Highway is the ultimate route for surf-casting, game fishing, and diving. Local knowledge is plentiful, and visitors can take a shortcut to success by contacting local fishing clubs or taking advantage of guides and charter services. Saltwater fishing does not require a license. For wilderness brown and rainbow trout fishing, call **Safari Adventures,** Taumata Road, Rere, Gisborne (✆ **06/867-0872;** www.nzsafari.co.nz), which also offers accommodations and saltwater game fishing.

The Motu, Waioweka, Hangaroa, and Ruakituri rivers offer some of the finest freshwater fishing. Licenses are required for all freshwater fisheries. Call **Fish & Game New Zealand's Trout Line** (✆ **0800/876-885** in NZ; www.fishandgame.org.nz). For the **Gisborne Fishery Office,** call ✆ **06/868-7160,** or check out www.fish.govt.nz.

GOLF   **Poverty Bay Golf Club,** Awapuni and Lytton roads, Gisborne (✆ **06/867-4402;** www.gisbornegolf.co.nz), is one of the top 10 18-hole courses in the country. Fees are NZ$35 for 18 holes and there is a pro shop on-site.

HORSE TREKKING One of the best horse-trekking operations around is **Eastender Horse Treks,** Rangitukia, Tikitiki (℃/fax **06/864-3033;** www.eastenderhorsetreks.co. nz), located near the top of East Cape. Their treks take you over beaches and through native bush and farmland and cost NZ$60. They also offer backpacker accommodations for NZ$25 per person.

HUNTING **New Zealand Safari Adventures,** Tangihau Station, Rere (℃ **06/867-0872;** www.nzsafari.co.nz), is an outdoor playground 30 minutes from the city where you can hunt trophy red deer, elk, mountain goat, or Hokonui ram with experienced guides.

SNORKELING WITH SHARKS Get face to face with mako sharks—from the safety of a cage, of course. **Surfit Shark Cage Experience** ★★★, 48 Awapuni Rd., Gisborne (℃ **06/867-2970;** www.surfit.co.nz), will take you out into reef waters teeming with the marine predators from November to April. The 5-hour experience costs NZ$300, which seems like a lot of money to terrify yourself—but think of the stories you can tell afterward. Spectators pay NZ$150. They also offer fishing charters. **Dive Tatapouri** ★★★, SH35, Tatapouri (℃ **06/868-5153;** www.divetatapouri.com), offers shark cage diving for NZ$250, and if you join their Reef Experience (NZ$40 adults, NZ$20 children), you can see guides feeding and interacting with wild stingrays, eagle rays, and other reef dwellers. Waders are provided.

SURFING The popular surf beaches are **Makorori Point** ★★, **Pouawa, Sponge Bay,** and **Kaiaua. Midway Beach** has the famous Gisborne pipe, known for its deep barrel rides, and **Waikanae** and **Wainui beaches** are also good for surfing and bodyboarding. **Kaiti Beach,** around the Gisborne Port and harbor area, offers excellent sailboarding and yachting. The visitor center staff will point you in the direction of numerous other surf breaks.

SWIMMING **Gisborne Olympic Pool Complex,** Centennial Marine Drive (℃ **06/867-6220;** fax 06/867-4953), is open daily from 6am to 8pm. It has indoor and outdoor pools, a dive pool, a Jacuzzi and therapy pool, a 98m (320-ft.) hydroslide, and a toddlers' pool.

WALKING Good walking abounds in this area. For an easy amble, pick up the free brochure *Gisborne, An Historic Walk,* which leads around the inner city on a 1- to 3-hour wander. *Walks of the Eastland Region* (available at the visitor center), is a more comprehensive appraisal of excellent walks in the whole region. Serious trampers who want to investigate the wilderness areas of the remote **Te Urewera National Park** should contact the Department of Conservation, Aniwaniwa Visitor Centre, Private Bag, Wairoa (℃ **06/837-3803**). Apart from the famous multiday Lake Waikaremoana Great Walk, there are at least 15 short and day walks in this area.

WHERE TO STAY
In Gisborne

There are a number of new accommodations providers in and around Gisborne that warrant a special mention. Top of the list is **Repongaere Estate** ★★★, 30 Repongaere Rd., Patutahi, Gisborne (℃ **06/862-7515;** www.repongaere.co.nz), which has two modern villas elevated above a boutique vineyard and olive estate just 15 minutes from the city. Each villa has two bedrooms and two bathrooms, and a chef can be arranged to produce gourmet meals in your villa. Rates range from NZ$310 to NZ$400. **Knapdale**

Eco Lodge, 114 Snowsill Rd., Waihirere, Gisborne (✆ **06/862-5444;** www.knapdale. co.nz), puts the emphasis on tranquillity and environmentalism. Set on a farm with a wide variety of animals, they have two rooms priced at NZ$305 to NZ$375. And if you'd like a beachfront stay, **Absolute Wainui B&B** ★, 69 Wairere Rd., Wainui Beach (✆ **06/ 867-0386;** www.absolutewainui.com), has two very nice rooms (single-party bookings only) just 5 minutes' drive from Gisborne, which cost NZ$200 to NZ$400. If you prefer a more traditional inner city stay, head for **Te Kura B&B,** 14 Cheeseman Rd. (✆ **06/ 863-3497;** www.tekura.co.nz), which has two modest rooms in a lovely Arts and Crafts house for NZ$120 to NZ$130. One room is en suite and one has a private bathroom. Budget beds can be found at **Gisborne YHA Hostel,** 32 Harris St. (✆ **06/867-3269;** yha.gisborne@clear.net.nz), which is close to town and offers 41 dorm beds for NZ$22 to NZ$26. All rates here and below include 12.5% GST and parking.

Portside Hotel ★★ (**Value**)   The Portside brings a new level of smart and much-needed apartment-style accommodations to Gisborne. Studio rooms are a little on the small side, but if you opt for the one-bedroom suite, you'll be more than happy. They have bigger kitchens, laundry facilities, and a big corner tub and shower. Two-bedroom suites sleep four, and connecting rooms mean flexibility. Prices are unbelievably good. The only downside is the lack of a restaurant, but there are plenty of choices close by.

2 Reads Quay, Gisborne. ✆ **06/869-1000.** Fax 06/869-1020. www.portsidegisborne.co.nz. 64 units. NZ$150 guest room; NZ$175 suite; NZ$420 penthouse. Long-stay rates and special breakfast packages. AE, DC, MC, V. **Amenities:** Airport transport; concierge; nearby golf course; very small gym; outdoor lit pool; room service. *In room:* A/C, TV/DVD, fridge, hair dryer, kitchen or kitchenette, minibar, Wi-Fi.

Around East Cape

I'm happy to report that the availability of accommodations around East Cape has improved greatly in recent years, which means you no longer have to rush around this spectacular knob of land in 1 day. At Te Kaha, 70km (43 miles) from Opotiki, you'll find the brand-new **Te Kaha Beach Resort** ★★, SH35, Te Kaha (✆ **07/325-2830;** www. tekahabeachresort.co.nz), which has 24 rooms on a spectacular site overlooking the bay, for NZ$160 to NZ$325. They have a pool and a restaurant on-site. Thirty kilometers farther on, you'll find **Stollies** ★, SH35, Waihau Bay (✆ **07/325-3603;** www.holiday homes.co.nz), which is a very nice new home with two guest rooms in a seaside suite and meals by arrangement. At the top of the Cape you'll find the much more modest **Hicks Bay Motor Lodge,** SH35, Hicks Bay (✆ **06/864-4880;** www.hicksbaymotel.co.nz), which has very dated rooms in need of work from NZ$100. Its singular advantage is that it is cheap and almost exactly halfway between Opotiki and Gisborne. And, saving the best till last—don't go past **Rangimarie Beachstay** ★★, 930 Anaura Rd., Anaura Bay (✆ **021/633-372;** www.anaura-stay.co.nz), which is situated above one of the cape's loveliest golden sand beaches. They have a romantic self-contained cottage for NZ$220 a night, a suite for NZ$200, a loft bedroom with private bathroom for NZ$200, and a fourth room (with private bathroom) for NZ$175. There are no restaurants in the bay (which is 67km/42 miles north of Gisborne), but hosts David and Judy Newell are happy to provide meals by arrangement.

WHERE TO DINE

In the post-millennium vacuum, Gisborne eateries seem to have declined rather than improved. Service is often near appalling and the meals are disappointing and entirely forgettable. All that saves some places is their location. But don't despair—there are one or two gems. **La Quay,** 6 Reads Quay (✆ **06/868-7578**), is slightly voluminous and lacking character, but I mention it here because this new cafe with a small delicatessen is handily located beside Portside Hotel. I enjoyed very good coffee here.

Bookshop Café ★★★ CAFE This is my new Gisborne favorite. The place's own billing says it all—"Serious food and serious coffee." Located above Muir's Bookshop, with plenty of good books and magazines to browse, it has fabulous counter food, a delightful little balcony overlooking the main street, and the best coffee in Gisborne. It's the perfect place for coffee or a light lunch.

62 Gladstone Rd. ✆ **06/869-0653.** Main courses NZ$12–NZ$20. AE, MC, V. Mon–Fri 8:30am–4pm; Sat–Sun 9:30am–3pm.

Ruba ★★ CAFE In the grand old Union Steamship Company building, this hidden-away treat is worth seeking out. It serves terrific breakfasts, excellent coffee, and a lunch menu that's more creative than that at some of the town's bigger eateries. They're also a little more adventurous with their menu than some. A long pine table covered in magazines sets the casual mood. You won't regret a visit.

14 Childers Rd. ✆ **06/868-6516.** Main courses NZ$15–NZ$22. AE, MC, V. Mon–Sat 7am–4pm; Sun 9am–3pm.

Verve Café ★ CAFE/INTERNATIONAL Not only is this one of those refreshingly scruffy local haunts that abounds in personality, but it's also a three-time winner of the Regional Best Café award. It comes minus pretensions, and you'll find an incredibly mixed crowd enjoying the excellent coffee and simple food. It's especially popular with backpackers and surfers, but all ages congregate here. The menu includes everything from antipasto platters and nachos to pastas, curries, salads, and preparations of fish, lamb, beef, and chicken. This is Gisborne at its laid-back best. You won't leave hungry, and you will have tasted the local culture. They also have live music every Friday night.

121 Gladstone Rd. ✆ **06/868-9095.** Reservations recommended for dinner. Main courses NZ$12–NZ$26. AE, MC, V. Mon–Sat 8:30am–10pm; Sun 8:30am–3pm.

The Wharf Café, Bar & Restaurant ★ ⓞverrated PACIFIC RIM The location is unbeatable, but sadly, neither the food nor the service lives up to the hype. The menu reads well—seared scallops, roasted pork loin, snapper filet with Gruyère potatoes—but the place begs for an overhaul of staff and delivery.

60 The Esplanade, Shed No. 1, The Wharf. ✆ **06/868-4876.** Reservations recommended. Main courses NZ$28–NZ$35. AE, DC, MC, V. Daily 9am–late. Closed Dec 25–26.

EN ROUTE TO NAPIER

The 216km (134-mile) drive along State Highway 2 from Gisborne to Napier passes through a wealth of picturesque natural scenery: rugged high-country sheep stations, lush native bush, Lake Tutira, and a breathtaking view of Poverty Bay from the top of the Wharerata Hills, 37km (23 miles) outside the city. Between Poverty and Hawke's bays, **Morere Hot Springs Scenic Reserve** ★ (✆ **06/837-8856;** www.morerehotsprings.com) is signposted on the highway. It makes a nice stop-off point for a bush walk—there are six tracks, which take from 10 minutes to 2½ hours round-trip—a picnic, or a soak in the pools (both thermal and cold). Admission to the public pools is NZ$5 for adults, NZ$3 for children; private pools cost NZ$3 extra. They're open daily from 10am to 7pm (till 5pm in winter).

2 HAWKE'S BAY ★★★

216km (134 miles) SW of Gisborne; 423km (262 miles) SE of Auckland; 228km (141 miles) SE of Rotorua

Napier is bursting at the seams with pride, and so it should be: It is the prettiest little city in New Zealand. It boasts an unbeatable combination of fabulous climate, elegant Art Deco architecture, as much award-winning wine as anyone could want, plus sea, surf, and pretty vineyards—and, combined with Hastings and Havelock North, the best selection of unique boutique accommodations in the country. A wealth of unexpected surprises awaits—it's one of my favorite places.

It hasn't always been this good. In 1931, a massive earthquake demolished the whole of Napier and nearby Hastings, killing hundreds of people. But like the phoenix, Napier rose again, this time on new ground lifted out of the harbor by the force of the earthquake. Rebuilt during the Depression, the town opted for the Art Deco and Spanish mission architecture so popular at the time. As a result, Napier (pop. 54,298) easily claims one of the world's largest collections of buildings in these styles.

Hastings (pop. 67,428) is something of a nonentity by comparison. It does have some fine Spanish mission architecture, plus Te Mata Peak, with the best views in the district, and it's closest to the famous gannet colonies. It also has excellent wineries and some great accommodations.

Havelock North (pop. 8,507) is a genteel community surrounded by wineries, farms, and fruit orchards. It boasts some of the best-regarded private schools and some of the oldest commercial wine cellars in the country.

ESSENTIALS

GETTING THERE & GETTING AROUND **By Plane** **Air New Zealand** (© 06/833-5400) provides daily service between Napier/Hastings and Auckland, Wellington, and Christchurch, with connections to other key centers. The airport is a 5-minute drive from Napier City and a 20-minute drive from Hastings. Shuttle service (© 06/879-9766) into Napier costs NZ$20.

By Coach (Bus) **InterCity** (© 09/623-1503) and **Newmans** (© 09/623-1504) provide daily bus service between Napier/Hastings and Auckland, Gisborne, Rotorua, Taupo, Tauranga, and Wellington. **Magic Travellers** (© 09/358-5600) and **Kiwi Experience** (© 09/366-9830) both include Napier/Hastings on their routes. Monday through Friday, **Coachrite Connections** (© 06/868-9969) operates regular bus service between Hawke's Bay towns.

By Car An extensive highway system links the region to key North Island cities: Wellington on State Highway 2; Rotorua/Taupo on State Highway 5; Gisborne on State Highway 2; and Auckland via Taupo on State Highway 1 and State Highway 5. The drive from Auckland is 5 hours; from Wellington, 4 hours; from Rotorua, 2½ hours; from Gisborne, 2 hours; and from Taupo, 1½ hours. Three excellent, free touring guides cover this area: *Pacific Coast Highway* (**www.pacificcoast.co.nz**), *Thermal Explorer Highway,* and the *Classic New Zealand Wine Trail* (www.classicwinetrail.co.nz). Pick up copies at any visitor center.

By Taxi A **Napier Taxis** (© 06/835-7777) stand is at Clive Square.

ORIENTATION   The pride of Napier is **Marine Parade,** a beautiful stretch of waterfront lined with stately Norfolk pines. **Kennedy Road,** the main thoroughfare, diagonally bisects the town. The fishing wharf suburb of **Ahuriri,** around **Bluff Hill,** is home to nice shops and restaurants. The best beach is **Westshore Beach** in Westshore Domain, part of the new-land legacy of the 1931 disaster.

Hastings lies 20 minutes south of Napier, and Havelock North is 5 minutes southeast of Hastings.

VISITOR INFORMATION   The **Napier i-SITE Visitor Centre,** 100 Marine Parade, Napier (✆ **06/834-1911;** fax 06/835-7219; www.visitus.co.nz), is open daily 9am to 5pm (closed Dec 25). It has extended hours from December 26 to March 31.

The **Hastings i-SITE Visitor Centre,** Russell Street North, Hastings (✆ **06/873-5526;** fax 06/873-5529; www.hastings.co.nz), is open Monday through Friday from 8:30am to 5pm, Saturday and Sunday from 9am to 3pm, with extended summer hours (closed Dec 25).

For a calendar of events in the area, check www.hawkesbaynz.com.

FAST FACTS   The chief **post office** is on Dickens Street, Napier (✆ **06/835-3725**). For Internet access, try **Cybers Internet Café,** 98 Dickens St., Napier (✆ **06/835-0125**), open daily 8:30am to midnight. The **Chemist Shop Napier,** 32 Munroe St. (✆ **06/834-0884**), is open daily 8am to 9pm.

SPECIAL EVENTS   The **Harvest Hawke's Bay Wine and Food Festival** ★★★ (✆ **06/834-1911;** www.harvesthawkesbay.co.nz), during the first week of February, provides an opportunity to sample a wealth of food and wine in one location. The **Art Deco Weekend** ★★★ draws up to 18,000 people for wining, dining, dancing, jazz, vintage cars, and special walks and tours. Most participants dress in 1920s and 1930s fashions. It's on the third weekend in February. For details, contact the **Art Deco Trust** in Napier (✆ **06/835-0022;** www.artdeconapier.com).

EXPLORING HAWKE'S BAY

Napier is the focus of most of the bay's paid attractions, but you'll find the bulk of the wineries in the Hastings/Havelock North area. *Tip:* Get a **4 in 1 Pass** from the visitor center. This gives you entry to four Marine Parade attractions including the National Aquarium, Hawke's Bay Museum & Art Gallery, Ocean Spa, and Par 2 Minigolf. The pass is also available from any one of the participating attractions.

In Napier

The **National Aquarium of New Zealand** ★★★, Marine Parade (✆ **06/834-1404;** www.nationalaquarium.co.nz), opened in March 2002. It includes a huge ocean tank

---

(Finds)   Classy Crafts

Statements Gallery ★★★, Tennyson and Hastings streets, Napier (✆ **06/834-1331;** www.statementsgallery.co.nz), is one of my favorite places for finding that extra-special piece of colorful New Zealand art glass, beautiful handcrafted New Zealand jewelry, and ceramics you'll want to take home. It also stocks paintings, prints, and sculptures.

Black Barn Vineyards Amphitheatre ★★★, Black Barn Road, Havelock North (© **06/877-7985;** www.blackbarn.com), is one of the best outdoor venues in the country; if you time it right (ring for the program), you could enjoy a fabulous live concert or an evening of open-air cinema. Sit on grass terraces surrounded by grapevines and enjoy one of your most memorable New Zealand nights. Make sure you book early.

with an acrylic tunnel, plus new themed exhibits. Napier opened the first public aquarium in New Zealand in 1956, and it now holds the most comprehensive collection. It's as close to the ocean as you can get without getting your feet wet, and the themed sleepovers for children and the interactive displays are a big hit.

The aquarium's magnificent architecture imitates the form of a stingray. Exhibits include tuatara, kiwi, piranha, crocodile, and every sea creature you could imagine. Kids have lots of hands-on activities, and feeding times (the reef tank at 10am, the ocean tank at 2pm) are always exciting. Allow 1 to 2 hours for a good visit. Admission costs NZ$16 for adults, NZ$8 for children 3 to 14, and NZ$44 for families. Diving in the oceanarium (certified divers only) costs NZ$68, plus NZ$7.30 for the tank and NZ$36 for dive gear. The Behind the Scenes Tour runs twice daily at 9am and 1pm and costs NZ$31 for adults, NZ$16 for children ages 3 to 14, including admission. The aquarium is open daily 9am until 5pm (till 7pm Dec 26–31). It's closed Christmas Day.

The Museums Chief among museum attractions is **Hawke's Bay Museum & Art Gallery** ★★, 65 Marine Parade (© **06/835-7781;** www.hbmag.co.nz). Check out the splendid semi-permanent, award-winning exhibition *Nga Tukemata—The Awakening,* which presents the art of local Ngati Kahungunu people. An audiovisual presentation tells the story of the 1931 earthquake, and there are ongoing New Zealand art and design exhibitions. Admission is NZ$10 adults and NZ$5 children 5 to 15; and it's open daily from 10am to 6pm (until 8pm on Thurs).

For something a bit different, look into the **British Car Museum,** 63 East Rd., Te Awanga (© **06/875-0561** or 025/231-3916), which parades more than 90 cars. It's open Saturday and Sunday from 10am to 4pm and by appointment. Admission is NZ$8 for adults, NZ$3 for children.

Not quite a museum, but almost, is **Trainworld and Lilliput,** 88 Dickens St., Napier (© **06/835-8045**). Up to 37 miniature trains operate on 800m (2,625 ft.) of track in one of the world's largest 00-gauge model railways. It's open daily from 10am to 5pm with reduced winter hours; admission is NZ$10 for adults, NZ$5 for children, and NZ$25 for families.

Fur, Fruit, Feathers & Wool For everything you ever wanted to know about the opossum but were afraid to ask, head for **Opossum World,** 157 Marine Parade (© **06/835-7697;** www.opossumworld.co.nz). See how the opossum trapper lives, look through a working boutique tannery, and buy furry crafts and souvenirs. They may be cute, but the animals are an ecological nightmare—over 70 million of them in the wild eat 21,000 tons of foliage each night. The museum is open daily from 9am to 5pm and admission is free.

A Taste of the Wineries

Hawke's Bay is home to New Zealand's oldest winemaking establishments, and with over 40 wineries to choose from, you're bound to find a glass of something pleasing. The conditions are ideal for late-maturing varieties such as cabernet sauvignon and Riesling. Chardonnay, sauvignon blanc, and sweet dessert wines from this area are also prized. Most wineries are open daily, with free tours, tastings, and sales. At least 10 also feature restaurants. Make sure you pick up the free *Hawke's Bay Winery Guide* and map from the visitor center. New vineyards and wineries are opening all the time; or carry a copy of the *Classic New Zealand Wine Trail.*

Craggy Range Winery ★★★, 253 Waimarama Rd., Havelock North (ⓒ **06/873-7126;** www.craggyrange.com), opened in 2003. It's the brainchild of Americans Terry and Mary Peabody and is already producing excellent chardonnay, sauvignon blanc, and merlot. **Te Mata Estate,** 349 Te Mata Rd., Havelock North (ⓒ **06/877-4399;** www.temata.co.nz), has been erected in stages since 1870. It's been voted New Zealand's top winery. **Trinity Hill** ★, 2396 Hwy. 50, Hastings (ⓒ **06/879-7778;** www.trinityhill.com), is a modern winery with picnic hamper-style food available during the summer. It has a bent toward chardonnay and bordeaux-style reds. **Te Awa Winery** ★★, 2375 Hwy. 50, Hastings (ⓒ **06/879-7602;** www.teawa.com), produces bordeaux-style reds and top label chardonnay and has one of the best winery restaurants, serving great lunches daily.

Vidal Wines ★★★, 913 St. Aubyn St. E., Hastings (ⓒ **06/876-8105;** www.vidal.co.nz), was founded in 1905 and produces many prizewinning wines. Its popular restaurant is open for lunch and dinner daily and is consistently rated one of the best. **Alpha Domus** ★★, 1829 Maraekakaho Rd., Hastings (ⓒ **06/879-6752;** www.alphadomus.co.nz), is a tiny boutique operation that makes outstanding bordeaux-style reds. **Clearview Estate** ★★, 194 Clifton Rd., Te Awanga, RD2, Hastings (ⓒ **06/875-0150;** www.clearviewestate.co.nz), has a very pretty lunch restaurant. Its blissful seaside location among grapevines and olive and avocado trees makes it a winner. **Brookfields Vineyards & Restaurant,** Brookfields Road, Meeanee, Taradale, Napier (ⓒ **06/834-4615;** www.brookfieldsvineyards.co.nz), is another popular restaurant and vineyard setting closer to town. Brookfields' wines are fruit driven and age well.

Mission Estate Winery, 198 Church Rd., Taradale, Napier (ⓒ **06/845-9350;** www.missionestate.co.nz), was founded by the Catholic Society of Mary in 1851. You can dine in the historic seminary building Monday through Satur-

Twenty-four kilometers (15 miles) south of Napier, visit **Pernel FruitWorld,** 1412 Pakowhai Rd., Hastings (ⓒ **06/878-3383;** www.pernel.nzliving.co.nz). You've tried wine tasting; now try fruit tasting in the fruit bowl of New Zealand. Pernel grows over 85 different varieties of pip and stone fruit. Leap aboard its unique apple wagon for a tour of the 32-hectare (79-acre) working orchard and fruit pack house. Visit during September or October, and you'll find the place a picturesque show of blossoms. On-site

day nights. **Church Road Winery** ★, 150 Church Rd., Taradale, Napier (☏ **06/ 845-9137;** www.churchroad.co.nz), is another of the older wineries. Established in the late 1890s, it contains the first wine museum in New Zealand. It also stages summer concerts; a restaurant serves daily lunches. **Sacred Hill Winery** ★★, 1033 Dartmoor Rd., Puketapu, Napier (☏ **06/844-0138;** www. sacredhill.com), occupies a divine hilltop setting and serves outdoor summer lunches on weekends from November to Easter.

A Total Wine & Food Destination   If you have a weakness for fine food and fine wines, you must visit **Sileni Estates Winery & Epicurean Centre** ★★★, Maraekakaho Road, Hastings (☏ **06/879-8768;** www.sileni.co.nz). You'll find a divine little gourmet-food store, a fabulous restaurant, the wine cellar, a culinary school, and more, all in a striking piece of architecture set among vineyards. The center is open daily from 10am to 5pm. The restaurant opens daily for lunch at 11am in summer. They offer a range of exciting culinary school packages from NZ$150 and vineyard and winery tours from NZ$15.

Wine Tours   One of the most down-to-earth and personalized tours is with **Grant Petherick Exclusive Wine Tours** ★★, 805 Fitzroy Ave., Hastings (☏/fax **06/876-7467;** www.flyfishingwinetours.co.nz). He takes two to six people at a time, and everyone raves about him. Tours cost NZ$100 per person per hour. **Grape Escape** (☏ **0800/100-489** in NZ; www.grapeescape.net.nz) puts you in the capable and experienced hands of Greg Beachen. His afternoon wine tour (1–5pm) takes in four to five wineries and costs NZ$60.

If you feel like exercising, call **On Yer Bike Winery Tours** ★★★, 121 Rosser Rd., Hastings (☏ **06/879-8735;** www.onyerbikehb.co.nz). Its flat-terrain tours are suitable for anyone and cycle past olive groves, orchards, ostrich farms, and horse studs (in addition to seven of the better Hastings wineries), giving you a back-road view of this charming region. You have a choice of rickshaws, tandem cycles, or mountain bikes; the tour team will collect any wine you purchase along the way. Tours are NZ$50 per person, and you should allow up to 5 hours. If you don't have time for a winery tour, head downtown to the **New Zealand Wine Centre** ★★, AMP Building, 1 Shakespeare Rd., Napier (☏ **06/ 835-5326;** www.newzealandwinecentre.co.nz), which features red and white aroma awareness rooms, cellar door wine sales, and the Big Picture Wine Theatre, where you can meet six local winemakers (on film) and taste their wines. It's open daily from 10am to 8pm and the full wine experience with tasting costs NZ$29 per person (NZ$15 for nondrinkers).

are a shop, cafe, and museum. It's open daily from 9am to 5pm. Regular tours (phone for times) cost NZ$16 for adults, NZ$8 for children 15 and under.

And if you still haven't learned all there is to know about sheep, visit **Classic Sheepskins Tannery,** 22 Thames St., off Pandora Road, Napier (☏ **06/835-9662;** www.classic sheepskins.co.nz). It offers free 25-minute tours through its tannery, daily at 11am and 2pm. The shop sells sheepskin products at factory prices and offers worldwide mailing service. The shop is open Monday through Friday from 8:30am to 5pm, Saturday and Sunday from 9am to 4pm. It is closed Christmas Day and Good Friday.

An Art Deco Amble   The city of Napier is virtually a museum of Art Deco and Spanish mission architecture, built from 1931 to 1933, after the earthquake. Over 70 years later, the buildings are remarkably unchanged. A map outlining a 1½- to 2-hour self-guided walk through the downtown area and another showing a more extensive scenic drive are available for NZ$5 each at the visitor center and at the **Art Deco Shop** ★★, 163 Tennyson St. (© **06/835-0022;** www.artdeconapier.com). Open daily from 9am to 5pm (closed Dec 25), it stocks a wide range of brochures and terrific Art Deco gifts.

Guided walking tours ★★ run all year. Bookings are not necessary; just go to the Art Deco Shop and inquire about the next tour. The 1-hour **Morning Walk** leaves from the visitor center daily at 10am (except Dec 25). It includes an Art Deco booklet and ends at the Art Deco Shop, where you can watch a video. This walk is NZ$15 for adults, free for children ages 5 to 15. The **Afternoon Walk** begins at the Art Deco Shop at 2pm, daily from October through June and on Wednesday, Saturday, and Sunday from July to September. The 2-hour program includes an introductory slide presentation, an Art Deco booklet, and a 1½-hour walk. The cost is NZ$20 for adults. A 1-hour vintage car tour of Art Deco landmarks in a 1934 Buick costs NZ$130, maximum three people. Ask about the new **Evening Walk** (NZ$18) and the **Deco Bus Tour** (NZ$38). You'll find more Art Deco and a whole cluster of new boutique stores, restaurants, cafes, and accommodations over at the portside village of Ahuriri (www.ahuriri.co.nz). Just follow Marine Parade around past the port and follow the signs. The visitor center also has an Ahuriri brochure detailing businesses and attractions.

In Hastings

The **Hawke's Bay Exhibition Centre,** 201 Eastbourne St. E. (©/fax **06/876-2077;** hbec@inhb.co.nz), is the region's major venue for touring exhibits of paintings, sculpture, crafts, and historical material. It has a cafe and a shop specializing in local crafts. The center is open Monday through Friday from 10am to 4:30pm; Saturday, Sunday, and holidays from 11am to 4pm (closed Dec 25). And make sure you pick up the **Public Artworks** brochure ★★, which details the large number of public sculptures (over a dozen) that have been installed in Hastings and Havelock North as part of an award-winning revitalization program.

Driving to the top of **Te Mata Peak** ★★★, about 11km (7 miles) from Hastings, is a must-do activity. Take Havelock Road to Te Mata Peak, then to Simla Avenue to Te Mata Peak Road, and ascend the 393m (1,289-ft.) peak. On a clear day, the grand limestone ridge between beach and city offers panoramic views across the Ruahine, Kaweka, and Maungaharuru ranges, with the volcano Ruapehu visible in the distance. There are also walking tracks in the forest as you ascend.

Gannet Gazing   Australian gannets have been nesting at **Cape Kidnappers** ★★★ since the 1870s, with numbers steadily increasing to around 6,500 pairs. This makes it the largest and most accessible mainland gannet colony in the world. The sanctuary affords stunning views and is open to the public from October to April. The best time to view the birds is from early November to late February. If you want to go it alone, drive 21km (13 miles) south to Clifton Domain; then it's a 2-hour walk along 8km (5 miles) of sandy beach. **_Note:_** The walk _must_ be done at low tide because the high tide rides all

---

ⓘ Tips   **Kidnappers Escape**

Stop by the visitor center to pick up the excellent free brochure and map *Kidnappers Escape* ★★★, which details all artists, craftspeople, accommodations, and tours in this especially picturesque area. The trail starts at Clive, which is a 5-minute drive from Napier, Hastings, or Havelock North, and covers the 12km (7¹⁄₂-mile) coastal stretch out to Clifton. A great day out. For more information, check **www.kidnappersescape.com**.

---

the way up to the base of steep cliffs. Be sure to check with the Napier or Hastings visitor centers or with the **Department of Conservation** (ⓒ **06/834-3111**) about tide times.

There are two main organized tours, which basically differ in the form of transport. **Gannet Safaris Overland** (ⓒ **0800/427-232** in NZ, or 06/875-0888; www.gannet safaris.co.nz) offers half-day tours in an air-conditioned coach from September to May; no walking is required. The 3½-hour trip departs daily at 9:30am and 1:30pm and costs NZ$65 per person. **Gannet Beach Adventures** (ⓒ **0800/426-638** in NZ, or 06/875-0898; www.gannets.com) transports you by tractor and trailer for NZ$38 adults, NZ$23 children ages 2 to 14. It includes 20 to 30 minutes of walking and lasts 4 hours. Tours operate from October through early May.

In Havelock North

At **Arataki Honey,** 66 Arataki Rd. (ⓒ **0800/272-825** in NZ, or 06/877-7300; www.aratakihoneyhb.co.nz), you can see into the world of the honeybee through glass walls. It's one of the largest beekeeping enterprises in the country. Visitors can take a tour of the honey factory (daily at 1:30pm), taste the honey, and browse in the gift shop. It's open daily 9am to 5pm, closed Christmas Day, Good Friday, Easter Sunday, and April 25. Entry is free but tours cost NZ$12 per person; call ahead to arrange a tour.

OUTDOOR PURSUITS

BALLOONING   Waft skyward from Hastings with **Early Morning Balloons** (ⓒ/fax **06/879-4229;** www.hotair.co.nz). Flight time is around 1 hour, but allow 4 hours total. Adults fly for NZ$360, children 10 to 12 for NZ$325. The cost includes breakfast.

CANOEING   **Sail 'n Surf,** Pandora Road and Humber Street, Ahuriri, Napier (ⓒ/fax **06/835-0684**), rents canoes and windsurfers for use in a safe tidal waterway. A single canoe costs NZ$25 for 1 hour.

FISHING   **Grant Petherick Fly Fishing,** 805 Fitzroy Ave., Hastings (ⓒ/fax **06/876-7467;** www.flyfishingwinetours.co.nz), caters to anglers of all abilities and offers full- and half-day trips for nymph and dry fly-fishing. He charges NZ$100 per person per hour.

GOLF   The **Napier Golf Club,** Waiohiki, State Highway 50, Taradale, Napier (ⓒ **06/844-7913**), is an excellent 18-hole course just minutes from the city. Greens fees are NZ$35 for affiliated members, NZ$55 for nonaffiliated players. **Cape Kidnappers Golf Course** ★★★, 446 Clifton Rd., Te Awanga (ⓒ **06/873-1018;** www.capekidnappers.com), is one of the finest courses in the world. You'll pay NZ$400 for a round.

(Kids) Especially for Kids

Treat yourself to a moment's rest by letting the kids loose at **Splash Planet** ★★, Grove Road, Hastings (© **06/876-9856;** www.splashplanet.co.nz). The park has everything from go-carts, bumper boats, a pirate ship, and a train to castles, a continuous river-raft ride, an activity pool, a safe toddlers' pool, miniature golf, and more. It's open daily October to April from 10am to 6pm (closed May–Sept). Admission is NZ$25 for adults, NZ$20 for children under 16, NZ$90 for families.

In Napier, you'll find lots of fun at **Napier Aquatic Centre,** Maadi Road, Onekawa (© **06/834-4150;** www.napieraquatic.co.nz). As well as swimming, you can play volleyball, miniature golf, touch rugby, and basketball. It's open daily from 6am to 9pm. For more watery fun, visit **Ocean Spa Napier** ★★★, 42 Marine Parade, Napier (© **06/835-8553**), which features toddler pools, lap pools, sauna and massage facilities, beauty therapy, and a cafe. It's open Monday through Saturday from 6am to 10pm, Sunday 8am to 10pm. Admission starts at NZ$8 for adults, NZ$5 for children, NZ$20 for families.

Another great place to burn off energy is **Kiwi Adventure Company** ★★★, 58 West Quay, Ahuriri, Napier (© **06/834-3500;** www.kiwi-adventure.co.nz). It has climbing walls for beginners to experts and also offers kayak lessons and rentals, plus custom-made adventure trips. It's open Tuesday through Friday from 3 to 9pm, Saturday and Sunday 10am to 6pm. For farmyard fun head for **Haumoana Farmyard Zoo,** 32 East Rd., Haumoana, Hastings (© **06/875-0244**). Kids can interact with alpacas, turtles, ostriches, and common farm animals, or take a pony ride. Zoo entry is NZ$8 for adults, NZ$5 for children, and NZ$25 for a family. It's open daily from October through February, from 10am to 5pm. Finish off at the **Summer Sweet Shop,** 298 Middle Rd., Havelock North (© **06/877-1397;** www.summersweetshop.co.nz). They stock more than 40 varieties of traditional boiled sweets, ice creams, and chocolates. They're open from mid-October through April daily 10am to 5pm.

WHERE TO STAY

Stylish accommodations abound in Hawke's Bay, as a stop at the visitor center will quickly confirm. The endless choices include dozens of gorgeous little self-contained cottages, many of them in association with vineyards. Rates listed below include 12.5% GST and parking.

In Napier

Summer visitors may well fancy camping in this balmy climate. If that's the case, head straight for **Kennedy Park Top 10 Park** ★, Storkey Street, off Kennedy Road (© **0800/457-275** in NZ, or 06/843-9126; www.kennedypark.co.nz), which has a grand history of treating generations of New Zealanders to a fabulous stay. Set on 2.8 hectares (7 acres) with a pool and a playground, it's a great place for kids. Backpackers will find good digs at **Napier YHA,** 277 Marine Parade (© **06/835-7039;** www.yha.co.nz), just across the road from major attractions and close to town; and you'll find B&B lodgings at **Mon**

Logis, 415 Marine Parade, Napier (✆ **06/835-2125;** www.babs.co.nz/monlogis), which has four upstairs rooms a few minutes' walk from town for NZ$260. **Scenic Hotel Te Pania,** 45 Marine Parade (✆ **0800/696-963** in NZ, or 06/833-7733; www.scenicgroup. co.nz), is also worth checking out. Its 114 bright, airy rooms (NZ$270–NZ$506) are a much more modern experience than the County Hotel (below) and it's within walking distance of most shopping.

For a touch of inner city history and luxury, I'd opt for the **Dome Penthouse Apartments** ★★, Top Floor, T&G Building, Marine Parade (✆ **06/835-0707;** www.the dome.co.nz), which has two superb, two-bedroom penthouses with amazing views; and, on the lower floor, another four double suites plus a plunge pool. The suites are incredible value at NZ$295 and the penthouses go for NZ$850. Across town you'll find a modern, luxurious apartment filled with leading New Zealand art and design at **Esther's Place** ★★, Apartment 504, the Waterfront, 7 Humber St., Ahuriri (✆ **06/875-1977;** www.millarroad.co.nz), which is all yours for NZ$500.

The County Hotel (Value) This is a very English-style boutique hotel in a faithfully restored Edwardian building right in the heart of Napier. There are plenty of more modern stays in town, but there's old-world charm and history here that many enjoy—it's one of only two major buildings that survived that 1931 earthquake. Service is attentive, rooms are good size, and there's a library filled with over 1,000 books. Best of all, town is just footsteps away. They have a bronze Green Globe benchmark.

12 Browning St., Napier. ✆ **06/835-7800.** Fax 06/835-7797. www.countyhotel.co.nz. 18 units. NZ$252–NZ$370 queen or Jacuzzi room; NZ$390–NZ$878 suite. Long-stay and off-peak rates. AE, DC, MC, V. **Amenities:** Restaurant (Chambers, Modern NZ); bar; airport transport; babysitting; bike rentals; concierge; gym; room service; nearby Ocean Spa pool and day spa w/saunas. *In room:* A/C, TV, fridge, hair dryer, minibar, Wi-Fi.

The Master's Lodge ★★ (Finds) Once owned by tobacco baron Gerhard Husheer (the master), the gracious home has been restored to its original splendor and is now under the ownership of Larry and Joan Blume—ex–New Yorkers who are among the best hosts I have encountered. The two large suites have million-dollar views over the city and bay, and their elegant appointments are faultless. One has a private bathroom, the other an unbelievably stylish en-suite bathroom with an elevated tub. Vibrant color prevails throughout, and you'll feel very much at home.

10 Elizabeth Rd., Bluff Hill, Napier. ✆ **06/834-1946.** Fax 06/834-1947. www.masterslodge.co.nz. 2 units. NZ$890 includes breakfast. Dinner at additional cost. Special deals. AE, MC, V. Closed in June. Children 11 and under not accepted. **Amenities:** Dining room; bar; airport transport NZ$30; nearby bike rentals; nearby golf course and tennis courts; access to nearby pool and spa. *In room:* Hair dryer, Wi-Fi.

In Hastings

The Farm at Cape Kidnappers ★★★ (Moments) Like its sister property Kauri Cliffs in Northland, this immaculate property leaves no stone unturned when it comes to comfort, service, and luxury. Every suite opens onto a private porch with panoramic views. If you want everything at your fingertips, opt for a lodge suite. Ridge suites—a short walk from the main lodge—are best if you want more privacy. There's also an Owner's Cottage, which can be rented as a two-bedroom or four-bedroom cottage. The overall mood is one of chic rural elegance, and you'll want for nothing at this sublime spot, which comes complete with its own Tom Doak–designed golf course, rated the world's 10th best outside the U.S. by *Golf Digest.*

446–448 Clifton Rd., Te Awanga, Cape Kidnappers. (©) **06/875-1900.** Fax 06/875-1901. www.cape kidnappers.com. 22 suites, 1 Owner's Cottage. Hilltop suite NZ$1,980; lodge or ridge suite NZ$2,678; 4-bedroom owner's cottage NZ$14,065. Off-peak rates. Rates include predinner drinks, gourmet dinner, full breakfast, complimentary minibar (excluding wine and liquor), and full use of lodge facilities excluding golf course. AE, DC, MC, V. Closed June. **Amenities:** Restaurant (Dining Room, Modern NZ); bar at clubhouse; airport transport NZ$135 each way; babysitting; free mountain bikes; concierge; 18-hole golf course on property; health club and spa; outdoor Jacuzzi in pool complex and 1 at owner's cottage; outdoor heated pool; room service. *In room:* A/C, TV/DVD, fridge, hair dryer, minibar, Wi-Fi.

Millar Road ★★ (Finds)   Millar Road is the quintessential Hawke's Bay experience. Perched high above a small vineyard and an adjacent persimmon orchard with views to die for, the two modern cottages feature outstanding New Zealand art and design, and hosts Ginny and Jeremy Collinge have a wealth of local knowledge. I fell in love with this peaceful spot and with a pool on hand and cottages that provide everything—including fabulous bathrooms. Why would you want to go anywhere else? It is comfort plus, the perfect hideaway.

83 Millar Rd., Hastings. (©) **06/875-1977.** Fax 06/875-1927. www.millarroad.co.nz. 2 cottages. NZ$500 per cottage; 2-night minimum stay. Rates include breakfast provisions. Long-stay and off-peak rates. AE, MC, V. **Amenities:** Bar; nearby golf course; outdoor heated pool. *In room:* TV/DVD, CD, fridge, hair dryer, Wi-Fi.

In Havelock North

This is where you'll find the biggest concentration of fabulous cottage, B&B, and new apartment accommodations. **Black Barn Vineyards** ★★★, Black Barn Road ((©) **06/ 877-7985;** www.blackbarn.com), offers the best among them. They include **Summerlee** from NZ$1,500 for three couples; **Rush Cottage** for NZ$350; the **Black Barn** for NZ$550, which sleeps four; and the **River Houses** for NZ$400 to NZ$500. All are seriously classy.

WHERE TO DINE

Including the wineries (see "A Taste of the Wineries," p. 264), Hawke's Bay has a number of good restaurants and cafes, but consistency of food and service is often an issue. Wineries are, in the main, concentrated around the Hastings/Havelock North area, while most good restaurants and cafes are in Napier. Of the wineries, **Sileni Estate, Clearview,** and **Vidal Estate** have excellent restaurants, and Craggy Range Winery's **Terroir** (see p. 272) is not to be missed.

In Napier

In addition to the establishments below, you'll eat well at **Provodore** ★★, 60 West Quay, Ahuriri ((©) **06/834-0189**), which offers modern New Zealand cuisine with Asian and Mediterranean influences. It's open for lunch and dinner Tuesday through Friday and is a popular meeting place for artistic locals. For good light meals at reasonable prices, try **Soak** ★★, at Ocean Spa Napier, Marine Parade ((©) **06/835-7888**), which is open daily from 9am to 9pm. It's a super place to enjoy a long, lazy brunch from the casual cafe-style menu, or an evening meal with a great choice of Hawke's Bay wines.

Ujazi ★★★ CAFE   Almost everyone loves Ujazi—there's just something warm and inviting about the place. It's all about shabby chic, great food, and excellent value for the money. It's considered *the* place for a hearty brunch, and with tables spilling out onto the pavement, it's a great people-watching spot. The menu includes soups, pastas, salads, focaccia melts, and a tasty range for vegetarians.

28 Tennyson St. (©) **06/835-1490.** Lunch main courses NZ$12–NZ$26. MC, V. Daily 8am–5pm (varies seasonally).

ⓜ Moments   Foodie Heaven

A wealth of local gourmet-food producers have joined forces to create the **Hawke's Bay Wine Country Food Trail** ★★★. Pick up the free map at the visitor center and make your way to some of the tastiest spots in these parts. The choices are endless—handmade chocolates, breads, olives, wine, ice cream, honey, and more. All this culminates in the **HB Food Group Farmers' Market** ★★★, held at the Hawke's Bay Showgrounds, Kenilworth Road, Hastings (ⓒ **06/877-1001;** www.savourhawkesbay.co.nz), every Sunday from 8:30am to 12:30pm, and behind the Daily Telegraph Building, Tennyson Street, Napier, every Saturday from 8:30am to 12:30pm.

The **Village Growers' Market** ★★★, held at the Sun Dial, Black Barn Vineyards, off Te Mata Road, Havelock North (ⓒ **06/877-7985;** www.blackbarn.com), is a colorful extravaganza of local food products in an idyllic vineyard setting. It's held Saturday mornings from early November through March from 9am to noon. Finish off the morning with a fabulous brunch at Black Barn Bistro (see below).

In Hastings

Your best bets in this area are the winery restaurants (see "A Taste of the Wineries," p. 264). **Sileni Estates Restaurant** ★★, 2016 Maraekakaho Rd. (ⓒ **06/879-8768**), is one of the most popular, although it's getting a run for its money from the new and very, very chic **Elephant Hill Estate Winery** ★★★, 86 Clifton Rd., Te Awanga (ⓒ **06/872-6060;** www.elephanthill.co.nz), which is open daily from 11am to 10pm. Its menu is inspired by contemporary European cuisine using the finest local products. **Vidal Winery Restaurant** ★★, 913 St Aubyn St. E. (ⓒ **06/876-8105;** www.vidal.co.nz), gets top votes among the locals for its consistently good lunches and dinners. It's open daily from 11:30am to 3pm for lunch and from 6pm for dinner. **Clifton Bay Café** ★★, 468 Clifton Rd. (ⓒ **06/875-0096**), is out of town on the way to Cape Kidnappers, but it's worth the trip. It serves terrific breakfast and lunch daily in summer from 10am to 4pm. Another great find is **River Bar Restaurant** ★★, Main Road, State Highway 2, Clive (ⓒ **06/870-0533**), which is bound to surprise with the quality of its food and its warm, lively atmosphere. It sits 10 minutes between Hastings and Napier and has a great local wine list. **Opera Kitchen** ★★, 312 Eastbourne St., Hastings (ⓒ **06/870-6020;** www.operakitchen.co.nz), is a great spot with local food and wine. It's one of the most popular cafes in all of Hawke's Bay—and for good reason—so expect a crowd. It's open 8am to 4pm Monday through Friday and 9am to 3pm on weekends.

In Havelock North

Black Barn Bistro ★★★, Black Barn Road (ⓒ **06/877-7985**), is my absolute favorite place—a stylish bistro set among vines, with a gorgeous outdoor courtyard sheltered by overhead vines. It's open for lunch Wednesday through Sunday noon to 2:30pm. There's no better place to admire the scenery and sample the fruit of the land. The good-value food and lively atmosphere at the **Rose and Shamrock Village Inn,** Napier Road and Porter Drive (ⓒ **06/877-2999**), styled after an authentic Irish bar, also gets the thumbs up. The nearby **Olive Tree Café,** 7 Joll Rd. (ⓒ **06/877-0222**), is a simple spot that serves excellent light lunches and delicious counter food. And **Diva Bar & Bistro,** Village Court, Napier Road (ⓒ **06/877-5149**), is a pleasant cafe bar for a light evening meal.

Terroir ★★★ FRENCH COUNTRY Big open fireplaces, soaring ceilings, and culinary drama underpin a French-style rustic menu that will have your mouth watering in minutes. Rated one of the top 13 winery restaurants in the world in 2004 by *UK Wine Spectator,* it's guaranteed to impress. You can watch your chickens on the open-fire rotisserie, swoon over wood-fired fish, or savor traditional coq au vin, spit-roasted lamb, and classic duck dishes. It's a big culinary adventure, and the high point of Hawke's Bay dining.

Craggy Range Winery, 253 Waimarama Rd. ℂ 06/873-0143. Main courses NZ$30–NZ$45. AE, DC, MC, V. Daily from noon; express dining 3–6pm; dinner 6pm–late. Closed Monday Easter to Labour Weekend (Oct).

NAPIER AFTER DARK

Night owls looking for a bit of action will do well to head for **Shed 2,** West Quay, Ahuriri (ℂ **06/835-2202**), which has lots of loud music, a big-screen TV, and good food at good prices. It's popular with a young crowd. Next door, there's a more sedate atmosphere in **Caution** ★★ (ℂ **06/835-0028**), a lounge bar serving great cocktails and vintage Hawke's Bay wines. **O'Flaherty's Irish Pub,** Hastings Street, has regular live Irish music and is big on atmosphere. More Irish fun is at **Rosie O'Grady's Irish Bar,** Hastings Street (ℂ **06/835-8689**). **Churchill's Champagne & Snug Bar,** in the County Hotel, 12 Browning St. (ℂ **06/835-7800**), is a small corner bar with over 100 wines and champagnes to choose from; but **Style Latinos** ★★, Hastings Street (ℂ **06/833-7500**), with its '70s and '80s dance music, is more popular with the younger dance crowd.

EN ROUTE TO NEW PLYMOUTH

Contrary to expectations you might have of simply driving east to west from Napier to New Plymouth, by far the quickest way is to drive *south* from Napier. Pass through Waipukurau and Dannevirke on State Highway 2, connecting with State Highway 3 at Woodville and traveling on to Palmerston North. Continue on State Highway 3 to Wanganui, and then up to New Plymouth. This 412km (255-mile) trip should take about 5 hours without stops. The roads are excellent, and you'll be driving through prime farmland for most of the journey.

Taranaki & Wanganui

Situated between Auckland and Wellington, Taranaki is the westernmost province of the North Island. Its major city is New Plymouth, a busy port on the coast of the Tasman Sea. Taranaki is a leading dairy-farming region, an energy center with major reserves of natural gas and oil, and home to Mount Egmont, now known as Mount Taranaki. The region is also famous for its lush gardens, beautiful parks, and world-class surf breaks. In 2008, the United Nations–endorsed Liveable Communities Award named New Plymouth the best city of its size in the world, and the city's Coastal Walkway the world's best environmental project.

Southeast of Taranaki is Wanganui, one of the major towns of the area now known as the River Region, which includes the provinces of Manawatu, Horowhenua, Tararua, Whanganui, and Rangitikei. Until recently, Wanganui did not play a significant part in overseas visitors' itineraries, but its leading light—the broody Whanganui River, the longest navigable river in New Zealand—is worth exploring. A number of good outdoor activities center on the river, and the town will give you an idea of the workings of small-town New Zealand.

1 NEW PLYMOUTH: GATEWAY TO EGMONT NATIONAL PARK

412km (255 miles) W of Napier; 164km (102 miles) NW of Wanganui; 369km (229 miles) SW of Auckland

You get the feeling that being left out on the western tip of the North Island has had benefits for New Plymouth. As if to compensate, the residents have provided themselves with excellent cultural amenities, stunning gardens, and fabulous nature walks.

Then there are the cows, the milk, the cheese, the world's biggest dairy factory at nearby Hawera, and some of the prettiest rolling green pasture you'll see anywhere in the country. Above all, literally, is Mount Taranaki, the Fuji-like jewel in the Egmont National Park crown, which attracts hundreds of trampers, mountaineers, rock climbers, and casual walkers. Be prepared to be surprised by this buzzy little city of 72,000 people.

ESSENTIALS

GETTING THERE & GETTING AROUND   **By Plane**   **Air New Zealand Link** provides daily flights from Auckland, Wellington, and Wanganui, with connecting service to other cities. Call ✆ **06/755-2250** for flight information. The New Plymouth Airport is approximately 8km (5 miles) from the city, a 10- to 15-minute drive. **Withers Coachlines** (✆ **06/751-1777;** www.withers.co.nz) provides shuttle service to and from the airport and they're much cheaper than taxis.

By Coach (Bus)   **InterCity** (✆ **09/623-1503**) and **Newmans** (✆ **09/623-1504**) provide daily coach service. **New Plymouth City Bus** (✆ **06/753-9646;** www.okatobus. co.nz) operates local city buses.

By Shuttle   **Cruise NZ Tours,** 8 Baring Terrace (© **06/758-3222**), departs New Plymouth daily at 7:30am for the North Egmont Visitor Centre at Egmont National Park, returning to the city at 4:30pm. Reservations are essential; the trip costs NZ$50 round-trip.

By Car   New Plymouth is reached on State Highway 3 from Wanganui via Stratford and from the north via Waitara; or on State Highway 45, the coastal highway, via Opunake. If you have plenty of time, enjoy history, and want to see a remote slice of "old New Zealand," take the **Forgotten World Highway 43** ★★★, which runs between Stratford in Taranaki to Taumaranui in the Ruapehu region. It's about a 3-hour trip. Most i-SITE Visitor centers carry the detailed, pictorial brochure of the trip, which includes all highlights along the way. Note that 12km (7½ miles) of the road are still unsealed and there are no petrol stations along the 155km (96-mile) route.

By Taxi   Call **New Plymouth Taxis** (© **06/757-3000**) or **Energy City Cabs** (© **06/757-5580**).

ORIENTATION   **Devon Street East** and **Devon Street West** are the main thoroughfares. Running parallel and to the north are the one-way streets **Powderham** and **Courtenay,** and to the west, **Vivian** and **Leach streets.** The main road into the city from the south is **Eliot Street.** Once you've memorized the one-way pattern, it's very easy to find your way around. The small towns of Stratford and Hawera lie to the south of New Plymouth.

VISITOR INFORMATION   The i-SITE **New Plymouth Visitor Centre,** Puke Ariki, 65 St. Aubyn St. (© **06/759-6060;** fax 06/759-6073; www.newplymouthnz.com), is open Monday through Friday from 9am to 6pm (Wed until 9pm), and Saturday, Sunday, and public holidays from 9am to 5pm (closed Dec 25). You can also find information on the area at www.taranaki.com.

  South Taranaki i-SITE Visitor Centre, 55 High St., Hawera (© **06/278-8599;** fax 06/278-6599; www.stdc.co.nz), is open Monday through Friday from 8:30am to 5:30pm, and weekends 9:30am to 4pm, December through April; and 10am to 3pm May to November (closed Dec 25).

SPECIAL EVENTS   During October's **Taranaki Rhododendron Festival,** more than 100 private and public gardens open their gates. The **TSB Bank Festival of Lights** ★★ (© **06/759-6060;** www.festivaloflights.co.nz) takes place in Pukekura Park, nightly from mid-December through early February, weather permitting. **WOMAD** (www.womad.co.nz) is a massive 3-day multicultural festival of world music and dance held in March at Brooklands Park; and **Parihaka** (www.parihaka.com) is a 3-day International Peace Festival featuring arts, music, and culture staged on the historic Parihaka Pa in January. Call the visitor center for details of other events, or check the events calendar on the website.

EXPLORING THE TOWNS
In New Plymouth

For thought-provoking contemporary art, head for **Govett-Brewster Art Gallery** ★★★, Queen Street (© **06/759-6060;** www.govettbrewster.com). You'll find major works by world-renowned New Plymouth–born kinetic artist Len Lye (who spent most of his life in New York), accompanied by an ongoing program of changing exhibitions. The gallery is open daily from 10am to 5pm. Entry is by donation.

The Taranaki Museum underwent massive renovations during 2001–02 and reopened in 2003 as **Puke Ariki** ★★★, 1 Ariki St. (✆ **06/758-4544;** www.pukeariki.com). The impressive two-wing complex rises up in the heart of the city, a groundbreaking knowledge center that houses the full public library, the museum, and the visitor information center. An air bridge connects the two wings. The museum showcases a major repository of Taranaki history, including many Maori treasures associated with the Taranaki tribes. "Treasures" is the name that encompasses all gallery spaces, each one focusing on different components of the Taranaki experience. Make sure you check out **Taranaki Stories,** which details the region's tumultuous Maori land wars, pioneer history, and current Taranaki life. The complex has two cafes (see "Where to Dine," below) and a large grass park. The museum is open Monday through Friday from 9am to 6pm, and Saturday, Sunday, and holidays from 9am to 5pm. Admission is free.

The **TSB Bank Bowls New Zealand Museum,** Dean Park, Brooklands Road (✆ **06/758-0284;** bowlsnzmuseum@xtra.co.nz), has the well-deserved distinction of being the only lawn-bowling museum in the world—over 8,000 entries on lawn bowling's history. The museum is open by appointment only; call first.

Three beautifully restored historic buildings you can visit are **Richmond Cottage,** Ariki Street; **Te Henui Vicarage,** 290 Courtenay St.; and the **Gables Colonial Hospital,** Brooklands Park Drive. The visitor center can supply details on their hours.

If you'd like to know more about the region's energy reserves, visit the **Maui Production Station Display Centre,** Tai Road, Oaonui, South Taranaki, on the west side of the mountain on State Highway 45 (✆ **06/757-7171;** www.stos.co.nz). It's New Zealand's largest gas processing plant and offers a host of information and interactive displays. The center is open daily, and admission is free. The **Methanex New Zealand Motunui Plant,** Main Highway, Motunui (✆ **06/754-9700**), is the world's first synthetic fuel plant. Its information center has models and a video display and is open daily 8am to 8pm.

Outdoorsy types might like to cruise the **Sugar Loaf Islands Marine Park,** off the coast of New Plymouth. **Chaddy's Charters** (✆ **06/758-9133;** fax 06/759-9095) will accommodate you on an English lifeboat. The 1-hour cruise takes you to the cluster of small islands, home to an astoundingly rich plant, bird, and wildlife population. The trip costs NZ$25 for adults, NZ$10 for children ages 5 to 12. Fishing trips cost NZ$60 per person and require a minimum of six people.

And if you want to explore a quaint slice of rural life, pick up the detailed brochure and map from the visitor center and drive around the little knob of coast, formally State Highway 45, otherwise known as **Surf Highway.** As well as the premier surf spots, you'll find many small towns, access to Egmont National Park walking tracks, and more. The area has suddenly taken off, and a number of excellent new attractions have sprung up. Make sure you also get the **Oakura Arts Trail** brochure, which details excellent studios like **Ringcraft Moana,** 109 Surrey Hill Rd., Oakura (✆ **06/752-7772;** www.natural pearl.co.nz), open Monday through Friday 9am to 4pm. **Emacadamia,** the Nutcracker Suite, 219 Surrey Hill Rd., Oakura (✆ **06/752-7793;** www.emacadamia.co.nz), is a macadamia-nut orchard offering factory tours and a delicious range of macadamia goodies. It's open Sunday from 1:30 to 4:30pm. The **Egmont Soap Factory,** 33 Tasman St., Opunake (✆ **06/761-8707**), produces environmentally friendly products, including vegetable oil and natural herbal soaps.

In Hawera

In Hawera, a 50-minute drive south of New Plymouth, you'll find what is widely acclaimed as the best private museum in New Zealand. The **Tawhiti Museum** ★★★,

401 Ohangai Rd. (© **0800/921-921** in NZ; www.tawhitimuseum.co.nz), is the brain-child of Nigel and Teresa Ogle. It uses life-size exhibits and scale models—all made by Nigel—to capture the history of South Taranaki. The Tawhiti Bush Railway operates on the first Sunday of each month, weather permitting. The museum, once a cheese factory, is open December 26 through January daily 10am to 4pm; June through August Sunday only 10am to 4pm; the rest of the year Friday through Monday 10am to 4pm. Admission is NZ$10 for adults, NZ$2 for children 5 to 15, and free for children 4 and under. The railway costs NZ$5 for adults, NZ$2 children. This amazing labor of love has won seven separate tourism awards and is definitely worth seeing.

VISITING GARDENS GALORE

The *Taranaki Visitor's Guide,* available free from any of the region's visitor centers, lists 25 public and private gardens that are open to the public. That's just the beginning. **Pukekura Park & Brooklands** ★★★, accessible from Fillis Street, Brooklands Road, or Victoria Road, is a double hit of exquisite parkland that includes walkways, the Brook-lands Zoo (daily 9am–5pm), playgrounds, a beautiful fernery (daily 8am–4pm), lakes, fountains, waterfalls, and specialist gardens. It's a free must-visit spot in any season. Between Christmas and February, try to visit the park at night to see the stunning **TSB Bank Festival of Lights** ★★.

The **Pukeiti Rhododendron Trust** ★★, 2290 Carrington Rd., RD4 (© **06/752-4141;** www.pukeiti.org.nz), has a world-class collection of rhododendron, azalea, and viraya set in centuries-old rainforest. It's a 30-minute drive from New Plymouth on Car-rington Road and is open September through March daily from 9am to 5pm (closed Dec 25); and April through August daily from 10am to 3pm. There is a cafe, shop, and dis-play center. Admission is NZ$10 adults, free for children 15 and under.

Two more must-see gardens offer free admission. **Tupare,** 487 Mangorei Rd. (© **06/765-7127;** www.tupare.info), is open daily from 9am to 5pm. **Hollard Gardens,** Upper Manaia Road, Kaponga (© **06/765-7127;** www.hollardgardens.info), is open daily from 9am to 5pm. Kaponga, a small rural village, is approximately 1 hour from New Plym-outh. From New Plymouth, head south on State Highway 3 to Stratford and turn right toward Dawson Falls. Take a left just past the village of Mahoe to get to Kaponga. The best season to visit is September through March.

EXPLORING EGMONT NATIONAL PARK

The 33,534-hectare (82,829-acre) area surrounding Mount Taranaki/Mount Egmont was established as Egmont National Park in 1900. Centered on the volcanic cone of Mount Taranaki, with more than 140km (87 miles) of walks and tracks, the area is made up of subalpine forest, volcanic landforms, mountain streams and waterfalls, rainforest, and alpine herb fields. There are panoramic views of Taranaki province from the summit of the mountain, which is just 30km (19 miles) from New Plymouth.

The North Egmont entrance to the park is a 25-minute drive from New Plymouth; for shuttle transport, see "Essentials," above. The **North Egmont Visitor Centre,** Egmont Road, Egmont Village (© **06/756-0990;** www.doc.govt.nz), displays geologic and botanic exhibits related to the park. It's open daily in summer from 8am to 4:30pm, and late March to late September Wednesday through Sunday from 9am to 4pm. *Warn-ing:* Mountain weather can be harsh and changeable; care is needed above the tree line at all times. Mount Taranaki may be pretty but it has accounted for more deaths than any other mountain in New Zealand. Always check conditions with the Department of Conservation, Stratford (© **06/765-5144**), before a climb or hike.

(Finds) Dawson Falls

Dawson Falls, off Manaia Road, Kaponga, is well worth a visit. The 17m (54-ft.) falls are just 20 minutes from the parking lot, along a safe and attractive path in the bush. The **Dawson Falls Visitor Centre** (© **027/443-0248**) has a public exhibit with information on the history of the mountain and its flora and fauna. The visitor center is open in summer daily from 8:30am to 4:30pm; winter Wednesday through Sunday from 8:30am to 4:30pm. You'll also find a lodge, a waterfall lookout, many walking trails, and picnic areas. The falls are a 1-hour drive from New Plymouth. Head south on State Highway 3 to Stratford and take the signposted right-hand turn to the falls.

If you want to stay on Mount Taranaki, **Rahiri Cottage,** Egmont Road, Ingle-wood (© **06/756-9093;** fax 06/278-6541; rahiri@taranaki-bakpak.co.nz), is a modest three-bedroom cottage set in Egmont National Park surrounded by native bush. It has two double rooms and one single room for NZ$225, and breakfast costs NZ$25 per person. A percentage of your rates goes toward kiwi conservation within the national park.

Major attractions in the park include walking tracks, rock-climbing areas, delightful picnic spots, and waterfalls. The **Maunganui Ski Fields** (© **06/756-5493**) are on the Stratford side of the park in the area known as East Egmont. Follow the signs off Pembroke Road in Stratford. The ski area has T-bar and rope tows, a canteen, a ski patrol, and instructors. For conditions, call **Snowphone** (© **06/767-7669**) or **Metphone** (© **0900/ 999-06;** NZ$1 per minute).

Mt Taranaki Guided Tours (© **027/441-7042,** or 06/765-6234 after hours; www. mttaranakiguidedtours.co.nz), offers 1- to 4-day guided hiking trips up the mountain, with prices starting at NZ$350 per person. If you'd like the local Maori perspective on Mount Taranaki, seek out **Taranaki Tours** ★★, 48 Buller St. (© **0800/886-877** in NZ, or 06/757-9888; www.macalpineguides.com), whose staff will talk about the spiritual significance of the mountain and the Taranaki Maori land wars. Their "Around Mt. Taranaki" tour costs NZ$155 per person and requires a minimum of two people. Make sure you take plenty of warm, waterproof clothing—even in summer!

OUTDOOR PURSUITS

BIKING **Cycletours Taranaki** (© **06/756-7727;** www.cycle-taranaki.co.nz) will tailor a tour of the region's quiet back roads to suit all ages and levels of fitness. **Joe's Cycles,** 27 West Quay, New Plymouth (© **06/754-7065**), rents mountain bikes and tandem cycles for NZ$20 to NZ$25 for 2 hours.

FISHING **Ultimate Fishing Adventures** (© **027/224-9992** or 06/759-2345) will take you game fishing, fresh- or saltwater fly-fishing, bottom fishing, or sea fishing. In summer it also has evening fishing packages.

GOLF Taranaki is home to 20 courses, including the **New Plymouth Golf Club Ngamotu Links,** Devon Road, Bell Block (© **06/755-1349;** www.golfer.co.nz). The

18-hole, par-72 championship course is on magnificent parklike grounds and has a pro shop, bar, and restaurant. Greens fees are NZ$30 for affiliated and NZ$60 for nonaffiliated players.

KAYAKING **Taranaki Outdoor Adventures** (© **0800/200-625** in NZ; www.toa. co.nz) is expert in sea, surf, and river kayaking. Throw in a bit of bridge-swinging, rock climbing, and rappelling, and you have the ideal one-stop shop.

SURFING **Tara Wave Surf School** (© **06/752-7474**; tarawave@xtra.co.nz), gives lessons at Oakura, one of the region's safest beaches. All gear is provided.

SWIMMING The **New Plymouth Aquatic Centre,** Kawaroa Park (© **06/759-6060**), is open Monday through Friday from 6am to 8:30pm, weekends and public holidays from 8:30am to 7pm (closed Dec 25). It offers a range of heated indoor and outdoor pools, hydroslides, and a steam room. **Taranaki Mineral Pools,** 8 Bonithon Ave. (© **06/ 759-1666;** www.windwand.co.nz/mineralpools), was established in 1914 and now provides a host of modern massage and beauty treatments to follow a hot soak in one of the private or group pools. They are open in summer Monday 9am to 8pm; Tuesday 9am to 5pm; Wednesday through Friday 9am to 9pm; Saturday noon to 9pm; and Sunday 2 to 8pm. Private pools cost NZ$35 per couple.

WALKING A wide range of walks, from easy to energetic, crisscross the New Plymouth area. The visitor center produces a super series of foldout pamphlets and maps that highlight the best walks, including a very good *Walk Taranaki* guidebook. Do try and experience at least some of the multi-award-winning **Coastal Walkway** ★★★, which runs 7km (4⅓ miles) from the mouth of the Waiwhakaiho River in the east to Port Taranaki in the west. You'll pass world-class surf beaches, public art, and great seascapes along the way. You can book a mobility scooter (reservations and bond required), which is free between 8am and noon and 1pm and 5pm. Contact © **06/759-6060** or www.new plymouthnz.com for details.

WHERE TO STAY

A lot of pleasant things have happened to the Taranaki accommodations scene in the last 2 years, chief among them the addition of the smart offerings described below. **Taranaki Country Lodge** ★★, 169 Hursthouse Rd. (© **0800/395-863** in NZ, or 06/755-0274; www.taranakicountrylodge.co.nz), has two suites set amid rolling Taranaki farmland; you'll pay NZ$20 to NZ$300 per night. Dinner is available on request and they offer free airport transport.pAll rates here and below include the 12.5% GST and parking.

Airlie House ★ (Value) This beautifully restored 112-year-old villa is tucked under big trees in the inner city, just a few minutes' walk from town and the popular mineral pools. The lovely downstairs Drawing Room is a big, sunny haven with a super-king-size bed, a window seat, and shower-only en suite. For the money, though, you can't beat the modern apartment upstairs, which has its own kitchen. There's a second downstairs suite with a private bathroom.

161 Powderham St., New Plymouth. © **06/757-8866.** www.airliehouse.co.nz. 3 units. NZ$155. Rates include breakfast. Long-stay rates negotiable. AE, MC, V. **Amenities:** Nearby golf course and tennis courts. *In room:* TV, hair dryer, Wi-Fi.

Nice Hotel & Bistro ★★★   New Plymouth's only small luxury hotel offers stylish rooms with individual charm. You'll find feather duvets, contemporary artwork, and generous bathrooms with double Jacuzzis or massage showers. The hotel is right in the heart of the city and it has a popular restaurant downstairs. The suite is divine, with its own private lounge, fireplace, and grand piano. It's a cut above the usual hotel room.

71 Brougham St., New Plymouth. (C) **06/758-6423.** Fax 06/758-6433. www.nicehotel.co.nz. 7 units. NZ$230 double; NZ$290 suite. Long-stay rates and special deals. AE, DC, MC, V. Head onto Leach St. and turn right onto Brougham. No children 11 and under. **Amenities:** Restaurant and private dining rooms; bar; free bikes; several nearby golf courses; gym across the street. *In room:* TV, fridge, hair dryer, minibar, Wi-Fi.

The Waterfront Hotel ★ (Value)   Location, location, location—this place has it, right beside the new museum and bustling inner city developments overlooking the ocean. Just 3 years old, the Waterfront has smart, uncluttered rooms (some connecting). Oceanview units are the most sought after. I fell in love with the three big, one-bedroom apartments, which have roomy bathrooms, Jacuzzis, leather furniture, modern kitchens, and laundry facilities—and yes, they overlook the ocean. Units on the top two floors of the three-story building have air-conditioning. Crisp design and unbeatable value make the hotel popular with corporate and international travelers.

1 Egmont St., New Plymouth. (C) **0508/843-928** in NZ, or 06/769-5301. Fax 06/769-5302. www. waterfront.co.nz. 42 units. NZ$150–NZ$500. MC, V. Long-stay and off-peak rates. **Amenities:** Restaurant; bar; airport transport; babysitting; free membership to town gym; nearby golf courses and tennis courts; room service. *In room:* TV/DVD, fridge, hair dryer, minibar, Wi-Fi.

WHERE TO DINE

Prepare to be surprised by the standard of cuisine in this provincial outback. For a town of its size, it has an unbelievable number of very good eateries. The Plymouth Hotel's **Orangery Restaurant** ★★ ((C) 06/758-0589) offers fine a la carte dining every night from 6pm. **Andre L'Escargot Restaurant & Bar** ★★, 37–43 Brougham St. ((C) 06/758-4812; www.andres.co.nz), is an elegant New Plymouth institution; it's still good dining, but it's now facing competition from a few other top choices. It's open Monday through Saturday from 11am until late and offers reliable classics like filet mignon, confit of duck, and venison rump.

Tables Bistro ★★, Nice Hotel ((C) 06/758-6423; www.nicehotel.co.nz), also gets lots of votes (see "Where to Stay," above). **Café Arborio** ★★, in Puke Ariki ((C) 06/758-4544), is an Italian cafe by day and licensed restaurant by night. It gets my vote as the best in town. It's on the first floor on the North Wing of the new museum and library complex and is one of the "in" spots. Open 9am to late, the food is divine. In the South Wing you'll find a great spot for coffee at **Daily News Café** ((C) 06/758-4544), an espresso bar with a great stack of newspapers and magazines to read.

Another top-quality new addition is **Pankawalla** ★★★, 85 Devon St. W. ((C) 06/758-4444; www.pankawalla.co.nz), a classy Indian restaurant that you wouldn't normally expect to find in the provinces. It's reasonably priced and is open daily from 6pm.

For the best coffee, head straight for **Mookai** ★, 67 Devon St. W. ((C) 06/759-2099), open daily 8am to late. **MacFarlanes Caffe,** 1 Kelly St., Inglewood ((C) 06/756-6665), 20 minutes southeast of New Plymouth, is popular for brunch. It has excellent coffee and a nighttime atmosphere that is about as raging as it gets in Taranaki. It's open Sunday through Thursday from 9am to 5pm, Friday and Saturday from 9am to late.

The 2½-hour drive from New Plymouth to Wanganui goes through some of the best dairy farmland in New Zealand. Regardless of the time of year, the rolling landscape is generally green and lush. You'll pass through the rural towns of Inglewood, Stratford, Hawera, and Waverley before reaching Wanganui.

2 WANGANUI ★

164km (102 miles) SE of New Plymouth; 141km (87 miles) SW of Tongariro National Park; 193km (120 miles) N of Wellington; 252km (156 miles) SW of Napier

There's tourism potential in Wanganui, and the town has finally become aware of it. In the past few years it has transformed itself from a rather grubby little river town to something much prettier. Now that the inner city has a smart face, attention is turning to the long-awaited beautification of the town's major beach suburb, Castlecliff.

The single-biggest draw in the area is the history-rich **Whanganui River.** This moody snake of a river is the second longest in the North Island and the longest navigable waterway in the country. It flows 290km (180 miles) from the upper reaches of Tongariro National Park to the Tasman Sea, where, at its mouth, you find **Wanganui township.** The river has always had a special place in Maori history. A long history of discontent between Maori and Pakeha over its use and ownership hopefully was settled with the mid-1999 Waitangi Tribunal decision to hand the river back to the Maori people. Now the controversy—still unresolved at time of writing—is over the name of the town. Local Maori won the argument to have the district and river spelling reverted to Whanganui (*whanga*=bay, *nui*=big) in 1991, but so far the town is split over changing the town's name Wanganui (wanga has no meaning in Maori) to Whanganui. The Whanganui River flows through **Whanganui National Park,** most of which is accessible only by boat or on foot. The population of the greater Whanganui District is 48,000, and the area is blessed with 2,084 hours of sunshine annually.

ESSENTIALS

GETTING THERE & GETTING AROUND   By Plane   Wanganui Airport, 10 minutes outside the town center, is served daily by **Air New Zealand** (© 0800/737-000 in NZ; www.airnz.co.nz).

By Coach (Bus)   InterCity (© 09/623-1503) and **Newmans** (© 09/623-1504) provide service between Wanganui and Auckland, New Plymouth, National Park Village (in Tongariro National Park), and Wellington. **White Star Passenger Services,** 161 Ingestre St. (© 06/347-6677), operates local town buses.

ⓘ Tips   Studio Arts

In late March, the town's many artists open their studios to visitors. It's a great chance to see artists in their working environments and you might even pick up some excellent original artworks—prints, paintings, ceramics, glassware, sculpture—at bargain prices. Visit www.whanganuiopenstudios.org.nz for more information.

TARANAKI & WANGANUI

11

WANGANUI

By Car   Wanganui is on state highways 3 and 4. It is 2½ hours from New Plymouth or Wellington, 3 hours from Taupo, and 4 hours from Rotorua.

By Taxi   Call **Wanganui Taxis** (✆ **06/343-5555**).

VISITOR INFORMATION   The **i-SITE Wanganui Visitor Centre,** 101 Guyton St. (✆ **0800/926-426** in NZ, or 06/349-0508; fax 06/349-0509; www.wanganuinz.com), is open in summer Monday through Friday from 8:30am to 5pm, Saturday and Sunday from 9am to 3pm. Hours may be extended in summer.

SPECIAL EVENTS   The **Billy Webb Regatta** is held in December. It features dozens of rowers on the Whanganui River (www.billywebbchallenge.co.nz). Art lovers are sure to enjoy the **Festival of Glass** in September (www.wanganuiglass.co.nz), which brings together the very best of the town's glass studios with workshops, demonstrations, and stunning glassworks for sale. **Celebrating Opera Week** (www.wow.gen.nz), occurs in January each year. Recitals, classes, and performances center on the Royal Wanganui Opera House.

WHAT TO SEE & DO
The Main Attractions

The **Sarjeant Gallery** ★★★, Queen's Park (✆ **06/349-0506;** www.sarjeant.org.nz), is one of the finest provincial galleries in the country. It boasts a large contemporary photographic collection and stunning architecture. The gallery is open daily from 10:30am to 4:30pm, holidays from 1 to 4:30pm. Admission is free and they are closed December 25 and Good Friday.

Nearby you'll find the **Whanganui Regional Museum** ★★, Watt Street (✆ **06/345-7443;** www.wanganui-museum.org.nz), which is renowned as New Zealand's finest provincial museum. It has rare collections of Maori canoes, artifacts, and moa bones. It's open daily 10am to 4:30pm, closed December 25 and Good Friday. Admission is NZ$5 for adults, and children 14 and under are free.

Ohorere Gardens, 1778 Papaiti Rd. (✆/fax **06/342-5848**), is a private garden on the banks of the Whanganui River, 4km (2½ miles) from the city center. You'll see camellias, rhododendrons, more than 100 varieties of old roses, and ponds. It's open September through April on Wednesday and Sunday from 10am to 4pm. The entry fee of NZ$7 includes tea and coffee but personally, I think you get better value at the free Virginia Lake (see below) and **Bason Botanic Gardens** ★★ (www.wanganui.co.nz), 11km (7 miles) out of town (pick up the brochure at the visitor center for directions). It's also free of charge and is open daily from 8am until dusk. There are picnic spots aplenty and a glorious rare orchid display.

If you feel up to climbing hundreds of steps, cross the river to **Durie Hill Elevator and Tower.** Located opposite the Wanganui City Bridge at the bottom of Victoria Avenue, it

---

 Tips   **Heart of Glass**

Chronicle Glass Studio & Tours, 2 Rutland St. (✆ **06/347-1921**), is a collective of local glass blowers. Watch them in action and browse in the contemporary mezzanine gallery, which features a wide range of collectible glass art produced by Wanganui glass artists. The studio is open Monday through Friday 9am to 5pm, weekends 10am to 4:30pm.

> **(Tips) A Traditional Marae Visit**
>
> If you would like to meet local Maori at the **Koriniti Marae,** Whanganui River
> Road, Wanganui (© **06/342-8198;** fax 06/348-0398; www.koriniti.com), call first
> to make sure you do not interrupt private events like *tangi* (funerals). Visitors are
> welcome to take photographs at the marae and to look through the Whare
> Toanga (museum). There is no charge, but a *koha* (donation) is welcome.

begins with a pedestrian tunnel that takes you to the historic elevator, which in turn rises
66m (216 ft.) through the hill to the summit. You can then take the 191 narrow spiraling
steps up the Memorial Tower for unparalleled views. Check with the visitor center for
hours. For a lovely, quiet wander close to town, it takes a lot to beat **Virginia Lake** ★,
on Great North Road on St. John's Hill. The lake is bordered by pleasant bush walks,
hundreds of ducks waiting to be fed, a free-flying bird aviary that you can walk through,
and a coin-operated fountain that shows off with brilliant colored displays at night.

If you are interested in the arts, you'll be pleased to hear that some of New Zealand's
top artists live in the area. Pick up the *Arts & Cultural Trail, Arts Guide,* and *Whanganui
Artists Open Studios* brochures from the information center. They cover a wealth of paint-
ers, printmakers, sculptors, jewelers, potters, and glass artists.

A Scenic Drive to Pipiriki

River Road, the only road that leads into Whanganui National Park from Wanganui, is
narrow and winding but very scenic. Staying on River Road for approximately 1½ hours
will lead you to the tiny settlement of Pipiriki, 79km (49 miles) upstream from Wanganui. Many marae lie along the river, and you'll pass the historic Maori mission of
Jerusalem, once home to the famous New Zealand poet James K. Baxter.

Exploring Whanganui River & Whanganui National Park

The Whanganui River has its origins high on Mount Tongariro. There the river is a mere
alpine stream, but it gathers water from Mount Ngauruhoe and Mount Ruapehu as it
descends through the Central Volcanic Plateau, toward Taumaranui, Wanganui, and
finally the Tasman Sea.

There are 239 listed rapids along the Whanganui, but it is a Grade II river and therefore popular with canoeists of all levels. Many begin their river adventures at the Taumaranui end, making their way south to Wanganui. This trip can take 5 to 6 days, and the
Department of Conservation maintains huts along the way for overnight stays.

In 1987, the huge, largely inaccessible, and remote bush areas surrounding the middle
reaches of the Whanganui River were designated a national park, becoming the second-
largest tract of native bush on the North Island. Several of the original routes for the early
Maori and European inhabitants have been cleared, providing some of the most isolated
wilderness tramping in New Zealand—the 3-day **Mangapurua** and **Matemateaonga
tracks** (see "On Foot," below) are accessible only by canoe or jet boat.

One of the most popular spots in the park is the **Bridge to Nowhere,** which was built
in 1935 deep in the bush across the Mangapurua Gorge to give access to the last pioneering settlement of the New Zealand government. The isolated settlement failed in 1942,
but the bridge remains. You'll need to travel upstream (see "By Jet Boat," below) and then
walk 40 minutes along some steep sections and narrow tracks to reach the bridge.

If you'd like to spend the day picnicking, head to **Hipango Park Reserve,** 26km (16 miles) upriver from Wanganui. The .8-hectare (2-acre) native bush reserve with recently upgraded barbecue pits and toilets is a popular destination for boat tours (see "By Riverboat," below). For details of **Journeys on the Whanganui,** a collection of river packages, visit www.whanganuiriver.co.nz.

There are a number of exciting ways to experience the Whanganui River and Whanganui National Park. Following are a few examples.

By Aerial Cableway   The **Flying Fox** ★★ (℃/fax **06/342-8160;** www.theflyingfox. co.nz), is a unique river experience. A little patch of civilization in the middle of nowhere is accessible by an aerial cableway, or "flying fox." Once you've negotiated this awesome swing across the river, you can enjoy charming cottage accommodations or bush campsites (see "Where to Stay," below). The Flying Fox is 45 minutes from Wanganui. To reach it, take a jet-boat tour or drive up River Road and cross the river on the aerial cableway. Several tours stop here (see "By Bus," below). They offer a half-day canoe journey for NZ$80 per person and a half-day jet boat trip for NZ$110.

By Bus   If a 14-seat air-conditioned bus is your style, you can join the popular **Whanganui River Road Mail Tour** ★★. Call **Whanganui Tours** (℃ **06/347-7534;** www. whanganuitours.co.nz). The tour runs from 7:30am to 2:30pm and covers 190km (118 miles), delivering mail to remote farms, schools, and marae. The mail tour costs NZ$55. You can also meet up with the **Bridge To Nowhere Jet Boat Tour** (℃ **0800/480-308;** www.bridgetonowhere.co.nz) and you can stay overnight at the Bridge To Nowhere Lodge, the Flying Fox, or at Jerusalem Backpackers, where Catholic nuns put you up for the night.

By Canoe   If you want to find out about Maori myths and legends of the river, go with Niko Tangaroa of **Waka Tours** ★★, 17a Balance St., Raetihi (℃/fax **06/385-4811;** www.wakatours.com). His 3-day guided canoe tour (Oct–Apr) takes you to historic sites with overnight stays at riverside marae. It's a rare experience that costs NZ$650 for adults, NZ$520 for students 12 to 16 years old, including all meals; children 11 and under are not permitted. A minimum of four people is required per tour, and 4- to 5-day packages are available. Another option is **Wades Landing Outdoors,** RD2, Owhango (℃/fax **07/895-5995;** www.whanganui.co.nz), which has a number of 3-, 4-, or 5-day trips canoeing the river from Taumaranui to Pipiriki. They're based at the Taumaranui end of the river.

By Jet Boat   **Bridge to Nowhere Jet Boat Tours,** Ramanui Landing, Whanganui River (℃ **0800/480-308** in NZ, or 06/385-4622; www.bridgetonowheretours.co.nz), operates in the most beautiful part of the river. Its most popular 4-hour tour to the Bridge to Nowhere costs NZ$95 and is suitable for all ages. There is also a jet boat/canoe option, which allows you to enjoy a leisurely paddle downstream. **Whanganui River Adventures,** 2513 RD6, Pipiriki (℃ **0800/862-743** in NZ, or 06/385-3246; www. whanganuiriveradventures.co.nz), also runs Bridge to Nowhere jet-boat rides for NZ$120 per person. Its 45-minute ride through deep, moss-covered ravines to the home of the endangered native blue duck costs NZ$75 per person.

By Riverboat   The Waimarie Paddle Steamer was built in 1890, sank in 1952, and was salvaged in 1993. Since then, it has been painstakingly rebuilt at the **Whanganui Riverboat Centre & Museum,** 1A Taupo Quay (℃/fax **06/347-1863;** www.riverboats. co.nz). Daily cruises (summer at 2pm, with reduced cruises in winter) travel 13km (8 miles) up the Whanganui River to Upokongaro, then return to the city. The cost is

> ⓘ **Tips** **The River Traders**
>
> Every Saturday, from 9am to 1pm, you'll find the colorful **River Traders Market** (ℭ **06/343-9795;** www.therivertraders.co.nz), beside the river. Go behind the Whanganui Riverboat Centre and turn right. You'll see the gathering of local artists, craftspeople, and organic produce sellers.

NZ$40 for adults and NZ$14 for children 5 to 15. They also offer lunch and barbecue packages. The center is open Monday through Saturday from 9am to 4pm, Sunday 10am to 4pm (free admission). Call for winter sailing times.

On Foot   Contact the **Department of Conservation,** Whanganui Area Office, 74 Ingestre St. (ℭ **06/345-2402;** www.doc.govt.nz), for information on a range of walks. In brief, the **Skyline Walk** requires 6 to 8 hours and affords views of Mount Ruapehu and Mount Taranaki. The **Matemateaonga Track** takes 3 to 4 days; the 3-day **Mangapurua Valley Walk** includes the Bridge to Nowhere. **Whanganui River Jet,** Wades Landing Outdoors, RD2, Owhango (ℭ **07/895-5995;** www.whanganui.co.nz), offers a complete charter service for trampers wanting to use either of these tracks. It will drop you off and pick you up at prearranged times on the riverbanks. Costs vary depending on which track you choose. Bridge To Nowhere Jet Boat Tours (see above) also offers a track transport service.

OUTDOOR PURSUITS

BEACHES   **Castlecliff Beach,** 9km (5½ miles) from the city center, is a typical West Coast beach with black-iron sand and lots of driftwood. It's good for swimming and surfing and is patrolled by professional lifeguards in summer. Wild **South Beach,** obviously to the south of the city, is great for long beachcombing walks, while **Mowhanau** is a pretty swimming beach surrounded by *papa* cliffs (a soft and slippery cross btw. a mudstone and sandstone formation). It has a playground and good picnicking areas. Head north on the highway to New Plymouth and turn left onto Rapanui Road; continue another 9km (5½ miles).

BIKING   **City Cycle Tours** (ℭ **06/343-7130**) offers cycle packages that include bikes and helmets.

FLIGHTSEEING   Get yourself into the bright-yellow **Wanganui Aero Work Tiger Moth** (ℭ **06/345-3994**) for a 20-minute flight over the city, river, and Tasman Sea.

GOLF   The **Wanganui Golf Club,** Belmont Links, Clarkson Avenue (ℭ **06/344-4481**), is an 18-hole championship course.

MOUNTAIN BIKING   **Lismore Forest,** just minutes from central Wanganui, has some of the best mountain bike tracks in the region. You can rent bikes from **Wanganui Pro-Cycle Centre,** 199 Victoria Ave. (ℭ **06/368-5459**). Rentals are around NZ$50 per day.

WHERE TO STAY

Accommodations are not Wanganui's strong point. There are no major hotels and nothing truly upmarket, probably no more than 30 motel complexes, around 30 homestays or farmstays, and fewer than half a dozen backpacker establishments.

If remote is what you're after, try the **Flying Fox** ★, P.O. Box 333, Wanganui (ⓒ **06/342-8160;** www.theflyingfox.co.nz), where two self-contained cottages and a gypsy cart go for NZ$150. Everything sits under old walnut trees, and hosts Annette and John make natural beers and organic meals. *Note:* You'll have to cross the river on a flying fox (see "By Aerial Cableway," above), and it's 45 minutes upriver from Wanganui.

Even more remote, for those who truly do want to get away from it all, is **Bridge to Nowhere Lodge** ★, Ramanui Landing, Whanganui River (ⓒ **0800/480-308** in NZ; fax 06/348-7133; www.bridgetonowheretours.co.nz), where rooms, breakfast, and dinner go for NZ$250, or self-catering with your own bedding (ideal for canoeists and trampers) for NZ$50 per person.

Arles Bed & Breakfast ★, 50 Riverbank Rd., RD3, Wanganui (ⓒ/fax **06/343-6557;** www.arles.co.nz), is a pretty upriver location with four units in a charming old home (two with shared bathroom) and one self-contained two-bedroom flat for NZ$140 to NZ$160.

All rates listed include the 12.5% GST and parking.

Rutland Arms Inn ★ This is one of the better hotel-style lodgings in Wanganui, and is a good budget option. All rooms are large and well appointed, with feather duvets and cotton sheets; four units have Jacuzzis. The Taylor Suite is my favorite—very big and very sunny. The original 1800s building was completely renovated in 1996. The Rutland has an English-style bar on the ground floor, along with a mediocre restaurant and the Courtyard Café.

48–50 Ridgway St., Wanganui. ⓒ **0800/788-5263** in NZ, or 06/347-7677. Fax 06/347-7345. www.rutland-arms.co.nz. 8 units. NZ$140–NZ$185. Rates include breakfast. AE, DC, MC, V. **Amenities:** Restaurant; bar; nearby gym; room service. *In room:* TV, fridge, hair dryer, minibar, Wi-Fi.

Siena Motor Lodge ★ This 1997 complex is definitely worth your attention. It's right on the main street, just down from the shopping center and near a number of eateries. The decor is a little dated, but all rooms have premium-quality beds and CD players. My pick for value and comfort is room no. 9, a corner studio with its own Jacuzzi and private courtyard.

335 Victoria Ave., Wanganui. ⓒ **0800/888-802** in NZ, or 06/345-9009. Fax 06/345-9935. www.siena.co.nz. 10 units. NZ$125–NZ$155. AE, DC, MC, V. **Amenities:** Nearby golf course; Internet; nearby tennis courts. *In room:* A/C, TV/DVD, hair dryer, kitchen, minibar.

Tamara Lodge Backpackers ★ Rory Smith believes in keeping things clean and comfortable, and providing a good kitchen and a friendly atmosphere. The house, once a maternity hospital and then a private hotel, overlooks the river and is an easy walk to town. The fabulous rear garden has hammocks under giant palm trees. No dorms have more than four beds.

24 Somme Parade, Wanganui. ⓒ **06/347-6300.** Fax 06/345-8488. www.tamaralodge.com. 40 beds. NZ$24 dorm bed; NZ$40–NZ$50 single; NZ$62 standard double; NZ$78 double with en suite. MC, V. **Amenities:** Free bikes; nearby golf course; Wi-Fi in reception area. *In room:* No phone.

WHERE TO DINE

Indigo ★★, Majestic Square (ⓒ **06/348-7459**), is one of the few cafes in town that hints at city style and it's been judged Best Cafe in Wanganui. It has a great setting in the heart of town and very nice outdoor areas. It's open daily from 8am until late. Service can be patchy, but that's not uncommon in the provinces, where good staff are hard to find.

I prefer **Big Orange/Ceramic Wine Bar** ★, 51 Victoria St. ((℘ **06/348-4449**), which operates as a lively cafe by day and a restaurant and bar by night. The lunch menu includes some excellent light meals, but the service is notoriously slow. They're open Monday through Friday 7:30am to 5pm, and weekends from 9:30am to 5pm.

Redeye Café ★, 96 Guyton St. ((℘ **06/345-5646**), has plenty of character, although it doesn't seem to appeal to a lot of the older locals, who classify it as noisy with bad service. It's certainly a student haunt that plays no-compromise music, but I wouldn't bypass it. It's open Monday through Friday from 8am until late, Saturday from 9:30am until late. **Jolt Coffee** ★, 19 Victoria Ave. ((℘ **06/345-8840**), has good coffee and a bit more style. It's open Monday through Friday 7:30am to 5:30pm, Sunday 1 to 5pm (closed Sat).

More popular with the over-35s is **Legends,** 25 Somme Parade ((℘ **06/345-7575**), overlooking the river. Although the meals are tasty and the surroundings pleasant, I prefer the grittiness of Redeye. Legends is open Wednesday through Friday 9am until late, weekends from 10am. **Vega** ★, Taupo Quay and Victoria Avenue ((℘ **06/345-1082**), is a popular fine-dining restaurant that many consider the best in town. **Stellar,** 2 Victoria St. ((℘ **06/345-7278;** www.stellarwanganui.co.nz), offers tasty meals for a good price (especially pizzas and desserts) Monday 3pm until late and Tuesday through Sunday 9am until late.

EN ROUTE TO WELLINGTON

You can get to Wellington in two ways—on State Highway 1 down the coast via Levin, Waikanae, and Paraparaumu (the better road), or via Palmerston North, the Wairarapa, through Masterton, Carterton, Greytown, and Featherston. Both trips take about 2½ hours, but the Wairarapa journey begs for a few stop-offs that may well eat up some of your time. If you go this way, I strongly suggest you spend a night in the area (see "Where to Stay" in the "A Side Trip to Wairarapa" section in chapter 12). The **i-SITE Palmerston North Visitor Centre,** 52 The Square, Palmerston North ((℘ **06/350-1922;** fax 06/350-1929; www.manawatunz.co.nz), can help with accommodations and local highlights.

If you travel down the coast road, be sure to drop by the **Southward Car Museum** ★★, near Paraparaumu, 45 minutes north of Wellington ((℘ **04/297-1221;** www. thecarmuseum.co.nz). Even if you're not auto-inclined, I think you'll find it interesting as it contains much more than just cars. The museum is open daily from 9am to 4:30pm and costs NZ$10 for adults and NZ$3 for children. A little farther south on the Kapiti Coast, it's worth making even a brief stop at the Lindale Centre, where you'll find the fabulous **Kapiti Cheese Company** ★★★ ((℘ **04/298-1352**), along with a range of New Zealand crafts stores. You must sample their divine ice cream! The **Kapiti Coast Visitor Information Centre,** Centennial Park, State Highway 1, Otaki ((℘ **06/364-7620;** www.kapiticoast.govt.nz), can provide accommodations and adventure details for this increasingly popular holiday area. It's open Monday through Friday 8:30am to 5pm, weekends 9am to 4pm.

12

Wellington

Wellington is, without doubt, my favorite New Zealand city. I've always seen it geographically as a miniature Hong Kong—there's a beautiful curved harbor surrounded by hillsides dotted with houses and elegant high-rises clustered into a central fist. There is an immediacy and a vibrancy here that you don't get in other New Zealand cities.

Once seen as a stuffy, bureaucrat-filled political capital, Wellington has reinvented itself to become New Zealand's entertainment and cultural capital and the fastest-growing weekend destination in the country.

With the opening of the long-awaited Te Papa, the national museum of New Zealand, the waterfront is alive again. The Courtenay Place neighborhood has one of the best bar, cafe, and restaurant scenes in the country, and galleries, theaters, and shops abound.

The beauty of Wellington is that so much is within walking distance. It's a compact place with a pronounced cosmopolitan elegance, and an exciting corporate component adds to the rich urban atmo-sphere: Morning, noon, and night, "the suits," as they are affectionately called here, crowd the streets.

The British originally called the harbor Port Nicholson, and it wasn't until after the 1839 visit of the Duke of Wellington that the city was renamed in his honor. The seat of government was moved here from Auckland in 1865.

Today's Wellington is diverse and sophisticated. The fact that it can be extremely cold and windy here in winter is understandable if you consider the fact that there's little between the capital and Antarctica to stop the gales. And the fact that so much of this city—filled with many glass-fronted high-rises—sits on a major fault line seems to be of such little concern to its inhabitants that I almost feel picky raising the issue. Speaking of raising, it's interesting to note that a large portion of Wellington's waterfront playground is on reclaimed land (just like Hong Kong)— much of it forced up by a giant 1855 earthquake and finished off by clever acts of reclamation.

1 ORIENTATION

ARRIVING

BY PLANE **Wellington International Airport** (www.wellingtonairport.co.nz), is 8km (5 miles) southeast of the city. The quickest route passes through Mount Victoria via a two-lane tunnel. A more circuitous, but more scenic, route travels via Oriental Parade. The trip usually takes 15 to 20 minutes, although it can exceed 30 minutes at peak traffic times.

Wellington Airport operates both international and domestic business from the same building. It is served by the following international airlines: **Air New Zealand** (✆ 0800/737-000 in NZ, or 04/388-9737; www.airnewzealand.com), **British Airways** (✆ 09/966-9777; www.ba.com), **Lufthansa** (✆ 0800/945-220 in NZ; www.lufthansa. com), **Qantas Airways** (✆ 0800/808-767; www.qantas.com), **Singapore Airlines**

($\textcircled{C}$ 0800/808-909; www.singaporeair.com), and **Polynesian Blue** ($\textcircled{C}$ 0800/670-000; www.polynesianblue.com).

The leading domestic airlines that fly into Wellington are **Air New Zealand** ($\textcircled{C}$ 0800/737-000; www.airnz.com), **Jetstar** ($\textcircled{C}$ **0800/800-995;** www.jetstar.com), and **Soundsair Ltd.** ($\textcircled{C}$ 0800/505-505; www.soundsair.com). For **arrival and departure information,** call $\textcircled{C}$ 04/388-9900.

The **Wellington Airport Visitor Information Centre** ($\textcircled{C}$ **04/385-5123;** fax 04/385-5137; www.wellingtonairport.co.nz) is on level one of the main terminal building. Staff members can assist with booking accommodations, TranzRail, Interislander ferries, and long-distance coaches. It's open daily from 7am to 8pm.

The terminal has nine cafes and restaurants in a large food hall that offer everything from pizza and pasta to wine and tapas. There are also car-rental desks, duty-free stores, gift shops, a Travelex Foreign Exchange service open during all international flight times, and ATMs. Coin-operated lockers can be found on the ground floor. Most retail outlets are open 6:30am to 7pm, some later. Duty-free stores are open for every international flight.

Super Shuttle ($\textcircled{C}$ **0800/748-885 in NZ** or 04/472-9552; www.supershuttle.co.nz) operates between the airport, the city, and the railway station Monday through Friday. It costs NZ$15 per person. Several shuttle operators provide door-to-door service at higher fares.

The **Airport Flyer,** the GO Wellington airport express bus **Metlink** ($\textcircled{C}$ **0800/801-700** in NZ; www.airportflyer.co.nz), goes right into the inner city and then on to Waterloo Interchange in Lower Hutt. It operates every 20 minutes, 365 days a year from 5:30am to 8:20pm. An All Day Star Pass costs NZ$12 per person and gives unlimited all-day travel on all Flyer, GO Wellington, and Valley Flyer services. It's available from bus drivers. Single-ride tickets are also available. The trip from the airport to central-city stops takes about 45 minutes. A new fleet of buses comply with the latest European emission standard, Euro 5, which means exhaust emissions are up to 90% lower than the older buses. The buses also have air-conditioning, free Wi-Fi, and lowered floors for wheelchair access.

A **taxi** between the city center and the airport costs NZ$25 to NZ$50, depending on the destination. The fare to Lower Hutt is approximately NZ$60 to NZ$70. Taxi stands are directly outside the main terminal. If you have any problems with your taxi driver, call **Wellington Airport Operation** ($\textcircled{C}$ **04/385-5124**).

BY TRAIN & COACH (BUS)   Most long-distance trains depart from the **Wellington Railway Station,** on Waterloo Quay. For long-distance rail information, call $\textcircled{C}$ **0800/802-802** in New Zealand or 04/495-0775, or visit www.tranzscenic.co.nz. Most major hostels and hotels are within a short taxi ride of the station.

For coach information, call **InterCity** ($\textcircled{C}$ **09/623-1503;** www.intercity.co.nz) or **Newmans** ($\textcircled{C}$ **09/623-1504;** www.newmanscoach.co.nz). Both of these coach lines operate out of the railway station. **Kiwi Experience** ($\textcircled{C}$ **09/366-1665**) and the **Magic Travellers Network** ($\textcircled{C}$ **09/358-5600**) also stop in Wellington.

BY CAR   Wellington is reached via highways 1 and 2. It's 195km (121 miles) from Wanganui (approx. 2 hr.); 460km (285 miles) from Rotorua (approx. 5 hr.); and 655km (406 miles) from Auckland (approx. 8 hr.). The motorway terminates right in the city.

BY FERRY   For information on the **Interislander** Wellington-Picton ferry, call $\textcircled{C}$ **0800/802-802** or check www.interislander.co.nz. Be aware that there are two ferry operators working between Wellington and Picton. The three Interislander ferries

WELLINGTON

12

ORIENTATION

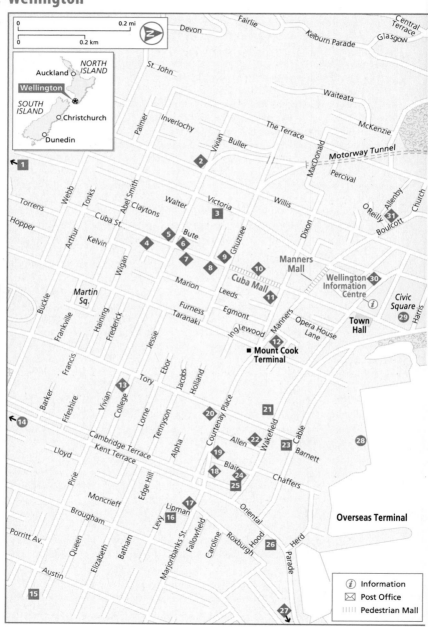

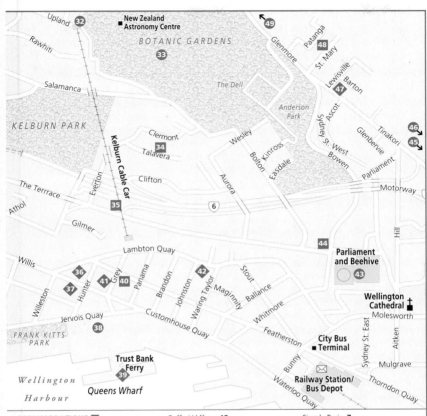

ACCOMMODATIONS ■
Bolton Hotel **44**
Booklovers Bed and Breakfast **15**
Duxton Hotel **21**
Gardens Homestay **48**
InterContinental Wellington **40**
James Cook Hotel Grand Chancellor **35**
Lambton Heights **34**
Mermaid Guesthouse for Women **1**
Mount Victoria Homestay **16**
The Museum Hotel **23**
Ohtel **26**
Victoria Court Motor Lodge **3**
Wellington City YHA **25**

DINING ◆
Arabica **41**
Boulcott Street Bistro **31**
Caffe Astoria **42**
Caffe Italiano **4**

Caffe L'Affare **13**
Café Bastille **17**
Chow **20**
Dixon Street Gourmet Deli **11**
Ernesto **9**
Floriditas **8**
Great India Restaurant **12**
Hummingbird **19**
Le Metropolitan **9**
Le Moulin **2**
Lido Café **30**
Logan Brown **5**
Martin Bosley's Yacht Club
    Restaurant **27**
Matterhorn Bar & Restaurant **10**
Midnight Espresso **6**
One Red Dog **24**
Pandoro **22**
Pravda **37**
Shed 5 **39**

Simply Paris **7**
Smith the Grocer **36**
The White House Restaurant **27**
Tinakori Bistro **47**
Zico Cucina & Bar **18**

ATTRACTIONS ●
Botanic Gardens **33**
City Gallery Wellington **29**
Katherine Mansfield Birthplace **46**
Kelburn Cable Car Top Station **32**
Museum of Wellington **38**
TheNewDowse **45**
The Parliament Buildings **43**
Pataka **45**
Museum of New Zealand–Te Papa
    Tongarewa **28**
Wellington Zoo **14**
ZEALANDIA: The Karori Sanctuary
    Experience **49**

> **(Tips) Public Relief**
>
> Free public toilets are at 69 sites throughout the city. Staffed facilities are at the
> ANZ Building (at the corner of Lambton Quay and Featherston St.). You'll also find
> restrooms at all major attractions and several department stores.

operate all year and take 3 hours to cross the strait. **Strait Shipping Ltd.,** Waterloo Quay
(© **0800/844-844** in NZ; www.bluebridge.co.nz), operates **Bluebridge Cook Strait
Ferry,** traveling to Picton daily at 3am and 1pm, and Picton to Wellington daily at 8am
and 7pm. There are no 3am or 8am sailings on Mondays. The Bluebridge trip is cheapest but it takes 3 hours 20 minutes. If you book either online you get the best fares—
especially if you book well ahead. Cook Strait can be notoriously rough in bad weather,
so if you get seasick, take your medication.

VISITOR INFORMATION

The **Wellington i-SITE Visitor Centre,** 101 Wakefield St., Civic Square (© **04/802-
4860;** fax 04/802-4863; www.wellingtonnz.com), is open Monday through Friday from
8:30am to 5:30pm (Tues till 5pm) and Saturday and Sunday from 9:30am to 4:30pm.
It provides details of regional attractions and has the best range of free guides in the
country. It also has a range of tiny pocket-size leaflets and cards on everything from
transport systems to shopping, art, fashion, and free walking tours. Staff members can
book accommodations and attractions, arrange transport, and sell stamps and phone
cards. It also has an e-mail center and cafe.

For information on Lower and Upper Hutt areas, contact **Hutt City i-SITE Visitor
Centre,** 25 Laings Rd., Lower Hutt (© **04/560-4715;** fax 04/570-3374; www.huttvalley
nz.com), or **Upper Hutt i-SITE Visitor Centre,** 84–90 Main St., Upper Hutt (© **04/
527-2141;** fax 04/527-9818; www.upperhuttcity.com).

The free weekly publications *Capital Times* and *City Voice* are available at the visitor
centers and leading hotels and cafes. Both have details on local happenings. If you're a
keen follower of the performing arts, check at the visitor center for availability of discounted day-of-performance tickets.

SPECIAL EVENTS

Wellington is home to the country's biggest cultural event, the biennial **New Zealand
International Arts Festival** ★★★ (© **04/473-0149;** www.nzfestival.telecom.co.nz). It
features international works and the best of New Zealand talent in everything from opera
to jazz, dance to comedy. The next festival will be staged in February and March 2010.
A major spinoff from the festival is the growth of the **Wellington Fringe Festival** ★★
(© **04/495-8015;** www.fringe.org.nz), which is a completely separate event run at the
same time. It's now an annual event celebrating offbeat productions and innovative art
forms.

Summer City Festival (© **04/801-3500;** www.wellington.govt.nz), staged during
January and February each year, launches Wellington's events calendar with more than
70 free activities such as the Teddy Bears' Picnic, the Rock Barge Concert on Oriental
Parade, a Pacific Islands Festival, and Summer Shakespeare in the Botanic Garden Dell.
Montana World of Wearable Art ★★★ (© **03/548-9299;** www.worldofwearableart.
com) is a theatrical costume spectacle not to be missed, now staged annually at the Events

Centre Wellington in mid-September and early October. This 2-hour visual extravaganza attracts international entrants and sell-out audiences of over 22,000—not bad considering it started in Nelson in 1987 in a leaky tent with just 200 people watching. **Montana Wellington International Jazz Festival** (www.jazzfestival.co.nz) features a superb roster of national and international jazz musicians performing modern jazz through the classics (mid- to late Oct at various city locations).

Martinborough Country Fair ★★ (© 06/306-9043; www.martinboroughfair.org.nz) is a popular gathering of crafts artisans from around the country. Held the first Saturday in February and the first Saturday in March, it attracts about 30,000 visitors. Martinborough is about an hour's drive northeast of Wellington. **Golden Shears** (© 06/378-7373; www.goldenshears.co.nz) is a 3-day international shearing contest that includes wool handling and sheep and goat shearing. It's held in late February or early March in Masterton, 103km (64 miles) northeast of Wellington. In November, catch a special 50-minute festival train from Wellington to the **Toast Martinborough Wine, Food & Music Festival** ★★★ (© 06/306-9183; www.toastmartinborough.co.nz). Shuttles run a continuous circuit within a 10km (6-mile) area of Martinborough's town square to Martinborough vineyards, where tastings take place with the winemakers.

CITY LAYOUT

The main focal point of the **inner city** is the harbor. The new Te Papa national museum fronts this water, as does the Queen's Wharf dining and shopping complex. Unlike the rest of the city, the central business district (CBD) is generally flat and easily negotiable. The best **shopping** is along Lambton Quay and Willis Street; Manners Street and Cuba Mall also have plenty of stores. They are less upmarket, but **Cuba Mall** especially is one of the hippest areas, known for its edgy boutiques, design stores, and excellent eateries. This is my favorite part of Wellington because it's always busy and interesting. The inner area of Lambton Quay, Willis Street, and The Terrace is home to many of the nation's **corporate headquarters** and thus is second home to "the suits." Several leading hotels and apartment complexes are also in this area, so if you base yourself here, you won't need a car to see most of the major attractions and shops—but you will need earplugs for a truly sound sleep.

The heaviest concentration of **bars** and **eateries** is between Courtenay Place and Wakefield Street and the lanes running between them, especially Blair and Allen streets. Most of the inner city is safe, but I wouldn't go lurking around Cuba Mall after closing time, especially the top end, which has always been seen as the heart of the seedier side of the sex industry. Manners Mall is no more appealing late at night. Courtenay Place on Thursday, Friday, and Saturday nights is the center of nightlife, but there are often numerous people about who have consumed more than their fair share of alcohol and who may not be entirely open to reason. Generally, though, personal safety rules are the same as in any other international city—use common sense and don't wander about dark places alone in the middle of the night. Many inner city areas are now under security camera surveillance.

THE NEIGHBORHOODS IN BRIEF

Thorndon This neighborhood sits right on the fault line, but that hasn't detracted from real estate values here. It's seen as one of the premier suburbs in Wellington because of its beautiful historic buildings, its views, and its proximity to the inner city. There are some excellent bed-and-breakfasts

WELLINGTON

12

ORIENTATION

within walking distance of Parliament Buildings, the city, the Botanic Garden, and Tinakori Village, a fashionable little spot for shopping and eating. The area's only downsides are the noise from the motorway, the heavy traffic on Tinakori Road, and the lack of both off- and on-street parking.

Mount Victoria This is where I would live if I thought I could afford anything bigger than a letter box. It's very close to the Courtenay Place end of town, everything is within walking distance, and it's filled with gorgeous (slightly less perfect) wooden houses. It's also quieter. Parking is generally earmarked for residents only during business hours, but you'll be fine after 6pm.

Kelburn Kelburn is easily accessed via the cable car from Lambton Quay, which runs up to the Botanic Garden and Victoria University. Homes in this area are sought after for their especially good harbor and city views.

Oriental Bay This part of town offers prime real estate just 800m (about ½ mile) around the water's edge from the inner city and Mount Victoria. Again, it's a great place to stay, with several hotels and private high-rise apartments stretched out along Oriental Parade, which is a favorite playground for in-line skaters, walkers, and runners. There are hints of San Francisco here, I'm told, plus a few excellent cafes and restaurants and beautiful city and harbor views.

Evans Bay This area is far less inspiring. It's farther out, around the point, and its prime attraction is its proximity to the airport.

Lower Hutt A city within a city— Lower Hutt is the ninth largest in New Zealand. It's across the harbor from Wellington proper and accessed via a short motorway drive, usually about 15 minutes in good traffic. This is where you'll find the fabulous New Dowse Art Museum, but I have to scratch my head to think of other reasons why you would stay here instead of the inner city.

2 GETTING AROUND

Wellington is blessed with an excellent public transport system, and you can easily see the best attractions without a car.

BY BUS Call **GO Wellington** (© 04/387-3224) for information on all urban services. Buses operate daily 7am to 11pm on most routes and the visitor center can give you a comprehensive city map that shows major bus routes and timetables. Timetables are also available from newsstands. The main city bus terminal, **Lambton Interchange,** is adjacent to the main railway station on the corner of Bunny and Featherston streets. The easiest places to catch buses in the inner city are Lambton Quay, Willis Street, Dixon Street, Cuba Mall, Courtenay Place, and the railway station.

The NZ$8 **Daytripper Pass** gives you unlimited 1-day travel on the GO Wellington, Valley Flyer, Airport Flyer, and After Midnight services. With this pass, you can also take two children 15 and under after 9am on weekdays and all day on weekends. The **STAR-Pass** is NZ$12 and gives one person a day's unlimited travel on all GO Wellington and Valley Flyer bus services. Both passes can be purchased from your bus driver. The NZ$16

> **(Tips) Have Scooter Will Travel**
>
> If you have limited mobility, you can enjoy central Wellington and the waterfront on a free mobility scooter. Book it for 4 hours and pick it up from one of four locations—**Freyberg Pool,** Oriental Parade (*©* **04/499-4444**); **Wellington City Council,** 101 Wakefield St. (*©* **04/499-4444**); **Fergs Kayaks,** Shed 6, Queens Wharf (*©* **04/499-8898**); or **Wellington Botanic Garden,** Tinakori Rd. (*©* **04/ 499-1400**).

Discovery Pass gives you a full day of unlimited travel after 9am on a wide range of train and bus services in and around Wellington, Hutt Valley, and the Kapiti Coast.

Newlands Coach Service operates bus routes 50 to 59 from central Wellington to the northern suburbs. Purchase tickets from the driver; these buses arrive on Featherston Street and leave from Lambton Exchange.

BY TAXI There are taxi stands in front of the railway station; in the Lambton Quay shopping area between Grey and Hunter streets; on Bond Street just off Willis Street; on Dixon Street between Cuba and Victoria streets; and on Cambridge Terrace near Courtenay Place. For service, call **Black & Gold Taxis** (*©* **04/388-8888**) or **Wellington Combined Taxis** (*©* **04/384-4444;** www.taxis.co.nz). You'll pay a NZ$1 surcharge if you phone for a taxi. Wellington Combined Taxis recently became the first taxi company in New Zealand to receive carboNZero certification, which means they are committed to reducing their greenhouse gas emissions. They use only hybrid, diesel, or LPG cars for their 442-strong fleet.

BY TRAIN **Tranz Metro** operates daily electric train service from Wellington to its outer suburbs. Trains arrive at the railway station on Bunny Street; everything is an easy walk or bus ride from there. You can save money with the purchase of a **Group Rover ticket,** which gives unlimited travel for a day for up to four people traveling together. Call *©* **0800/801-700** in New Zealand, or check www.metlink.org.nz for timetable information and discount fares.

BY CAR If you can avoid using a car in downtown Wellington, do so; you'll save yourself a lot of hassles and steep parking fees. Traffic congestion is significant during the week and parking can be a problem. If you do drive, there are 10 major parking buildings in the inner city. All are well signposted and are open 24 hours. Rates range from NZ$4 to NZ$15 per hour. There are also pay-and-display parking areas, where a machine dispenses a ticket to be displayed in your car window. On Saturday and Sunday, parking is free in all metered pay-and-display areas and in council parking buildings, but the time limits still apply. If you exceed them, you can expect a fine. Parking in resident parking zones is also a costly business if you get caught. *Tip:* If you park in the Te Papa carpark, you pay NZ$4 per hour up to a daily maximum of NZ$12, so it works out cheaper to leave your car there all day and walk to your chosen spots.

BY CABLE CAR The cable car takes you from Lambton Quay straight up to the Botanic Garden, with a Victoria University stop on the way. It runs daily every 10 minutes from 7am to 10pm Monday through Friday, 8:30am to 10pm Saturday, 9am to 10pm Sunday and public holidays. A round-trip ticket costs NZ$6 for adults, NZ$3 for

WELLINGTON

12

GETTING AROUND

children 5 to 15. Family and senior discounts are available. For information, call ✆ **04/ 472-2199.**

BY FERRY The **Dominion Post Ferry** runs daily between Queen's Wharf, Somes Island, Eastbourne, and Days Bay Wharf. The trip to Days Bay takes 30 minutes one-way, and Eastbourne Village is a good 10- to 15-minute trip from Days Bay. The one-way fare costs NZ$12 for adults and NZ$6 for children; a family pass is NZ$50. Call ✆ **04/ 494-3339** or 499-1282, or check www.eastbywest.co.nz for timetable information.

(*Fast Facts*) **Wellington**

American Express The foreign exchange bureau is in the Cable Car complex, 280–292 Lambton Quay (✆ **04/473-7766;** fax 04/473-7765). It's open Monday through Friday from 8:30am to 5pm.

Area Code Wellington's telephone area code (STD) is **04.**

Babysitters Most hotels and B&Bs can arrange babysitters, or you can call Wellington Nannies College at ✆ **04/384-5888** or visit www.wnc.co.nz.

Dentist For 24-hour service, phone ✆ **04/801-5551.**

Doctor For emergency doctor referrals, call ✆ **04/472-2999.**

Embassies & Consulates The **U.S. Embassy** is at 29 Fitzherbert Terrace, Thorndon (✆ **04/462-6000**); the **Canadian High Commission** is at Lvl 11, 125 The Terrace (✆ **04/473-9577**); and the **British High Commission** is at 44 Hill St. (✆ **04/924-2888**).

Emergencies Dial ✆ **111** to call the police, report a fire, or request an ambulance.

Hospitals **Wellington Hospital** is on Riddiford Street, Newtown (✆ **04/385-5999**).

Internet Access The **Email Shop,** 175 Cuba St. (✆ **04/384-1534**), has a full range of Internet and computer services; it's open daily from 9am to 10pm. It also has outlets at the **Wellington i-SITE Visitor Information Centre** (see "Visitor Information," above). For other options, try **Cybernomad,** 43 Courtenay Place (✆ **04/801-5964**), which offers high-speed Internet service, or **Cyber Spot Internet,** 180 Lambton Quay (✆ **04/473-0098**).

Newspapers Wellington's morning newspaper, the *Dominion,* and evening paper, the *Evening Post,* are both published Monday through Saturday. On Sundays, get the best paper in the country, the ***Sunday Star Times.*** Overseas newspapers are sometimes available at newsstands and in the reading room of the National Library, Molesworth Street (✆ **04/474-3000**).

Pharmacies There are late-night pharmacies at 17 Adelaide Rd., Wellington (✆ **04/385-8810**), and 729 High St., Lower Hutt (✆ **04/939-6669**).

Police See "Emergencies," above.

Post Office The main post office is at 7 Waterloo Quay (✆ **0800/501-501;** www. nzpost.co.nz). Collect poste restante mail at NZ Post, 43 Manners St. (✆ **04/473-5922**). New Zealand post shops are open Monday through Friday from 9am to 5pm.

Everything in Wellington is geared for the corporate market. Hotel and motel rates are significantly higher Monday through Thursday, but you can pick up exceptionally good deals on the weekends, especially during the off season. There has been a big increase in inner city apartment developments, and some exceptional values rise right off the heart of Lambton Quay and The Terrace, placing you perfectly in the heart of everything. Although there is a wide range of homestay options farther out, I'm always disappointed to discover that there are not as many upmarket B&Bs in the inner suburbs as there are in, say, Christchurch or Auckland.

All rates include 12.5% GST and free off-street parking unless otherwise stated.

IN THE INNER CITY
Expensive

Duxton Hotel ★★   So you want style, service, award-winning cuisine, and a great location all wrapped up in one? The Duxton delivers. Ideally located across the street from Te Papa and the Michael Fowler Centre, it offers nine levels of comfort and attracts everyone from leisure and corporate travelers to international dignitaries. Built in 1987, all rooms are large and have either harbor or city views. The club-level suites go up another notch in comfort and are well worth the extra price—especially if you get a weekend deal. A total hotel upgrade, due for completion at the end of 2010, will give this popular choice a slick new look.

170 Wakefield St., Wellington. © **0800/655-555** in NZ, or 04/473-3900. Fax 04/473-3929. www.duxton hotels.com. 192 units. NZ$185–NZ$475 deluxe; NZ$285–NZ$575 club; NZ$435–NZ$725 club suite; NZ$1,238 presidential suite. Extra person NZ$30. Long-stay rates. AE, DC, MC, V. Valet parking NZ$25. **Amenities:** Restaurant; bar; babysitting; concierge; club-level rooms; well-equipped gym; room service. *In room:* A/C, TV w/pay movies, fridge, hair dryer, minibar, Wi-Fi.

InterContinental Wellington ★★★   Seen as Wellington's most luxurious hotel, this is the sort of place where you could rub shoulders with the rich and famous—or at least the cosmopolitan and corporate. Now 19 years old, it's right in the heart of the central business district, and if you give in to indulgence, you'll love the top service and classy environment. The higher the price, the better it gets—and there's no doubt in my mind that the top-floor Club rooms are pampering at its best. These have divine bathrooms with huge Jacuzzis and lots of other perks, including access to the Club Lounge. I like staying here because my favorite cafe, Arabica, is right across the street and it's close to the best shopping. The hotel has a Qualmark Enviro-Gold rating and participates actively in water- and energy-saving measures and recycling.

Grey and Featherston sts., Wellington. © **0800/442-215** in NZ, or 04/472-2722. Fax 04/472-4724. www. ihg.com. 232 units. NZ$249 classic queen; NZ$289 superior; NZ$369 club king; NZ$550 club executive; NZ$1,900 presidential suite. Extra person NZ$35. Children 15 and under stay free in parent's room. Long-stay, off-peak rates, and special deals. AE, DC, MC, V. Valet parking NZ$30. **Amenities:** 2 restaurants (Chameleon Restaurant [Contemporary NZ] and Arizona Bar & Grill [Tex-Mex]); 2 bars; charged airport transfers; babysitting; concierge; club-level rooms; well-equipped gym; Jacuzzi; high-rise heated indoor pool; room service; sauna; day spa and beauty treatments; Wi-Fi in public areas. *In room:* A/C, TV, fridge, hair dryer, Internet, minibar.

Moderate

Bolton Hotel ★★ (Finds)   Brand-new in 2005, this multistory, apartment-style hotel has an elegance and style that exceeds some of its bigger capital city cousins. The hotel

(Tips) **All-Girl Guesthouse**

If you want to stay in an all-girls environment, consider the **Mermaid Guest-house for Women,** 1 Epuni St., Aro Valley, Wellington (📞/fax **04/384-4511;** www.mermaid.co.nz). Rates in the restyled Victorian villa are NZ$115 to NZ$150. It's walking distance to the central city, and buses stop right outside the gate.

was built with energy and water conservation in mind, and its Qualmark Enviro-Gold rating indicates a commitment to all avenues of sustainable tourism. Owners have paid meticulous attention to guest preferences, and rooms abound with luscious textural fabrics and unexpected extra touches—a comprehensive minibar, for instance, that includes an umbrella and disposable raincoat, the importance of which can't be overestimated in Wellington. It's colorful, crisp, modern, and close to the heart of the city. Above all, its rates are enticing. Ask about their classy Bolton suite if you want to indulge; it's very reasonably priced and ideal for families or couples traveling together.

Corner of Bolton and Mowbray sts., Wellington. 📞 **0800/996-622** in NZ, or 04/472-9966. Fax 04/472-9955. www.boltonhotel.co.nz. 142 units. NZ$275–NZ$315 studio; NZ$385–NZ$435 1-bedroom suite; NZ$500 2-bedroom suite. Long-stay, off-peak, and special deals. AE, DC, MC, V. Valet parking NZ$25. **Amenities:** Restaurant (Mediterranean/NZ) and tiny lobby cafe; bar; airport transfer NZ$35; babysitting; concierge; excellent gym; Jacuzzi; heated indoor lap pool; sauna. *In room:* A/C, TV/DVD/pay movies, fridge, hair dryer, kitchen (in most), minibar, Wi-Fi throughout.

James Cook Hotel Grand Chancellor ★ (Value) This 38-year-old hotel has earned its reputation for great rates in a prime location with friendly staff. Some locals aren't enamored of it, but I have a real soft spot for this hotel's liveliness and great value. Club Rooms on Level 26 provide complimentary breakfast and extra amenities in the Club Lounge. For the little extra you pay, these 17 slick rooms are the pick of the bunch. With its views of the bustling city, direct access to shopping on Lambton Quay, and commerce on The Terrace, this hotel is the perfect base for business or pleasure—and don't forget to ask about the cheaper weekend rates. The hotel runs recycling and power-saving programs.

147 The Terrace, Wellington. 📞 **0800/699-500** in NZ, or 04/499-9500. Fax 04/499-9800. www.ghihotels.com. 260 units. NZ$185–NZ$450. Long-stay, off-peak, and special deals. AE, DC, MC, V. Valet parking NZ$18. **Amenities:** 2 restaurants; 2 bars; babysitting; concierge; limited gym on-site w/use of full-size off-site gym; day spa and beauty treatments. *In room:* A/C, TV/DVD/pay movies, fridge, hair dryer, minibar, Wi-Fi throughout.

The Museum Hotel ★ Perfectly located on the waterfront, across the road from Te Papa and close to dozens of restaurants, the Museum Hotel offers both modern apartments and hotel rooms in two separate wings. You'll enjoy the opulent mood and the big, slightly eccentric New Zealand art collection, which gives it a funkier character than the nearby classic Duxton. The two-bedroom apartments are a good option for families and couples traveling together. Staff are very friendly.

90 Cable St., Wellington. 📞 **0800/994-335** in NZ, or 04/802-8900. Fax 04/802-8909. www.museumhotel.co.nz. 160 units. NZ$190 classic; NZ$212 harbor; NZ$235 premier studio; NZ$235 twin studio; NZ$268 1-bedroom suite; NZ$325 2-bedroom suite. Long-stay and special deals. AE, DC, MC, V. Valet parking NZ$20. **Amenities:** Restaurant; 2 bars; babysitting; concierge; well-equipped gym; Jacuzzi; heated indoor lap pool; room service; sauna. *In room:* A/C in most, TV/pay movies, DVD in some, fridge, hair dryer, kitchen in some, minibar, Wi-Fi throughout.

WELLINGTON

12

WHERE TO STAY

Victoria Court Motor Lodge ★ (Finds) Stay in this tidy, convenient complex and **299**
you can forget all about driving your car. It's just a hop, skip, and jump from central
shopping and restaurants. What's more, the 25 units have much to offer in terms of value
and comfort. The two-bedroom units especially are a gift for families or two couples
traveling together, and when you see the smart kitchens, you might even feel inclined to
cook. Best of all, it's just behind my favorite part of town—Cuba Mall.

201 Victoria St., Wellington. © **04/472-4297.** Fax 04/385-7949. www.victoriacourt.co.nz. 25 units.
NZ$145–NZ$200. Extra person NZ$20. AE, DC, MC, V. Long-stay, off-peak, and weekend rates. Victoria St.
is one-way heading west so enter it off Vivian or Dixon sts. **Amenities:** Babysitting. *In room:* TV, fridge,
hair dryer, kitchenette or kitchen, Wi-Fi throughout.

Inexpensive

Wellington City YHA This is without doubt the best backpacker establishment in
Wellington. It hums with activity as guests of all ages settle into crisp, colorful rooms—
private or bunk style—and the international staff seems to know everything there is to
know about the city. Location is a prime attraction, and rooms are well situated for
sunshine and harbor views. Internet and postal services are available, and a lounge acts as
a great social spot. There is a well-equipped kitchen, plenty of quiet intimate spaces, and
a supermarket just across the road. All transport and other YHA bookings can be made
on the premises.

Cambridge Terrace and Wakefield St., Wellington. © **04/801-7280.** Fax 04/801-7278. www.yha.co.nz.
320 beds. NZ$28–NZ$32 multishare; NZ$110 double with en-suite bathroom; NZ$85 double with shared
bathrooms. Nonmembers pay additional NZ$3 per person per night. Off-peak rates. MC, V. Carpark build-
ing nearby. **Amenities:** Dining room; Internet room. *In room:* Hair dryer on request.

IN THORNDON/KELBURN

Lovers of heritage homes and a good view will enjoy the comforts of three lovely rooms
at **Lambton Heights** ★, 20 Talavera Terrace, Kelburn (© **04/472-4710;** fax 04/472-
4715; www.lambtonheights.co.nz), priced from NZ$180 to NZ$285. It's just 5 minutes
from the inner city.

Gardens Homestay ★ Neil Harrap and Sally Guinness like to say that guests are
simply friends they haven't met yet. As the inventor of New Zealand's Fly By Wire ride,
Neil has an extensive knowledge of tourism, which he delights in sharing with those
lucky enough to score a bed in this grand 1892 Victorian home filled with antiques. The
large two-bedroom, upstairs suite (one smallish bathroom) is ideal for two couples or
family members traveling together. It's quiet and private, and has lovely views over one
of Wellington's premier residential areas.

11 St. Mary St., Thorndon, Wellington. © **04/499-1212.** www.gardenshomestay.co.nz. 1 2-bedroom
suite. NZ$265. Long-stay and off-peak rates. Rates include breakfast. MC, V. **Amenities:** Free bikes; heated
outdoor pool. *In room:* A/C, hair dryer, Wi-Fi.

IN MOUNT VICTORIA/ORIENTAL PARADE

Booklovers Bed and Breakfast ★★ (Finds) Journalist and author Jane Tolerton
offers four large rooms in her two-story Victorian home, and she's a terrific and knowledgeable hostess who knows just when to leave you alone. My pick is the downstairs
room, but all are lovely. The whole place heaves with books—if you dabble in the book-
shelves you may never want to leave! It's just a short walk from Courtenay Place, or hop
on one of the buses that stop right outside the gate.

123 Pirie St., Mount Victoria. ☏ **04/384-2714.** www.booklovers.co.nz. 4 units. NZ$220. Long-stay and off-peak rates. Rates include breakfast. MC, V. **Amenities:** Babysitting. *In room:* A/C, TV/DVD, guest fridge, hair dryer, free Wi-Fi throughout.

Mount Victoria Homestay   The visitors' book at Bill and Coral Aitchison's inner city home is filled with glowing reports on their hospitality and generosity—"hosts from heaven," they're called. Their 1920s villa was completely restored in 2002 and every-thing—from the Wedgwood and Spode dinnerware to hearty breakfasts to the tranquil garden courtyard where guests enjoy evening drinks—illustrates Coral's attention to detail. Two upstairs guest rooms are quiet and private, yet just a few minutes' walk from some of the capital's best restaurants and nightlife. Guests can participate in the Aitchi-sons' voluntary carbon-offset program to benefit a 100-acre conservation reserve.

11 Lipman St., Mount Victoria, Wellington. ☏ **04/802-4886.** Fax 04/802-4877. www.mountvictoria.co.nz. 2 units. NZ$315. Rates include breakfast, canapés, and predinner drinks. MC, V. **Amenities:** Babysitting. *In room:* TV/DVD, fridge, Wi-Fi.

Ohtel ★★★ (**Value**)   I love this small, new, chic boutique hotel for its great location, its striking individuality, and its total commitment to sustainability. Stylishly furnished throughout with the owner's collection of Mid-Century Modern furniture and German ceramics, it is perfectly placed, overlooking Te Papa and Oriental Parade. All rooms are large, but the six front-facing are definitely the best if you like a view. You'll get all the mod-cons here and they take a proactive ecofriendly stance with solar-powered showers and recycling within rooms. Best of all, the intimate scale makes it feel like home. It's a full sensory experience; I still dream about their gorgeous big bathrooms.

66 Oriental Parade, Mount Victoria. ☏ **04/803-0600.** Fax 04/803-0611. www.ohtel.com. 10 units. NZ$534 rear studio; NZ$591 front studio; NZ$669 suite; NZ$55 each extra person. Long-stay and off-peak rates. AE, MC, V. Valet parking NZ$28. **Amenities:** Lobby cafe for breakfast and cabinet food; bar; airport trans-fers NZ$45; babysitting; concierge; small cardio/weights gym and full-size gym nearby; nearby pool; room service; infra-red sauna; Wi-Fi in lobby. *In room:* A/C, LCD TV/digital movies, fridge, hair dryer, free Internet, minibar.

NEAR THE AIRPORT

Brentwood Hotel, 16 Kemp St., Kilbirnie, Wellington (☏ **0508/273-689** in NZ, or 04/920-0400; fax 04/920-0401; www.brentwoodhotel.co.nz), is a modest yet practical airport choice if all you want is a bed before an early departure. Rooms range from NZ$135 to NZ$250.

Home Stay at Evans Bay   Multilingual Leisha Schuitema has traveled extensively, adores meeting people, and doesn't feel alive until she has dipped her hands into her cooking bowls. She'll spoil you with edible delicacies and a warm welcome. Two upstairs rooms are sunny and bright. One has its own en-suite bathroom (shower only), the other a private bathroom with tub and shower. This modern home is filled with Leisha's own paintings and collections of china. It's just 5 minutes from the airport and city, it enjoys beautiful harbor views, and the city bus stops nearby.

4/378 Evans Bay Parade, Evans Bay, Wellington. ☏ **04/386-1504.** Fax 04/386-1503. www.home stayevansbay.co.nz. 2 units. NZ$190–NZ$250. Rates include breakfast. Long-stay and off-peak rates. AE, MC, V. **Amenities:** Airport transport; Internet; nearby pool, golf course, and tennis courts. *In room:* TV, hair dryer.

Wellington used to have the best concentration of restaurants and cafes of any city in New Zealand, but Auckland has edged it out. However, it's still crammed with a variety that reflects its cosmopolitan population. Everything is within walking distance and priced for all budgets. The visitor center's *Wine & Food Guide* gives an excellent introduction to many of the leading lights. Ethnic restaurants—Turkish, Greek, Indian, Thai, Mongolian, Japanese, Malaysian, Chinese, Korean, and more—abound and are found in the biggest concentration around Cuba Street and Courtenay Place. Cuba Street has become one of the hippest places to eat and a number of excellent restaurants and cafes have loyal followers among locals. And don't forget the suburbs: Thorndon, Mount Victoria, Oriental Parade, and Eastbourne, just for starters, have little pockets of culinary magic.

Situated strategically between the ever-expanding winegrowing regions of Marlborough and Wairarapa, Wellington couldn't be better placed to introduce you to the sublime delights of New Zealand's finest wines. It's wall-to-wall food and wine out here—go for it!

IN THE INNER CITY
Expensive
Boulcott Street Bistro ★★★ CONTINENTAL   A French-inspired menu will please lovers of classic cuisine with a contemporary twist—served to perfection in a cute little Victorian house right in the heart of the city. Small, intimate, and formal, it's elegance par excellence, and classic dishes like lamb shank, filet béarnaise, and crème brûlée will delight the testiest palate. It's popular so you may not get in the first time. Keep trying—if only for the lobster ravioli!

99 Boulcott St. ℂ **04/499-4199.** www.boulcottstbistro.co.nz. No reservations. Main courses NZ$35–NZ$45. AE, DC, MC, V. Mon–Fri noon–2pm; Mon–Sat 6pm–late.

Logan Brown ★★★ INTERNATIONAL   Ask about Wellington's best restaurant, and the name Logan Brown will be mentioned consistently. It's all leather-upholstered booths, white-clothed tables, Corinthian pillars, and chandeliers big enough to swing on in what was once a banking chamber. The food is billed as "honest and simple" and focuses on fish and game. The wine list is lengthy with an uneven balance between French (they win) and New Zealand offerings. Funnily enough, you'll find this culinary star cast adrift in the city's red-light area—not that that should affect your decision to try the epicurean offerings of the most splendid a la carte restaurant in town. Service is impeccable, but it can be stuffy. If you want to sample Logan Brown without emptying your wallet, go for the bistro lunch.

Tips   The Top Four

For the very best in fine dining, Wellington's top four restaurants are Boulcott Street Bistro, Logan Brown, the White House Restaurant, and Martin Bosley's Yacht Club Restaurant—all reviewed below and all seriously expensive.

Cuba and Vivian sts. © **04/801-5114.** www.loganbrown.co.nz. Reservations recommended. Main courses NZ$40–NZ$45. AE, DC, MC, V. Mon–Fri noon–2pm; daily 5:30pm–late.

Moderate

If you enjoy Indian food, **Great India Restaurant** ★, 141 Manners St. (© **04/384-5755**), comes highly recommended; it's open for lunch Monday through Friday midday to 2pm, and for dinner daily 5pm until late. Reservations are advised. I recommend **Ernesto** ★, 132 Cuba St. (© **04/801-6878**), if you want a relaxed, sunny cafe to read the morning paper. It's a little more relaxed than nearby Floriditas (see below), but the service can be patchy.

Caffe Astoria ★ MODERN CAFE/LIGHT FARE This upmarket cafe has a prime setting in the center of Lambton Quay's little green space, and it's well patronized by businesspeople and earnest-looking Wellingtonians with a slightly professorial image about them. It's a great place to unwind with a bottle of wine, a good coffee, or a delicious snack. Its big interior is always full and buzzing, and it's a popular brunch spot on weekends. There's something quintessentially Wellington about it that shouldn't be missed. It's always my first stop when I arrive in the capital.

159 Lambton Quay. © **04/473-8500.** Main courses NZ$15–NZ$26. MC, V. Mon–Thurs 7am–7:15pm; Fri 7am–8:15pm; Sat–Sun 9am–4pm.

Chow ★★ SOUTHEAST ASIAN The fact that Chow now has two inner city locations is an indication of its popularity. It has a casual, modern interior and its extensive range of noodles, grills, steamed dishes, and salads combined with wine, sake, cocktails, or teas, have made it a winner with busy professionals. Servings are tapas style, so order two or three menu choices. It's the sort of place I keep going back to because I know I'll always leave happy.

45 Tory St. and 11 Woodward St. © **04/382-8585** or 473-4474. www.chow.co.nz. Main courses NZ$16–NZ$24. AE, MC, V. Daily noon–midnight.

Floriditas ★ EUROPEAN A simple one-page menu makes for easy choices in this paisley-embellished corner retreat. European-inspired dishes like vegetable and ricotta lasagna and polenta-dusted calamari make a delicious lunch or light dinner, and the generally friendly staff are knowledgeable about their good wine list. It's also an excellent coffee stop, and daily sweet treats lining the countertop are there to be eaten. Don't resist the urge. I like the buzzy atmosphere here and it's a favorite with all ages.

(Tips) **Quick Caffeine Fixes**

Apart from the other cafes reviewed in this section, you'll find excellent coffee and good atmosphere at **One Red Dog,** 9–11 Blair St. (© **04/384-9777**); **Caffe L'Affare** ★, 27 College St. (© **04/385-9748**), which has a fabulous humming atmosphere; and **Starbucks** (© **04/472-4861**), now firmly ensconced in several city locations, including the Old Bank Arcade & Chambers, on Lambton Quay (© **04/922-0624**), and also on The Terrace and on Willis Street. And for constant reliability, you can't go past my busy little favorite, **Arabica** ★ (© **04/473-7697**), opposite the InterContinental hotel on Grey Street, where people pour in like ants to a new food source.

ⓕ Finds   Deli Fixings

Whether you want to stock up on picnic food or just sit and enjoy coffee with a fine range of edibles, don't miss these inner city delis and bakeries. **Dixon Street Gourmet Deli,** 45 Dixon St. (ⓒ **04/384-2436**), has a glowing reputation as long as my arm; and **Smith the Grocer,** in the Old Bank Arcade, Lambton Quay (ⓒ **04/473-8591**), is a surprise tucked in between leading fashion stores. Both have a wide range of specialty items to take home, plus delicious ready-to-eat treats for the moment. **Bordeaux Bakery,** 220 Thorndon Quay (ⓒ **04/499-8334**), and **Le Moulin,** 248 Willis St. (ⓒ **04/382-8118**), are two superlative French bakeries; and for Italian-style breads, try **Pandoro,** 2 Allen St. (ⓒ **04/385-4478**).

161 Cuba St. ⓒ **04/381-2212.** Reservations recommended for dinner. Main courses NZ$18–NZ$25. AE, MC, V. Mon–Sat 7am–11pm; Sun 8am–5pm.

Hummingbird ★ PACIFIC RIM   With a superbly broody, moody interior—all chocolate brown, dark timber, and leather—Hummingbird has always been a big favorite for lunches, and the chef presents a wide range of appetizer-size dishes in the belief that we should all eat like hummingbirds—savoring small amounts regularly. It's loud and relaxed when full and a good choice for a quick snack before going on to the movies or the theater. For the real fun stuff, come at night for a lively bar scene. There's also a popular late supper every night until 3am and live music on Sundays.

22 Courtenay Place. ⓒ **04/801-6336.** www.hummingbird.net.nz. Reservations recommended. Main courses NZ$19–NZ$38. AE, DC, MC, V. Daily 10am–late; light snacks to 3am.

Lido Café ⓥ Value CAFE   No matter what time of day you come here, you'll find a decent smattering of people to make things interesting. Lido has always been popular for its tasty meals, and its location opposite the City Council makes it a favorite lunch spot with the working crowd. This is a laid-back place, far from formal, and you can sit inside or out—see and be seen. The interior is looking a little tatty, but the place still tickles my taste buds with a menu that scans the continents.

Wakefield and Victoria sts. ⓒ **04/499-6666.** Main courses NZ$15–NZ$26. AE, DC, MC, V. Mon–Fri 7:30am–late; Sat–Sun 9am–late.

Pravda ★ CONTEMPORARY EUROPEAN   The name, the pictures of Lenin, the sparkling chandeliers, the dark-wood paneling, and long, dining hall style all suggest something Russian, but the big brasserie menu takes a broader leap. Expect quality mid-price dishes like seared salmon or grouper with fennel and potato purée. It's sophisticated and doubles as a terrific cafe.

107 Customhouse Quay. ⓒ **04/801-8858.** Main courses NZ$24–NZ$28. AE, MC, V. Mon–Fri 11:30am–5pm; Sat 9am–3pm.

Shed 5 ★★ CONTEMPORARY SEAFOOD   As the name implies, this is a huge restaurant, but its popularity and award-winning status are such that, even on a quiet night, there is a decent crowd. If you like good seafood, this is the place to find it—right on the edge of the wharf. The menu also includes lamb, beef, venison, and chicken, and the service is friendly and unobtrusive.

(Finds) Cuba Character

This is my favorite bohemian part of Wellington with great food joints that shouldn't be missed. Top of the list is **Midnight Espresso** ★, 178 Cuba St. ((*C*) **04/384-7014**), an iconic, slightly scruffy melting pot of people and color. Quintessentially Cuba Street, it serves fabulous counter food and espresso late into the night. **Simply Paris** ★, 181 Cuba St. ((*C*) **04/801-5486**), is a French-owned cafe and patisserie with cakes to die for; I can never walk past it. **Caffe Italiano,** 229 Cuba St. ((*C*) **04/385-2703**), has an excellent deli and a lively week-end brunch scene that often includes the Italian community; and farther down, the French-owned bistro, **Le Metropolitain,** 146 Cuba St. ((*C*) **04/801-8007**), has legions of fans who love the authentic provincial dishes and noisy atmosphere. **Matterhorn Bar & Restaurant** ★★★, 106 Cuba St. ((*C*) **04/384-3359**), is a pop-ular, award-winning choice that everyone I met recommended. It's "the place of the moment" and meals are outstanding.

Shed 5, Queen's Wharf. (*C*) **04/499-9069.** Reservations recommended. Main courses NZ$32–NZ$36. AE, DC, MC, V. Daily 11am–late.

Zico Cucina & Bar ★ (Finds) ITALIAN CAFE   Franco Zanotto left his role as execu-tive chef at the famous Il Casino restaurant to start up this divine little cafe, and for that we can all be truly thankful. He's created just the right mix of relaxed informality, great-tasting food, and fun service. It's a family affair—his wife and sons also attend to your culinary needs—and the menu is so vast I had forgotten the first offerings before I read through to the last. Pizzas, seafood and veal dishes, and numerous pastas all deserve sampling. It's very popular, so be prepared to queue.

8 Courtenay Place. (*C*) **04/802-5585.** Reservations required. Main courses NZ$24–NZ$30. AE, DC, MC, V. Mon–Fri 10:30am–late; Sat–Sun 5:30pm–late. Closed Dec 25–26 and Jan 1–3.

Inexpensive

New Dynasty, 25 Tory St. ((*C*) **04/384-3288**), is a great place for traditional Chinese *yum cha* lunch—fat little dumplings and the like. The **Green Parrot,** Taranaki and Wakefield streets ((*C*) **04/384-6080**), is a backpacker regular that's been serving up big, old-fash-ioned meals for the past 31 years. On Courtenay Place are numerous **kabob houses** that stay open late. **One Red Dog,** 9–11 Blair St. ((*C*) **04/384-9777**), has cheap wood-fired pizzas and good service.

IN THORNDON/KELBURN

For a laid-back spot to put a smile on your face, head for **Backbencher Pub & Café,** 34 Molesworth St. (opposite Parliament; (*C*) **04/472-3065**), where you'll find a great pub atmosphere that lightheartedly mocks the local parliamentarians. It's best summed up as cheap and cheerful. In Kelburn, seek out the pocket-size delights of **Kelburn Café,** 87–89 Upland Rd., Kelburn ((*C*) **04/475-8381**), which is open daily 9am to 5pm, serv-ing great coffee and fabulous cakes. **Red Tomatoes** ★, 87–89 Upland Rd., Kelburn ((*C*) **04/475-7123**), has some of the most delicious thin-crust wood-fired pizzas I've ever tasted. They also do great Malaysian curries and Greek salads. They're open Monday through Saturday 4 to 10pm and Sunday 4 to 9pm, with live jazz every Tuesday night.

Maria Pia's ★★ ITALIAN COUNTRY This gorgeous little family-owned and -operated trattoria was an instant success from the minute it opened its doors. Sited in an old building, it has a warm, low-key interior that doesn't distract you in any way from the divine fresh pasta that is made, by hand, by Italian-born Maria every day. Located close to Parliament, it's invariably busy and the food is wholesome and authentic. The minestrone is a must and lemon sorbet a great way to finish.

55–57 Mulgrave St., Thorndon. ℭ **04/499-5590.** Reservations required. Main courses NZ$25–NZ$32. AE, MC, V. Tues–Fri 11:30am–2:30pm; Mon–Sat 6–11pm.

Tinakori Bistro ★ MODERN NEW ZEALAND This cute restaurant, right in the heart of Tinakori Village, is a delightful place for an evening meal, and it's been getting good reviews for years. You probably won't have a wild time here—the mood is generally pretty restrained—but the food is very good. I favor their fish of the day baked in an olive crust with fennel bulb tomato jus, but they also do a very good chargrilled beef filet with béarnaise sauce.

328 Tinakori Rd. ℭ **04/499-0567.** Reservations recommended. Main courses NZ$25–NZ$32. AE, DC, MC, V. Tues–Fri noon–2pm; daily 6–10:30pm.

IN MOUNT VICTORIA/ORIENTAL PARADE

Café Bastille ★★ PROVENÇAL Business is brisk in this award-winning restaurant, and you might have to queue if you want to savor old favorites like French onion soup, coq au vin, and Provençal fish soup. You might also consider the rabbit kidneys, chicken livers, and pigs' ears. With its sunny yellow interior, timber floors, French posters, and mirrors, it feels like a friendly neighborhood cafe. It's sometimes a squeeze but worth it for the rich, succulent tastes.

16 Marjoribanks St., Mount Victoria. ℭ **04/382-9559.** No reservations. Main courses NZ$22–NZ$28. AE, DC, MC, V. Mon–Sat 5:30pm–late.

Martin Bosley's Yacht Club Restaurant ★★★ MODERN NEW ZEALAND Previously reserved as the exclusive dining domain of members of the Royal Port Nicholson Yacht Club, this bright and classy spot has opened its doors to the wider public—and for that we can be truly thankful. You'll get some of the best dishes in Wellington here—luscious seafood served in myriad ways from an all-around creative menu. Try the smoked eel mousse or the oyster broth. Service is pleasant and confident and the waterside location is almost unbeatable. The menu changes daily, so there are always pleasant surprises.

Royal Port Nicholson Yacht Club, 103 Oriental Parade, Oriental Bay. ℭ **04/385-6963.** www.martinbosley.com. Reservations recommended. Main courses NZ$35–NZ$45; degustation NZ$100–NZ$170. AE, DC, MC, V. Mon–Fri noon–3pm; Tues–Sat 6pm–late.

WELLINGTON

12

WHERE TO DINE

Ⓣⓘⓟⓢ **Food Courts**

Wellington has good food courts. The best is **Gourmet Lane,** in the BNZ Centre, 1 Willis St. This place is a dream for dollar-wise travelers, as even NZ$10 will fill the gaps. The choices include Chinese, burgers, gourmet pies, barbecue, and more. It's open Monday through Thursday from 8am to 5pm, Friday from 8am to 8pm, and Saturday from 10am to 3pm. Another popular choice is the **Reading Food Court** at Reading Cinema, Courtenay Place Central (ℭ **04/801-4601**).

(Finds) **A Taste of France**

La Cloche ★★, 134 Hutt Rd., Kaiwharawhara, Wellington ((✆ **04/473-4892;**
www.lacloche.co.nz), sits at the bottom of the Ngaio Gorge beside a BMW showroom. It's there that you'll find the two Francois's—French business partners who
have Wellingtonians lining up for all things French and edible in a former warehouse jammed with goodies to eat in or take away—over 40 French cheeses for
a start, and their fresh breads are scrumptious. Open Monday to Friday 9am to
5pm; weekends 9am to 3pm.

The White House Restaurant ★★★ MODERN NEW ZEALAND   This is a top-
priced option you'll hear recommended time and again. It draws the corporate crowd and
the romancers and serves fine New Zealand food with great sea views. Flavors are mixed
to perfection here and taste-teasers like spinach and oyster soup will leave you begging
for more—grilled venison with mushrooms perhaps. They have excellent options for
vegetarians and the fish is always perfect.

232 Oriental Parade (upstairs), Oriental Bay. (✆ **04/385-8555.** www.whr.co.nz. Reservations essential.
Main courses NZ$39–NZ$45. AE, DC, MC, V. Daily 6pm–late; Fri noon–3pm.

NEAR THE AIRPORT

To call this area a culinary backwater is an understatement, and restaurants here seem to
change like the weather. If you're staying in this area, consult with the locals. The best
option I found is **Maranui Café,** the Parade, Lyall Bay ((✆ **04/387-2829**), which is a
quirky joint located in the distinctive Maranui Surf Life Saving Club building on the
windy waterfront. It's a terrific place for coffee, big cakes, and light lunches and with gulls
soaring just outside the upstairs windows at table level, you'll soon forget all about the
rush of the city. It's open daily 7:30am to 5pm. Make sure you check out the historic surf
club photos in the stairwell. **Soi Café & Bar,** 305 Evans Bay Parade, Haitaitai ((✆ **04/
386-3830;** www.soicafebar.co.nz), is a new addition to Great Point Wharf. It's light,
bright, and contemporary, and a lovely place to unwind over fish and salad or risotto
before hitting the airport 5 minutes away. As the name suggests, there's an Asian under-
tone to the menu.

5 EXPLORING WELLINGTON

THE TOP ATTRACTIONS

Museum of New Zealand—Te Papa Tongarewa ★★★ (Kids)   New Zealand's
largest cultural investment and Wellington's most exciting attraction, Te Papa opened in
1998. It has since played a major role in increasing visitor numbers to the capital city.
One of the largest national museums in the world, Te Papa is redefining the word
museum. Built at a cost of NZ$317 million, it is believed to be 5 years ahead of anything
of its kind in the world, combining interactive technology with stunning world-class
displays that tell the story of New Zealand—its history, art, and natural environment.
Advanced motion simulators take visitors back in time to the explosive formation of New

Zealand and the prehistoric landscape, and in the present you can try virtual-reality bungy jumping, sheep shearing, or whale riding.

Te Papa is also a partnership between Pakeha (the majority culture of European descent) and Maori culture. It includes a range of magnificent exhibitions featuring **Manu Whenua** ★★, some of the country's most significant Maori treasures, as well as **Te Marae** ★★, a unique 21st-century carved meetinghouse. Visitors can share in formal Maori welcomes and *iwi* (tribal) ceremonies, see how the Maori navigated the Pacific, and learn the stories behind the carvings and the Treaty of Waitangi.

The second level contains **Mountains to Sea,** which puts the spotlight on the natural world. From minuscule insects to a slightly creepy colossal squid specimen, with computer-generated interactive displays and 3-D animation to keep people of all ages amused, it presents both the familiar and the bizarre of New Zealand's natural inhabitants. The part I love best, though, is **Our Space** ★★★, which is a spectacular multimedia adventure. It includes a walk-on satellite map of New Zealand that triggers images; and the **Wall,** a fabulous interactive space where you can upload your own images to the Te Papa database and create works of art that merge with everyone else's.

On Level 4, **Tangata o le Moana: The Story of Pacific People of New Zealand** explores how Pacific Island cultures have influenced and affected New Zealand—and kids will love the hologram movie of their early exploration. **Golden Days** is a captivating animated junk shop that comes alive, and **Passports** ★★ explores the migrant story of New Zealand in a fantastic exhibition and audiovisual presentation that is one of the highlights of the museum. Spread over five levels, the museum includes much more and warrants at least half a day's exploration. It's playful, imaginative, bold, and more than impressive. It is an essential destination if you're keen to learn more about New Zealand. Few people leave unmoved. It's stunningly high-tech and loads of fun. On top of that, the architecture isn't bad, either.

Special guided tours must be prebooked. These are priced from NZ$11 to NZ$30 for adults, and NZ$5.50 to NZ$20 for children 15 and under. The 60-minute **Introducing Te Papa Tour** is an excellent choice if you're short on time. It runs hourly from 10am to 3pm November through March, and twice daily at 10:15am and 2pm in winter, with a 7pm Thursday tour year-round. The tour costs NZ$11 for adults and NZ$5.50 for children 15 and under. Request foreign-language guides at the time of booking. A self-guided tour booklet is available at the information desk for NZ$3, an excellent investment. Audio guides in several languages are also available.

Te Papa has two eateries: Te Papa Café (Level 1), serving excellent New Zealand cuisine; and Espresso Bar (Level 4), for coffee and snacks. It also has a superb gift shop, **Te Papa Store,** featuring original crafts and top Maori designs.

Cable St., on the Waterfront. ✆ **04/381-7000.** Fax 04/381-7070. www.tepapa.govt.nz. Free admission; fees for some activities, guided tours, and short-term exhibitions. Interactive displays NZ$8–NZ$10; children's rides NZ$5–NZ$9. Daily 10am–6pm (Thurs till 9pm). Parking NZ$4 per hour up to daily maximum of NZ$12, or NZ$6 for evening if you arrive after 5pm.

Wellington Cable Car ★ ⓜ**Moments**   This splendid little 4½-minute trip takes you to some of the best views you'll see anywhere. Pray for fine weather, as Wellington city and the harbor look spectacular from up here on a cloudless day. It's also the best way to access the Wellington Botanic Garden (see below); and there is a fine little Cable Car Museum (✆ **04/475-3578;** www.cablecarmuseum.co.nz) at the top, detailing the 100-year history of the service. The museum has free admission and is open daily in summer from 9:30am to 5:30pm and in winter from 9:30am to 5pm (closed Dec 25).

Cable Car Lane, 280 Lambton Quay (next to McDonald's) and Upland Rd., Kelburn, Wellington. ℭ 04/472-2199. www.wellingtonnz.com/cablecar. Round-trip fare NZ$5 adults, NZ$3 children, NZ$12 families. Mon–Fri 7am–10pm; Sat 8:30am–10pm; Sun and holidays 9am–10pm. Car runs every 10 min.

Wellington Botanic Garden ★   The Botanic Garden brochure and map available at the Wellington visitor center or Treehouse Visitor Centre within the gardens will help you make the most of your time in this leafy enclave. Established in 1868, the gardens have been managed by the Wellington City Council since 1891. They cover 25 hectares (62 acres), presenting a mix of protected native forest, conifer varieties, and plant collections with seasonal floral displays. The Lady Norwood Rose Garden is a colorful spectacle from November to May, with blooms flourishing in 106 formal beds. The Begonia House shows off tropical and temperate plants, including orchids and waterlilies, with a gift shop and Picnic Café adjacent. The Bolton Street Memorial Park includes a heritage rose collections and a historic cemetery. The chapel is open daily from 10am to 4pm.

The **Carter Observatory** (ℭ **04/472-8167;** www.carterobservatory.org) is another key attraction within the gardens. This is your chance to see the wonders of the Southern Hemisphere's night sky. From November through April, it's open Sunday through Tuesday from 10am to 5pm, Wednesday through Saturday from 10am until late; from May through October, Sunday through Thursday 11am to 4pm, Friday through Saturday 11am until late.

Access to the gardens is from the Cable Car or Centennial entrance on Glemore St., Thorndon. ℭ **04/499-1400** for Treehouse Visitor Centre. www.wellington.govt.nz. Free admission. Daily sunrise–sunset. Karori Bus 12 from Lambton Quay stops outside Founders entrance on Glenmore Rd. Parking available along Glenmore Rd. and in the public lot adjacent to the Lady Norwood Rose Garden.

Wellington Zoo ★★ (Kids)   Wellington Zoo is renowned for its work with endangered species, such as the Sumatran tiger, chimpanzee, white-cheeked gibbon, and Malayan sun bear. It's also the only place in the capital to see the famous brown kiwi (the Kiwi House is open daily 9:30am–5pm) and the tuatara. The Tropical River Trail highlights a rainforest habitat, bird life, and several species of primates. In February and March, look out for **Wild Summer Nights** ★★, when you can spend an evening at the zoo with a picnic (food outlets are available on the grounds) and listen to jazz or blues among the animals. Another interactive feature is the **Close Encounters** program ★★★, which offers the chance to hand-feed a red panda (must be 6 and over), a giraffe (7 and over), the big cats (12 and over), or to spend a full day with a zookeeper tending the animals (18 and over). All proceeds from Close Encounters go toward conservation projects.

200 Daniell St., Newtown. ℭ **04/381-6755.** Fax 04/389-4577. www.wellingtonzoo.com. Admission NZ$18 adults, NZ$9 children 3–16, NZ$36–NZ$54 family; NZ$65–NZ$500 for Close Encounters, bookings required. Daily 9:30am–5pm. Closed Dec 25. Bus: 10 or 23 to Newton Park from the railway station.

The Parliament Buildings ★★   New Zealand's Parliament Buildings are on Molesworth Street in the city center and include the distinctive beehive-shaped building that is the administrative headquarters. You can visit Parliament daily free of charge. The 1-hour tours include the Edwardian neoclassical **Parliament House,** the Victorian-Gothic **Parliamentary Library,** and, if the group is not too large, the 1970s-style **Beehive.** If you want to see and hear history in the making, call first to check when the House is sitting. The Debating Chamber makes for fascinating spectator sport.

The refurbished buildings also present outstanding examples of New Zealand art. The most impressive of all is the spectacular work by Malcolm Harrison, which occupies the

(Value) **Wellington for Free**

- **Take in the Scenery from Mount Victoria:** Take a leisurely drive to the top and enjoy the spectacular views in all directions, or allow an hour or so to walk up the well-marked tracks, enjoy the sights, and return down a different route.
- **Savor Botanic Beauty:** Enjoy the lush greenbelt in the heart of the city. Check out the Carter Observatory and the sculptures in the gardens.
- **Explore Te Papa:** Don't overlook the possibility that one visit to the stunning Te Papa National Museum of New Zealand simply may not be enough!
- **Tour the Beehive:** Hope that a Parliamentary session coincides with your visit and stay and listen to the debates. Enjoy the artwork, too.
- **Wander Along Oriental Parade:** Amble along the waterfront, enjoying the architecture, the cafes, the views, and the buzz of activity as Wellingtonians race past on in-line skates and bikes.
- **Get Wet in the Bucket Fountain:** A popular city landmark since 1969 when it was unveiled as the centerpiece of the new Cuba Mall, the fountain surprises, soaks, and delights adults, children, and dogs alike.

three-story height of the new Galleria. The Maori Affairs Select Committee Room, at the front of Parliament House, is another interesting feature, worth visiting for the remarkable carvings and weavings specially commissioned for it.

Across the road, the **Old Government Building** is also worth a look. It's the second-largest wooden building in the world and now houses the University Law Faculty. And since you're in the vicinity, you could also check out the **National Library of New Zealand,** 70 Molesworth St. (© **04/474-3000;** www.natlib.govt.nz). The ground-floor National Library Gallery showcases the art and history collections of the Alexander Turnbull Library and is open Monday through Friday from 9am to 5pm, Saturday from 9am to 4:30pm, and Sunday from 1 to 4:30pm. The **Alexander Turnbull Library,** in the same building, is the research wing of the National Library, specializing in New Zealand and the Pacific. Books, serials, recordings, manuscripts, and archives are on the first floor and newspapers on the lower ground floor. On the second floor, visitors can peruse files of photographs. Drawings, paintings, and maps are available for research by appointment.

Parliament Buildings, Molesworth St. © **04/471-9503.** www.parliament.nz. Free admission. Tours given hourly Mon–Fri 10am–4pm; Sat 10am–3pm; Sun noon–3pm. Closed Dec 25–26, Good Friday, New Year's Day, Jan 2, and Waitangi Day (Feb 6). City Circular Bus stops at gates of Parliament.

MORE ATTRACTIONS

The Weta Cave ★★ (Kids) When Weta Workshop created the special effects for the *Lord of the Rings* trilogy (and many other movies), they initiated an enduring phenomenon. People still flock to the movie's locations and now, for the first time, they can get an inside look at the multi–Academy Award–winning Weta operation in this cavelike minimuseum. Close encounters with characters, props, and displays from the movies will give you a unique perspective on Middle Earth and other well-known movies like *King*

Kong and *Narnia*—and like everything Weta does, it's memorable. Kids will love it; but so will Mum and Dad. There's also a terrific concept store where you can buy a range of pop culture and collectible items, including limited editions and hard-to-find miniatures.

Corner of Camperdown Rd. and Weka St., Miramar. © **04/380-9361.** www.wetanz.com. Free admission. Daily 9am–5:30pm. Closed Jan 1, Apr 25, Dec 25–26. Take bus route 2 toward Miramar and get off at Camperdown Rd.

ZEALANDIA: The Karori Sanctuary Experience ★ Opened to the public at the beginning of 2001, this 252-hectare (623-acre) reservoir catchment was the world's first urban sanctuary. Only minutes from the inner city, it is home to rare native wildlife such as kiwi, saddlebacks, and tuatara, which were reintroduced after all pests and predators had been removed from the valley. Enjoy a 1½-hour guided bush walk and learn about the history of the area as well as plans for the continuing development of this unique urban greenbelt. Tracks are steep and require moderate fitness and sensible shoes, but if you explore alone you can take your time. The Sanctuary by Night tours are a real treat, and they depart daily 30 minutes before sunset. A new education center under construction at the time of writing is due for completion in 2010. It will detail the story of the successful ecological restoration in the heart of the nation's capital, and will showcase New Zealand's natural history and the threats it faces. Allow half a day at least to get the most from the sanctuary.

31 Waiapu Rd., Karori. © **04/920-9200.** Fax 04/920-9000. www.visitzealandia.com. Admission NZ$14 adults, NZ$6 children, NZ$34 family. NZ$28–NZ$60 guided tours. Daily 10am–5pm. Closed Dec 25. Access is from Waiapu Rd.; turn left when emerging from the Karori side of the Karori Tunnel. Bus: 12, 17, 18, 21, 22, or 23; travel past the entrance to Waiapu Rd. and disembark at the 1st stop after Karori Tunnel; the Sanctuary is an easy 5-min. walk at the end of Waiapu Rd.

Museum of Wellington ★ (Kids) Housed in a historic icon, the 1892 Bond Store, this museum presents the history of the area in six galleries with audiovisual displays, cinema screens, and traditional exhibitions of memorabilia and photographs. Make sure you see **Wahine Gallery,** which is a memorial to the 1968 marine tragedy in Cook Strait; and **A Millennium Ago,** where Maori legends are combined with special effects. If you want an intense glimpse into Wellington's past, this is the place to get it. Holograms and interactive displays are great for kids. The museum also runs themed birthday parties for kids and there are free kids' activities every day.

The Bond Store, Queens Wharf. © **04/472-8904.** Fax 04/496-1949. www.museumofwellington.co.nz. Free admission. Short tours NZ$8; free at 2pm on Sun. Specialized tours NZ$30–NZ$40. Daily 10am–5pm. Closed Dec 25. City Circular bus.

City Gallery Wellington ★ City Gallery has a reputation for challenging viewers with the best of contemporary visual art—everything from painting, sculpture, film, and video to industrial and graphic design and architecture. It's not everyone's cup of tea, but if you want to find out what's happening in the New Zealand world of contemporary art, it's one of the best places to start. The gallery has a fully licensed cafe, bar, and restaurant.

Civic Sq., 101 Wakefield St. © **04/801-3021.** Fax 04/801-3950. www.citygallery.org.nz. Admission by donation; some international exhibitions may carry an entry charge. Daily 10am–5pm. Free exhibition tours Sat–Sun at noon. Closed Dec 25.

TheNewDowse ★★ If you found City Gallery a bit too intellectual (some people do), it will be well worth your while taking a trip out to TheNewDowse art museum, which has the best collection of New Zealand craft art in the country. They have regularly changing shows in a lively, colorful environment, generally with a broader appeal than

Especially for Kids

If you're ready to let the kids loose, head for **Capital E,** Civic Square, Victoria Street (*C* **04/913-3740;** www.capitale.org.nz), daily from 10am to 5pm. This wonderful place combines a varied program of exhibitions, events, and theater especially designed for families. It's all about fun, entertainment, and education. Call for current programs and admission prices.

Lollipop's Playland & Café, Station Village, Hutt Road, Lower Hutt (*C* **04/566-6677;** www.lollipops.co.nz), is another fantasyland that has been created to entertain children up to age 12. It has a wide range of children's activities including a merry-go-round, dress-up clothes, climbing frames, and facilities for drawing and collage-making. Children need to be supervised, or you can hire a "playcarer" to make sure the kids are safe while you enjoy a break in the cafe. Admission is NZ$3 adults, NZ$10 for ages 3 to 11, NZ$7 for ages 12 months to 23 months. They're open Sunday through Friday 10am to 6pm and Saturday 9:30am to 6pm.

Story Place, at Te Papa, Cable Street (*C* **04/381-7000;** www.tepapa.govt. nz), is a magical world of dress-ups, storytelling, songs, and art activities for children 5 years and under. There are daily 45-minute sessions from 10:15am to 4:30pm and admission is NZ$5. Tickets can be purchased at Te Papa's Information Desk on Level 2 of the museum.

Older kids will get a buzz out of **Wet & Wild,** Frank Kitts Park, the Waterfront (*C* **04/235-9796**), where they can let loose on in-line skates, in paddleboats, or on water bikes. It's open daily December through February, weather permitting.

WELLINGTON

12

EXPLORING WELLINGTON

those at the City Gallery. Exhibitions feature contemporary ceramics, jewelry, glass, textiles, wood, sculpture, and photography, most of it exceedingly pleasing to the eye.

45 Laings Rd., Lower Hutt. *C* **04/570-6500.** Fax 04/569-5877. www.newdowse.org.nz. Free admission; fees for some special exhibitions. Mon–Fri 10am–4:30pm; Sat–Sun and holidays 10am–5pm. Closed Dec 25. Situated 20km (12 miles) from Wellington city. Take the train to Waterloo Station and walk down Knights Rd. to the museum, or catch the Eastbourne/Big Red bus, which departs hourly from Courtenay Place to Queensgate.

Pataka ★★ This modern gallery, 15 minutes north of the city, in Porirua, celebrates the cultural diversity of the region. It showcases the very best of Maori, Pacific Island, and New Zealand art, all of which gives you excellent insight into the region's heritage. If you're interested, there's also a chance to buy a piece of New Zealand art from their very good sales gallery.

Corner of Norrie and Parumoana sts., Porirua City. *C* **04/237-1511.** Fax 04/237-4527. www.pataka. org.nz. Free admission. Mon–Sat 10am–4:30pm; Sun 11am–4:30pm. Take the motorway heading north and exit at Porirua. Free parking.

Katherine Mansfield Birthplace ★ **Finds** Anyone of a literary bent will get a great deal of pleasure from a visit to Katherine Mansfield's restored birthplace. New Zealand's most distinguished author and a short-story writer of world renown, Mansfield was born into the Beauchamp family in 1888. She left Wellington at age 19 for Europe, where she

(Moments) **Island Sanctuary** ★★★

Kapiti Island is a conservation lover's paradise. Managed by the New Zealand government as a nature reserve for over 100 years, it is known for its well-protected native flora and fauna. The island has always been important to a number of different Maori tribes, and of the total 1,965 hectares (4,854 acres), 13 hectares (32 acres) at Waiorua Bay is still designated Maori land. This is where you'll find **Kapiti Nature Lodge** and **Kapiti Island Alive** ((C) **06/362-6606;** www.kapitiislandalive.co.nz), owned by John and Susan Barrett and John's sister, Amo Clark. John's *whanau* (family) has lived on Kapiti since the 1820s, and they have a wealth of historical and conservation knowledge about the island, which you'll discover if you take one of their guided walks. Their lodge offers cabins (each with four bunks) set in native bush, plus some oceanview accommodations with en suites. There's a dining room in the central lodge and a wealth of activities from nature and history walks to weaving weekends, amazing photo opportunities, night kiwi spotting, and the chance to swim, snorkel, or scuba dive in Kapiti Marine Reserve. The lodge has a capacity for just 10 overnight guests and 24 day visitors.

Every person visiting Kapiti Island must have a permit, and extra permits are required to enter the Department of Conservation land on either side of Kapiti Nature Lodge. These can be acquired through the Wellington DOC office (www.doc.govt.nz) and cost NZ$11 for adults and NZ$5 for children. Ferries to the island, departing from Kapiti Boating Club at Paraparaumu just north of Wellington, depart each day at 9am and 2:30pm, and cost NZ$55 for adults and NZ$30 for children. The trip takes 15 minutes, and because Kapiti is a strictly controlled conservation area, you will be asked for a bag check to eliminate the possibility of pests and predators getting onto the island. The team at Kapiti Island Alive can help you organize permits. They also offer a day tour to the island if you're short on time.

kept company with the likes of Virginia Woolf, T. S. Eliot, and D. H. Lawrence. The Beauchamp house has been meticulously restored. If you're familiar with Mansfield's stories, you'll get a sense of what inspired them as you walk about the family home.

25 Tinakori Rd., Thorndon. (C)/fax **04/473-7268.** www.katherinemansfield.com. Admission NZ$6 adults, NZ$4 seniors and students, NZ$2 children. Victorian teas by arrangement. Tues–Sun 10am–4pm. Closed Dec 25 and Good Friday. Bus: 14 Wilton (stops at nearby Park St.).

ORGANIZED TOURS & CRUISES

If your time is limited, you'll get a comprehensive view of Wellington by booking with **Hammond's Scenic Tours** ((C) **04/472-0869;** www.wellingtonsightseeingtours.com). Their Wellington CityTour covers the financial and commercial area, Parliament buildings, and Botanic Garden; they also go up to Mount Victoria lookout and then around the coastal bays, returning to the city via View Road. It costs NZ$50 for adults and NZ$25 for children ages 4 to 14. Wally and his son Lance run the operation, giving it a personalized flavor with good commentary. Their 2½-hour tours depart daily at 10am and 2pm.

Flat Earth ★★ (© **0800/775-805** in NZ, or 04/977-5805; www.flatearth.co.nz) has a range of excellent specialty tours, including very interesting Maori Treasures tours priced from NZ$145 per person for a half-day, and excellent Capital Arts Tours that immerse you in the city's art and architecture for NZ$145 per person for a half-day.

Zest Food Tours ★★ (© **04/801-9198;** www.zestfoodtours.co.nz) is another excellent business and is a real hit with foodies. Its Walking Gourmet (daily 9:30am–1:30pm) costs NZ$210 per person and introduces you to the capital's lively food scene and hard-to-find places. Taste Wellington (daily 9:30am–3pm) costs NZ$395 per person and includes coffee roasting, top specialty food stores, a wine-matched lunch at an award-winning restaurant, and a visit to the home of a local food writer. Chocolate Espresso (9:30am–noon) is a behind-the-scenes look into Wellington's chocolate hot spots for NZ$99 per person. Tours can be tailored to specific interests.

Wild About Wellington ★★ (© **027/441-9010** in NZ; www.wildaboutwellington. co.nz) has a fabulous Boutique Beer Tasting Tour, which is hosted by local beer expert/ writer Neil Miller. The 1-hour walking day tour is great value at NZ$180; and a 3-hour evening tour is NZ$165 per person. Fashion lovers should ask about their equally good City of Style Tour, which takes you to meet local fashion designers for NZ$125 per person.

Seal Coast Safari ★ (© **0800/732-527** in NZ, or 04/801-6080; www.sealcoast.com) offers a completely different outing that departs daily from the visitor center at 10:30am and 1pm. For NZ$99 for adults (children 14 and under half-price), you'll spend 2¾ hours taking the coastal road to the seals at Red Rocks. **Walk Wellington** (© **04/384-9590;** www.walk.wellington.net.nz), on the other hand, gives you a fabulous value introduction to the city. The Essential Wellington tour is NZ$20 per person and departs from the visitor center daily, rain, hail, or shine at 10am. Additional afternoon walks are offered in summer at 5:30pm Monday, Wednesday, and Friday. Call © **04/802-4860** for bookings and departure times.

Wellington Movie Tours (© **027/419-3077** in NZ; www.movietours.co.nz) will give you a comprehensive overview of the Wellington movie scene, including visits to *The Lord of the Rings* locations, the Weta Cave, on-site movie clips, and movie props. Tours range from NZ$40 to NZ$110 per person.

On the Water

Take a Somes Island excursion with the **Dominion Post Ferry** (see "Getting Around," earlier in this chapter). Simply take the ferry and stop off on the island, picking up a return ferry a few hours later. The island recently reopened to the public after 100 years of restricted access. In recent times, it has served as a quarantine station and before that as a prisoner-of-war camp. It has been replanted and developed as a wildlife refuge and has walking tracks and great views.

6 OUTDOOR PURSUITS

GOLF   There are a number of courses within 25 minutes of Wellington city. **Paraparaumu Beach Golf Club,** 376 Kapiti Rd., Paraparaumu Beach (© **04/298-4561;** www. paraparaumubeachgolfclub.co.nz), is an 18-hole, par-71 course rated one of the top 50 courses in the world by *Golf Digest*. Greens fees are NZ$110, club rental is NZ$45, and carts are NZ$40. Reserve well in advance. **Hutt Golf Club,** Military Road, Lower Hutt (© **04/567-4722;** www.huttgolfclub.co.nz), is an 18-hole, par-70 course where you'll pay NZ$75 for a round. **Karori Golf Club,** South Makara Road, Wellington (© **04/ 476-7337;** www.karorigolf.co.nz), is an 18-hole, par-70 course; a round costs NZ$40 during the week and NZ$50 on weekends.

IN-LINE SKATING   This is a great way to explore Oriental Parade. Skates can be hired from **Fergs Kayaks,** Queens Wharf (© **04/499-8898;** www.fergskayaks.co.nz), for NZ$7 per half-day. Daily rates available.

KAYAKING   **Fergs Kayaks** (see above) is owned by New Zealand's legendary canoeist and Olympic gold medalist Ian Ferguson. You can either do the self-paddle thing for NZ$15 per hour, or join a guided group. Try the night harbor tour, NZ$70 per person for 2½ hours of paddling, with soup and snacks at the end. **Tamarillo Sea Kayaking,** Kapiti (© **025/244-1616;** fax 04/239-9789), offers a more remote, nature-based sea-kayak experience around Kapiti Island, one of New Zealand's most famous conservation reserves. Instruction is given to those with no previous experience. The all-day adventure includes a chartered launch trip to and from the island and costs NZ$185. Birders will love this one.

MOUNTAIN BIKING   This is one group that truly celebrates Wellington's hilly terrain. You have the choice of everything from a leisurely ride around the bays to a spine-chilling route that includes a vertical cliff face. For bike rentals, contact **Penny Farthing Cycles,** 89 Courtenay Place (© **04/385-2279;** www.pennyfarthing.co.nz). **Mud Cycles** (© **04/ 476-4961;** www.mudcycles.co.nz), which is next to Wellington's Mountain Bike Park in Karori, offers guided tours and instruction for all abilities.

SWIMMING   The **Wellington Regional Aquatic Centre,** 62 Kilbirnie Crescent, Kilbirnie (© **04/387-8029**), has four heated pools: a lap pool, a learners' pool, and adjoining junior and toddler pools with an access ramp for people in wheelchairs. There are also diving facilities, Jacuzzis, saunas, a sun deck, a cafe, and a YMCA fitness center. The **Freyberg Pool,** 139 Oriental Parade (© **04/384-3107**), is an easy walk from most inner city accommodations.

TENNIS   The **Wellington Renouf Tennis Centre,** 20 Brooklyn Rd., Central Park (© **04/384-6294;** www.wellingtontennis.org.nz), has 14 outdoor courts and four indoor courts. It's open Monday through Friday from 6am to 11pm, Saturday and Sunday from 8am to 11pm. A cafe and bar are on the premises.

WALKING   There are endless walking opportunities in Wellington. The most obvious that spring to mind are a quiet amble through the **Botanic Garden** or around **Oriental Parade,** or a more taxing climb up any one of the many **Mount Victoria** tracks. The visitor center has a wide range of excellent Heritage Trail brochures, which give you the chance to learn and discover as you go. They also have a terrific range of more than 10 Explore Wellington brochures, which detail various themed walks in different areas of the city. Included is the popular Five Lunchtime Walks, all of 40 or 50 minutes' duration within the inner city area.

7 SHOPPING

Wellington is such a compact city that it's easy for visitors to find their way around and to wander at ease. You can pick up the free guides, *The Fashion Map* and *The Arts Map,* at the visitor center. From the department and designer stores of Lambton Quay (nick-named the Golden Mile) up Willis Street to the funkier side of town on Cuba Street,

Shopping for Souvenirs

The always-popular **Simply New Zealand,** 13 Grey St. (℗ **04/472-6817**), has a huge range of gifts, jewelry, and crafts as well as wool knitwear, Maori carvings, and America's Cup souvenirs. **Te Papa Store** ★★★, Te Papa, Cable Street (℗ **04/381-7000;** mail@tepapa.govt.nz), has one of the best selections of New Zealand arts, crafts, and souvenirs in the city. Everything is top quality and attractively laid out, and you don't pay local tax (GST) if you're mailing gifts overseas. **Ora** ★, 23 Allen St., Courtenay Place (℗ **04/384-4157;** www.ora.co.nz), open daily 9am to 4pm, features a big range of top-quality handmade New Zealand artworks in glass, fiber, ceramics, native timbers, and mixed media. They post goods overseas tax-free.

Other worthy places to browse top-notch arts, crafts, and jewelry are **Tamarillo,** 102–108 Wakefield St., opposite the visitor center (℗ **04/473-6095**); **Avid,** 48 Victoria St. (℗ **04/472-7703**); **Kura,** 19 Allen St. (℗ **04/802-4934;** www.kuragallery.co.nz); and **Vessel,** 87 Victoria St. (℗ **04/499-2321**). And for all things woolly, drive around the bays to **Sheepskin Warehouse,** Evans Bay Parade, Greta Point (℗ **04/386-3376;** fax 04/386-3379). New Zealand has the best technology in the world for sheepskin products, and if you doubt that, come here. An overseas shipping service is available and GST is deductible.

you'll find markets, alternative boutiques, secondhand stores, and great cafes. It's all easy and shopper-friendly. Store hours are usually Monday through Friday from 9am to 5:30pm, Saturday from 9am to 4:30pm, and Sunday from 10am to 2pm.

The best place to start is **Lambton Quay,** which has three linked arcades, and **Capital on Quay,** at 250 Lambton Quay (℗ **04/473-8868**). There are boutiques, a heap of shoe stores, music shops, and excellent bookstores. It's also where you'll find Wellington's most famous department store, **Kirkcaldie & Stains** (℗ **04/472-5899**), offering traditional service and quality merchandise since 1863. **Jumpers,** Harbour City Centre (℗ **04/499-9915**), has Wellington's largest range of New Zealand knitwear.

The historic Bank of New Zealand building on Lambton Quay is now the **Old Bank Arcade & Chambers,** a retail arcade after the style of Sydney's Queen Victoria Arcade. It has attracted interest from top national and international retail stores and includes cafes, restaurants, and designer clothing stores.

As you move onto **Willis Street,** you'll find more fashion, books, and music. Turn down **Manners Street** and make your way into the weird and wonderful **Cuba Street** area, which gets more interesting the higher up the mall you go. If you want your future predicted, your sexual preferences catered to, your body pierced or tattooed, or just crave a cup of damn good coffee, you're in the right area.

Another good specialty-store area is the **Tinakori Road Village.** Much more upmarket than Cuba Street, it's not overly big, just a few smart, little gift stores, galleries, and the like. My favorite is **Millwood Gallery,** 291b Tinakori Rd., Thorndon (℗ **04/473-5178**), an art-and-book boutique filled to the gills with divine papery offerings. It specializes in original works of art based on Wellington and has a range of cards and gift

---

(**Tips**) **The Markets**

Moore Wilson Fresh Food Market, at Moore Wilson's on Lorne Street (© **04/384-9906**), is where you'll find a wealth of organics, fish, flowers, breads, and other edibles. **Jackson Street Market,** corner of Jackson and Elizabeth streets, Petone (© **04/939-2811**), features fine goods and gourmet products and is held Sunday mornings from 9am to 1pm.

---

wraps. Antiques fans will love **Tinakori Antiques** ★★, 291a Tinakori Rd. (© **04/472-7043**), which has two small stores crammed with collectibles, furniture, and antique jewelry. I spent far too much time here. **Groom** ★, 306 Tinakori St. (© **04/472-5605**), will appeal to the men. This tiny little squeeze of a store is home to barber and stylist, ex–All Black Johni Rutene, who has covered the walls in rugby paraphernalia. Complete with an old-fashioned barber chair, it is one of the few barbershops offering hot towel cutthroat shaves.

8 WELLINGTON AFTER DARK

This is one city where you won't run out of things to do after dark. Start by checking the current issues of *Capital Times* and *What's On,* both free and available at visitor centers and many cafes.

THE PERFORMING ARTS

Wellington is home to the largest performing-arts festival in the country (see "Special Events," earlier in this chapter); it is also home to the National Orchestra and Opera, the Royal New Zealand Ballet, and four thriving professional theater companies. In addition, you'll find the National Dance and Drama Centre, the New Zealand School of Dance, and the New Zealand Drama School, all based in the capital.

A rejuvenated **Westpac St. James Theatre,** 77–87 Courtenay Place (© **04/802-4060;** www.stjames.co.nz), opened its doors in 1998 after a NZ$21-million refurbishment project, and this fine Edwardian venue now combines a preserved heritage theater with state-of-the-art technology. Apart from staging top-quality musical shows, it is also the new and permanent home of the Royal New Zealand Ballet Company.

The city has a healthy professional theater scene. The **Downstage Theatre,** in Hannah Playhouse, Courtenay Place, corner of Cambridge Terrace (© **04/801-6946;** www.downstage.co.nz), presents first-rate theater in an exciting, award-winning structure. Downstage's year-round season presents its own productions and the best touring shows, including classics, contemporary drama, comedy, and dance, with an emphasis on quality New Zealand works. Tickets are NZ$35 to NZ$40 for most shows.

Circa Theatre, 1 Taranaki St. (© **04/801-7992;** www.circa.co.nz), sits grandly beside Te Papa. It produces quality and generally innovative productions. You can enjoy a pre-show meal at its licensed cafe. Tickets are NZ$38. **Bats Theatre,** 1 Kent Terrace (© **04/802-4175;** www.bats.co.nz), is seen as the country's top developmental theater, presenting new and experimental plays and dance at great prices (NZ$18–NZ$25). **Embassy Theatre,** 10 Kent Terrace (© **04/384-7657;** www.deluxe.co.nz), was refurbished for the

world premiere of *The Lord of the Rings: The Return of the King.* The combination of **317**
sumptuous 1920s decor with a giant screen and state-of-the-art digital sound, not to
mention its cafe and bar, makes it well worth a visit. There are summer screenings of *The
Lord of the Rings* every Sunday afternoon.

THE CLUB & BAR SCENE

It's simple: When it gets dark, the party starts, and again, the compact nature of the city
is a blessing for those looking for a good time. There are late-night bars and dance venues
aplenty, and if you want to bypass the quiet start and head straight for the action, then
Courtenay Place it is. I have to say, though, that the large number of drunken youths in
this area on Thursday, Friday, and Saturday nights is almost enough to put me off—
almost. The reality is that there are enough bars in this part of town for all ages to find a
comfortable niche, and anyone over 25 who has outgrown the vomiting-in-the-street
trick need only look around for a place that suits his or her mood. Be warned though—
the Wellington bar scene is ever-changing and venues listed here may have changed
names and owners by the time you arrive. The best bars are also typically in tiny, tucked-
away places, so ask the locals about the latest hot spots.

The closing time for bars and clubs varies wildly in New Zealand. It depends on
whether you're in the provinces or a major city, whether it's summer or winter, and what
type of liquor license the establishment holds. In a major city like Wellington, it is safe
to assume that most stay open in summer until between midnight and 2am. Many have
24-hour licenses.

The "in" places for the older crowd (that's 30 plus) are always changing, but you'll be
safe if you start with trendy **Zibibbo,** 25–29 Taranaki St. (© **04/385-6550**), which
inhabits the old central police building. You can get great Spanish-Italian tapas here along
with sophisticated nightlife. One of the coolest new places to be seen at is the very posh
Arbitrageur ★★★, 125 Featherston St. (© **04/499-5530**), where you'll find sophisticated club style, over 60 of the best wines, and an interior that will win over any wine
purist's heart. It's open Monday through Thursday from 11:30am till late and on Saturdays from 5pm. **Beaujolais Wine Bar** ★, 11 Woodward St. (© **04/472-1471**), is tucked
away in the thoroughfare connecting Lambton Quay and The Terrace. It's well known
for its exceptional cellar and is open Monday through Friday, from midday till late and
on weekends by appointment.

Matterhorn ★★★, 106 Cuba St. (© **04/384-3359**), serves great cocktails, and once
the restaurant crowd is satisfied, it turns into a funky bar deserving of its accumulated
awards. **Mighty Mighty** ★, Level 1, 104 Cuba St. (© **04/385-2890**), has gone retro

WELLINGTON

12

WELLINGTON AFTER DARK

Ⓣ **Tips**   **A Night at the Movies**

All Wellington cinemas offer discounted tickets for daytime and Tuesday-night
screenings. Students and seniors also get a discount. Look in the newspapers for
schedules. Try the **Embassy Theatre,** 10 Kent Terrace (© **04/384-7657**), with a
giant screen and a new sound system; **Hoyts Cinemas,** which has two multiscreen complexes in Manners Mall and Manners Street; or **Rialto Cinemas,** Cable
Street and Jervois Quay (© **04/385-1864**), a three-theater complex. **Penthouse
Cinema & Café,** 205 Ohiro Rd., Brooklyn (© **04/384-3157**), is the city's only suburban theater and draws a loyal local crowd.

(Tips) **Beer Literacy**

If you're a beer lover, Wellington will please you to no end. I'd start with **Tasting Room,** 2 Courtenay Place (✆ **04/384-1159**), which is New Zealand's 10th Monteith's Craft Beer Bar. They know all about creative beer and food matching. **Bodega,** 101 Ghuznee St. (✆ **04/384-8212**), is Wellington's original ale house serving the city's only hand-drawn ales. It has 17 different tap beers and a massive selection of imports. **Mac's Brewery,** corner of Taranaki and Cable streets (✆ **04/802-1956**), has great harbor views where you can sit back and see why these beers are international award winners. Take one of their beer- and food-matching evenings or a brewery tour. The **Courtenay Arms,** 26–32 Allen St. (✆ **04/385-6908**), is a real English ale house with premium imported British ales on tap. And no beer section would be complete without the **Malthouse** ★, 48 Courtenay Place (✆ **04/802-5484;** www.themalthouse.co.nz), which has New Zealand's largest range of beers—over 150 local and international brews.

with menus on old record covers and cocktails that will get your evening off to a good start. **Concrete Bar** ★, Level 1, Cable Car Lane, Lambton Quay (✆ **04/473-7427**), is a sophisticated joint with a great wine-and-beer list and cocktails to get any evening off to a good start. **Motel** ★★, Forrester's Lane (✆ **04/382-8585**), creates an exotic mood with a retro twist that includes sculptures and oriental lamps. It's very suave and runs adjacent to the ever-popular Chow restaurant. **Red Square** ★★, 8–20 Blair St. (✆ **04/802-4244**), has one of those sumptuous, moody interiors that instantly puts you in a party mood, helped greatly by a head-spinning vodka list. It attracts a mixed crowd—as does nearby **Ponderosa**, 28 Blair St. (✆ **04/384-1064**), which, as the name suggests, has let loose with a cowboy-themed lounge bar. If you can overlook corny names like Stubborn Mule and Randy Ranger, you'll have a great time with their delicious cocktail list.

Molly Malones, Taranaki Street and Courtenay Place (✆ **04/384-2896**), is the biggest and busiest Irish bar in town, with live music every weekend. Also in this area is the hugely popular **Coyote,** 63 Courtenay Place (✆ **04/385-6665**), which attracts a mixed and generally rowdy crowd.

There are also interesting bar and dance choices in the Cuba and Willis streets area, which tend to be a bit less concerned with fashion and making an appearance.

THE GAY SCENE

The visitor center has folders full of information related to the gay scene, including gay-friendly accommodations and nightspots other than those listed here. **Sanctuary,** Courtenay Place (✆ **04/384-1565**), is a men's cruise club open Tuesday through Sunday from 8pm. There's a gay sauna at **Checkmate,** 20 Garrett St. (✆ **04/385-6556**), and another at **Wakefield Health Club,** 15 Tory St. (✆ **04/385-4400**). If you want to find out more about the gay scene, call the **Gay Switchboard** (✆ **04/473-7878**). The line is open nightly from 7:30 to 10pm for information and support. **Gay Line Wellington** (www.gayline.gen.nz) is also a useful first stop. **Lesbian Line** (✆ **04/499-5567**) operates Tuesday, Thursday, and Saturday 7:30 to 10pm, offering information on accommodations, sporting events, and counseling services.

9 A SIDE TRIP TO WAIRARAPA ★★★

Don't be fooled by the quiet rural exterior and quaint, sleepy villages; there's a lot happening in the Wairarapa. This is the place of wine, warmth, and more wine. And I'm not talking hobby vineyards—Wairarapa is home to some of the world's finest boutique vineyards, and built around that draw card is the biggest array of boutique accommodations you'll find anywhere in New Zealand.

Just over an hour's drive from Wellington across the winding Rimutaka Hills (take care driving in winter), you'll find a spread of productive farmland hemmed in by the rugged Tararua Ranges to the west and the dramatic Pacific Ocean to the east.

Twenty years ago, Wellingtonians scarcely gave Wairarapa a second look; now it's one of their hottest weekend getaway spots. Most of the activity is centered on **Greytown,** which has become a haven of boutique stores and cafes; and in **Martinborough,** where Hong Kong businessman Mike Laven bought the old **Martinborough Hotel** (p. 323) and turned it on its head. It's now one of the premier accommodations in the area. Not content to rest on his laurels, our Mr. Laven simply picked up the old Station Hotel in **Masterton,** a little farther north, moved it to Martinborough, and turned it into a restored office, retail, and wine complex.

It's entrepreneurial action and foresight such as these that have seen Martinborough and its southern neighbors, **Featherston** and **Greytown,** really take off. Wharekauhau Country Estate at Palliser Bay is a stunning addition to the Small Luxury Hotels of the World group, and there are new shops, cafes, and lodgings opening all the time. The **Toast Martinborough Wine, Food & Music Festival** attracts over 9,000 fans every year, the Martinborough Craft Fair is an annual favorite, and there are numerous outdoor activities to keep you amused if you ever run out of wine to taste.

ESSENTIALS

GETTING THERE From central Wellington, take the northern motorway, driving around the harbor toward Lower Hutt, and follow the signs to Wairarapa. Once on this route, you head over the Rimutaka Hills and arrive in Featherston, the southernmost village in Wairarapa, around 1½ hours later.

If you're entering the area from the north, it takes 3 hours from Napier and 1 hour from Palmerston North to reach Masterton. Flying to Martinborough from Wellington by helicopter takes just 15 minutes.

VISITOR INFORMATION In Masterton, the **Masterton Visitor Centre,** corner of Dixon and Bruce streets (✆ **06/370-0900;** fax 06/378-8451; www.wairarapanz.com), is open daily Monday to Friday 9am to 5pm, and weekends 10am to 4pm, with extended hours in summer. If you don't intend to drive the extra 30 minutes north from Featherston/Martinborough, check out the office at 18 Kitchener St., Martinborough (✆ **06/ 306-5010**). It's open the same hours.

EXPLORING THE AREA

About 27km (17 miles) north of Masterton on State Highway 2, **Pukaha Mount Bruce National Wildlife Centre** ★★ (✆ **06/375-8004;** www.mtbruce.org.nz) is New Zealand's main center for the captive breeding of endangered species. Wheelchair-accessible walkways wind through rainforest and aviaries where threatened birds such as the kiwi and stitchbird are making a comeback. Make your first stop the excellent audiovisual display, which will help you understand what the center is all about, and then pick up the free walkway guide. Make sure you see the live nest-cam film. Admission is NZ$15 for adults, NZ$4 for children 5 to 15, and NZ$38 for a family. It's open daily from 9am to 4:30pm (closed Dec 25); the monster eels are fed at 1:30pm and the kaka (native parrots) at 3pm.

The artistically minded might like to investigate **Aratoi-Wairarapa Museum of Art & History,** Bruce and Dixon streets, Masterton (© 06/370-0001; www.aratoi.co.nz), which is open daily from 10am to 4:30pm, showcasing local talent.

Fifteen minutes from Martinborough, you'll find **Kahutara Canoes** (© 06/308-8453; www.wairarapa.co.nz/kahutara), where John and Karen McCosh offer a variety of trips on the scenic Ruamahanga River. Canoes range from large Canadian craft down to one- and two-person kayaks. Trips last from 1 to 5 hours and cost NZ$30 to NZ$60 adults, NZ$15 to NZ$25 children ages 5 to 15, for a half-day excursion. John is likely to introduce you to his **Taxidermy Gallery,** a log cabin containing a veritable zoo of animals that no longer need feeding—everything from lions and tigers to alligators, deer, turtles, and birds. This costs NZ$5 for adults, NZ$1 for children, and NZ$10 for a family.

Heading south toward Cape Palliser, look out for **Putangirua Pinnacles** ★★★, a world-class example of badlands erosion. The pinnacles were formed in the past 120,000 years by heavy rain eroding an ancient gravel deposit, and it's worth the 30-minute walk off the road to see these spectacular formations. Quite eerie, and great photographic material. Farther around the coast, you'll find the cute fishing village of **Ngawi** and the country's largest breeding area for **New Zealand fur seals.**

The **Hau Nui Wind Farm,** New Zealand's first commercial wind farm, is 21km (13 miles) southeast of Martinborough on White Rock Road. Huge turbines are spaced along a 540m (1,770-ft.) ridge and make a dramatic silhouette against the skyline. The site itself is not open to the public, but you can check out a viewing area with information about the project.

Patuna Chasm Walkway ★★★ (© 06/306-9966; www.patunafarm.co.nz), 17km (11 miles) from Martinborough, is the region's best natural attraction. A 4-hour tramp through farm and bush takes you to a fascinating limestone gorge filled with fossils, ferns, stalactites, waterfalls, and eels. Take the map, which shows you the best swimming spots; your swimsuit; sturdy shoes; and spare clothes. The walk is open October through April and costs NZ$15 for adults, NZ$10 for children ages 5 to 12. Bookings are essential. You'll find an adventure ropes course and horse trekking at the same base.

If walking is your thing, consider the 3-day **Tora Coastal Walk** (© 06/307-8115 or 307-8862; www.toracoastalwalk.co.nz), which takes you through native bush and river valleys, staying at a different hill-country farm each night. It costs NZ$375, which includes accommodations and luggage cartage. It's open from October through April and bookings are essential.

There are also numerous fine **gardens** in the Wairarapa. The visitor center's *Wairarapa Escape Planner* lists great gardens along with other attractions of the region. The *Garden Trails* brochure lists 10 South Wairarapa gardens. There's very good value in **Wairarapa Garden Gourmet Escape** ★★ (© 0800/471-227 in NZ; www.tranzit.co.nz), which takes you from Wellington or Lower Hutt by train to the Wairarapa, where you join a coach and visit two extraordinary gardens, the very formal Richmond (www.boxwood. co.nz) in Carterton (a Garden of National Significance), and the hillside garden of Assisi (www.assisigardens.co.nz). Lunch, wine tasting, and a wander though the village of Greytown are also included. The total package costs NZ$160.

The Wairarapa is also a major orchard area. If you feel like fresh fruit while you're in Greytown, go to **Murphys Orchard,** 67 Reading St. (✆ **06/304-9551**), which produces nectarines, apricots, peaches, and 14 plum varieties in January and February; **Palmers Berryfruit Gardens,** Main Road North (✆ **06/304-9125**), which grows almost every berry fruit you can name; and **Pinehaven Orchards,** Udy Street (✆ **06/304-9699**), home to the now-famous Gala apple variety, developed in the 1940s.

The Wineries

The high sunshine hours and low autumn rainfall of the Martinborough region have been major factors in the international success of the small boutique wineries in this area. It is distinguished from other New Zealand wine areas by the high proportion of red-wine grape plantings and by its reputation for quality pinot noir. Most wineries are open for tastings while stocks permit, and some are open year-round. There are over 30 vineyards in the Martinborough area alone, and large tracts of grapes have also been planted at Gladstone and Masterton. The best time to visit is from late October to early March, when new wine stocks have been released. The best way to explore the area is to pick up a copy of the *Classic New Zealand Wine Trail Guide* ★★ (www.classicwinetrail.co.nz) from an i-SITE Visitor Centre. It links five of New Zealand's best wine regions, including the Wairarapa, and adds in sights, shopping, and dining opportunities so you can get the most from the regions it covers. To find out more about winemaking in this region, go to www.nzwine.com. Conducted group tours to area wineries can be made only by prior arrangement. Contact the Martinborough visitor center (✆ **06/306-9043**), which can also supply the free brochure *Martinborough & Wairarapa Wine Trails.*

When it comes to selecting the best of the bunch, it's pretty subjective, but local opinion consistently swings in the direction of **Dry River Wines,** Puruatanga Road (✆ **06/306-9388;** fax 06/306-9275), a small low-tech winery specializing in the Alsace varietals pinot gris, Gewürztraminer, and Riesling as well as chardonnay, pinot noir, and sauvignon blanc. The majority of its wines are sold by mail order within a few weeks of release, so it's unlikely you'll find the place open.

Ata Rangi Vineyard ★★, Puruatanga Road (✆ **06/306-9750;** www.atarangi.co.nz), maker of an internationally acclaimed pinot noir, has been operating for almost 27 years. It has an excellent tasting room for sampling the flagship pinot noir along with sauvignon blanc, chardonnay, and a summer rosé.

Palliser ★★, Kitchener Street (✆ **06/306-9019;** www.palliser.co.nz), is a leading force in this area. It features a purpose-built winery and a large barrel hall, and it has an excellent reputation for its award-winning pinot noir, chardonnay, sauvignon blanc, and Riesling. Wines are produced under the Palliser Estate and Pencarrow labels. Palliser is open daily for cellar sales.

Martinborough Vineyard, Princess Street (✆ **06/306-9955;** www.martinborough-vineyard.co.nz), was one of the original four vineyards in the area and was set up by a group of six investors who bought 6.4 hectares (16 acres) in one of the few zones in New Zealand with similar climactic conditions to Burgundy. It's open daily from 11am to 5pm for tasting and is dedicated to producing pinot noir, chardonnay, Riesling, sauvignon blanc, and pinot gris. Its star is the award-winning pinot noir.

Te Kairanga, Martins Road (✆ **06/306-9122;** www.tekairanga.co.nz), open daily from 10am to 5pm, is one of the founding and most popular vineyards in this area. Established over 20 years ago, it now has six vineyards in the region, each with its own distinctive qualities, and it is a key venue in the annual Toast Martinborough celebrations. It

(Finds) **Quirky Shopping**

The **Paua World,** 54 Kent St., Carterton (✆ **06/379-4222;** www.pauaworld.com), is an attraction in its own right. It gets over 50,000 visitors a year and has a huge range of jewelry and souvenirs at factory prices. It's open daily and there are factory tours and video presentations to enjoy. **Martinborough Cheese Shop,** 8 Kitchener St., Martinborough (✆ **06/306-8383**), features specialty cheeses and local delicacies, including wines and olive oils, and is open daily from 10am to 5pm. **Saratoga Dairy Goats,** Caveland Road, Gladstone, Masterton (✆ **06/372-7074;** www.saratoga.co.nz), produces handcrafted goat cheeses, while **Kingsmeade Cheese,** Olivers Road, Masterton (✆ **06/377-5252;** www.kingsmeade cheese.co.nz), is the medal-winning maker of sheeps' milk cheese. **Olivo Olive Grove,** Hinakura Road, Martinborough (✆ **06/306-9074;** www.olivo.co.nz), has award-winning extra-virgin and infused olive oils, with tastings and sales most weekends.

produces a wide range of wines, including pinot noir, chardonnay, cabernet sauvignon, and sauvignon blanc.

Others worth visiting are the very pretty **Gladstone Vineyard** ★, Gladstone Road, RD2, Carterton (✆ **06/379-8563;** www.gladstone.co.nz), which has weekend lunches between November and March; **Margrain Vineyard,** Ponatahi Road (✆ **06/306-9292;** www.margrainvineyard.co.nz), with rather divine villa accommodations; and **Walnut Ridge Vineyard,** 159 Regent St. (✆/fax **06/306-9323;** www.walnutridge.co.nz).

Martinborough Wine Centre, in Martinborough Village (✆ **06/306-9040;** www. martinboroughwinecentre.co.nz), represents 30 of the region's 40 vineyards. If you're short on time, or visiting out of the main wine season, this is the perfect place to get a comprehensive overview. Tastings cost NZ$10 to NZ$15 per person. A delightful cafe/delicatessen and retail store are on-site. Every Sunday from 10am to 2pm, the center stages the **Martinborough Country Market**—the perfect place for wines, breads, organic produce, fish, local cheeses, preserves, and much more. If you're interested in wine tours of this region, leave your car in Wellington and leap on the train for the **Tranz Metro Gourmet Wine Escape** ★★ (✆ **0800/471-227** in NZ; www.tranzmetro.co.nz). You'll connect with a coach tour in the Wairarapa and have tastings at four vineyards, a vineyard lunch, and a visit to the Martinborough Wine Centre for just NZ$140 round-trip per person from Wellington and Hutt Valley. For a smaller, more personal outing, join **Zest Food Tours** ★★★ (✆ **04/801-9198;** www.zestfoodtours.co.nz), for one of their excellent gourmet wine tours (NZ$230–NZ$325 per person), which takes you behind the scenes of top food producers.

Museum Mania

There's no shortage of museums in the Wairarapa. Here are a few to investigate. The **Fell Locomotive Museum,** Fitzherbert Street, Featherston (✆ **06/308-9379;** www.fell museum.org.nz), houses the only remaining Fell engine in the world. It's open daily 10am to 4pm. Admission is NZ$5 adults, NZ$2 children, NZ$12 family. Next door is the **Heritage Complex** (✆ **06/308-9458**), which displays early settler memorabilia and the Japanese POW camp history. It's open daily 10am to 4pm; entry is by donation.

Cobblestones Museum, 169 Main St., Greytown (℃ **06/304-9687**), has historic displays and a blacksmith's shop. It's open daily from 9am to 4:30pm. Admission is NZ$5 for adults, NZ$3 for children. **Martinborough Colonial Museum,** the Square, Martinborough (℃ **06/306-9736**), is open Saturday and Sunday from 2 to 4pm. Admission is by donation. **Mount Bruce Pioneer Museum,** 18km (11 miles) north of Masterton on State Highway 2 (℃ **06/372-5859;** h.christensen@xtra.co.nz), is Wairarapa's largest working museum with over 3,000 items on display. It's open daily from 9am to 4:30pm; admission is NZ$5 for adults, NZ50¢ for children 5 to 12.

WHERE TO STAY

You'll be spoiled for choice here. This region is one of the best in the country when it comes to terrific accommodations. There are over 100 self-contained cottages alone, most of them cute as buttons. There are endless numbers of homestays and several top-quality upmarket options as well. The visitor center has two excellent booklets, *A Taste of Greytown* and *Martinborough Accommodation.*

The 12.5% GST is included in the rates below.

Very Expensive

Wharekauhau Country Estate ★★★ Set amid 2,000 hectares (5,000 acres) of a working sheep station, this little piece of paradise sits in splendid isolation overlooking the rugged seas of Palliser Bay. It's highly rated by Andrew Harper (www.andrewharper travel.com), among others, and you'll be paying top dollar for the sublime comforts of a cottage suite with all the best trimmings—big four-poster beds, dressing room, luxurious bathrooms with great views, and private verandas. It's a member of Small Luxury Hotels of the World and has won several New Zealand Tourism Awards. This is warmth, elegance, and style at its best. You'll be pleased you went the distance.

Western Lake Rd., Palliser Bay, RD3, Featherston. ℃ **06/307-7581.** Fax 06/307-7799. www.wharekauhau. co.nz. 18 units. NZ$2,172 cottage suites; NZ$4,613 2-bedroom Chateau Wellington; NZ$6,497 3-bedroom; NZ$1,772 Wharepapa 3-bedroom cottage. Cottage suite rates include breakfast, predinner drinks, canapés, and 4-course gourmet dinner. Off-peak rates and special deals. AE, DC, MC, V. Closed mid-July for 3 weeks. **Amenities:** Bar; babysitting; free bikes; concierge; gym; outdoor Jacuzzi; heated indoor pool; day spa; all-weather tennis court. *In room:* LCD TV, fridge, hair dryer, Internet, MP3 docking station, mini-bar.

Moderate to Inexpensive

In Greytown, you'll find four delightful rooms at **Westwood,** 82 West St. (℃ **06/304-8510;** www.westwood.greytown.co.nz), priced from NZ$200 to NZ$300. In addition, the lovely three-bedroom Cherry Cottage sits in Westwood's garden and sleeps six. **Parehua Country Estate** ★★, New York Street, Martinborough (℃ **06/306-8405;** www. parehua.co.nz), has 28 gorgeous new cottages and villas set on 2 hectares (5 acres) of parklike grounds. They have all the mod-cons and an outdoor pool, restaurant, bar, tennis courts, free Wi-Fi throughout the property, and rental bikes complete the picture. Rates are very reasonable, from NZ$320 to NZ$600. Literally dozens of superb self-contained cottages are listed at the visitor center.

Peppers Martinborough Hotel ★★ This old beauty has been given a new life and a brush of contemporary interior design. It's a favorite weekend spot with Wellingtonians and a fine place to base yourself for vineyard exploration. Each of the large guest rooms has a different decor. There are nine units in the main hotel building and seven luscious new rooms in the garden courtyard; all have excellent bathrooms and king-size beds. The upstairs units in the main hotel open onto the balcony and have outdoor seating; the Riddiford and the Weld rooms are especially charming. The courtyard rooms are bigger and more modern; of these, my favorites are the Barton and Sheko.

The Square, Martinborough. (C) **306/306-9350.** Fax 06/306-9345. www.peppers.co.nz. 16 units. NZ$320 garden and veranda room; NZ$385 Sheko suite. Off-peak rates and special wine escape packages. Rates include breakfast. AE, DC, MC, V. **Amenities:** Restaurant; 2 bars; babysitting; bike rentals; nearby golf course; room service; tennis courts; Wi-Fi in lobby and library. *In room:* A/C (in suite), TV, fridge, hair dryer, minibar, Wi-Fi in veranda rooms.

WHERE TO DINE

The **Slow Food Café & Restaurant** ★, 290 High St. ((C) **06/377-5100**), is a welcome addition to the sleepy culinary scene of Masterton. It has great wood-fired pizzas and tasty dishes cooked according to slow food principles. It's open daily from 9am till late. Also in Masterton, **Café Cecille** ★, Queen Elizabeth Park ((C) **06/370-1166**; www. cafececille.co.nz), has a great reputation for its good service and lamb and beef dishes. Set in the middle of a leafy park, it's open Monday through Friday 10am until late, and weekends 9am until late.

In Greytown, **Main Street Deli Café,** 88 Main St. ((C) **06/304-9022**), is open daily for all meals and continues to attract a team of happy regulars. Across the road you'll find a fabulous array of baked goods and good coffee at the **French Baker** ★★, 81 Main St. ((C) **06/304-9569**).

Just out of Featherston village, the **Tin Hut** ★, State Highway 2, Tauherenikau ((C) **06/308-9697**), gets rave reviews from the locals for its excellent pub-style fare in a revamped interior—traditional Kiwi pub meets French Country—and barnyard animals will be a hit with the kids.

In Martinborough, the **Village Café,** the Wine Centre, Kitchener Street ((C) **06/306-8814**), serves up tasty food and some of the region's best wine and cheeses. Don't overlook the divine meals at the **Bistrot** ★★, Martinborough Hotel ((C) **06/306-9350**). You'll also want to consider the new **Wendy Campbell's French Bistro** ★★, 3 Kitchener St. ((C) **06/306-8863**), which is a small, charming spot with a menu that changes daily. It's open Wednesday through Sunday from 6pm. **Est Wine Bar** ★★, 8 Memorial Sq. ((C) **06/306-9665;** www.est.org.nz), is another culinary gem that shouldn't be missed. It has an innovative menu and a great wine list; it's open Wednesday through Friday 11am until late. Try their rabbit flavored with thyme and juniper.

Marlborough & Nelson

So, here you are on the South Island—the Mainland—home to around a million people. (Over three million live on the North Island and two-thirds of them north of Taupo, so there will be days when you think you have the huge and spectacular South Island all to yourself.) There's less traffic here, but you'll be traveling greater distances between major towns, and when you arrive at a few places, you may well think you have stepped back in time.

The stunning southern landscape—big, majestic, unforgiving—is dominated by the central spine of the Southern Alps, and anyone who lives here has enormous respect for its grandeur. You'll soon see why.

If you cross over from Wellington on the Cook Strait ferry, your introduction to the south will be at Picton, which sits at the head of the beautiful Marlborough Sounds. Nearby is Blenheim, at the heart of Marlborough's famous winemaking province. To the west lies Nelson, the sunniest place in New Zealand and home to more vineyards, fine beaches, and the most accessible concentration of top artists and craftspeople in the country.

The greater Nelson province is geographically made up of five distinct areas, each with its own character: Nelson-Richmond, the urban heart; Motueka, the horticultural heartland; Abel Tasman National Park, a paradise of bush-wrapped beaches and crystal-clear waters; Golden Bay, heaven cast between two great national parks; and St. Arnaud–Murchison, an alpine-lakes area in the heart of Nelson Lakes National Park.

1 PICTON & BLENHEIM ★★

Picton: 146km (91 miles) E of Nelson; Blenheim: 117km (73 miles) SE of Nelson

Picton and Blenheim are the two main towns of Marlborough province, an area best known as New Zealand's largest and most spectacular wine region. Both townships are quiet and easygoing. Blenheim, the larger of the two, has a population of 29,700. Picton, a quaint waterfront village at the head of Queen Charlotte Sound, has a population of just 4,300, and its main claim to fame is that it's the arrival point for ferries from Wellington. Unfortunately, many travelers think that's the end of its attributes, when in fact it is also the stepping-off point for the unspoiled tranquil charms of the Marlborough Sounds. With over 1,500km (930 miles) of shoreline, the sounds—Queen Charlotte, Kenepuru, and Pelorus—are ideal for sailing, kayaking, fishing, and bush walking. You'd be silly to miss them. There's also something to look forward to: By 2010, Picton's London Quay (the main waterfront area), should be completely redesigned as part of a multimillion-dollar landscaping program. The plan includes a new promenade, a large car-parking zone, a new floating jetty, and a town square. Wellington Street will become one-way and the town should benefit greatly from having a more focused heart.

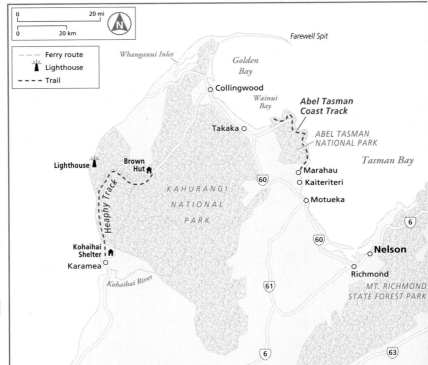

(Map legend)
- – – Ferry route
- Lighthouse
- - - - Trail

Whanganui Inlet

Golden Bay

Farewell Spit

Collingwood

Wainui Bay

Abel Tasman Coast Track

Takaka

ABEL TASMAN NATIONAL PARK

Lighthouse

Brown Hut

Tasman Bay

Marahau 60
Kaiteriteri

K A H U R A N G I
N A T I O N A L
P A R K

Motueka

6

Heaphy Track

60

Kohaihai Shelter
Karamea

Nelson

Richmond

MT. RICHMOND STATE FOREST PARK

Kohaihai River

61

6

63

ESSENTIALS

GETTING THERE & GETTING AROUND   **By Plane**   Air service to Picton from Wellington is provided by **Soundsair** (© **0800/505-005** in NZ; www.soundsair.com). **Air New Zealand Link** (© **0800/737-000;** www.airnewzealand.co.nz) flies into nearby Blenheim. The Picton Airport (also known as Koromiko Airport) is approximately a 10-minute drive from Picton's town center. The Blenheim Airport is 10km (6 miles) from the town center. **Marlborough Shuttle Services** (© **03/572-9910**) provides airport and ferry transport in Picton and Blenheim.

By Train   The TranzCoastal provides daily rail service between Picton and Christchurch. The trip takes about 5½ hours. Contact **Tranz Scenic** (© **0800/872-467** in NZ; www.tranzscenic.co.nz) for more information.

By Coach (Bus)   Coach service into both Picton and Blenheim is provided by **Inter-City** (© **09/623-1503**). The trip from Christchurch takes 5 hours; from Nelson, 2 hours. Picton, and Kaikoura farther south, are both included in the routes of **Magic Travellers** (© **09/358-5600**) and **Kiwi Experience** (© **09/366-9830**).

By Car   Most rental-car companies request that you turn in one car in Wellington (on the North Island) and pick up a new one in Picton. However, you can take cars and

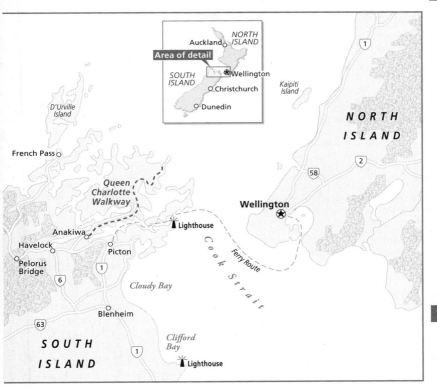

campers on the ferry should the need arise. If you're driving from Nelson, the trip takes about 2 hours; from Christchurch, 4 to 5 hours.

By Ferry   For timetables and information on the **Interislander,** call 🕾 **0800/802-802.** For information on **Bluebridge** ferries, call 🕾 **0800/844-844.** See also "Orientation" in chapter 12.

By Water Taxi   Picton doesn't have a local bus system, but water taxis from the **Cougar Line** (🕾 **0800/504-090** in NZ, or 03/573-7925; www.cougarlinecruises.co.nz) provide regular service throughout Queen Charlotte Sound. **Endeavour Express** (🕾 **03/573-5456;** www.boatrides.co.nz) also has regular service; or call **West Bay Water Transport** (🕾 **03/573-5597;** www.westbay.co.nz) each way.

By Taxi   **Blenheim Taxis** (🕾 **0800/802-225** or 03/578-0225) serves Blenheim, Picton, and the Sounds. It has cars, 10-seater vans, and a wheelchair hoist available.

ORIENTATION   It's difficult to get lost in Picton. The town faces Queen Charlotte Sound and the small shopping area is centered on High Street. London Quay runs along the foreshore, with the ferry terminal at one end and the town wharf at the other.

Blenheim is not quite so straightforward, despite its small size. Its layout has always puzzled me and no matter how many times I visit, I always go around in circles. Be sure to pick up a map at the visitor center!

VISITOR INFORMATION   The **Picton i-SITE Visitor Centre,** the Foreshore (✆ **03/ 520-3113;** fax 03/573-5021; www.destinationmarlborough.com), is in the same building as the **Department of Conservation** (the latter only in the building Oct–Apr), and is open daily 8:30am to 6pm in summer, 8:30am to 5pm in winter. The Blenheim office is at the Railway Station, Sinclair Street, State Highway 1 (✆ **03/577-8080;** fax 03/577-8079). It's open December to March from 8:30am to 6pm Monday to Friday, and weekends from 9am to 5pm; March to November, it's open weekdays from 8:30am to 5pm, and weekends from 9am to 3pm.

Other useful websites: www.marlborough.co.nz, www.picton.co.nz, and www. marlborough4fun.co.nz (for events listings).

EXPLORING BLENHEIM & PICTON
Wet Adventures: Getting Out on the Water

It's not a question of *whether* you'll go out on the water in Marlborough Sounds, but rather *which* vessel you'll be on. The ferries from Wellington provide a good introductory view as they make their way toward Picton, but for a closer look you'll need to go out on a smaller, more specialized boat. The **Cougar Line,** the Waterfront, Picton (✆ **0800/ 504-090** in NZ, or 03/573-7925; www.cougarlinecruises.co.nz), has a range of cruise options in Queen Charlotte Sound. If your time is limited, take the short cruise, which departs daily from Picton at 10am and returns at 1:30pm; or the One Hour Hidden Bays Cruise (NZ$46) which departs Picton daily at 11:30am and 2:30pm October to April (2pm May–Sept). This is a good way to fill in time if you're waiting for the ferry. Also offered are a twilight cruise during peak season and popular cruise-and-walk options to suit all levels of fitness. All-day tours cost NZ$70 to NZ$80 per person.

Another option is the 4-hour Queen Charlotte Sound **Magic Mail Run Cruise** operated by **Beachcomber Cruises,** London Quay, Picton (✆ **03/573-6175;** www.mailboat. co.nz), for NZ$83 adults and NZ$41 for children. Or try the **Pelorus Mail Run** (✆ **03/574-1088;** www.mail-boat.co.nz), which departs Tuesday, Thursday, and Friday from Havelock at 9:30am and costs NZ$125 for adults, free for children. Tea and coffee are supplied, but bring your lunch. A courtesy coach is available to and from Picton.

Sea kayaking is one of the best ways to get intimate and up close to the Sounds. I had my first-ever kayaking experience here and now I'm hooked. Two recommended outfitters to go with are **Sea Kayak Adventures,** Anakiwa Road, RD1, Picton (✆ **0800/262-5492** in NZ, or 03/574-2765; www.nzseakayaking.com), which has day trips from NZ$85; and **Marlborough Sounds Adventure Company** ★★★, London Quay, Picton (✆ **0800/283-283** in NZ, or 03/573-6078; www.marlboroughsounds.co.nz). The latter company is the larger of the two and has more boats, more extensive trips, and the most central Picton base. Its most popular trip is the 1-day excursion for NZ$105 per person. For those who like sailing, **Compass Charters,** 20 Beach Rd., Waikawa Marina, Picton (✆ **0800/101-332** in NZ, or 03/573-8332; www.compass-charters.co.nz), is the South Island's largest charter company. They have budget to luxury-yacht and launch cruises—skippered or self-driven—priced according to the vessel and duration. Renwick-based **Affinity Cruises** (✆ **0800/862-334** in NZ, or 03/572-7223; www.affinitycruises. co.nz) offers excellent 2-, 5-, or 7-day cruises with private cabins, including a lovely 4-night cruise for NZ$1,500.

(Kids) Especially for Kids

There's a treat in store for young and old alike at **Eco World Aquarium & Terrarium** ★★, Picton Foreshore (✆ **0800/800-081** in NZ, or 03/573-6030; www.ecoworldnz.co.nz). Watch tiny, mysterious sea horses court and dance, see thousands of babies at various stages of growth, and find out about the mysteries of the male pregnancy. On top of that, there's a 6m (20-ft.) preserved giant squid—only one of two examples in the Southern Hemisphere. Kids can also get up close and personal with crayfish, sharks, stingrays, and the multitudes of fishes that thrive in New Zealand waters. Fish are fed at 11am and 2pm and there are free guided tours (excluding entry fee) at 10am, noon, 1pm, and 3pm. It costs NZ$17 for adults, NZ$9 for children, and NZ$44 for a family pass. There's more fishy business at **Eyes on Nature Fish Museum,** 61 Main Rd., Havelock (✆ **03/574-1256;** www.eyesonnature.co.nz), which presents life-size models of New Zealand fish in a darkened environment in the old Havelock Post Office. If you're driving to Nelson, call in on the way and let the kids loose with a torch.

Bird-watchers will love the remote Chetwode and Outer Island Bird Tour run by **French Pass Sea Safaris** ★★, French Pass, Marlborough Sounds (✆ **03/576-5204;** www.seasafaris.co.nz), which takes you to a closed nature reserve (Feb–Apr only), to see a diverse mix of birds and marine mammals for NZ$160 per person.

If you're a food, wine, and water lover, opt for the **Marlborough Travel Greenshell Mussel Cruise** ★★★ (✆ **0800/990-800** in NZ, or 03/577-9997; www.marlboroughtravel.co.nz). This terrific half-day outing takes you into the stunning Sounds environment, visiting a Greenshell mussel farm, where you'll be treated to a feast of yummy, freshly steamed mussels with a complimentary glass of Marlborough Sauvignon Blanc. The tour operates November through March, departing Havelock and Picton at 1:30pm daily and from Portage Resort Hotel at 3pm daily. It costs NZ$110 from Portage and Havelock and NZ$140 from Picton, and is worth every cent. Children travel for NZ$35.

Although passengers on any of these vessels may see dolphins, **Dolphin Watch Ecotours,** Picton Foreshore (✆ **0800/945-3543** in NZ, or 03/573-8040; www.naturetours.co.nz), makes these lovely creatures the focus of its naturalist tours. A Dolphin Swimming Ecotour costs NZ$145 per person, and a Dolphin Viewing Ecotour costs NZ$95 for adults and NZ$55 for children. They also have an excellent bird-watcher's tour for NZ$95 per person.

If you have fishing on your mind, call up Havelock-based **Captain Clay's Snapper Fishing Charters** (✆ **03/574-2911;** bluecottage@actrix.co.nz), or **Sounds Connection,** 10 London Quay, Picton (✆ **0800/742-866;** www.soundsconnection.co.nz), which offers a half-day fishing adventure for NZ$79 per person, departing Picton at 1pm.

The Queen Charlotte Walkway ★★★

If you're like me and love walking but hate carrying things, the Queen Charlotte Walkway is just for you. It's a 1- to 4-day experience with amazing views and not a pack in sight. That's because kind people in boats do all the pack lifting and transferring of your goodies for you. Even better, you don't have to stay in cramped huts or tents, as there are smart lodgings along the way. There's lots more information about this walk in the

Sleeping Among the Grapes

There are a growing number of vineyard accommodations for visitors to choose from. **Walnut Block Cottages** ★, 43 Blicks Lane, Blenheim (© **03/577-9187;** www.walnutblock.co.nz), has two lovely, one-bedroom, self-contained cottages right beside vines, for just NZ$250 per night, which is a great value. Another option is **Straw Lodge** ★★, 17 Fareham Lane, Blenheim (© **03/572-9767;** www.strawlodge.co.nz), where three lovely private vineyard suites have their own courtyard and facilities. Rooms cost from NZ$295 to NZ$395 and the property has a Qualmark Enviro-Silver rating. **Vintners Retreat Resort** ★★★, 55 Rapaura Rd., Blenheim (© **03/572-7420;** www.vintnersretreat.co.nz), has a wide range of stylish one-, two-, and three-bedroom self-contained villas nestled among the vines, ranging in price from NZ$295 to NZ$600. At **St. Leonards Vineyard Cottages** ★★, 18 St. Leonards Rd., Blenheim (© **03/577-8328;** www.stleonards.co.nz), choose from five delightful self-contained cottages for the incredibly good value price of NZ$100 to NZ$370.

"Tramping" section in chapter 5, but briefly, the 71km (44-mile) walking track passes through lush coastal forest, around coves and inlets, and along skyline ridges with breathtaking views of Queen Charlotte and Kenepuru sounds. If you've got time, try the excellent kayak/walk combos offered by **Wilderness Guides,** 3 Auckland St., Picton (© **0800/266-266** in NZ, or 03/573-5432; www.wildernessguidesnz.com), from NZ$150 per day up to NZ$1,850 for a guided multiday experience. You can also tackle the track on mountain bikes. **Cycle Adventure Tours Downunder,** 1 Auckland St., Picton (© **03/573-8565;** www.cyclenz.com), has 1-day bike rentals from NZ$45 and 1- to 3-day guided tours from NZ$415, which includes transport, gear, and accommodations. You need a reasonable level of fitness.

Wine, Wine & More Wine

It doesn't matter what time of year you visit Marlborough, because the weather is invariably balmy (with a few frosty winter mornings), and there's always wine to drink if all else fails. If you stand on any high point, you'll see grapevines spread across the rolling landscape in all directions as far as the eye can see—vines now cover approximately 23,000 hectares (57,000 acres). In just over 25 years, Marlborough has established itself as one of the world's premier wine-producing regions, responsible for over 50% of New Zealand's total wine production. There are around 110 wineries in the area; many have restaurants, most have tastings, and some have galleries or crafts shops. Pick up the free *Marlborough Winemakers* map and the *Top of the South Wine Guide* from the visitor center before setting off, or check out www.winemarlborough.net.nz. You would also be wise to get a copy of *The Classic New Zealand Wine Trail* from visitor centers throughout the country. Following are a few wineries of note.

More than 30 years ago, **Montana Brancott Winery,** State Highway 1, Main Road South, Riverlands (© **03/577-5775;** www.montana.co.nz), planted the first vines in the region, and today it's New Zealand's largest winery. Tours leave Monday through Saturday from 10am to 3pm. The wine shop and the huge (and sometimes noisy) Montana Brancott Restaurant are open daily from 10:30am to 3pm.

(Finds) Taste Sensations

Marlborough is home to around 120 olive groves and a number of commercial presses. At the first New Zealand Extra Virgin Olive Oils Awards in 2002, Marlborough growers won more than 30% of all awards. A number of growers welcome visitors and you can get a list of their names from the visitor center, or contact the Marlborough branch of **Olives New Zealand** (www.olivesnz.org.nz). You can also visit the **Village** ★, 193 Rapaura Rd. (*(C)* **03/579-3520;** www.thevillage.co.nz), for a wide range of wines, olive oils, schnapps, liquors, and a cafe. And to satisfy your sweet tooth, you can now visit Northland's **Makana Confections** ★★, premier chocolate makers, which has set up a not-to-be-missed shop on the corner of Rapaura and O'Dwyers roads, Blenheim (*(C)* **03/570-5370;** www.makana.co.nz), open daily 9am to 5:30pm.

Those with an eye for good wines will be familiar with **Cloudy Bay** ★★★, Jacksons Road, Blenheim (*(C)* **03/520-9147;** www.cloudybay.co.nz). Its name is well known internationally, and 75% of its acclaimed sauvignon blanc is exported. It also produces chardonnay, cabernet merlot, and a sparkling wine, Pelorus. It's open for tasting and sales daily from 10am to 5pm (closed Dec 25).

Allan Scott Wines & Estates ★★, Jacksons Road, Blenheim (*(C)* **03/572-9054;** www.allanscott.com), is just across the road and has a good vineyard restaurant called Twelve Trees. The winery produces chardonnay, sauvignon, and Riesling. The cellar is open for tasting daily from 9am to 4:30pm; the restaurant opens daily for lunch at noon.

Hunter's Wines, Rapaura Road, Blenheim (*(C)* **03/572-8489;** www.hunters.co.nz), is home to Jane Hunter, acclaimed as one of the five best women winemakers in the world. The winery is hugely popular with tour groups. The restaurant is open daily from 10:30am to 4:30pm; the wine shop, daily from 9:30am to 4:30pm.

Grove Mill ★★★, Waihopai Valley Road, Renwick (*(C)* **03/572-8200;** www.grovemill.co.nz), is well worth a visit, especially if you're also an art lover. In addition to producing medal-winning chardonnay, Riesling, and cabernet sauvignon, its gallery features exhibitions of nationally recognized New Zealand artists. In 2006, it became the world's first carbon neutral winery. It follows the carboNZero program and is a member of Sustainable Winegrowing New Zealand. It's open daily from 11am to 5pm. **Highfield Estate** ★★, Brookby Road, Blenheim (*(C)* **03/572-9244;** www.highfield.co.nz), which produces classic varietal wines, has wine tastings, cellar door sales, and a restaurant with stunning views. It's open daily from 10am to 5pm.

Wairau River Wines ★★★, corner of Rapaura Road and State Highway 6, Blenheim (*(C)* **03/572-9800;** www.wairauriverwines.com), has one of the best winery restaurants in the Marlborough region—a reliable brasserie with an innovative blackboard menu at reasonable prices. It's housed in a charming mud-brick building, has cellar-door sales, and is open daily 10am to 5pm. **Mahi Wines** ★★, Terrace Road, Renwick (*(C)* **03/572-8859;** www.mahiwine.co.nz), has a delightful cafe. French winemaker Daniel Le Brun established the vineyard in 1980, and with 12 generations of champagne making behind him, he's truly established in his new venture. It's open 10am to 4:30pm.

Johanneshof Cellars, State Highway 1, Koromiko (*(C)* **03/573-7035;** www.johanneshof.co.nz), has spectacular underground wine cellars blasted into the hillside.

WINERY TOURS The **Sounds Connection** ★★★, 10 London Quay, Picton (© **0800/742-866** in NZ, or 03/573-8843; www.soundsconnection.co.nz), has half- and full-day tours from NZ$65. Its groups are smaller than some larger companies, and you can choose the vineyards. If you want some exercise while you see the wineries, call **Wine Tours By Bike** ★★★, 191 Bells Rd., Blenheim (© **03/577-6954;** www.wine toursbybike.co.nz), which will take you on an exploration of its favorite cycling roads, scenic spots, vineyards, wineries, arts, crafts, and olive or fruit farms. Stop at a vineyard for lunch (extra cost) and soak up the quiet calm of this divine area. A tour of up to 4 hours costs NZ$40 per person; from 4 to 8 hours costs NZ$55 per person. You can find five leading Marlborough wineries represented in one handy cellar door location at the **Wine Room** ★★, SH1, Grovetown, Blenheim (© **03/570-5490;** www.thewineroom. net.nz). It offers blind tastings, sells gourmet products like chocolate and olive oil, and will organize shipping of any wine you purchase.

WHERE TO STAY

Book early if you want to stay in Picton, which is a busy place during the summer months. Blenheim has a larger range of accommodations, including many delightful self-contained cottages and vineyard stays (see "Sleeping Among the Grapes," above).

In Picton & the Sounds

In addition to Picton township, there are quite a few lodgings waiting for you in the Marlborough Sounds. Prime among them is the very stylish **Bay of Many Coves Resort** ★★★, Queen Charlotte Sound (© **0800/579-9771** in NZ, or 03/579-9771; www.bayofmanycovesresort.co.nz), which has one-, two-, and three-bedroom self-contained apartments priced from NZ$500 to NZ$950. It also has an excellent restaurant open to casual diners. **Craglee Lodge** ★, Bay of Many Coves (© **03/579-9223;** www. craglee.co.nz), has three delightful rooms from NZ$450 a night. This good-value stay includes breakfast, lunch, dinner, fresh baking, fruit, and predinner drinks in the tariff.

In Picton itself, **McCormick House** ★★, 21 Leicester St. (© **03/573-5253;** www. mccormickhouse.co.nz), is hard to beat for character and charm. It has three beautiful rooms for NZ$300 to NZ$430. The **Gables,** 20 Waikawa Rd. (© **03/573-6772;** www. thegables.co.nz), has three more modest rooms plus two cottage suites (NZ$140–NZ$175). For great-value backpacker accommodations, the **Villa Backpacker's Lodge,** 34 Auckland St., Picton (© **03/573-6598;** www.thevilla.co.nz), is hard to beat. It has dorm beds for NZ$24 and double rooms for NZ$66.

Escape To Picton Boutique Hotel ★★ (Finds) Killian and Juliearna Kavanagh know all about satisfying the needs of international travelers, and at this classy little boutique operation in the heart of Picton, they do it with style and aplomb. It's one of my best discoveries; I love the way this old bank building has been converted into a modern stay that offers the best of everything. My favorite is the large, formal upstairs suite, but all three rooms are bound to please with their classic style, spaciousness, and soundproofing.

33 Wellington St., Picton. © **0800/693-7227** in NZ, or 03/573-5573. www.escapetopicton.com. 3 units. NZ$450–NZ$600. Long-stay and off-peak rates. AE, DC, MC, V. No children 11 and under. **Amenities:** Restaurant (Escape To Picton [Modern NZ]); bar; nearby bike rentals; nearby golf course; room service; nearby watersports activities. *In room:* A/C, TV/DVD, hair dryer, free high-speed Internet.

The Portage Resort Hotel ★ (Finds) The Portage has been providing hospitality for more than 100 years, but in its latest revamped guise there's much to be recommended

For a start, the Kenepuru Sounds setting is breathtaking. The rest of the world may as well not exist. All rooms—from backpacker style to deluxe suites—look out over the water. They're simple, fairly uninspired rooms and the bathrooms may be a little small in some cases, but this is offset by splendid public areas and a location to die for, just 10 minutes from Picton by water taxi.

Kenepuru Sound, Marlborough. (C) **0800/762-442** in NZ, or 03/573-4309. Fax 03/573-4362. www. portage.co.nz. 41 units. NZ$245–NZ$355. Off-peak and long-stay rates. AE, DC, MC, V. **Amenities:** 2 restaurants (Te Weka [contemporary NZ]; Snapper Café [light meals]); 2 bars; babysitting; bike rentals; children's program/adventure center; nearby 9-hole golf course; Jacuzzi; outdoor pool; watersports equipment rentals. *In room:* TV/DVD (in some), fridge, hair dryer, minibar on request.

In Blenheim

If you're looking for a place with individuality and style, try **Hotel d'Urville** ★★, 52 Queen St. ((C) **03/577-9945;** www.durville.com), which has 11 lovely themed rooms priced NZ$185 to NZ$285. **Old St. Mary's Convent** ★★, 776 Rapaura Rd. ((C) **03/570-5700;** www.convent.co.nz), is a unique stay—albeit a slightly overpriced one—in a restored 100-year-old convent. Its five rooms are vast and cost between NZ$600 and NZ$800. The honeymoon suite is gorgeous, and there's even a small church on the property. I think you get better value at the stunning new property, **BEC Spa Resort** ★★★, 81 Cob Cottage Rd., Blenheim ((C) **03/579-4446;** www.becspa.com), where three richly appointed, modern suites go for NZ$515 to NZ$715—and that includes a four-course dinner with wine. (At Old St Mary's the higher tariff only includes full breakfast.) **Uno Piu** ★, 75 Murphys Rd. ((C) **03/578-2235;** www.unopiu.co.nz), offers lovely bed-and-breakfast homestead accommodations plus a delightful, self-catering, two-bedroom mud-block cottage set in its own garden. You can also frolic in the home swimming pool.

WHERE TO DINE

As well as the cafes and restaurants reviewed below, don't forget about all the winery restaurants. You'll find them listed on the free winery map from the visitor center.

In Picton

Picton eateries come and go, but one enduring favorite is **Le Café,** London Quay ((C) **03/573-5588)**—casual, friendly, reliable, and open daily. If you'd like a special dining experience, get a water taxi and head for Portage Resort's **Te Weka Restaurant** ★★ ((C) **03/573-4309**), which serves divine New Zealand food—salmon, mussels, tuna, lamb, venison—and wine in a gorgeous bush-clad setting adjacent to their funky Retro Lounge Bar.

Escape to Picton Restaurant ★★★ CONTEMPORARY NEW ZEALAND   This classy little restaurant with touches of Hollywood glamour highlights local delicacies like fresh scallops, mussels, and fish. Their Thai fish curry is one of the most popular choices on the menu, but I opted for one of their big main course platters. These come in Mediterranean, seafood, spicy, or vegetarian options and serve as many people as you like. My spicy choice included everything from Thai spring rolls to chorizo, duck leg, and assorted other delicious nibbles.

33 Wellington St., Picton. (C) **03/573-5573.** www.escapetopicton.com. Reservations recommended for dinner. Main courses NZ$33–NZ$49. AE, DC, MC, V. Daily noon–late.

(Moments) World-Class Wining & Dining

If you feel like a drop of one of the world's most sought-after wines—Chateau de Valandrand—Hanz and Therese Herzog of **Herzog Winery & Restaurant** ★★★, 81 Jeffries Rd., Blenheim (© **03/572-8770**; www.herzog.co.nz), can oblige. *Wine Spectator* has recognized Herzog for having one of the best wine lists in the world, and if you visit this little culinary paradise, you'll be reluctant to leave. Luckily you don't have to. As well as a divine Cellar Door & Bistro and a fine-dining restaurant with Michelin star-rated chefs, they also have a gorgeous little vineyard cottage for two restaurant guests at NZ$380 per night. Factor in an exciting range of cooking classes (from NZ$180 per person), and you'll think you've died and gone to heaven. Herzog Cellar Door is open weekdays 9am to 5pm; the bistro Tuesday to Sunday for lunch; the restaurant Tuesday to Sunday from 6:30pm. Restaurant main courses start at NZ$24 and a three-course set menu is NZ$99.

In Havelock

The highlight in Havelock is the delightful **Slip Inn Café Restaurant & Wine Bar** ★★, Havelock Marina (© **03/574-2345**), which is open daily from 7am until late. It offers unimpeded views over the marina and Pelorus Sound, as well as great value with seafood dishes and pizza priced around NZ$18 to NZ$22.

The Mussel Pot ★ SEAFOOD   The giant mussel shells on the restaurant roof are a dead giveaway—this is the place for the freshest, tastiest mussels you'll find anywhere. They're grown locally and treated with the utmost culinary care. Fresh steamers are served whole in their shell in special pots; fresh flats are grilled on the half shell and topped with something tasty; and the mussel chowder alone is worth the drive. Mmmmm. Need I say more?

73 Main Rd., Havelock. © **03/574-2824.** Reservations required for dinner. Main courses NZ$18–NZ$32. MC, V. Summer daily 11am–9:30pm; winter Sun–Thurs noon–7pm, Fri–Sat open late. At Havelock, St. Hwy. 6, 40 min. from Picton.

In Blenheim

Hotel d'Urville Restaurant & Bar ★, 52 Queen St. (© **03/577-9945**), established itself early as a place for top, innovative cuisine and after a couple of jaded years, seems to have made a comeback. It offers an impressive local wine list (more than 60 selections) and is a good place for cocktails. Open daily for dinner 6:30 to 10pm; bookings are essential. **Bacchus** ★★, 3 Main St. (© **03/578-8099**), is widely considered to be the most reliable restaurant in town. It's open daily from 6pm.

For coffee to jump-start your day, try **CPR @HQ,** 18–20 Wynen St. (© **03/579-5030;** www.cprcoffee.com), where they roast their own beans. Also check out **Figaro's,** 8 Scott St. (© **03/577-7277**), to find more excellent coffee along with great snacks, salads, and a menu that changes daily. It's open Monday to Friday 7:30am to 3:30pm, Saturday 9am to 1pm. And a reminder that some of the area's best restaurants are actually in the wineries (see above), although many are only open for lunch.

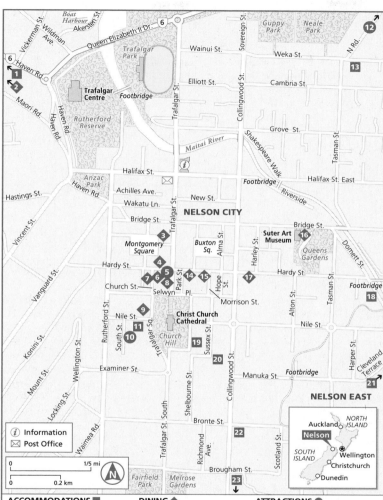

ACCOMMODATIONS ■
Baywick Inn **18**
Consulate Apartments **19**
Grampian Villa **22**
The Little Retreat **11**
Long Lookout Gardens **21**
Paradiso Backpackers **13**
Shelbourne Villa **20**
Te Puna Wai Lodge **1**
39 Russell **1**
Warwick House **23**

DINING ◆
Boatshed Café **2**
Cocoa **4**
Harry's Bar **17**
Hopgoods **8**
Lambretta's Café Bar **14**
Miyazu **9**
Morrison Street Café **15**
Penguino Gelato Café **3**
Stingray **7**
Suter Art Gallery Café **16**
Zest Deli & Café **6**

ATTRACTIONS ●
Founder's Heritage Park **12**
Nelson Provincial Museum **5**
South Street Historic Precinct **10**

HEADING SOUTH: EN ROUTE TO CHRISTCHURCH

If you're going south, the drive to Christchurch is approximately 4 hours. This is a perfect opportunity to stop off in Kaikoura or the winegrowing area of Waipara in North Canterbury. If you plan to do either, allow a whole day for the trip. For details on Kaikoura and its famous whale-watching excursions, see section 9, "Side Trips from Christchurch," in chapter 14.

HEADING NORTH: EN ROUTE TO NELSON

The **Queen Charlotte Drive** offers wonderful views of the Marlborough Sounds, but it's a narrow, winding road that needs to be driven with great care. It's a drive worth doing, with several good lookout stops along the way. The road meets up with State Highway 6 at the little village of Havelock; you then continue east to Nelson. The whole trip should take about 2 hours.

2 NELSON, RICHMOND & MOTUEKA ★★★

144km (89 miles) W of Picton; 226km (140 miles) NE of Westport; 424km (263 miles) N of Christchurch

Nelson is the sunniest playground in New Zealand. Its 2,500 hours of annual sunshine, tranquil waters, gold-sand beaches, vineyards, and craft activities make it one of the most popular destinations in the country. And the good thing is, this applies to winter as well. While the rest of the country is lashed with foul winter chills, Nelson sits in a sheltered haven, blissfully unaware of everyone else's discomfort.

Perhaps this accounts for why the area is one of the last bastions of alternative lifestylers, especially in the Takaka–Golden Bay area. Immigrating Europeans and Americans have sought it out, too, so you'll find plenty of mixed accents among the locals.

The combined population of Nelson City and nearby Richmond is about 45,000, and for the whole Nelson-Tasman region, 87,500. An hour's drive east is the small town of Motueka, population 12,000, and between the two is an area rich in tourist pickings. This is where you'll find most of the 300 full-time artists and craftspeople. It's thick with orchards, vineyards, galleries, quaint shops, and cafes, and a visit here should not be rushed. It's a laid-back province that quickly convinces you that laid-back is best. The region's tourism body, Latitude Nelson, is also right behind keeping it that way. It operates the Nelson Tasman Sustainable Tourism Charter to improve the environmental performance of all its members. You can find out who is working to protect this beautiful region by checking www.nelsonnz.com/sustainable.tourism.

ESSENTIALS

GETTING THERE   **By Plane   Nelson City Airport** is the fourth-busiest airport in New Zealand, with regular direct flights to and from Auckland, Wellington, Christchurch, and major provincial centers. It's serviced by **Air New Zealand** (✆ **0800/737-000**; www.airnewzealand.co.nz). **Super Shuttle** (✆ **0800/748-885** in NZ; www.supershuttle.co.nz), operates regularly between the airport and the city center for NZ$22 to NZ$25 one-way.

By Coach (Bus)   InterCity, 27 Bridge St., Nelson (✆ **03/548-1538;** www.intercity.co.nz or www.nelsoncoaches.co.nz), connects Nelson to Christchurch via Kaikoura/Marlborough or the Lewis Pass. Both **Kiwi Experience** (✆ **09/366-9830**) and the

are several local bus companies that link all towns within the region. Details are available from the visitor center.

By Car   The scenic drive from Picton to Nelson, via Queen Charlotte Sound (narrow and winding), or State Highway 6 (more direct), takes approximately 2 hours without stops. (The scenic route takes about a half-hour longer than the State Highway.) If you're coming from the West Coast, the drive from Westport takes approximately 3½ hours; from Christchurch via Lewis Pass, about 5 hours, or via Kaikoura-Blenheim, 6 hours.

By Taxi   Taxis pick up passengers outside the Majestic Theatre on Trafalgar Street and on Bridge Street opposite the Suburban Bus Company. For pickup, call **Nelson City Taxis** ((C) **03/548-8225**), **Sun City Taxis** ((C) **03/548-2666**), or **Motueka Taxis** ((C) **03/528-7900**).

ORIENTATION   Two landmarks will keep you oriented in Nelson: Trafalgar Street (the main street) and Church Hill, owned by Christ Church Cathedral and surrounded by lush lawns. The steps leading up to the church are a local gathering point. If there is any trouble at all to be had in Nelson, you'll usually find it in this area after dark.

Most shops, cafes, and restaurants are at Trafalgar and Halifax streets, although you'll find a few eateries around the bay on the waterfront. The waterfront road leads to Richmond township, which is 14km (8½ miles) and approximately a 10-minute drive away.

Past Richmond, you turn right over the railway bridge and take the Coastal Highway (St. Hwy. 60) to Motueka township, a 1-hour drive. Motueka itself is a straightforward little town built around the main highway at the mouth of the Motueka River. On the way to Motueka, stop off at the delightful little village of Mapua—it's just 5 minutes off the main highway. The wharf area particularly is home to a number of excellent cafes, galleries, and attractions.

VISITOR INFORMATION   The **Nelson i-SITE Visitor Centre,** at 77 Trafalgar St. ((C) **03/548-2304;** fax 03/546-7393; www.i-sitenelsonnz.com), is open Monday through Friday from 8:30am to 5pm, and 9am to 5pm on weekends and public holidays (closed Dec 25). It occupies a stylish complex that incorporates a large gift store and a display center. Make sure you watch the fabulous video of the region's attractions. Major bus lines also arrive and depart from here. The **Department of Conservation** counter at the visitor center is staffed only from October to Easter. The **Motueka i-SITE Visitor Centre** is on Wallace Street, Motueka ((C) **03/528-6543;** fax 03/528-6563; www.motueka isite.co.nz). Pick up a copy of the free newspaper *Discover the Top of the South* at either visitor center. It details many local attractions.

FAST FACTS   The post office is at the corner of Halifax and Trafalgar streets, diagonally opposite the visitor center. There is handy Internet access at the visitor center, or at **Boots-Off Travellers Centre,** 53 Bridge St. ((C) **03/546-8789**).

SPECIAL EVENTS   Sadly, the **Montana World of Wearable Art Awards** (www.world ofwearableart.com) are no longer held in Nelson; they've transferred to Wellington in the interests of coping with larger audiences. (See "Special Events" in chapter 12.) The **Nelson Jazz Festival** (www.nelsonjazzclub.co.nz) runs from late December to early January. The **Nelson Arts Festival** (www.nelsonartsfestival.co.nz), in late October, celebrates the region's diverse creativity over 11 days. For details on the wide range of Nelson regional events, contact the visitor center or check www.nelsonfestivals.co.nz.

The **Summertime Bus** is an excellent way to see Nelson's best attractions. Tickets and bus stops are available from the visitor center, or from the bus driver: NZ$6 for a circuit, NZ$12 for an all-day pass, and NZ$25 for a family day pass. The double-decker bus leaves from the visitor center on the hour from 10am to 4pm. It operates weekends only from November 6 until December 5; every day (except Dec 25) from December 11 until February 6; and then weekends only until March 27.

Nelson's Top Museums & Historic Buildings

Nelson Provincial Museum ★★, Trafalgar and Hardy streets (✆ **03/548-9588;** www. museumnp.org.nz), relocated to its original 1842 site in October 2005 and now the treasure-filled museum is welcoming in a new era of fascinating permanent displays and changing exhibitions. Look out for the fabulous silver collection, antique furniture, historical books, and Maori artifacts—not to mention the new stained-glass window featuring native birds and plants. Its research center in the former museum building in Isel Park, Stoke, houses one of the largest historical photographic collections in the country, and a comprehensive reference library on local history. The museum is open Monday to Friday 10am to 5pm (weekends and public holidays until 4:30pm); the Research Facility is open Saturdays 10am to 2pm, and Tuesday through Friday by appointment. Museum admission is by donation; the research facility is free.

In Stoke, a suburb of Nelson, you'll find the **Broadgreen Historic House** ★, 276 Nayland St. (✆ **03/547-0403;** fax 03/547-0409), a restored two-story cob house built in the mid-1850s. This New Zealand Tourism Award winner has 11 rooms furnished to faithfully represent a family home of the period. It's open daily from 10:30am to 4:30pm; call for winter hours. Admission is NZ$6 for adults and NZ$2 for children 14 and under.

In central Nelson, it's worth visiting the **South Street Historic Precinct** ★★★. Just off Nile Street West behind the Rutherford Hotel, this cute little street captures the feel of a past era. Sixteen working-class cottages built between 1863 and 1867 remain intact and are still inhabited. Nearby, on top of Church Hill, is **Nelson Cathedral,** 367 Trafalgar St. (✆ **03/548-1008;** nelson.cathedral@clear.net.nz). It's open daily free of charge to visitors, in summer from 8am to 6pm and in winter from 8am to 5pm. Built of local Takaka marble, the cathedral is known for its striking stained glass, carved features, and unique free-standing organ. Car and fashion buffs—jointly or separately—will enjoy the **World of Wearable Art & Classic Cars Museum** ★★★, 95 Quarantine Rd. (✆ **03/ 547-4573;** fax 03/547-0856; www.wowcars.co.nz), which presents around 50 collectible cars and motorbikes, as well as a stunning collection of past entries and winners of the internationally renowned World of Wearable Arts Awards. It's open daily from 10am to 6pm in summer and from 10am to 5pm in winter. Admission is NZ$18 for adults, NZ$14 for seniors, and NZ$7 for children ages 5 to 14. They also offer family concessions and there's a shop, cafe, and gallery on-site.

Across town, the **Founder's Heritage Park,** 87 Atawhai Dr. (✆ **03/548-2649;** www. nelsoncitycouncil.co.nz/founders-heritage-park), is a replica of a historic village containing many of the old buildings and artifacts of Nelson. Special attractions include Dr. Bush's Windmill, the Port Nelson Exhibition, vintage and horse-drawn vehicles, fire engines, and a working train. It's open daily from 10am to 4:30pm (closed Good Friday and Dec 25); admission is NZ$5 for adults, NZ$2 for children, and NZ$13 per family. Train rides run daily between December 26 and January 10. Look out for the interesting organic brewery complex on-site, and they stage a farmers' market from 3 to 6pm on Friday evenings.

> **(Tips) Liquid Sunshine**
>
> Nelson olive oils are rapidly gaining recognition nationally and internationally as some of the best you'll taste anywhere. If you're a fan of dipping, drizzling, and pouring, give in to temptation and visit some of the following. *Note:* It pays to call first to make sure they're open for direct sales. **Moutere Grove,** 979 Central Rd., Upper Moutere (✆ **03/543-2232;** www.mouteregrove.co.nz), has a free tour and organic olive oil tastings by appointment only. **Hau Plains Olive Oil,** 543 High St., Motueka (✆ **03/528-6391;** www.hauplains.co.nz), is open most days for sales and tastings. Others to look out for are **Frog's End Estate,** Westdale Road, Richmond (✆ **03/544-0570;** frogsend@ts.co.nz); **Tasman Bay Olives,** Horton Road, Tasman (✆ **03/540-2084;** www.olivesnewzealand.com); and **Mount Heslington Olives,** 89 Mount Heslington Rd., Brightwater (✆ **03/542-3727;** mt.heslington@clear.net.nz).

Last, but definitely not least, is the **Suter Te Aratoi o Whakatu** ★★, 208 Bridge St. (✆ **03/548-4699;** www.thesuter.org.nz), the region's public art museum. Collections include works by 19th-century New Zealand artists with strong Nelson ties, such as Gully, Lindauer, and Van der Velden. There's an excellent crafts shop and a bush-clad cafe overlooking Queens Gardens. It's open daily from 10:30am to 4:30pm (closed Good Friday, Dec 25, and Jan 1), and admission is NZ$3 adults, NZ$1 for students and children.

The Moutere Hills Wineries

Most of Nelson's 18 or so wineries are scattered along the rolling Moutere Hills and the alluvial Waimea Plains. The wines—Riesling, chardonnay, sauvignon blanc, Gewürztraminer, cabernet franc, merlot, cabernet sauvignon, and pinot noir—have intense fruit flavors, good acidic balance, and weight. A number of wineries have tasting rooms and restaurants. For more details on Nelson wineries, tap into the **Nelson Winemakers Association** website at www.nelsonwines.co.nz, or www.eatdrinknelson.co.nz.

The visitor center has a leaflet and a very clear map pinpointing the best of the area's wineries, or you can take a wine tour with **JJ's Quality Tours** ★★, 31a Stansell Ave., Nelson (✆ **0800/229-868** in NZ, or ✆/fax 03/546-5470; www.jjstours.co.nz). It costs from NZ$75 for a half-day tour. They also offer a tour of local breweries, or a mix of breweries and wineries. For a similar price (NZ$78), **Bay Tours,** Nelson (✆ **0800/229-868** in NZ, or 03/548-6486; www.baytoursnelson.co.nz), also offers an excellent range of gourmet wine tours that include either food or art stops. If you're short on time, hotfoot it straight to the **Regional Wine Centre** ★★, 67 Aranui Rd., Mapua (✆ **03/540-2526;** fax 03/540-2561), which features a showing of the region's best wines, olive oils, beers, and gourmet foods. It includes a wine and taste center, a cafe, and a restaurant. Or, in Nelson City itself, **Casa del Vino** ★★, 214 Hardy St. (✆ **03/548-0088;** www.casadelvino.co.nz), stocks a huge range of Nelson and New Zealand wines and holds regular wine tastings in summer. You can also pick up wine maps of the region here and take advantage of the worldwide shipping service. They're open Monday to Thursday 10am to 6:30pm and Friday and Saturday 10am to 7:30pm, except in December and January, when they're only open on Sundays 10am to 3pm.

Moments   To Market, to Market

You'll gain a terrific insight into local activities if you go to the **Nelson Market** ★★★, in Montgomery Square (📞 **03/546-6454**). It's held every Saturday from 8am to 1pm and offers fine crafts, fresh food and produce, and a whole heap of the unexpected. **Monty's Sunday Market** is held every Sunday from 8:30am to 1pm in the same place and features more bric-a-brac, clothing, and oddments. The **Motueka Sunday Market** ★, in the carpark behind the Motueka Visitor Centre in Wallace Street, Motueka (📞 **03/540-2709**), is held every Sunday from 8am to 1pm. Stalls here include fresh produce, clothing, crafts, and jewelry.

One of the best-known producers is **Neudorf Vineyards** ★★★, Neudorf Road, Upper Moutere (📞 **03/543-2643**; www.neudorf.co.nz). Set in a picturesque vineyard, the winery offers prearranged tastings of its prizewinning chardonnay, Riesling, pinot noir, and sauvignon blanc. It's open daily September through May from 11am to 5pm; June through August from 8:30am until 4pm, Monday to Friday. **Siefried Estate Vineyard and Restaurant,** Main Road, Appleby, Richmond (📞 **03/544-1555**; www.seifreid. co.nz), has a large restaurant and tasting room, open daily from 10am to 5pm. A winery tour and tasting is NZ$12 per person, by appointment, Monday through Saturday. Dinner is available in the restaurant Friday and Saturday evenings from 6pm; reservations are recommended.

Moutere Hills Vineyard ★★, Eggers Road, Upper Moutere (📞/fax **03/543-2288**; www.mouterehills.co.nz), serves beautifully presented light meals in its converted-woolshed winery, along with Riesling, sauvignon blanc, and chardonnay. It's open October 24 to Easter, Tuesday through Sunday, from 11am to 6pm.

Waimea Estates, 22 Appleby Hwy., Hope (📞 **03/544-4963**; www.waimeaestates. co.nz), produces all the main wine types, and their cafe and cellar door are open in summer daily 11am to 5pm; in winter, Wednesday to Sunday until 4pm. **Woollaston Estates** ★★★, School Road, Mahana (📞 **03/543-2817**; www.woollaston.co.nz), has a fabulous underground complex complete with a contemporary art gallery. They offer wine tasting and live music on the first Sunday of each month in summer. They're open daily, 11am until 4:30pm from mid-October through April.

Shopping for Arts & Crafts

The essence of Nelson province is found in its abundance of top-quality arts and crafts—by far the best concentration anywhere in New Zealand. There are over 300 practicing artists and 40 galleries and studios. Start by purchasing a copy of *Nelson Art Guide Book,* which is a terrific take-home, ring-bound volume available at the Nelson visitor center, which also distributes the free *Tourist Guide to Nelson Potters, Nelson Inner City Shopping Guide,* and *Nelson City Art Trail.* If you're driving to Motueka, pick up the free *Nelson's Coastal Way–Mapua & Coastal Villages,* a brochure that highlights top craftspeople, vineyards, and cafes. And check out www.nelsonarts.org.nz.

South Street Gallery, 10 Nile St. (📞/fax **03/548-8117**; www.nelsonpottery.co.nz), is well stocked with work by 25 top potters; it's open Monday through Friday from 9am to 5pm and weekends 10am until 4pm. **Jens Hansen Gold & Silversmith** ★★★, 320 Trafalgar Sq. (📞 **03/548-0640**; www.jenshansen.com), is a name associated with fine-quality New Zealand–made gold and silver jewelry—*and* the handmade rings and

---

Finds   Cool Crafts

One of the loveliest little galleries around is the **Coolstore Gallery** ★★★, 7 Aranui Rd., Mapua (✆ **03/540-3778;** www.coolstoregallery.co.nz), located in a converted apple cool store on Mapua Wharf. It displays a wide range of contemporary art and crafts from the region's best artisans. It's open daily in summer from 11am to 5pm, and Wednesday through Sunday in winter from 11am to 4pm. Just down the road, you'll find it hard to suppress a smile at **Laughing Fish Studio,** 24 Aranui Rd., Mapua (✆ **03/540-3940;** www.laughingfishstudio.co.nz), where large ladies cavort across everything from plates to wall works. And hat lovers will rejoice at **Serious Straw** ★★, 144 Aranui Rd., Mapua (✆ **03/540-3262;** www.hats.co.nz), which makes and imports a gorgeous range of fashionable and funky straw hats. If you can't make it to Mapua, they have a stall at Nelson's Saturday and Sunday markets.

---

jewelry used in the trilogy *The Lord of the Rings.* It's open Monday through Friday 9am until 5:30pm, Saturday 9am to 2pm, and Sunday 10am to 1pm. **RED** ★★, 1 Bridge St. (✆ **03/548-2170;** www.redartgallery.com), is a terrific place for contemporary fine art, jewelry, and New Zealand crafts. **Flame Daisy,** 324 Trafalgar Sq. (✆ **03/548-4475;** www.flamedaisy.com), is a new glass art gallery, with a wide variety of items, many at cheaper prices than the gorgeous Höglund Glass (see below). It's open Monday through Friday 10am until 5pm, and weekends 10am to 4pm.

Farther afield, potter **Steve Fullmer** ★★★, Baldwin Road, Tasman (✆ **03/526-6765;** fullmer.gallery@xtra.co.nz), is one of the country's best. His gallery is open daily 10am until 5pm in summer, and Wednesday through Sunday in winter. **Royce McGlashen Pottery** ★★★, 128 Ellis St., Brightwater (✆ **03/542-3585;** www.royce mcglashen.co.nz), is another high point. When it comes to color, some of the nicest pottery around is produced by **Katie Gold** ★★★, 1380 Main Rd., Upper Moutere (✆ **03/543-2544;** katie_gold@paradise.net.nz).

If you like beautiful glass pieces, drive 20 minutes out of Nelson to **Höglund Art Glass International Glass Centre** ★★★, 62 Lansdowne Rd., Richmond (✆ **03/544-6500;** www.hoglundartglass.com). Ola and Marie Höglund trained at Orrefors and Kosta Boda before emigrating from their native Sweden, and their skills have translated into stunning, colorful handblown glassware. You can watch the action in the studio by joining a guided studio tour (Dec 15–Apr 15; NZ$20 adults, free for kids 13 and under) that enlightens you to the history of glass and its processes; or you can make your own glass beads (NZ$70 per hour) or a paperweight (NZ$185 per person). And don't worry about having to cart your favorite piece home—they offer an international shipping service. Open daily from 10am to 5pm (closed Dec 25–26 and Good Friday). They have a second gallery in Nelson's Rutherford Hotel on Trafalgar Square.

Especially for Kids

Give the kids their own timeout at **Nelson Fun Park** (✆ **03/548-6267**), adjacent to Tahunanui Beach, just a 5-minute drive from Central City. They can unwind on the hydroslide, play miniature golf, or have fun on bumper boats. **Natureland Zoo** (✆ **03/548-6166;** www.naturelandzoo.co.nz) is also at Tahunanui Beach, open daily from

(Tips) **Six Times the Fun**

If you want to try a bit of everything and save money at the same time, check out combo deals with the Nelson Visitor Centre. If you invest in several activities, you'll pay far less, which is a big consideration when you're traveling with a family.

9:30am to 4pm. It gives children a chance to get up close to wallabies, meerkats, otters, monkeys, and exotic birds; it costs NZ$5 for adults and NZ$3.50 for children.

Touch the Sea Aquarium ★★, 8 Aranui Rd., Mapua (℃/fax **03/540-3557**; seatouch@tasman.net), is a charming little aquarium on Mapua Wharf. Kids get to put their hands in special tanks to discover the mysteries of sea urchins, starfish, and various shells and fish. It's worth the admission of around NZ$8 for adults, NZ$6 for children. There's also a playroom and an excellent gift store.

Outdoor Pursuits

For a complete overview of outdoor activities in the region, it's best to start at one of the visitor centers, which have a wide range of brochures. There are three national parks within easy driving distance; that alone raises dozens of outdoor possibilities.

BEACHES Nelson has dozens of fabulous beaches. Close to the city, the best bet is **Tahuna Beach,** which offers excellent swimming. Farther afield, just past Motueka, you'll find the hugely popular **Kaiteriteri Beach** ★★★, a favorite with Christchurch holidaymakers.

CAVING Lovers of dark underground spaces will enjoy exploring **Ngarua Caves,** Takaka Hill, Motueka (℃ **03/528-8093;** janetdavid@paradise.net.nz). These marble caves feature the skeletal remains of New Zealand's extinct flightless bird, the moa, and a 45-minute guided tour is offered on the hour from 10am to 4pm (closed July–Sept). Entry is NZ$15 for adults and NZ$7 for children ages 5 to 15. The caves are 70km (43 miles) from Nelson and 20km (12 miles) from Motueka. There are more caves at Takaka (see "Exploring Golden Bay" in section 3).

FISHING Bait up those hooks and get out there! The fish are awaiting in lakes, rivers, streams, and the ocean. There's good onshore fishing at Connolly's Quay on Rocks Road, the western end of Tahuna Beach, Boulder Bay, and Cable Bay. When it comes to stalking trout, call John Brunwin of **Fly Fishing New Zealand,** 97 Murphy St., Nelson (℃ **03/548-9145;** www.flyfishnewzealand.com).

FLIGHTSEEING When you get up in the air over this stunning province, you'll truly understand why so many people love it. **Abel Tasman Air** ★★, Motueka Airfield, Motueka (℃ **0800/304-560** in NZ, or 03/528-8290; www.abeltasmanair.co.nz), offers a range of scenic flight packages. One of the nicest is Fly & Dine, which delivers you to some of the region's special spots. Helicopter fans should buzz into the skies with **Nelson Helicopters,** Tangmere Place, Nelson Airport (℃ **0800/450-350** in NZ, or 03/547-1177; www.nelsonhelicopters.co.nz). Try their Nelson Lakes scenic tour, or visit *The Lord of the Rings* filming sites.

FOUR-WHEEL-DRIVE ADVENTURES Just 10 minutes from central Nelson, you can don your helmet, get on a 4×4 motorbike, and go for it over your choice of testing tracks.

or 03/545-0304; www.happyvalleyadventures.co.nz), is the place to call. Prices range
from NZ$75 to NZ$150 per rider (NZ$20 extra for pillion passengers). Or you can fly
on a Skywire for over 3km (1¾ miles) for NZ$85 adults, NZ$55 children 16 and under.

GOLF   **Nelson Golf Club,** Bolt Road, Tahunanui, Nelson (✆ **03/548-5028;** www.
nelsongolf.co.nz), is an 18-hole course open daily. Greens fees are NZ$50 for nonaffili-
ated members. **Greenacres Golf Club,** Best Island, Richmond (✆ **03/544-6441;** fax
03/544-8420), also has 18 holes and is open daily; nonaffiliated members pay NZ$40.

HORSE TREKKING   **Stonehurst Farm Horse Treks** ★★, Stonehurst Farm, 165 Hay-
cock Rd., Hope (✆ **0800/487-357** in NZ, or 03/542-4121; www.stonehurstfarm.co.nz),
gives visitors the chance to enjoy the freedom of 320 hectares (800 acres) of wide-open
spaces on a working farm. The 1- to 4-hour treks explore varied scenery (hill country,
river areas, plains, and farmland), and cost from NZ$40 to NZ$120.

KAYAKING   If you don't have time to kayak in the unforgettable Abel Tasman, at least
take to the waters near Nelson with **Cable Bay Kayaks,** Cable Bay Road, Nelson
(✆ **0508/222-532** in NZ, or 03/545-0332; www.cablebaykayaks.co.nz). They specialize
in half- and 1-day tours that take in bird colonies, caves, and coves for NZ$90 to
NZ$120 per person.

MOUNTAIN BIKING   **Natural High,** 52 Rutherford St., Nelson (✆ **0800/444-144** in
NZ, or 03/546-6936; www.cyclenewzealand.com), offers guided bike excursions, from a
2-hour tour of the city sights and waterfront to multiday South Island tours and off-road
adventures.

ROCK CLIMBING   **Vertical Limits Climbing & Adventure Centre,** 34 Vanguard St.
(✆ **0508/837-842** in NZ, or 03/545-7511; www.verticallimits.co.nz), is the largest
indoor climbing center in New Zealand. It offers indoor rock climbing, rappelling, and
guided climbing and caving adventures with qualified instructors. A shot at the climbing
walls costs NZ$18 for adults, NZ$15 for students, and NZ$12 for children 9 and under.
It's open Monday through Friday from 10am to 9pm and weekends from 10am to 6pm.

SKY DIVING   **Skydive Abel Tasman,** 16 College St., Motueka Airport (✆ **0800/422-
899** in NZ, or 03/528-4091; www.skydive.co.nz), has free-fall tandem sky dives with
instructors priced NZ$279 to NZ$299.

WALKING   Just about anywhere in Nelson is suited to walking. From a leisurely stroll
to full multiday treks, you'll be in your element. For information on multiday walks, see
"Tramping" in chapter 5. Also check out section 3, "Abel Tasman National Park &
Golden Bay," later in this chapter.

For a charming city walk, find the Maitai River off Nile Street and follow the signposted walkway to the locals' favorite swimming spot—Girlie's Hole. Another good
45-minute walk traces Nelson's old water system up through the native bush to dams

MARLBOROUGH & NELSON

13

NELSON, RICHMOND & MOTUEKA

Ⓜ**Moments**   **A Walk to Remember**

A walk along **Boulder Bank**—the thin strip of land that reaches out from Nelson
into the sea—is an unusual and exhilarating experience. Take water, sun protection, and a windbreaker for this 2¹/₂-hour, 8km (5-mile) walk, which begins and
ends at Boulder Bank Drive.

built in the 1870s. Go to Brook Motor Camp; there's a parking area by the dam, and the trail leads on from here. Within 5 minutes, you'll be in native bush and a quiet valley. There are steps and handrails on the trail.

If you'd like to walk with the birds, go along Motueka Sandspit and enjoy the views across Tasman Bay to D'Urville Island and Nelson City. This is an internationally important seabird habitat and is home to many varieties that come here to breed. (Please keep dogs away from the southern end of the spit.) It's part of the Motueka Walkway, which is detailed in a brochure available at the visitor center. Access the walkway from the end of Staples Street.

WHITE-WATER ADVENTURES Ultimate Descents New Zealand, Motueka (© **0800/748-377** in NZ, or 03/523-9899; www.rivers.co.nz), seems to have every possible white-water activity covered. It offers a wide range of outings by kayak, raft, or river bug (also known as a sled; this involves going through white water lying facedown on the sled), from Grade II to the savage Grade V on rivers throughout the greater Nelson province. Half-day to multiday rafting and kayaking trips for all ages cost from NZ$130 to NZ$550.

WHERE TO STAY

Nelson isn't short of beds, but if you're visiting over the December-to-January period, you'll be competing with thousands of New Zealanders who descend upon the area. Book early! There is a wide range of accommodations—including lots of smart B&Bs and excellent backpacker offerings—and with one or two exceptions, most are incredibly well priced. The rates given below include 12.5% GST and free parking.

In Nelson

At **Te Puna Wai Lodge** ★★, 24 Richardson St. (© **03/548-7621;** www.tepunawai.co.nz), consummate hosts James Taylor and multilingual Richard Hewitson attend to every comfort. They offer two rooms and an apartment in a lovely 1857 home filled with antiques, art, and beautiful ocean views. Rooms range from NZ$195 to NZ$325, and the apartment NZ$325 to NZ$345. There's another unique stay at **Warwick House** ★, 64 Brougham St. (© **03/548-3164;** www.warwickhouse.co.nz), where five rooms in a historic Victorian home go for NZ$295 to NZ$395. The Bayview Suite is the best of them.

Expensive

Consulate Apartments ★★★ Elegant, sophisticated, and understated, these three large apartments make the most of what was once the base for an Italian consul. Each apartment has modern facilities of the highest quality. Apartment Due, the largest and by far the most opulent of the three, even has a piano for your use. Its size and style make it a much better value than rooms at many larger lodges. Two apartments have two bedrooms and the other has one, and they're just a 2-minute walk from the main street. They are tidied by staff each day using environmentally friendly cleaning products, and they use solar energy and carry out recycling.

353 Trafalgar Sq., Nelson. © **03/545-8200.** Fax 03/548-7156. www.consulateapartments.co.nz. 3 units. NZ$695 Uno; NZ$1,195 Due; NZ$895 Tre. Minimum 2-night stay. Long-stay and off-peak rates. Rates include breakfast provisions. AE, DC, MC, V. Beside the Cathedral. Children 11 and under only by special approval. **Amenities:** Airport transfers (charge); nearby golf course; free high-speed Internet. *In room:* A/C, TV/DVD/CD, hair dryer, full kitchen.

> ## (Value) Backpacker Beds
>
> Nelson is blessed with quality accommodations at affordable prices—there are at least 10 backpacker establishments in the town. In addition to Paradiso (see below), you'll find good value at **Nelson City YHA,** 59 Rutherford St. ((📞 **03/545-9988;** www.yha.co.nz); and the **Green Monkey,** 129 Milton St. ((📞 **03/545-7421;** www.thegreenmonkey.co.nz). **Club Nelson,** 18 Mount St. ((📞 **03/548-3466;** www.nelsonbackpackers.co.nz), is in a sunny, quiet street and a swimming pool is among its excellent facilities.

39 Russell ★★★ (Moments)   I have enormous pleasure in announcing the return of this sublime self-contained hillside cottage, where acclaimed artist Jane Evans has used her creative talents and good taste to create a place you'll never want to leave. Folding doors and windows open to sea views and a divine courtyard; and with two guest rooms (both with bathrooms), it's an ideal stop for two couples. Suffused with color, original art, fabulous books, and a bulging pantry, it is one of the best-value B&B stays in the country. Jane does her part for the environment by utilizing solar energy and environmentally friendly cleaning products. Make sure you arrange a studio visit so you can see into Jane's creative world.

39 Russell St., Port Nelson. (📞 **03/548-7621.** www.nelsonluxuryaccommodation.co.nz. 1 2-bedroom cottage. NZ$495; NZ$25 each extra person. Minimum 2-night stay. Rates include self-catered breakfast. Long-stay and off-peak rates. MC, V. From Haven Rd., turn onto Russell St. and go uphill, keeping to the steep left-hand road; halfway up is a private road—it's the first house on the left. No children 11 and under. **Amenities:** Nearby golf courses, Wi-Fi in lounge. *In room:* TV/DVD, hair dryer, full kitchen w/ stocked pantry, minibar.

Moderate

Baywick Inn ★ (Value)   Canadian Janet Southwick and her New Zealand husband Tim Bayley have been doing a fabulous job of hosting guests at terrific prices long enough to be considered experts. Upstairs rooms in their 119-year-old home have plenty of space and character; the Parkdale has a huge step-down bathroom complete with claw-foot tub and shower, plus its own sunroom. And they've just built a new, ecofriendly cottage in the garden, with two further rooms—one up and one down—overlooking the stream and garden. These will be ideal for families or two couples who like to be close to each other. Expect terrific breakfasts. All this just 5 minutes' walk from town.

51 Domet St., Nelson. (📞 **03/545-6514.** Fax 03/545-6517. www.baywicks.com. 5 units. NZ$150–NZ$250. Long-stay and off-peak rates. Rates include breakfast. Dinner by arrangement. MC, V. Children 11 and under by arrangement. **Amenities:** Free bikes; nearby golf course. *In room:* TV, hair dryer, Wi-Fi.

Grampian Villa ★★   John and Jo Fitzwater take to the role of hosts like ducks to water, and their two-storied historic Victorian villa reflects the passion they have for the tourism industry. All four rooms are large, with excellent bathrooms and balconies, or veranda access. The upstairs Observatory room has the biggest bathroom, but my personal favorite is the luscious burgundy-and-gold downstairs Mr. Gibbs room. They also have four lower-priced rooms in a separate house across the street.

209 Collingwood St., Nelson (📞 **03/545-8209.** Fax 03/548-7888. www.grampianvilla.co.nz. 4 units. NZ$250–NZ$350. Rates include breakfast. Dinner on request. MC, V. Closed June–July. No children 11 and under. **Amenities:** Nearby golf course. *In room:* TV, fridge, hair dryer, minibar, Wi-Fi.

The Little Retreat ★★ (**Moments**) This little gem is right in the heart of Nelson's historic South Street area, and owner Angela Higgins also owns the natural health center located directly beneath—just the place for a soothing shiatsu massage after a day of sightseeing. She leaves you entirely to yourself but not before you have experienced her terrific hospitality. The modern, open-plan apartment has a king-size bed, leather chairs, full kitchen and laundry, two private balconies, and a barbecue. Waking up to a hearty breakfast, eating out on the balcony, and watching the world go by are what a holiday is all about.

22 Nile St. W., Nelson. ✆ **03/545-1411** or 021/247-1891. Fax 03/545-1417. www.nelsongetaways.co.nz. 1 unit. NZ$195–NZ$240. Rates include breakfast provisions. Long-stay and off-peak rates. AE, DC, MC, V. **Amenities:** Babysitting; nearby golf course; health center below. *In room:* A/C, TV/DVD, hair dryer, kitchen.

Long Lookout Gardens ★★ (**Finds**) David and Yvonne Trathen are not wrong when they say that the hardest thing you'll ever have to do is leave Long Lookout Gardens. As a lover of old homes, I find it very easy to recommend this gorgeous 1864 homestead set in English-style gardens. The two suites are elaborate and luscious with their rich silks and satins, and beautiful modern bathrooms are a big plus. It's hard to choose between the ground-floor Richmond and the first-floor Hunter-Brown suites. Both are exquisite. Breakfasts also get rave reviews.

60 Cleveland Terrace, Nelson. ✆ **03/548-3617.** Fax 03/548-3127. www.longlookoutgardens.co.nz. 2 units. NZ$325. Long-stay and off-peak rates. Rates include breakfast. MC, V. **Amenities:** Airport transfers; bike rentals; nearby golf course. *In room:* TV, fridge, hair dryer.

Shelbourne Villa ★★ Wayne and Val Ballantyne have converted their two-story 1929 villa into a pleasurable oasis offering four lovely room choices. I'd opt for the Loft if you like a modern look, plenty of space, and balcony views; like the Master Suite, it has its own fireplace and king-size bed. The downstairs Garden Suite is also very appealing and has a separate living room and kitchenette. Wherever you end up sleeping, you won't be disappointed. The property has a Qualmark Enviro-Gold rating and is a member of the Nelson Sustainable Tourism Charter.

21 Shelbourne St., Nelson. ✆ **03/545-9059.** Fax 03/546-7248. www.shelbournevilla.co.nz. 4 units. NZ$275–NZ$385. Long-stay and off-peak rates. Rates include breakfast. AE, DC, MC, V. **Amenities:** Airport transfers for fee; nearby golf course. *In room:* A/C (deluxe room only), TV/DVD, fridge, hair dryer, kitchenette (Garden Suite), Wi-Fi in some areas.

Inexpensive

Paradiso Backpackers ★ (**Finds**) You can expect a crowd at Paradiso—it's definitely the most popular Nelson backpacker stay. One look at its fabulous pool, its conservatory kitchen/dining room, and its quirky lounge set up in an old bus, and you realize why. Bedrooms might be pretty standard and boring, but they're comfortable, and with all the other luxuries on hand, who cares?

42 Weka St., Nelson. ✆ **0800/269-667** in NZ, or 03/545-7128. Fax 03/546-7533. www.backpackernelson. co.nz. 95 beds with shared bathrooms, 9 en suites, 10 apts. NZ$20 dorm; NZ$60 double; NZ$80–NZ$150 apt. Long-stay and off-peak rates. AE, MC, V. **Amenities:** Jacuzzi; outdoor heated pool; sauna. *In room:* A/C (apts only), high-speed Internet.

In Tahunanui-Richmond

Tahuna Beach Holiday Park, 70 Beach Rd., Tahunanui (✆ **0800/500-501** in NZ, or 03/548-5159; www.tahunabeachholidaypark.co.nz), is the largest motor camp in New

> **Tips** **Top Tastes**
>
> Pick up a free copy of *Eat Drink Nelson* from the visitor center, or check www.eat drinknelson.co.nz for all the best restaurants and boutique food producers in the region.

Zealand, accommodating several thousand travelers a night during the summer months. It has motel units, tourist and standard cabins, and tent sites—not to mention a fabulous atmosphere.

In Motueka/Mapua

Motueka township itself doesn't contain an abundance of nice accommodations, but outlying areas have rich pickings for those wanting a peaceful country stay. **Bronte Country Estate** ★★, Bronte Road East, near Mapua (✆ **03/540-2422;** www.bronte lodge.co.nz), is one such place, with two luxury suites (NZ$520) and three villas ranging from NZ$650 to NZ$1,000. A lovely new discovery in this area is **Neudorf Hall** ★, 252 Neudorf Rd., Upper Moutere (✆ **03/543-2252;** www.neudorfhall.co.nz), which is just a short stroll from nearby Neudorf Vineyard. They have two rooms for NZ$195 to NZ$295. A lovely vineyard stay is **Ruby Bay Lodge and Vineyard** ★★, 271 Pomona Rd., Ruby Bay (✆ **03/540-3938;** www.rubybayvineyard.co.nz), where a romantic two-bedroom cottage goes for NZ$375, and two lodge suites are NZ$450 (2-night minimum stay). At the top end of the market, **Eden House** ★★★, Orinoco Valley, Motueka (✆ **03/526-8174;** www.edenhouse.co.nz), provides two top-quality suites for NZ$952, which includes dinner and breakfast. There are several vineyards close by and they're just 30 minutes from beautiful Abel Tasman National Park.

Expensive

Wairepo House ★★ In a fourth-generation apple and pear orchard, this big colonial homestead oozes romance. With nearly a hectare (2½ acres) of woodland gardens (including a giant chess set), this peaceful, rural oasis begs a lingering stay. Richard and Joyanne Easton will make sure it's everything you hoped for, starting with the fresh produce from their organic gardens and orchard they use for the gourmet breakfasts. The big two-bedroom top-floor suite is the most spacious and has a double Jacuzzi, lounge, kitchen, and balcony. Others open onto the pool and garden.

22 Weka Rd., Mariri, Tasman. ✆ **03/526-6865.** Fax 03/526-6101. www.wairepohouse.co.nz. 4 units. NZ$450–NZ$595. NZ$55 per person for extra adults. Long-stay rates. Rates include breakfast, canapés, and predinner drinks. MC, V. Closed Dec 24–Jan 12. **Amenities:** Airport transfers; babysitting; nearby bike rentals; nearby golf course; outdoor heated pool; grass tennis court. *In room:* TV/CD, fridge, hair dryer, kitchenette (in 1 suite), minibar, Wi-Fi.

Moderate

Aporo Pondsiders ★★ **Finds** Mike and Marian Day have come up with a gem of an idea—two supercute, self-contained, environmentally friendly cottages overhanging an ornamental pond in a peaceful rural environment. You'd be silly to miss them! Staggered for privacy, they have king-size beds and modern furnishings with a small kitchen, living room, and balcony overlooking the water. Pick up the binoculars and watch herons and shags, row in the dinghy, or walk in the woods.

23 Permin Rd., Tasman. (Ⓒ **03/526-6858.** Fax 03/526-6258. www.aporo.co.nz. 2 units. NZ$300. Long-stay and off-peak rates. Rates include breakfast provisions. MC, V. 30-min. drive from Nelson and 10 min. from Motueka. **Amenities:** Free bikes. *In room:* TV/CD, hair dryer, kitchen, Wi-Fi.

Inexpensive

Bakers Lodge, 4 Poole St., Motueka (Ⓒ **03/528-0102;** www.bakerslodge.co.nz), has 75 beds in 17 rooms priced at NZ$23 for dorms and NZ$76 to NZ$145 for doubles and rooms with en-suite bathrooms. They employ sustainable practices like recycling and there is an organic vegetable garden for guests' use.

WHERE TO DINE

Nelson is the seafood capital of New Zealand, so it isn't unreasonable to expect top seafood in the area's restaurants. Combine that with a wealth of horticultural produce, world-renowned wines, and a casual atmosphere, and the stage is set for some memorable dining. There's been a rush of new cafes—not all worth visiting—and you won't be short of an opportunity to dine well.

In Nelson

For the best coffee in Nelson, go to **Morrison Street Café** ★★, 244 Hardy St., Nelson (Ⓒ **03/548-8110;** www.morrisonstreetcafe.co.nz). It's open Monday through Friday from 7:30am until 4:30pm, Saturday from 8:30am until 4:30pm, and Sunday from 9am until 4:30pm. I had a divine seafood *laksa* here on my recent visit. Table service can be erratic, but their food is generally worth waiting for and there's always an interesting mix of people. **Lambretta's Café Bar** ★, 204 Hardy St. (Ⓒ **03/545-8555**), remains popular for light meals (especially their pizzas), and a good time. It's invariably packed with people enjoying pastas, pizzas, and seafood dishes daily from 8:30am until late. The **Suter Art Gallery Café,** Suter Art Gallery, 208 Bridge St. (Ⓒ **03/548-4040**), looks out into the leafy environs of Queen's Gardens. They have delicious counter food, with lots of vegetarian, gluten-free, and dairy-free options to choose from. They're open daily from 9am to 4pm in summer (until 3:30pm in winter).

There's excellent Japanese cuisine at **Miyazu Japanese Restaurant** ★★★, Rutherford Hotel, Nelson (Ⓒ **03/548-2299;** www.rutherfordhotel.co.nz), where you can watch slick Japanese chefs preparing your meal in front of you. They're open Monday through Saturday from 6pm. For a quick sushi fix, you can't go past **Haroo Sushi,** 50 Bridge St., Nelson (Ⓒ **03/546-6123**).

> ### (Finds) Mouthwatering Morsels
>
> For the best and biggest range of ice cream in town, head for **Penguino Gelato Café** ★★★, 85 Montgomery Sq., Nelson (Ⓒ **03/545-6450;** www.penguino. co.nz), where you'll find 18 flavors made from traditional Italian recipes. Try the gelato, sorbet, sundaes, "bambinos" for children, and big four-flavor cone for the ambitious. They're open daily in summer, 11am to 6pm. Chocoholics should celebrate the arrival of **Cocoa** ★★, 173 Hardy St. (Ⓒ **03/539-1080;** www.cocoa chocolate.co.nz), and in Richmond Mall, Richmond (Ⓒ **03/544-9030**). They combine Belgian chocolate with local Prenzel liqueurs to make sticky perfections you'll want to take home by the case. The Nelson store is open Monday through Saturday 9am to 5pm, and in Richmond daily 9am to 5pm.

ⓘ Tips Raise Your Glass

With a strong hop-growing history, it's not surprising that Nelson delivers on the beer front. Two to visit are **Founders Organic Brewery** ★★★, Founders Historic Park, 87 Atawhai Dr., Nelson (© **03/548-4638**; www.biobrew.co.nz), the country's first certified organic brewery complete with a cafe that serves great lunches; and **The Vic Brew Bar** ★★★, 281 Trafalgar St., Nelson (© **03/548-7631**; www. macs.co.nz), where they serve a range of premium, award-winning beers. They're open daily from 11am until late.

Boatshed Café ★ SEAFOOD   The over-the-water setting of this busy Nelson landmark is a terrific feature, and while it continues to deliver good seafood meals in a memorable location, the service and staff's attitudes fluctuate a little more than is desirable. You can handpick your own wriggly crabs or lobster and have them delivered to the pot for the chef's attention, or select from a large seafood menu.

350 Wakefield Quay. © **03/546-9783.** www.boatshedcafe.co.nz. Reservations required for dinner. Main courses NZ$28–NZ$32. AE, DC, MC, V. Daily 9am–late.

Harry's Bar ★★ PACIFIC/ASIAN   Locals seem very happy with Harry's and that's usually a good sign. Sited in old legal chambers, it has a reputation for serving consistently excellent meals with an emphasis on Asian flavors—crispy, red-braised duck and chili-salt squid are two favorites. The modern interior, built around glass and lighting effects, can distract you from the sometimes patchy service. It's lively, especially in the early evening when locals gather for predinner drinks.

306 Hardy St. © **03/539-0905.** Reservations recommended. Main courses NZ$22–NZ$32. AE, MC, V. Tues–Sat 5pm–late.

Hopgoods ★★★ MODERN NEW ZEALAND   Kevin Hopgood has worked with the Ruex brothers and Gordon Ramsey in London, and he brings a welcome style and professionalism to Nelson with this calm, cream, contemporary addition to the main street. Expect a showcase of local produce at great prices and a hoard of returning locals.

284 Trafalgar St. © **03/545-7191.** Reservations essential. Main courses NZ$26–NZ$38. AE, MC, V. Tues–Sat 9am–late; Mon 5:30pm–late.

Stingray ★ CAFE   It's a smart operator who can successfully combine fabulous organic and healthy vegetarian fare with a diverse menu that includes steaks, Thai-marinated chicken, and pizza in one of the hippest meeting places in town. Come here for amazing smoothies, fresh juices, organic salads, coffee, or champagne and tapas at the start of an evening out. As the evening progresses there's a distinct nightclub feel about the place.

8 Church St. © **03/545-8957.** www.stingraycafe.com. Main courses NZ$16–NZ$26. AE, MC, V. Daily 8am–late.

Zest Deli & Café ★ CAFE/DELI   You won't know where to start when you walk through the doors of this "giant food basket." It's a great little find, tucked between Hardy Street and Selwyn Place, just across the street from the equally delicious Stingray. This place—with fresh food (especially the pies and pastries) and coffee, plus a wide range of gourmet gift products—is worth looking for. And look out for their second deli

MARLBOROUGH & NELSON

13

NELSON, RICHMOND & MOTUEKA

on Bridge Street. I'm not sure I enjoy the coffee as much now that it's under new ownership, but it's definitely still worth visiting for its terrific deli and picnic foods.

5 Church St.; 56 Bridge St. (C) **03/546-7064** or 546-6332. NZ$10–NZ$20. MC, V. Church St.: Mon–Fri 7:30am–4:30pm; Sat 8am–4pm. Bridge St.: Mon–Sat 8:30am–4:30pm.

In Richmond

One of the popular casual favorites in the area is the **Honest Lawyer Country Pub** ★, 1 Point Rd., Monaco (C) **03/547-8850**; www.honestlawyer.co.nz), which is not actually in the country at all, but near Nelson Airport. It's a replica of a classic English pub, offering breakfast, lunch, and dinner daily from 7am till late. But by far the nicest Richmond eatery is **Bouterey's Restaurant** ★★★, 251 Queen St., Richmond (C) **03/544-1114;** www.bou500.co.nz). It's open Monday to Saturday for dinner and features fresh and organic local produce whisked into edible delicacies by Michelin-trained owner/chef, Matt Bouterey. Before coming to Nelson he ran the famous Sugar Reef Restaurant in London and cooked for celebrities like Angelina Jolie and Michael Caine. His international menu will seduce you in seconds.

In Motueka/Mapua

The **Smokehouse** ★★, Shed 3, Mapua Wharf, Mapua (C) **03/540-2280**; www.smokehouse.co.nz), hangs out over the turquoise depths of Mapua Estuary, and the menu is completely dominated by fish dishes, many of them using the smoked product prepared on the premises. It's well signposted from the main highway and worth the sidetrack. It's open daily from 9am to 9pm. The **Naked Bun Patisserie** ★★, 66–68 Aranui Rd., Mapua (C) **03/540-3656;** www.thenakedbun.co.nz), is a European-style patisserie, where you'll get not only divine sweet things but also organic breads and savory snacks. It's open Monday through Friday from 7:30am to 4:30pm; and weekends 8am to 4:30pm, and has indoor and outdoor dining. There are also dining opportunities at some of the local wineries (see "The Moutere Hills Wineries," earlier in this chapter).

3 ABEL TASMAN NATIONAL PARK & GOLDEN BAY ★★★

Marahau, the southern gateway to the park: 67km (42 miles) NW of Nelson; Takaka, the gateway to Golden Bay: 109km (68 miles) NW of Nelson

Abel Tasman is New Zealand's smallest national park. It protects 23,000 hectares (57,000 acres) of easily accessible coastline, offering unbeatable gold-sand beaches and forested headlands. Marahau and Totaranui are the main gateways to the park, a 1½- and 2½-hour drive, respectively, from Nelson.

Farther north, Golden Bay sits peacefully beyond the twists and turns of Takaka Hill, opening out in a spread of forested parks and golden beaches. The scenery is breathtaking, and the area draws many visitors keen to hike the Abel Tasman's Coastal Track and Kahurangi's Heaphy Track. Today, it is a fertile mix of dairy farming and arty alternative lifestyles—a reflection of the number of people who've reached this corner of the world and found they didn't want to leave.

ESSENTIALS

GETTING THERE & GETTING AROUND   **By Plane**   **Capital Air** (C) **0800/588-885;** www.capitalair.co.nz), has scheduled flights between Wellington and Takaka, plus

to Golden Bay takes just 50 minutes. Several other small operators, including **Abel Tas-man Air** (© **0800/304-560** in NZ; www.abeltasmanair.co.nz), also service this area.

By Coach (Bus) Abel Tasman Coachlines, 27 Bridge St., Nelson (© **03/548-0285** in Nelson or 528-8850 in Motueka; www.abeltasmantravel.co.nz), operates year-round daily service from Nelson to Kaiteriteri, Marahau, Totaranui, and Abel Tasman National Park. It also provides connecting service to Kahurangi National Park and the north entrance to the Heaphy Track. They offer a number of well-priced 1-day Abel Tasman packages. **KBus,** P.O. Box 1079, Blenheim (© **0508/458-835** in NZ, or 03/358-8355; www.kbus.co.nz), has scheduled service between Picton, Blenheim, Motueka, Nelson, Abel Tasman, Golden Bay, and Heaphy Track, plus service between Collingwood and Takaka.

By Shuttle Trek Express (© **0800/128-735** in NZ, or 03/540-2042; www.trek express.co.nz) operates a four-wheel-drive shuttle to Kahurangi Park and all other major hikes in the area.

By Car The trip from Nelson to Takaka via State Highway 60 takes about 2 hours and includes a long, steep, winding section crossing Takaka Hill. To reach Marahau, turn right at the bottom of Takaka Hill, just past Motueka (don't go over Takaka Hill), and drive through Kaiteriteri. The trip takes about 1½ hours.

VISITOR INFORMATION The **Department of Conservation,** 62 Commercial St., Takaka (© **03/525-8026;** www.doc.govt.nz), provides information on the national parks and huts available on the tracks. It's open Monday through Friday from 8:30am to 4pm. The **Golden Bay i-SITE Visitor Centre,** Willow Street, Takaka (© **03/525-9136;** www. nelsonnz.com), is open summer daily from 9am to 5pm, and winter daily from 9am until 4pm (closed Dec 25). The **Farewell Spit Visitor Centre & Paddlecrab Kitchen,** RD1, Collingwood, Golden Bay (© **03/524-8454;** www.farewell-spit.co.nz), is open daily most of the year and has informative displays on the upper reaches of Golden Bay. Further information on Golden Bay can be found at www.goldenbaynz.co.nz.

EXPLORING ABEL TASMAN NATIONAL PARK ★★★

Abel Tasman is the jewel among popular national parks. It's a sea kayaker's paradise, and it's great for swimming and fishing. The **Abel Tasman Coastal Track** is one of the Department of Conservation's eight identified Great Walks and the only coast track of its kind in the country. It can be done in 3 to 5 days, or combined with water taxis or sea kayaks for added interest. See p. 92 for more details.

Sea kayaking is probably the best way to see the area, and **Abel Tasman Kayaks** ★★★, Main Road, Marehau (© **0800/732-529** in NZ, or 03/527-8022; www.abeltasmankayaks.co.nz), pioneered the activity in this region. It has a large base with secure car parking and hot showers. A range of guided trips are available year-round and they'll give you an insight into the Maori and European history of the area. The most popular are the full-day guided excursions, which can include guided walks or swimming with seals, or both. Prices for 1-day tours range from NZ$175 to NZ$220. They also have a 3-day kayak-camping tour (catered) for NZ$575, departing Monday, Wednesday, and Friday. You must be 14 and over for all tours. Prices include pickup and transport from Motueka. Return transport to Nelson costs NZ$25. **Ocean River Sea Kayaking** ★★, Main Road, Marehau (© **0800/447-352** in NZ, or 03/527-8340; www. oceanriver.co.nz), specializes in unguided rentals from NZ$65 per person per day. They'll give you all the instruction you need and you can unwind at the end in the company's hot tub! *Note:* If you're being picked up from Nelson for any of these park excursions, you'll have to allow 1½ hours each way on a bus. You'll leave Nelson at 7:15am, 8:30am, or 3:40pm, returning 1:55pm, 5:15pm, 6pm, or 7:15pm. There's only one bus in from late April to October, leaving Nelson at 8:30am, returning at 6pm.

Abel Tasman Wilson's Experiences ★★★, 265 High St., Motueka (© **0800/223-582** in NZ, or 03/528-2027; www.abeltasman.co.nz), operates buses, launches, and beachfront lodges. It's an award-winning family-owned business run by the Wilson family, who pioneered tourism in the park in 1977. They arrange 1- to 5-day guided walks and sea-kayaking trips that include stays at their Torrent Bay Lodge and Meadowbank Homestead-Awaroa. All trips can be arranged as walking only, or walking/sea kayaking combinations, and skilled guides and chefs provide quality experiences and meals. During high season, a 1-day guided sea kayaking trip costs NZ$120 adults and NZ$90 children ages 10 to 14; the 3-day guided walk is NZ$1,200 for adults, NZ$985 for children 8 to 14; the 5-day guided kayak and walk trip costs NZ$1,820 for adults only. Rates are lower from mid-April to mid-October. Scenic cruises are also offered on the company's **Vista Cruises,** in the new catamaran *Abel Tasman Voyager.* It carries 140 passengers and makes three trips a day. The Southern Cruise and Walk package costs NZ$62 for adults and NZ$31 for children 5 to 14 years. The Northern Cruise and Walk costs NZ$70 for adults and NZ$35 for children.

Abel Tasman Aqua Taxi ★, Main Road, Marahau (© **0800/278-282** in NZ, or 03/527-8083; www.aquataxis.co.nz), has a 3-hour cruise that visits points of interest along the park beaches and the fur-seal colony on Tonga Island. The price ranges from NZ$65 to NZ$85. If you're short on time, do the cruise if nothing else, or you'll miss seeing this spectacular unspoiled coast. Another lovely way to experience the best of the Abel Tasman is to join **Abel Tasman Cruises** ★, Port Nelson (© **0508/488-066** in NZ; www.abeltasmancruises.co.nz), in Nelson, for their day trip to Awaroa. You see all the gorgeous golden sand beaches on the way and have a fabulous lunch at Awaroa Lodge before returning to Nelson on their fast catamaran. This costs NZ$215 per person and runs November through April.

For a terrific guided walk, look no further than **Kahurangi Guided Walks** ★★, Dodson Road, Takaka, Golden Bay (© **03/525-7177;** www.kahurangiwalks.co.nz). They offer 1-, 3-, or 5-day walking trips in the Abel Tasman and Kahurangi National Parks. There are excellent half-day trips for those on a tight schedule, for NZ$35 to NZ$75 per person. **Bush and Beyond Guided Walks** ★★, 35 School Rd., Motueka (© **03/528-9054;** www.bushandbeyond.co.nz), has day and multiday walks priced from NZ$195.

Where to Stay

Kaiteriteri Beach has a wealth of accommodations, but you'll have to book months in advance. At Marahau Beach, backpackers and campers should check out the **Barn,** Harvey Road, Marahau (© **03/527-8043;** fax 03/527-8440), the closest lodgings to the park, with a shared dorm, double and twin rooms, and motor-home or tent sites from NZ$25 to NZ$75. **Marahau Beach Camp,** Franklin Street, Marahau (©/fax **03/527-8176;** www.abeltasmanmarahaucamp.co.nz), also has backpacker and camping facilities. There are smarter rooms at the ecofriendly **Abel Tasman Ocean View Chalets,** 305 Sandy Bay Rd., Marahau (© **03/527-8232;** www.accommodationabeltasman.co.nz), with rates of NZ$138 to NZ$255 for their one- and two-bedroom chalets. They are a member of the Nelson Sustainable Tourism Charter.

My pick for this area is ecofriendly **Awaroa Lodge** ★★★, Abel Tasman National Park (© **03/528-8758;** www.awaroalodge.co.nz), which has 26 modern rooms from NZ$275 to NZ$400. It's tucked into the northern end of the park, is a feature destination of the Abel Tasman Coastal Track, and has its own restaurant, which serves food grown in their amazing organic garden. It has won a New Zealand Tourism Innovation in Ecotourism award for its sound ecological practices, which include a sophisticated, sustainable waste-management system. There is no road access. You reach the lodge via foot, kayak, water taxi, catamaran, helicopter, or small, fixed-wing aircraft. Another ecofriendly choice is **Abel Tasman Marahau Lodge** ★, Marahau Beach (© **03/527-8250;** www.abeltasman marahaulodge.co.nz), which has 14 smart studio units with en-suite bathrooms for NZ$165 to NZ$280. It's not the Hilton, but you do get great service, a magical setting, and incredible silence; and it has a Qualmark Enviro-Silver rating.

EXPLORING GOLDEN BAY ★★★

The main town near Golden Bay is Takaka, which has an astoundingly small population of 1,100. Another 28km (17 miles) north is Collingwood, which is even smaller. While in Takaka, you can peek in at the **Golden Bay Museum & Gallery,** Commercial Street (© **03/525-6268** or 525-9990), open daily in summer from 10am to 4pm (closed Sun in winter). There are also several working artists in the area, and the free brochure *Arts of Golden Bay,* available from the visitor center (© **03/525-9136**), details the locations and visiting hours of some of the best.

Golden Bay is rich in natural attractions, and one of the best known is **Te Waikoropupu Springs** ★★, called Pupu Springs by the locals. Here you'll find rushing water claimed to be the clearest fresh water in the world. It's signposted just north of Takaka township.

Cave formations are also common; one of the most famous, **Harwood's Hole,** plummets an awesome 180m (600 ft.) straight down. The visitor center can supply you with details. There are three other cave systems worth investigating. **Ngarua Caves,** 20km (12 miles) from Motueka on Takaka Hill (© **03/528-8093**), are easily negotiated and feature stalactites aplenty and the skeletal remains of the extinct moa. Guided tours are given on the hour between 10am and 4pm from mid-September to June 7. Admission is NZ$15. **Te Anaroa & Rebecca Caves,** Rockville, Golden Bay (© **03/525-6044**), have easy access and the best glowworms. They're very beautiful, but some of the rooflines are low and narrow, which may put you off if you're claustrophobic. Admission is NZ$15 for adults and NZ$6 for children ages 5 to 15; call for tour times. **Rawhiti Caves,** also in Golden Bay (© **03/525-7177**), cost NZ$15 for adults and NZ$7 for children ages 5 to 15. It takes a 40-minute bush walk to reach the caves, where you're greeted with a huge entrance and a steep descent. You need to be agile for this outing, and it's not recommended for children 4 and under.

Local rock climbers know all about the many attributes of **Payne's Ford Scenic Reserve,** near Takaka. The limestone bluffs they favor dominate the area; a track through the reserve follows an old tramway line. You'll find excellent swimming holes in the nearby Takaka River.

All along the road from Takaka to Collingwood, you'll see signs pointing to the coast. Each beach is different, but much of the bay is shallow; swimming at high tide involves a lot less walking. Tata Beach is deeper.

Another 26km (16 miles) north of Collingwood is the base of **Farewell Spit,** a unique sand spit 35km (22 miles) long and nearly a half-mile wide. All along its length are sand dunes as high as seven- to eight-story buildings. The bird life here is amazing, as it is a migratory stopover for several species. **Farewell Spit Eco Tours** ★★, 6 Tasman St., Collingwood ((C) **0800/808-257** in NZ, or 03/524-8257; www.farewellspit.co.nz), has a range of superb tours to Farewell Spit. Most popular is the Lighthouse trip, a 4½-hour excursion that costs NZ$120 for adults, NZ$50 children 15 and under. There are also special bird-watching trips by arrangement that range from NZ$120 to NZ$145 for adults, NZ$50 to NZ$55 children 15 and under. Bring binoculars and a camera.

For information on the **Heaphy Track** and **Kahurangi National Park,** see "Tramping" in chapter 5. And pick up the two free guides *Bike Tasman* and *Walk Tasman* from any Nelson visitor center.

Where to Stay

Sans Souci Inn ★, 11 Richmond Rd., Pohara Beach ((C)/fax **03/525-8663;** www.sans souciinn.co.nz), is an ideal beach stay near Takaka if you're into simplicity and style. The seven-unit grass-roofed inn, run by a young Swiss couple with a strong interest in sustainable tourism, is a divine hideaway with a Japanese feel. Mediterranean floor tiles, low futon-style beds, and scented Lawson cypress ceilings give it a unique character. They use solar energy and recycle all waste. Doubles are NZ$105 and a restaurant is on-site. If you'd like a big, self-contained holiday home, **Villa on the Bay** ★, Beachfront, Pohara Beach ((C) **03/525-8465;** www.villaonthebay.co.nz), will be hard to beat. It has five lovely rooms, modern facilities throughout, and it comes with a car—all for NZ$790 per night (minimum 2-night stay).

Farther north, **Collingwood Homestead** ★★, 15 Elizabeth St., Collingwood ((C) **03/524-8079;** www.collingwoodhomestead.co.nz), is one of the best homestays in the region. It's hard to find fault with the personalized hospitality and three large bedrooms with modern bathrooms. The rate is NZ$265, which includes a wonderful breakfast. If you'd like to rent a holiday home in this region, contact **Golden Bay i-SITE,** Willow Street, Takaka ((C) **03/525-9136;** fax 03/525-9288; www.nelsonnz.com). They manage over 60 holiday homes and can point you in the direction of a unique stay. But get in early, as New Zealand holidaymakers love this area too.

Where to Dine

It's easy to recommend the **Wholemeal Café** ★★, 60 Commercial St., Takaka ((C) **03/525-9426**). It has the best food in the area, and you can't help feeling it's horrendously healthy as well as delicious. It's also a great place to pick up picnic fare. The cafe is open in summer daily from 7:30am to 9:30pm, and, after Easter, Sunday through Tuesday from 8:30am to 5pm, Thursday through Saturday from 8:30am until late.

Near Collingwood, **Paddlecrab Kitchen,** Farewell Spit, Puponga ((C) **03/524-8708**), will surprise you with the standard of its food. It may be well out on a geographical limb, but combine its incredible location with inventive cuisine, courteous service, and good-value dining and you'll find it was worth the extra miles. It's open daily October through April from 8am until 10pm, and August through September from 10am until 4pm. It's closed June and July. At Pohara, enjoy a wide choice of seafood and gourmet pizzas at **Penguin Café & Bar,** 818 Abel Tasman Dr. ((C) **03/525-6126**). It's open daily in summer from 9am.

Christchurch & Canterbury

Christchurch may have a reputation for being the most English and the most conservative of New Zealand's major cities, but it's far from quiet and subdued—and let's not get carried away with hype: It's not *that* English. A river, a few parks, and old buildings do not England make. That said, it's a picturesque city that's worth more than a cursory glance. I've lived here for 20 years and I'm pleased to say Christchurch can still surprise me.

Christchurch's modern airport provides the gateway to the South Island, affectionately known as "The Mainland" by those who live here. It is the third-largest city in New Zealand—a prosperous place that is home to 370,000 people who enjoy the lowest annual rainfall of any of the four major cities, the greatest temperature extremes, and 2,120 hours of sunshine annually.

With one-eighth of its area devoted to public parks, reserves, and recreation grounds, and with the 186-hectare (459-acre) Hagley Park smack in its center, you

shouldn't be surprised to find Christchurch tagged New Zealand's Garden City. This verdant core, along with the Avon River, a spread of Victorian architecture, and the avenues and squares, is almost entirely responsible for the reputation of "Englishness." Plus, with a multitude of adventure packages to offer, the city is a mecca for anyone who likes a racy edge to his or her holiday. Whether you choose leisurely days discovering the city's cultural foundation or adrenaline-pumping outdoor activities, you'll find that conservative old Christchurch can dish up a few surprises.

The province of Canterbury, stretching from the Southern Alps to the Pacific Ocean, has legendary physical attractions, from ski fields and fishing rivers to the Port Hills tramping tracks and east coast beaches. Day-trip options from Christchurch include Kaikoura, Akaroa, Hanmer, Arthur's Pass, and Methven—each presenting its own version of provincial hospitality, rural escapism, and heart-stopping outdoor adventure.

1 ORIENTATION

ARRIVING

BY PLANE Christchurch has frequent air service from all major centers via Air New Zealand (© **0800/737-000;** www.airnewzealand.co.nz) and Air New Zealand Link. **Christchurch International Airport** is 10km (6 miles) from Cathedral Square and it receives direct flights from several countries. The international terminal features everything travelers will need, including boutique shopping and a **visitor information center** (© **03/ 353-7783;** www.christchurchairport.co.nz). A massive upgrade is now underway and the first stage—a new covered carpark—is already completed. Further plans include the integration of international and domestic terminals with improved services and retail outlets. The

CHRISTCHURCH & CANTERBURY

14

ORIENTATION

ACCOMMODATIONS ■
Base Backpacker **28**
The Charlotte Jane **2**
Christchurch City
    Central YHA **26**
Coastal Cliffs Bed &
    Breakfast **52**
Crowne Plaza Christchurch **18**
Elm Tree House **2**
The George Christchurch **5**
Hadleigh **15**
The Heritage Christchurch **38**
Hotel SO **42**
Orari Bed & Breakfast **32**
Otahuna Lodge **14**
Springfield Cottage **15**
Stonehurst **24**
The Weston House **4**
The Worcester of Christchurch **7**
YMCA **11**

DINING ◆
Ace Wasabi **16**
Aiki Japanese
    Organic Kitchen **49**
Bodhi Tree **21**
Cafe Metro **20**
Caffe Roma **34**
C1 Espresso **47**
Canterbury Tales **18**
Dux de Lux **33**
Flying Burrito Brothers **25**
The Globe Café **48**
The Honey Pot Café **45**
Joe's Garage **41**
Le Café **8**
Little India Bistro & Tandoor **27**
Lotus Heart **50**
Oasis **23**
Pedro's **40**
Pescatore **5**
Portofino **30**
Raj Mahal **39**
Retour **22**
Rotherams **12**
Saggio di Vino **1**
Sala Sala **29**
Simo's **43**
Sticky Fingers Restaurant & Bar **36**
Two Fat Indians **46**
Underground Coffee **19**
Vic's Café & Bakehouse **3**

ⓘ Information
░ Pedestrian Mall
✉ Post Office
– – – – Tramway

Bealey Ave.
Harper Ave.
Dublin St.
Victoria St.
Dorset St.
Park Terrace

**NORTH
HAGLEY PARK**

*Victoria
Lake*

Avon River

Conservatories

Park Terrace

Gloucester St.

CHRIST'S COLLEGE

BOTANIC GARDENS

Canterbury
Museum **6**

Avon River

Riccarton Ave.

Rolleston Ave.

ARTS CENTRE

Cashel St.

**CHRISTCHURCH
HOSPITAL**

Cambridge

Oxford

Antigua St.

ATTRACTIONS ●
Air Force Museum of New Zealand **13**
The Arts Centre **10**
Canterbury Museum **6**
Christchurch Art Gallery **31**
Christchurch Casino **17**
Christchurch Cathedral **37**
Court Theatre **9**
Christchurch Gondola **53**
Ferrymead Heritage Park **53**
Science Alive **51**
South of Lichfield (SOL) **44**
Southern Encounter Aquarium & Kiwi House **35**

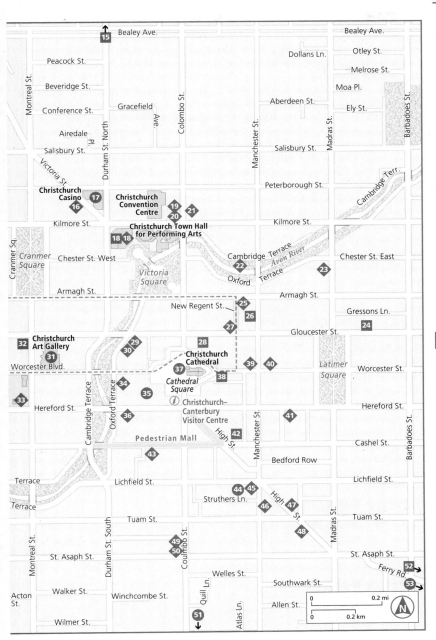

airport will function as usual throughout the upgrade, scheduled for completion in mid-2012. The **visitor information center** in the domestic terminal (✆ **03/353-7774**) will book accommodations and transportation at no charge. Also here are car-rental firms, baggage wrapping and storage facilities, a bank, a florist, a bookstore, a confectionery store, a hair salon, Internet kiosks (including 15 min. free wireless access), a restaurant, a souvenir shop, and a duty-free store. For further international airport details, check www.christchurchairport.co.nz.

Several shuttle companies operate between the airport and Central City. **Super Shuttle** (✆ **0800/748-885** in NZ; www.supershuttle.co.nz) runs daily 24 hours and charges NZ$18 to NZ$20. The **Red Bus City Flyer** (✆ **0800/733-287** in NZ; www.redbus.co.nz) departs from the airport and from Worcester Street, near the Square, opposite Regent Theatre and calls at the Bus Exchange before returning to the airport. It leaves on the half-hour Monday through Friday, on the hour Saturday and Sunday, and costs NZ$7 one-way. For a 20-minute taxi ride, call **First Direct** (✆ **03/377-5555**). The fare to Central City should be NZ$25 to NZ$40.

By Train & Coach (Bus)   Train service to and from Christchurch has been greatly reduced as railway companies consolidate their operations. The TranzAlpine (Greymouth), and the TranzCoastal (Picton) are the only two still running. For information, call **Tranz Scenic** at (✆ **0800/872-467** in NZ, or 03/341-2588; www.tranzscenic.co.nz). The **Christchurch Railway Station** is on Clarence Street, in Addington. Regular shuttles run from the station to the city. The Metro 51 Bus to Tower Junction is the closest bus service.

InterCity (✆ **0800/468-372** in NZ, or 03/377-0951; www.intercity.co.nz) covers most of the South Island, offering service between Christchurch, Dunedin, Fox and Franz Josef Glaciers, Greymouth and the West Coast, Wanaka, Queenstown and Mount Cook, Invercargill, Timaru, Picton, and Kaikoura. If you prefer something cheaper, go with **Kiwi Experience** (✆ **09/369-9410**; www.kiwiexperience.com).

BY CAR   If you're coming from the north, you'll drive in on State Highway 1 and enter the city through the northwest suburbs of Papanui and Merivale. It's 4 to 5 hours from Picton and 2½ hours from Kaikoura. From Dunedin, via Timaru and Ashburton, you'll also be on State Highway 1. It takes 5 hours from Dunedin, 2 from Timaru. From the southwest, via Lake Tekapo and Geraldine, travel on Highway 79 to Highway 77 and then Highway 73; this takes you to Mount Hutt and over the Rakaia River. If you're coming from the West Coast, you'll go over Arthur's Pass and enter Christchurch at Upper Riccarton. This trip takes 4 hours. Christchurch is 366km (227 miles) north of Dunedin, 350km (217 miles) south of Picton, and 254km (157 miles) southeast of Greymouth.

VISITOR INFORMATION

The **Christchurch & Canterbury i-SITE Visitor Centre** is in the Old Chief Post Office Building, Cathedral Square West (✆ **03/379-9629**; fax 03/377-2424; www.christchurchnz.com). It's open 7 days from 8:30am to 5pm (closed Dec 25 only). Useful websites are www.bethere.org.nz or www.whatsonchristchurch.co.nz.

SPECIAL EVENTS

Christchurch is the festival capital of New Zealand—no matter when you visit, it's bound to coincide with a festival of some sort. The **World Buskers Festival** ★★★ (✆ **03/377-2365**; www.worldbuskersfestival.com), from mid- to late January, is the largest street performance festival in the Southern Hemisphere. You'll be treated to jazz and comedy shows, as well as acts of juggling, contortionism, and more. In February, the city bursts into bloom with the **Festival of Flowers** (© 03/365-5403; www.festivalofflowers.co.nz) and the **Ellerslie International Flower Show** (© 03/379-4561; www.ellerslieflower show.co.nz). The **Christchurch Arts Festival** ★★★ (© 03/365-2223; www.artsfestival. co.nz) is staged every 2 years in July and showcases international talent. The next one will be held in 2011. **Showtime Canterbury** ★★, featuring the **Canterbury A & P Show** (© 03/343-3033; www.theshow.co.nz), is an absolute tradition in this part of the world. Staged the second week of November, it features thoroughbred and standard-bred racing.

CITY LAYOUT

Cathedral Square (also known as the Square) is the center point around which the main roads are laid out in a grid system, surrounded by four main avenues—Bealey, Moorehouse, Deans, and Fitzgerald. The winding Avon River meanders 24km (15 miles) from the west of Christchurch, through the city and out to sea. The Port Hills, south of the city, are an ever-present landmark from which you can always get your bearings. Colombo Street is the main street running north-south to the Port Hills.

THE NEIGHBORHOODS IN BRIEF

Fendalton This is the heart of Christchurch conservatism and money—the southern equivalent of Auckland's Remuera. You'll find wonderful old homes and beautiful tree-lined streets, but its retail center is small, unimaginative, and easily bypassed altogether in favor of Merivale shopping. There are few accommodations in this area.

Merivale Those among the moneyed set who consider themselves a little more contemporary throng to Merivale to shop and dine. Located between Papanui and the inner city, it is an attractive suburb, close to the heart of things, and it offers a good number of B&Bs along with "Motel Mile," which stretches south along Papanui Road from Merivale Mall to Bealey Avenue. Always safe, in all senses of the word, it is a pleasant place to be, and you can walk here from the heart of the city in about 30 minutes.

St. Albans This older suburb lies adjacent to Merivale to the east—some would call it the poor man's Merivale, but now that most of the old villas have

been significantly renovated, real-estate prices are a little out of the "poor" league. There is no real retail heart here and just a few lodgings—predominantly at the Bealey Avenue end of the suburb, where there is another good selection of motels.

Inner City I recommend finding accommodations in the inner city area, which generally consists of the area within the four main avenues: Deans, Bealey, Moorehouse, and Fitzgerald. Most of the major hotels are close to Cathedral Square (known as the Square) and the shopping on Colombo Street, City Mall (the pedestrian-only zone of Cashel St.), and Manchester and High streets. The main restaurant/bar zone is situated on Oxford Terrace, which borders the Avon River and connects with the lower end of City Mall. Hagley Park is a short walk.

Hagley Park/Botanic Gardens Theoretically still the inner city, this compact area just west of the central business district is easily defined by its proximity to Hagley Park and the

Botanic Gardens. It is generally the area west of Montreal Street, along Park Avenue, and through to Deans Avenue on the west side of the park. You'll find excellent accommodations and some of the major attractions, such as the Canterbury Museum, the Arts Centre, and the new Art Gallery. It's a 5- to 10-minute walk along Worcester Boulevard (serviced by the tram) to the Square and the visitor center.

Riccarton/Ilam Riccarton is on the western side of Hagley Park, and apart from its huge shopping mall, a proliferation of cheap Asian restaurants, and a Sunday market, it has little for me to recommend. The area between Riccarton and Fendalton is known as Ilam, and this is where you'll find Canterbury University tucked into a beautiful leafy enclave.

Sumner Once a holiday spot for Christchurch residents, Sumner has long since become a suburb of the city itself. It's a delightful place about 15 to 30 minutes from the city depending on traffic. The neighborhood is characterized by steep hillsides dotted with prime real estate with stunning views of the city and coast, as well as by quaint holiday homes that still sit near the beach. It's easily accessed by bus, has a cute village feel, and offers a thriving social life with at least 20 cafes and restaurants. In summer, the young surfing crowd gathers on The Esplanade, and there's generally volleyball and beach fun aplenty.

Lyttelton This is a quaint port village over the Port Hills from Christchurch, a 20- to 30-minute drive away. You'll either love it or hate it; Lyttelton seldom gets reactions in between. Quaint, to some, turns out to be ugly and gray to others. It has few lodgings and is considerably less convenient for Christchurch sightseeing. However, a visit here makes for a nice drive and their Saturday farmer's market is the best in Christchurch. Head out to Sumner and go up over the Port Hills and down into Lyttelton. You can then return to the Central City via the tunnel. (Of course, you can use the tunnel both ways for a quicker trip.)

2 GETTING AROUND

BY PUBLIC BUS All local buses operate out of the **Bus Exchange,** Colombo and Lichfield streets (✆ **03/366-8855;** www.metroinfo.org.nz). North-south buses are based on Colombo Street; east-west buses are based within the building. **Red Bus Limited** (✆ **0800/733-287** in NZ, or 03/379-4260; www.redbus.co.nz) operates the majority of these urban bus services, with others provided by **Leopard Coachlines (Urban Cat;** ✆ **03/73-8100).** The **Bus Info Centre** is on the second level of the building for details on the complete service. Zoned fares range from NZ$3 to NZ$10. For information and details on all-day passes, contact **Bus Info** (✆ **03/366-8855;** www.metroinfo.org.nz).

Check out the advantages of a **Metrocard All Day Pass,** which costs NZ$4 for adults and NZ$2 for children, and gives as many trips as you like in a day. Purchase it from your bus driver or Metro Info in the Bus Exchange, which is open daily 7:30am to 6pm Monday through Friday and 9:30am to 5:30pm weekends. If you're planning an evening out, consider the **Midnight Express Service** ★★, which leaves on four major suburban routes on the hour between midnight and 4am. Just look out for the distinctive purple buses, or call Bus Info (see above) for route details. It will save you the hassle of finding carparks and it costs just NZ$6, or you can use your Metrocard.

A suburban bus system, the **Orbiter,** allows you to travel around the outskirts without having to go into Central City. The bright-green buses run every 15 minutes during the day and every half-hour in evenings and on weekends. They cost NZ$3 and you can use your Metrocard. The **Metro Star** is an extension of that cross-suburban service, linking all the major suburban shopping malls. Its orange buses run every 15 minutes Monday through Friday and every 30 minutes on evenings and weekends. It uses a long-term electronic card system, which is prepaid and can be used on all other buses. Cash is accepted, but it's more expensive and you only get one free transfer, as opposed to unlimited transfers with Metrocards.

The upstairs information center at the Bus Exchange has takeaway timetables and all the information you'll need.

BY SHUTTLE   The free central-city electric shuttle is bright yellow; its pickup points are designated by bright-yellow street towers. The shuttle travels between the Casino, Town Hall, Victoria Square, Cathedral Square, City Mall, South City, Smiths City, and Hoyts 8 on Moorehouse Avenue at 10-minute intervals during the day, 15-minute intervals at night. The service does not operate on December 25, Boxing Day, New Year's Day, or Good Friday.

BY PRIVATE BUS   The **Best Attractions Bus** (✆ 0800/484-485; www.leisuretours. co.nz) offers transportation to the area's most popular attractions: The **Must See Four** goes to Willowbank Wildlife Reserve, the International Antarctic Centre, Air Force Museum, and Christchurch Tram. It takes 6 hours and costs NZ$125 per person, which includes all transportation and admission prices. The **Big Five** includes Willowbank, the Antarctic Centre, Christchurch Tram, a Lyttelton Harbour excursion with Christchurch Wildlife Cruises, and a ride on the Christchurch Gondola. It takes 8 hours and costs NZ$185 per person.

BY TRAMWAY   Christchurch's short but pleasant tramway (✆ 03/366-7830; www. tram.co.nz) runs from Cathedral Square down Worcester Boulevard, crossing the Avon River to the Arts Centre. From here, it turns right to Rolleston Avenue and travels on to Armagh and New Regent streets and back to the Square. It operates from 9am to 9pm in summer and until 6pm in winter; one circuit takes 25 minutes and there are 11 stops along the route. Tickets, which can be purchased on the tram, are NZ$15 for adults, NZ$5 children ages 5 to 15, NZ$35 for a family, and you can hop on and off the tram as often as you like for 2 days.

ⓘ Tips   A Note on Safety

Like any large city, Christchurch has its criminal element, but if you use common sense, there's no reason why you should see any evidence of it. It's generally considered not a good idea to wander about in Cathedral Square alone after midnight, and most inner city streets east of Manchester Street need a little more caution. It also pays to give Latimer Square a wide berth if you're alone after dark. The inner city, especially around City Mall and Oxford Terrace, is generally safe, as there are always plenty of people about at all hours, and security cameras now operate in some areas.

Tips **An Easy Introduction**

If you're in town for a few days and want to get a feel for the inner city, head for the Square and look for the red-and-black **Personal Guiding Service** kiosk. Trained guides—they're in red and black, too—offer daily 2-hour walking tours at 10am and 1pm from October through April, and at 1pm from May through September. Tours also depart 15 minutes earlier from outside the nearby visitor center. For more information, call 📞 **03/379-9629.**

BY TAXI   There are taxi stands scattered around the inner city and at all transport terminals. **First Direct** (📞 **03/377-5555**) has a reputation for being the best priced. For taxis that can accommodate wheelchairs, call 📞 **03/379-9788.**

BY CAR   If you want to see only the main central-city sights, you probably won't need a car; you can make the most of free shuttles and cheap tour buses for those farther-afield destinations. And don't forget the Midnight Express bus (see above) if you're staying late in the city. If you do have a car, driving in Christchurch is straightforward. Most on-street parking is metered or has time limits. It's a good idea to make use of the centrally located municipal parking buildings, most of which offer your first hour's parking free. They are well signposted on Kilmore Street over the Crowne Plaza Hotel; in Cashel Street near the Grand Chancellor Hotel; on Lichfield Street near the Durham Street intersection; on Oxford Terrace near the Main Library; on Manchester Street near the intersection with Armagh Street; and under the new Art Gallery on Gloucester Street. You'll find free car parking in Hagley Park during the day—entrance is at the end of Armagh Street.

BY BICYCLE   Christchurch is a biker's heaven—it's flat (except for the Port Hills), and motorists are used to a high volume of bicycle traffic. There are cycle lanes set aside in many areas, especially in the northwest suburbs, where there's quite a bit of university bike traffic. For information on rentals, see "Outdoor Pursuits," later in this chapter.

ON FOOT   Most of the main central-city attractions are well placed for easy walking—especially in the Arts Centre/Botanic Gardens area. Shopping areas are fairly far-flung, but you can make use of the free electric shuttle or the very reasonably priced tram to take the load off your feet every so often.

Fast Facts   **Christchurch**

American Express   The office at 773 Colombo St. (📞 **0800/656-660** in NZ) accepts mail for cardholders, issues and changes traveler's checks, and replaces lost and stolen traveler's checks and American Express cards.

Area Code   The telephone area code (STD) is **03.**

Babysitters   **Tuam Street Early Learning Centre,** 161 Tuam St. (📞 **03/941-8055**), open Monday through Friday from 8am to 5:30pm, can be contacted for babysitting services. Many hotels can also furnish evening babysitters.

Currency Exchange The **ANZ Bank Bureau de Change,** at Hereford and Colombo streets, in Cathedral Square (℡ **0800/269-296**), is open Monday through Friday from 9am to 4:30pm, Saturday 10am to 3pm.

Doctors For referrals, emergencies, or medical care, contact **After Hours Surgery,** Colombo Street and Bealey Avenue (℡ **03/365-7777**).

Emergencies Dial ℡ **111** to call the police, report a fire, or request an ambulance.

Hospitals **Christchurch Hospital,** Oxford Terrace and Riccarton Avenue (℡ **03/364-0640**), has an Accident and Emergency Department.

Internet Access There are several Internet providers located around Cathedral Square. Try e Blah Blah, Crystal Plaza, 77 Cathedral Sq. (℡ **03/377-2381**), which is open daily 8:30am till late. They also rent mobile phones.

Pharmacies Go to **Urgent Pharmacy,** 931 Colombo St. (℡ **03/366-4439**).

Post Office The **Christchurch Mail Centre** is at 53–59 Hereford St. and is open Monday through Friday from 9am to 5pm. For all post offices, call ℡ **0800/501-501.**

Services for Travelers with Disabilities Contact **Disability Information Service,** 314 Worcester St. (℡ **03/366-6189;** fax 03/379-5939; dis@disinfo.co.nz), open Monday through Friday from 9am to 4:30pm.

3 WHERE TO STAY

I recommend staying in the inner city or near Hagley Park, within the four major avenues (see "City Layout," above), so you're within walking distance of the main attractions. All rates quoted include the 12.5% GST and free off-street parking unless otherwise stated.

IN THE INNER CITY
Expensive

Crowne Plaza Christchurch ★★★ The Crowne Plaza is still seen by many as Christchurch's number-one luxury hotel. It's hard to miss its architectural dominance of Victoria Square, and what really sells the place is its central-city location and its unquestionably high level of service. All rooms are well maintained with elegant contemporary furniture; many units have excellent city views. The Club rooms occupy the two top floors and have extra touches and access to Club Lounge with free breakfast and cocktails. It's worth paying the extra to get the space and bigger bathrooms they offer. Although in my view not quite as refined or as intimate as the George (see below), it's still a good choice—and 71% of hotel energy consumption is carbon neutral certified. It is a Green Globe benchmarked property and works hard to conserve water and energy.

Kilmore and Durham sts., Christchurch. ℡ **03/365-7799.** Fax 03/365-0082. www.crowneplaza.co.nz. 298 units. NZ$170–NZ$350 standard; NZ$215–NZ$395 park view; NZ$265–NZ$445 club king; inquire for rates in premier suites. Long-stay and special deals. AE, DC, MC, V. Valet parking NZ$20. **Amenities:** 3 restaurants; 3 bars; babysitting; free bikes; concierge; nearby golf course; small gym; room service; Wi-Fi in lobby. *In room:* A/C, TV w/pay movies, fridge, hair dryer, Internet, minibar.

Inner City Backpackers

New and improved backpacker stays have sprouted in the inner city region. The best is the highly awarded **Stonehurst** ★★★, 241 Gloucester St. (© **0508-786-633** in NZ, or 03/379-4620; www.stonehurst.com), which has a wide range of accommodations from dorms to tourist motels and flats. **Christchurch City Central YHA,** 273 Manchester St. (© **0800/278-299** in NZ, or 03/379-9535; www.yha.co.nz), has 166 beds in dorm and double arrangements. **Base Backpackers** ★★, 56 Cathedral Sq. (© **0800/227-369** in NZ, or 03/982-2225; www.stayatbase.com), is perfectly located in Cathedral Square and has a popular bar and theme nights.

Moderate

The Heritage Christchurch ★★ At the Heritage, you have the choice of charm and character from the colonial past in the Old Government Building, or contemporary indulgence in the large rooms of the adjacent Heritage Tower. In the tower, I especially like the split-level one-bedroom suites, which have a separate lounge, walk-in wardrobe, and mezzanine bedroom. The sought-after heritage suites in the OGB also feature mezzanine bedrooms, along with open dining areas, kitchens, and laundry facilities, making them ideal for long stays. The marvelous location puts you close to everything, but I like the Crowne Plaza rooms better.

28 Cathedral Sq., Christchurch. © **0800/936-936** in NZ, or 03/377-9722. Fax 03/377-9881. www.heritagehotels.co.nz. 175 units. NZ$210–NZ$240 deluxe; NZ$240–NZ$270 executive; NZ$295–NZ$325 penthouse studio; NZ$425–NZ$475 suite. Long-stay and special deals. AE, DC, MC, V. Valet parking NZ$20. **Amenities:** Restaurant; bar; babysitting; concierge; nearby golf course; well-equipped gym and day spa; Jacuzzi; heated indoor lap pool; room service; sauna; Wi-Fi in lobby and 1st floor of Tower Building. *In room:* A/C (in some), TV w/pay movies, fridge, hair dryer, Internet, minibar.

Inexpensive

A new inner city hotel that's big on economy, style, and environmental sustainability is **Hotel SO** ★★, 165 Cashel St. (© **0508/165-165** in NZ, or 03/968-5050; fax 03/968-5051; www.hotelso.co.nz), which regularly offers rooms under NZ$100 along with great perks like free wireless Internet, a funky virtual concierge, a revolutionary wake-up system, and colorful compact rooms. It's my pick for the best value-for-money in the city and it has a great central location. Almost every aspect of the hotel is geared toward environmentally friendly practices.

Living Space ★ (**Value**) A funky cross between a hotel and an independent apartment block, Living Space is ideal for families, or couples traveling together. It offers basic studios, roomier apartments from one to four bedrooms, and secure access via swipe cards. You'll be right in the heart of the city, a step away from the Bus Exchange, in one of the brightest, most colorful stays in town. There are communal kitchens, theaters, a library, dining rooms, laundries, and masses of art on the walls.

96 Lichfield St., Christchurch. © **0508/454-846** in NZ, or 03/964-5212. Fax 03/964-5245. www.livingspace.net. 110 units. NZ$99–NZ$120 studio; NZ$150–NZ$270 apt. Long-stay rates. AE, DC, MC, V. **Amenities:** Internet. *In room:* TV, fridge, kitchenette.

Expensive

The George Christchurch ★★★ (Value) The George is a member of the Small Luxury Hotels of the World group, and its attention to detail is hard to fault. Sleek, cool, and modern, it typifies the new breed of boutique hotels that focus energy on individual guest needs. The George has also annexed an old adjacent homestead, which is now the Residence; it has two luxury suites and one studio apartment, plus a formal dining room, lounge, and kitchen for those booking the whole property. I can think of no better place in town to indulge yourself—you get everything you pay for. It's quieter and more elegant than the Crowne Plaza. The hotel is active in recycling, reducing its carbon footprint, and conserving water and energy. It also supports numerous local, national, and international charities.

50 Park Terrace, Christchurch. (℃) **0800/100-220** in NZ, or 03/379-4560. Fax 03/666-747. www.thegeorge. com. 53 units in hotel; 3 units in the Residence. NZ$309 standard; NZ$341 executive; NZ$537 junior suite; NZ$617–NZ$747 suite. Residence rooms can be booked individually, or the entire property can be booked for exclusive use. Long-stay rates and special deals. AE, DC, MC, V. **Amenities:** 2 restaurants; bar; babysitting; free bikes; concierge; concierge-level rooms; nearby 9-hole golf course; access to off-site gym w/Jacuzzis and sauna; room service; floodlit AstroTurf tennis court; Wi-Fi in lobby. *In room:* A/C, TV w/pay movies, fax, fridge, hair dryer, minibar, Wi-Fi.

The Weston House ★★ Few have been disappointed with the architectural splendor of this Georgian-style home, a Category 1 Historic Places Trust building. Ideally located just across from Hagley Park, it offers two large rooms in what were once the servants' quarters—one upstairs, one down. Guests are spoiled with extras such as heated bathroom floors, a private sitting area upstairs, and a walk-in wardrobe downstairs. The house is divine, no question; although I think bedrooms at the Worcester, a few blocks away, have more style.

62 Park Terrace, Christchurch. (℃) **03/366-0234.** Fax 03/366-5254. www.westonhouse.co.nz. 2 units. NZ$395–NZ$450. Rates include airport transport. Long-stay rates and special deals. AE, DC, MC, V. Children 11 and under by arrangement. **Amenities:** Nearby golf course and tennis courts. *In room:* TV, fridge, hair dryer, minibar, Wi-Fi.

(Moments) **A Rare Privilege**

Otahuna Lodge ★★★, Rhodes Road, Tai Tapu, Christchurch ((℃) **03/329-6333;** www.otahuna.co.nz), is my favorite place on earth! This magnificent 1895 mansion, 20 minutes out of the city, gives you an insight into the life of the Victorian landed gentry—a life of privilege and luxury that has been accentuated by the clever hands and good taste of owners, Hall Cannon and Miles Refo. The seven magnificent suites are gigantic and get my pick for the best accommodations in Canterbury. It is one of the grandest homes in the region and the level of craftsmanship and architectural detail is awe inspiring. You won't regret a stay here. The meals are divine, and the rural setting and 12 hectares (30 acres) of gardens have much to offer. Stay at least 2 nights to make the most of it. The wholly inclusive rate for suites is NZ$1,238 to NZ$1,688, and for master suites NZ$1,800 to NZ$2,250. Every comfort is assured

Moments Historic Retreat

You'll have to be in quick if you want to stay in the divine little gem that is **Jack's Cottage** ★, Taunton Gardens, Governor's Bay Road, Governor's Bay (☎ **03/329-9746;** fax 03/329-9546; www.tauntongardens.co.nz). Located in the middle of Barry Sligh's beautiful, 1-hectare (2-acre) woodland garden, this little 1860s cottage has been fully restored into the quaintest sleep you'll find anywhere. It has its own kitchen and a beautiful bathroom, and you can roam the gardens at will. It's about a 25-minute drive over the Port Hills from Christchurch and about a 15-minute drive around the bays from Lyttelton. It costs NZ$250 to NZ$330, which includes breakfast supplies and laundry service.

The Worcester of Christchurch ★★ (Value) This superb B&B is the only one in Christchurch with its own gallery. Host Maree Ritchie has been an art dealer for the past 22 years, and the home she shares with her husband, Tony Taylor, is filled with paintings, sculpture, and antiques. Rooms are well appointed with fine furnishings, fresh flowers, and chocolates. The Worcester suite overlooks Worcester Boulevard and has its own dressing room, while the Godley suite has its own lounge. This gem of a Victorian house is directly across from the Arts Centre; you couldn't wish for a better location.

15 Worcester Blvd., Christchurch. ☎ **0800/365-015** in NZ, or 03/365-0936. Fax 03/364-6299. www.worcester.co.nz. 2 units. NZ$450; extra person NZ$185. Rates include breakfast and predinner drinks. AE, DC, MC, V. No children 11 and under. **Amenities:** Nearby golf course and tennis courts. *In room:* TV, fridge, hair dryer.

Moderate

Orari Bed & Breakfast ★ (Value) Directly across Montreal Street from the Christchurch Art Gallery and right in the heart of the cultural precinct, Orari gets top marks for perfect positioning. It's a fabulous, big, old house, built in 1893, and its splendid timbers have been beautifully restored. Rooms are clean-cut, spacious, and comfortable. All but two have en-suite bathrooms. Big, stylish living rooms and a yummy breakfast add to its charms. The addition of five modern, three-level apartments next door—perfect for two to three couples and long stays—makes this one of the best value options in this area.

Gloucester and Montreal sts. ☎ **0800/267-284** in NZ, or 03/365-6569. Fax 03/365-2525. www.orari.co.nz. 10 units. NZ$160–NZ$230 B&B, rates include breakfast; NZ$300–NZ$350 apt. Minimum 3-night stay in apts. Off-peak and long-stay rates. AE, MC, V. **Amenities:** Nearby golf course and tennis courts; Wi-Fi. *In room:* Hair dryer, full kitchen (in apts).

Inexpensive

YMCA ★ (Value) Three words spring instantly to mind—value, location, and liveliness. There's a constant flow of traffic of all ages here, and the modern six-story building is perfectly situated just across from the Arts Centre and Botanic Gardens. The apartments have kitchenettes, while the deluxe units have bathrooms and TVs. Each person in a 5-, 6-, or 10-bunk room gets a locker with a key. Overall, this is probably the most upmarket of Christchurch's hostels.

12 Hereford St., Christchurch. ☎ **0508/962-224** in NZ, or 03/365-0502. Fax 03/365-1386. www.ymcachch.org.nz. 42 dorm beds, 34 units with shared bathrooms, 25 units with private bathrooms. From NZ$25 dorm bed; NZ$65 standard room; NZ$95 deluxe room; NZ$160–NZ$180 apt. Long-stay rates. AE,

DC, MC, V. **Amenities:** Cafe; dining room; babysitting; children's school holiday programs; nearby golf course; full-scale gym; discount on fitness classes and climbing wall; Internet; sauna; nearby tennis courts. *In room:* Fridge (in deluxe and apts), hair dryer (in deluxe rooms), kitchen (in 2 apts), no phone.

IN FENDALTON/MERIVALE/ST. ALBANS
Expensive
Motels abound in this area and most offer good deals.

The Charlotte Jane ★★   At this smart boutique hotel, no stone is unturned when it comes to comfort. This stunning old mansion—formerly a Victorian school for young ladies—has been converted into a haven of period luxury, and if you like big rooms, you'll be in your element here. Bathrooms are equally huge, some with monster Jacuzzis. They have a sustainability program in place and as part of that, they source local wine and produce for their restaurant. The restaurant sits between the main Charlotte Jane homestead and Henderson House, which was added to the property to provide extra guest accommodations. It's just a 5-minute walk to Merivale and approximately 15 minutes to the city.

110 Papanui Rd., Merivale. (C) **03/355-1028.** Fax 03/355-8882. www.charlotte-jane.co.nz. 12 units in the Charlotte Jane; 2 units in Henderson House. NZ$515 deluxe; NZ$555 luxury room; NZ$660 luxury and honeymoon suite; NZ$815 2-bedroom suite. Off-peak rates available. Rates include gourmet breakfast. MC, V. No children 11 and under. **Amenities:** Restaurant; bar; concierge; nearby golf course. *In room:* TV/VCR, hair dryer, kitchen (in 2-bedroom town-house suite), minibar (in suites), Wi-Fi.

Moderate
Elm Tree House ★   Built in 1920, this lovely two-storied home is just a few steps from Merivale Mall and numerous cafes and restaurants. Rooms are big—all with en-suite bathrooms, one with a bathtub—and the original wood paneling throughout gives it a warm, intimate old-world feeling. The Honeymoon and Franz Josef suites are the

---

(Moments)   Rural Retreats

Imagine total silence, snowcapped mountain peaks, and an endless spread of perfect rolling green. This is what you get when you stay at **Terrace Downs High Country Resort ★★**, Coleridge Road, Rakaia Gorge, Canterbury ((C) **0800/465-373** in NZ, or 03/318-6943; fax 03/317-9372; www.terracedowns.co.nz), which is located 45 minutes northwest of Christchurch. Complete with a new day spa and one of New Zealand's top 18-hole golf courses, it provides accommodations in stylish villas and chalets, beautifully crafted from local stone and timber. It's close to Mount Hutt ski fields and some of the best fishing around. Rates range from NZ$390 to NZ$850. I found the terrace villas just perfect.

For something more modest and closer to Christchurch, visit Merrilies Rebbeck, who will welcome you at **Ballymoney Farmstay ★**, Wardstay Road, RD, Christchurch ((C) **03/329-6706;** fax 03/329-6709; www.ballymoney.co.nz), located in the very pretty Tai Tapu area, just 15 minutes from central Christchurch. She has two guest suites (NZ$230–NZ$270, breakfast included), a gorgeous garden, and a small farm filled with an amazing array of special animals. Look out for the stunning white peacock.

sunniest and nicest (upstairs), but I can't imagine anyone complaining about any of the accommodations here.

236 Papanui Rd., Merivale. ✆ **03/355-9731.** Fax 03/355-9753. www.elmtreehouse.co.nz. 6 units. NZ$395; NZ$80 each extra person. Long-stay and off-peak rates. Rates include breakfast and predinner drinks. AE, MC, V. Children 11 and under by arrangement only. **Amenities:** Airport transfers NZ$32; nearby golf courses; nearby gym; Internet; nearby tennis courts. *In room:* TV, hair dryer.

Hadleigh ★ Located on a quiet, residential street, this gorgeous two-storied home exudes charm. The gold Goddard Room is the biggest, but it only has a queen-size bed. I prefer the sunny Cartwright Room, which has a much bigger bathroom, a tub, and a king-size bed. I think it's the pick of the bunch. Two other more modest suites have two bedrooms and a shared bathroom each. I think Elm Tree House bedrooms are the best value for your money, but Hadleigh has lovelier living rooms and shared spaces—and let's not forget that the owner, Jon Warring, is a New Zealand Porsche racing champion and you can hire his Porsche 996 Carrera for the day. Hadleigh has a Qualmark Enviro-Silver rating for its ecotourism practices.

6 Eversleigh St., St. Albans. ✆/fax **03/355-7174.** www.hadleigh.co.nz. 4 units. NZ$308–NZ$425; NZ$60 each extra person. Rates include breakfast. MC, V. **Amenities:** Babysitting; nearby golf course; Wi-Fi. *In room:* TV, hair dryer, kitchen (in apt).

Springfield Cottage ★ (Moments) My own home is only a few blocks from this darling, heritage award-winning place, but I want to shift here immediately. Built in the 1870s and renovated with a modern kitchen, it's a romantic stopover that I'm sure you'll love. It has a big back garden, a barbecue for your use, and two lovely little sitting rooms. If you're the independent type, it will suit you perfectly. If this one is taken, ask about their nearby Camellia Cottage.

137 Springfield Rd., St. Albans. ✆ **03/377-1368.** www.springfieldcottage.co.nz. 2 self-contained cottages for 2 people each. NZ$190–NZ$200. Minimum 2-night stay. Long-stay and off-peak rates. MC, V. No children 11 and under. **Amenities:** Nearby golf course. *In room:* A/C (in 1 cottage), TV/DVD/CD, hair dryer, full kitchen, Wi-Fi (in 1 cottage).

IN SUMNER

Coastal Cliffs Bed & Breakfast ★ (Value) Glenda Proko is a natural hostess, and you'll love the creative home she and architect husband Rick have established overlooking McCormack's Bay. There are two upstairs rooms (one en-suite bath, one private) featuring king-size and single beds; and a third, larger room with a queen-size bed downstairs. I like this creative patch the best—it has fantastic mirrored mosaic walls created by Glenda, and it opens onto the deck and heated pool. All rooms have their own separate entrances, and breakfasts are made with fresh, local, organic produce.

11 Balmoral Lane, Redcliffs, Christchurch. ✆ **03/384-2247.** Fax 03/384-2205. www.coastalcliffs.co.nz. 3 units. NZ$180–NZ$200. Long-stay rates. Rates include breakfast. V. Children 11 and under on request. **Amenities:** Nearby golf course; outdoor solar-heated pool; nearby all-weather tennis court; nearby watersports rentals. *In room:* TV/DVD (in some), fridge, hair dryer, kitchenette (in 1 room), Wi-Fi.

NEAR THE AIRPORT

If you've just landed in Christchurch and urgently need sleep, try **Copthorne Hotel Commodore** ★, 449 Memorial Ave. (✆ **0508/266-663** in NZ, or 03/358-8129; www.commodore.net.nz), which has 135 rooms from NZ$220 for a premium room to NZ$295 for very good business rooms.

Peppers Clearwater Resort ★★ (Value) Much nicer than other airport-hotel options, Clearwater has the advantage of a rural situation, not to mention its 18-hole international golfing resort facilities—and all for a very pleasing price. Set amid 186 hectares (465 acres) of greenery, golf courses, and trout-filled lakes, it's a short drive to the airport and rooms are modern, chic, individual, and beautifully cantilevered out over the water. The hotel rooms and suites are great value, and the eight larger terrace apartments are perfect for long stays, sharing with friends, or families. It opened in 2003 and construction on future facilities—including a swimming pool and health spa—is still underway.

Clearwater Ave., Harewood, Christchurch. (C) **0800/555-075** in NZ, or 03/360-1000. Fax 03/360-1001. www.clearwaternz.com or www.peppers.co.nz. 97 units. NZ$236 lakeside room; NZ$293 lake-view suite; NZ$351 lakefront and quay suite; NZ$491 lakeside villa; NZ$562 apt and terrace villa. Long-stay, off-peak, and special rates. AE, DC, MC, V. **Amenities:** Restaurant; bar and wine cellar; free airport transfers; babysitting; bike rentals; concierge; 18-hole championship golf course (home of Clearwater Classic Australasian PGA tournament); gym; room service; spa; 2 outdoor lit tennis courts; on-site freshwater fishing guide and lessons; Wi-Fi. *In room:* A/C, TV/VCR/DVD, fridge, hair dryer, minibar.

---

4 WHERE TO DINE

You can make a pig of yourself in a region renowned for its lamb, seafood, produce, and world-class wines. Christchurch has the highest ratio of eateries per capita of any New Zealand city—though it's not the only city to claim that. You'll get a bunch of options in one spot at Oxford Terrace, known to locals as "The Strip." Lunchtime is the most crowded; after 11pm, it transforms itself into more of a nightclub scene. The best restaurants, though, tend to be tucked away in more low-key places.

IN THE INNER CITY
Expensive

Canterbury Tales ★★★ MODERN NEW ZEALAND Canterbury Tales presents you with edible works of art that taste just as good as they look. This is a forever-award-winning establishment where you can feel completely at ease with the friendly service. It's not big on atmosphere (it has no windows) and though the regularly changing menu is far from cheap, you'll be offered the best of everything. The menu tends toward the long-winded, but in the end plates are a skillful blend of flavors, textures, and tastes. North Atlantic scallops, truffled mushroom tortellini, butternut volute, and pancetta is just one sampling.

> (Finds) **Currying Favor**
>
> Indian restaurants have popped up all over Christchurch like *pappadums* in hot oil. The **Raj Mahal** ★★, at Manchester and Worcester streets ((C) **03/366-0521**), is considered the best of the bunch. A few of the best of the rest are **Little India Bistro & Tandoor** ★★, Gloucester and New Regent streets ((C) **03/377-7997**); **Tulsi** ★, Gloucester and Manchester streets ((C) **03/377-8999**); and **Two Fat Indians** ★, 112 Manchester St. ((C) **03/371-7273**).

> **(Finds) Classy Cafe**
>
> If you've stepped out on the trendy retail strip of Victoria Street, make sure you take a side step near the clock tower and veer over to **Blax Espresso Bar** ★★ corner of Montreal and Victoria streets (✆ **03/366-8982**). It's all white and bright, and you need to be in early to snare one of their delectable *pain au chocolat,* or their fought-over small cakes. Blax is open Monday through Saturday 7:30am to 4pm. And feast your eyes on the huge range of yummy products in their delicatessen in the same building.

Crowne Plaza Christchurch, Kilmore and Durham sts. ✆ **03/365-7799.** Reservations required. Main courses NZ$32–NZ$48. AE, DC, MC, V. Summer Tues–Sat 6pm–late; winter Thurs–Sat 6pm–late.

Pedro's ★★ SPANISH   For nearly 30 years, Pedro Carazo has been bringing the best of the Basque region to Christchurch. Market-fresh seafood forms the core of the menu, with *lots* of garlic. Regulars keep coming back to enjoy the noisy, relaxed atmosphere and the always charming Pedro, who likes to mingle with his guests. Food is divine, from the paella to the *gambas al ajillo* (garlic prawns). And it's all served up on the traditional Spanish crockery that Pedro buys on his regular trips home.

143 Worcester St. ✆ **03/379-7668.** www.pedrosrestaurant.co.nz. Reservations recommended. Main courses NZ$33–NZ$36. DC, MC, V. Tues–Sat 6–11pm.

Moderate

Bodhi Tree ★★ **(Value)** BURMESE   You'll have to beat back the crowds to get into what the owners claim is New Zealand's only Burmese restaurant. It's a place of humble decor, small taste plates, and sensational flavors that you'll remember for hours after. Make sure you try the pickled tea salad and the sautéed squid with chili and basil. You can keep ordering as many little dishes as you like until you're full.

808 Colombo St. ✆ **03/377-6808.** Reservations essential. Main courses NZ$15–NZ$20. AE, DC, MC, V. Tues–Sun 6pm–late.

Flying Burrito Brothers ★ MEXICAN   This is the place to indulge your love of chilies, burritos, and enough tequila to float a small ship. Quite apart from the super-tasty, chili-laden menu, this fine and lively little den has the biggest selection of tequila in New Zealand and you can indulge in a tasting tray to pinpoint your favorite. The two-leveled interior is subdued, but the crowds who come here for the terrific hot food don't seem to mind that.

Armagh and New Regent sts. ✆ **03/377-7626.** www.flyingburritobrothers.co.nz. Reservations recommended. Main courses NZ$20–NZ$32. AE, DC, MC, V. Daily 4pm–late.

Portofino ★★ ITALIAN   I personally celebrated when Auckland's Portofino made an appearance in Christchurch. The chain has a long history of polished restaurant service and excellent, well-priced fare. In Christchurch, it has established a sexy little restaurant—all mood and mirrors—with a bountiful wine display, cute Italian waiters, and all the edible favorites from calzone and linguine through scampi, veal, scallops, prawns, and pastas.

182 Oxford Terrace. ✆ **03/377-2454.** www.portofino.co.nz. Reservations recommended for dinner. Main courses NZ$20–NZ$45. AE, DC, MC, V. Wed–Fri 11:30am–11:30pm; Sat–Tues 4:30–11:30pm. Closed Dec 24–Jan 3.

Simo's ★★ MOROCCAN   Finding Simo's is like finding Aladdin's Cave. It's a treasure-trove of North African and Middle Eastern flavors woven together with passion and creativity by Moroccan-born chef Mohamed Abbari, who advocates that his food be savored slowly and with immense pleasure. It's not hard. His rich, authentic dishes—everything from traditional, melt-in-the-mouth lamb tagine to lemon chicken and spicy Berber brochette—make for a culinary adventure you'll remember long after. I still dream of his spicy couscous and honeyed fruit.

Upstairs, 114 City Mall. ✆ **03/377-5001.** www.simos.co.nz. Reservations recommended. Main courses NZ$30–NZ$36. AE, DC, MC, V. Tues–Sat 6:30pm–late.

Sticky Fingers Restaurant & Bar ★ MODERN NEW ZEALAND   Big umbrellas mark the entrance to this popular spot, and you'll find all types enjoying the interior (which tries hard to be sleek, but falls a bit short). If you can, grab one of the comfortable booths. The menu includes salads, steak, lamb, fish, pasta, and pizza in generous servings. It's a popular haunt for lunching businessmen and after-work drinkers. Service can be patchy, but Sticky Fingers isn't alone in that, I'm sorry to say.

Clarendon Towers, Oxford Terrace. ✆ **03/366-6452.** www.stickyfingers.co.nz. Reservations recommended for dinner. Main courses NZ$22–NZ$39. AE, DC, MC, V. Daily 8am–very late.

Inexpensive

Ace Wasabi ★★ JAPANESE   The night I discovered this wee gem I thought I had fallen down a time tunnel and landed back in Japan. This small, immensely personable place serves up all the traditional favorites from sushi and sashimi to noodles (udon and soba) to tempura and teriyaki—and all of it with the impeccable manners and service the Japanese are known for. I thought it was going to be expensive and I felt an inner panic rising with every dish I ordered; so I fell a little bit in love when I was presented with one of the smallest Japanese restaurant bills I've ever had.

55 Victoria St. ✆ **03/365-0762.** www.acewasabinz.com. Reservations recommended. Main courses NZ$16–NZ$40; set meals NZ$12–NZ$40. AE, MC, V. Mon–Fri 5:30–10pm; Sat–Sun 5:30pm–late.

The Globe Cafe ★ (Value) CAFE   If you want to throw yourself into the center of student and arty life, this is the place. Situated in the older, funkier part of town near Christchurch Polytechnic's Schools of Jazz and Fashion, and tucked between quaint secondhand stores and designer boutiques, the Globe is always busy. The interior is low-key, and the portions generous. Sought out for its coffee, it also does a hearty breakfast. It has the best vegan muffins in town and a good range of vegetarian and gluten-free food

CHRISTCHURCH & CANTERBURY

14

WHERE TO DINE

Ⓣ**ips   Espresso Hits**

Gasping for a good coffee? Then head for **Joe's Garage** ★★, 194 Hereford St. (✆ **03/366-8317;** www.joes.co.nz), which is a popular haunt for the business crowd and those looking for big brunches. **C1 Espresso** ★, 150 High St. (✆ **03/366-7170**), is more funky and rough around the edges, but it has excellent coffee. **Underground Coffee** ★★, 791 Colombo St. (✆ **03/982-8394;** www.underground coffee.co.nz), combines funky street art with superb coffee; and **Vic's Café & Bakehouse** ★, 132 Victoria St. (✆ **03/366-2054**), combines good coffee with an award-winning array of freshly baked European breads.

> **(Finds) Meals on Wheels**
>
> For Christchurch's most moving dining experience, leap aboard the **Tramway Restaurant,** in Cathedral Square near the Police Kiosk (© **03/366-7511;** www. tram.co.nz for reservations). It operates one departure daily, September to May at 7:30pm and June to August at 7pm, and does about five circuits of the tramway during your meal. Main courses are priced from around NZ$32 and meal packages start at NZ$70 per person for a four-course meal. There are better dining experiences, but this one has novelty value.

that includes salads, pastas, panini, and more. Licensed for wine drinkers, it's a great place for people-watching and a favored hangout for many artists.

171 High St. © **03/366-4704.** Main courses NZ$15–NZ$25. AE, DC, MC, V. Mon–Fri 7am–4pm; Sat–Sun 8am–4pm.

The Honey Pot Café ★ CAFE   If you're in the mood for a big, wholesome breakfast, stop by the Honey Pot. It has a warm, casual atmosphere, and if you can get through its "Full Breakky" of two eggs with house sausages, grilled tomatoes, bacon, fried mushrooms, onions, hash browns, and an espresso, you're doing better than me. The lunch and dinner menus offer pizzas, gourmet sandwiches, and desserts. It's not salubrious, but if you're on a budget it can fill the gaps.

114 Lichfield St. © **03/366-5853.** Main courses NZ$15–NZ$22. MC, V. Mon–Fri 7am–late; Sat–Sun 8am–late.

NEAR HAGLEY PARK
Expensive

Pescatore ★★★ PACIFIC RIM   Pescatore has an established reputation for innovative cuisine. It even boasts a mention in the *New York Times.* Thankfully, it has now had a designer makeover to create an elegant ambience equal to a superb menu offering—the star of which is the 10-course Evolution degustation menu featuring Canterbury lamb, Akaroa salmon, Golden Bay crab, and scallops. Pescatore is a pricey option, but it's popular with local foodies, and the chance to sit back and enjoy a myriad of tastes cleverly matched with award-winning wines is too good to pass up. The service is very attentive.

The George Hotel, Park Terrace. © **03/371-0257.** www.thegeorge.com. Reservations required. Main courses NZ$39–NZ$45; degustation menu from NZ$120, with suggested wines from NZ$195. AE, DC, MC, V. Oct–May daily 6–10pm; June–Sept Wed–Sun 6–10pm.

Rotherams ★★★ (Moments) INTERNATIONAL   This is a tucked-away culinary jewel in the midst of Riccarton retail heartland. It's most definitely worth searching out and savoring. You'll get some of the best meals in the most romantic ambience of almost any restaurant in the city. Personally, I like it best of the top-rated restaurants. Service is attentive, presentation first class, flavors divine, and the wine list impressive. If you have something special to celebrate (and who needs a reason?), let Swiss owner/chef Martin Weiss spoil you to bits.

42 Rotheram St. © **03/341-5142.** Reservations required. Main courses NZ$35–NZ$40. AE, DC, MC, V. Tues–Sat 6pm–late.

Inexpensive

Dux de Lux ★ BREWPUB   If you're young and looking for a good time, head for the Dux, especially Thursday, Friday, and Saturday nights when it features live bands; there's live jazz on Tuesdays. The Dux is an avid supporter of the New Zealand music scene and hosts the best talent in town, from loud guitar rock to smooth drum-and-bass grooves. It batch-brews its own beers and has won best lager at the Australian International Beer Awards. When it comes to food, it features satisfying meals at a decent price. Vegan and most cultural dietary requests can be accommodated. Now 30 years old, the Dux has a superb laid-back weekend atmosphere, as people crowd into the courtyard and watch the activity of the nearby market stalls.

The Arts Centre, Montreal and Hereford sts. © **03/366-6919.** www.thedux.co.nz. Main courses NZ$20–NZ$24. AE, DC, MC, V. Mon–Thurs 10:30am–11pm; Fri–Sat 10:30am–11:30pm; Sun 10:30am–10pm.

Le Café ★ (Kids) CAFE   This is a popular spot for coffee after a show at Court Theatre, and a great place for people-watching, but things get pretty hectic at times, so expect to wait. The quality of service can also be variable. The menu includes light meals—nachos, focaccia, pizza, burgers, Caesar salad. Le Café's bakery is another choice farther into the Arts Centre. Everything is made fresh daily—Italian ciabatta, German-style sourdough and rye, and traditional Kiwi meat pies—and makes good picnic fare if you're heading for the gardens.

The Arts Centre, Worcester Blvd. © **03/366-7722.** Reservations accepted for breakfast only. Main courses NZ$15–NZ$22. AE, DC, MC, V. Sun–Thurs 7am–midnight; Fri–Sat 24 hr.

IN FENDALTON/MERIVALE

In heartland Merivale (just behind the mall on Aikmans Rd.), you'll find a fistful of swanky eateries rubbing shoulders in a sunny, shared courtyard filled with grassy patches, potted trees, and grape vines. It becomes quite a party on a warm summer's day.

Brigittes Espresso Bar ★ (Kids) CAFE   Half the population of Merivale seems to enjoy weekend brunch at Brigittes, so make sure you book ahead. The homey interior looks out onto the street and opens up to a sheltered courtyard. You'll find all the usual breakfast options, including eggs Benedict and eggs Florentine, plus lunch and dinner choices such as honey-glazed chicken on salad greens served with lime-ginger soy dressing. The service can be decidedly half-hearted but the atmosphere is always good.

Aikmans Rd. and Papanui Rd. © **03/355-6150.** Reservations recommended. Main courses NZ$16–NZ$26. AE, DC, MC, V. Mon 8:30am–6pm; Tues–Sat 8:30am–10pm; Sun 10am–4pm; public holidays 10am–late.

(Finds)   **Vegetarian Hits**

Head down Colombo Street to find the **Lotus Heart,** 595 Colombo St. (© **03/379-0324**), for plenty of vegan and gluten-free options. Just a few doors away is **Aiki Japanese Organic Kitchen** ★, 599 Colombo St. (© **03/366-1178**), which combines 99% health with inventive Asian favorites.

CHRISTCHURCH & CANTERBURY

14

WHERE TO DINE

JDV ★★ MODERN NEW ZEALAND   This is where fashionable black garb and gold jewelry are ranked as highly as the coconut-and-ginger duck curry with sticky rice cake, steamed bok choy, lychees, and charred lime. Movers and shakers (along with the rich and slothful), gather here to pay homage to the chefs' penchant for unexpected flavor mixes and reliably delicious meals. I've had to wait too long for service here, but I had no complaints about the food once it finally arrived.

The Mall, Aikmans Rd. (✆ **03/964-3860.** Reservations recommended. Main courses NZ$25–NZ$35. AE, DC, MC, V. Daily 11:30am–late.

Tutto Benne ★★ (Value) ITALIAN   Felice and Paulette Mannucci have run a succession of excellent eateries in Christchurch for nearly 3 decades. This latest effort is a little gem—it's one of my favorite Christchurch restaurants. At this pizzeria-meets-small-neighborhood-restaurant, the full menu gallops across 15 pizza types, pastas, risottos, and traditional delicacies like veal saltimbocca with prosciutto, sage, and Marsala. And while we should never forget the Italian cassata, the tiramisu is to die for!

192 Papanui Rd. (✆ **03/355-4744.** Reservations recommended. Main courses NZ$20–NZ$32. AE, DC, MC, V. Daily 5pm–late.

IN SUMNER

A trip to Sumner wouldn't be complete without a visit to **Coffee Culture Ltd.** ★★, 28 Mariner St. (✆ **03/326-5900**). Desserts and coffee are their specialty. The **Cornershop Bistro** ★, 32 Nayland St. (✆ **03/326-6720**), is an excellent neighborhood restaurant that's casual and competent, presenting everything from racks of lamb to fresh grouper filets. By the time this goes to press, there will be further dining options in a new commercial development in the center of Sumner.

OTHER PALATABLE CONSIDERATIONS

Caffe Roma ★, 176 Oxford Terrace (✆ **03/379-3879**), is popular for breakfast and lunch. The **Metro** ★, Kilmore and Manchester streets, opposite the Town Hall (✆ **03/374-4242**), is great for after-show coffee. You'll find a classy little wine bar at **Saggio di Vino** ★★★, on the corner of Victoria Street and Bealey Avenue (✆ **03/379-4006**).

Sala Sala ★★, 184 Oxford Terrace (✆ **03/379-6975**), is one of the best Japanese restaurants in town. **Retour** ★, Cambridge Terrace (✆ **03/365-2888**), is a delicious dining experience in a unique band rotunda setting; and for good-value meals in a contemporary setting, go to **Oasis** ★, at the corner of Madras and Chester Street East (✆ **03/363-2800**).

> (Tips) **Gourmet Takeaway**
>
> For the best gourmet takeout meals in Christchurch, go to **Traiteur of Merivale,** at the corner of Papanui and Aikmans roads (✆ **03/355-7750**). Its menu changes weekly with several starters, mains, and desserts, plus pasta and salad options, all well priced.

(Finds) **Berry, Berry Nice**

You get two chances to pick fresh berries and then sit down in smart little on-farm cafes for a meal, or coffee and berry-based treats. Take a drive through the pretty lanes of the Halswell area and find **Otahuna Berries Raspberry Café** ★, Rhodes Road, Tai Tapu (✆ **03/329-6687**). It's about a 20-minute drive out of town. Head out toward Tai Tapu on the main highway to Akaroa, and you'll see it signposted down Rhodes Road on your left. Pig out on *the* most divine cakes when you get there. **Berryfields' Sweethearts Restaurant** ★, 161 Gardiners Rd., Harewood (✆ **03/359-5630**), is in the opposite direction, near the airport. It's more of a restaurant experience and attracts a more mature crowd.

5 EXPLORING CHRISTCHURCH

Christchurch prides itself almost equally on its arts, sports, history, and gardens. There are a number of theaters and art galleries, along with several excellent museums, parks, and gardens to explore. Attractions and events are listed in the daily newspaper, *The Press,* and in the monthly *Tourist Times,* available free at the visitor center.

THE TOP ATTRACTIONS

The hub of the city center and an excellent starting point is **Cathedral Square.** There are several restaurants, hotels, duty-free shops, and attractions within an easy stroll. It's also where you'll find the **Wizard of Christchurch,** who performs daily at 1pm in summer and when the weather cooperates in winter. The Wizard stands above the crowd on a ladder, ranting and raving about all things from bureaucracy, love, and religion to Americans and politicians. He's an essential Christchurch personality—quirky, smart, and not to be trifled with intellectually. Be sure you know what you're talking about if you pick an argument. You'll also find *Chalice* ★★ here. It's a massive new sculpture created by internationally renowned, Christchurch-based sculptor Neil Dawson.

Canterbury Museum ★★ (Kids) Perfectly placed on the edge of the Botanic Gardens within a stone's throw of the Arts Centre, the Canterbury Museum has something for everyone. Check out the excellent Antarctic display, a must-see before going out to the International Antarctic Centre. Also look for the superb Natural History Discovery Centre, where you can happily pull open drawers and inspect the contents of jars and cases. The quaint Victorian Canterbury street is interesting, and there's an excellent Maori section. Allow 2 hours.

Rolleston Ave. ✆ **03/366-5000.** Fax 03/366-5622. www.canterburymuseum.com. Free admission; Discovery Centre NZ$2; fees for special exhibits. Oct–Mar daily 9am–5:30pm; Apr–Sept daily 9am–5pm. Free guided tours Tues–Thurs 3:30–4:30pm (meet in museum foyer). Closed Dec 25.

Arts Centre ★ (Kids) You can't go to Christchurch and not visit the Arts Centre. Originally home to Canterbury University College from 1873 to 1975, it begs leisurely exploration. Quite apart from the lovely Gothic architecture, it presents a rabbits' warren of over 40 retail outlets selling New Zealand–made arts and crafts and heaps of things to interest kids, including great weekend food stalls. You'll find some rather bizarre goods, but overall the standard is high. There are excellent buys in leather, wool, wood, and crafts. It's best to visit on weekends when it's much busier and around 80 stalls are open.

Court Theatre is housed in the original Engineering Building and Hydraulics Lab, the **Academy Cinema** is in the old Boys' High Gym, and the **Southern Ballet** now occupies the Electrical Engineering Lab and the Mechanical Engineering Lab. There are several good eating spots (Dux de Lux and Le Café are described on p. 373; the Boulevard Cafe, E-Caf Internet Café, and Annie's Wine Bar & Restaurant are also popular). Buskers and performers add color to the weekend market, and you can take an NZ$8 tour daily or by appointment (☎ 03/363-2836).

Bounded by Worcester Blvd., Rolleston Ave., Hereford St., and Montreal St. ☎ 03/363-2836. www. artscentre.org.nz. Free admission. Most crafts and retail outlets daily 10am–4pm; market and food fair Sat–Sun 10am–4pm; restaurant and cafe hours vary. Free guided tours daily.

Christchurch Art Gallery Te Puna o Waiwhetu ★★★

I love the flashiness of this new and sparkling architectural icon that has rapidly established itself as the place to go since its 2003 opening. Curving glass facades and spectacular outdoor sculpture aside, it has one of the largest permanent collections in New Zealand, and with eight new gallery spaces, there's plenty of room for both contemporary and historic displays. The collection of over 5,500 paintings, sculptures, prints, drawings, and crafts emphasizes work from the Canterbury region, but there are regular touring international and national shows as well.

And don't overlook the new book and gift shop. It has some terrific New Zealand–made goods—as does the in-house craft gallery, **Form.** A cafe/restaurant completes the picture, making this a must-visit attraction. Next door is the **Centre of Contemporary Art** (☎ 03/366-7261), which is also worth a visit for its exhibitions of New Zealand contemporary art.

Worcester Blvd. and Montreal St. ☎ 03/941-7300. Fax 03/941-7301. www.christchurchartgallery.org.nz. Free admission; fees for special exhibits. Daily 10am–5pm (Wed till 9pm). Free guided tours daily at 11am and 2pm, Wed at 6:30 and 7:30pm. Closed Dec 25. Underground parking, entrance off Gloucester St.

Christchurch Botanic Gardens ★ Kids

The turquoise-and-yellow Peacock Fountain just inside the main gate on Rolleston Avenue is a handy marker that can't be missed. This is the best point of entry to the lush 23 hectares (57 acres) of deservedly world-renowned gardens. Even if you've never considered yourself the slightest bit green-thumbed, there's something magical about this place. Sweeping lawns, fragrant rose gardens, and some of the oldest exotic trees in New Zealand provide spectacular displays year-round. The Avon River and its huge duck population add interest. The kids can run loose, feed the ducks, and frolic in the playground. Don't miss the lush tropical greenhouse, or the heavenly scented rose gardens adjacent to it. I also love the little alpine garden area and the two ponds that border the rhododendron and azalea gardens.

Rolleston Ave. ☎ 03/941-8999. www.ccc.govt.nz/parks. Free admission. Grounds daily 7am to 1 hr. before sunset; conservatories daily 10:15am–4pm; information center Mon–Fri 9am–4pm, Sat–Sun 10:15am–4pm. Caterpillar garden tours every 30 min., NZ$15 adults, NZ$6 children 5–18, daily at 10am–4pm (departing from both Canterbury Museum entrance and Gardens Kiosk). Bus 17 and the tram provide convenient access to the Rolleston Ave. entrance.

International Antarctic Centre ★★★ Kids

If you've always wanted to romp with penguins, stroke a leopard seal, climb aboard a snowmobile, explore a snow cave, and feel the icy wind chills of Antarctica, this is probably as close as you'll ever get. Everything about this attraction is of superb value and you'll get a particular thrill from the live penguin display. It takes more of a geographic/natural history approach than the Canterbury Museum's Antarctic exhibition, and if you see both, you'll have a healthy appreciation for life on the ice. Considered one of New Zealand's leading attractions, it gives you a feel for modern Antarctic life through sophisticated sound-and-light shows, a spine-tingling audiovisual presentation, and interactive exhibits. The center is suitable for visits of 30 minutes or half a day, but spending 1 to 2 hours is ideal. Two wheelchairs are available for use by the public.

The newest attraction here is the **Antarctic Hagglund Ride** ★★, the only one of its type in the world. Its 15-minute tour gives you a unique insight into the planning of Antarctic journeys. It's well worth the extra money and a big hit with kids.

38 Orchard Rd., adjacent to the Christchurch International Airport. © **0508/736-4846** in NZ, or 03/353-7798. Fax 03/353-7799. www.iceberg.co.nz. Admission NZ$50 adults, NZ$38 children 5–15, NZ$150 families; group rates available. Audio tour available in 6 languages for NZ$8. Oct–Mar daily 9am–7pm; Apr–Sept daily 9am–5:30pm. The center is a 15-min. drive from Central City and an 8-min. walk from the Christchurch Airport Terminal. The city/airport bus runs to the center every half-hour; the complimentary Super Shuttle runs from the airport to the center. Free parking.

Christchurch Cathedral ★   If you want a bird's-eye view over the square and the inner city, climb the 133 steps in the 37m (120-ft.) Christchurch Anglican Cathedral tower. You won't be alone—well over 300,000 visitors per year wend their way into the cathedral, making it one of the South Island's most visited attractions. Construction was begun in 1864, just 14 years after the first settlers arrived, and was completed in 1904. Today, it's New Zealand's most famous Gothic Revival church and Christchurch's most important landmark. The cathedral is open for prayer during the weekdays; Holy Communion is celebrated daily. The Rose Window above the main entry is especially beautiful.

Cathedral Sq. © **03/366-0046.** www.christchurchcathedral.co.nz. Free admission to cathedral; tower NZ$5 adults, NZ$2 children, NZ$6 for guided tour. Summer 8:30am–7pm; winter daily 9am–5pm. Guided tours 11am–2pm. Cathedral choir sings a half-hour choral evensong Tues–Wed 5:15pm, Fri 4:30pm, Sun 10am; young choristers sing service Fri 4:30pm (except during school holidays). Most buses pass through the square.

Southern Encounter Aquarium & Kiwi House ★ **Kids**   Visit this attraction if you won't get a chance to swim with dolphins or whale-watch in Kaikoura. It's all here on film in a fascinating 25-minute sequence that takes in the mysteries of underwater Fiordland and New Zealand bird life as well. You can get your hands wet in the touch tank, see fly-tying demonstrations in the fishing lodge, and gaze upon the engineering marvel that holds 92 tons of seawater behind four glass panels, each weighing 750 kilograms (1,660 lb.) and leaning out at a 45-degree angle. A diver gets in with giant eels at feeding time (11am, but subject to change); marine species are fed at 3pm. Well-situated near the visitor center, it makes a good diversion; however, if you're short on time, opt for the International Antarctic Centre or Orana Park instead.

Cathedral Sq. © **03/359-7109.** Fax 03/359-4330. www.southernencounter.co.nz. Admission NZ$16 adults, NZ$6 children 5–14, NZ$38 families, free for kids 3 and under. Group discounts available. MC, V. Daily 9am–5pm. Feeding times: trout and salmon 1pm, marine fish 3pm, special feeds 11am. Kiwi on display 10am–4:45pm. Closed Dec 25. Enter through Christchurch Visitor Centre or T&Ski Shop.

ADDITIONAL ATTRACTIONS

Animal lovers who are short on time may have to choose between Orana Park and Willowbank Wildlife Reserve. Both are closer to the airport than to Central City, so either could make a good last-minute stop. Personally, I'm a big-cat fan, so I'd opt for Orana,

Moments   Crossing the Harbor

Take the stunning scenic drive over the Port Hills to Lyttelton, and once you've explored the little village, leap aboard the **Diamond Harbour Ferry** (✆ **03/366-8855**), located on Lyttelton Wharf. For the small sum of NZ$10 for adults and NZ$5 for children ages 5 to 15, you can travel across to the other side of the harbor and back. It's a walk uphill once you get there, but you can catch your breath over coffee or a cool beer at historic **Godley House** (✆ **03/329-4880;** www.godley house.co.nz). A ferry run can also drop you off at **Quail Island** for the day. This former quarantine station and leper colony was also used by Scott and Shackleton as home base for their Antarctic expeditions. It abounds with interesting walks and historic points of interest. Get dropped off by **Black Cat Cruises,** B Jetty, Port of Lyttelton (✆ **0800/436-574;** www.blackcat.co.nz).

where things African are to the fore. But if you want a guaranteed sighting of a kiwi before you leave New Zealand, go to Willowbank.

Orana Park ★★ (Kids   There's something quite magical about getting up close and personal with Rothschild giraffes. You can feed them and fondle their ears and they won't mind a bit, but don't try that with the park's lions, tigers, and cheetahs. Set in 80 attractively laid-out hectares (198 acres), the park is New Zealand's largest wildlife reserve. You'll see few fences and cages here—the emphasis is on a natural environment, which seems to agree with the cheetahs, the only successfully breeding ones in Australasia (over a dozen new cubs in the past 16 years). At 3:55pm daily, you can see them make a dash for their raw-meat supper, which is attached to a fast-moving lure. The main lion feeding time is 2:30pm daily. This is the only place in Christchurch to see a tuatara, and there's a nocturnal kiwi house as well, but the one at Willowbank is bigger and better. If you're in a hurry, take the park's 40-minute free shuttle circuit.

743 McLeans Island Rd. ✆ **03/359-7109.** Fax 03/359-4330. www.oranawildlifepark.co.nz. Admission NZ$24 adults, NZ$8 children 5–14, NZ$56 families. Group rates available. MC, V. Daily 10am–5pm. Closed Dec 25. The park is a 25-min. drive from Central City and is well signposted from the airport. Free parking.

Willowbank Wildlife Reserve ★ (Kids   Willowbank is a good place for children to get close to relatively tame animals of all sorts, but it doesn't have the impact of Orana's exotic animals. It has the country's largest collection of kiwis, and you won't find any glass between you and the feathers. It takes a few minutes for your eyes to adjust to the dimly lit nocturnal house, but if you're patient and quiet, you will see a kiwi. This is guaranteed if you take a guided tour at 11:30am or 2:30pm. I'd recommend paying the extra for the Kiwi Breeding Tour—it's the best thing about Willowbank in my view. Night tours of the New Zealand Kiwi Experience are at 7:30, 8:30, and 9:30pm. Another feature is the Ko Tane Cultural Performance at 5:30 and 6:30pm, which is a fun introduction to things Maori.

60 Hussey Rd. ✆ **03/359-6226.** Fax 03/359-6212. www.willowbank.co.nz. Admission and Kiwi Tour NZ$27 adults, NZ$12 children 5–15, NZ$60 families. Ko Tane NZ$48 adults, NZ$23 children 5–15. Group discounts available. AE, DC, MC, V. Daily 10am–10pm. Take Harewood Rd. and turn right on Gardiners Rd.; turn right again on Hussey Rd. It's a 15-min. drive from the city. The Best Attractions bus also calls here.

Science Alive ★ (Kids) This is a thinking person's outing, and it may be the quietest your children ever get on your entire holiday. Adults seem to have as much fun as the kids as they come to grips with tsunami makers, tightropes, and a host of interactive exhibits. It's educational and entertaining at the same time. Stop by the excellent gift shop, which stocks great science kits and games; or take in a movie on one of the eight screens across the foyer.

392 Moorehouse Ave. (C) **03/365-5199.** Fax 03/365-5189. www.sciencealive.co.nz. Admission from NZ$14 adults, NZ$10 children 2–5, NZ$35 for 4 people. Group discounts available. Mon–Fri 1–9pm; Sat–Sun and public holidays 10am–9pm. Located within the Hoyts 8 complex. The free, yellow electric shuttle stops here every 10 min. Free parking at rear of complex.

Air Force Museum of New Zealand If you've got a hankering to indulge your passion for flight, this past winner of Best New Zealand Attraction is your place. Two hours will give you a good overview of flight simulators, the history hall, the restoration hangar, and displays of planes—everything from Spitfires and Skyhawks to Tiger Moths.

45 Harvard Ave., Wigram. (C) **03/343-9532.** Fax 03/343-9533. www.airforcemuseum.co.nz. Free admission. NZ$8 Restoration Tour, NZ$5 Children's Air Force experience, NZ$10 Discover Wigram Historic Walking tour. AE, MC, V. Daily 10am–5pm. Closed Dec 25. Take the City Circuit Bus or bus 5, 51, 81, or 82 from Central City. Located at Wigram Air Base, a 15-min. drive from the center, via Riccarton Rd. or Blenheim Rd., both of which merge into Main South Rd.

Ferrymead Heritage Park (Kids) The 8-hectare (20-acre) historical park offers a look at life in early colonial Christchurch, with buildings, streets, fashions, and other paraphernalia of a bygone era. There's a schoolhouse, jail, houses, printery, church, and operating bakery, along with tram and train links between the two main areas of the park. This could be a stopover to or from the Mount Cavendish Gondola, which is also accessed off Bridle Path Road.

Ferrymead Park Dr., Ferrymead. (C) **03/384-1970.** Fax 03/384-1725. www.ferrymead.org.nz. Weekend admission NZ$15 adults, NZ$5 children 5–15, NZ$35 families. Rates are almost half-price on weekdays. Tram runs Sat–Sun for small fee. Daily 10am–4:30pm. Closed Dec 25. Take Ferry Rd. east and take the 1st right after Heathcote Bridge, or take bus 35.

Christchurch Gondola ★ (Kids) The Christchurch Gondola may not have quite the same breathtaking impact as the Queenstown equivalent, but for unparalleled views westward over the city and the Canterbury Plains to the Southern Alps, and for the full sweep of Pegasus Bay and the Pacific Ocean all the way up to the Kaikoura Ranges, you can't beat it. Perched on the crater rim of an extinct volcano, 445m (1,460 ft.) above sea level, the Gondola complex features the Time Tunnel Heritage Show, with a Canterbury video presentation and a walk-through exhibition.

If you want to take the Freedom Walk in the Port Hills, pay for the gondola ride up and then walk down any of the numerous hill tracks to Sumner Beach (allow 2 hr.), from

---

(Value) **Double Deal**

Get two rides for the price of one with the **Double Deal** offered by **Christchurch Gondola** ((C) **03/384-0700**) and **Christchurch Tramway** ((C) **03/366-7830**). Pay just NZ$35 for adults and NZ$20 for children ages 4 to 14.

which you can catch a bus back to the city, or to Lyttelton, also about 2 hours. Wear sturdy walking shoes—the tracks are steep and can be slippery. The **Mountain Bike Adventure Co.** (© **0800/424-534;** www.cyclehire-tours.co.nz) is another option for your descent. Reservations are essential and can be made at the visitor center (© **03/379-9629**).

10 Bridle Path Rd. © **03/384-0310.** Fax 03/384-0757. www.gondola.co.nz. Admission NZ$24 adults, NZ$10 children 5–15, NZ$58 families. Discounts for seniors and students. Oct–Apr daily 10am–midnight; winter daily noon–10pm. The lower terminal is 15 min. from the city center. Take Ferry Rd. and head east; take the 1st right over the Heathcote Bridge, or take the Best Attractions bus or bus 28 Lyttelton. Free parking.

Tamaki Heritage Village ★★   *The Chronicles of Uitara—Lost in Our Own Land* is a night of drama and action set in a re-created Maori village, fortified *pa*, and colonial village. Replicating the changeable, uncertain times from 1820 onward, this experience relives the impact of civil war and colonization on indigenous peoples. You can travel by tram through the village, walk through the *pa* to experience Maori life of the period; and then feast on a selection of Maori and colonial banquet food. See this evening show and visit nearby Ferrymead Heritage Park by day for a comparative look at customs, values, and lifestyles of the 1820s.

Ferrymead Park Dr. © **03/366-7333.** Fax 03/366-4333. www.globalstorytellers.com. Admission NZ$130 adults, NZ$76 children 5–15, NZ$380 families. V. Daily 10am–10pm.

Yaldhurst Museum ⎛Value⎞   Transport and classic car lovers will enjoy this 40-year-old museum with its collection of over 400 vehicles, plus one of the country's largest collections of horse-drawn vehicles and associated memorabilia. From an 1810 American buggy, a unique 1860 Phaeton, an 1866 glass-sided hearse, fire engines, and carriages, there's something for vehicle fans of all sorts. Set in the grounds of an 1876 colonial homestead and run by Grant Cooper, great grandson of the original owner, it's a great value rural outing.

School Rd., Yaldhurst. © 03/342-7914. Fax 03/342-7916. www.yaldhurstmuseum.co.nz. Admission NZ$15, NZ$5 children 5–14, NZ$30 families. Daily 10am–5pm. Closed Dec 25 and all of June. Near the airport and 20 min. from city center. Take St. Hwy. 73 and take 1st turn right past Yaldhurst Hotel.

PARKS & GARDENS

Christchurch isn't called the Garden City for nothing, and taking pride of place among them all are the **Botanic Gardens** ★★★, described under "The Top Attractions," earlier in this chapter.

Mona Vale ★, 63 Fendalton Rd. (© **03/941-8999;** www.ccc.govt.nz/parks/garden city), has 5.5 hectares (14 acres) of rolling lawns, rose gardens, fountains, and a grand turn-of-the-20th-century homestead, all open to the public free of charge. The homestead restaurant serves lunch from noon to 2pm, morning and afternoon teas from 10am to 3:30pm. Reservations are essential. Guided garden tours are held daily from November through March.

The **Avon River** runs along the border of Mona Vale, and a punting excursion will give you a peek into some of the beautiful private gardens on the river. The punts operate October through April, daily from 9am to 4:30pm, or on request. The cost is NZ$25 for 20 minutes, NZ$30 for 30 minutes.

The 2½-hour **Garden Drive,** described in *Christchurch Scenic Drive Guide* brochure at the visitor center, includes both the Botanic Gardens and Mona Vale. Although much of the tour highlights architecture rather than actual gardens, it will give you a good look around the northwest suburbs, where there are many exquisite private home gardens.

Two other self-guided drives in the same brochure cover the **Port Hills Drive** ★★★ and the **Avon River Drive,** which are not exactly garden tours, but will give you an excellent overview of the city and its natural landscape. The Port Hills Drive is especially worth doing for its spectacular views from Alps to ocean.

During the 4-day **Cathedral Garden Festival,** many of Christchurch's private gardeners throw open their gates. It's held annually in late November. Ask at the visitor center for more information.

If you take the spectacular drive up Dyer's Pass Road and over the Port Hills to Governor's Bay, you'll find a cluster of private gardens open to the public (ask at the visitor center for details). Barry Sligh at **Taunton Gardens** ★★ (© 03/329-9746) is an enthusiastic plant breeder whose stunning 2 hectares (5 acres) of woodland gardens are open September to April Tuesday through Sunday for NZ$15. Just down the road is one of the most famous structured gardens in New Zealand: **Ohinetahi** ★★★ (© 03/329-9852), owned by architect Sir Miles Warren and open by appointment for NZ$30.

THE WINERIES

There are now over 80 wineries in the Canterbury region, making this the fourth-largest winemaking area in the country. The combination of long hours of sunshine; stony, free-draining soils; low rainfall; extended autumns; and cool winters produces grapes with complex and developed flavors. The region is well suited to the production of red wines such as cabernet, merlot, and pinot noir. The main growing areas are Waipara, Christ-church, and Banks Peninsula. Look out for the development of the **Waipara Wine Village & Day Spa.** It was expected to open in 2009, but because of delays, earthworks had just begun at time of writing. The attraction will include a 132-room Grand Mercure hotel, a wine bar and restaurant, international ale house, wine-tasting facilities, and a luxury day spa.

For details on March's **Waipara Wine & Food Festival,** call © 0800-166-071 in New Zealand.

The visitor center's brochure on the *Waipara Valley Wineries Wine Trail* has a map showing the main wineries. Or pick up a copy of the very informative ***North Canterbury Food & Wine Trail*** ★ guide from Kaiapoi Visitor Information Centre © 03/327-3134; it details wineries, food suppliers, and farmers' markets. Here are a few suggestions to whet your appetite.

The **Mud House Winery & Cafe,** State Highway 1, Waipara (© 03/314-6900; www. mudhousewineryandcafe.co.nz), planted their first vines in 1994 and pinot noir is their flagship. They're open daily from 10am to 5pm for tastings and they also have a large restaurant. **Daniel Schuster Wines** ★, 192 Reeces Rd., Omihi, North Canterbury (© 03/314-5901; www.danielschusterwines.com), is one of my personal favorites. It's a few kilometers north of Waipara Valley in the Omihi area, and international wine consultant and owner Danny Schuster is well worth meeting. You can visit the tasting room and peruse wine for sale, or take a more comprehensive cellar tour and enjoy barrel tastings

CHRISTCHURCH & CANTERBURY

14

EXPLORING CHRISTCHURCH

ⒻFinds   **Well Oiled**

If you're in the Waipara Valley, make sure you visit **Athena Olive Groves,** 164 MacKenzies Rd. (© **03/314-6774;** www.athenaolives.co.nz), and try their fabulous range of extra-virgin and flavored olive oils, plus their pickled olives. Open daily from 10am until 5pm.

Wine Tours

Canterbury Wine Tours (✆ **0800/081-155;** www.waiparavalley.co.nz) has a range of options from half-day Waipara Valley wine tours starting at NZ$65. Its tours operate year-round and include wine tasting at three award-winning wineries. **Canterbury Leisure Tours** (✆ **0800/484-485** in NZ; www.leisure tours.co.nz) has a half-day tour of the Waipara winery region that explores four leading wineries and costs NZ$80 per person.

If you need transport from Christchurch to Waipara, take the **Hanmer Connection** shuttle (✆ **0800/377-378** in NZ) for NZ$25 one-way. It leaves from the Christchurch visitor center, with hotel pickups by arrangement.

Rossendale Wines, 168 Old Tai Tapu Rd., Halswell (✆ **03/322-9684;** www. rossendale.co.nz), is located in the charming Tai Tapu Valley area, on the perimeter of Christchurch. It has an established tradition of good wine and good food. Wines available here including Riesling, Gewürztraminer, sauvignon blanc, merlot, and pinot noir. **Trents Estate Vineyard & Restaurant,** Trents Road, Templeton (✆ **03/349-6940;** www.trentsvineyard.co.nz), is a charming setting built around a 125-year-old historic chicory kiln, which has been cleverly converted into a rustic restaurant. It is surrounded by pinot noir, chardonnay, and Riesling grapes. **Waipara Springs Winery & Restaurant** ★, State Highway 1, Waipara (✆/fax **03/314-6777;** www.waiparasprings.co.nz), is one of the oldest vineyards in the Waipara region. It produces premium-quality sauvignon blanc, Riesling, chardonnay, cabernet sauvignon, and pinot noir grapes from its own 20 hectares (50 acres). It has accumulated numerous medals overseas and in New Zealand, including a Gold Medal for its 1996 cabernet sauvignon, a Silver Medal for the 1997 sauvignon blanc, and a Gold for its 1997 Riesling.

with the winemaker by prior arrangement. The vineyard produces pinot noir, chardonnay, and Riesling. Open daily 10am to 5pm.

Pegasus Bay Winery & Restaurant ★★, 263 Stockgrove Rd., Amberley (✆ **03/314-6869;** www.pegasusbay.com), is a small vineyard and winery run by the Donaldson family, who have been seriously involved with wine for over 30 years. A 100-seat restaurant serves top-quality cuisine. Specialties include sauvignon/semillon, chardonnay, merlot cabernet, pinot noir, and Riesling. Open daily, tasting room 10am to 5pm, restaurant noon to 4pm.

If you'd like to stay in the Waipara Wine Region, I highly recommend **Claremont Country Estate** ★★★, 828 Ram Paddock Rd., Waipara Gorge, Amberley (✆ **03/314-7559;** fax 03/314-7065; www.claremont-estate.com), which offers fantastic tours on its 960-hectare (2,400-acre) working station and nature reserve, complete with 65-million-year-old fossils. They have B&B rates from NZ$880 and lodge rates from NZ$1,120. Tours cost extra. A more moderately priced option—but also divine—is **Dry Paddocks Country Retreat** ★★, 325 Purchas Rd., Waipara Valley, Amberley (✆ **03/314-9639;** fax 03/314-9637; www.drypaddocks.co.nz), which has a beautiful, modern, self-contained cottage for NZ$295 to NZ$395. It's closer to Christchurch than Claremont.

For a good overview of Akaroa and Banks Peninsula, call **Canterbury Trails** (✆ **03/337-1185;** www.canterburytrails.co.nz), which offers comprehensive day tours to the area that include a nature harbor cruise or an opportunity to swim with dolphins. If mountain scenery is more your thing, take the trip to Arthur's Pass National Park, which can also include a ride on the TranzAlpine train (one-way). Prices begin around NZ$280.

Unlimited New Zealand (✆ **03/960-9119;** www.unlimitednz.co.nz) will get you out into the wide-open spaces of Arthur's Pass for a firsthand experience in Canterbury's magnificent high country. Their walk up Bealey Valley takes in several different ecosystems, right up to the sub-alpine zone. It's a full day out and you return to Christchurch on the Tranz Alpine. You need warm, wet-weather gear and good boots, and it costs NZ$325 per person.

In the food and drink line, **Taste Canterbury** ★ (✆ **03/326-6753;** www.goodthings.co.nz) offers a terrific set of personalized gourmet food and wine tours of the greater Canterbury region. Mavis Airey is a knowledgeable guide and food writer, and her half-day tours cost NZ$140 per person for two (less if there are more of you), or NZ$240 per person for a full day. You'll get a lovely overview of rural Canterbury on the Akaroa and Ellesmere tours. I strongly recommend them—and all the goodies you get to sample and buy.

And for something entirely different again, allow a full day for the **TranzAlpine & High Country Explorer** ★★ (✆ **0800/863-975;** www.high-country.co.nz). You'll never forget this standout adventure. You'll leave Christchurch on the TranzAlpine, traveling to Arthur's Pass where you'll be picked up by a 4WD tussock buggy for the trip to Flock Hill Lodge and a hearty three-course lunch. Then it's a 22km (14-mile) safari into spectacular and otherwise inaccessible areas of Flock Hill sheep station. The last leg of the journey is an exhilarating jet-boat ride down the Waimakariri River to Woodstock sheep station for afternoon tea. A coach returns you to the city. It's a big day but one you'll love. Make sure you take warm clothes as the high country can be chilly, even in summer. This superb tour costs NZ$375 for adults and NZ$188 for children ages 4 to 14. Don't forget your camera. There's dynamite scenery along the way!

Canterbury Leisure Tours (✆ **0800/484-485** in NZ, or 03/384-0999; www.leisure tours.co.nz) has a comprehensive selection of half- and full-day tours that cover everything from whale-watching in Kaikoura (see "Side Trips from Christchurch," later in this chapter) to wine trails, sheep-farm tours, horse trekking, Mount Cook, Hanmer Springs (see "Side Trips from Christchurch," later in this chapter), and more.

And if you *still* haven't gotten *The Lord of the Rings* out of your system—and believe me, plenty haven't—you're a sure thing for **Hassle-Free Tours'** adventures. Call ✆ **0800/427-753** in New Zealand, or 03/385-5775, or visit the website at www.hasslefree.co.nz to find out about their 4WD excursions that deposit you in the thick of Edora, the

---

(Ⓜ**oments** **Maori Magic**

Tucked away in suburban Christchurch sits the largest urban marae and carved ancestral house (Aoraki) in New Zealand. **Nga Hau E Wha National Marae,** 250 Pages Rd., Wainoni (✆ **03/382-6628**), offers a number of daytime and evening cultural experiences; you'll be impressed by the bounty of fine Maori carving on-site. This is the best place in the South Island to enjoy a traditional hangi and cultural experience.

(**Moments**) **An Unforgettable Train Trip**

The **TranzAlpine** ★★★ is rated as one of the five most spectacular train journeys in the world, and you can't fail to be impressed by the scenery as you make your way from Christchurch in the east to Greymouth in the west. The train travels over the Canterbury Plains; through the heart of the Southern Alps; and through tunnels, beech forests, and massive river gorges to the West Coast. It's a must-do for anyone visiting the South Island.

The round-trip excursion costs NZ$150 to Arthur's Pass and NZ$199 to Greymouth, with cheaper rates for children—and cheaper specials if you book online. If you take the Arthur's Pass option, you'll have 5 hours there before the train returns, but there are many excellent bush walks in the area and a couple of nice cafes (see "Side Trips from Christchurch," later in this chapter).

If you go to Greymouth, you'll have only 1 hour in the township before the train returns to Christchurch—not a lot of time to do much more than wander about. Check out the "Greymouth & Lake Brunner" section in chapter 15 for possible activities.

The train leaves from Christchurch's main railway station at 1 Clarence St., Addington. For reservations and further information, contact **Tranz Scenic** (© **0800/872-467** in NZ; www.tranzscenic.co.nz). Food is available on the buffet car, or you can bring your own picnic. The train makes six stops during the journey.

capital city of the Rohan people of the film trilogy. The cost is NZ$215 adults, NZ$150 children.

Adventure Canterbury (© **0800/847-455** in NZ; www.adventurecanterbury.co.nz) and **Tuatara Tours** ★★ (© **0800/377-378;** www.tuataratours.co.nz) are two more excellent companies offering a wide range of half-day, 1-day, and multiday tours into the wider Canterbury landscape. I can personally recommend Tuatara Tours' 3- to 4-day Akaroa Walk, which takes you into spectacular landscapes—make sure you're fit, as it involves a *lot* of uphill walking. Or try their much less taxing 4-day West Coast Trail, which is a truly beautiful introduction to things West Coast. The great thing about these tours is that, in addition to excellent guides, you only have to carry a small day pack, you eat well, and you sleep in comfortable beds.

6 OUTDOOR PURSUITS

BEACHES Christchurch has three main beaches—Sumner, Taylor's Mistake, and New Brighton. Originally a quiet holiday suburb, **Sumner** ★ is now favored by city dwellers on weekends. Its attractive beach is a magnet for swimmers, surfers, and volleyball players. There are plenty of good cafes, restaurants, and bars (see "Where to Dine," earlier in this chapter). Lots of families, lots of young people.

Taylor's Mistake is a surfer hangout with some quaint old holiday homes tucked into the cliffs. There's a good walk around the cliff tops from Taylor's Mistake to Boulder Bay.

Directions are on a big board to the right of the parking area behind the surf club. The beach is over the hill from Sumner and is best accessed by car. Once past Scarborough Hill, there's no place else to go but down to Taylor's Mistake.

There has been a rush of redevelopment at **New Brighton.** It's a good place to take the kids for fishing, safe swimming, and surfing. All in all, a better beach experience awaits at Sumner.

BIKING   Christchurch has a reputation as a cyclist's paradise because of its overall flat terrain. Bike lanes are marked off in several parts of the city, and parking lots provide bike racks. For rentals, contact **City Cycle Hire** (✆ **0800/343-848** in NZ, or 03/339-4020; www.cyclehire-tours.co.nz), which will deliver bikes to your accommodations. They have road and mountain bikes plus tandems, and all are supplied with licks and helmets. Half-day, 1-day, and long-term hires are available.

BOATING   **Punting** is a fun activity, especially since someone else is doing all the work. You'll spot the young men from **Punting on the Avon** (✆ 03/353-5944; www.punting. co.nz) in straw hats pushing their way up the Avon River at the junction of Oxford Terrace and Worcester Boulevard. You can reserve a ride at the visitor center and pay NZ$12 per person for a 20-minute round-trip to the Town Hall, NZ$16 for a 30-minute round-trip to the Retour Restaurant. You can also get tickets from the landing stage at Worcester bridge. Punts depart daily 9am to dusk. Punting is also available at Mona Vale Gardens (see "Parks & Gardens," earlier in this chapter).

If canoeing is your thing, rent one from **Antigua Boatsheds,** 2 Cambridge Terrace (✆ 03/ 366-6768; www.boatsheds.co.nz), for NZ$10 per hour. It opens at 9am; the last boats go out at 5pm.

CLIMBING   Get the inside scoop at **Bivouac Outdoor,** 76 City Mall, near the Bridge of Remembrance (✆ 03/366-3197; www.bivouac.co.nz), where you can also buy *Port Hills Climbing* for NZ$25. **Castle Rock** and the **Tors** are good for all levels; **Rapaki** is good for beginner to intermediate climbers; and **Lyttelton Rock** is for the more adventurous. **Castle Hill** in Arthur's Pass has hundreds of climbs for mixed levels and is excellent for boulder climbing. Or head to the **YMCA Indoor Rock Climbing Wall,** 12 Hereford St. (✆ 03/366-0689; www.ymcachch.org.nz), which is open daily from 8am to 10pm and costs NZ$12 for adults, NZ$8 for children; it's an extra NZ$5 for harness hire and NZ$5 for shoe hire.

DOLPHIN-WATCHING   **Christchurch Wildlife Cruises,** 17 Norwich Quay, Lyttelton (✆ 0800/436-574 in NZ, or 03/328-9078; www.blackcat.co.nz), has an afternoon dolphin-watching cruise, departing daily at 1:30pm all year. It costs NZ$60 for adults and NZ$25 for children ages 5 to 15. They also operate dolphin-watching cruises in Akaroa (see "Side Trips to Christchurch," later in this chapter). You'll find free parking near the wharf, or you can catch the no. 28 bus from the city to Lyttelton. A free shuttle also connects with each cruise.

GOLF   The Canterbury region boasts over 40 courses. **Russley Golf Club,** 428 Memorial Ave., near the airport (✆ 03/358-4748), has reasonably flat, well-bunkered greens and is one of the premier courses in New Zealand. It is open by arrangement. Greens fees are around NZ$60. **Harewood Twin Courses,** 371 McLeans Island Rd. (✆ 03/359-8843; www.harewoodgolf.co.nz), is the largest golf club in the South Island, with two 18-hole courses. Greens fees are NZ$20 to NZ$40. **Christchurch Golf Club** (sometimes referred to as Shirley), 45 Horseshoe Lake Rd. (✆ 03/385-2738), has well-groomed,

Taking to the Slopes

There are excellent ski fields within 2 hours of Christchurch. Closest among them are the five main fields of the Arthur's Pass area—Porter Heights, Mount Cheeseman, Broken River, Craigieburn Valley, and Temple Basin—all 1 to 1½ hours from the city. **Porter Heights** (© 03/318-4002; www.skiporters.co.nz) is the closest commercial field. It has the longest downhill drop in New Zealand, and although the facilities are pretty basic, it has a variety of terrain and stunning views. It's good for all skill levels. **Mount Cheeseman** (© 03/379-5315; www.mtcheeseman.com) is a club field and the second closest to Christchurch. It's good for all skiers and snowboarders, but it's not as big as the others. **Broken River** (© 03/318-7270; ski@brokenriver.co.nz) is another club field and a bit more rugged; it has rope tows only. **Craigieburn Valley** (© 03/365-2514; www.craigieburn.co.nz) is a club field 1¼ hours away, perfect for intermediate and advanced skiers. **Temple Basin** (© 03/377-7788; www.templebasin.co.nz), a club field beyond Arthur's Pass, has the most reliable snow in Canterbury facing the sun. It's a steep and enclosed field, and skiers say that if you can ski at Temple Basin, you can ski anywhere in the world. It's a snowboarder's paradise, too.

North Canterbury also has **Mount Lyford** (© 03/315-6178; www.mtlyford.co.nz), a privately owned commercial field 1 hour from Kaikoura and 1½ to 2 hours north of Christchurch; and **Mount Olympus** (© 03/318-5840; www.mtolympus.co.nz), a club field in the back of the Craigieburn range, set in a wide south-facing basin, that offers a variety of runs on uncrowded slopes.

Farther afield is **Mount Hutt Ski Area,** Main Road, Methven (© 03/302-8811; www.nzski.com). Right in the heart of the Southern Alps, Mount Hutt is recognized internationally as having the longest number of skiable days in Australasia. It's located 90 minutes south of Christchurch by car. Although it's the most developed commercial field in Canterbury, Mount Hutt is very popular because it's well serviced by T-bars and chairlifts, and good shuttles are available. It's quite crowded here, and it isn't every skier's favorite. It doesn't have the same good fall line as Porter Heights, but it does have much better après-ski and on-field facilities. *Note:* It's important to read all signs here. If they say CLOSED, they mean it—it can get dangerous here because the weather closes in very quickly. It's a long haul up the mountain, and chains are necessary for a good part of the season. For a snow report, call © **0900/99-SNO [99-766].**

Addicted skiers tell me you should never go anywhere in the Porter Heights range or Mount Hutt when Canterbury's infamous nor'west wind blows; apparently it's often raining in the mountains then and you'll be plagued by horrendous winds.

primarily flat fairways. It's open most days; greens fees are around NZ$95. **Clearwater Resort,** Johns Road (© **03/360-1003;** www.clearwaternz.com), is a par-72 course and players will pay around NZ$135 for a round of golf. The **Terrace Downs Country Resort and Golf Club** (© **0800/465-373** in NZ, or 03/318-6943; www.terracedowns.co.nz) has opened in Rakaia, a 50-minute drive from Christchurch, at the base of the Mount Hutt ski field and on the banks of the Rakaia Gorge. The par-72 course has 70 bunkers, eight lakes, rolling fairways, and spectacular views; nonaffiliated fees are around NZ$120.

HORSE TREKKING   Head over the Port Hills to Charteris Bay and join a farm and bush trek with **Orton Bradley Horse Treks,** Orton Bradley Park (℃ **03/329-4900;** www.obhorsetreks.co.nz). They're 30 minutes from the city and you'll see terrific harbor views along the way. A 1-hour ride is NZ$50 per person and return transport from the city can be arranged for NZ$30 per person (minimum two people).

HOT-AIR BALLOONING   There is no other place in the world where it's possible to fly from the center of a city, in view of the ocean, toward snowcapped mountains. **Up, Up and Away** (℃ **03/381-4600;** www.ballooning.co.nz) charges NZ$300 for adults and NZ$260 for children ages 5 to 11 for a special first-light experience. Free transport is provided from city locations.

JET-BOATING   Several operators offer exhilarating spins up the Waimakariri River. The longest established is **Waimak Alpine Jet** (℃ **0800/263-626** in NZ, or 03/318-4881; www.alpinejet.co.nz). It's a little farther out of town than **Jet Thrills** (℃ **0800/847-455** in NZ; www.adventurecanterbury.com), a 15-minute drive away, but both give you something to squeal about. Prices are NZ$90 to NZ$300 per person.

MOUNTAIN BIKING   The Port Hills are a favorite place for mountain biking. The **Mountain Bike Adventure Co.** (℃ **0800/424-534** in NZ) makes it possible to take the Christchurch Gondola to the top and then bike down one of the hill tracks or the road. The cost is NZ$65. The gondola operates daily October through April from 10am to midnight, in winter from noon to 10pm. Mountain-biking reservations can be made at the visitor center.

PARAGLIDING   Nimbus Paragliding ★★ (℃ **0800/111-611** in NZ; www.nimbus paragliding.co.nz) was the early pioneer of Canterbury paragliding and has pilots who will assist you in leaping off one of three superb Port Hills sites. Four to 10 minutes of flying will cost NZ$160 tandem. A paragliding school with 1- to 11-day courses is also available. Seriously addicted paragliders could consider **Nimbus Paragliding Adventure Tours,** which provides all flying equipment, campervans, and a New Zealand–wide itinerary covering the best flying sites (see chapter 5).

SKY DIVING   If you feel ready for that ultimate adrenaline rush, ring **Skydivingnz. com** (℃ **0800/697-593** in NZ; www.skydivingnz.com). You'll be attached to its highly experienced tandem instructor. Free-fall sky diving over Hagley Park costs NZ$330 from 2,700m (9,000 ft.). Courtesy transport is provided from the city.

SWIMMING   Get your head wet at **QEII Park,** Travis Road, on the way to New Brighton (℃ **03/383-4313;** www.ccc.govt.nz). There are four heated indoor pools, including a crazy hydroslide made up of 220m (722 ft.) of twisting tubes. Right in town is the new **Centennial Leisure Centre,** Armagh Street (℃ **03/941-6853**), which has a gym, lap pool, leisure pools, spas, and saunas.

WALKING   The visitor center has several brochures detailing city walks. One of the best is *Christchurch City Walks* ★, which gives three easy, 45-minute options that take in city landmarks. *River Walks of Christchurch* ★★ details 13 walks for all ages; and *Christchurch Central City Lanes Walk* introduces you to many historic buildings in the now-trendy lanes off Lichfield Street. There is also a network of good walking tracks through the Port Hills that you can enjoy on your own, free of charge.

The more energetic will find the 4-day, 35km (22-mile) **Banks Peninsula Track** ★★ worthwhile (see "Akaroa" under "Side Trips from Christchurch," later in this chapter); there's also the 3-day, 43km (27-mile) **Kaikoura Coast Track ★★**. **Arthur's Pass National Park,** 150km (93 miles) west of Christchurch, is another tramper's heaven (see "Side Trips from Christchurch," later in this chapter). Or call **New Zealand Hiking Safaris** (✆ **0800/697-232** in NZ; www.hikingnewzealand.com), which has a range of superb multiday treks. It's based in Lyttelton but offers treks all over New Zealand.

WHITE-WATER RAFTING **Rangitata Rafts** (✆ **0800/251-251** in NZ, or 03/696-3735; www.rafts.co.nz) will take pleasure in introducing you to the Rangitata River's Grade V rapids. You'll start the adventure with a relaxed lunch rather than hard work. That comes later as you go through safety briefs, practical training, and a natural progression to the intense Grade IV and V section. End with hot showers and a barbecue. All this will cost NZ$210. The day trip includes transport from Christchurch.

7 SHOPPING

THE MALLS

The city has a number of suburban malls. **Westfield Riccarton** (✆ 03/348-4119) has more than 100 shops; the bus stops right outside the door. **Northlands Mall,** in Papanui (✆ 03/352-6535), has 67 stores. The **Palms,** in Shirley (✆ 03/385-3067), has more than 85 stores, a big entertainment complex, and good bus services. The recently revamped, upmarket **Merivale Mall ★** (✆ 03/355-9692) is smaller, but features a more expensive range of designer stores and boutiques. All malls are open daily.

THE MARKETS

The **Arts Centre,** on Worcester Boulevard (p. 375), offers a good range of everything from quirky to quality, especially during the open market weekends when the courtyard swells with purveyors of all things.

Riccarton Rotary Market ★★ (✆ 03/339-0011; www.riccartonmarket.co.nz), which you'll find Sundays from 8am at Riccarton Racecourse, on Racecourse Road, Upper Riccarton, is supposedly New Zealand's biggest outdoor market and attracts over 300 vendors. Arrive early to get the best bargains. The goods are predominantly second-hand, but there are some good buys in sheepskin products and crafts. You'll need to sift

---

ⓘ Tips Made in New Zealand

Head for **Untouched World ★★★**, 155 Roydvale Ave. (✆ **03/357-9399;** www.untouchedworld.com), where you'll find a stunning range of top-quality, New Zealand–made wool garments. It has a delightful setting with a top-end restaurant and native garden. They have another outlet at the Arts Centre, 301 Montreal St. (✆ **03/962-6551**). Phone for courtesy transport. **Wild South Adventure Clothing,** 685 Colombo St. (✆ **03/379-7330**), also sells excellent garments in natural fibers.

Finds   **Retail on High**

Some of my favorite stores are on High Street. **One Big Sugar Bowl** (☎ **03/377-3600**) will appeal to all your senses with lovely costume jewelry, underwear, and accessories. **Decodence,** 151 High St. (☎ **03/982-8332**), is a good place for Art Deco finds; and **inform** ★★, 158 High St. (☎ **03/366-3893**), is where you'll find more beautiful contemporary jewelry by Koji Miyazaki (owner of Form in the Christchurch Art Gallery) and other reputable New Zealand jewelers.

through everything as there's a lot of junk, but it's a good cultural study. Bus no. 83 from central city drops you at the main gate.

CITY SHOPPING SPOTS

Back in the city, **New Regent Street** ★ is an architectural highlight on the central-city tram route. It features a mix of boutique stores, restaurants, and cafes and is generally very lively. If you're walking, it runs between Gloucester and Armagh streets.

For antiques and interesting secondhand stores, walk the length of **High Street** between Litchfield and Tuam streets. My favorite is **Chaos** ★, 180 Tuam St. (☎ **03/366-8651**). It always has a great array of the unexpected and it shares the space with a vintage clothing and jewelry dealer. **W. Holliday & Sons** ★★★, 20 Papanui Rd., St. Albans (☎ **03/355-4117**), is a fifth-generation enterprise with the best imported antiques. **Wayne Wright Antiques** ★, 88 Victoria St. (☎ **03/366-1116**), is a close second.

Victoria Street, north of the Crowne Plaza through to Bealey Avenue, is now home to a lovely range of boutique gift, fashion, design, furniture, and interior decor stores, with plenty of cafes and restaurants along its length for a much-needed shopper's rest.

A new shopping and entertainment heart has sprung up at **South of Lichfield (SOL)** ★★, a classy alley off Lichfield Street, which mixes popular cafes, bars, and nightclubs with boutique stores. This theme continues in nearby **Poplar Lane** ★, which can be accessed off Lichfield Street (a couple minutes' walk to the east), or off High Street. And **High Street** ★★ itself is certainly the fashion center. You'll also find a number of leading art galleries in the High and Manchester streets area.

Top-quality New Zealand arts, crafts, and jewelry can be found at **Form Gallery** ★★★, in the new Christchurch Art Gallery (☎ **03/377-1211;** www.form.co.nz). If you don't find what you want, **Cave Rock Gallery** ★, on the Hereford Street side of the Arts Centre (☎ **03/365-1634**), will almost certainly fill some gaps.

There is a **Regency Duty-Free Shop** at 736 Colombo St. (☎ **03/379-1923**). And it's in this area and into the Square that you'll find a wide range of gift stores selling souvenirs and clothing.

J. Ballantyne & Co., at City Mall and Colombo Street (☎ **03/379-7400**), is still seen as *the* department store in Christchurch. It has been operating with distinctive style for over 100 years and its newly opened Contemporary Lounge is a good spot for top international clothing and accessories brands that can't be found elsewhere on the South Island.

For excellent New Zealand–made contemporary gifts, go to the **Vault** ★ (☎ **03/379-5399**), which is also in this area, or **Wild Places** (☎ **03/365-2533**).

Map World ★, 173 Gloucester St. (℃ **03/374-5399;** www.mapworld.co.nz), is New Zealand's most comprehensive specialty map shop, stocked to the brim with guidebooks and topographic maps.

8 CHRISTCHURCH AFTER DARK

Christchurch has a variety of nightlife, but lacks the range and color of Wellington and Auckland. Find out about weekend happenings by reading the "Entertainment" section of Friday's *Press,* or consult the "What's On" section of the *Tourist Times.*

THE PERFORMING ARTS

The city has a regular program of concerts, plays, musicals, and dance performances held at the **Town Hall,** on Kilmore Street (℃ **03/377-8899**), and the **Theatre Royal,** 145 Gloucester St. (℃ **03/366-6326**).

The **Court Theatre,** in the Arts Centre, Worcester Boulevard (℃ **0800/333-100** in NZ, or 03/963-0870; www.courttheatre.co.nz), is the home of the best professional theater company in New Zealand. Shows range from Shakespeare to contemporary American and British theater to the best New Zealand plays. Tickets for most shows are NZ$30 to NZ$42.

THE CLUB & BAR SCENE

The most visible evidence of Christchurch nightlife is to be found along Oxford Terrace, or **"The Strip"** ★, as it's known locally. This is the most established hub of the cafe-and-bar scene. Come 11pm, the mood changes as the place is infiltrated by the 18-to-30 age group and the music is pumped up accordingly. If you're single, under 40, hungry for the inebriated attention of the opposite sex, and ready for just about anything, you'll have a great time here; if you're none of the above, you'll probably get the urge to move on around midnight. In this area, **Liquidity** ★ (℃ **03/365-6088**), has the most style; **Coyote** (℃ **03/366-6055**) and **Viaduct** (℃ **03/377-9968**) have popular dance floors,

---

Hedging Your Bets

The **Christchurch Casino,** Victoria Street, across from the Crowne Plaza (℃ **0800/227-466** in NZ, or 03/365-9999; www.christchurchcasino.co.nz), opened in 1994 and was New Zealand's first. Since then, it's had several million visitors (60% local). It's probably the only boutique casino in Australasia that features a more classical European style, setting it apart from its Auckland equivalent's money-churner atmosphere. You'll find over 350 gaming machines as well as blackjack, baccarat, Caribbean stud poker, American roulette, keno, and tai sai. Café Caesars is open for light meals; there are several bars; and the Grand Café is worth a visit in itself for its excellent food. You must be at least 20 to enter; dress codes are strict—no jeans or denim of any kind, and no thongs, T-shirts, or active sportswear. Free shuttles operate to and from local hotels and motels. Open 24 hours a day, 7 days a week.

> (i) **Tips**   **The Gay Scene**
>
> Christchurch is a very "polite" city, and its gay scene is less overt than in the big-ger cities. Here's what I've unearthed: **Heaven's Above,** corner of Tuam and Colombo streets (📞 **03/365-5648**), is open Thursday and Friday 7pm to late, Sat-urday 8pm until late, and Sunday 3pm until late. **Cruz,** upstairs, Ministry Night-club complex, 90 Lichfield St. (📞 **03/379-2910**), is Christchurch's only gay bar nightclub and is open Tuesday through Sunday 7pm until late. **Menfriends,** upstairs, 83 Lichfield St. (📞 **03/377-1701**), is a sauna and cruise club; the **Box,** upstairs, 146a Lichfield St. (📞 **03/377-4748**), is a gay video and cruise lounge; and **Divas Boutique,** 146a Lichfield St. (📞 **03/379-3446**), is a social lounge where cross-dressers and transvestites can meet, Tuesday through Saturday, noon until 9pm. They have regular cross-dressing parties every Saturday night. For more information, check www.gaynz.com.

which get so packed you can barely move. Next door to Viaduct is its partner, **Di Lusso** (📞 **03/377-9968**), which presents a stylish little lounge bar that mixes good music and cocktails—chiefly for the 30s crowd. The **Tap Room** (📞 **03/365-0547**) attracts a wider age group.

Personally, I think there are better options in the **South of Lichfield (SOL)** ★★ (www.sol.net.nz) area. SOL has over a dozen creatively themed bars, and the place is pulsing with people and atmosphere from Thursday through Saturday nights. And if you're in Christchurch on New Year's Eve, this is the place to be. In this area, the ever-popular steak lover's **MU Bar** ★, 92 Lichfield St. (📞 **03/377-0681**), has the distinction of delivering both terrific steak meals and a lively night out. And if you feel like kicking your heels up afterward, you need only walk around the corner to **Base Bar & Night-club,** 92 Struthers Lane (📞 **03/377-7149**), or any of the many bars adjacent. I like the classy-but-tiny champagne cafe, **La Petite Croix** ★★, 3 Sol Sq. (📞 **03/964-5260**), and the all-pink **Minx Bar** (📞 **03/374-9944**). **His Lordship's Bar,** 110 Lichfield St. (📞 **03/366-3225**), is a good bet if you favor European beers; and you'll get proper English beers at the very pleasant **Twisted Hop Microbrewery,** 6 Poplar Lane (📞 **03/962-3688**). Nearby **Poplar Lane** ★, in fact, is also blessed with several good bar options.

Lime, 817 Colombo St. (📞 **03/365-2393**), is an intimate, late-night hangout; and good times are had by all at the **Flying Burrito Brothers** ★, corner of Armagh and New Regent streets (📞 **03/377-7626**), in the company of New Zealand's biggest tequila selection.

If sports bars are more your style, you won't find one bigger than **Holy Grail,** 98 Worcester Blvd. (📞 **03/365-9816**), which has huge screens and a 24-hour license. **Leg-ends,** 46 Bedford Row (📞 **03/366-5596**), is another in this vein; and the **Loaded Hog,** Manchester and Cashel streets (📞 **03/366-6674**), is a popular starting point for the 20- to 30-something crowd. Also in this area is the raging dance club, the **Concrete Club,** 132 Manchester St. (📞 **03/366-0438**), where the cool crowd hangs out; and just around the corner and just as cool, is **Double Happy,** in Cashel St. (📞 **03/374-6463**).

A good jazz bar is **Sammy's Jazz Review** ★, 14 Bedford Row (📞 **03/377-8618**).

In Merivale, **Aikmans** ★★, 154 Aikmans Rd. (📞 **03/355-2271**), hums on Thursday through Saturday nights, and it has a fabulous outdoor courtyard with fireplace and leather sofas. Next door, **Ivy,** 150 Aikmans Rd. (© **03/355-5577**), is also lively though it's more of a "meat market." Adjacent **JDV,** Aikmans Road (© **03/964-3860**), has a gorgeous little martini bar that rocks until late, especially on Thursday nights; and **No. 4 ★★**, 4 Mansfield Ave. (© **03/355-3720**), generally attracts a wide age group looking for a good time—and in Merivale that tends to mean a clubby-style bar with free-flowing alcohol and lots of beautiful people doing things they might regret in the morning.

The **Dux de Lux,** in the Arts Centre (p. 373), is the place to be if you're into loud local bands and a pretty full-on bar environment. It's a favorite for 20- and 30-year-olds, who spill out into the paved courtyard area. Great boutique brews, too.

MOVIES

Currently, the biggest multiplex is **Hoyts 8,** 392 Moorehouse Ave. (© **03/366-6367**). The **Regent on Worcester,** 94 Worcester St. (© **03/377-8095**), is a fine, centrally placed four-cinema complex right beside the Square. And the **Academy ★** (© **03/366-0167**) and the **Cloisters** (© **03/366-0167**), located in the heart of the Arts Centre, show national and international art-house films. An eight-theater complex opened at the **Palms** in Shirley in late 2003 and another at **Westfield Riccarton** (see "Shopping," above).

9 SIDE TRIPS FROM CHRISTCHURCH

AKAROA ★★★

There's a rather off-putting, winding hill road between Christchurch and Akaroa—but the scenery is wonderful and you shouldn't let a few steep twists and turns deter you from visiting this little French-inspired whimsy on the shores of Akaroa Harbour.

From the time you reach the breathtaking setting of the **Hilltop Café & Bar** (© **03/ 325-1005**), a country pub overlooking Akaroa and the harbor, you'll be seduced by this dramatic volcanic landscape. Jean Langlois, an early French explorer, took word of it back to France, and in 1840, two ships and a handful of settlers arrived to colonize the site. They were too late—the British had beaten them to it when they signed the Treaty of Waitangi the year before. The French abandoned their plan, but the settlers stayed on, casting about names such as Le Bons Bay, Duvauchelle, and French Farm. Today, you'll still find "rues" here, not streets.

In recent years, the community of about 1,000 residents has pulled up its promotional socks, and you'll find a growing number of excellent lodgings, restaurants, and shops. The Maori word *akaroa* means "long harbor," and that's exactly what dominates the village and its activities.

ⓕFinds   Pit Stop

If you feel like a break before crossing the hill, stop at the **Little River Gallery ★**, Main Road, Little River (© **03/325-1944;** www.littlerivergallery.com), where you'll find a wide range of New Zealand–made arts and crafts. And right beside the gallery is the excellent **Little River Store & Café.** Both are open daily—the gallery from 9:30am to 5:30pm, the store from 7:30am to 7:30pm, and the cafe from 9am to 6pm.

> **(Finds) The Big Cheese**
>
> As you drop down from the hills into Barrys Bay on your drive to Akaroa, keep an eye out on the left for **Barrys Bay Cheese** ★★★ (☎ **03/304-5809;** fax 03/304-5814), makers of mouthwatering traditional cheeses—everything from award-winning cheddars to Maasdam, Gouda, Edam, and havarti, to name just a few. During the cheesemaking season (usually Oct–Apr), you can watch cheesemaking activities every second day, through the viewing gallery window. There's a shop and I advise you to stock up! They're open daily.

Essentials

GETTING THERE   From Christchurch, follow State Highway 75 to Akaroa, passing through Halswell Village and Little River, up over the hills and down around Akaroa Harbour. Two shuttle companies operate regularly from Christchurch. Akaroa **French Connection** (☎ **0800/800-575** in NZ, or 03/366-4556; www.akaroabus.co.nz) has daily departures from Christchurch Visitor Centre and a complimentary pickup service from inner city accommodations. They charge NZ$49 round-trip. The **Akaroa Shuttle** (☎ **0800/500-929;** www.akaroashuttle.co.nz) charges NZ$45 per person round-trip (cash only) for the direct shuttle service. Both make the 1-hour trip daily, and both also offer scenic tours; reservations are essential.

VISITOR INFORMATION   The **Akaroa Visitor Centre** is in the old post office building, 80 Rue Lavaud (☎/fax **03/304-8600;** www.akaroa.com). It's open daily in summer 9am to 5pm; and in winter, Monday to Friday 9am to 5pm, and weekends 10am to 4pm.

Exploring the Town & Harbor

A small **museum,** made up of four historic buildings on Rue Lavaud (☎ **03/304-1013;** akaroa.museum@ccc.govt.nz), has lively displays and good Maori collections. It's open daily from 10:30am to 4:30pm. The **Langlois-Eteveneaux Cottage** was partly prefabricated in France around 1846 and is probably the oldest in Canterbury. The **Old French Cemetery** was the first consecrated burial ground in Canterbury and is just off Rue Pompallier. The old **lighthouse,** which was in service from 1880 to 1980, is also interesting. Admission is NZ$4 adults and NZ$8 families.

If you're artistically inclined, pick up the brochure for the self-guided **Akaroa & Bays Art Trail** ★, which leads to the homes and studios of 18 local artists and craftspeople. You'll need at least a day, as many of them are scattered farther afield in the surrounding bays. One of the most striking and unusual artist environments is the **Giant's House—Linton** ★★★, 68 Rue Balguerie (☎ **03/304-7501;** www.linton.co.nz), where sculptor Josie Martin has created one of the wackiest and most inspiring gardens you'll find anywhere. She's surrounded her gorgeous historic home (B&B accommodations also provided), with landscaped gardens and a myriad of amazing mosaic sculptures that are bound to delight. Children will love it, and it's bound to be one of your lasting Akaroa memories, too. The garden is open daily from noon to 4pm December to March, and from 2 to 4pm from April through November. Admission is NZ$15 for adults and NZ$7 for children. Josie also has a cafe on-site. For a sample of local village culture, you can't go past **Akaroa Cinema & Café** ★, 4 Selwyn Ave. (☎ **03/304-7678;** www.cinecafe.

co.nz), which has two tiny theaters showing the latest foreign and art-house films. It's a great experience!

One thing every visitor should do is experience the harbor firsthand. **Pohatu Sea Kayaking** ★★ (✆ 03/304-8552; www.pohatu.co.nz), offers excellent guided kayak tours in the Flea Bay Marine Reserve and you should see lots of penguins. Your tour guide is one of the volunteers working on penguin conservation and protection, and the evening tours cost NZ$75 per person.

Akaroa Harbour Nature Cruises ★★ *The Cat* takes 90 people and offers great views throughout the 2-hour scenic cruise, which visits a salmon farm, a *paua* pearl farm, and bird-life sites. You have to be quite unlucky on this trip *not* to see the charming Hector's dolphins. The company's 3-hour dolphin-swimming trip gives you a chance to have a close encounter. See the section on sustainable tourism in chapter 3 for more information on swimming with dolphins.

Main Wharf. ✆ 0800/436-574 in NZ, or 03/304-7641. Fax 03/304-7643. www.blackcat.co.nz. Scenic nature cruise NZ$60 adults, NZ$30 children 5–15. YHA discounts available. May–Sept daily 1:30pm; Oct–Apr daily 11am and 1:30pm. Dolphin swimming NZ$130 adults, NZ$110 children 5–15. May–Sept daily noon; Oct–Apr 8:30am, 11:30am, 1:30pm, and 3:30pm. Parking at base of wharf and along the waterfront.

Walking the Walk

Consider this: 35km (22 miles) of unspoiled coastal farmland scenery; undisturbed colonies of fur seals, penguins, and dolphins; sheltered turquoise bays; the rustic comforts of trampers' huts; and enough moderate exertion to keep you honest. This is what you get with the **Banks Peninsula Track** ★★ (✆ 03/304-7612; www.bankstrack.co.nz). The track twice climbs to 600m (1,970 ft.) and features rugged, exposed headlands, so a reasonable level of fitness is required. The season runs from October through April. The cost is NZ$230, which includes transport from Akaroa to the first hut, 4 nights' accommodations, track registration, and landowners' fees. The 2-day tramp is recommended only for those with a high level of fitness and costs NZ$150 per person.

The **Southern Bays Track** (✆/fax 03/329-0007) offers three unguided and guided options over the southern coastlines, cliffs, valleys, bush, and peaks of Banks Peninsula, descending into the Little River village via the Okuti Valley. For those who like challenge without the hassle, the guided walk, with packs carried by someone else, has got to be a dream option. The season runs from mid-October to the end of May. Call for prices.

Moments   On the Run

One adventure that shouldn't be missed is the **Eastern Bays Scenic Mail Run** ★★ (✆ 03/304-8526, or call the visitor center; www.akaroa.com). Join mailman Robin and Jo, who make this 120km (74-mile), 4-hour journey around some hair-raising Banks Peninsula roads every day. They deliver mail, papers, and freight to the isolated farms and communities of the peninsula, and they'll take up to eight passengers along for the ride. They'll even stop to let you take photos—and believe me, you'll want to. The Mail Run departs from the visitor center Monday through Saturday at 9am. It costs NZ$60; reservations the day before travel are essential.

(Finds) A Beach Diversion

On the way to or from Akaroa on State Highway 75, take a detour to **Lake Elles-mere.** It measures 287 sq. km (111 sq. miles), but it's only 2m (6½ ft.) deep at its deepest point and is home to thousands of Australian black swans and other birds. And for a dramatic seascape, don't go past **Birdlings Flat** ★★, in the same area. The seas are very dangerous on this stone-covered beach, so don't attempt swimming under any conditions. It's signposted off the main highway about 30 to 40 minutes from Christchurch.

Where to Stay

In addition to those listed below, I recommend the following options. **Garthowen on the Waterfront,** 7 Beach Rd. (© **03/304-7419;** www.garthowen.co.nz), is centrally located opposite the main beach and has four good-size bedrooms with en suites. **Chez la Mer Backpackers,** 50 Rue Lavaud (©/fax **03/304-7024;** www.chezlamer.co.nz), has shared bunkrooms for NZ$28 per person, and twins/doubles for NZ$70 to NZ$90. But if you truly want to get away from it all, stay at one of my favorite old country homes, **Rowandale Homestead** ★★, 894 Okains Bay, Banks Peninsular (© **03/304-8615;** www.rowandalehomestead.co.nz). It's 20 minutes from Akaroa, and with a tariff of just NZ$165 to NZ$295 and some of the best food and hospitality in a unique setting, it's a must-stay in my view. Hostess Angela Thacker will spoil you with fresh, organic produce straight from her large garden. Beyond those recommended here, Akaroa now has ump-teen lovely accommodations offerings.

Rates given include 12.5% GST.

Maison de la Mer ★★★ (**Moments**) Bruce and Carol Hyland's last B&B in Devon-port was my favorite in all of New Zealand. Their Akaroa venture has all that same romance, class, and hospitality transferred south. For privacy, opt for the Boathouse, a self-contained apartment set apart from the main house that has its own kitchen. Two luscious rooms in the main house have wide sea views. The Fleur de Lys has a private sunroom.

1 Rue Benoit, Akaroa. © **03/304-8907.** Fax 03/304-8917. www.maisondelamer.co.nz. 3 units. NZ$400– NZ$450. Rates include breakfast. AE, MC, V. Closed July–Aug. No children 11 and under. **Amenities:** Free bikes; nearby golf course; Internet. *In room:* TV/DVD, fridge, hair dryer, kitchen (in the Boathouse), mini-bar, free Wi-Fi.

Wilderness House ★★ (**Value**) This big two-storied home, set in a large garden, is just a short stroll from the heart of the village. It oozes old-world charm and, of the four rooms, I like the elegant botanically themed Nalder Room the best. Mind you, the claw-foot tub was a draw card in the Walker Room, and the private balcony and French Provincial style of the Shepherd Room were just as appealing. You even get to wander in a tiny private vineyard as part of the deal.

42 Rue Grehan, Akaroa. © **03/304-7517.** Fax 03/304-7518. www.wildernesshouse.co.nz. 4 units. NZ$290. Long-stay and off-peak rates. Rates include breakfast. MC, V. No children 11 and under. **Amenities:** Nearby golf course. *In room:* Fridge, hair dryer, free Wi-Fi.

Hot & Steamy

Hanmer Springs Thermal Pools & Spa, 42 Amuri Ave. (📞 **0800/442-663** in NZ, or 03/315-0000; www.hanmersprings.co.nz), has attracted visitors for over 125 years. The complex boasts nine open-air thermal pools, three sulfur pools, sauna and steam rooms with plunge pool, four private thermal suites, a 25m (16-ft.) heated freshwater pool, a family activity pool with two water slides, a gym, and therapeutic massage facilities. The water in the pools is maintained at a temperature between 90°F and 104°F (32°C–40°C). The Garden House Café overlooks the whole complex. The pools are open daily from 10am to 9pm. Adults pay NZ$14 admission; children pay NZ$7. Hanmer Springs is 1¹/₂ hours northeast of Christchurch. It's a picturesque drive, but be careful in winter, when icy conditions can make the roads dangerous. Take Highway 1 out of Christchurch and go 45 minutes to the left-hand Hanmer turnoff just over the Waipara River Bridge. It's well signposted the rest of the way. If you don't have a car, call the **Hanmer Connection** (📞 **0800/242-663** in NZ; www.atsnz.com), which operates daily between Christchurch and Hanmer. Bookings are essential. It costs NZ$33 one-way, NZ$60 same-day round-trip. They also offer package deals that include a swim at the pools.

The **Hanmer Springs i-SITE Visitor Centre,** 42 Amuri Ave. (📞 **03/315-7128;** fax 03/315-7658; www.alpinepacifictourism.co.nz), is open daily from 10am to 5pm in winter and 9:30am to 5:30pm in summer.

If you'd like to stay overnight in Hanmer Springs, try the **Cheltenham House** ★★, 13 Cheltenham St. (📞 **03/315-7545;** www.cheltenham.co.nz). Len and Maree Earl have 38 years' worth of local knowledge and an elegant 1930s home with six sunny, spacious bedrooms; central heating and electric blankets

Where to Dine

For excellent picnic fare, head to **Akaroa Bakery,** 51 Beach Rd. (📞 **03/304-7663**), open daily from 7:30am to 4pm. It has specialty breads, sandwiches, pies, and cakes baked fresh each day. It's always surprises me that good restaurants come and go with frightening regularity in Akaroa. I think it says something about the service and the winter downturn in tourism. That said, of those that endure, **Ma Maison** ★, 2 Rue Jolie (📞 **03/304-7668;** www.mamaison.co.nz), is a good bet for a tasty meal without too many frills. Set away from the main street, it's a great place to look out over the water.

Bully Hayes Bar & Café MODERN NEW ZEALAND This one is right on the promenade—a modern spot that maximizes its waterfront location with lots of glass and a big terrace where you can enjoy a glass of Canterbury wine. The menu is concise and seafood is a strength. Their seafood chowder is a great lunchtime filler; and come evening you can enjoy mains like seared salmon filet, seafood risotto, or braised venison shank.

57 Beach Rd. 📞 03/304-7533. www.bullyhayes.co.nz. Reservations recommended. Main courses NZ$24–NZ$28. AE, DC, MC, V. Daily 8:30am–late. Closed Dec 25.

C'est La Vie Bistro/Café ★ FRENCH You'll pay city prices here and I'm not entirely sure they're always justified. The menu generally includes seafood specialties and

will insulate you against those icy, 14°F (–10°C) winter mornings. The house is set in large gardens, a 2-minute stroll to the Hamner Springs Thermal Pools and Spa. This is great style at an unbelievably good price—NZ$220 to NZ$260 a night. Another good B&B option is **Rippinvale Retreat** ★, 68 Rippingale Rd., Hanmer ((℃ **0800/373-098** in NZ, or 03/315-7139; www.rippinvale.co.nz), where John and Helen Beattie offer two beautiful full suites, each with its own sitting room and kitchen, each NZ$355. The **Heritage Hanmer Springs** ★, 1 Conical Hill Rd. ((℃ **0800/368-888** in NZ, or 03/315-0060; www.heritagehotels.co.nz), is another excellent choice, with 64 stylish rooms from NZ$235 to NZ$425.

For a host of excellent, fast-paced activities all centered in one place, contact **Thrillseekers Canyon Adventure Centre** ★★, 839 Main Rd., Hanmer Springs ((℃ **03/315-7046;** www.thrillseekerscanyon.co.nz), which is open daily 9am to 5:30pm offering everything from bungy jumping and jet-boating to river rafting and assorted combos. Walkers *must* investigate **Hanmer Forest** ★★★, which provides a web of pretty walkways through stunning collections of exotic trees. There's an excellent forest brochure at the visitor center that outlines the best woodland, forest, and alpine walks. Make sure you take your camera!

There are now a host of excellent eateries in Hanmer. One I always enjoy is **Malabar** ★★, Alpine Pacific Centre, 5 Conical Hill Rd. ((℃ **03/315-7745**), which has a delicious Asian-Indian menu; and for the best coffee, go straight to **Powerhouse Café** ★, 8 Jack's Pass Rd. ((℃ **03/315-5252**), or **Springs Deli Café** ★, 47 Amuri Ave. ((℃ **03/315-7430**). The latter has a fabulous range of takeout picnic food.

treats such as quail wrapped in speck and sauce burgundy. The duck à l'orange is legendary. The 16-year-old bistro has an intimate interior with space for 24 in two seatings.

33 Rue Lavaud. (℃/fax **03/304-7314.** Reservations essential. Main courses NZ$28–NZ$38. MC, V. Daily 6pm–late. Closed July–Sept.

ARTHUR'S PASS ★★

Arthur's Pass, named after Arthur Dudley Dobson, who discovered it in 1865, connects Canterbury and Westland. Nestled in the Southern Alps on State Highway 73, the pass has become a destination in its own right, and Arthur's Pass village (pop. minuscule) has a growing range of modest accommodations. The area has several ski fields (see "Taking to the Slopes," on p. 386) and many short walks; Arthur's Pass National Park is a favorite with trampers. If you like a dramatic landscape and weather conditions to match, this is the place for you.

Essentials

GETTING THERE   From Christchurch, take State Highway 73 to Arthur's Pass National Park. The alpine village of Arthur's Pass is 2 hours from Christchurch and your halfway mark to the West Coast. You can also go by train on the TranzAlpine (see "An

Finds   Wine on High

Make sure you don't drive past **Kaikoura Winery,** 140 St. Hwy. 1 ((℃) **03/319-7966;** www.kaikourawinery.co.nz), perched high above the ocean on limestone cliffs, to the south of the town. It's worth a stop for some of the most scenic wine tasting you'll ever experience. The ocean views are wonderful and they have a very impressive underground cellar and a cafe. You're welcome to have a picnic there, and they have gourmet food available. It's open daily from 10am until 5:30pm and tours are held on the hour for NZ$15 per person. Wine tasting costs NZ$5.

Unforgettable Train Trip" on p. 384) or by shuttle with **West Coast Shuttles** ((℃) **03/768-0028;** www.westcoastshuttle.co.nz). Another option is a 1-day tour from Christchurch with **Travel Pioneer** ((℃) **0800/808-070** in NZ) or **Peninsula & Alpine Tours** ((℃) **03/384-3576;** fax 03/384-3971). The only daily afternoon service is provided by **Alpine Coaches** ((℃) **0800/274-888** in NZ).

VISITOR INFORMATION   The **Arthur's Pass Visitor Centre,** State Highway (73 Main Rd.), P.O. Box 51008, Arthur's Pass ((℃) **03/318-9211;** fax 03/318-9093; www.doc.govt. nz), is a good place to start. The weather in this area can be extremely changeable—never underestimate the danger; people can die when they are ill-prepared and ignore warnings. The center staff will be able to advise you on all safety issues related to walking tracks. Open daily, except December 25.

Walking on the Wild Side

Snow, avalanches, and over 4,000 millimeters (160 in.) of rain a year have their impact on the walking tracks here. Despite these changing conditions, the area has numerous 2- to 3-day tramps and many shorter walks that bring you up close to thundering waterfalls, wild rivers, dripping beech forests, and a wealth of bird life.

A lot of them are also tough going and require a degree of skill in personal navigation using maps and compasses. Make sure you're tackling something within the range of your ability, and no matter what the weather is like when you set off, *always* bring plenty of warm clothing. Pick up the Department of Conservation's two brochures, *Walks in Arthur's Pass National Park* and *Arthur's Pass Village Historic Walk,* at the visitor center.

Two short walks worth doing are **Devil's Punchbowl Waterfall** ★ and **Bridal Veil.** Each takes 1 to 1½ hours. The **historic village walk** ★ is a pretty 1½-hour wander that can be accomplished easily if you've stopped off at Arthur's Pass on the return TranzAlpine journey.

Where to Stay

For the modest sum of NZ$120 to NZ$150, you can take a bed at **Arthur's Pass Chalet Restaurant & Accommodation,** Main Road ((℃) **03/318-9236;** www.arthurspass.co.nz). Its 11 units are right in the heart of the little township.

Grasmere Lodge ★★★ **(Moments**   This is the New Zealand equivalent of an English country-house hotel where an intimate number of guests receive the very best personal service. It's also a member of the Small Luxury Hotels of the World group and owner Tom Butler makes sure your stay is first-rate. The original homestead is the center of lodge activities and modern, alpine-styled chalets spread around it. All of the spacious rooms offer every comfort and bathrooms are fabulous. I love the pool complex here; there's nothing better than floating in the middle of this magnificent landscape.

St. Hwy. 73, Cass. ✆ **03/318-8407.** Fax 03/318-8263. www.grasmere.co.nz. 13 units. NZ$1,400 lake-view room; NZ$1,843 mountain-view room; NZ$2,173 chalet and cottage suite. NZ$197 per person surcharge Dec 25. Rates include breakfast, predinner canapés, 5-course dinner, and transport from TranzAlpine stop at Mount White Bridge. AE, MC, V. Located 120km (74 miles) from both Greymouth and Christchurch. Inquire in advance about acceptance of children 11 and under. **Amenities:** Restaurant; bar; free bikes; concierge; limited fitness equipment; heated outdoor pool; tennis court; canoes; Wi-Fi in main reception. *In room:* A/C, fridge, hair dryer, minibar.

Wilderness Lodge ★★   Nature lovers will want to stay at this wonderful high-country lodge, where hosts Gerry McSweeney, ecologist/conservationist extraordinaire, and his wife Anne Saunders have developed a very special experience. Although it's not nearly as luxurious as Grasmere, the lodge offers superior outdoor activities and informed, guided nature tours—all of which highlight environmental conservation practices on the property. All rooms overlook the Waimakariri valley and mountain peaks and there are four new alpine lodges for a bit of extra pampering. I recommend a 2-night minimum stay to fully enjoy the property. It has a Qualmark Enviro-Gold rating for its excellent conservation and recycling measures, and it has its own hydro-power scheme.

St. Hwy. 73, Arthur's Pass. ✆ **03/318-9246.** Fax 03/318-9245. www.wildernesslodge.co.nz. 24 units, all with private bathroom. NZ$780–NZ$980. Surcharge for Dec 25 and 31 and Jan 1. Off-peak rates. Rates include breakfast, dinner, use of lodge facilities, and guided nature and farm activities. MC, V. **Amenities:** Restaurant; bar; babysitting by prior arrangement; room service on request; canoe trips; Wi-Fi in lounge. *In room:* Fridge, hair dryer.

KAIKOURA ★★★

The seaside settlement of Kaikoura is located halfway between Christchurch and Picton on the rugged east coast. Waves lap at its toes and huge mountains stretch away from its shoulders. It's a stunning combination that never fails to impress and these days the population of approximately 4,000 never misses a beat in capitalizing on natural attributes. Chief among them is the marine bounty—several breeds of whales, dolphins, seals, and thousands of seabirds. Once a sleepy hollow that virtually closed down in the winter, Kaikoura is now a thriving little town that is especially energetic and interesting during the tourist season. It was also the first local authority in the world to achieve Green Globe 21 certification, proving the town's commitment to reducing environmental impacts.

Essentials

GETTING THERE   Traveling on State Highway 1, Kaikoura is an easy 2½-hour drive from Christchurch—unless you use this opportunity to stop over in the Waipara wine region, in which case you should allow a whole day. It is approximately 2 hours south of Blenheim. You can also go by train and the **TranzCoastal** (✆ **0800/872-467** in NZ; www.tranzscenic.co.nz) is certainly a lovely trip. As a round-trip day trip from Christchurch, it costs NZ$88 for adults and NZ$62 for children ages 2 to 14, but remember to check online for cheaper fares. That gives you around 5½ hours to explore Kaikoura or go whale-watching. It departs Christchurch at 7:30am and returns at 7pm. One-way fares are also available. **ATSNZ Hanmer Connection** (✆ **0800/242-663;** www.atsnz.com) provides a shuttle service to Kaikoura via Hanmer Springs on Tuesday, Thursday, and Saturday; and **InterCity** (✆ **09/623-1503**) and **Newmans** (✆ **09/623-1504**) both pass through the township.

Marine Experiences in Kaikoura

Whales and other marine mammals are the primary draw of Kaikoura, but be aware that you'll be fighting for a place with hundreds of others *and* that it's all weather dependent. **Whale Watch Kaikoura** ★★★ (℃ **0800/655-121** in NZ, or 03/319-6767; www.whalewatch.co.nz) gives you a close encounter with the giant sperm whale. Book well ahead for this awesome adventure. It offers four 2¹/₂-hour tours daily on two types of vessels. The fare is NZ$145 for adults, NZ$60 for children ages 3 to 15 (not suitable for kids 2 and under). You may also spot dolphins, fur seals, and seabirds. If you're prone to seasickness, make sure you take the appropriate medication because even the sight and smell of others being sick around you is enough to upset the sternest gut. This is a slick, well-managed operation, the films and videos first-rate, but I found there was something slightly manic about it all and you spend most of the trip waiting to see a whale's tail from about 30m (100 ft.) away.

Wings Over Whales (℃ **0800/226-629** in NZ, or 03/319-6580; www.whales.co.nz) offers an airborne perspective to whale-watching via a 30-minute flight that costs NZ$165 per person. If you're short on time, this is probably the best alternative.

Encounter Kaikoura ★★ (℃ **0800/733-365** in NZ, or 03/319-6777; www.encounterkaikoura.co.nz) has tours for watching and/or swimming with Dusky dolphins, the most playful and acrobatic of all the dolphins. The cost is NZ$165 for adults, NZ$150 for children 14 and under. Reserve well in advance. I'd also recommend their **Albatross Encounter** ★★, which gets you up close and personal with the area's astounding seabird population. Make sure you take your camera for this one. It costs NZ$110 for adults and NZ$55 for children ages 8 to 14. **Seal Swim Kaikoura** (℃ **0800/732-579** in NZ, or 03/319-6182; www.sealswimkaikoura.co.nz) operates October through May and has seal swims priced from NZ$70 to NZ$90.

Kaikoura Kayaks ★★★ (℃ **0800/452-456** in NZ, or 03/319-7118; www.kaikourakayaks.co.nz) provides one of the loveliest ways of getting a feel for the richness of Kaikoura's marine environment. You'll have fur seals diving around your kayak and seabirds diving down from above. This is definitely what I'd be doing if I only had a day in Kaikoura. They offer half-day trips for NZ$85 for adults and NZ$75 for children 12 and under.

VISITOR INFORMATION The **Kaikoura i-SITE Visitor Centre** is located at the south end of the town's main carpark, Westend (℃ **03/319-5641;** www.kaikoura.co.nz or www.naturallykaikoura.co.nz). It has comprehensive displays of all the town's attractions and can organize transport.

SPECIAL EVENTS Do your utmost to be in Kaikoura for the first week of October, when the town hosts **Seafest** ★★★ in Takahanga Domain (℃ **0800/473-2337;** www.seafest.co.nz), a crazy and delicious celebration of the ocean and its extravaganza of tastes.

The **Kaikoura Coast Track** ★★, Medina, 210 Conway Flat Rd., Cheviot (🕾 **03/319-2715**; www.kaikouratrack.co.nz), begins almost an hour south of Kaikoura and takes you across a historic sheep station, up into tussock land, down into bush valleys, and along a beach beneath cliffs embedded with 8,000-year-old tree stumps and fossils. It's 3 days in country otherwise inaccessible to you and for NZ$185 per person, it's money very well spent. You sleep in farm cottages along the way and home-cooked meals can be provided.

Kaikoura Wilderness Walk ★★★ (🕾 **0800/945-337** in NZ, or 03/319-6966; www.kaikourawilderness.co.nz), is a comfortable 2-day hiking experience over 17km (11 miles) in the Puhi Peaks Nature Reserve, a remote area that is home to rare wildlife. You'll overnight at Shearwater Lodge, which was built in 2004 on a precipitous location that has to be seen to be believed. The 2- to 3-day guided walk, all meals, and accommodations cost from NZ$795 to NZ$995 per person. Only available from October through April, this is a more mountainous, wilderness experience than the more farm-based Kaikoura Track. Both are well worth doing.

Where to Stay

Nikau Lodge ★, corner of State Highway 1 and Deal Street, Kaikoura (🕾 **03/319-6973**; www.nikaulodge.com), has six B&B rooms (five with en-suite bathrooms, one with a private bathroom), plus a two-bedroom cottage, with prices ranging from NZ$165 to NZ$225.

All rates quoted below include the 12.5% GST and free off-street parking unless otherwise stated.

Hapuku Lodge ★★★ (**Value**)   You won't believe your eyes when you see the level of style and quality you get here for the oh-so-reasonable price. It is, without doubt, one of the smartest small contemporary lodges in the country and you'll love the deep, restful silence of nights spent in this out-of-town location. Handcrafted furniture; big, well-designed bathrooms; and generous beds all add up to a fantastic stay. If you want extra space and privacy, opt for the apartment above the olive mill. But my favorite spot is tucked up in one of the exquisite new treehouses.

Hapuku Rd., just off St. Hwy. 1, Kaikoura. 🕾 **0800/521-568** in NZ, or 03/319-6559. Fax 03/319-6557. www.hapukulodge.com. 14 units. NZ$394–NZ$462 lodge room; NZ$655–NZ$855 treehouse. NZ$75 each extra person. Off-peak rates and special rates. Rates include breakfast. AE, MC, V. Located 12km (7¹⁄₂ miles) north of Kaikoura township. **Amenities:** Restaurant; bar; airport transport to Kaikoura; free bikes; small gym; room service; Wi-Fi. *In room:* A/C (in treehouses), TV/DVD/CD, fridge, hair dryer, minibar, Wi-Fi.

(**Moments**)   **A Cultural Exchange**

Maurice and Heather Manawatu of **Maori Tours Kaikoura** ★★ (🕾 **0800/866-267** in NZ, or 03/319-5567; www.maoritours.co.nz) will send you away with some of your loveliest New Zealand memories. They'll take you on a journey through Kaikoura's rich Maori history to ancient Maori sites, and you'll explore a beautiful stand of native bush, learning about the traditional uses of plants by Maori. Wear sensible walking shoes and take along a sense of humor and a willingness to participate. The 3- to 4-hour tour costs NZ$115 for adults and NZ$65 for children ages 5 to 15.

Kincaid Lodge ★ Located 6km (3¾ miles) north of Kaikoura, this old farm home-stead, built in 1903, now has a new life. New owners Greg and Jessica Frost have exten-sively updated this pretty property set in a peaceful garden well back from the main highway, with farm animals peering over the fence. If you like a little more privacy, take the self-contained two-bedroom cottage; but lodge rooms are spacious with nice bath-rooms. I think you get better value at the much more stylish Hapuku Lodge up the road, but it's a lovely stay nonetheless and it's more intimate than Hapuku.

611 Main North Rd., Kaikoura. ✆ **03/319-6851.** Fax 03/319-6801. www.kincaidlodge.co.nz. 4 units. NZ$545. Long-stay rates. Rates include breakfast. MC, V. **Amenities:** Free bikes; nearby golf course; out-door tennis court; watersports equipment; Wi-Fi in lounge. *In room:* TV/DVD, fridge, hair dryer.

Where to Dine

New cafes and restaurants are popping up in Kaikoura like mushrooms on a damp day, but they're variable in service and all-around quality, and there's a definite lack of any-thing really classy. For the size of the place, though, there are more than enough casual options to choose from. **Hislops Wholefoods Café** ★, 33 Beach Rd. (✆ **03/319-6971**), is an excellent cafe. It has an organic focus and the food is always great. **Encounter Kaikoura** ★, West End (✆ **03/319-6777**), is my preferred hit for a delicious lunch, or coffee and a snack. They have an excellent menu, fabulous counter food, and a busy, modern environment that teems with people of all nationalities. **Craypot Café** ★, Westend (✆ **03/319-6027**), is well placed on the main street opposite the carpark and it's a good relaxed spot for lunch. Service can be patchy but I always enjoy their seafood chowder. Another fun, casual choice is **Kaikoura Seafood Barbecue** ★, Jimmy Armers Beach, near the end of Fyffe Quay (✆ **027/433-9691**), which is a little-known treat for seafood lovers. They serve fresh scallops, mussels, whitebait, and crayfish for under NZ$25; and their stand and outdoor, umbrella-covered tables are open daily year-round from 10am until dark—unless it's raining.

EN ROUTE TO THE WEST COAST & THE GLACIERS

From Christchurch, take State Highway 73 through the magnificent landscape of Arthur's Pass National Park. In 2 hours, you'll get to the village of Arthur's Pass, your halfway point to the West Coast. You'll then pass over the new Otira Viaduct, which takes care of the worst and most dangerous part of the journey. Continue to proceed with caution, though, especially when it's snowing. From Otira, it's another 1 to 1½ hours to Greymouth on the West Coast. If you're traveling straight down to Franz Josef and Fox glaciers, follow State Highway 6 all the way. You can expect the drive to the glaciers to take another 3 to 5 hours, depending on how often you stop.

West Coast & the Glaciers

This is a unique part of New Zealand, where people approach life with a laid-back attitude and a strong sense of community. It's a place of majestic landscapes, rich history, and colorful characters, and you'll be hard-pressed to find anything slick or superficial here.

Greenstone was the first treasure of these wild and beautiful shores. It's still the best place in the country to purchase contemporary jade carvings. Gold and timber have also shaped the course of coast history, and both continue to figure prominently in what you'll experience here.

More than anything, though, the dramatic landscape draws visitors. Almost 80% of the West Coast land area is protected under the Department of Conservation, and 5 of the country's 13 national parks are wholly or partially in the region. The rainforests of the West Coast are among the most diverse in New Zealand, and few places in the temperate world contain such a variety of vegetation. Naturally, these forests are well sustained by the West Coast's notoriously high rainfall, so bring a raincoat, lots of insect repellent, and a sense of humor—you'll need all three!

From its subtropical north to its rainforested south, the West Coast is diverse and always interesting. Where else in the world could you find an icy glacier just a few kilometers from a sandy beach?

1 WESTPORT ★ & KARAMEA ★★★

Westport: 101km (63 miles) N of Greymouth; 226km (140 miles) SW of Nelson

The drive to **Westport** (pop. 11,000) is better than actually arriving here. This funny little township is slightly shabby and smells of coal. I think calling it the "Adventure Capital of the West Coast" is stretching it a bit, but the area's mild climate and coastal to subtropical mountain scenery do provide an ideal setting for outdoor activities such as white-water rafting, jet-boating, horse trekking, caving, and rock climbing. For the not-so-adventurous, there are excellent sea and river fishing, gold panning, and a variety of scenic and historic walks.

Traveling 1½ hours north to **Karamea** is worth the time and effort. This little corner of paradise is snuggled into the warm northwest part of the South Island and is, in fact, much farther north than Wellington. It is the terminal point of the Heritage Highway, the gateway to the Kahurangi National Park—the beginning of a natural heaven. It's my favorite part of the West Coast—all those nikau palms are just so unexpected.

ESSENTIALS
GETTING THERE & GETTING AROUND **By Plane** **Air New Zealand Link** (© **0800/737-000** in NZ; www.airnewzealand.co.nz) flies daily to Westport from Wellington.

(Tips) **The Long Road**

The West Coast is the longest region in New Zealand—550km (340 miles)—which is roughly equivalent to driving from Auckland to Wellington. In many ways—certainly geographically—it is an epic journey and it is important that you don't underestimate driving times. Take care at all times and stop to enjoy the quaint townships and spectacular scenery along the way.

By Coach (Bus)   Westport is serviced daily by **InterCity** (℃ **09/623-1503.** Both **Magic Travellers** (℃ **09/358-5600**) and **Kiwi Experience** (℃ **09/366-9830**) also include Westport on their schedules.

To get from Westport to Karamea, go with either **Cunningham's Coaches** (℃ **03/789-7177**), which charges NZ$25 per person one-way, NZ$12 for bikes; or **Karamea Express** (℃ **03/782-6757**), which charges NZ$25. Both make the trip Monday through Friday and connect with other bus services to Nelson, Greymouth, Hokitika, and Christchurch. **Drive Me Wild Hikers' Transport** (℃ **0800/945-369** in NZ, or 03/546-8876; www.drivemewild.co.nz) offers transport on both sides of Heaphy Track. From Karamea, they travel to Nelson via Westport and Motueka on the day you finish walking.

By Car   Westport can be reached on Highway 6 from Greymouth in the south in about 2 hours, or from Nelson via the Buller Gorge in approximately 3½ hours. All roads are good, but look out for single-lane bridges and those that share the bridge with trains—a unique West Coast feature.

Karamea is just 100km (60 miles) north of Westport, but you should allow 1½ to 2 hours for the trip, as at least 25km (15 miles) of it is steep and winding. It's a beautiful drive over the Karamea Bluff, descending into bush landscape and then along the coast. And look out for truck drivers who dominate the road!

VISITOR INFORMATION   The **Westport i-SITE Information Centre,** 1 Brougham St. (℃ **03/789-6658;** fax 03/789-6668; www.westport.org.nz), opposite the post office, is open in summer daily from 9am to 5:30pm, and in winter Monday through Friday from 9am to 4pm (closed Dec 25).

The **Karamea Visitor Information Centre,** Market Cross (℃ **03/782-6652;** fax 03/782-6654; www.karameainfo.co.nz), is opposite the Karamea Store in the tiny village of **Market Cross.** From November to April, it's open daily from 9am to 5pm; May to October, Monday through Friday from 9am to 5pm, Saturday 9am to 1pm. There is also a post office here along with a garage, crafts outlet, and cafe. Just beyond Market Cross are the Karamea Tavern, a supermarket, general store, the police station, motels, and the **Last Resort** (p. 409). Everything is within walking distance, but the entrance to the Heaphy Track and Kahurangi National Park is another 15km (9 miles) farther on at the end of State Highway 67. For more information, check **www.west-coast.co.nz.**

EXPLORING WESTPORT

Coal Town Museum, 165 Queen St. (℃/fax **03/789-8204**), gives you the chance to walk through a true-to-life coal mine, complete with sound effects from the deep bowels of the earth. Even if you're not lured here by these promises, you'll find an interesting repository of historical artifacts. Check out the new displays of maritime and pioneering

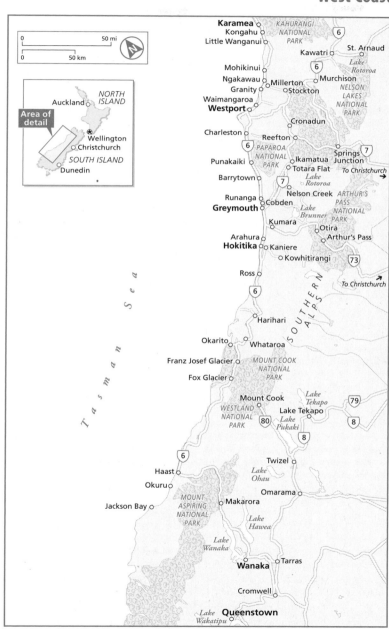

history. The museum is open daily 9am to 4:30pm (Jan till 5pm; closed Dec 25). Admission is NZ$10 for adults, NZ$5 for children.

If you want an insight into the rugged history of the Westport area, try the local guides at **Outwest Tours** (© **0800/688-937** in NZ; www.outwest.co.nz), who will take you on personalized tours of old coal mining and off-the-beaten-track areas, like **Stockton Mine ★★**, New Zealand's largest coal mine, 750m (2,500 ft.) above sea level on the Stockton Plateau. You'll travel in 4×4 Unimog vehicles, traversing rivers and generally taking on everything in your path. It won't always be smooth, but it will be exciting.

Outdoor Pursuits

ABSEILING (RAPPELLING) & ADVENTURE CAVING **Norwest Adventures Ltd. ★★**, Main Road, Charleston (© **0800/116-686** in NZ, or 03/788-8168; www.caverafting.com), can introduce you to the mystery and intrigue of the underworld. The Adventure Caving trip costs NZ$295 and requires high levels of fitness for people ages 16 and over—don't try it if you get claustrophobic or are afraid of heights. The Glow Worm Cave Tour (NZ$90) is the dry, passive version of the Underworld Rafting tour (below). You travel by Rainforest Train to the huge Nile River glowworm caves, where you get to see amazing stalactites and stalagmites. You need to be able to walk unassisted on uneven surfaces, and robust footwear and warm clothing are advised. The Underworld Rafting experience involves making your way by raft along underground stream passages and out into the Nile River rapids. Some consider it a tamer adventure than that offered by Wild West Adventure in Greymouth (p. 413). It's a 4- to 5-hour trip that costs NZ$145 per person.

ECORAFTING For multiday white-water rafting expeditions, check out **Eco-Rafting Adventures NZ ★★**, 108 Mawhera Quay, Greymouth (© **0508/669-675**; www.ecorafting.co.nz). They offer a range of adventure packages on different West Coast rivers priced from NZ$500 to NZ$2,000, depending on the river and length of the trip.

KAYAKING **Ultimate Descents,** Buller Gorge (© **0800/748-377**; www.rivers.co.nz), offers three types of kayaks for all skill levels on Grade II to III rivers. You must be 13 years and over to participate in the 4½-hour trips.

SURFING Chief among the best beaches is **Tauranga Bay,** 15 minutes south of Westport.

SWIMMING There are just two phrases to sum up swimming on any of the West Coast beaches—*extreme care* and *are you mad?* Undertows are common and an ever-present hazard on beaches exposed to the westerly swell. Always seek local advice about safe areas. If you're uncertain, *never* get wet!

SWING BRIDGE If you haven't found enough ways to test your nerves already, enlist in a walk across New Zealand's longest swing bridge. **Buller Gorge Swingbridge & Adventure Park ★**, State Highway 6, Buller Gorge (© **03/523-9809**; www.bullergorge.co.nz), offers a heart-pumping distraction 1 hour from Westport.

WALKING **Tauranga Bay ★★★** is a popular place to explore beaches, coastline, and seal colonies. There is a good-quality short track through the area, specially designed to accommodate wheelchairs. The seal-colony walk is 20 minutes round-trip, and the Cape Foulwind Walkway ★★★ is 1½ hours. The Department of Conservation's brochure with maps of both walks is available at the visitor center.

(© **0800/697-286** in NZ, or 03/789-7286; www.adventuretours.co.nz), which also offers jet-boating and horse-trekking tours. Eco- and white-water rafting start at NZ$120, horse treks at NZ$80, and jet-boating at NZ$79.

Where to Stay

If you're looking for classy, upmarket accommodations in Westport, stop now—you won't find any. You will, however, find one or two smart, moderately priced options that are bound to bring a satisfied smile to your face. Campers can head for **Westport Holiday Park,** 31–37 Domett St. (© **03/789-7043;** www.westportholidaypark.co.nz), which has chalets, tent and caravan sites, and bunk rooms in a native bush setting. **Chelsea Gateway Motor Lodge** ★, 330 Palmerston St. (© **0800/660-033** in NZ, or 03/789-6835; fax 03/789-6379; www.chelseagateway.co.nz), lacks inspiration, but it's clean, comfortable, and reasonably priced with 20 one-, two-, and three-bedroom units from NZ$128 to NZ$230. It also has a Qulamark Enviro-Bronze rating. **River View Lodge,** State Highway 6, Buller Gorge Road, Westport (© **03/789-6037;** www.rurallodge.co.nz), has four en-suite B&B rooms for NZ$250.

All rates quoted below include the 12.5% GST and free off-street parking unless otherwise noted.

Rough and Tumble Bush Lodge ★★ (Value) Don't be fooled by the name—this new, purpose-built, ecofriendly property on the banks of the Mokihinui River 50km (31 miles) north of Westport is worth traveling the extra distance. It's definitely off the beaten track, but if you're keen hikers, or just want total solitude, this will be perfect. They have five comfortable, well-equipped rooms looking out into native bush, and owners Marion Boatwright and Susan Cook are both keen hikers and NZ Mountain Safety Council Bush I instructors, so you'll be in safe hands. Susan is also a terrific cook and caters to any health requirements. The property has a Qualmark Enviro-Silver rating.

Mokihinhui Rd., Seddonville, Westport. © **0800/333-746** in NZ, or 03/782-1337. www.roughandtumble.co.nz. 5 units. NZ$225; NZ$175 each additional person; NZ$85 each child sharing with adults. Long-stay and off-peak rates. Rates include all meals and use of bikes and kayaks. AE, MC, V. Take St. Hwy. 67 from Westport to Seddonville. Drive right through Seddonville. At the last house on your left the road turns to gravel. Proceed 1.7km (about 1 mile). Cross the ford and follow signs to lodge 800m (2,624 ft.) away. **Amenities:** Airport transfers from Westport booked in advance; free bikes; high-speed Internet in main lodge; free kayaks. *In room:* Hair dryer on request.

Where to Dine

The notion of culinary excellence and innovation has yet to hit Westport, and if it's your first West Coast destination, it will give you the chance to get used to the West Coast dining style, which, at best, can be described as laid-back. **Serengeti Restaurant,** Westport Motor Hotel, 207 Palmerston St. (© **03/789-7889**), is open daily for a la carte meals and Sunday smorgasbords. **Yellow House Café** ★, 243 Palmerston St. (© **03/789-8765;** www.currtinos.co.nz), is as close as I get to putting the flicker of a star on anything in town—spice-rubbed pork served with apple chutney indicates they're at least trying, and they have good options for vegetarians. It's open daily from 8am until 10pm in summer; winter hours vary.

Bay House Café & Restaurant ★★ (Finds) PACIFIC RIM This is definitely the little dining gem of the West Coast. Situated about 15 minutes southwest of Westport at Tauranga Bay, it has a dramatic location overlooking the beach, and food that more than

> **Tips   Filling Up**
>
> Before you leave Westport, heading to either Nelson or Greymouth, fill your car with petrol. There are no more petrol stations until you hit Murchison, or 87km (54 miles) south near Greymouth.

measures up. Try the seafood salad, featuring smoked salmon, king prawns, and sautéed calamari in a citrus dressing. Steamed Thai mussels, open steak sandwiches, pastas, and chicken satay are other menu offerings. Eat your fill, then walk around to view the seal colony.

Tauranga Bay. ✆/fax **03/789-7133.** www.thebayhouse.co.nz. Reservations required. Main courses NZ$27–NZ$32. AE, MC, V. Daily 11am–late (until 7:30pm in winter).

EXPLORING KARAMEA ★★★

Caught between the wild Tasman Sea on one side and the bush-clad mountains of Kahurangi National Park on the other, Karamea (pop. 650) is a thin slither of subtropical paradise. As the gateway to the Kahurangi, it offers a host of natural attractions, and it is to Karamea that Heaphy Track walkers go at the end of their 4- to 6-day tramp. Much of the coastline is wild and rugged, with rocky points and narrow beaches backed by steep cliffs. Nikau palms, rainforest, and dairy-farm pastures all flourish in the warm temperatures, and the limestone landscape contains many spectacular caves.

Tops on your list should be a visit to **Oparara Arch** ★★★, the biggest limestone arch of its type in the Southern Hemisphere. The drive to the arch takes approximately 1 hour through rainforest. If you're short on time, go straight to **Oparara Basin Guided Tours** (✆ 03/782-6652; www.oparara.co.nz). They take you into to the restricted **Honeycomb Cave area** ★★★, which was discovered in 1980. Now managed by the Department of Conservation, it's in pristine condition, complete with moa bones. Most people are completely blown away by the experience. The full 5-hour **Grand Eco Tour** includes an extensive tour of the Basin and arches with the choice of either a Honeycomb Hill cave tour or a kayak trip. It costs NZ$200 per person. *Please note:* These caves are protected and access is by guided tour only. You'll need warm clothing and a good degree of fitness, and no walking sticks are allowed in the caves.

Outdoor Pursuits

CANOEING   Hire a canoe from the **Last Resort** (✆ 03/782-6617; www.lastresort. co.nz) for NZ$35; or **Karamea Motors** (✆ 03/782-6757). Paddle in the safe estuaries, but be aware of tidal changes and keep away from river mouths. The Last Resort also hires kayaks from NZ$25.

FISHING   There are over 320km (200 miles) of accessible heli-fishing on several back-country rivers. The 40km (25 miles) of coastline are suitable for surf-casting, and the Karamea River is a trout fisherman's heaven. Trout licenses can be obtained from the **Karamea Hardware Store,** State Highway 67, Market Cross, on a daily, weekly, or annual basis.

The whitebait season is from September 1 to November 14. Whitebait are the young of three main species of migrating fish. They're considered a delicacy and found pre-dominantly on the West Coast. There are special rules and regulations for whitebaiters, so make sure you get a copy of them from the Department of Conservation or the Karamea Information & Resource Centre.

MOUNTAIN BIKING   Mountain biking is prohibited in Kahurangi National Park, but if you'd like to ride in other areas, the **Last Resort** and **Karamea Motors** (see "Canoeing," above) have bikes for rent.

WALKING   There are two major hikes in this area—the famous **Heaphy Track ★★★**, which is suitable for trampers of all ages, and the **Wangapeka Track,** which is better suited to the well-equipped tramper. Both tracks take about 4 days, and both require hut ticket passes available from the Karamea Information & Resource Centre. Parts of the Wangapeka Track have been washed out by flooding, so always check first with the information center to make sure it is open. For more information on the Heaphy track, see "Tramping" in chapter 5.

There are also many excellent short walks. For the **Nikau Loop Walk,** drive to the Kohaihai River mouth at the start of the Heaphy Track. The walk is suitable for all ages and takes 40 minutes. **Heaphy Hut Walk ★★★** gives you a 5-hour taste (round-trip) of the Heaphy Track. Guided walk companies operating in this area include **Kahurangi Guided Walks,** Dodson Road, Takaka, Golden Bay (© 03/525-7177; www.heaphytrack.co.nz), and **Bush and Beyond Guided Treks,** 35 School Rd., Motueka (© 03/528-9054; www.naturetreks.co.nz).

Where to Stay

Karamea River Motels (© 03/782-6955; fax 03/782-6944; www.karameamotels.co.nz), 31 Bridge St., just over the Old Karamea Bridge, 500m (1,600 ft.) from the township, is ideal for families or travelers aiming to spend a few days in the area. Studio and one- and two-bedroom units are NZ$120 to NZ$160.

The Last Resort ★★ (Finds)   This grass-roofed complex may well surprise you. First opened as budget accommodations in 1991, they now offer another tier of comfort in en-suite units and three cottages. The latter are the biggest, with full cooking facilities and two bedrooms each. There is also a good restaurant and bar, following the same Mediterranean style and incorporating huge native timber beams from the forest floor.

71 Waverly St., P.O. Box 31, Karamea. © 0800/505-042 in NZ, or 03/782-6617. Fax 03/782-6820. www.lastresort.co.nz. 30 units. NZ$30–NZ$35 shared backpacker rooms; NZ$75 lodge room with shared bathroom; NZ$95–NZ$105 lodge room with en-suite bathroom; NZ$125 studio with en-suite bathroom; NZ$150 cottage. Long-stay and off-peak rates. AE, DC, MC, V. Less than 1km (1/2 mile) from local shops, 5km (3 miles) from beach. Bus service from door. **Amenities:** Restaurant; cafe; 2 bars; bike rentals; nearby golf course; miniature golf; Jacuzzi; watersports rentals. *In room:* TV, hair dryer, kitchen (in cottages), no phone in some units.

EN ROUTE TO GREYMOUTH: PUNAKAIKI

The drive between Westport and Greymouth is simply stunning, with some of the best coastal views in the country. There are many walkways leading to a variety of natural attractions. Chief among them is the world-famous **Punakaiki Pancake Rocks and Blowholes ★★★**, the main feature of the 10-minute **Dolomite Walk** in the heart of the **Paparoa National Park.** These strange pancakelike limestone formations were pushed up from the ocean floor by seismic action 30 million years ago. For the best show, try to visit the rocks at high tide with a westerly swell running; water comes surging into the deep caverns below and can spout up to 9m (30 ft.) in the air. The rocks are 45km (28 miles) north of Greymouth on the coast section of State Highway 6. If you're on an

InterCity coach, the bus will stop here to enable you to do the 20-minute round-trip walk. The track is wide, well maintained, easily negotiable, and there are opportunities for great photos. But expect crowds here in mid-summer.

Across the road from the track entrance, you'll find a busy gathering of little cafes and crafts stores, along with the **Punakaiki-Paparoa National Park Visitor Centre,** P.O. Box 1, Punakaiki (✆ **03/731-1895;** fax 03/731-1896; www.punakaiki.co.nz). The **Department of Conservation** (✆ **03/731-1895;** www.doc.govt.nz) is in the same building; it is open daily in summer 9am to 6pm, and in winter to 4:30pm. **Punakaiki Crafts** ★★ (✆/fax **03/731-1813;** www.punakaikicrafts.co.nz) is a cooperative with the best, most innovative arts and crafts on the coast. It's open daily from 8:30am to 6pm. There's an excellent espresso outlet here, too but expect a bit of a queue during peak tourist season.

There are plenty of other excellent short walks in the area. Both the **Truman Track** ★★ and the **Punakaiki Cavern** are under 1 hour and suitable for the entire family. The Truman includes a stroll through coastal forest to a beach with caves and a waterfall. The **Pororari River Walk** is another beautiful walk. I did this last year as part of a guided walking tour run by Christchurch-based **Tuatara Tours** (www.tuataratours. co.nz). It's part of their excellent **West Coast Trail,** an easy 4-day experience that introduces you to some of the best highlights between Porter's and Arthur's Passes, and the West Coast from Greymouth to Punakaiki. You get to the Punakaiki area on day 3 of the tour, and for 2 days your guide will lead you through the Punakaiki Pancake Rocks Track, the Truman Track, the Fox River or Cave Creek Track (depending on weather), and the Pororari River Walk.

All of these afford you a terrific insight into the Paparoa National Park area, which is often overlooked in favor of the better known, longer tracks elsewhere in the South Island. It's an area filled with dramatic limestone cliffs, towering bluffs, and dense subtropical forest filled with coastal broadleaf plants, nikau palms, incredible tree ferns, and immense rata trees.

There is also rich bird life here, and if you go quietly, your guide will point out the friendly plump wood pigeons; tomtits; our favorite songbirds, the tui and the bellbird; and the very friendly New Zealand robins that will hop right up to your feet. The tour is one I recommend constantly. Apart from the stunning scenery, you get to stay in comfortable accommodations along the way, and you only have to carry a day pack. It is rugged country though, so you do need excellent hiking boots and a reasonable level of fitness.

Punakaiki Horse Treks (✆ **03/731-1839;** www.pancake-rocks.co.nz) offers a variety of activities exploring the rich park environment, including nature tours of the magnificent Punakaiki Valley in an eight-wheeled amphibious vehicle, and horse treks through bush and beach environments. The latter start at NZ$125 per person for a 2½-hour ride. They're open for business from the third week of October through to June.

Punakaiki Canoes ★★, State Highway 6, Punakaiki (✆ **03/731-1870;** www. riverkayaking.co.nz), will take you upstream on the Pororari River, through a stunning gorge cut from limestone cliffs. It's suitable for all ages and experience levels and costs NZ$55 per person for half-day rental; guided trips start at NZ$85.

Where to Stay

Many travelers now stop over in Punakaiki on the trip from Nelson to the West Coast. It's an excellent place for a rest before heading south to the glaciers, but accommodations options are fair to middling at best.

Punakaiki Resort, State Highway 6 ((C) 0800/624-646 in NZ, or 03/731-1168; www. punakaiki-resort.co.nz), opened in 2001 with bright, new rooms right on the beach. It's a stunning location, and while rooms are comfortable, I have found the service here to be less than impressive, especially in the restaurant. But it's the closest to the Pancake Rocks and the prime location may make up for other flaws. The 61 rooms range in price from NZ$140 to NZ$350. **Paparoa Park Motel,** State Highway 6 ((C) 0800/727-276 in NZ, or 03/731-1883; www.paparoa.co.nz), is just a short distance south of the Pancake Rocks over the Punakaiki River. It has tidy native-timber studios and family units.

The **Rocks Homestay** ★, 33 Hartmount Place ((C) 0800/272-164 in NZ, or 03/731-1141; www.therockshomestay.com), is 3km (2 miles) north of Punakaiki; their three rooms cost from NZ$170 to NZ$210. Farther south, 29km (18 miles) from Punakaiki and 15km (9 miles) north of Greymouth, **Breakers Boutique Accommodation** ★, 9 Mile Creek, State Highway 6 ((C) 0800/350-590 in NZ, or 03/762-7743; www.breakers. co.nz), has four en-suite rooms for NZ$200 to NZ$330. Ask for the Breakwater Room for fabulous views. Breakers has a Qualmark Enviro-Silver rating.

2 GREYMOUTH & LAKE BRUNNER

101km (63 miles) SW of Westport; 45km (28 miles) N of Hokitika; 290km (180 miles) SW of Nelson

I've always felt Greymouth was rather well named. Personally, it's never been a town to inspire a long stopover, despite the fact that it is centrally placed and has the best access to Nelson and Christchurch. It has had a bit of a face-lift recently, though, and in mid-summer it's a busy stopover for international visitors.

It is also part of a rich history. The Grey River was the landing place for Maori canoes on the hunt for greenstone, or *pounamu*—the jade that was Westland's most prized possession. Even today, the Grey River gap has great significance in Maori myth, and greenstone is just as prized as ever. The discovery of gold in the 1860s also left its mark on the area.

With a population of 11,000, Greymouth is kept busy with coal and timber exports. It is the largest town and the commercial heart of the West Coast, and most goods and services are available here—although some of them could do with a bit of a crank-up. If you're trying to decide whether to stay in Greymouth or travel another 45km (28 miles) to Hokitika, keep in mind that Greymouth has better food outlets, while Hokitika has a greater range of attractions, better accommodations, and tourist shopping.

ESSENTIALS

GETTING THERE & GETTING AROUND **By Plane** Daily flights between Christ-church and Hokitika are operated by **Air New Zealand** ((C) 0800/737-000 in NZ; www. airnewzealand.co.nz). A shuttle service carries visitors the extra 30 minutes by road to Greymouth.

By Train The **Tranz Scenic** TranzAlpine route ((C) 0800/872-467 in NZ; www.tranz scenic.co.nz) runs daily between Christchurch and the Greymouth railway station on Mackay Street and will stop in Moana (at Lake Brunner) on request. This is New Zealand's best rail experience (see p. 384 for more details).

By Coach (Bus) **InterCity** ((C) 09/623-1503, or 03/768-7080) buses reach Greymouth from Queenstown, Fox Glacier, Franz Josef, Nelson, and Westport. Both **Kiwi Experience** ((C) 09/366-9830) and **Magic Travellers** ((C) 09/358-5600) include Greymouth on their routes. A daily shuttle bus stops at Lake Brunner en route to Christchurch.

By Car   Greymouth is reached via Highway 6 from both the north and the south. Highway 7 brings travelers from the east coast via Lewis Pass, and Highway 73 takes you through Arthur's Pass National Park on the road from Christchurch. The trip from Nelson takes approximately 4 to 5 hours; from Christchurch, 4 hours.

VISITOR INFORMATION   The **Greymouth i-SITE Visitors Centre,** in the Regent Theatre Building, at Herbert and Mackay streets (✆ **0800/473-966** in NZ, or 03/768-5101; fax 03/768-0317; www.greydistrict.co.nz), is open in summer Monday through Friday from 8:30am to 7pm, Saturday 9am to 6pm, Sunday and public holidays 10am to 5pm (closed Dec 25). It has reduced hours in winter, closing at 5:30pm Monday through Friday. It also functions as the Department of Conservation agency for the region.

EXPLORING GREYMOUTH

If you're a history buff, you'll find that **Shantytown** ★ (✆ **0800/807-787** in NZ, or 03/762-6634; www.shantytown.co.nz) has been rather well done. Situated amid native bush, the replica West Coast gold-mining town includes over 30 historic buildings, a collection of over 10,000 historic objects, photographs, archives, and textiles. A steam train operates on a 20-minute bush track, and a stagecoach will rattle you over an old bush road. You can also pan for gold, and the new sawmill experience takes you through what appears to be an operating sawmill, complete with historical film footage. It's open daily from 8:30am to 5pm. Admission is NZ$25 for adults, NZ$12 for children 5 to 17, with family concessions (this includes a steam train ride and gold panning). To get here, drive 8km (5 miles) south of Greymouth to Paroa, make a left, and go another 3km (2 miles) inland.

For a summary of the region's artistic talents, head for **Left Bank Art Gallery** ★, 1 Tainui St. (✆ **03/768-0038;** www.leftbankart.co.nz), Monday through Friday from 10am to 5pm; and weekends 10am to 2pm. It has changing exhibitions (NZ$2 admission), an excellent shop featuring the work of 70 West Coast artists, and the New Zealand Pounamu Jade Collection. It's closed Sunday and Monday in winter.

If you prefer something a little more intoxicating, go to **Monteith's Brewery** ★★, 60 Herbert St. (✆ **03/768-4149;** www.monteiths.co.nz), to book the NZ$15 brewery tour and tasting. Daily tours are given at 11:30am, 2pm, 4pm, and 6pm (closed Easter Friday and Saturday, Dec 25, and Jan 1).

OUTDOOR PURSUITS

CAVE RAFTING   **Wild West Adventure Company** (✆ **0800/122-283** in NZ, or 03/768-6649; www.fun-nz.com), has a 5-hour Dragon's Cave Rafting Trip for NZ$165

ⓕFinds   A Blackball Experience

Go off the beaten path and discover the quaint historic village of Blackball, 28km (17 miles) northeast of Greymouth in the Grey Valley. Started as a base for transient gold seekers in 1864, it's a lingering testimony to the way life used to be on the coast. Visit the "famous" **Formerly the Blackball Hilton,** 26 Hart St. (✆ **03/732-4705;** www.blackballhilton.co.nz), an original West Coast pub, for a beer, a casual meal, or a low-key overnight stay; and stop off at the award-winning **Blackball Salami Company,** Hilton Street (✆ **03/732-4111**), which makes sausages and salami—low-fat venison and beef versions are a specialty.

(i) **Tips** **Shopping for Greenstone**

You can hold out and peruse a far wider range of greenstone options in Hokitika, or you can accept local word that **Jade Boulder Gallery,** 1 Guinness St., Greymouth (📞 **0800/523-326** in NZ, or 03/768-0700; www.jadeboulder.com), is the best source of quality jade carving on the West Coast. Owner Ian Boustridge's work is in collections all around the world. He carves the bigger pieces on display at the gallery. You'll also see other souvenir items such as wooden bowls, hand-knit sweaters, and furniture. Light meals are available at the Jade Boulder Café. If you're looking for top-quality New Zealand jade, I'd recommend you start here. The gallery is open daily in summer from 8:30am to 9pm and in winter 8:30am to 5pm.

(NZ$245 with rappelling), taking you deep into a subterranean wonderland of lakes, glowworms, and waterfalls.

GOLF **Greymouth Golf Club,** Golf Links Road, Kaiata (📞 **03/768-5332**), is 3km (1¾ miles) from town, has 18 holes, and welcomes visitors. Greens fees are from NZ$20.

OFF-ROAD ADVENTURES Five kilometers (3 miles) north of Greymouth, you can experience an off-road adventure with **On Yer Bike** (📞 **0800/669-372** in NZ, or 03/762-7438; www.onyerbike.co.nz) on either a four-wheeled bike or the amphibious eight-wheeled Argo. A 1-hour Explorer bike ride costs NZ$95. One hour on a go-cart will set you back NZ$115 plus NZ$60 for passengers.

SURFING The main breaks are on **Cobden** and **Blaketown** beaches, both signposted about 5 minutes north of central Greymouth, and farther north at **9-Mile Beach.**

WALKING The **Point Elizabeth Walkway** ★★ starts at Rapahoe and follows the coast south around the headland to the Cobden Beach road end. The track takes under 2 hours one-way. If the tide is low, return along the beach. Go in early evening to enjoy one of Greymouth's fabulous sunsets.

Wild West Adventure (📞 **0800/122-283** in NZ, or 03/768-6649; www.fun-nz. com), has details on 83 walks within **Te Ara Pounamu** ★★★, the Greenstone Pathway—a spectacular 720km (450-mile) route that has been followed for hundreds of years by Maori traders. Walks range from 30-minute wanders to multiday options; some are guided. **Walks & Drives** (📞 **03/768-4090**) has a wide range of guided walks from a few hours to several days anywhere on the West Coast or the greater South Island.

WHITE-WATER RAFTING **Wild West Adventure Company** (see above) has a wide range of rafting packages that can include trail rides, helicopters, walking, or drinking champagne in natural hot pools surrounded by rainforest. There are three popular Hot Rock options. The 5-hour guided walk, raft, and hot pools trip costs NZ$205 per person. If you include a helicopter ride, the price rises to NZ$415.

ORGANIZED TOURS

Kea Heritage Tours, 152 Golf Links Rd. (📞 **0800/532-868** in NZ, or 03/768-9292; www.keatours.co.nz), has a number of tours to the glaciers, Punakaiki, Shantytown, and Blackball. These range in price from NZ$70 per person to NZ$260 per person for the Twin Glaciers and Lake Matheson Tour.

Off Beat Tours (🕿 **0800/270-960** in NZ, or 03/731-1424; www.offbeattours.co.nz) goes all the way south to the glaciers and all the way north to Karamea and the spectacular Oparara Limestone Arches. Prices range from NZ$90 for a half-day tour to NZ$240 for the full-day glacier trip.

For one of the best-value scenic flights, seek out **Air West Coast** ★★★ at Greymouth Airport (🕿 **03/738-0524;** www.airwestcoast.co.nz). The four-seater Cessna 172 takes you all the way down to Milford Sound. It's a full figure-eight trip that also covers the glaciers, Mount Cook, valleys, rivers, forests, and lakes. They also connect with cruise boats at Milford Sound and helicopter flights at Franz Josef to land on the snow. To fly to Mount Cook, the glaciers, Milford, and back to Christchurch (an advantage if you've traveled to Greymouth via the TranzAlpine and need to get back for connecting flights), costs NZ$875 per person (minimum two people). Keep in mind that you'll pay close to that for some of the scenic flights out of Queenstown that are shorter and cover far less territory. A shorter flight to Mount Cook and the glaciers will cost NZ$295 per person, minimum two people.

WHERE TO STAY

Greymouth Seaside Top 10 Holiday Park, 2 Chesterfield St. (🕿 **0800/867-104** in NZ, or 03/768-6618; www.top10greymouth.co.nz), has tent and caravan sites, cabins, motel units, and a backpacker bunkhouse. Backpackers have some fun choices in the fish-themed **Neptunes,** 43 Gresson St. (🕿 **0800/003-768** in NZ, or 03/768-4425; www. neptunesbackpackers.co.nz), which has a free Jacuzzi; the animal-themed **Noahs Ark Backpackers,** 16 Chapel St. (🕿 **0800/662-472** in NZ, or 03/768-4868; www.noahs. co.nz); and **Global Village Backpackers,** 42–54 Cowper St. (🕿 **03/768-7272;** www. globalvillagebackpackers.co.nz), which has a charming riverside setting and has been completely refurbished with new beds throughout.

All rates given here include the 12.5% GST and free off-street parking.

Kingsgate Hotel ★ (Value) This is my choice for the best lodging in Greymouth, but don't get too excited, it's nothing special. It offers tidy, spacious guest rooms with everything you'll need on-site. The six-floor hotel tower contains 42 premium rooms, and seven family suites are available as well. The property is within walking distance of restaurants and attractions; it has a better in-house restaurant than Hotel Ashley. Many tour groups and business travelers frequent the place.

32 Mawhera Quay, P.O. Box 337, Greymouth. 🕿 **0800/805-085** in NZ, or 03/768-5085. Fax 03/768-5844. www.kingsgategreymouth.co.nz. 102 units. NZ$105 standard and premium room; NZ$165 family suite; from NZ$195 suite. Off-peak and long-stay rates. AE, DC, MC, V. **Amenities:** Restaurant; bar; babysitting; concierge; gym; high-speed Internet; room service; some Wi-Fi hot spots. *In room:* TV, fridge, hair dryer, minibar.

Rosewood Bed & Breakfast ★ This restored 1920s home is minutes from the town center. Four big bedrooms have en suites. The Mona room upstairs is the nicest and has the best bathroom, although the front room downstairs is very pleasant, with a window seat looking out into the garden. Overall, it's a pleasing stay and you'll be close to everything.

20 High St., Greymouth. 🕿 **0800/185-748** in NZ, or 03/768-4674. Fax 03/768-4694. www.rosewoodnz. co.nz. 4 units. NZ$200–NZ$250. Off-peak rates. Rates include breakfast. MC, V. **Amenities:** Nearby golf course. *In room:* TV, hair dryer, Wi-Fi.

Apart from the eateries reviewed below, the restaurants at Quality Kings Hotel and Hotel Ashley also serve good meals. Both veer toward the more formal—or as formal as things get on the West Coast. For good coffee, Internet, and adventure atmosphere, try **dp: one café** ★, 108 Mawhera Quay (✆ **03/768-4005**), which is my pick for the best relaxed cafe environment. If you prefer a less-funky interior, you'll be happier at **Café 124 on Mackay,** 124 Mackay St. (✆ **03/768-7503**), which has reasonable all-day food, but the service is patchy at best. **Trawlers Seafood Restaurant,** 14–16 Tarapuhi St. (✆ **03/768-9254**), has the smartest restaurant interior and good meals, but the service is often hopeless. I'll say it again: Don't expect dining miracles on the West Coast. For pizza try **Friar Tuck Pizza,** 1 Marsden St. (✆ **03/768-066**).

Jones's Café ★★ CAFE/LIGHT MEALS   Locals will tell you this little cafe offers the best food, the best service, and the best atmosphere. The interior is unremarkable, but the coffee is the most consistent in town.

37 Tainui St. ✆ **03/768-6468.** Main courses NZ$16–NZ$26. No credit cards. Daily 11am–9pm.

The Smelting House Café Value CAFE/LIGHT MEALS   I appreciate the laid-back atmosphere of this cafe, situated in the old bank building. It's gained a solid reputation for good coffee and tasty snacks. There's a range of pasta dishes, soups, and salads for lunch or a light early-evening meal, plus delicious cakes. Appetizing, affordable, and always filled with travelers, cyclists, and families.

102 Mackay St. ✆ **03/768-0012.** Main courses NZ$10–NZ$25. No credit cards. Daily 8am–5pm.

A SIDE TRIP TO LAKE BRUNNER ★★

Lake Brunner and the little township of Moana, situated on its northern shore, lie 30 minutes east of Greymouth. It's a peaceful, scenic diversion serviced by both the Tranz-Alpine train and a daily shuttle bus—and, I regret to say, great clouds of greedy sand flies that you'll spend your hours swatting away. Access by road is via Arthur's Pass or Lewis Pass, which makes it a good stopover point if you're heading north or south.

The lake and surrounding rivers have some of the best trout fishing in the South Island. The prime time for fishing is between October and April. The Greymouth i-SITE Visitor Centre has a big list of guides and will point you in the right direction for the best spots. Just make sure you get a license first.

If you find the tranquil nature of this location appealing and you decide to stay over, you'll find a motel complex, a motor camp, and the old **Moana Hotel,** Ahau Street, Moana (✆ **03/738-0388;** www.moanahotelmotel.co.nz), which offers inexpensive motel/hotel rooms and cabins. If you prefer a more upmarket option, stay at **Lake Brunner Lodge** ★★, Mitchells, RD1, Kumara, Westland (✆/fax **03/738-0163;** www.lake brunner.com), on the unpopulated side of the lake. It has 11 rooms and has recently been upgraded. Rates run from NZ$440 to NZ$555 and a five-course dinner costs NZ$110 per person on top. It's looking very smart, and this spot is a great hit with fishermen.

Dining out is a little more limited. Your best option is **Stationhouse Café,** Koe Street, Moana (✆ **03/738-0158**), where pastas, steaks, and roast lamb range from NZ$16 to NZ$32. It's a pretty setting overlooking tiny Moana Railway Station and the lake, but a trifle overpriced and you have to take the service as you find it. It's open daily from 10:30am until late.

This 45km (28-mile), 30-minute drive south follows the coastline closely along mostly flat farmland. Nothing too inspiring, but there are hints of the Southern Alps that await when you turn away from the Tasman Sea farther south. About 30km (20 miles) from Greymouth, you'll cross the **Arahura River,** where Maori found huge supplies of greenstone.

3 HOKITIKA: GREENSTONE, GLOWWORMS & GOLD

45km (28 miles) S of Greymouth; 147km (91 miles) N of Franz Josef Glacier

As you drive into the quiet, rather forlorn-looking township of Hokitika, you'll find it hard to believe that it was once a boisterous "Goldfields Capital," where more than 35,000 miners and prospectors patronized more than 102 hotels and kept the dance halls roaring. As many as 80 boats would be docked at the wharves, many of them waiting to transport gold out of the area.

Sadly for Hokitika, the gold supply was finite; when the rush died, so did the wild, carefree days. The economy took a downward turn, and the livelihood of most of today's 4,000 residents is based on farming, forestry, and tourism. But the town is renowned for the Wildfoods Festival, held each March, and it is *the* place to buy crafts on the West Coast. During the summer months, it's probably the cheeriest and busiest of the West Coast towns. It has 1,850 sunshine hours annually and 2,783 millimeters (110 in.) of rainfall—keep your wet-weather gear handy if you're staying for any length of time.

ESSENTIALS

GETTING THERE   **By Plane**   There is air service via **Air New Zealand Link** (✆ **0800/ 737-000** in NZ; www.airnewzealand.co.nz) between Hokitika and Christchurch.

By Train   Access to the nearest rail service is in Greymouth (see "Greymouth & Lake Brunner," earlier in this chapter).

By Coach (Bus)   InterCity (✆ **09/623-1503**) has daily departures from Hokitika to Nelson, Westport, Greymouth, and Fox Glacier. Both **Magic Travellers** (✆ **09/358-5600**)

(**Moments**) **Wildfoods Festival**

If you're in the area around the second Saturday in March, stop in Hokitika for the **Hokitika Wildfoods Festival** ★ ★ ★ (✆ **03/756-9048** or 756-9045; www.wild foods.co.nz). On the easy side of things, you'll be able to sample wild pig, veni-son, wild herbs, honey, and fish from local waters; the much braver visitor might like to try possum pâté, wild goat, wriggling grubs, and the unmentionable parts of a variety of animals. The general motto here is close your eyes, swallow, and ask questions later! Admission is NZ$30 for adults, NZ$5 for children, and ticket numbers are limited to 17,000 each year. It's a crazy get-together that will give you a real insight into the quirky character of the West Coast. Not to be missed if you're in the area.

> ⓜ **Moments**   **Bright Lights: Spotting Glowworms for Free**
>
> When people talk about the bright lights of Hokitika, they don't mean a dazzling display of neon and inner city activity. It's much more likely that they're referring to the largest outdoor gathering of glowworms in New Zealand. Head north, to the edge of the town, and there, right on the edge of the main road (St. Hwy. 6), is a charming, easily accessed dell that shines bright every evening. The glowworms thrive in the moist atmosphere of the wooded banks. Make sure it's properly dark before you visit, speak quietly, and don't turn on torches (flashlights), or these shy critters will vanish. It's free, quite magical, and well worth the effort of groping your way through darkness.

and **Kiwi Experience** (ⓒ **09/366-9830**) pass through Hokitika on their way from Greymouth to the glaciers.

By Car   Hokitika is reached from the north and south via Highway 6.

VISITOR INFORMATION   The **Westland Visitor Information Centre,** Carnegie Building, Tancred and Hamilton streets, Hokitika (ⓒ **03/755-6166;** fax 03/755-5011; www.hokitika.org), is open December through April daily from 8:30am to 6pm, May through November Monday through Friday from 8:30am to 5pm, and Saturday and Sunday from 10am to 4pm. Twenty-five minutes south of Hokitika, the **Ross Goldfields Information & Heritage Centre,** 4 Aylmer St., Ross (ⓒ **03/755-4077;** www.ross.org.nz), is open daily in summer from 9am to 4pm, and in winter from 9am to 3pm. Try your hand at gold panning for NZ$10.

Note: If you're traveling farther south, Hokitika is the last stop for banks, ATMs, pharmacies, and major supermarkets until you reach Wanaka, 450km (279 miles) away. For more information on this area check www.hokitika.com and www.westlanddc.govt.nz.

EXPLORING HOKITIKA

To gain insight into the history of this little town, pick up the *Hokitika Heritage Walk* brochure at the visitor center or the West Coast Historical Museum.

The **West Coast Historical Museum,** Tancred and Hamilton streets (ⓒ **03/755-6898;** enquiries@hokitikamuseum.co.nz), features reconstructions and artifacts of the 19th-century "Alluvial placer" gold-mining era on the West Coast. Wood and slab dwellings display household furnishings. A typical bar, horse-drawn vehicles, mining tools, and pictorial records of the harbor's maritime history are among the wealth of items you'll see. Gold panning is an all-weather attraction in the miner's hut. The museum is open daily from 9:30am to 5pm. Admission is NZ$10 for adults, NZ$5 for children.

If you're traveling with kids, the **National Kiwi Centre** ★, 64 Tancred St. (ⓒ **03/755-5251;** natkiwi@xtra.co.nz), is worth a visit. The stars here are the 63 rather repulsive, but nonetheless fascinating, giant eels. The eldest is over 80 years old, and some weigh up to 25 kilograms (55 lb.). Try to visit during their feeding (ring ahead for times), and try a spot of hand-feeding. It also features Australasia's largest tropical aquarium, with an indoor lake, giant trout, birds, reptiles, and, of course, the kiwi. It is open daily from 9am to 5pm. Admission is NZ$20 for adults, NZ$10 for children ages 5 to 14, and NZ$40 for families.

Take to the water on a Scenic Waterways **Paddle Boat Cruise** ★, Main Road South (✆ **03/755-7239** or 755-6166; www.paddleboatcruises.com). A dreamy tour down tranquil Mahinapua Creek is just the thing to do on a leisurely afternoon (Jan–Apr daily at 2pm). Keep a look out for the beautiful white herons that may be in residence. The 1½-hour cruises cost NZ$25 for adults and NZ$12 for children ages 5 to 14. Make reservations in advance at the visitor center.

EXPLORING LAKE KANIERE SCENIC RESERVE ★★★

This beautiful nature reserve, centered on one of the South Island's largest lakes, is just 18km (11 miles) from Hokitika. If you don't have time to stay and explore, there's a lovely 58km (36-mile) circular scenic drive past the lake and back through Kakatahi Valley farmlands.

Lingering, however, will be rewarded by vistas of the lake ringed by unspoiled forests with a backdrop of distant mountains. You'll find an information kiosk and toilets at the landing, where the road first comes to the water's edge. There are picnic tables, fireplaces, and toilets at Sunny Bight. This is also the starting point for two walks: the **Kahikatea Forest Walk** ★, a 10-minute stroll through the forest; and the **Lake Kaniere Walkway** ★★, a 3½-hour trek that features beaches, rainforest, and bird life. Pick up advance information on the walks at the visitor center in Hokitika.

SHOPPING

In peak season, shopping takes on the nature and dimensions of a sport in Hokitika, as the human contents of buses spill out into the vicinity of Tancred Street. All of the following stores are open daily (usually 10am–5pm). At the **Gold Room,** 37 Tancred St. (✆ **03/755-8362;** www.thegoldroom.co.nz), you'll see gold in every form—from raw nuggets and flakes to top-quality crafted jewelry. **Hokitika Craft Gallery,** 25 Tancred St. (✆ **03/755-8802;** www.hokitikacraftgallery.co.nz), features the work of 19 of the West Coast's top artisans under one roof. Look out for contemporary works in fiber, wood, pottery, jade, leather, wool, glass, and bone. My pick is the furniture by top craftsman Marc Zuckerman. **Hokitika Glass Studio,** 28 Tancred St. (✆ **03/755-7775;** www.hokitikaglass.co.nz), is home to more glass penguins than the average person could cope with; but beyond that, there are some stunning glassworks here. Bowls, platters, and gorgeous perfume bottles are my picks. **House of Wood,** 29 Tancred St. (✆ **03/755-6061**), has the best range of handcrafted wooden items. Browse the creative boxes, lovely bowls, and wooden toys. You can also watch wood-turners at work in the studio. **Jade Factory,** 41 Weld St. (✆ **03/755-8007;** www.jadefactory.com), generally has up to seven carvers at work. A big selection of excellent-quality jewelry is for sale. **Westland Greenstone Ltd,** 34 Tancred St. (✆ **03/755-8713**), is a good place to see greenstone and *paua* jewelry being made. The showroom has a wide range of the finished products at factory prices.

WHERE TO STAY

Campers will find a good deal at the **Hokitika Holiday Park,** 242 Stafford St. (✆ **0800/465-436** in NZ, or 03/755-8172; www.hokitika.com/holidaypark). It has tent and caravan sites, cabins, and flats. **Mountain Jade Backpackers,** 41 Weld St. (✆ **0800/838-301** in NZ, or 03/755-8007; fax 03/755-7804), has roomy dorms with beds costing from NZ$55 to NZ$95. One of the nicest things to happen to the accommodations scene here is the massive upgrade of the old Southland Hotel. It's now the **Beachfront Hotel** ★, 111 Revell St. (✆ **0800/400-344** in NZ, or 03/755-8344; fax 03/755-8258;

for the new Ocean View rooms, which are far nicer and better equipped than the older Driftwood rooms. They are also just a few steps from the beach.

Moderate

Rimu Lodge ★★ (Value)   Peter and Helen Walls have built a real gem on the top of a spur, overlooking bush-clad slopes and the Hokitika River. You'll be hard-pressed to find a more serene and tranquil setting, or better views. Four big suites (two up, two down) will bring an instant smile to your face. They're modern, spacious, and gorgeous. The two upstairs rooms have bigger bathrooms.

33 Seddons Terrace Rd., Hokitika. ℂ **03/755-5255.** Fax 03/755-5237. www.rimulodge.co.nz. 4 units. NZ$295–NZ$365. AE, MC, V. Long-stay rates. Rates include breakfast, canapés, and predinner drinks. Drive south over the Hokitika River Bridge and turn left on Arthurstown Rd.; travel 4km (2¹/₂ miles) to a T-junction and turn right; pass Rimu Hotel on the right, go uphill, and Seddons Terrace Rd. is the 1st on your left. No children 11 and under. **Amenities:** Nearby golf course. *In room:* Hair dryer, fridge.

Teichelmann's Bed & Breakfast ★ (Value)   Brian Ward and Frances Flanagan transformed this iconic Hokitika B&B, making it lighter, brighter, and lovelier. The upstairs Wilson room—creamy and luscious—is my favorite. The sun pours in, and the room has a king-size and larger-than-normal single beds plus a private bathroom. Four other in-house rooms have en suites. If you're lucky, you might be able to nab the cute garden suite with its big Jacuzzi. Overall a terrific stay for the price.

20 Hamilton St., Hokitika. ℂ **0800/743-742** in NZ, or 03/755-8232. Fax 03/755-8239. www.teichelmanns. co.nz. 6 units. NZ$215–NZ$260. Long-stay and off-peak rates. Rates include breakfast. MC, V. Directly opposite the visitor center. No children 9 and under. **Amenities:** Airport transport; nearby golf course. *In room:* Hair dryer, Wi-Fi.

WHERE TO DINE

Pounamu Kai, 23 Weld St. (ℂ **03/755-8581**), serves light lunches, including vegetarian, vegan, and gluten-free fare and some of the best coffee in Hokitika. **Ocean View Restaurant,** in the Beachfront Hotel, 111 Revell St. (ℂ **03/755-8344**), is a great spot for balcony dining overlooking the beach. They serve breakfast, lunch, and dinner, and are open from 7am until late; and **Stumpers Bar and Café** ★★, corner of Weld and Revell streets (ℂ **0800/788-673;** www.stumpers.co.nz), gets the most local votes for the most consistently good meals. It's open daily from 7am until late.

   Café de Paris ★, 19 Tancred St. (ℂ **03/755-8933**), seems like it has been around forever. It provides reasonably good meals; the French owner has always swung his menu in favor of things European. When service is not patchy, you'll dine well. They're open daily, 7:30am till late. For tasty treats to eat in or takeaway, visit **Hokitika Cheese & Deli** ★, Revell Street (ℂ **03/755-5432**). They stock an excellent range of imported and local cheeses, fresh and cured meats, and delicious cabinet food for light lunches or picnics.

EN ROUTE TO FRANZ JOSEF & FOX GLACIERS

There are no banks or ATMs in either glacier village, so remember to get money before going south—you won't be able to do so again until you get to Wanaka, some 450km (280 miles) away. Credit cards are accepted in most places, though. If you're driving nonstop to Wanaka, allow 6 to 7 hours. The drive to Franz Josef from Hokitika takes about 2 hours.

   If you're in the **Whataroa** area (35km/22 miles north of Franz Josef) during the November-to-February nesting season of the *kotuku* (white heron), book one of the

> ### (Tips) Kiwi Spotting
>
> Okarito is also the only place in the South Island where you can venture into bush at night in the hope of spotting kiwi in their natural habitat. **Okarito Kiwi Tours,** The Strand, Okarito (© **03/753-4330;** www.okaritokiwitours.co.nz), offers a low-impact, ecominded jaunt into the night bush for NZ$55 per person. Numbers are limited to eight and the tour takes 2 to 3 hours, leaving just before sunset.

White Heron Sanctuary Tours ★★★ (© **0800/523-456** in NZ, or 03/753-4120; www.whiteherontours.co.nz). Entry to the country's only white-heron nesting colony is by permit and starts with a 20-minute jet-boat ride. You then walk through native rain-forest accompanied by a guide. The excursion costs NZ$110 for adults, NZ$45 for children 12 and under.

A little farther west, **Okarito Lagoon,** 10km (6 miles) off State Highway 6, is a beautiful spot where **Okarito Nature Tours** ★★ (© 03/753-4014; www.okarito.co.nz) can introduce you to the wonders of New Zealand's largest unmodified wetland—home to over 70 species of birds including the Great White Heron and the Royal Spoonbill. Its guided kayak tours have fabulous photo opportunities and are priced from NZ$75 per person. Kayak rental is NZ$40 per person for 2 hours, NZ$60 per person for a full day.

4 FRANZ JOSEF & FOX GLACIERS ★★★

Franz Josef: 188km (117 miles) S of Greymouth; 24km (15 miles) N of Fox Glacier

It seems improbable that you could find a glacier on a South Pacific island and ice in a temperate rainforest, but that's New Zealand for you—full of surprises. Nowhere else in the world outside arctic regions will you find glaciers just 300m (1,000 ft.) above sea level and just 12km (7½ miles) from the sea.

The two glaciers are just a small part of the 115,000-hectare (284,000-acre) **Westland National Park,** an impressive area of high mountains, glacial lakes, and rushing rivers. The park is popular for tramping, mountain climbing, fishing, canoeing, hunting, and horse trekking. In 1990, the combined Mount Cook/Westland National Parks, Fiordland National Park, Mount Aspiring National Park, and all the significant adjacent natural areas were incorporated into a single vast **Southwest New Zealand World Heritage Area (Te Wahipounamu),** which contains about 10% of New Zealand's total land area, or 2.6 million hectares (6.4 million acres). The World Heritage Highway traverses the northern third of this region and is largely confined to the West Coast side of the Main Divide.

So what are the differences between Franz Josef and Fox glaciers and their townships? Fox Glacier is longer and has better helicopter and walking options; Franz Josef village has a better visitor center and is busier overall, with superior food and lodging options. Just a short distance apart, the drive should nonetheless be undertaken with care.

ESSENTIALS

GETTING THERE **By Coach (Bus)** InterCity (© 09/623-1503) provides regular transport to the glaciers from north and south. Both **Magic Travellers** (© 09/358-5600) and **Kiwi Experience** (© 09/366-9830) include the glaciers on their itineraries as well.

By Car   The World Heritage Highway (St. Hwy. 6) follows the coast from Whataroa to Franz Josef Glacier to Fox Glacier to Haast and over the Haast Pass. The Department of Conservation's *World Heritage Highway Guide* suggests places to stop along the way. Roads in this area should always be treated with respect, especially in wet or icy conditions.

GETTING AROUND   I'd be surprised if you can't walk the full length of either village in just 10 minutes. Bike rentals are available in both, and you can travel between the two via InterCity coach.

VISITOR INFORMATION   The **Westland National Park Visitor Centre and i-SITE,** State Highway 6 (℃ **03/752-0796;** www.doc.govt.nz), is in the center of the village. Their displays, literature, and activities are essential to a full appreciation of the area and they're open daily in summer 8:30am to 6pm, and in winter 8:30am to 5pm. For additional information check www.glaciercountry.co.nz.

EXPLORING THE GLACIERS

Ask at the visitor center about the schedule for nature lectures, slide presentations, and guided walks—and see the excellent *Flowing West* movie at the **Alpine Adventure Centre,** Main Street, Franz Josef (℃ **03/752-0793**), or at **Fox Heli Services,** Alpine Guides Building, Fox Glacier (℃ **03/751-0866**). It runs daily continuously from 10:30am and it will take your breath away.

The visitor center administer the alpine and tramping huts available for overnight hikers, and keep track of trampers and climbers as well—it is essential to check conditions and register your intentions before setting out. The center's displays give a complete rundown on the formation of glaciers, the movement of ice, the mountains, the history of the region, and more.

Your sightseeing at the glaciers can be as costly or as inexpensive as your budget dictates. There are several options that can put a rather unfriendly hole in your budget, but these are among the most spectacular travel experiences in the world and are therefore worth every cent. If you'd rather, there are plenty of self-guided walks in the area, many of which give good views of the glaciers.

The silence of any fine morning in glacier country is ruptured by the frenetic buzz of **helicopters.** It's one of the best ways to see and appreciate the natural splendor of this area. Equally amazing are the **guided glacier walk** and the **heli-hike,** which combines both.

ⓘ Tips   Ice is Nice

If you don't have time to go to the glaciers, make time to visit the new multimillion-dollar **Hukawai Glacier Centre** ★★★, Cowan and Cron streets (℃ **0800/485-2921** in NZ, or 03/752-0600; www.hukawai.co.nz). Complete with a 10m-high (33-ft.) ice-climbing wall—the only one in the Southern Hemisphere—it offers a full interpretive glacier experience and a very nice cafe. It's a fabulous experience for all ages (climbing optional), and if it's too wet for glacier trips, it's a superb alternative. It's open daily in summer 9am to 7pm (last climb at 6pm), and in winter 9am to 6pm (last climb 5pm). Admission to the interactive glacier display costs NZ$20 for adults and NZ$7.50 for children. Ice climbing costs NZ$95 for adults and NZ$75 for children (14 and under), for 2 hours inclusive of all gear and instruction.

The choice of what to do may not turn out to be as agonizing as you think—the weather could very easily decide for you. To say that the weather here is unpredictable is an understatement, and even when it appears fine and sunny on the ground, conditions up on the glacier may preclude a helicopter landing. If your time is short, take the first flight available lest you miss out.

Several operators offer glacier hikes. The **Helicopter Line** ★★★ (✆ 0800/807-767 in NZ, 03/752-0767 in Franz Josef, or 751-0767 in Fox Glacier; www.helicopter.co.nz) is the biggest heli-tourism operator in New Zealand. Its most popular trip is the 30-minute twin glacier option with snow landing for NZ$275. Mention you saw them in Frommer's and you'll get a 10% discount when booking direct. **Glacier Helicopters** (✆ 0800/800-732 in NZ, 03/752-0755 in Franz Josef, or 751-0803 in Fox Glacier; www.glacierhelicopters. co.nz), has a 30-minute twin glacier trip with an 8- to 10-minute névé landing from NZ$270. They also give Frommer's readers a 10% discount when booking direct. **Fox and Franz Josef Heliservices** (✆ 0800/800-793 in NZ, 03/751-0866 in Fox Glacier, or 752-0793 in Franz Josef; www.scenic-flights.co.nz) also offers a comprehensive range of flights, with a 30-minute flight going for NZ$245. Remember that flight routes and snow landings are always weather dependent and at the pilot's discretion.

Another option that everyone raves about is the **heli-hike** ★★★, which you can do with either the Helicopter Line (see above for contact information) or **Fox Glacier Guiding** ★★★ (✆ 0800/111-600 in NZ, or 03/751-0825; www.foxguides.co.nz). If you have deep pockets and love adventure, set NZ$395 aside for Fox Glacier Guiding's Flying Fox Helihike. They fly you to a high glacier level to spend 3½ hours exploring spectacular ice formations. The helicopter then returns to pick you up. It's suitable for all fitness levels, but does require some agility.

There are less taxing options, like guided glacier walks, for families and the less fit. Fox Glacier Guiding (see above) has both half- and full-day options on Fox Glacier. An expert guide will lead the way, chipping steps in the ice for you; you'll go up into the icefall, walk among the crevasses, and listen to the deep-throated grumble of the moving glacier. Hobnailed boots, waterproof parkas, heavy socks, and a walking stick are provided. The Fox Trot Half Day Walk costs NZ$95 for adults, NZ$75 for children (16 and under), or NZ$273 for a family.

In Franz Josef, **Franz Josef Glacier Guides** (✆ 0800/484-337 in NZ, or 03/752-0763; www.franzjosefglacier.com) offers half-day hikes from NZ$100; a full-day glacier adventure from NZ$160; glacier valley ecotours from NZ$65 for adults, NZ$50 for children ages 6 to 16 (no children 5 and under); and heli-hike options from NZ$395. It also has a slower, more informative half-day walk for the less agile.

Last but not least, **Mount Cook Ski Planes** ★★ (✆ 0800/368-000 in NZ, 03/752-0714 on the West Coast, or 430-8034 at Mount Cook; www.mtcookskiplanes.com) offers a fabulous-value specialist experience. This is New Zealand's only fixed-wing glacier landing, and when you land up on the snow and the engines are switched off, you're in total silence. This makes for a very different experience compared to a helicopter glacier landing. The twin glacier excursion takes 50 minutes and costs from NZ$315. The 60-minute Glacier Magic trip costs from NZ$395. This one will give you fantastic close-up views of Aoraki/Mount Cook and Mount Tasman, from both the eastern and western sides of the Southern Alps.

BEYOND THE GLACIERS: WHAT TO SEE & DO

Skydive NZ ★★★ (✆ 0800/751-0080 in NZ, or 03/751-0080; www.skydivingnz. co.nz) takes you up around the side of Mount Cook and over some of the most awesome scenery in the country. Then lucky you gets to jump 2,700m (8,900 ft.) for NZ$295.

(Moments) Lake Matheson & Lake Mapourika

Lake Matheson, 5km (3 miles) from Fox Glacier township, shows up on all the postcards, but what the pretty pictures don't show is the wonderful **Lake Matheson Walk** ★★, an easy track around the lake that takes about 1¹/₂ hours. You'll enjoy great views of Mount Cook (on the right) and Mount Tasman (to the left), and if you go to the lake before dusk, you can watch the mountains turn pink in the sunset—along with plenty of other sightseers doing exactly the same thing. When the lake and air are still, you'll be able to get one of those famous photographs of the mountains perfectly reflected in the water. **Café Lake Matheson** is at the parking area where the walk starts; it's open daily from 7am to 5pm.

Lake Mapourika, 9km (5¹/₂ miles) north of Franz Josef, is the largest lake in Westland National Park and deserves attention for its arresting reflections and setting. You can swim and fish, or opt for a peaceful cruise (see Glacier Country Lake Tours under "Beyond the Glaciers: What to See & Do," above).

Glacier Country Lake Tours ★, 64 Cron St., Franz Josef (© **0800/525-386** in NZ, or 03/752-0244; www.laketours.co.nz), takes cruises on nearby, mirrorlike Lake Mapourika. Bird-watchers will love this one, as the lake edge is home to some of New Zealand's rarest species. Photographic opportunities abound here, so make sure you have your camera ready. The scenery is beautiful. They operate daily at 9:30am, 11:30am, 1pm, and 3pm all year, with additional cruises at 5pm and 7pm from October through March. The ecocruise costs NZ$98 for adults, NZ$49 children (4–12), and NZ$245 for a family.

The West Coast's wet weather is great news for rafters; if you want to see how brave you really are, join **Eco Rafting Adventures** ★★, 2087 Whataroa (north of Franz Josef) (© **0508/669-675** in NZ, or 021/523-426; www.ecorafting.co.nz), for an unforgettable day on otherwise inaccessible Grade IV and V rivers. You'll get there by helicopter, and multiday hike and raft options cost NZ$250 to NZ$1,500. It's your best chance to get into an untouched wilderness

Walkers and trampers should stop by either visitor center to collect Department of Conservation material on the numerous tracks in the area. The **Copland Track** ★★ is a popular overnight round-trip that gives you a glimpse of Westland's spectacular scenery, with the natural hot pools at Welcome Flat an added attraction. Rainfall in the area is high, so come well equipped and always sign in (and out) before undertaking any hike.

Another walk takes you to a **seal colony at Gillespies Beach** ★★★, a 21km (13-mile) drive from Fox village. Take Cook Flat Road–Lake Matheson Road from the village and follow the signs to the beach. The last 11km (7 miles) of the road are unpaved. Allow 3 hours round-trip.

If all this exercise seems positively tedious, why not take a quiet after-dark amble to Fox's mini **glowworm dell?** Wait until it's very dark, and keep quiet. There is a short track just off the main road opposite the BP gas station. There is a small charge for adults, but children enter free. The ultimate way to relax after all this adventure, though, is to soak in divine hot pools at the new complex, **Glacier Hot Pools** ★★★, Cron Street,

Franz Josef (© **0800/044-044** in NZ, or 03/752-0161; www.glacierhotpools.co.nz), set in native rainforest. They have three lovely fern-enclosed public pools, three private pools, and lovely massage facilities; they're open from noon to 10pm (closed Dec 25). Admission to the public pool (for an unlimited duration) is NZ$23 for adults and NZ$16 for children (16 and under). Private pools (for 45 min.) cost NZ$40 per person. Massage rates range from NZ$80 (30 min.) to NZ$170 (1½ hr.).

WHERE TO STAY

During peak season, accommodations are woefully short in these parts. You'll be competing for rooms with lots of tour groups. On top of that, some hotels are overpriced for what they offer. My best advice is to book well ahead or travel outside the summer months; otherwise, you may find yourself staying as far away from the glaciers as Greymouth. You can experience the glaciers without staying overnight in Fox or Franz Josef townships, but the advantage of sleeping here is being close enough to jump on flights when there's a break in the weather. By the time this guide hits the shelves, the Scenic Hotel Group's brand-new, NZ$25-million, ecofriendly, sustainable hotel, **Te Waonui Forest Retreat** (© **09/377-5767** for national sales office; www.scenicgroup.co.nz), will be open for business. It's right beside the Glacier Hot Pools (above) and it will certainly outclass all existing accommodations in the area.

In Franz Josef

The **Franz Josef Top 10 Holiday Park,** Main Road (© **0800/467-897** in NZ, or 03/752-0735; www.mountainview.co.nz), has tent and powered sites, cabins, a lodge, tourist cabins, and flats. **Rainforest Retreat & Backpackers** ★, 46 Cron St. (© **0800/873-346** in NZ, or 03/752-0220; www.rainforestretreat.co.nz), is nestled in native rainforest and provides some lovely, reasonably priced options for travelers on a budget. Another smart new option for a few more dollars is **Glenfern Villas** ★, State Highway 6 (© **0800/453-633** in NZ, or 03/752-0054; www.glenfern.co.nz), where you'll find very comfortable one- and two-bedroom villas with fully equipped kitchens. Plus, they're just a short walk to village shops and cafes. There are good hotel-style B&B digs at **Franz Josef Glacier Country Retreat,** State Highway 6, Lake Mapaourika (© **0800/372-695;** www.glacier-retreat.co.nz), which has 10 rooms for NZ$395, and two suites priced NZ$495 to NZ$595.

The rates provided here include 12.5% GST and free off-street parking.

Holly Homestead ★★   Gerard and Bernie Oudemans have renovated and extended their gracious 1926 homestead to include five very nice guest rooms with en suites. The superior rooms with king-size beds are more spacious; and the suite has a private lounge. There's a new upstairs deck to take in those wonderful southern sunsets, and an overall mood of warmth and hospitality prevails. It's just a few minutes north of the township.

St. Hwy. 6. © **03/752-0299.** Fax 03/752-0298. www.hollyhomestead.co.nz. 5 units. NZ$200–NZ$400. Off-peak rates. Rates include full breakfast. MC, V. No children 11 and under. *In room:* TV, fridge (in suite), hair dryer, Wi-Fi.

Punga Grove Motor Lodge ★★ (Value   This gorgeous spot surrounded by huge tree ferns and rainforest is my pick for the best value in the area. The seven rainforest studios built in 2003 are the best of all. They have big Jacuzzis and leather furnishings, and look directly into the forest. Among the original choices, the two-bedroom suite is especially appealing, with a big kitchen. Four other units have two levels with rooms looking directly into the treetops. They're shady, inviting, and well situated for long stays.

The complex is in a quiet location, 150m (500 ft.) from shops and restaurants and just across the road from the new Glacier Hot Pools.

40 Cron St., Franz Josef. © **0800/437-269** in NZ, or 03/752-0001. Fax 03/752-0002. www.pungagrove. co.nz. 20 units. NZ$190 standard studio; NZ$250 executive studio; NZ$200 1-bedroom suite; NZ$275 2-bedroom suite. NZ$25 each extra person. Off-peak rates. AE, DC, MC, V. Turn off St. Hwy. 6 to Cowan St., then left to Cron St. Children 11 and under in family units only. **Amenities:** Babysitting; Internet. *In room:* TV, fridge, hair dryer, kitchenette.

In Fox Glacier

Heartland Hotel Glacier Country, State Highway 6 (© **0800/696-963** in NZ, or 03/ 751-0847; www.scenicgroup.co.nz.), is the baby of the Scenic Hotel Group. You can expect modest accommodations at affordable prices, often well below the rack rates. Built in the late 1960s, it's right in the heart of the village and is the smaller and older of the two Scenic Hotel Group hotels in Fox Glacier. You'll find new motel rooms at the **Westhaven** (© **0800/369-452** in NZ, or 03/751-0084; www.thewesthaven.co.nz), right in the heart of the action.

Te Weheka Inn ★   These central accommodations opened in two stages in 2001 and 2002, and provide one of the nicer stays in Fox Glacier. Rooms are spacious with king-size or twin beds and they have balcony views toward the village. Bathrooms are also a decent size and have a bathtub as well as a shower. There's an upstairs guest lounge and library where you can relax and a sunny dining room for breakfast.

St. Hwy. 6, Fox Glacier. © **0800/313-414** in NZ, or 03/751-0730. Fax 03/751-0731. www.teweheka.co.nz. 21 units. NZ$360–NZ$400. Extra adult NZ$75. Off-peak rates. Rates include breakfast. MC, V. **Amenities:** Free bikes; Internet in lounge. *In room:* TV, fridge, hair dryer.

WHERE TO DINE

In Franz Josef

If you've decided to do your own cooking, head for **Fern Grove Food Centre,** Main Road (© **03/752-0177**), open from 7:45am until late, especially for fresh bread and Mrs. Mac's famous meat pies. The **Blue Ice Restaurant & Bar** ★, Main Road (© **03/ 752-0707**), serves pizza, is fully licensed, and gets raves for the best cafe atmosphere in glacier country. It turns into a party venue as the night wears on. **Beeches Café & Bar,** Main Road (© **03/752-0721**), is a more expensive option with reasonably good food, a big wine list, and all-day service.

The **Landing** ★, Main Road (© **03/752-0229**), is a popular sports bar serving pizza, snacks, and platters. It's nothing fancy, but service is good (mostly) and it's a good value-for-money option; it's open daily in summer 10am till late, and in winter 4 to 10pm. My choice for the best coffee, though, goes to **Full of Beans Café** ★, Main Road, Franz Josef (© **03/752-0139**). It's open daily from 7am, and in addition to home-baked cabinet food, they'll also serve you home-style roast meals. Don't expect anything posh, but if you like good organic, free-trade coffee, this is the place.

In Fox Glacier

The **Fox Glacier General Store** ★, Main Road (© **03/751-0829**), sells everything from foodstuffs and hot meat pies to camping supplies, hardware, and boots. It's open daily from 8am till late. **Hobnail Café** ★, Main Road (© **03/751-0005**), right next to the Alpine Guides booking office, has a constant traffic of eager adventurers. It's open for breakfast, lunch, and all-day snacks, and the simple timber-tabled interior is always bustling and sunny. It's open daily from 7:30am to 4pm.

(Finds) **Back to Nature**

Nature lovers will get a real thrill out of spending a few nights at **Wilderness Lodge Lake Moeraki,** 30km (19 miles) north of Haast (© **03/750-0881;** www.wildernesslodge.co.nz), which has forged a solid international reputation in eco-tourism. Rates range from NZ$780 to NZ$980 and include accommodations, breakfast, dinner, use of lodge facilities, and daily guided nature trips. Expect a NZ$80 per person surcharge if you're staying here on December 25 and 26, January 1 and 2, Good Friday, and Easter Monday. There are numerous outdoor activities available, from kayaking, walking, and fishing to seal- and bird-watching. The big attractions here are the free daily guided nature activity program and newer rooms that opened in 2006. There is a minimum 2-night stay requirement between December 23 and March 1.

Café Neve ★★, Main Road (© **03/751-0110**), has a terrific range of pizzas along with delicious counter food and dinner dishes such as venison *osso buco* served on a Kumara (sweet potato) mash with steamed vegetables. Another possibility is the traditional West Coast whitebait omelet with fresh herbs. It's open from 8am till late and is definitely one of the nicest options. **Matheson Cafe** ★, Lake Matheson Road (© **03/751-0878**), has a fabulous aspect beside the lake, a nice "woody" interior, and great-value light meals. Take a walk around the lake first to work up an appetite. They're open daily from 7:30am until late in summer (from 8am with reduced hours in winter).

Cook Saddle Café and Saloon, Main Road (© **03/751-0700**), is a Tex-Mex favorite with backpackers. It has good ambience in true eclectic West Coast style—a trophy head here, an animal skin there. Venison burgers, Boss Hogg ribs, and Texas T-bone all speak of a slightly displaced sense of geography, but if a full stomach and a good night are your intention, then you've come to the right place. The **Plateau Café & Bar,** corner of Sullivan Street and State Highway 6 (© **03/751-0058**), is a nice spot in the Glowworm Forest Building, open for lunch and dinner daily with homemade baking all day.

EN ROUTE TO HAAST

Just 1 hour south of Fox Glacier (62km/38 miles) is the **Salmon Farm Café,** State Highway 6, South Westland (© **03/751-0837**). The menu is predictably "fishy," with both fresh and smoked salmon dishes in abundance. It's open daily from 7am to 7pm, with shorter winter hours. It's a popular stop for tour buses, so try to avoid the main lunch hour or you'll face a long queue. The food here is still fine, but the place is definitely looking a little shabby from the outside and could do with a makeover.

Farther south, the magnificent vistas from the **Knight's Point View Point** are worth a stop to take in sandy coves, bush-clad hillsides, rocky headlands, and ocean views.

Haast itself is 121km (75 miles) south of Fox Glacier. The **South Westland World Heritage Visitor Centre** is at the junction of State Highway 6 and Jackson Bay Road (© **03/750-0809;** fax 03/750-0832; haastvc@doc.govt.nz). The center has excellent exhibits on coastal highlights. It's open daily from 8:30am; mid-April to early November, until 4:30pm; early November to December 25 and February 7 to mid-April, until 6pm; and December 26 to February 6, it closes at 7pm.

The highway between Haast and Wanaka is magnificent, moss-covered, and often misty. It follows the course of the Haast River for much of the way. High peaks rise up on either side of the road. The route took 40 years to build and is 563m (1,847 ft.) above sea level. The Department of Conservation has created many walks along the way. Traveling non-stop, the trip to Wanaka should take 2 to 3 hours. Be prepared to make camera stops along the way of stunning waterfalls and river views.

EN ROUTE TO QUEENSTOWN

Highway 6 is good traveling all the way to Wanaka. From there, the trip to Queenstown will take around 1½ hours. You drive around the edge of Lake Dunstan, which was formed behind the Clyde Dam. Bypassing Cromwell township, you then travel through the stone fruit orchards of the Cromwell area. After passing through the Kawarau River Gorge, you come into Gibbston Valley and on into Queenstown.

If you're a competent driver, you could also go to Queenstown via the Crown Range. It's unsuitable for caravans and can be slippery and icy in winter, but the views from the top are stunning, and it's 30 minutes shorter than State Highway 6. If you are crossing the Crown Range in winter, it is now a legal requirement to carry chains. If you don't have them, expect a NZ$150 fine. They are available for hire from most gas stations in the Wanaka/Queenstown area.

Queenstown & Environs

The southwestern section of the South Island holds some of New Zealand's greatest natural beauty. At its heart, the Fiordland National Park is but a small portion of Te Wahipounamu, the South West New Zealand World Heritage Area—2.6 million hectares (6.4 million acres) that make up about 10% of New Zealand's total landmass.

The area gives a whole new meaning to the word "wilderness," and you don't have to be a pack-carrying tramper to appreciate its grandeur. From mountain peaks, lakes, and rivers to native bush, waterfalls, rural towns, and more organized tours and adventures than anywhere else in New Zealand, you'll find plenty to satisfy your recreational appetite.

Before you hit Queenstown farther south, you'll come to Wanaka, a lakeside settlement that serves as the gateway to the Mount Aspiring National Park and World Heritage Area. It's a pretty town that quickly seduces you into a state of total relaxation. Mount Cook, which the Maori named *Aoraki* ("the cloud piercer"), is the highest

point in New Zealand. It lies close to the West Coast, but the only road access is from the south, turning off State Highway 8, approximately 2 hours north of Wanaka.

Queenstown is undeniably the hub of it all. Spreading out from the foot of the Remarkables on the northeastern shore of Lake Wakatipu, it's an international resort, and ever since gold was discovered in the region in the 1860s, the town has been on a winning streak. Today it is booming and spreading in every direction—and Queenstown real estate values are the highest in New Zealand.

Just over the hill as the crow flies, Te Anau is the hub for exploring Fiordland National Park. Situated on the tranquil shores of Lake Te Anau, this little township is renowned as a walking capital. It is the stepping-off point for several world-famous tracks—the Milford, Routeburn, Hollyford, Greenstone, Kepler, and Dusky. It is also the departure point for explorations of Milford Sound, once astutely described by Rudyard Kipling as the eighth wonder of the world.

1 WANAKA: GATEWAY TO MOUNT ASPIRING NATIONAL PARK ★★

145km (90 miles) S of Haast; 117km (73 miles) N of Queenstown

Either you warm to Wanaka (pop. 5,000), or you don't. It's often seen as a very quiet, less self-important version of Queenstown, or to put it another way, as Queenstown was 20 years ago. Often overlooked by visitors on the move between the West Coast and Queenstown, Wanaka is the perfect place to spend a couple of days recharging. There has been a huge amount of growth in the town in the last 10 years, with much-needed new accommodations, restaurants, shops, and tourism operators opening for business.

And one last key thing to remember about Wanaka, which is often overlooked in favor of Queenstown in relation to Milford Sound: If you plan to fly to Milford, keep in mind that if you fly from Wanaka instead of Queenstown, you will get a longer flight over a different route—one that takes in great swaths of the Mount Aspiring National Park, not seen on the Queenstown flights.

Lake Wanaka Tourism is another of the six members of the government's Environmentally Sustainable Tourism Project. Sustainable Wanaka has over 65 registered charter members in accommodations, retail, transportation, and activity businesses. Check www. sustainablewanaka.co.nz for charter member listings.

ESSENTIALS

GETTING THERE **By Plane** **Air New Zealand** (© 0800/737-000 in NZ; www. airnewzealand.co.nz), provides a daily service from Christchurch. **Aspiring Air** (© 0800/ 100-943 in NZ, or 03/443-7943; www.aspiringair.com) has three flights a day from Queenstown.

By Coach (Bus) **InterCity** (© 09/623-1503) provides coach service linking Wanaka to the West Coast, Christchurch, Dunedin, Mount Cook, Queenstown, Te Anau, and Milford Sound. **Kiwi Experience** (© 09/366-9830) and **Magic Travellers** (© 09/358-5600) both include Wanaka on their routes. **Wanaka Connexions** (© 0800/244-844 in NZ, or 03/477-2224; www.time2.co.nz) runs between Wanaka and Queenstown several times a day, and also has a daily service to Invercargill, Dunedin, and Christchurch.

By Car Wanaka is reached via the Haast Pass from the West Coast. It's a 4-hour drive from the glaciers. State Highway 6 connects it to Cromwell and Queenstown, 1½ hours to the south. State Highway 89, the Cardrona Road over the Crown Range, is a more direct and impressive route that takes around 1 hour (if you stop to admire the views). Once narrow, winding, and treacherous, it's now fully paved and is, in fact, the highest tar-sealed road in Australasia. Keep in mind that if you travel the Crown Range Road in winter, you are now legally required to carry chains (available for hire from service stations). If you're caught without them, you'll get a NZ$150 fine. Wanaka is a 5-hour drive from Christchurch and 3½ hours from both Dunedin and Te Anau.

VISITOR INFORMATION The **Lake Wanaka i-SITE Visitor Centre,** 100 Ardmore Rd., is in the log cabin on the lakefront (© 03/443-1233; fax 03/443-1290; www. lakewanaka.co.nz). It's open daily May to mid-September from 8:30am to 5pm, mid-September through April from 8:30am to 6pm (closed Dec 25). The **Department of Conservation,** Ardmore Street and Ballantyne Road (© 03/443-7660; fax 03/443-8777; www.doc.govt.nz), provides information on Mount Aspiring National Park and all DOC tracks in the area. The DOC is open November through mid-April daily from 8am to 5pm, and in winter Monday through Friday from 8:30am to 4:30pm, Saturday from 9:30am to 4pm (closed Sun and noon–12:30pm daily).

FAST FACTS The fastest and cheapest Internet access is offered by **Dub Dub Dub,** corner of Helwick and Brownston streets (© 03/443-7078). For medical matters, go to **Wanaka Medical Centre,** 21 Russell St. (© 03/443-7811). The **Post Office,** Ardmore Street, as you drive into Wanaka (© 03/443-8211), is open 8:30am to 5pm, Monday through Friday.

SPECIAL EVENTS **Wanaka Rodeo** (© 03/443-7736) is held in early January. **Rippon Open-Air Music Festival** (© 03/443-1833; www.ripponfestival.co.nz) is a biennial open-air music festival in a vineyard in early February; the next festival is in 2010. April's

Warbirds Over Wanaka International Air Show (www.warbirdsoverwanaka.com) combines classic vintage and veteran aircraft, machinery, fire engines, and tractors with dynamic Air Force displays and aerobatic teams in the natural amphitheater of the Upper Clutha Basin. It's one of the top four Warbirds Airshows in the world and is held every second Easter in even-numbered years. The next show is April 2 to April 4, 2010. In autumn, celebrate the **Festival of Colour** (www.festivalofcolour.co.nz), 5 days of intense arts, dance, theater, and music. The next festival will be held in April 2011. There are also numerous ski festivals during winter; the visitor center has details.

EXPLORING WANAKA

There's fun to be had at **Stuart Landsborough's Puzzling World** ★★, on State Highway 89, 2km (1¼ miles) from Wanaka (✆ 03/443-7489; www.puzzlingworld.co.nz). Since 1973, Stuart Landsborough (also known as Professor Puzzle) has drawn thousands of visitors to the confusing passageways of his elaborate Great Maze. The crazy Tilted House and Leaning Clock Tower will further test your perceptions. Admission to both the Great Maze and the Illusion Rooms is NZ$13 for adults and NZ$9 for children, and it's open daily from 8:30am to 5:30pm (until 6pm in summer). Allow 1 to 2 hours for your visit.

The **New Zealand Fighter Pilots' Museum** ★★★, Skyshow Centre, Wanaka Airport, 10km (6 miles) southwest of Wanaka (✆ 03/443-7010; www.nzfpm.co.nz), is home to the largest collection of flyable World War II fighter planes in the Southern Hemisphere. It's currently in the middle of a NZ$10-million redevelopment program and it will be opening in a new building in 2011. In the meantime, you can continue to investigate the airplanes, interactive displays, film footage, and scale model aircraft. The Skyshow Centre is also home to a collection of alpine fighter aircraft, Biplane Adventures, Tandem Skydive, Wanaka Helicopters, Aspiring Air, and the Flight Deck Café. Admission is NZ$10 for adults, NZ$5 for children, and NZ$25 for families. It's open daily from 9am to 4pm (till 6pm Dec 27–Jan 27).

Take a break at **Wanaka Beerworks** ★, State Highway 6 (✆ 0800/273-9754 in NZ, or 03/443-1865; www.wanakabeerworks.co.nz), which is wedged between two museums. This little boutique brewery with a cozy bar and tasting room is open daily from 9am until 4pm (tours and tastings daily at 2pm).

Rippon Vineyard ★★★, Mount Aspiring Road (✆ 03/443-8084; www.rippon.co.nz), is run by Rolfe and Lois Mills, pioneer grape-growers in Central Otago, and their vineyard location overlooking Lake Wanaka is simply stunning. It's open for free tastings and sales November through April, daily from 11:30am to 5pm; and July through October, daily from 1:30 to 5pm.

ORGANIZED TOURS

Camera buffs will enjoy an outing with photographer and naturalist Gilber van Reenen of **Clean Green Phototours,** 641 Ballantyne Rd., Wanaka (✆ 03/443-7951; www.cleangreen.co.nz), who will tailor a photographic expedition to suit your interests. You'll pay from NZ$300 per person for a 2-hour tour for up to three people. For some of the most dramatic landscapes and photographic opportunities, join **Ridgeline Adventures** ★★, Wanaka (✆ 0800/234-000 in NZ; www.ridgelinenz.com), which will take you up into the high country surrounding Lake Wanaka. A 3-hour trek will cost NZ$179 for adults and NZ$70 for children. You'll be taken into the hills by 4WD transport and there's just a short walk before you enjoy the views, good coffee, and tasty treats. Wine lovers can explore some of Central Otago's premier wineries with **Wanaka Wine Tours**

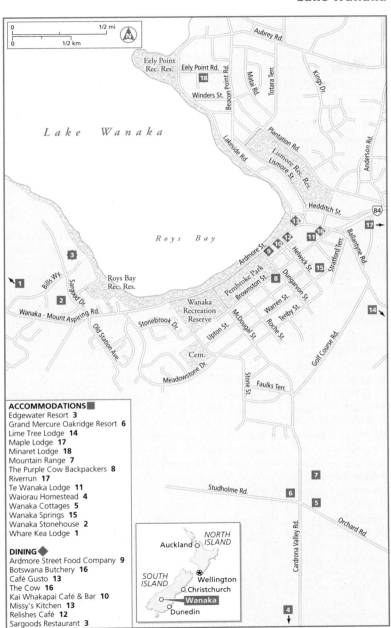

ACCOMMODATIONS ■
Edgewater Resort **3**
Grand Mercure Oakridge Resort **6**
Lime Tree Lodge **14**
Maple Lodge **17**
Minaret Lodge **18**
Mountain Range **7**
The Purple Cow Backpackers **8**
Riverrun **17**
Te Wanaka Lodge **11**
Waiorau Homestead **4**
Wanaka Cottages **5**
Wanaka Springs **15**
Wanaka Stonehouse **2**
Whare Kea Lodge **1**

DINING ◆
Ardmore Street Food Company **9**
Botswana Butchery **16**
Café Gusto **13**
The Cow **16**
Kai Whakapai Café & Bar **10**
Missy's Kitchen **13**
Relishes Café **12**
Sargoods Restaurant **3**

> ## (Moments) The Big Screen
>
> Get real local flavor at **Cinema Paradiso** ★★★, 1 Ardmore St. (✆ **03/443-1505;** www.paradiso.net.nz), Wanaka's only movie theater. It's quite possibly the wackiest place you'll ever experience. Seats take the form of old sofas and cushions in the aisles, and a Morris Minor car has been installed for a drive-in feel. You'll get a personalized, off-the-wall introduction from the owner, and there's a 30-minute intermission for quick cafe meals—and yes, they will hold the movie until you're finished eating. Showtimes are at 6 and 8:30pm daily; admission is NZ$15 for adults, NZ$10 for children.

(✆ **027/534-8388;** www.wanakawinetours.com). Their full-day tour takes in a number of wineries and includes a winery lunch. It runs daily from 10am to 4:30pm and costs NZ$195 per person.

OUTDOOR PURSUITS

CANYONING   Contact **Deep Canyon** (✆ **03/443-7922;** www.deepcanyon.co.nz), pioneers of the sport in New Zealand. You'll get a tobogganing, rappelling, and swimming adventure guaranteed to thrill. The 7½-hour Niger Stream adventure costs NZ$225, which includes lunch. They operate November through April and offer a range of day trips, including an introduction to rock climbing, which costs NZ$190 (NZ$120 for half-day).

CLIMBING   There's a lot of excellent, stable climbing in the area. **Wanaka Rock Climbing,** 7 Apollo Place St. (✆ **03/443-6411;** www.wanakarock.co.nz), can introduce you to all the best places. You'll pay from NZ$110 for a range of options.

ECORAFTING   This is an easy adventure for less active people. It's all about learning as you paddle, and guides will enlighten you about flora and fauna along the way. From September to April, **Pioneer Rafting** ★★ (✆ **03/443-1246;** www.ecoraft.co.nz) conducts half- and full-day excursions down the Upper Clutha. This is not white-water rafting, and the trip is suitable for anyone from ages 8 to 80. A half-day trip costs NZ$135 for adults and NZ$75 for children ages 5 to 15 (no kids age 4 and under).

FISHING   Opportunities abound in the Wanaka area, with plenty of guides operating on the rivers and lakes. **Lakeland Adventures** (✆ **03/443-7495;** www.lakelandadventures. co.nz) charges from NZ$305 for guided trout fishing for three people. **Southern Lakes Fishing Safaris** (✆/fax **03/443-9121;** www.southernlakesfishing.co.nz) specializes in fly-fishing for all levels of experience and charges from NZ$650 for a full day for one to two people.

FLYING   **Aspiring Air** (✆ **0800/100-943** in NZ, or 03/443-7943; www.nz-flights. com) has a variety of scenic flights in the Mount Aspiring area from NZ$160 per person. Their Milford Sound flight with included boat cruise costs NZ$445 for adults and NZ$300 for children ages 3 to 13. **Alpine Helicopters** (✆ **03/443-4000;** www.alpine heli.co.nz) can give you a scenic flight over Wanaka for NZ$170 per person; and **Aspiring Helicopters,** Cattle Flat Station (✆ **03/443-7152;** www.aspiringhelicopters.co.nz), has a 50-minute Mount Aspiring and Glacier trip with snow landing for NZ$450. **Wanaka Flightseeing,** Wanaka Airport (✆ **0800/105-105** in NZ, or 03/443-8787; www.flightseeing.co.nz), has an excellent range of options from short flights at NZ$99 to a Milford Sound flight-and-cruise option for NZ$445 for adults and NZ$300 for children. It takes 4 hours, and if you mention Frommer's you'll get a 10% discount.

GOLF   **Wanaka Golf Club,** Ballantyne Road (© **03/443-7888;** www.wanakagolf.co. nz), is a challenging 18-hole course with astounding views. There is a well-stocked pro shop and it costs NZ$55 for 18 holes, or NZ$35 for 9 holes.

JET-BOATING   The best jet-boating is with **Wilkin River Jets** ★★★, State Highway 6, Makarora (©/fax **03/443-8351;** www.wilkinriverjets.co.nz), which is between Fox Glacier and Wanaka. Locals say it's better than the much-lauded Dart River experience at Glenorchy, near Queenstown. Priced at NZ$95 for 1 hour, it's also cheaper and offers a mix of thrill riding and the softer approach, so you get a good feel for this remote region. They also offer combos that include a helicopter flight, bush walk, and river jet from NZ$330 per person. **Wanaka River Journeys** ★★ (© **0800/544-555** in NZ, or 03/443-4416; www.wanakariverjourneys.co.nz), explores the braided Matukituki River and includes a wilderness walk into native beech forest to a waterfall. You have the option of being met at the top of the river by helicopter for a flight into Mount Aspiring's magnificent glacial areas. The river journey with a wilderness walk is NZ$220 for adults, NZ$129 for children 15 and under; the jet/heli combo is NZ$570 for adults, NZ$339 children 15 and under.

KAYAKING   **Alpine Kayak Guides,** 119 Main Rd., Luggate (© **03/443-9023;** www. alpinekayaks.co.nz), has half- and full-day trips on three rivers, ranging in difficulty from beginner to experienced. Trips last 5 to 8 hours and run daily from November to April. Costs start at NZ$135 for adults and NZ$75 for children, and include equipment, lessons, and lunch. You can rent kayaks for a lake paddle from **Lakeland Adventures** (© **03/443-7495**), on a per-hour basis.

MOUNTAIN BIKING   The Department of Conservation's leaflet on bike trails in the Wanaka area is available from its office at Ardmore Street and Ballantyne Road (© **03/ 443-7660**). Mountain bikes can be rented from **Racer's Edge/Mountain Bikes Unlimited,** 99 Ardmore St. (© **03/443-7882;** www.racersedge.co.nz), for NZ$50 to NZ$60 per day. Good bikes are also available from **Lakeland Adventures,** next door to the information center (© **03/443-7495**), for about NZ$12 per hour, and there are excellent (and easy) biking tracks around the lake.

QUAD BIKES   For rugged outdoor fun, **Cardrona Adventure Park** ★ (© **0800/102-122** in NZ, or 03/443-6363; www.adventurepark.co.nz) offers tours on four-wheel all-terrain quad bikes priced from NZ$165 for a 2-hour tour. You must be at least 16 and have a driver's license. They also have a crazy range of monster trucks that you can ride in or drive.

SKIING   **Cardrona Ski Field** is 40 minutes from Wanaka on State Highway 89. The more challenging **Treble Cone Ski Field** is also 40 minutes away. In addition, you'll find cross-country skiing and heli-skiing in the Harris Mountains. And for Nordic skiing, head to the **Waiorau Nordic Field,** in the Cardrona Valley. For further information on all ski fields in this area, see chapter 5.

WALKING   Walking opportunities in Mount Aspiring National Park vary from easy strolls through lowland forest to tramps on mountain tracks that may take several days. Brochures and information can be obtained from the Department of Conservation office. **Eco Wanaka Adventures** ★★, 5 Rimu Lane (© **03/443-2869;** www.ecowanaka. co.nz), has a guided Rob Roy Glacier Valley Trek priced from NZ$235 per person. At

Diamond Lake, 20 minutes from town, you'll find the Diamond Lake and Rocky Mountain Track, which takes 1½ hours from the carpark to the summit. For a more remote walk, call **Siberia Experience** ★★★ (✆ **0800/345-666** in NZ, or 03/443-4385; www.siberiaexperience.co.nz), offering a combo of scenic flight, jet boat, and a 3-hour walk in remote beech forests for NZ$310 for adults and NZ$260 for children ages 3 to 13. Their guided experiences are unique and some of the best in the region. Just make sure you take plenty of insect repellent to keep the notoriously greedy sand flies at bay! Fit, adventurous travelers might like to be tested by a remote wilderness experience with **Wild Walks** ★★, Level 1, 99 Ardmore St. (✆ **03/443-9422;** www.aspiringguides. com). Their specialist mountain guides take just five people maximum into remote back-country locations. Overnight trips range in price from NZ$1,350 to NZ$2,130.

But if all you really want is a light amble, follow my footsteps around the lovely, tree-covered tracks of the lake. Start at the information center and simply follow your nose. Even if you don't exert yourself, it will leave your conscience clear for dinner.

WHERE TO STAY

If you're looking for accommodations with style and character, you'll definitely find them in the Wanaka area. There has been a lot of development in the township itself, especially around the lake edge. Quality lodges and bed-and-breakfasts are increasing in numbers, and you won't be short of a good stop here, but you will need to book well ahead if you're planning to stay between November and March. Wanaka is a favorite playground for New Zealanders.

All rates quoted include the 12.5% GST and free off-street parking unless otherwise noted.

Very Expensive

Whare Kea Lodge ★★★ (Finds) Tucked away from the public eye, Whare Kea offers style and luxury at its most sublime. Walk through the door and you'll be overwhelmed by one of the most remarkable residential views in the country. This monster of a house has huge bedrooms with verandas, deep bathtubs, dual-sided showers, and top-quality furnishings. A classy hideaway for those who want to indulge. As an added bonus, they have a fabulous alpine chalet in the heart of the Southern Alps, accessible only by helicopter. It accommodates six, but all facilities are shared with a qualified mountain guide and staff member, and access is weather dependent. The property also boasts a Relais & Châteaux Environmental Award.

Mount Aspiring Rd., P.O. Box 115, Wanaka. ✆ **03/443-1400.** Fax 03/443-9200. www.wharekealodge.com. 6 units, 1 chalet. NZ$1,100–NZ$1,400 deluxe; NZ$1,400–NZ$1,700 master suite; NZ$5,500–NZ$6,800 chalet 1-night stay. Off-peak rates. Lodge rates include breakfast, dinner, and use of all facilities; chalet rates include helicopter and mountain guide. AE, DC, MC, V. Follow signs on Mount Aspiring Rd., 5 min. west of Wanaka township. No children 13 and under. **Amenities:** Bar; charged airport transfers; nearby golf course; Jacuzzi. *In room:* TV, fridge, hair dryer, minibar, Wi-Fi.

Expensive

Wanaka Cottages ★★, 11 Orchard Rd. (✆ **0800/292-6252** in NZ; www.wanaka cottages.co.nz), offer a luxurious four-bedroom house and a new two-bedroom cottage in a new residential suburb for NZ$495 and NZ$395, respectively. **Lime Tree Lodge** ★★★, Ballantyne Road, RD2, Wanaka (✆ **03/443-7305;** www.limetree lodge.co.nz), is a gorgeous spot with six beautiful suites that range in price from NZ$495 to NZ$695. It's set on 4 hectares (10 acres) just out of Wanaka, and you'll be spoiled rotten here with meals based on organic garden produce (dinner NZ$150 per person) to die for. They are charter members of Sustainable Wanaka.

Minaret Lodge ★★ (Finds) Open since 2002, this smart B&B option is full of surprises (and that includes a *Lord of the Rings* room), and exceeds all expectations. The dining and living room facilities are contained within a stylishly renovated home in a peaceful residential neighborhood, and three purpose-built chalets are set in a .8-hectare (2-acre) garden with an attractive spa and sauna complex a short stroll across the lawn. Chalet beds are big and bathrooms are well appointed—the suite chalet is the biggest and includes a tastefully finished lounge and en suite with both bathtub and shower. There is a greater sense of privacy here than at other similarly priced B&B options in Wanaka. The property plays an active role in sustainable tourism and is a charter member of Sustainable Wanaka.

34 Eely Point Rd., Wanaka. ✆ **03/443-1856.** Fax 03/443-1856. www.minaretlodge.co.nz. 5 units. NZ$450–NZ$550. Rates include predinner drinks and full gourmet breakfast. Off-peak rates. MC, V. No children 11 and under. **Amenities:** Airport transfers NZ$10 per person; free bikes; nearby golf course; Jacuzzi; sauna; all-weather tennis court. *In room:* TV/DVD/CD, fridge, hair dryer, minibar, Wi-Fi.

Riverrun ★★★ (Value) When you see the facilities at environmentally aware Riverrun, you'll know you've got one of the best lodge deals in the country. John Pawson and Meg Taylor have built with imagination and flair: Everything smacks of originality and every room is arranged with comfort in mind, with generous beds, fine linens, and superb marble bathrooms. John and Meg are outdoor types who love mountaineering and climbing, and John also tends their 170-hectare (420-acre) mixed farm that borders the Clutha River. Riverrun is a heavily hosted experience and Meg is a superb chef.

Halliday Rd., RD2, Wanaka. ✆ **03/443-9049.** Fax 03/443-8454. www.riverrun.co.nz. 5 units. NZ$485–NZ$525. Dinner by arrangement. Winter packages during ski season. AE, MC, V. 6-min. drive east of central Wanaka. Turn off St. Hwy. 6 to Halliday Rd.; continue to stone gates and drive through to Riverrun. No children 8 and under. **Amenities:** Bar; free bikes; outdoor Jacuzzi. *In room:* TV/DVD, fridge, hair dryer, Wi-Fi.

Moderate

Wanaka Stonehouse ★, 21 Sargood Dr. (✆ **03/443-1933;** www.wanakastonehouse.co.nz), is a quiet, residential B&B with four light, airy alpine-style en-suite rooms; a bigger ground-floor suite is ideal for families. There's a Jacuzzi and sauna to help you unwind at the end of the day. Prices range from NZ$345 to NZ$395. **Te Wanaka Lodge,** 23 Brownston St. (✆ **03/443-9224;** www.tewanaka.co.nz), is a small boutique hotel with 13 rooms and lots of charm. Rooms are a great value at NZ$210 to NZ$275, and if you get in quick, you might be able to score the garden cottage for a little more privacy.

Edgewater Resort ★★ (Value) Situated right on the shores of Lake Wanaka, this Green Globe affiliate and Sustainable Wanaka charter member property is a favorite with New Zealanders who like resort-style accommodations. There's a welcoming atmosphere here and style tends toward that of a high-country fishing lodge. All the one- or two-bedroom suites, which have been extensively upgraded recently, offer balconies or terraces. In short, it's a friendly, comfortable 23-year-old development that has aged well and oozes Kiwi atmosphere. If you like space and value, go for the one-bedroom suites, which have bigger bathrooms with double tubs. It's not as new as Oakridge and it doesn't have their hot pools, but it has a much friendlier, more intimate atmosphere.

Sargood Dr., P.O. Box 61, Wanaka. ✆ **0800/108-311** in NZ, or 03/443-8311. Fax 03/443-8323. www.edge water.co.nz. 65 units. NZ$325–NZ$525. Package deals and off-peak rates. AE, DC, MC, V. 20-min. stroll to town center. **Amenities:** 2 restaurants (Sargoods [Modern New Zealand a la carte]; Wineglass Café [snacks]); bar; free transfers from Wanaka Airport if booked; babysitting; bike rentals; children's playground; concierge; nearby golf course and 9-hole putting green on-site; Jacuzzi; room service; sauna; all-weather tennis court; kayaks hire. *In room:* LCD TV, hair dryer, kitchens or kitchenettes, minibar on request, Wi-Fi.

Grand Mercure Oakridge Resort ★★ (Value)

There have been extensive developments at Oakridge, as blocks of new apartments spread out from the main complex. They're new, modern, and very pleasing, and the complex has a beautiful hot pool complex and day spa, but I can't help feeling they've lost something in the expansion—a sense of intimacy for one thing. All up though, they are able to offer great-value packages, and the one-bedroom apartments (some up, some down) are the best. The complex is a charter member of Sustainable Wanaka.

Corner of Cardrona Valley Rd. and Studholme Rd. ✆ **0800/869-262** in NZ, or 03/443-7707. Fax 03/443-7750. www.oakridge.co.nz. 173 units. NZ$125–NZ$240 resort room; NZ$190–NZ$305 studio suite; NZ$235–NZ$465 apt. NZ$25 each extra person. Off-peak rates and special packages. AE, DC, MC, V. **Amenities:** Restaurant (The Poolhouse [contemporary New Zealand]); 2 bars; charged airport transfers; babysitting; children's play area; nearby golf course; large gymnasium; 7 outdoor Jacuzzis; 2 outdoor heated leisure pools; 1 heated lap pool; room service; sauna; day spa beauty treatments. *In room:* TV/DVD, hair dryer, kitchen or kitchenette, minibar, Wi-Fi.

Maple Lodge ★★ (Value)

Paul and Bernadette Raymont's purpose-built, Qualmark Enviro-Gold-rated lodge is set amid a 2.8-hectare (7-acre) maple tree plantation 4 minutes from Wanaka. Seven modern suites open onto private balconies or patios; and heated floors, de-misting mirrors, great views, and big beds are indicative of the attention to detail. All rooms are in a separate wing of the house, and a large guest lounge and library is the meeting spot for predinner drinks and afternoon tea. This is a great-value stay that definitely deserves a 2-night stay minimum. They are also charter members of Sustainable Wanaka.

Halliday Rd., Wanaka. ✆ **03/443-6275.** Fax 03/443-6274. www.maplelodgewanaka.co.nz. 7 units. NZ$295–NZ$335. MC, V. **Amenities:** Free Wanaka airport transfers; nearby golf course; Jacuzzi. *In room:* A/C, TV/DVD/CD, hair dryer, Wi-Fi (in suites).

Mountain Range ★

If you want breathtaking views of three mountain ranges, peace and quiet, and spacious rooms with beautiful bathrooms, Mountain Range delivers. Chris Shaw and Erica Wymore are terrific young hosts, and they go out of their way to make you comfortable. They're newer to the game than Wanaka Springs (and their rooms are bigger), but there's a sense of understated service and comfort that makes them one of my favorite Wanaka spots. Ask for the McKerrow room if you want a giant bathtub, or the loft room for coziness and great views.

Heritage Park, Cardrona Valley Rd., Wanaka. ✆ **03/443-7400.** Fax 03/443-7450. www.mountainrange. co.nz. 7 units. NZ$305–NZ$340. Long-stay, off-peak, and special deals. Rates include breakfast. MC, V. Just off Cardona Valley Rd., 2km (1¼ miles) outside Wanaka. No children 11 and under. **Amenities:** Free bikes; nearby golf course; outdoor Jacuzzi. *In room:* TV/DVD, hair dryer, free Wi-Fi.

Waiorau Homestead ★★ (Finds)

This gorgeous old homestead, tucked into an idyllic rural setting near Cardrona Alpine Resort, has had a modern makeover that attends to every traveler's needs. Blyth Adams (a chef) and Anne Lockhart have four large, beautifully appointed guest rooms (three en suite; one private bathroom). The room with the private bathroom is the largest; and the separate smaller room right beside the swimming pool is the most fun. They are 20 minutes from Wanaka, but once you get here you won't want to leave anyway—especially once you sit down to one of Blyth's meals. It's farther out than Riverrun or Maple Lodge and has a more intimate B&B atmosphere.

2127B Cardona Valley Rd., Wanaka. © **03/443-2225.** www.waiorauhomestead.co.nz. 4 units. NZ$320. Each extra person NZ$70. Long-stay and off-peak rates. Dinner by arrangement. MC, V. Take Cardona Valley Rd. from Wanaka. Approx. 20 min. on, turn left into Snow Farm Rd. Turn immediately right a few meters along and follow yellow signs. The homestead driveway is 300m (984 ft.) ahead on your left, just before the farm buildings. **Amenities:** Charged transfers to Queenstown and Wanaka airports; babysitting; free bikes; outdoor Jacuzzi; outdoor heated pool. In room: TV/DVD/CD, hair dryer, Wi-Fi.

Wanaka Springs ★ Wanaka Springs is a purpose-built lodge on a quiet residential street. Rooms here envelope you in warmth and rich color, and garden views (with decks) add a restful quality. Bathrooms are big and modern, and the main living spaces are lovely. At the end of a hard day, there's nothing better than relaxing in their eight-seater Jacuzzi in the garden. They're a member of Sustainable Wanaka and have a Qualmark Enviro-Silver rating. They also give NZ$1 of every booking to the Te Kakano Aotea Trust, which is developing a native nursery for community and reforestation projects.

21 Warren St. © **03/443-8421.** Fax 03/443-8429. www.wanakasprings.com. 8 units. NZ$320–NZ$355. Rates include breakfast. Long-stay rates. AE, DC, MC, V. **Amenities:** Free transfers from Wanaka airport; free bikes; nearby golf course; outdoor Jacuzzi. In room: TV, DVD (in some), hair dryer, Wi-Fi.

Inexpensive

The **Purple Cow Backpackers,** 94 Brownston St. (© **0800/772-277** in NZ, or 03/443-1880; www.purplecow.co.nz), is frequented by budget-minded travelers from throughout the world. It's just a step or two from town and has dorm beds from NZ$18 to NZ$28 per person and doubles from NZ$78 to NZ$84.

WHERE TO DINE

There are plenty of places to eat in Wanaka. **Sargoods Restaurant** ★, Edgewater Resort (© **03/443-8311**), serves remarkably good international cuisine from an a la carte menu with main courses priced from NZ$32. You'll find excellent picnic foods (and light meals) at **Ardmore Street Food Company** ★, 155 Ardmore St. (© **03/443-2230**); and you'll always get great pizzas, pasta, and atmosphere at the **Cow,** Post Office Lane (© **03/443-4269**), which is open daily from noon to midnight. **Post Office Lane** ★★ off Ardmore Street near the Post Office (www.goodbars.co.nz), is a small, well-designed cluster of bars and restaurants that is worth seeking out if you want to socialize with locals and international travelers alike. They all open onto a big courtyard complex with a roaring fire and outdoor tables. This is where you'll find **Botswana Butchery** ★★★, upstairs (© **03/443-6745;** www.goodbars.co.nz), which specializes in specialty meat cuts cooked to perfection. Take a fat wallet, because it's the most expensive in town. It has a sister restaurant in Queenstown.

Café Gusto MODERN NEW ZEALAND Right next to Lakeside Apartments under the very popular Missy's Kitchen, Gusto draws you in with bright yellow furniture on a sunny patio overlooking the lake. It has delicious lunch and casual evening dining selections: Moroccan lamb salad, pumpkin and spinach risotto, curries, and delicious soups, to name a few. Colorful, bright, and popular with locals and visitors alike, it's a great place to start.

1 Lakeside Dr. © **03/443-6639.** Main courses NZ$18–NZ$25. AE, MC, V. Daily 8am–late.

Kai Whakapai Café & Bar ★ (Value) NEW ZEALAND/CAFE The most visible and definitely the most popular of Wanaka's casual cafes, this one is oozing with smiles and good food at sensible prices. Quite apart from the divine pizzas, burgers, croissants, and fresh pastas, much of it with a vegetarian slant, this place comes alive as a bar in the early evening. And what I like best about it is that it's open nice and early for coffee. It could do with a spruce-up inside, but otherwise it's one of my favorites.

Lakefront. (✆ **03/443-7795.** Main courses NZ$12–NZ$24. AE, DC, MC, V. Daily 7am–late.

Missy's Kitchen ★★ PACIFIC RIM Always broad in its focus, Pacific Rim cuisine comes peppered with a few international touches at this extremely popular award-winning Wanaka restaurant. This is where you can savor braised lamb shoulder stuffed with olives, or beef sirloin served with mushroom ragout and caramelized shallots. Casual by day and moody by night, with a menu that combines a wealth of interesting flavors and a big wine list, Missy's is sure to endure. It has the best wine list in Wanaka and reliable, professional service.

Level 1, 80 Ardmore St. (✆ **03/443-5099.** www.missyskitchen.com. Reservations recommended. Main courses NZ$23–NZ$32. AE, MC, V. Mon–Fri 6pm–late; Sat–Sun 10am–late.

Relishes Café ★★ INTERNATIONAL Relishes has been a top spot for years and I've had some of my nicest fish meals here. If you need proof of popularity, people are turned away in droves for lack of space. It's a simple, country-style interior, nothing flashy, but the baked blue cod served with hazelnut and lemon butter left a memorable impression. It's one of the most consistent places in town and many prefer its relaxed atmosphere and friendliness over the much-touted Botswana Butchery.

1/99 Ardmore St. (✆ **03/443-9018.** Reservations recommended. Main courses NZ$25–NZ$32. AE, MC, V. Daily 7:30am–late (dinner from 6pm).

EN ROUTE TO MOUNT COOK

If you plan to drive to Mount Cook from Wanaka, expect to get there in 2½ hours on excellent roads. Rejoin State Highway 6 and travel south to State Highway 6A, which links you to State Highway 8. From Queenstown, the trip to Mount Cook takes about 4 hours.

2 MOUNT COOK ★

263km (163 miles) NE of Queenstown; 331km (205 miles) SW of Christchurch

Mount Cook Village is known throughout the world for its alpine beauty and remoteness. It sits within the 70,000 hectares (173,000 acres) of **Mount Cook National Park,** some 753m (2,470 ft.) above sea level and surrounded by 140 peaks over 2,100m (6,888 ft.) high, 22 of which are over 3,000m (9,840 ft.). Most famous of all is **Aoraki–Mount Cook,** which rises 3,695m (12,120 ft.) into the sky. *Aoraki* means "cloud piercer" in Maori. A third of the park is permanent snow and ice, and the **Tasman Glacier,** at 29km (18 miles) long and 3km (2 miles) wide, is the longest known glacier outside arctic regions. More difficult to get onto than Fox or Franz Josef glaciers, it's still accessible for exhilarating downhill skiing.

ESSENTIALS

GETTING THERE There is a daily **InterCity** (✆ **09/623-1503**) link between Mount Cook and Christchurch, Queenstown, and Timaru. The **Cook Connection,** Twizel

> **Tips** **Be Prepared**
>
> If you're driving up to Mount Cook Village during winter, make sure you have antifreeze fluid in your car radiator.

(© **0800/266-526** in NZ; www.cookconnect.co.nz), offers daily trips from Lake Tekapo and Twizel to Mount Cook from October through May between 7:30am and 9pm. By car, Mount Cook is reached via State Highway 80 and great care should be taken on all roads in the area during autumn and winter when surfaces become icy and slippery. Twizel is 45 minutes from Mount Cook World Heritage Park and is the base for a number of tourism businesses operating in the Mount Cook area.

ORIENTATION A T-intersection at the end of the highway marks the entrance to Mount Cook Village. Turn left and you'll pass Glencoe Lodge, a modern motor hotel, the youth hostel, Alpine Guides Mountain Shop, and finally the Aoraki–Mount Cook National Park Visitor Centre. Turn right at the intersection and you'll pass Mount Cook Chalets before reaching the peak-roofed, internationally famous Hermitage Hotel, which now includes a modest grocery store and post office.

VISITOR INFORMATION The **Aoraki–Mount Cook National Park Visitor Centre,** 1 Larch Grove, Mount Cook Village (© **03/435-1186;** fax 03/435-1080; www.doc.govt.nz), is open daily in summer from 8:30am to 6pm and in winter until 5pm (closed Dec 25). Department of Conservation officers can give you the latest information on weather, track, and road conditions. Trampers and mountaineers must check in and sign the intentions register before entering the park. Officers can also fill you in on high-altitude huts, hut passes, picnic grounds, and recommended walks in the area.

The **Lake Pukaki Visitor Centre,** State Highway 8, Pukaki (© **03/435-3280;** fax 03/435-3283; www.mtcook.org.nz), is another good resource. **Alpine Guides,** Main Road, Mount Cook (© **03/435-1834;** fax 03/435-1898; www.alpineguides.co.nz or www.heliskiing.co.nz), can also provide a wealth of information on alpine activities, schedules, and fees. For information on Mount Cook ski areas, connect to www.nzski.com and www.mtcooknz.com.

EXPLORING THE AREA

Clearly, the mountains are the main attraction here. Before you get out onto the ice and snow, make your way to the **Sir Edmund Hillary Alpine Centre** ★★, the Hermitage (© **0800/686-800** in NZ, or 03/435-1641; www.hillarycentre.co.nz), which showcases the Mount Cook area. It features a 3-D movie, New Zealand's first full dome, a digital planetarium, a museum, and gallery that documents the pioneering heart of the region and Sir Edmund's long association with the Mount Cook region. Museum admission is NZ$25 for adults, NZ$13 for children, and NZ$50 for families. There are combo packages that include the planetarium, movie, and wine tasting in the cafe.

The Mount Cook area is also the access point for the beautiful **Tasman Glacier.** If you missed the scenic glacier flights at Fox and Franz Josef, you'll have another chance here. Go with award-winning **Air Safaris** ★★ (© **0800/806-880** in NZ, or 03/680-6880; www.airsafaris.co.nz). Its 50-minute Grand Traverse leaves from Lake Tekapo and flies over the McKenzie Basin and lakes, around Mount Cook, over 12 major glaciers, across the Main Divide to the Westland World Heritage National Parks, to the West Coast

(**Moments**) **Night Skies**

The skies above Lake Tekapo are renowned as some of the clearest in the world. That's why the top of Mount John is dotted with assorted international observatories. Visit this unique and fascinating spot for extraordinary night skies (and breathtaking daytime views) with **Earth & Sky Observatory** ★★★, Mount John, Tekapo (✆ **03/680-6960;** www.earthandsky.co.nz). Their 1-hour day tour costs NZ$30 for adults and NZ$15 for children ages 5 to 15. The 2-hour night tour costs NZ$75 for adults and NZ$45 for children ages 5 to 15. Either should be on your must-do list.

Glaciers, and back to Lake Tekapo. This stunning flight costs NZ$285 for adults and NZ$210 for children ages 3 to 13. **Mount Cook Ski Planes,** Mount Cook Airport (✆ **0800/800-702** in NZ, or 03/430-8034; www.mtcookskiplanes.com), is the only company licensed to land scenic flights on Tasman Glacier and in Mount Cook National Park. Their stunning fixed-wing flights cost NZ$230 to NZ$450.

The **Helicopter Line** (✆ **0800/650-651** in NZ, or 03/435-1801; www.helicopter. co.nz) has several tours, such as the Alpine Wonderland, a 45-minute flight which covers Mount Cook, the Main Divide, and Tasman Glacier for NZ$420 per person. This includes a glacier landing. Mention Frommer's and you'll get a 10% discount when booking direct. All helicopter operations in the Mount Cook area are based at Glentanner Helicopter Base, 15 minutes from Mount Cook Village. All fixed-wing craft operate from Mount Cook Airport.

Skiers will head for the Tasman Glacier during the June-to-October season, but know in advance that skiing here is neither cheap nor for novices. Skiing on the glaciers involves two runs of about 11km (7 miles) each, with ski planes returning you to the top after the first run and flying you out at the end of the day. The glacier is perfect for intermediate-grade skiers; it's a long distance, but not steep. The full-day excursion costs from NZ$850 and can be booked through **Alpine Guides** (✆ **03/435-1834;** www. alpineguides.co.nz), which also rents ski and climbing equipment and can organize guides to take you **mountain climbing** as well. Their 6- to 10-day guided ascents and courses cost from NZ$2,000 to NZ$5,000.

If you prefer something a little less expensive, park conservation offices can furnish a map of easy walks, which take anywhere from half an hour to half a day—you'll be able to commune with Mother Nature to your heart's content.

Glacier Explorers ★★★, Mount Cook Village (✆ **0800/686-800;** www.glacier explorers.com), can take you on an unbelievable 3-hour boat ride on Tasman Glacier Lake for NZ$120 for adults and NZ$60 for children ages 4 to 15. These tours only operate from mid-September through May (providing the lake is not frozen), and they include a 15-minute drive followed by a 30-minute walk to the lake.

WHERE TO STAY & DINE

Almost all of the accommodations in Mount Cook Village are owned by the same company, so you'll have minimal bargaining power, but call before you arrive as there are daily specials available, especially at the very ecofriendly **Hermitage Hotel, Motels & Chalets,** Terrace Road (✆ **0800/686-800** in NZ, or 03/435-1809; www.hermitage.co.nz). This old-faithful complex is an uneven mix of older motel units, chalets, and new and old hotel rooms, but recent renovations have made it more cohesive; and the on-site restaurants have greatly improved. The hotel has rates of NZ$130 to NZ$560; motel rooms are NZ$150 to NZ$255; and chalets are NZ$140 to NZ$225—but don't forget those specials. And this is one hotel where I would be prepared to spend extra for views, because they are simply breathtaking. In addition, the hotel also takes part in local native planting programs and a gene conservation program for native flora in the area.

Aoraki/Mount Cook Alpine Lodge ★, 101 Bowen Dr., Mount Cook (✆ **0800/680-680** in NZ, or 03/435-1860; www.aorakialpinelodge.co.nz), is a much-needed new, independent addition to the village accommodations scene. Its 16 rooms are much more reasonably priced at NZ$159 to NZ$225.

The **Mount Cook YHA Hostel,** Bowen Drive and Kitchener Avenue (✆ **0800/278-299** in NZ, or 03/435-1820; www.yha.co.nz), has 70 beds in 17 rooms, including six twins and two doubles. The cost is NZ$26 per dorm bed, NZ$70 for a twin or a double. It has the best shop in the village, plus a sauna, video library, TV lounge, luggage lockers, and a ski drying room. Reservations are essential from November to April.

Camping and **caravanning** are permitted in Mount Cook National Park at designated sites; water and toilets are available. If you use these facilities, remember that fires are prohibited within park boundaries. Check with the park visitor center for locations and conditions. Hikers and mountaineers have the use of 12 huts in the park, which have bunks and emergency radios. Only the Mueller Hut is within easy reach of the casual tramper. The others are at high altitudes and you need to be an experienced expert climber to reach them. The fee for overnight use of the huts is NZ$25 to NZ$30 per person, and arrangements must be made at the National Park Visitor Centre.

Rather than staying in Mount Cook Village itself, you might prefer to spend the night in one of the surrounding towns: Twizel, Fairlie, Tekapo, Omarama, and Kurow are all within a 2-hour drive and have motels, B&Bs, and homestays aplenty. Best among them is **Peppers Bluewater Resort** ★★, State Highway 8, Tekapo (✆ **0800/680-570;** www.peppers.co.nz/bluewater), which offers 142 very reasonably priced, brand-new rooms and villas, from NZ$237 to NZ$394. And if you stay in Tekapo, don't miss a visit to the new **Alpine Springs Spa & Winter Park** ★★, 150 Lakeside Dr., Tekapo (✆ **0800/235-3823** in NZ; www.winterpark.co.nz), which features delicious hot pools, a day spa, an ice rink, snow tubing, and curling. They have skates for hire. Admission to the hot pools area is NZ$16 for adults, NZ$9 for children, and NZ$49 for a family.

EN ROUTE TO QUEENSTOWN

State Highway 6 is good traveling all the way from Wanaka to Queenstown; the trip takes around 1½ hours. You'll drive around the edge of Lake Dunstan, which was formed behind the Clyde Dam. Bypassing Cromwell township, you then travel through the stone fruit orchards of the Cromwell area. As an introduction to the rapidly expanding wine industry in this area, stop at the **Big Picture** ★★, State Highway 6, Cromwell (✆ **03/445-4052;** www.wineadventure.co.nz). It has an excellent interactive wine film and tasting auditorium, a good cafe and restaurant, and a tasty selection of goodies from the area's wineries and boutique culinary producers. It's past the Cromwell turnoff on the left and open daily from 9am until 8pm. After passing through the winding Kawarau River Gorge, you come into Gibbston Valley—awash with vineyards—and on into Queenstown.

You could also go to Queenstown via the Crown Range. You'll be rewarded by spectacular views and a slightly shorter travel time than on the State Highway 6 route.

3 QUEENSTOWN ★★★

404km (250 miles) SW of Franz Josef; 263km (163 miles) SW of Mount Cook; 117km (73 miles) S of Wanaka; 172km (107 miles) NE of Te Anau

Queenstown has over one million visitors a year and you don't have to be a genius to figure out why. We've all heard the endless hype about it being the adventure capital of the world, and there are certainly enough crazy activities here to challenge the strongest, but Queenstown offers much more. Don't be put off by comments that it's touristy, un-Kiwi, crowded, and overrated. Sure, the streets are dominated by booking offices, but Queenstown has excellent shopping, restaurants, cafes, and clubs as well. And in many adrenalin-seeking ways, it encapsulates much of what New Zealand is about.

Famed for its international winter ski profile, Queenstown is also a brilliant spring, summer, and fall destination. This is when you get the best of its scenic beauty, easy walks, and endless opportunities to relax. Thrill seeking may be touted as the major attraction, but you can just as easily go fishing, golfing, gold panning, wine tasting, or boating. One thing is certain: You won't run out of things to do.

It seems as though the whole world suddenly wants to live in Queenstown, and the town has experienced a phenomenal growth in development in the last 5 years. The inner commercial area has several new retail, office, and restaurant complexes, with more under construction. Residential expansion is also obvious, although the current worldwide economic recession has stalled a number of major developments, including the new town of Five Mile, which was being developed near the airport at Frankton. It has gone into receivership, and there is a question mark over the future of the large hole in the ground that sits unattended. The big news of the moment, though, is the uncertain future of the NZ$1-billion Kawarau Falls Station hotel development that was to see four major hotel chains—Quay West, Westin, Quadrant, and Intercontinental—entering the Queenstown accommodations market. It went into receivership in May 2009, and at time of writing, no decision had been made about the completion of stage one of the development, which was to see the Quadrant opening at the end of 2009 and the Westin in April 2010.

ESSENTIALS

GETTING THERE & GETTING AROUND **By Plane** Queenstown is well serviced by **Air New Zealand National** and **Air New Zealand Link** (✆ **0800/737-000** in NZ; www.airnewzealand.co.nz) from such cities as Christchurch, Auckland, Wellington, and Rotorua. Air New Zealand also has a weekly flight from Sydney year-round and a weekly flight from Brisbane during ski season. The Air New Zealand Travel Centre is at 41 Shotover St., Queenstown (✆ **03/441-1900**). **Qantas** (✆ **0800/808-767** in NZ; www.qantas.com) also has a weekly flight direct from Sydney and Brisbane in winter. **Jetstar** (✆ **0800/800-995** in NZ; www.jetstar.com), also flies into Queenstown. You'll find more flight details at www.queenstownairport.co.nz.

Super Shuttle (✆ **03/442-3639;** www.supershuttle.co.nz) will drop you off downtown for NZ$15 per person; the **Connectabus** (✆ **03/441-4471;** www.connectabus.com) goes between the airport, Queenstown, Arrowtown, major attractions, hotels, shopping centers, and Millbrook Resort. A Day Pass costs NZ$13 for adults and NZ$6.50 for children, and buses run from 6am to midnight. A **taxi** (✆ **03/442-7788**) to the town center costs NZ$25 to NZ$35 depending on your final destination.

QUEENSTOWN & ENVIRONS

16

QUEENSTOWN

ACCOMMODATIONS ■
A Boutique Hotel
    Queenstown House **4**
Brown's Boutique Hotel **8**
Crowne Plaza Queenstown **10**
The Dairy Private Luxury Hotel **9**
Eichardt's Private Hotel **14**
Garden Court Suites &
    Luxury Apartments **26**
The Heritage **13**
Millbrook Resort **1**
Pencarrow **25**
Pinewood Lodge **2**
Queenstown Top 10
    Holiday Park Creeksyde **3**
The Rees Hotel & Luxury
    Apartments **27**
Remarkables Lodge **27**
Scenic Suites Queenstown **25**
Sofitel Queenstown **16**
White Shadows Country Inn **1**

DINING ◆
Bella Cucina **15**
Boardwalk Seafood
    Restaurant **12**
Botswana Butchery **23**
The Bunker **20**
The Cow **20**
Eichardt's House Bar **14**
Fishbone Bar & Grill **19**
Joe's Garage **21**
Skyline Gondola
    Restaurant **5**
Tatler **22**
True South **28**
Wai Waterfront
    Restaurant **12**
Vesta **24**
Vudu Café **18**

ATTRACTIONS ●
Department of
    Conservation **17**
Kiwi & Birdlife Park **7**
Skyline Gondola **6**
Steamer Wharf &
    TSS *Earnslaw* **11**

By Coach (Bus) InterCity (© 09/623-1503) runs between Queenstown and Christchurch, Dunedin, Fox Glacier, Franz Josef, Invercargill, Milford Sound, Mount Cook, Te Anau, and Wanaka. The InterCity depot is at the visitor center, Camp and Shotover streets (© 03/442-2800). **Kiwi Experience** (© 09/366-9830), **Magic Travellers** (© 09/358-5600), and **Backpackers Express** (© 03/442-9939) all service Queenstown as well.

The **Original Arrowtown Bus** (© 03/442-1900; www.arrowtownbus.co.nz) provides transportation between Queenstown and Arrowtown. Queenstown pickup is outside O'Connell's Centre on Camp Street at 9:45am, 11am, 1pm, 3:15pm, and 5:15pm; in Arrowtown catch the bus behind the Museum on Ramshaw Lane at 8:30am, 10:30am, noon, 2pm, and 4:30pm. The round-trip costs NZ$25, and they make two photo stops along the way.

By Car Allow a full day (6 hr.) from Christchurch, 3½ hours from Dunedin, 5½ hours from Franz Josef, 2½ hours from Te Anau, 5 hours from Milford Sound, and 2½ hours from Invercargill. All roads leading into town are excellent. All major rental-car companies have offices in Queenstown.

By Taxi Call **Queenstown Taxis** (© 03/442-7788) or **Alpine Taxis** (© 03/442-6666). Fares from the town center to most accommodations are between NZ$5 and NZ$15.

ORIENTATION Queenstown is a compact town, with most shops, restaurants, and amenities within easy walking distance. There is no public bus system, but the Connectabus (see above) provides excellent all-day service. The central shopping area is bordered by Marine Parade on the lakefront, Camp Street to the north of that, and Shotover Street, which runs into Lake Esplanade. Focus on Beach Street, Rees Street, and The Mall for shopping. If you have a car, keep in mind that parking in Queenstown is limited and expensive. Save yourself a lot of time and frustration and head straight for the new carpark on Man Street (beside the Sofitel). It has space for 400 vehicles and everything is within easy walking distance.

The historic village of Arrowtown is 20km (12 miles) to the northeast. A calm counterbalance to the frenetic pace of Queenstown, Arrowtown is one of New Zealand's last little frontier towns. Glenorchy, now billed as the "Gateway to Paradise," is a 45-minute drive around the west arm of Lake Wakatipu.

VISITOR INFORMATION The **Queenstown i-SITE Visitor Centre,** Clocktower Centre, Shotover and Camp streets (© 0800/668-888 in NZ, or 03/442-4100; fax 03/442-8907; www.queenstown-vacation.com), is open in summer daily from 7am to 7pm, and from Easter to the end of October from 7am to 6pm. It sells stamps; sends faxes and e-mail; exchanges currency; and makes reservations for accommodations, transport, and activities. The **Real Journeys Visitor Centre** is on the Steamer Wharf, Beach Street (© 0800/656-503 in NZ, or 03/442-7500; fax 03/442-7504; www.realjourneys.co.nz). The **Department of Conservation Information Centre,** 37 Shotover St. (© 03/442-7933), is the place to go for information on walking trails and national parks.

While at the visitor center, pick up a copy of the *Queenstown Today & Tonight* brochure. For a critical lowdown on what to do, get *Itag* and the *Backpackers' Guide to Queenstown*. Also look for the two free tourist papers, *The Mountain Scene* and *Qt Visitor Information*.

Get an online introduction to the area at www.newzealand-vacation.com, www.queenstownnz.co.nz, www.queenstownadventure.com, www.queenstownvisitorguide.com, www.arrowtown.org.nz, and www.centralotagonz.com.

SPECIAL EVENTS The visitor center can provide details on a vigorous program of **445** special events held in the area throughout the year. Here's a small sampling of what you can expect.

In January, riders from all over the South Island participate in the famous **Glenorchy Races,** which include bareback riding and attract thousands of spectators. The **Queenstown Jazz Festival** (© 03/442-9516; www.asbjazzfest.co.nz), presents 10 days of top jazz. The **Arrowtown Autumn Festival** (© 03/442-0809; www.arrowtownautumn festival.org.nz) runs the week after Easter. The festival celebrated its 25th anniversary in 2009, and it features market days and street entertainment celebrating the gold-mining era. The **Queenstown American Express Winter Festival** (© 0800/337-8482; www. winterfestival.co.nz) is the perfect excuse for 9 days of unadulterated madness and mayhem in July. It features a big opening ceremony and Mardi Gras, ski events, and street entertainment, and just about anything goes. The **Spring Carnival** (© 03/442-4615; www.nzski.com), held in mid-September at the Remarkables Ski Resort, presents a feast of snow-related sports and social activities.

QUEENSTOWN & ENVIRONS

16

QUEENSTOWN

(*Fast Facts*) Queenstown

American Express The office is at 59 Beach St. (© **03/442-7730**).

Area Code The telephone area code (STD) for Queenstown is **03**.

Currency Exchange Try **Thomas Cook,** 34 Camp St. (© **03/442-6403**), or **BNZ Bureau de Change,** 11–13 Rees St. (© **03/442-5810**).

Dentists For 24-hour service, call © **03/442-7274,** 442-8580, or 442-2711.

Doctors The **Queenstown Medical Centre** is at 9 Isle St. (© **03/441-0500**).

Emergencies For police, fire, or ambulance services, dial © **111.**

Internet Access **Internet Outpost,** 26 Shotover St. (© **03/441-3018**), open daily from 8:30am to 11:30pm, charges NZ$6 per hour. **Budget Communications,** above McDonald's in O'Connell's Mall (© **03/441-1562**), is open daily from 9am until 11pm and charges from NZ$3 per hour.

Pharmacy **Bradley's Pharmacy,** 19 Rees St. (© **03/442-8338**), is open daily from 8am to 10pm. After hours call © **03/442-9140.**

Post Office The post office is tucked away behind the Pig & Whistle on Ballarat Street (© **03/442-7670**). It's open Monday through Friday from 8:30am to 8pm, Saturday from 9am to 8pm, and Sunday 10am to 6pm.

EXPLORING THE AREA
In Queenstown

There is no better place to appraise Queenstown than from the **Skyline Gondola** ★★★ (© 03/441-0101; www.skyline.co.nz), which takes you up to **Bob's Peak.** The view is well worth the effort. You can stay for lunch or dinner at the buffet restaurant or cafe (see "Where to Dine," later in this chapter). The gondola operates from daily 9am until the restaurant closes around midnight, with a round-trip fare of NZ$22 for adults, NZ$10 for children ages 5 to 14. The complex includes a very good souvenir shop and a nearly 1km (½-mile) luge for the brave-hearted. From the top of the gondola you can then take a free

(Kids) Especially for Kids

Many of the adventures have high minimum age requirements, but one that doesn't is **Family Adventures** ★★★ ((C) **03/442-8836;** www.familyadventures. co.nz), which encourages families to take part in its scenic four-wheel-drive excursion into Skipper's Canyon to see old mining relics and jet boats in action, before embarking on a 1½-hour gentle rafting tour down the safest section of the Shotover River. The cost is from NZ$165 for adults and NZ$115 for children ages 3 to 16 (no kids 2 and under allowed).

Caddyshack City ★, 25 Brecon St. ((C) **03/442-6642**), is an indoor minia-ture-golf experience that makes for lots of laughs. Open daily from 10am to 8pm, it costs NZ$18 for adults, NZ$12 for children 5 to 14, and NZ$50 for fami-lies. Kids 4 and under cannot play, but strollers are provided.

Off-Road Adventures Kids Quads, 61a Shotover St. ((C) **03/442-7858**), has a family tour for NZ$139; and **Strikebowl Queenstown,** Coronet Alpine Hotel, 161 Arthurs Point Rd. ((C) **03/409-2135;** www.strikebowl.co.nz), has child-friendly equipment and before 5pm it costs just NZ$12 for adults and NZ$10 for children (includes shoes).

Kiwi & Birdlife Park ★ (see below) gives kids a good introduction to conser-vation and New Zealand bird life. The **Skyline Luge** ★★★ (see "Outdoor Pur-suits," later in this chapter) is great fun for all ages, as is Real Journey's **Walter Peak Farm Excursion** ★★ (see "Lake Cruises," below), which includes a steam-ship cruise and a farmyard tour where children can help feed the animals.

The **Underwater Observatory,** Main Pier ((C) **03/442-6142**), will also amuse the kids. Fish are fed each day and eels should also make an appearance. Admission is NZ$5 for adults, NZ$3 for children, and a mere NZ$10 for a family pass, which probably makes it Queenstown's cheapest attraction. Take some NZ$1 coins for the fish feeding machine, which attracts some huge specimens.

If you're traveling with kids, pick up the free guide, *Kidz Go!* at visitor centers.

chairlift another 100m (330 ft.) higher for even better views, and then walk the short dis-tance down to the complex to enjoy the 30-minute Maori cultural performance by Kiwi Haka. The combo ticket for both the gondola and Kiwi Haka costs NZ$53 for adults, NZ$27 for children, and NZ$134 for a family pass.

The **Kiwi & Birdlife Park** ★, Brecon Street ((C) **03/442-8059;** www.kiwibird.co.nz), is in tranquil 3-hectare (8-acre) surroundings near the base of the gondola. Allow 30 to 40 minutes to see the bird life and reptiles close at hand. Along with daily conservation shows (11am and 3pm), they have several rare birds that can't be seen anywhere else. A recent addition is the early Maori hunting village, and you can watch Maori dance per-formances at 11am and 3pm. Admission (including shows) is NZ$35 for adults and NZ$15 for children. The park is open 9am to 6pm in summer (open until 5pm in winter).

Goldfields Mining Centre, in Kawarau Gorge ((C) **03/445-1038;** www.goldfields mining.co.nz), is open daily from 9am to 5pm. The gold fields of this region were among the richest in the world in the early 19th century, and Goldfields is the official gold-mining demonstration site. It's a 40-minute drive through the Kawarau Gorge on the way to Cromwell, so if you're on your way to Wanaka or Dunedin, stop in. You have to walk over a narrow but stable bridge that crosses high above the river; and if you've got a fear of heights like me, you might shake in your boots a bit. But if I can do it, so can you. A self-guided tour costs NZ$16 for adults and NZ$8 for children.

If you have an interest in the arts, take the self-drive **Wakatipu Arts Trail,** which takes you through the pretty back roads between Queenstown and Arrowtown, visiting eight well-known artists and craftspeople. Pick up the brochure from the visitor center and allow at least a morning to appreciate fine watercolors, oils, wood art, and jewelry.

If you're not in the mood for paid adventures, there is always plenty to see by wandering around the compact center of Queenstown itself. You can sit on the little beach and have a picnic; on Saturdays you can visit the **Queenstown Art & Craft Market** at Earnslaw Park, which runs near Steamer Wharf from 9am to 4:30pm; and you can explore the **Steamer Wharf complex** itself. Designed by a local architect, Michael Wyatt, Steamer Wharf is home to restaurants, cafes, and TSS *Earnslaw* (see below), one of the last remaining coal-fired passenger-carrying vessels operating in the Southern Hemisphere. It's always fun to take a seat on the wharf and watch the *Earnslaw* and other boats coming and going.

In Nearby Arrowtown

For an enjoyable outing and a less hectic pace, drive out to the once-thriving gold-mining town of Arrowtown. It sprang up on the banks of the Arrow River when gold was discovered here in 1862. Many of the quaint original buildings remain, along with stunning avenues of trees planted in 1867. In autumn, the whole town glows with colorful foliage. To get a better understanding of the town's history, go to the **Lakes District Museum** ★, 49 Buckingham St. (© **03/442-1824;** www.museumqueenstown.com). Admission is NZ$6 for adults, NZ$1 for children ages 5 to 14; it's open daily from 8:30am to 5pm.

Although there is no longer a Chinese community in Arrowtown, you can take a stroll in the restored **Chinese Camp,** on Bush Creek at the northern end of town. The camp was once occupied by the Chinese gold-mining community in the late 19th century. Look out for **Ah Lum's General Store** and the tiny dwellings tucked under rocky outcrops.

Other places to explore include the **Royal Oak Hotel,** 47 Buckingham St. (© **03/442-1700**), one of the oldest licensed hotels in Central Otago, where you can still enjoy a drink and a hearty round of pub food; the **Old Gaol,** on Cardigan Street; and **St. John's Presbyterian Church,** which dates back to 1873, at Durham and Berkshire streets. Overall, Arrowtown is very pretty, but in peak tourist season it's about as "touristy" as touristy gets. It's much better in autumn when the crowds have dissipated and the leaves are falling. If you have time on your hands, catch a movie at **Dorothy Brown's Boutique Cinema** ★★, 144 Buckingham St. (© **03/442-1964;** www.dorothybrowns.com), which is a fabulous little den of art-house movies with a bar, bookstore, and lounge. It's open 11am to 11pm and reservations are recommended.

ORGANIZED TOURS

Start with the sedate **Queenstown-Arrowtown Double Decker Bus Tour** ★★ (© **03/441-4471;** www.doubledeckerbus.co.nz), which gives a bird's-eye view of the Wakatipu Basin without leaving the ground. It includes a 1-hour stop in Arrowtown; you can also leave the bus there in the morning and go back to Queenstown on the afternoon return trip. It costs NZ$48 for adults and NZ$20 for children 14 and under and departs daily from the top of Camp Street at 9:30am and 1:30pm, returning at 1 and 5pm. Allow 3 hours and purchase tickets from the visitor center, or on the bus.

For information on **Wine Trail** tours, see "The Wineries," below.

A Side Trip to Skippers Canyon ★★

Skippers Canyon, 22km (13 miles) from Queenstown, at the head of the Shotover River, was made famous by the discovery of gold there in 1862; within 4 months of that first find, over 10,000 miners were in the canyon. A settlement quickly sprang up to accommodate the miners, and at one time there were four hotels there. Today, among the few reminders of that bustling era are an old schoolhouse and the incredible narrow, winding road that was carved out of the rock faces by Chinese laborers. It can be a hair-raising journey, and I'd think twice about doing it under your own steam. Instead, I recommend you join one of the experienced tour operators who know this iconic route well.

Of the operators taking four-wheel-drive tours into Skippers Canyon, **Queenstown Heritage Tours** ★★★ (℃ 03/442-5949; www.qht.co.nz) is one of the best. The half-day tour is limited to four to six people and culminates in a delicious picnic on the edge of the cliff. The cost is from NZ$150 for adults and NZ$75 for children. **Nomad Safaris** (℃ 0800/676-264; www.nomad safaris.co.nz) offers a 4-hour 4WD safari into the canyon for NZ$140 for adults and NZ$70 for children. You can also go into the canyon with **Skippers Canyon Jet** (℃ 0800/226-966), for NZ$99 for adults and NZ$69 for children; some operators include a little gold panning in their excursion.

Trilogy Trail (℃ **0800/676-264** in NZ, or 03/442-2207; www.trilogytrail.com) is operated by people who were involved in the making of *The Lord of the Rings* trilogy, and they'll give you an insight into Middle Earth, visiting filming locations by air or road. Tours run from 2½ to 5 hours. A 4WD tour costs NZ$145 for adults, NZ$75 for children 13 and under. A flying/landing tour runs from NZ$350 to NZ$1,250 for adults, NZ$175 to NZ$665 for children 13 and under.

Nomad Safaris ★★ (℃ **0800/688-222** in NZ, or 03/442-6699; www.nomadsafaris. co.nz) has exclusive rights to guide in the old mining towns of Macetown and Sefferstown, taking you through spectacular Otago scenery along the way. They also offer two 4WD "Safari of the Rings" tours, visiting *The Lord of the Rings* filming locations. Several of their drivers were extras in the film trilogy, and all have an in-depth knowledge of Tolkien's work that is bound to satisfy the most dedicated fans. They are the only company offering dedicated *The Lord of the Rings* tours, and their experience is by far the best. For the most landscape diversity, take the Wakatipu Basin tour; for the most film locations and more remote scenery, take the Glenorchy tour. Both are 4 hours long and cost NZ$150 for adults, NZ$75 for children ages 4 to 14.

If, like me, you're not given to throwing yourselves off high places for the hell of it, take the excellent Secrets of the Bungy Tour ★★, **Kawarau Bungy Centre** (℃ **0800/ 286-495** in NZ, or 03/442-4007; www.bungy.co.nz), which gives you a 45-minute behind-the-scenes insight into this iconic New Zealand activity. Pricing for the Secrets of Bungy tour (self-drive to the bungy site) is adults NZ$20, children NZ$15, NZ$50 for a family. If you would like to be picked up in central Queenstown and transported to the site, ask for prices that include transport.

If you want to tour in style, contact **Limousine Line** (© **03/442-2040;** www. limousineline.co.nz). Its knowledgeable drivers give clients a unique, personal experience based on their interests and time constraints.

Lake Cruises

If you need a moment of serenity, get aboard the 1912 vintage steamship **TSS *Earnslaw*** and cruise across Lake Wakatipu in style. Affectionately known as the "Lady of the Lake," the 97-year-old *Earnslaw* was built to service the remote farming communities around Lake Wakatipu. She could carry 1,500 sheep and 30 cattle on her decks. Today, she carries up to 350 passengers on daily scheduled excursions and makes around 2,000 trips per year. To keep up with the times, the vessel had a short "holiday" in 2009, when she underwent her regular survey and also had combustion fans fitted on both main steam boilers to optimize her coal-burning efficiency and reduce emissions. Some of the older decking was also replaced. In 2012, the steamship's entire forward deck section will be replaced, once the correct timber has been sourced, cured, and prepared.

The **TSS *Earnslaw*** departs on 1½-hour cruises to Walter Peak up to six times a day, year-round (with a reduced winter schedule). Cost is NZ$48 for adults and NZ$20 for children ages 5 to 14. Passengers with more time can disembark at Walter Peak on the 3½-hour farm excursion, which includes a country-style morning or afternoon tea (NZ$68 adults, NZ$20 children ages 5–14). Alternatively, from October to mid-April, you can take a 40-minute horse trek across the foothills, enjoy a delicious Walter Peak barbecue, learn about the area's history on a Heritage Excursion, or splurge on the evening dining excursion, which features a three-course carvery buffet and a shortened farmyard tour. Contact **Real Journeys,** Steamer Wharf (© **0800/656-503** in NZ, or 03/442-7500; www.realjourneys.co.nz).

Sail Queenstown ★★★, Steamer Wharf (© **03/442-7517;** www.sailqueenstown. co.nz), gives you the chance to sail on former America's Cup vessel, *NZL14,* which was skippered by Russell Coutts. You can sit back and enjoy the ride, or act as part of the crew. No former experience is needed and you'll pay NZ$150 for the pleasure (children NZ$110). Allow 2 hours for high-level excitement.

THE WINERIES

There's new gold in this picturesque valley—liquid gold, in the form of prizewinning wine! Central Otago's rugged hillsides are clad in lush vineyards that produce some of the country's most distinctive wines. Pinot noir (85% of the total plantings), chardonnay, sauvignon blanc, pinot gris, and Riesling varieties are well suited to the hot summer days and cool nights. Since 1990, Central Otago pinot noir has topped its class five times in national wine competitions. Pick up the free brochure *The Central Otago Wine Map,* which locates the major wineries. Study it carefully and choose the wineries that best suit your preferences. It's by far the best, most concise overview of the entire wine industry in this region.

New vineyards are coming on stream all the time as the region's 686 hectares (1,694 acres)—and expanding—mature and many are developing new winery and restaurant complexes. There are now over 71 vineyards in the region. The Queenstown and Wanaka visitor centers can provide a comprehensive map and brochure of the Central Otago wine industry to make your self-drive exploration more satisfying and straightforward. For more information check **www.otagowine.com** or **www.cowa.org.nz.**

Start your wine exploration at the very classy **Amisfield Winery** ★★★, 10 Lake Hayes Rd. (✆ **03/442-0556;** www.amisfield.co.nz), where you'll find one of the best restaurants in the region, along with an underground barrel hall and cellar door. They're just 10 minutes from Queenstown and are producers of pinot noir, aromatic whites, and *méthode traditionelle* wines. **Chard Farm Vineyard** ★, State Highway 6, just past the Kawarau bungy bridge, 20 minutes from Queenstown (✆ **03/442-1006;** www.chard farm.co.nz), is one of the most spectacularly situated vineyards in the country. Straddling a narrow ledge between rugged mountains and the Kawarau River Gorge, it's reached via a narrow, unpaved road 100m (330 ft.) above the river. Available wines include chardonnay, pinot noir, Riesling, sauvignon blanc, pinot gris, and Gewürztraminer.

GVW Winery ★★, State Highway 6, 25 minutes from Queenstown (✆ **03/442-6910;** www.gvwines.com), is a popular lunch stop. It's the most visited winery in Australasia, with not only great food but also a divine setting. As pioneers of winemaking in Central Otago, Gibbston has set high standards. Many of its wines are stored in the climatically controlled wine cave, which was blasted out of a rocky outcrop behind the restaurant. Connoisseurs will enjoy the tour through the caves and the tasting of four wines. There is also a large gift store and delicatessen on-site, and next door, **Gibbston Valley Cheesery** ★★ (✆ **03/441-1388;** www.gvcheese.co.nz) makes and sells top-quality regional cheeses.

Just down the road you'll find **Peregrine** ★★★ (✆ **03/442-4000;** www.peregrine wines.co.nz). Named after the falcon now found only in the Central Otago region, Peregrine is a relatively new player on the scene. Success has come early, though, and its 1998 sauvignon blanc won New Zealand, Australian, and United Kingdom trophies. The opening of its new architecturally designed restaurant complex, with a distinctive curved wing-shaped roof, has cemented it as one of the classiest wineries to visit. They produce good pinot noir, pinot gris, Riesling, sauvignon blanc, chardonnay, and rosé.

You won't regret a trip into the Bannockburn area, either. Drive through the Kawarau Gorge and just before Cromwell, and you'll see Bannockburn signposted to your right. This is where you'll find **Mt. Difficulty Wines** ★★, Felton Road, Bannockburn

---

ⓘTips   The Wine Tours

Queenstown Wine Trail ★★ (✆ **0800/827-8464** in NZ, or 03/442-3799; www. queenstownwinetrail.co.nz), offers a 5-hour tour with an informed commentary and tastings at four wineries. The cost is NZ$114 and it operates all year. If you can't get into this one, try **Appellation Central Wine Tours** ★★ (✆ **03/442-0246;** www.appellationcentral.co.nz), which will take you to the rapidly expanding Bannockburn and Cromwell vineyard regions, where you'll explore many of the best new vineyards. It has two daily options, one including lunch in the historic town of Clyde. Prices range from NZ$155 to NZ$195 per person. If you don't have time to get the vineyards at all, visit **Wine Tastes New Zealand Wine Experience,** 14 Beach St., Queenstown (✆ **03/409-2226;** www.winetastes.com), which carries a selection of over 600 of New Zealand's best wines, over 80 of them available to taste by the glass. They're right in the center of town and are open daily from 10am until late. They can also organize the packaging and shipment of your purchased wines to your home.

For an unforgettable adventure, call up experienced Queenstown helicopter pilot Louisa "Choppy" Patterson at **Over the Top** ★★★, the Blue Hangar, Tex Smith Lane, Queenstown Airport (② **0800/123-359** in NZ, or 03/442-2233; www.flynz. co.nz). Something of a legend in these parts, Choppy knows all the magic picnic spots thousands of feet up in the mountains. She can land you there, leave you with a champagne lunch in total solitude, and return later to drop you back into civilization. This truly memorable excursion will start at around NZ$800 per person, depending on where you decide to fly. Don't miss this unique chance for adventure! As well as investing in quieter aircraft, Over the Top partnered with the Department of Conservation and the University of Otago to sponsor two eco projects donating helicopter time to help ensure this unique World Heritage area remains pristine.

(② **03/445-3445;** www.mtdifficulty.co.nz), which produces excellent pinot noir, Riesling, chardonnay, sauvignon blanc, pinot gris, and merlot. They also have a very pleasant cafe open for lunch at noon.

You could easily spend a whole day in the Bannockburn area alone, as there are dozens of wineries here. If you're on a tight schedule, though, and want to maximize your time, I suggest you take a wine tour. The two outlined below are the best.

SIDE TRIPS TO MILFORD SOUND ★★★

If you don't have time to make the long drive to Milford Sound (see "Milford Sound," later in this chapter), there are numerous operators offering trips from Queenstown. Flying is money well invested, as the long 1-day coach trips can be exhausting and you'll spend most of your time on a bus. If you are planning to drive yourself, I definitely recommend spending a night at Te Anau before undertaking the journey to Milford Sound. That way, your Milford trip can be taken at a leisurely pace, and you can stop along the way to enjoy the scenery. Otherwise it can be an arduous journey.

There are numerous suppliers of fixed-wing scenic flights from Queenstown to Milford. You'll get 10% discount if you mention Frommer's to either **Air Fiordland,** Queenstown Airport (② **0800/103-404;** www.airfiordland.com), or **Milford Sound Scenic Flights,** Queenstown Airport (② **0800/207-206;** www.milfordflights.co.nz). They're similarly priced, offering flights and inclusive boat cruise options for around NZ$425 to NZ$450 for adults and NZ$255 to NZ$260 for children. Their longer fly/cruise/coach options are a little cheaper and will give you the opportunity for an on-the-ground look at this remarkable landscape. But if you're short on time and you can afford to fly both ways, it's definitely the way to go. You'll see many hidden valleys and lakes never seen from the road and the flight only takes around 35 minutes from Queenstown to Milford.

If flying and driving are not options, don't despair. **Great Sights** (② **0800/744-487;** www.greatsights.co.nz) and **Real Journeys** (② **0800/656-503;** www.realjourneys.co.nz) both offer coach trips from Queenstown. Allow at least 12 hours for a trip of this nature, of which approximately 10 hours will be spent on the bus. A better option is to coach in and fly out, which saves time and lets you see the landscape from two different perspectives, but if the weather closes in—and it often does—you'll end up coaching both ways.

Real Journeys also offers a flight and scenic-cruise option priced at NZ$435 for adults and NZ$283 for children. Their Coach and Nature Cruise (all year) from Queenstown is NZ$230 for adults, NZ$115 for children ages 5 to 14. The vessel is designed along the lines of a traditional trading scow and there's an onboard nature guide. A coach/ nature cruise/fly package (all year) from Queenstown is NZ$540 for adults, NZ$317 for children ages 5 to 14. A coach/scenic cruise/fly package (all year) from Queenstown costs NZ$586 for adults, NZ$47 for children ages 5 to 14. You can book all Real Journey excursions at the visitor center at Steamer Wharf (© 03/442-7500; fax 03/442-7504). It has excellent coaches, comfortable cruising vessels, informed drivers, and interpretation in seven languages other than English.

OUTDOOR PURSUITS
In Queenstown

There's no doubt Queenstown has more crazy, boundary-testing activities per square mile than anywhere else in New Zealand.

BIKING **Queenstown Bike Hire,** 23 Beach St. (© 03/442-6039), rents road and mountain bikes, tandems, and scooters; ask for a map that details the popular rides around town. **Outside Sports,** 36 Shotover St. (© 03/441-0074; www.outsidesports. co.nz), rents road and mountain bikes. It also supplies mountain-bike trail maps. Rentals range from NZ$50 to NZ$120 per day. Serious mountain bikers should consider the guided tours provided by **Gravity Action** (© 03/442-5277; www.gravityaction.com), and **Vertigo Bikes,** 4 Brecon St. (© 03/442-8378; www.vertigobikes.co.nz), which can arrange heli-biking in the Remarkables.

BUNGY JUMPING There are three bungy-jumping sites in Queenstown. So what's the difference between them all? **A. J. Hackett Bungy ★★★** (© 0800/286-4958 in NZ, or 03/442-4007; www.bungy.co.nz) now operates them all.

Kawarau Suspension Bridge, at 43m (140 ft.) high, was the world's first commercial bungy operation, and since it was the "original," it seems to hold a special place in jumpers' hearts. It's great for water touches in the Kawarau River and is 23km (14 miles) from Queenstown. The full package, including jump, T-shirt, video, photos, and transport, costs NZ$170. Allow 1 to 3 hours. At the top of Bob's Peak, the **Ledge** is 47m (155 ft.). This is what you might call an urban bungy experience that has two angles—the Wild Side and the Mild Side. You can also jump at night. You'll pay NZ$170 for the jump, a T-shirt, and the gondola ride; allow 1 hour. The **Ledge Sky Swing** also operates here and costs NZ$125. The **Nevis Highwire Bungy ★★★** is Hackett's big daddy of bungy. At 134m (440 ft.) over the Kawarau River, it is the tallest bungy site in New Zealand. The full pack here costs NZ$250. The **Nevis Arc** is the latest addition to this thrill seekers' heaven. It's right beside Nevis Bungy. You'll walk across a 70m (230-ft.) suspension bridge to the launchpad, and then decide which way you're going to free fall 160m (525 ft.) through the air above Doolan's Creek Gorge. This crazy adventure will cost you NZ$175 and the minimum age is 10. Don't forget to check out the A. J. Hackett combos, which offer several thrills at a reduced cost. The minimum age for all bungy jumps is 13.

CANYONING **Canyoning NZ** (© 03/441-3003; www.canyoning.co.nz) does half-day trips for NZ$155 to NZ$225. Allow 3 hours, 1½ of them wet. They also offer a heli-canyon combo, and operate from mid-October through to mid-April.

FISHING The visitor center can advise you on several recognized trout-fishing operators with prices ranging from NZ$85 per hour to NZ$800 or more for a full day.

Queenstown Fishing Guides & Charters (© 03/442-5363; www.wakatipu.co.nz),
offers lake trolling, fly-fishing, and lure fishing. Or try **Over The Top Fly Fishing**
(© **0800/123-359** in NZ, or 03/442-2233; www.flynz.co.nz) for a truly out-of-the-way
guided heli-fly-fishing experience.

GOLF   The ultimate in Queenstown golf is **Millbrook Resort** ★★★, Arrowtown
(© **0800/800-604** in NZ, or 03/441-7010; www.millbrook.co.nz), where you'll pay
NZ$70 to NZ$175 for the par-72, Bob Charles–designed course. Carts, equipment,
instruction, and a free shuttle from Queenstown are available. The 18-hole **Queenstown
Golf Club,** Kelvin Heights (© **03/442-9169;** www.queenstowngolf.co.nz), is a full-
service course with NZ$70 greens fees and NZ$65 for club rental.

HORSE TREKKING   There are a number of horse-trekking operators who charge from
NZ$50 to NZ$120. **Moonlight Stables** (© **03/442-1229;** www.moonlightcountry.
co.nz) is on the 325-hectare (800-acre) Doonholme Farm, 15 minutes from Queenstown. Well-mannered horses and experienced guides offer full- or half-day treks through
spectacular landscapes and deer farms. **Shotover Stables** (© **03/442-9708**) is just 6
minutes out of town at Arthur's Point.

HOT-AIR BALLOONING   **Sunrise Balloons** ★★ (© **0800/468-247** in NZ, or 03/
442-0781; www.ballooningnz.com) will give you a memorable experience floating
silently over the Wakatipu Basin at dawn. The price—NZ$375 for adults, NZ$245 for
children 11 and under—includes a champagne breakfast after landing.

JET-BOATING   **Shotover Jet** ★★★ (© **0800/746-868** in NZ, or 03/442-8570;
www.shotoverjet.com) is perhaps the best-known operator and the biggest adrenaline
rush. You'll pay from NZ$109 for adults and NZ$69 for kids ages 5 to 15 to blast
through narrow rocky canyons in as little as 10 centimeters (4 in.) of water for 30 minutes. **Kawarau Jet** (© **0800/529-272** in NZ, or 03/442-6142; www.kjet.co.nz) departs
from the main town pier and skates across Lake Wakatipu to the Kawarau and Shotover
rivers. The 45- to 60-minute trip costs NZ$95 for adults, NZ$55 for children (see
"Money-Saving Combos," below, for other options).

LUGE   The **Skyline Luge** ★★★ (© **03/441-0101;** www.skyline.co.nz) is nearly 1km
(½ mile) of downhill fun. There are various packages on offer, including several rides and
gondola transport. The gondola and a single luge ride costs NZ$29 for adults and
NZ$19 for children. It operates daily from 9am to dusk; and tickets are available from
the Skyline Gondola terminals.

PARAPENTING/HANG GLIDING/PARAGLIDING   Queenstown Paragliding
School (© **0800/727-245** in NZ; www.extremeair.co.nz) will give you a day's course in
the basics for NZ$195. There are approximately 15 **tandem parapente** operators, most
working above the gondola on Bob's Peak; prices are NZ$185 to NZ$250 for an introductory tandem flight.

RIVER BOARDING/RIVER SURFING   If you thought surfing was restricted to the
ocean, forget it. Now you can cling to a specially designed boogie board, don a helmet,
and go for it down churning river rapids. **Serious Fun River Surfing** (© **0800/737-468**
in NZ, or 03/442-5262; www.riversurfing.co.nz) goes down a 7km (4-mile) stretch of
the Kawarau River for NZ$155. You'll progress from flat water to Grade IV rapids with
instruction as you go along. No experience is necessary, but confidence in the water is.
Trips are conducted from October to May.

SKIING From late June to September, the international ski crowd flocks to Queenstown to enjoy the accessible slopes of **Coronet Peak;** the least-crowded slopes of the **Remarkables;** the best family fields at **Cardrona;** and the most challenging slopes at **Treble Cone.** For the ultimate rush, try a day of heli-skiing or heli-boarding with **Harris Mountains Heliski** (© **03/443-7930;** www.heliski.co.nz), **HeliGuides** (© **03/442-7733;** www.flynz. co.nz), or **Glacier Southern Lakes Heliski** (© **03/442-3016;** www.heli-flights.co.nz). For more information on skiing and snowboarding in the area, see chapter 5.

SKY DIVING For NZ$265 to NZ$399, **NZONE** (© **03/442-5867;** www.nzone.biz) will fly you over awesome scenery and then drop you out to fall at speeds of up to 200kmph (124 mph).

WALKING Three well-known multiday walks start in the Queenstown vicinity. See "Tramping" in chapter 5 for information on the **Routeburn,** the **Greenstone Valley,** and the **Grand Traverse Tracks.** Each starts near the little township of Glenorchy, at the far end of Lake Wakatipu, 47km (29 miles) from Queenstown. It's also possible to sample these great walks by going in several hours and back out again on the same day. Alternatively, you can do the **Routeburn Encounter Guided Day Walk** ★★ (© **0800/768-832** in NZ, or 03/442-8200; www.ultimatehikes.co.nz) from November to April, with transport from Queenstown provided. The track rises 230m (755 ft.) over 6.5km (4 miles) and is suitable for reasonably active people. Take warm and waterproof clothing and good boots. Ultimate Hikes offers a similar 1-day guided walk on the Milford Track, plus multiday guided options.

The **Department of Conservation Information Centre,** 37 Shotover St. (© **03/442-7935**), open daily from 8am to 8pm, can furnish details on short walks around Queenstown as well as those farther afield. There are at least 10 walks of 1 to 8 hours in and around town. One of the most testing is the 2- to 3-hour, uphill **Queenstown Hill Track,** which starts and finishes on Belfast Terrace. You'll be rewarded by great views and photo opportunities if you make it to the top. There are also several excellent walks around **Lake Wakatipu,** including the pleasant and easy **Bobs Cove Track and Nature Trail** ★★, which starts 14km (9 miles) from Queenstown on the road to Glenorchy. Experienced naturalist Richard Bryant of **Guided Walks of New Zealand** ★★★ (© **0800/455-712** in NZ, or 03/442-7126; www.nzwalks.com) specializes in treks with nature interpretation. He offers half- and full-day options with a maximum of seven people, costing from NZ$100 to NZ$435.

There are also pleasant walks and trails in and around **Arrowtown.** Pick up the Department of Conservation brochure, which details all these walks, their conditions, and fitness requirements. For weather forecast information, call **MetPhone** (© **0900/99-903** in NZ; www.metservice.co.nz).

WHITE-WATER RAFTING The Shotover and Kawarau rivers are top spots for white-water rafting. The Kawarau trips are generally better for those who are rafting for the first time. The Shotover trips are much more challenging and are usually accompanied by safety kayaks. **Challenge Rafting** ★★ (© **0800/442-7318** in NZ; www.raft.co.nz), has half- and full-day rafting trips from NZ$175. Mention Frommer's and you'll get a 10% discount when booking direct. **Queenstown Rafting** (© **0800/723-846** in NZ; www.rafting.co.nz) operates similar trips priced from NZ$175. They also have a multiday rafting trip for NZ$1,495. **Extreme Green Rafting** ★★★ (© **03/442-8517;** www.nzraft.com) is a smaller operator with more competitive prices. It also has an Upper Shotover Scenic option, which includes a flight or drive to the top of the river. This

> (Tips) **Money-Saving Combos**
>
> If you want to try a variety of activities, look into money-saving combos. Most booking agents around Queenstown can fill you in on all the details and several adventure operators have their own money-saving combinations. The **Shotover High Five** ★★, combines the Shotover Jet with a helicopter ride, luge, and gondola rides. **Queenstown Combos** (© **0800/423-836** in NZ, or 03/442-7318; www.combos.co.nz) has about 14 different packages and can make reservations for you. Prices start at NZ$220. Mention Frommer's and you'll get a 10% discount if you book direct. **Extreme Combos** (© **03/442-8517;** www.nzraft.com) offers a range of rafting-based combos that include bungy, helicopter rides, sky diving, and jet boats.

full-day outing is a passive rather than high-adrenaline activity, suitable for all ages and levels of fitness. It's also priced at NZ$175.

In Nearby Glenorchy

Glenorchy is a tiny village surrounded by rugged high country, mountains, glacier-fed lakes, and ancient beech forests—*The Lord of the Rings* country, in fact. Much of the filming was done in this remote area. It's also the latest hot spot in southern tourism. Just 40 minutes away, it's now a base for several tour operators, all of which offer transport from Queenstown.

FUNYAKING   Sitting in an inflatable Canadian-style canoe and floating downstream at 8kmph (5 mph), enjoying the scenery, is my idea of a sensible adventure. With **Funyaks** ★★★ (© **03/442-9992;** www.dartriver.co.nz), you'll jet-boat up the Dart River for 75 minutes (or you can go by 4WD vehicle, if you prefer), then canoe back down to Glenorchy in stable inflatable canoes. No need for daredevil confidence—it's a family trip guaranteed to please everyone. The price is from NZ$279 for adults, NZ$179 for children ages 3 to 15, and NZ$749 for a family, including transport, guides, and lunch.

HORSE TREKKING   The **Dart Stables** ★ (© **0800/474-3464** in NZ, or 03/442-5688; www.dartstables.com) has exclusive riding territory in the high country of the 200-hectare (500-acre) Wyuna Station and sole rights to trek through Department of Conservation areas. Treks are available for all abilities and range from 2 hours to overnight excursions, priced from NZ$110 to NZ$255 per person.

JET-BOATING   **Dart River Safaris** ★★★ (© **0800/327-8538** in NZ, or 03/442-9992; www.dartriverjetsafaris.com) provides one of the best jet-boating experiences in New Zealand. The Safari combines jet-boating with walks in ancient forests and visits to *The Lord of the Rings* sites at Paradise. It departs Glenorchy daily at 9am and 1pm (Queenstown 8am and noon). Allow 6 hours in total and expect to pay NZ$199 for adults and NZ$99 for children ages 3 to 15.

WALKING   Glenorchy is the departure point for the **Routeburn,** the **Greenstone and Caples,** and the **Rees and Dart** tracks, all of which are internationally renowned. Get information at the **Department of Conservation,** Glenorchy Visitor Centre (© **03/442-9937;** www.glenorchyinfocentre.co.nz). See also "Tramping" in chapter 5.

Queenstown has an excellent range of New Zealand–made goods, from sheepskin products, leather, and outdoor wear to fine crafts, pure wool hand-knits, and jewelry. Most shops are open daily to 10pm, and many offer overseas packaging and postal services. Pick up the free *Queenstown Dining & Shopping Guide* at the visitor center.

Several new upmarket shopping complexes have opened since 2007, and you can expect much more in the next 2 years as new shopping centers and town developments come on-stream.

O'Connells Shopping Centre, Camp and Beach streets (© 03/442-7760), has 25 stores offering everything from food and fashion to knitwear, jewelry, and contemporary art. If you missed **Canterbury New Zealand** (© 03/442-4020) in other major centers, you'll find it here.

Bonz Gallery, upstairs in **Bonz New Zealand** ★, 8–10 The Mall (© 03/442-5398; www.bonz.com.au), is a top outlet for original designs in 100% merino wool hand-knit sweaters and jackets. **Goldfields Jade and Opal,** top of The Mall (© 03/442-9356), and the **Opal Centre,** Beach and Rees streets (© 03/442-8239; www.opalsnz.com), have the finest collections of investment opal jewelry.

For one of the biggest selections of sheepskins, woolen jerseys, leisurewear, jewelry, wooden carvings, confectionery, and local honeys and jams, go to **DF Souvenirs,** 32 The Mall (© 03/442-5275). Another good source of all of the above is the **Mountaineer Shop,** Beach and Rees streets (© 03/442-7460). And if you have a sweet tooth, don't miss the **British Lolly Shop,** Church Lane (© 03/441-2274; www.thebritishlollyshop. com), which seems an awfully long way from home to me, but some among you may be glad of that. You'll find another very cute little gift store at **Vesta** ★, Williams Cottage, 19 Marine Parade (© 03/442-5687), which is hardly bigger than a doll's house, yet manages to present some excellent New Zealand art, design work, and a tiny cafe.

(Moments) Body Business

When the stress of being a tourist gets the better of you, turn your attention to one of Queenstown's new pampering services. Among them all, **Body Sanctum Day Spa** ★★, Level 2, 50 Stanley St. (© 03/442-8006; www.bodysanctum.co. nz), comes most highly recommended. Men and women alike can feel the benefits of aromatherapy, sports massage, shiatsu, reflexology, and a wide variety of beauty therapy services. You can also unwind at the **Millbrook Resort Day Spa** ★★★, Malaghan Road (© 03/441-7000; fax 03/441-7007); it's the biggest and classiest, and offers a full range of wet and dry massage therapies, a hair salon, facials, beauty treatments, manicures, and pedicures—all set within the restful acres of Millbrook. **Aspects Day Spa,** 53 Shotover St. (© 03/442-7389; www.aspectsdayspa.co.nz), can rejuvenate the weariest traveler with a wide range of massage therapies, body wraps, Jacuzzis, and manicures. **Hush Spa** ★★, Level 2, the Junction, corner of Gorge and Robins roads (© 03/409-0901; www. hushspa.co.nz), will soothe you with exotic body therapies, massage rituals, and facial treatments. **Le Spa at Sofitel** ★★, Sofitel Hotel (© 03/450-0045; www. lespaqueenstown.co.nz), is the latest addition and its classy spa suites and gorgeous French products are well worth indulging in.

Untouched World ★★★, The Mall (✆ **03/442-4992;** www.untouchedworld.com), is a fabulous source of exclusive men's and women's apparel—especially merino mink garments that combine 100% New Zealand merino wool with possum fur for pure luxury. If you'd like to take home a special memento of your time in New Zealand, visit **Toi o Tahuna Fine Art Gallery** ★★★, Church Lane, Queenstown (✆ **03/409-0787;** www.toi.co.nz), which has a great range of original art, sculpture, ceramics, glass, and jade.

WHERE TO STAY

There are now over 20,000 visitor beds in this small town, ranging from backpackers to new apartments, international-class hotels, and luxury lodges, yet still they keep coming. Even with multiple new additions, it still pays to book well in advance. If you're looking for something extra special, refer to the Queenstown luxury concierge company, **Touch of Spice** ★★★ (✆ **03/442-8672;** www.touchofspice.co.nz), listed in the "Planning Your Trip to New Zealand" chapter. They provide a luxury concierge service for their Private Villa Collection—everything from rustic cottages to country lodges and luxury penthouses. The rates below include 12.5% GST and free off-street parking unless otherwise noted.

In Queenstown
Very Expensive
Eichardt's Private Hotel ★★★ (Finds) Voted the Best Small Hotel in the World by Andrew Harper (www.andrewharpertravel.com) in 2003, Eichardt's takes on the best of any luxury accommodations in New Zealand and comes up trumps. It's one of my favorite places in New Zealand. It's small, but first class in every respect. The large rooms have luxurious bathrooms, and you'll get all the modern conveniences in an exquisite interior that draws on the original building's history. Service is detailed, interior design mouthwatering, and its central location a bonus. Just be sure to pack earplugs as noise in this central location can sometimes be an issue. And check out their new Lakefront Cottage with four two-bedroom suites, just down the street.

Marine Parade, Queenstown. ✆ **03/441-0450.** Fax 03/441-0440. www.eichardts.com. 9 units. NZ$1,164 lakefront family; NZ$1,519 lakefront cottage; NZ$1,603 mountain view; NZ$1,850 lake view. NZ$250 each extra person; NZ$200 per person Christmas/New Year supplement. Long-stay rates. Rates include breakfast and cocktails. AE, DC, MC, V. **Amenities:** Restaurant; bar; airport transfers at charge; babysitting; bike rentals; concierge; 5 nearby golf courses; room service. *In room:* A/C, TV/DVD/CD, fridge, hair dryer, kitchenette, minibar, Wi-Fi.

Sofitel Queenstown ★★★ This is New Zealand's first Sofitel hotel—and with bigger rooms, wired concierge, and espresso machines in every room, it's setting a new standard for service. Rooms are classic yet sensual, bathrooms are orchid-filled and complete with LCD screens over the bathtub. It's right in the center of town surrounded by new shops and restaurants. A sophisticated stay for the discerning traveler. I love it, and with a new day spa now open, there's even more reason to treat yourselves!

8 Duke St., Queenstown. ✆ **0800/444-422** in NZ, or 03/450-0045. Fax 03/450-0046. www.sofitel.co.nz. 82 units. NZ$315–NZ$415 superior; NZ$515–NZ$615 suite; NZ$2,750 penthouse. Long-stay, off-peak, and special packages. AE, DC, MC, V. Valet parking NZ$17. **Amenities:** Restaurant (Vie [Contemporary French]); bar; airport transport; nearby bike rentals; Les Clefs d'Or Concierge; executive-level rooms; nearby golf course; gym; Jacuzzi (in penthouses); room service; infra-red sauna; steam room; day spa and beauty treatments. *In room:* A/C, TV/DVD/CD, fridge, hair dryer, kitchen (in penthouses), minibar, Wi-Fi.

A Boutique Hotel Queenstown House ★★

In addition to remodeling this unique stay into something between a small boutique hotel and a B&B, owner Louise Kiely gave it a big revamp in 2009. The property has seven delightful rooms in the main house and seven new villa suites in an adjacent building. Each has its own special charm—I especially love the Hunting Room—but for the best views, go for the larger Baron Room. Apartment suites in the new block are much bigger and have their own decks, large sitting rooms, and a modern kitchen. Louise has personality-plus and encourages guests to meet for predinner drinks in the cozy living room. A delicious breakfast is served in the dining room overlooking the lake and township, which is only a short walk downhill.

69 Hallenstein St., Queenstown. ✆ **03/442-9043.** Fax 03/442-8755. www.queenstownhouse.co.nz. 15 units. NZ$250–NZ$395 in main house; NZ$395–NZ$595 villa. Long-stay and off-peak rates, special deals. Rates include breakfast and predinner drinks. AE, DC, MC, V. **Amenities:** Babysitting; nearby golf course. *In room:* TV/DVD, fridge (in some), hair dryer, kitchen (in suites), Wi-Fi.

The Dairy Private Luxury Hotel ★★

Once a 1920s general store, the Dairy has grown beyond a simple B&B and is now a small, boutique hotel. Bedrooms are beautifully decorated and there are excellent social spaces, including a roaring fire and reading room. Best, your hostess Elspeth will spoil you with delicious afternoon tea scones. Always a well-loved spot just a stroll from town, it has a stronger hosting presence than Browns and Queenstown House, but the latter both have bigger rooms. The premier rooms have the best views.

10 Isle St., Queenstown. ✆ **03/442-5164.** Fax 03/442-5166. www.thedairy.co.nz. 13 units. NZ$450–NZ$480. Long-stay and off-peak rates. Rates include breakfast. AE, MC, V. Limited off-street parking. It's a 150m (490-ft.) uphill walk from town center. **Amenities:** Bar; free bikes; Jacuzzi. *In room:* TV, hair dryer, high-speed Internet.

Pencarrow ★★ (Value)

Bill and Kari Moers' outstanding service and value put them in a class of their own when it comes to B&Bs; in fact, they rival many more expensive options in their attention to detail and the warmth of their welcome. Factor in four fabulous big rooms and a collection of Persian rugs to die for—not to mention great views and a breakfast you'll never forget, and you'll see why I rate this as one of the best B&B stays in the country.

678 Frankton Rd., Queenstown. ✆ **03/442-8938.** Fax 03/442-8974. www.pencarrow.net. 4 units. NZ$595 suite. Rates include breakfast. AE, DC, MC, V. Turn off Frankton Rd. btw. the Remarkables and Greenstone apartment complexes and head straight up the central (and steep) gravel driveway. No children 11 and under. **Amenities:** Nearby golf course (free clubs available); small fitness room; Jacuzzi. *In room:* A/C (in 2 upstairs rooms), TV/VCR, fridge, hair dryer, kitchen (in 1 suite), minibar, Wi-Fi.

Moderate

Brown's Boutique Hotel (Value)

You'll be right at home at Brown's if you want a good-value stay with character and friendly, knowledgeable local hosts. The hillside, Tuscan-style property with great views offers spacious rooms with big bathrooms and luxurious beds. Size-wise, it's on a par with the Dairy and Queenstown House, although being purpose-built, it has a more distinct small hotel character. It's now 9 years old and there are five rooms on two levels, with generous living areas and patios on the ground floor. Town is just a 4-minute walk downhill.

26 Isle St., Queenstown. ✆ **03/441-2050.** Fax 03/441-2060. www.brownshotel.co.nz. 10 units. NZ$315. Long-stay and off-peak rates. Rates include breakfast. AE, DC, MC, V. **Amenities:** Nearby golf course. *In room:* TV/DVD, fridge, hair dryer, free Wi-Fi.

Crowne Plaza Queenstown ★★ After a NZ$12-million upgrade in 2006–07, this central hotel has moved several notches higher in the style and service stakes. All of its 139 rooms were completely refurbished and its chic, innovative lobby, bars, and restaurant make a fabulous first impression. Rooms here are lake view, mountain view, or courtyard view, and they're priced accordingly. In reality, they're all exactly the same—pleasantly decorated in crisp white and earth-toned color schemes, with good bathrooms and excellent desks. I love the sleek, contemporary look of this place and it's in a great spot within walking distance of all downtown shopping.

Beach St., Queenstown. ℂ **0800/801-111** in NZ, or 03/441-0095. Fax 03/442-8895. www.crowneplaza queenstown.co.nz. 139 units. NZ$160–NZ$350 standard; NZ$250–NZ$600 suite. Off-peak rates. AE, DC, MC, V. Valet parking NZ$7. **Amenities:** Restaurant (Three-Sixty [Fusion Cuisine]); bar; babysitting; concierge; nearby golf courses; room service; sauna; Wi-Fi in public areas. *In room:* A/C, TV/DVD, fridge, hair dryer, minibar.

Garden Court Suites & Apartments ★ Ⓥalue Once an average motel, Garden Court has taken itself into a new league with the addition of fabulous contemporary apartments at a reasonable price. On top of that, the existing studios have also been revamped. They slope down, away from the road, so there's no traffic noise; among these, the two-bedroom apartments are the best value, with a cozy living area, kitchen, and bathroom downstairs and two bedrooms and a second toilet upstairs. If you want style and comfort, you won't find much to complain about in the new apartment block. Its bathrooms are simply great—well lit, spacious, and with combination tub/showers. Fourteen new one-bedroom apartments overlook the lake and are the quietest.

41 Frankton Rd., Queenstown. ℂ **0800/427-336** in NZ, or 03/442-9713. Fax 03/442-6468. www.garden court.co.nz. 54 units. NZ$169–NZ$187 studio suite; NZ$226–NZ$247 1-bedroom apt; NZ$282–NZ$360 2-bedroom apt. Extra person NZ$36. Long-stay and off-peak rates. AE, DC, MC, V. .5km (¼ mile) from town center, opposite Millennium Hotel; on Shopper Bus route. **Amenities:** Breakfast restaurant; bar; bike rentals; nearby golf course; Jacuzzi. *In room:* TV/VCR, fridge, hair dryer, kitchen (in studio suites and apts), Wi-Fi.

The Heritage ★★ This is a big hotel with an intimate boutique feel. Just 14 years old, it's idyllically set in an alpine forest and offers traditional hotel-style rooms as well as apartment-style suites with kitchen and laundry facilities. Accommodations are in three wings, with uncovered walkways between them and the main lodge (umbrellas are provided). The staff is incredibly friendly, the property is quiet, and you'll quickly get that home-away-from-home feel. Twenty large, stylish new villas came on stream in 2003, and these are terrific value for families and long-stayers. The property is Green Globe benchmarked and has a Qualmark Enviro-Gold rating.

91 Fernhill Rd., Queenstown. ℂ **0800/368-888** in NZ, or 03/442-4988. Fax 03/442-4989. www.heritage hotels.co.nz. 213 units. NZ$235–NZ$285 deluxe; NZ$315–NZ$510 suite; from NZ$535–NZ$605 villa. NZ$80 surcharge on lake-view rooms. Long-stay and off-peak rates and special deals. AE, DC, MC, V. Drive through town and go up the hill at the Fernhill roundabout; 20-min. walk to town. **Amenities:** Restaurant; bar; babysitting; concierge; small exercise room; Jacuzzi; indoor/outdoor heated pool; room service; sauna; spa; Wi-Fi in reception and restaurant. *In room:* TV/DVD, fridge, hair dryer, high-speed Internet, kitchenette (in suites), minibar.

The Rees Hotel & Luxury Apartments ★★★ This brand-new, ecofriendly combination of hotel-style rooms and fabulous one- to four-bedroom apartments is terraced down the banks of Lake Wakatipu midway between the airport and the town. I fell in love with the sense of privacy, the staggering views, the first-class restaurant, and the exceptionally friendly service delivered here. You'll love the extra touches like the library of rare books, a wine cellar featuring New Zealand's best collection of Bordeaux wines, the gallery of original paintings, and an overall sense of being safely in the capable hands of someone who really knows how to look after you. Sixteen executive residences with access to a butler and chef are also planned.

377 Frankton Rd., Queenstown. ℂ **03/450-1100.** Fax 03/409-2852. www.therees.co.nz. 142 units. NZ$295–NZ$345 Rees room; NZ$405–NZ$455 1-bedroom apt; NZ$480–NZ$635 2-bedroom apt; NZ$655–NZ$855 3-bedroom apt; NZ$995 4-bedroom apt. Long-stay and off-peak rates and special deals. AE, DC, MC, V. **Amenities:** Restaurant (True South [Modern NZ]); bar (Bordeau wine lounge w/platter food); airport transfers NZ$15; babysitting; bike rentals; nearby golf courses; gymnasium; room service; sauna; Wi-Fi in reception. *In room:* TV/DVD, fridge, hair dryer, high-speed Internet, kitchen (in apts).

Scenic Suites Queenstown (Value) Bright, new, contemporary—with big living areas, good-size bathrooms, and lovely kitchens—the apartments here are roomy and they have proximity to town on their side. Great value, great views. The Aurum shares reception and gym facilities with its sister property, the adjacent A-Line Hotel, which also has good value, but older rooms.

27 Stanley St., Queenstown. ℂ **0800/696-963** in NZ, or 03/442-4718. Fax 03/442-4719. www.scenic group.co.nz. 84 units. NZ$315 superior room; NZ$383 1-bedroom suite; NZ$584 2-bedroom suite. Long-stay and off-peak rates. AE, DC, MC, V. Shopper Bus stops nearby. **Amenities:** Restaurant (Hillside Brasserie [Modern NZ]); bar; babysitting; nearby golf course; room service; Wi-Fi in reception. *In room:* TV, fridge, hair dryer, kitchen (suites only), minibar.

Inexpensive

Queenstown Top 10 Holiday Park Creekside, 54 Robins Rd. (ℂ **03/442-9447;** www. camp.co.nz), is definitely the Mercedes of campgrounds, situated in what was once a nursery—so there are trees and plants aplenty, plus room for 90 campervans, all with power outlets and water (solar heating) and waste hookups. There are also completely self-contained units and budget lodge rooms. They have a Green Globe Gold certificate and it's within a 5-minute walk of town. The charge is NZ$47 for powered sites; NZ$63 for lodge rooms; NZ$110 to NZ$200 for holiday units; NZ$120 for motel rooms; and NZ$183 for motel apartments. **YHA Queenstown Lakefront** ★, 88–90 Lake Esplanade, Queenstown (ℂ **0800/278-299** in NZ, or 03/442-8413; fax 03/442-6561; www. yha.co.nz), has 147 beds—dorm beds from NZ$30 and doubles from NZ$75.

Pinewood Lodge ★ (Value) Rob and Roz Greig have created one of the best budget options on the South Island. The series of little houses dots a tree-covered hillside, and brand-new complexes, housing a dorm area, kitchens, and lounges, rival many pricier operations. There's a real family feel about this place, the perfect choice if you want quality budget digs and a sociable atmosphere.

48 Hamilton Rd., Queenstown. ℂ **0800/746-3966** in NZ, or 03/442-8273. Fax 03/442-9470. www.pinewood. co.nz. 26 units. From NZ$28 dorm bed; NZ$60–NZ$90 double/twin; NZ$80–NZ$95 standard; NZ$100–NZ$120 en-suite unit. Extra person NZ$20. AE, DC, MC, V. **Amenities:** Children's playground; Jacuzzi. *In room:* TV (in some), no phone.

Just Out of Town
Very Expensive
Remarkables Lodge ★★ (Value) Brian Savage and Colleen Ryan sailed around the world chartering their yacht for 10 years, and then bought Remarkables Lodge, which they have infused with new life and style. With a big extension and a total makeover, this lovely property has been brought back from the brink and you'll love its quiet, understated, rural charm. Standouts here are the friendly staff, the fabulous meals, and some of the best beds I've slept in. They also offer some terrific exclusive tours—Cascade Hut,

for instance—that you won't want to miss. They have a Qualmark Enviro-Gold rating and are Green Globe benchmarked.

595 Kingston Rd., Queenstown. (C) **03/442-2720.** Fax 03/442-2730. www.remarkables.co.nz. 7 units. NZ$1,090–NZ$1,390. Long-stay and off-peak rates, special deals. Rates include breakfast, afternoon tea, predinner drinks and canapés, and 4-course dinner. AE, MC, V. Located 10 min. south of Queenstown, a few minutes after the entrance to Remarkables Ski Field. **Amenities:** Bar; free airport transfers; free bikes at nearby Jack's Point; nearby golf course (Jack's Point greens fees included in tariff); small fitness room; Jacuzzi; outdoor pool; room service; sauna; asphalt tennis court. *In room:* TV/DVD, fridge, hair dryer, free minibar, free Wi-Fi.

Near Arrowtown
Very Expensive
Millbrook Resort ★★★ (Value) I would like to live at Millbrook permanently! I love its minivillage feel and its dramatic location. I can't fault the quantity and quality of facilities here. It has luxury accommodations and international-caliber golf at unbeatable rates, plus the best giant bathtubs in the country. Opened in 1992, this award-winning resort is a destination in itself. The pricier cottages and villas are ideal for families or friends traveling together, while the generously sized village inn rooms offer the best value. Every comfort is attended to with 2m-wide (7-ft.) beds, fireplaces, and walk-in wardrobes. All this overlooks one of the best championship golf courses in the country. There are good walks between restaurants, spa facilities, and your room. One of the best-value stays you'll find.

Malaghans Rd., Arrowtown, Private Bag, Queenstown. (C) **0800/800-604** in NZ, or 03/441-7000. www.millbrook.co.nz. 170 units. NZ$215–NZ$435 village inn; NZ$315–NZ$535 villa suite; NZ$445–NZ$665 hotel villa; NZ$445–NZ$935 cottage; NZ$900–NZ$1,600 Fairway Home. Rates include breakfast. Special deals available. AE, DC, MC, V. 20 min. from Queenstown and 3 min. from Arrowtown. **Amenities:** 3 restaurants; bar; babysitting; bike rentals; children's programs; concierge; 18-hole golf course designed by Bob Charles, pro shop, driving and putting greens; extensive gym; 2 Jacuzzis and 1 Japanese hot pool; heated indoor pool; room service; saunas; day spa; 3 tennis courts (1 all-weather, 2 grass). *In room:* TV/DVD, fridge, hair dryer, high-speed Internet, kitchen (in some), minibar.

Expensive
White Shadows Country Inn ★★ (Moments) Set on 4 hectares (10 acres) of terraced gardens, lawns, and ponds, this romantic hideaway opened in 1999. Since then, hosts William Bailey and Michael Harris have impressed hundreds of international guests. Two guest suites are in a separate, secluded stone cottage with its own private courtyard. Rooms are plush and en-suite bathrooms have glass roofs. Wood beams, stone fireplaces, fine linens, and gourmet breakfasts are just a few of the reasons you should stay here.

58 Hunter Rd., RD1, Queenstown. (C) **03/442-0871.** Fax 03/442-0872. www.whiteshadows.co.nz. 2 units. NZ$695 suite. Long-stay rates. Rates include breakfast, predinner drinks, and hors d'oeuvres. AE, MC, V. Closed mid-Apr to mid-Oct each year. No children 12 and under. **Amenities:** Free airport transfers; free bikes; several nearby golf courses; outdoor Jacuzzi. *In room:* A/C, TV/DVD, fridge, hair dryer, free minibar, free Wi-Fi.

Moderate
Arrowtown House Boutique Hotel ★★ I have followed Steve and Jeanette Brough to their third highly successful lodging. Like the two previous, this one is quite delicious, and Steve and Jeanette are the best and friendliest hosts you'll find anywhere. They've traveled extensively themselves, and they've applied that experience to providing first-rate rooms (upstairs and down) in a modern building beside the main lodge. All have balconies or patios, and you'll never know anyone else is around. It's just a 5-minute walk into town. They're both superb cooks, too, so expect a breakfast to remember.

10 Caernarvon St., Arrowtown. ℂ **03/441-6008.** Fax 03/441-6015. www.arrowtownhouse.com. 5 units. NZ$445 standard suite; NZ$495 superior suite. Long-stay and off-peak rates, special deals. Rates include gourmet breakfast, predinner drinks, and canapés. MC, V. As you drive into Arrowtown, turn left into Caernarvon St. by the small church. **Amenities:** Bar; charged airport transfers; babysitting; nearby golf courses. *In room:* TV, fridge, hair dryer, minibar, free Wi-Fi.

Inexpensive

Arrowtown Lodge ★, 7 Anglesea St., Arrowtown (ℂ **0800/258-802** in NZ, or 03/442-1101; fax 03/442-1108; www.arrowtownlodge.co.nz), has four semidetached cottages that replicate something of Arrowtown's gold-rush heritage. You'll get charm and 21st-century comfort here for the very reasonable rate of NZ$150 to NZ$200.

In Nearby Glenorchy

There's a bit of everything in Glenorchy, from cheap backpackers to a very upmarket lodge. **Glenorchy Hotel** (ℂ **03/442-9902;** fax 03/442-9912; www.glenorchynz.com) is a classic Kiwi country-style hotel with nine rooms and backpacker accommodations; **Glenorchy Holiday Park & Backpackers** (ℂ **03/442-7171;** glenpark@queenstown.co.nz) has the usual campground facilities, plus lodge rooms and cabins; and gorgeous little **Kinloch Lodge** ★ (ℂ **03/442-4900;** www.kinlochlodge.co.nz), located between the Greenstone and Routeburn tracks, offers bunks and private rooms with shared facilities (NZ$80–NZ$195), in a setting you'll always remember. Drive 45 minutes out to Glenorchy, then take a 3-minute boat ride across the lake to the low-cost comforts of this outback gem.

Very Expensive

Blanket Bay ★★★   This is luxury at its most sublime. Opened in December 1999, this Small Luxury Hotels of the World member is set on sprawling grounds on the bush-clad fringes of Lake Wakatipu. At the heart of the lodge is a 9m-high (30-ft.) great room with a massive log fireplace and antique wooden floors. No expense has been spared in the construction of the spacious guest rooms. All beds are king-size, and all bathrooms have double sinks and separate showers and tubs. High-fidelity sound systems and private balconies are in every room. Designed as an exclusive haven, Blanket Bay promises a lot—and delivers. A big bonus here is the award-winning cuisine.

Blanket Bay, Glenorchy. ℂ **03/442-9442.** Fax 03/442-9441. www.blanketbay.com. 12 units. NZ$1,451 lodge room; NZ$2,150 suite; NZ$2,750 stateroom. Extra person NZ$345. Off-peak rates. Rates include breakfast, predinner cocktails, and dinner. AE, DC, MC, V. Closed June. Near Glenorchy, a 45-min. drive from Queenstown. Water and helipad access and limousine transport can be arranged. No children 13 and under. **Amenities:** 2 dining rooms; bar; airport transfers NZ$200 each way; free bikes; concierge; nearby golf course; well-equipped gym; Jacuzzi; heated outdoor pool; room service; 2 steam rooms; free watersports equipment. *In room:* A/C, TV/DVD, fridge, hair dryer, minibar, free Wi-Fi.

WHERE TO DINE

Queenstown is filled with an ever-changing array of good cafes and restaurants. The **Skyline Gondola Restaurant** (ℂ **03/441-0101**) is as much an experience as a meal. Enjoy lavish lunch and evening buffets accompanied by spectacular views. A buffet dinner including gondola ride is NZ$72 and lunch is NZ$47. The restaurant is huge and tour groups are seated in a separate area. Bookings are essential.

In Queenstown

Expensive

Boardwalk Seafood Restaurant ★ SEAFOOD   After 15 years in operation, but now with a new owner, this upstairs spot has a new lease on life. It's always been recognized for its excellent seafood—in partnership with New Zealand beef and lamb—and

ⓘ Finds Winning Wines

Gantley's Restaurant, 172 Arthur's Point Rd., Arthur's Point (ⓒ **03/442-8999**), has an extensive wine list with over 250 selections, showcasing some of the most outstanding wines produced in New Zealand. One of only a few New Zealand restaurants to win an Award of Excellence from *Wine Spectator* magazine for "having one of the most outstanding restaurant wine lists in the world," Gantley's is favored for its romantic interior and superior wine selections. Main courses range from NZ$35 to NZ$45, and they're open daily from 6pm; they offer courtesy transport from Queenstown.

that hasn't changed. The big seafood platters are always popular; daily fish specials are innovatively presented; and the roasted rack of lamb wins fans every time. Despite the competition from new fine-dining players, award-winning Boardwalk is always mentioned in top recommendations.

Steamer Wharf, Beach St. ⓒ **03/442-5630.** www.boardwalk.net.nz. Reservations recommended. Main courses NZ$40. AE, DC, MC, V. Daily 6pm–late.

Botswana Butchery ★★ CONTEMPORARY NEW ZEALAND/EUROPEAN Chef Leungo Lippe's opulent little restaurant on the waterfront is Queenstown's newest upmarket eatery. It's a meat-eater's heaven where they specialize in fine beef cuts, wild game, and organic foods. All meat cuts are aged and are served either wood-grilled or pan-seared to your liking. My only gripe about the place is that in addition to expensive plates, they charge extra for even a flicker of a green vegetable—a trick I find pretentious in the extreme.

Marine Parade. ⓒ **03/442-6994.** www.botswanabutchery.co.nz. Reservations recommended. Main courses NZ$34–NZ$80, vegetables NZ$6–NZ$15 extra. AE, DC, MC, V. Daily noon–late.

Eichardt's House Bar ★★★ ⓘ Finds CONTEMPORARY NEW ZEALAND   For a sublime lunch experience (or just coffee and cake), treat yourself to the oh-so-classy environs of Eichardt's House Bar, in the private hotel building on the ground floor. Just five tables add to the air of exclusivity, so be in quick. New Zealand crab and scallop cake, wild pork pies, Moroccan chicken, and delicious vegetarian dishes have all been featured on this top menu. Small, but big on atmosphere, it's a must. It's also a great cocktail spot at night, before or after dinner.

Ground Floor, Eichardt's Private Hotel, Marine Parade. ⓒ **03/442-0450.** www.eichardtshotel.co.nz. Reservations recommended. Main courses NZ$26–NZ$34. AE, DC, MC, V. Lunch daily noon–2pm. Bar daily 11am–11pm.

True South ★★ CONTEMPORARY EUROPEAN   I like a restaurant that offers you lots of choices, and here at True South you can take your pick from a truly memorable 10-course degustation menu, two-or three-course set menus, or a la carte, all of which include delectable treats like poached blue cod with fennel, gnocchi, and ratatouille; or wild venison braised and roasted with red cabbage and chocolate. It's an adventurous menu and visually stunning, and I for one think that "food as theater" is a very important component of dining out.

The Rees Hotel, 377 Frankton Rd. ⓒ **03/450-1100.** www.therees.co.nz. Reservations essential. Main courses NZ$32–NZ$38; 10-course degustation menu NZ$85; 2-course set menu NZ$45; 3-course set menu NZ$55. AE, DC, MC, V. Daily 6pm–late.

(Finds) **Treasure Hunt**

Every city has them—those luscious little culinary secrets that locals like to keep for themselves. I won't win friends in Queenstown for this, but I'm going to tell you about the **Bunker** ★★★, Cow Lane (📞 **03/441-8030;** www.thebunker.co.nz). And don't think that just because I've given you the address, you're going to be able to find it easily. It hides behind a very unassuming door and just assumes that people who are hungry and passionate enough will find it. And once you do unearth it, you won't regret the hunt. It's a tiny restaurant with a huge reputation for classy haute cuisine, an intimate atmosphere, and an impressive collection of single malt whiskeys. Venison, lamb, scampi, quail, and duck all take their place on an innovative menu that most definitely will make a hole in your wallet. It's open from 5pm until 5am, by which time you'll probably be bankrupt but hugely satisfied. Reservations are essential, and main courses range from NZ$44 to NZ$50.

Moderate

Bella Cucina ★★ ITALIAN COUNTRY   This little gem was opened by the people who brought us Wai Waterfront (see below), and it's quickly established itself as a local favorite. They have great wood-fired pizzas, and pasta is made on-site each day. Factor in seafood and slow-cooked meat dishes—all at very affordable prices—and you have a little winner. The menu changes every day, based on available fresh ingredients, and the mood is relaxed and intimate.

6 Brecon St. 📞 **03/442-6762.** www.bellacucina.co.nz. Reservations recommended. Main courses NZ$18–NZ$31. AE, DC, MC, V. Daily 11am–11pm.

The Cow ★ PIZZERIA   A big fire roars in this dark little den of delicious, great-value tastes. It's all wood, moody, and very, very popular. It's less authentically Italian than Bella Cucina, but it invariably has a great atmosphere. If your budget has taken a beating, this is a great place to fill up on treats like pepperoni pizza, Bolognese with fresh green salad, or homemade soups and crusty bread. It's a good family stop, too.

Cow Lane. 📞 **03/442-8588.** www.goodbars.co.nz. No reservations. Main courses NZ$18–NZ$32. AE, MC, V. Daily noon–late.

Fishbone Bar & Grill ★★ SEAFOOD   If I could have a restaurant in my backyard, it would be this one. It's wacky and colorful, the decorative fish-filled interior is a joy, and the seafood meals rate among the best I've had. Fresh fish is sourced daily and the South Island salmon smoked over Canadian sycamore wood chips is an eternal favorite. The blue cod dishes are also reliably good; and for a well-priced fill-up, you can't pass up their seafood chowder.

7 Beach St. 📞 **03/442-6768.** Reservations recommended. Main courses NZ$20–NZ$32. AE, DC, MC, V. Daily 5pm–late.

Tatler ★ INTERNATIONAL   This is one of the justifiably favored restaurants in Queenstown. The dark-timbered interior sets up an instant atmosphere and meals are consistently well flavored and tasty. I can't always say the same about the service—like most New Zealand restaurants, it has peaks and troughs—but I always enjoy a meal here. Whether it's roasted duck with *boniato rosti* and cherry glaze, Moroccan spiced lamb filet, or spinach cannelloni, Tatler is what I call a sure thing. I go there every time I'm in Queenstown.

5 The Mall. ℂ **03/442-8372.** www.tatler.co.nz. Reservations recommended for dinner. Main courses NZ$28–NZ$38. AE, MC, V. Daily 10am–late.

Wai Waterfront Restaurant ★ MODERN NEW ZEALAND Wai (Maori for "water") was a winner from the beginning. Its heavy focus on fresh seafood and oysters is well complemented by the water lapping directly outside its doors, and summer outdoor tables give it a festive feel. If you like fresh oysters, you'll be in seventh heaven (when they're in season, that is), and you should try them with lime sorbet and vodka, or baked in an herb Parmesan crust. Beyond that, venison, beef, lamb, duck, and ostrich also feature on an exciting menu; or you can treat yourself to the nine-course degustation menu.

Steamer Wharf, Beach St. ℂ **03/442-5969.** www.wai.net.nz. Reservations required, especially for a waterfront table. Main courses NZ$38–NZ$42; NZ$135 degustation menu. AE, DC, MC, V. Daily noon–late.

Inexpensive

Joe's Garage ★ (Finds) CAFE Although trendily hard to find, you *must* seek out Joe's because in my mind, it is the best coffee provider in QT. It's a case of American roadie-style cafe meeting Queenstown hip—and strangely, it works. It's virtually unadorned but for the buzzy atmosphere and chatty locals. Sit up at the counter while you wait for a strong espresso, bacon and bun, panini, or burger. This is my favorite Queenstown cafe; I just can't keep away from it. Look out for their Arrowtown cafe on Arrow Lane—it's just as good.

Searle Lane. ℂ **03/442-5282.** Most menu items under NZ$20. AE, MC, V. Daily 7am–5pm.

Vesta (Finds) CAFE For a truly unique coffee experience mixed with history, contemporary design, and quirky retail opportunity, head for Vesta. This tiny espresso bar (with snacks and light meals) is tucked into the back of Queenstown's oldest house (1864), and modern art and design appear against a backdrop of the original, peeling 1800s floral wallpapers. Don't miss it and be prepared to loosen your wallet on goodies to take home.

Williams Cottage, Marine Parade. ℂ **03/442-5687.** Menu items NZ$5–NZ$20. AE, MC, V. Daily 9am–5pm.

Vudu Café ★ CAFE Vudu Café is one that has endured for years, so it must be doing something right. I know the divine almond croissant I had there recently certainly guaranteed a return visit for me. It's small and it can be hard to get a seat (another good sign), but keep persisting, because they make excellent coffee and have delicious cabinet food. It always has a buzzy atmosphere and they offer organic options.

23 Beach St. ℂ **03/442-5357.** Menu items NZ$5–NZ$20. AE, MC, V. Daily 8am–late.

(Finds) **Market Treats**

The best place for delicious treats, picnic food, and fabulous tastes to take home is **Mediterranean Market** ★★★, 53 Robins Rd., Queenstown (ℂ **03/442-4161;** www.mediterranean.co.nz). Head out on Gorge Road, turn down the hill beside the supermarket, and then hard left into the lower carpark. It's home to Squisito Café, and if you come out empty-handed, I'll be surprised. Open Monday to Saturday 8am to 6:30pm, Sunday 10am to 6pm.

> **Tips** **For Chocolate Lovers**
>
> **Patagonia Chocolates** ★★★, Lakeside, 50 Beach St., Queenstown (✆ **03/442-9066**), and Ramshaw Lane, Arrowtown (✆ **03/409-8584**); www.patagonia chocolates.com), are must-stop/must-eat destinations. They're open daily from 8am to 10pm.

In Nearby Arrowtown

Amisfield Winery & Bistro ★★★ MODERN NEW ZEALAND   I've never heard a bad word about Amisfield Bistro. It's been *the* lunch spot of choice ever since it opened a few years ago. Just about as classy—and somewhat bigger—than Eichardt's, it features a daily changing menu based on local, fresh, and organic ingredients. Corn-fed chicken with garlic butter and watercress; Serrano ham, steamed asparagus and poached egg; or seared salmon with cumin, couscous, tomato, and yogurt are just some of the temptations on offer. And don't pass up their spectacular wine-tasting room.

10 Lake Hayes Rd. (btw. Queenstown and Arrowtown). ✆ **03/442-0556.** www.amisfield.co.nz. Reservations recommended. Main courses NZ$18–NZ$30. AE, DC, MC, V. Tues–Fri 11:30am–8pm; Sat–Sun 9am–8pm.

Pesto ⓥ **Value** ITALIAN/PIZZA   Baby sister to Saffron, Pesto offers a copper-clad casual setting in which to bite into some of the most succulent pizzas in this part of the world. Pasta with anchovies, tomato, Italian sausage, spinach, and lemon chili oil will also tempt. All ages gather in the sunny courtyard and the super-cool interior.

18 Buckingham St. ✆ **03/442-0885.** Reservations recommended. NZ$18–NZ$30. AE, DC, MC, V. Daily 5pm–late.

Postmaster's House ★★ CONTEMPORARY NEW ZEALAND/EUROPEAN This is another feather in Arrowtown's rather surprising culinary cap. Who would have expected this tiny village to dish up another top eatery after Saffron? Come here to enjoy a restored historic building, an elegant interior, and delicious meals that might include pan-roasted white veal; lamb rack; prime beef-eye filet with béarnaise, merlot, and mushroom jus; or a simple-yet-delicious crispy roast duck salad with fennel. Sink back in your leather chair with a glass of the region's best wine and resign yourself to indulgence.

Buckingham St., Arrowtown. ✆ **03/442-0991.** Reservations essential. Main courses NZ$28–NZ$38. AE, DC, MC, V. Daily 11:30am–late.

Saffron ★★★ **Finds** MODERN NEW ZEALAND   When you're named in *Condé Nast Traveler*'s list of the 100 Best Tables in the World (2001), you've got a lot to live up to, but Saffron seems to have managed the stress rather well. It's currently considered one of the most serious fine-food places in the region. Book ahead, because people are coming from miles around to enjoy Bollinger by the fireside before meals such as Thai duck and lemon-grass curry with two rices.

18 Buckingham St. ✆ **03/442-0131.** www.saffronrestaurant.co.nz. Reservations required. Main courses NZ$29–NZ$40. AE, DC, MC, V. Daily 11am–late.

In Nearby Glenorchy

Glenorchy is a bit lean on dining options, but you won't starve. **Glenorchy Hotel** (✆ **03/442-9902**) has a terrace cafe and restaurant with a la carte, stone grill, and bistro dining; and **Glenorchy Café** (✆ **03/442-9958**) can fill the gaps with snacks and light

meals in a casual atmosphere. **Kinloch Lodge** ★ (© **03/442-4900**) has the best menu,
with the likes of Mediterranean baked lamb, seared grouper, or homemade meatballs.

QUEENSTOWN AFTER DARK
Midwinter in Queenstown is a night owl's paradise. There's plenty happening all year, of
course, but once the town fills up with international visitors, anything can, and often
does, happen.

Queenstown now has two casinos. **SKYCITY Queenstown Casino,** 16–24 Beach St.
(© **03/441-0400;** www.skycityqueenstown.co.nz), has over 80 gaming machines and
the usual table games such as roulette, blackjack, and baccarat. Also here are Wild Thyme
Bar & Restaurant and live entertainment on Friday and Saturday nights. It's open daily
from noon to 4am and they have a free courtesy shuttle. **Lasseters Wharf Casino,**
Steamer Wharf (© **03/441-1495;** www.lasseterswharfcasino.co.nz), is a boutique operation with much the same on offer in the way of games. It's open daily from 11am to 3am.
In both cases, you must be 20 and over and smartly dressed to enter.

Those with wild times on their mind head for **Chico's Restaurant & Bar,** on The
Mall (© **03/442-8439**). It has great food, live entertainment, and dancing from
10:30pm until late. The **Edge Niteclub,** Camp and Man streets (© **03/442-4144**), and
the **World,** Shotover Street (© **03/442-6757**), are part of the recognized backpacker
scene. **Shooters Bar,** 10 Brecon St. (© **03/442-4144**), is dominated by pool tables and
a football crowd. The **Dux de Lux** ★, 14 Church St. (© **03/442-9688**), draws big
crowds with its specialty beers and great atmosphere, and next door is the ever-popular
Monty's Bar ★★, 12 Church St. (© **03/441-1081**), which offers a full range of Mon-
tieth's beers. Not far away, the **Pig & Whistle Pub** ★, 19 Ballarat St. (© **03/442-9055**),
has had a serious makeover and, as an English-themed pub, is doing a roaring trade. They
also have excellent pub meals at reasonable prices.

You can freeze your tail off in the name of a good time at **Minus 5,** Steamer Wharf
(© **03/442-6050**), in the company of hand-sculpted ice and their famous vodka cocktails.

Those of you who like a sense of discovery in your nightlife may want to hunt for "the
B bars"—a cluster of nightspots all beginning with the letter B. The **Bunker** ★★★,
Cow Lane (© **03/441-8030**), is favored by a 20s-to-40s crowd and plays on no advertising, no signs, and the fact that it's hard to find. (It will also make a handsome hole in
your wallet.) Equally obscure is **Bardeaux** ★★, Eureka Arcade, off The Mall or Searle
Lane (© **03/442-8284**), a sophisticated late-night wine and cocktail bar, with a huge
range of local pinot noir and champagne. **Barup,** next to Bardeaux and upstairs from
Minibar (© **03/442-7707**), is an exclusive Swiss chalet–type of wine and cocktail bar
where locals of mixed ages head for a good time. **Barmuda,** Searle Lane (© **03/442-
7300**), has a big cocktail list and a gorgeous private lounge to enjoy it in. **MiniBar** ★★,
Eureka Lane (© **03/441-3212**), is, as the name suggests, tiny, but it has over 100
premium beers and a whole lot of atmosphere. **Buffalo Club,** 8 Brecon St. (© **03/442-
4144**), is all about DJs, live music, and late nights.

It's all class and cocktails at **Eichardt's House Bar** ★★★, Marine Parade (© **03/441-
0442**), which is one of most people's favorites—again, expensive but, like owning a Louis
Vuitton suitcase, it must be done.

EN ROUTE TO TE ANAU
Te Anau is a 172km (107-mile) drive from Queenstown on excellent roads. Follow State
Highway 6 to Kingston at the south end of Lake Wakatipu, where you'll have the option of
taking a ride on the historic **Kingston Flyer** (© **03/248-8848;** www.kingstonflyer.co.nz), a

pre-1930s passenger train pulled by steam engines. The train departs daily at 10:15am and 3:45pm from October through April. The round-trip takes 1½ hours and costs NZ$45 for adults, NZ$23 for children ages 5 to 14. The train is owned and operated (on track set in 1878) by TranzRail.

Continue on State Highway 6 through the tiny township of **Athol** and then turn west onto State Highway 94 over the summit of **Gorge Hill,** along the **Mararoa River,** and through sheep and cattle country to **Te Anau,** nestled beside the largest lake on the South Island.

4 TE ANAU ★★

172km (107 miles) SW of Queenstown; 116km (72 miles) S of Milford Sound; 157km (97 miles) NW of Invercargill

Te Anau is the hub of Fiordland National Park, a magnificent 1.2-million-hectare (3-million-acre) World Heritage Site filled with scenic wonders, serenity, mystery, and some of the best walking tracks in the world. The little resort township is built around the foreshore of Lake Te Anau, the largest of the South Island lakes. It has a permanent population of about 4,000, which swells to over 10,000 in summer. If you're coming to explore Fiordland's waterfalls, virgin forests, mountains, rivers, and lonely fiords, this is the place to base yourself.

Lake Te Anau is a wonder in itself. Its eastern shoreline, where the township is located, is virtually treeless, with about 76 centimeters (30 in.) of annual rainfall, while its western banks are covered in dense forest nurtured by more than 254 centimeters (100 in.) of rain each year. What attracts visitors to New Zealand's second-largest lake are the opportunity for watersports and the proximity to Milford Sound, 116km (72 miles) away. The sound, which is actually a fiord, reaches 23km (14 miles) in from the Tasman Sea, flanked by sheer granite peaks and traced by playful waterfalls. Its waters and surrounding land have been kept in as nearly a primeval state as humans could possibly manage without leaving them totally untouched. In fine weather or pouring rain, Milford Sound exudes a powerful sense of nature's pristine harmony and beauty.

Milford Sound may be the most famous and accessible of the fiords, but Doubtful Sound is the deepest and, according to some, the most beautiful. Even farther south, Dusky Sound may well qualify as the most remote and mysterious of the famous trio.

Fittingly, as one of the most pristine regions in New Zealand, Destination Fiordland (with Venture Southland), is one of the six regions participating in the government initiative, the Environmentally Sustainable Tourism project. As in the other five participating regions, the Southland/Fiordland project encourages tourism operators to focus on energy efficiency, waste reduction, recycling, water quality, and conservation. You can check charter members at www.southlandnz.com or www.fiordland.org.nz.

ESSENTIALS

GETTING THERE   By Plane   Air services to Te Anau and Fiordland are provided by **Air Fiordland Ltd.** (© **0800/107-505** in NZ, or 03/249-6720; fax 03/249-6721; www.airfiordland.com). Charter flights are also available.

By Coach (Bus)   Daily coach service runs between Te Anau and Christchurch, Dunedin, and Invercargill via **InterCity** (© **09/623-1503**). Daily service also runs to Te Anau

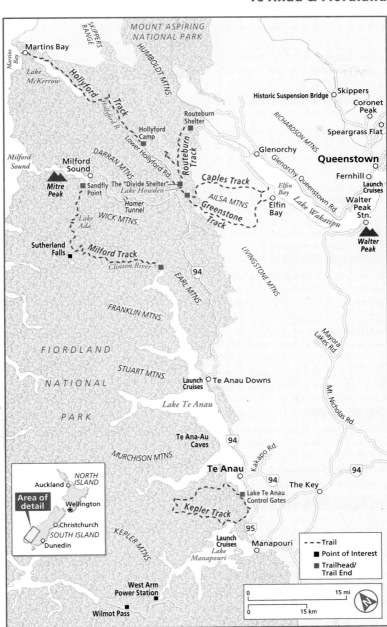

MOUNT ASPIRING
NATIONAL PARK

SKIPPERS RANGE

Martins Bay

Martins Bay

Lake McKerrow

Hollyford Track

Hollyford R.

HUMBOLDT MTNS.

Historic Suspension Bridge

Skippers

Coronet Peak

Speargrass Flat

RICHARDSON MTNS.

Hollyford Camp

Routeburn Shelter

Lower Hollyford Rd.

Routeburn Track

Glenorchy

Glenorchy Queenstown Rd.

Queenstown

Fernhill

DARRAN MTNS.

Milford Sound

Milford Sound

Mitre Peak

Sandfly Point

The "Divide Shelter"

Lake Howden

Caples Track

AILSA MTNS.

Elfin Bay

Launch Cruises

Walter Peak Stn.

Homer Tunnel

Greenstone Track

Elfin Bay

Lake Wakatipu

WICK MTNS.

Lake Ada

Walter Peak

Sutherland Falls

Milford Track

Clinton River

EARL MTNS.

94

LIVINGSTONE MTNS.

FRANKLIN MTNS.

FIORDLAND

STUART MTNS.

Mayora Lakes Rd.

NATIONAL

Launch Cruises

Te Anau Downs

Mt. Nicholas Rd.

PARK

Lake Te Anau

MURCHISON MTNS.

Te Ana-Au Caves

94

Te Anau

94

Kakapo Rd.

94

The Key

NORTH ISLAND

Auckland

Area of detail

Wellington

Lake Te Anau Control Gates

Christchurch

SOUTH ISLAND

Dunedin

Kepler Track

95

KEPLER MTNS.

Launch Cruises

Lake Manapouri

Manapouri

West Arm Power Station

Wilmot Pass

- - - Trail
■ Point of Interest
■ Trailhead/ Trail End

0 _____ 15 mi

0 _____ 15 km

N

> **(Tips) Natural Mystery**
>
> For an excellent cinematic introduction to the greater Fiordland region—much of which you will never lay eyes on otherwise—make sure you see **Ata Whenua-Shadowland** ★★★, a stunning and unforgettable cinematic journey. Call **Fiordland Cinema,** The Lane, Te Anau (𝄐 **03/249-8812;** www.fiordlandcinema.co.nz), for session times. It costs NZ$10.

and Milford Sound from Queenstown. And numerous shuttle bus companies make daily trips, too. Information is available at the visitor centers in Queenstown, Invercargill, and Te Anau.

By Car   From Queenstown, take State Highway 6, then State Highway 94 (see "En Route to Te Anau," above, for details).

ORIENTATION   Te Anau's main street is State Highway 94, called Milford Road within the township, with the post office, restaurants, grocery stores, and most shops. The majority of hotels and motels are on Lakefront Drive, which stretches attractively around the lake. The township is tiny and very easy to negotiate on foot or by car.

VISITOR INFORMATION   The **Fiordland i-SITE Visitor Centre,** Lakefront Drive, Te Anau (𝄐 **03/249-8900;** fax 03/249-7022; fiordland-isite@realjourneys.co.nz), sits at the lake end of Milford Road. It shares the same office as **Real Journeys** (𝄐 **0800/656-501** in NZ, or 03/249-7416; www.realjourneys.co.nz). Hours are daily from 8:30am to 6pm in summer and 8:30am to 4:30pm in winter. The **Fiordland National Park Visitor Centre,** Lakefront Drive, Te Anau (𝄐 **03/249-7924;** fax 03/249-8515; www.doc.govt. nz), is a must for anyone contemplating doing either short walks around Te Anau or the well-known multiday tramps—Hollyford, Routeburn, Milford, Kepler, and Caples. It's open daily in summer from 8:30am to 6pm, and in winter until 4:30pm. It operates 8:30am to 1pm on December 25. For more information, go to www.fiordland.org.nz or www.fiordlandnz.com.

SPECIAL EVENTS   The **DOC Fiordland Summer Nature Programme** (𝄐 **03/249-7921**) presents a wide range of adventures in the national park during the summer months, and encourages people to explore some of the park's lesser known beauties. Details are available from the National Park Visitor Centre. The **Kepler Challenge** and the **Luxmore Grunt** (𝄐 **03/249-9596;** www.keplerchallenge.co.nz) are tough international ultra-marathon races held in December each year.

EXPLORING TE ANAU & THE SOUNDS

Milford and Doubtful sounds are the primary draws of this area, and in Te Anau you'll discover a number of options for exploring one or both. You can drive, fly, or take a coach to Milford Sound from Te Anau (see "Milford Sound" below), and you can fly over or take a scenic cruise through Doubtful Sound.

You'll quickly discover that people in Te Anau are reluctant to recommend one sound or one excursion above another, so explore the choices carefully. Consider your available time and the amount of money you want to spend. My advice would be to drive to Milford and, if you can, overnight on one of the boats; then, if you're still keen to see Doubtful and Dusky sounds, take the 40-minute flight. Not only does this take just a fraction of the cruise time, but you also get a thrilling perspective of otherwise inaccessible areas. Either way, don't try to see everything in 1 day. It is definitely worth staying in this area for 2 to 3 days if you can.

Air Fiordland, Manapouri Airport, Te Anau (✆ **0800/107-505** in NZ, or 03/249-6720; www.airfiordland.com), has several Milford Sound flight packages, some combining cruise options, plus an excellent 40-minute flight over Doubtful Sound.

Southern Lakes Helicopters, Lakefront Drive (✆ **03/249-7167;** www.southernlakes helicopters.co.nz), has a 50-minute flight over Doubtful Sound that passes soaring peaks and waterfalls. The highlight is the flight into Campbell's Kingdom, which is accessible only by helicopter. Call for prices of all their flights. **Fiordland Helicopters,** Te Anau Airport (✆ **03/249-7575;** www.fiordlandhelicopters.co.nz), offers trips that range from 15 minutes to 1½ hours. It's a little cheaper than Southern Lakes, but it's based farther out of town.

If a full-day bus tour (from Te Anau) is more your style, join the "Discover Milford Sound" tour run by **Great Sights** (✆ **0800/744-487** in NZ; www.greatsights.co.nz). It runs daily, departing 10:15am from Te Anau Travel Centre and returns at 5:15pm. It costs NZ$145 for adults and NZ$73 for children ages 5 to 14. You can include lunch for an extra NZ$30 per person. Another good option is the popular **Milford Sound Barbecue Bus** ★★ (✆ **0800/421-045;** www.milford.net.nz), which departs from either Queenstown or Te Anau. It's a smaller group tour and includes a classic barbecue lunch in spectacular Hollyford Valley rather than on the cruise boats. It links with the 2pm Milford Sound cruise, which is the off-peak and therefore less crowded time; and if you like you can fly back to Queenstown.

Doubtful Sound ★★★

Doubtful Sound makes an idyllic day excursion from Lake Manapouri. At 21m (69 ft.), it's the deepest of the fiords. Filled with ancient rainforest, cascading waterfalls, towering peaks, and abundant wildlife, it's an unforgettable experience. An air of complete silence, broken only by birdcall, adds to the mystery.

Doubtful Sound is 10 times bigger than Milford, and although it can't boast Mitre Peak, its still waters mirror 1,200m (3,900-ft.) **Commander Peak.** Another difference between the two sounds is that you always know Milford is close to civilization because of the buzz of aircraft going to and from the airstrip and the multitude of buses that make their way there on a daily basis. Doubtful is much more remote.

There's no way to get to Doubtful Sound on your own. Real Journeys (see "Visitor Information," above) transports visitors from Manapouri, then takes a launch trip to the

---

ⓘ Tips **A Sound Difference**

Real Journey's Doubtful Sound cruise has English-only commentary and two styles of picnic lunches available. It's a longer cruise than the Milford Sound option and much more remote. You'll see far fewer people at Doubtful—and given that there are around 100 buses a day going into Milford, that says a lot. Milford Sound is more dramatic and awe-inspiring, but Doubtful is a lot more untouched and remote. You're also far more likely to see wildlife at Doubtful—not that the dolphins are on the payroll!

West Arm, followed by a 20km (12-mile) coach trip to Deep Cove in Doubtful Sound. The coach takes you up and over Wilmot Pass, 662m (2,171 ft.) above sea level, stopping on the way to visit **Manapouri Power Station,** where you spiral 225 eerie meters (750 ft.) downward to view the seven immense underground turbines. A second launch then takes you out into the sound, and if you're lucky, you'll spot the resident pod of 60 or more dolphins, fur seals, and rare crested penguins. You'll get close enough to waterfalls to feel the spray, and you'll be able to savor total silence when the captain shuts off the engine.

Real Journey's Doubtful Sound day excursions use a modern, purpose-built catamaran, *Patea Explorer.* It carries 150 passengers over two decks and departs daily from Manapouri with connecting coaches from Queenstown or Te Anau. Visitors can self-drive from Queenstown in 2½ hours and from Te Anau in 40 minutes. Reservations are essential. From Manapouri, the Wilderness trip costs NZ$275 for adults, NZ$60 for children ages 5 to 14. From Te Anau, add about NZ$20, and about NZ$70 from Queenstown. Preordered picnic lunches start at NZ$15. From October to May, Real Journeys offers overnight cruises on the *Fiordland Navigator.* Prices vary depending on the season, starting at NZ$473 for an off-peak cruise from Manapouri; children's fares start at NZ$237.

The Milford Track & Other Walks

Most dedicated trampers consider the famous **Milford Track** ★★★ among the finest anywhere in the world. Four days are required to walk the 54km (33 miles) from Glad Jetty at Lake Te Anau's northern end to Sandfly Point on the western bank of Milford Sound. If you're short on time, you could join the **Real Journeys Milford Track Day Walk** (✆ **0800/656-501;** www.realjourneys.co.nz), which includes a Lake Te Anau cruise, coach transfers, lunch, and a nature guide. The minimum age is 10 years and the excursion will cost NZ$190 for adults and NZ$124 for children. Other popular walks in this area are the **Hollyford Valley,** the **Routeburn,** and the **Kepler.** For more information, see "Tramping" in chapter 5.

Other Outdoor Pursuits

FISHING   Fiordland offers unsurpassed opportunities for wilderness trophy trout fishing. The best fishing is in the Eglinton Valley. Ian Murray of **Fish 'n' Trips** (✆ **03/249-7656;** www.fiordland-flyfishing.co.nz) clearly has a sense of humor. If you want a guided

---

⒨ Moments   All A-Glow

The **Te Anau Glowworm Caves** ★★ excursion on Lake Te Anau is operated by **Real Journeys,** Lakefront Drive, Te Anau (✆ **0800/656-501** in NZ, or 03/249-7416; www.realjourneys.co.nz). This adventure runs year-round and includes an underground boat ride into the glowworm grotto. The geologically young caves (only about 15,000 years old) have 200m (660 ft.) of passages, which are still being formed by water cascading down the cave tiers at a rate of 55,000 gallons per minute. On the second level of the water bed, you'll see the glowworm grotto. A major upgrade of the caves excursion was completed in October 2006. This includes a new multimillion-dollar catamaran for accessing the caves across Lake Te Anau. If you want to make the most of the 15km (10-mile) scenic lake cruise, take the daylight option (NZ$63 for adults, NZ$20 for children ages 5–14). Alternatively, evening options provide an interesting nocturnal experience from October to April.

wilderness fishing experience, call him. He charges NZ$300 for a half-day trip and NZ$550 for a full day. **Fiordland Guides** ★★, 472 Te Anau-Milford Hwy. (✆ **03/249-7832;** www.fiordlandguides.co.nz), can take you on a terrific fishing trip for NZ$780 per day for two people.

HORSEBACK RIDING   Pay NZ$80 for a horse trek through beautiful landscapes with **High Ride Adventures,** 865 Wilderness Rd. (✆ **03/249-8591;** www.highride.co.nz). They pick up tours at 9:30am and 2pm, and in summer at 6pm; and they have a variety of horses to suit all levels of experience.

KAYAKING   **Fiordland Wilderness Experiences,** 66 Quintin Dr. (✆ **03/249-7700;** www.fiordlandseakayak.co.nz), offers guided sea-kayaking options ranging in length from 1 to 6 days. It goes to Milford, Dusky, and Doubtful sounds and Lake Manapouri. See the section on "Milford Sound," below, for further kayaking options.

WHERE TO STAY

Reserve well ahead for visits between Christmas and February. Once the peak season is over, you can expect to get some incredibly good deals. There are numerous motel complexes along the waterfront, and backpackers are well served in Te Anau. One of the nicest is **Te Anau Backpackers Lodge,** 48 Lakefront Dr. (✆ **0800/200-074** in NZ, or 03/249-7713; www.teanaubackpackers.co.nz), where dorm beds are from NZ$25 to NZ$28 and doubles cost NZ$75 to NZ$85.

Very Expensive

Fiordland Lodge ★★★   Ron and Robynne Peacock are responsible for this gem of a rural lodge that sits on a tussock-covered ridge overlooking Lake Te Anau. Think stylish treehouse and you won't be far wrong. Wood is the focus, and although the rooms are simply dressed, I'll be amazed if you don't come away impressed. I especially love the creative way they use logs to support the bathroom basins. Take one of the smart lodge rooms for in-house comforts, or opt for the privacy and romance of one of the two quaintest little log cabins. The lodge participates in recycling and energy conservation activities.

472 Te Anau-Milford Hwy., Te Anau. ✆ **03/249-7832.** Fax 03/249-7449. www.fiordlandlodge.co.nz. 12 units. NZ$880 lodge room; NZ$1,800 executive suite; NZ$680 log cabin. Off-peak rates. Rates include breakfast and dinner. AE, DC, MC, V. 5km (3 miles) from Te Anau. Turn right onto no. 472; when road forks into 3, take the center driveway and follow to top. **Amenities:** Restaurant; bar; airport transfers by arrangement; nearby golf course. *In room:* TV/DVD, fridge, hair dryer, Wi-Fi.

Moderate

Blue Ridge Bed and Breakfast ★★, 13–15 Melland Place (✆ **03/249-7740;** fax 03/249-7340; www.blueridge.co.nz), has four sunny rooms with mountain views, en-suite bathrooms, big beds, and kitchenettes. Breakfast is included for the very reasonable tariff of NZ$250 to NZ$275. The old-world charms of **Te Anau Lodge** ★★, 52 Howden St. (✆ **03/249-7477;** www.teanaulodge.com), are also worthy of your attention. Originally a convent, this grand old building has been relocated to a new garden and restored to offer eight rooms—seven with en-suite bathrooms, for NZ$225 to NZ$350. I'd also like to recommend a brand-new spot, **Dock Bay Lodge** ★★, 192 William Stephen Rd., Te Anau (✆ **03/249-7709;** www.dockbaylodge.co.nz), which has five big, modern suites right beside Te Anau Golf Course, for NZ$350 to NZ$550—definitely the nicest rooms in Te Anau township.

The dining scene is slowly improving, but there's still room for innovation and snappier service. Just remember that if you come here out of the main tourist season, several eateries close for the winter months. Apart from the listings below, try **La Toscana** ★, 108 Town Centre (© **03/249-7756**), one of the town's better culinary bets. It's open from 5:30pm.

The Fat Duck Café & Restaurant ★ (Kids) CAFE/NEW ZEALAND   The terms laid-back, casual, and friendly were invented for this place. They cater to everyone, including the kids, who can choose from their own kids'-size menu. Don't expect anything fancy, but big servings of blue cod, beef filet, or salmon will certainly fortify you after a hard day in the national parks. You can opt for venison burgers, calamari, or minted lamb sausages if you'd rather. They also serve good breakfasts.

124 Town Centre, Te Anau. © **03/249-8480.** Main courses NZ$17–NZ$34. AE, DC, MC, V. Daily 8am–late.

Recliff Café ★★ NEW ZEALAND/INTERNATIONAL   Step into a cute old cottage refitted with a contemporary bar and moody little dining rooms. The menu here is fresh and inviting, incorporating all food types in a healthy, modern way. You'll find it frequented by backpackers and older folks alike, who come to enjoy a lively atmosphere that includes guitar music. Offerings range from Fiordland venison to orange roughy grilled with a chili-and-coriander-herb crust and served with a fresh Greek salad and tzatziki. Vegetarians and vegans are well taken care of.

12 Mokonui St. © **03/249-7431.** Main courses NZ$24–NZ$36. MC, V. Summer daily 4pm–1am; call for winter hours.

Sandfly Café ★★ CAFE   You know you're in the deep south when a cafe decorates its computers with possum fur! Quirky, charming, and friendly, this is my favorite Te Anau cafe. People of all ages and walks of life congregate here on stools and sofas for the excellent coffee, tasty salads, soups, and hot paninis. They definitely make the best coffee in Te Anau, and when it's sunny you can sit outside.

9 The Lane. © **03/249-9529.** Main courses NZ$15–NZ$25. MC, V. Daily 8am–6pm (reduced hours in winter).

EN ROUTE TO DUNEDIN

If you've already visited Milford Sound and are planning to travel to Dunedin from Te Anau, the drive will take about 4½ hours over good roads. Take State Highway 94 across Gorge Hill into Lumsden, across the Waimea Plains to the milling center of Gore, through farmlands to Clinton, and across rolling downs to Balclutha. From there, take State Highway 1 north along the coast past Milton and Lookout Point, where you'll get your first look at Dunedin.

5 MILFORD SOUND ★★★

119km (74 miles) NE of Te Anau; 286km (177 miles) NW of Queenstown

No matter when you visit or what the weather is like, your memories of Milford Sound are bound to be special. Its 14 nautical miles leading to the Tasman Sea are lined with mountain peaks that rise sharply out of the water to heights of 1,800m (5,900 ft.). Forsters fur seals laze on rocky shelves, and dolphins play in water that reaches depths of

> ## (Tips) Warning
>
> During the winter months, take the NO STOPPING—AVALANCHE ZONE signs along the Milford Road very seriously. No matter how much you want to stop and take a photograph, don't—it could cost you your life.

600m (2,000 ft.). The sound's entrance is so hidden when viewed from the sea that Captain Cook sailed right by without noticing it when he charted the waters some 200 years ago.

It rains a lot in Milford Sound, and that's an understatement. And while I'm on negatives, it can't be stressed enough that weather in this area is extremely changeable, even in summer, so come prepared. As many have found, reading about the cold and rain in midsummer is one thing, experiencing it quite another. Over 927 centimeters (365 in.) fall annually, so be prepared to get wet. The sound is a mystical, moody place when it rains. You may not glimpse the mountaintops or Mitre Peak through the mist, but you'll see hundreds of waterfalls cascading down spectacular cliff faces. In dry conditions, there are only three or four permanent waterfalls in the sound.

In summer, coaches pour in at a rate of 100 per day for the launch cruises—that's up to 5,000 people joining you for a look at this special place. If you're prepared to overlook this rather cramped state of affairs, you'll be rewarded with grand, unforgettable landscapes.

THE MILFORD ROAD

The road to Milford Sound is world-famous. Although it can be completed in 2 hours, allow at least 3 so you can stop to look at the many natural attractions along the way. Highway 94 from Te Anau leads north along the lake, with islands and wooded distant shores on your left. The drive is often a slow one, especially in wet conditions, as you make your way through steep gorges and between walls of solid rock and moss-covered inclines. I would discourage anyone from taking a motor home on this road as it is narrow, steep, and winding with a lot of bus traffic—and if that doesn't put you off, the dark, narrow tunnel will. The road is usually very busy in summer and there can be delays, especially at Homer Tunnel. *Remember:* There are no fuel stops between Te Anau and Milford, so make sure your tank is full. This is *not* a road you want to be "marooned" on—in any season. During the winter months, all drivers on Milford Road are required by law to carry chains for their vehicles. Road conditions can be checked on www.milfordroad.co.nz, or by calling (©) **0800/444-449** in New Zealand, or check www.transit.govt.nz/projects/milfordroad.

Be sure to stop for pictures at the **Mirror Lakes.** The road winds down the **Eglinton** and **Hollyford valleys,** through the astoundingly narrow and steep **Homer Tunnel,** and down into the majestic **Cleddau Valley,** to Milford Sound. Before you go, stop by the **Fiordland National Park Visitor Centre,** Lakefront Drive, Te Anau ((©) **03/249-7921;** fax 03/249-7613; www.doc.govt.nz), for information on Fiordland National Park. Ask specifically for the pamphlet *The Road To Milford* (NZ$4), which describes each mile of the journey. It's not a bad idea to go armed with sand fly repellent, too.

Homer Tunnel, about 100km (65 miles) into the journey, is a major engineering marvel: a 1.2km (¾-mile) passageway first proposed in 1889, begun in 1935, and finally opened in 1940. It wasn't until 1954 before a connecting road was completed and the first private automobile drove through. There's no lighting in the tunnel and it's very narrow. Drive with extreme care!

About 6km (3¾ miles) past the tunnel, stop and walk to the **Chasm.** The pleasant 15-minute round-trip goes through mossy undergrowth and beech forest to see a rather wonderful feat of natural erosion on the **Cleddau River.**

EXPLORING THE SOUND

To be fully appreciated, Milford Sound must be seen from the deck of one of the cruise vessels. **Real Journeys,** Lakefront Drive, Te Anau (© **0800/656-502** in NZ, or 03/249-7416; www.realjourneys.co.nz), operates a bewildering array of cruises—both daytime and overnight options. Prices differ depending on whether you join the activity in Queenstown, in Te Anau, or at Milford Sound, and whether you have coach, car, fixed-wing, or helicopter connections. A popular day option is the **Coach and Nature (or Scenic) Cruise,** which departs Queenstown daily at 7:30am and returns at 8:30pm; the cost is NZ$230 (NZ$226 scenic) for adults, NZ$115 (NZ$113 scenic) for children ages 5 to 14. If you go coach both ways, don't expect to be back in Queenstown until around 8pm, but also be aware that flights in and out of Milford are completely dependent on the weather and you may have to bus it if your flight is canceled. If you choose to fly one-way you will pay close to twice the above prices. The scenic cruises tend to have more tour groups on board.

You can overnight on Milford Sound in Real Journey's *Milford Mariner,* which features 30 en-suite cabins and includes kayaking and trips in tender vessels, a three-course buffet, and breakfast; rates are from NZ$470 for adults, NZ$235 for children. The *Milford Wanderer* sleeps 61 in quad-share bunk-style compartments; NZ$230 quad-share for adults, NZ$115 quad-share for children.

Milford Sound Red Boat Cruises (© **0800/264-536** in NZ, or 03/441-1137; www.discovermilfordsound.co.nz) has been a tradition here since 1957. It has four boats operating day cruises only. The cost of NZ$65 to NZ$95 for adults and NZ$15 for children ages 4 to 14 gets you a cruise lasting 1 hour and 45 minutes. Preordered picnic lunch options are available and Great Sights coaches from Queenstown and Te Anau connect with all cruises.

Both of the above cruise companies will take you to **Milford Deep Underwater Observatory** ★★ (© **0800/264-536** in NZ, or 03/441-1137; www.discovermilford sound.co.nz), where you'll descend over 10m (33 ft.) beneath the fiord surface to observe the vibrant underwater community. It costs NZ$30 extra above your cruise price for adults and NZ$14 extra for children. **Mitre Peak Cruises** (© **0800/744-633** in NZ, or 03/443-8787; www.mitrepeak.com) operates two small vessels for smaller, more personalized 2-hour cruises. They travel farther out than the other boats—all the way to the Tasman Sea, past St. Annes Point Lighthouse. Their prices are NZ$65 to NZ$75.

Walking is another marvelous activity in this area if you have the time. The Fiordland National Park Visitor Centre in Te Anau (see "Te Anau," earlier in this chapter) will furnish you with details on guided outings that climb into the peaks, meander along the shore, or take you close to waterfalls. One to consider is the much-praised **Trips 'n' Tramps** (© **0800/305-807** in NZ, or 03/249-7081; www.tripsandtramps.com), which has a 1-day walk on the Milford Track as part of a small group of 12 for NZ$175 per person.

Kayaking may be the most popular activity here after the cruises. Your best bet is **Rosco's Milford Sound Sea Kayaks,** State Highway 94, Deepwater Basin, Milford Sound (© **0800/476-726** in NZ; www.roscosmilfordkayaks.com). These easygoing

> **Tips Avoiding the Crowds**
>
> If possible, avoid going into Milford Sound at the peak tourist times of 12:30 to 1:30pm. Cruise sailings during the lunch period are the prime tour-bus time, and you will face long queues and higher prices.

excursions offer an extraordinary way to experience the sound. You don't have to be super-fit or have previous kayaking experience. One of the most popular is the Milford Track Paddle 'n Walk trip, which departs daily at 2:30pm and returns by 7:30pm. This costs NZ$179 per person and includes an easy walk through pristine rainforest. For people traveling out of peak tourist season, keep in mind that Rosco offers several excellent winter kayaking options. **Adventure Kayak & Cruise ★**, 33 Waiau St., Manapouri (© **0800/324-966** in NZ, or 03/249-6626; www.fiordlandadventure.co.nz), offers a stunning guided day tour on Doubtful Sound for NZ$220 per person.

WHERE TO STAY

The historic Mitre Peak Lodge provides accommodations only to members of guided Milford Track parties. The hotel dates from 1891, when Elizabeth Sutherland (wife of the sound's first settler) established a 12-room boardinghouse to accommodate seamen who called into the sound.

Milford Sound Lodge You'll need to enjoy communing with nature to savor a stay here. It's the only land-based lodge in Milford Sound and it is basic, no-frills, and generally filled with young backpackers, but the complex is set in splendid surroundings and was refurbished in 2007. Four new riverside chalets allowing a little more privacy are the best option here. Most of the simple rooms have four beds and little else. There are a lounge, cooking, and laundry facilities.

St. Hwy. 94 (Private Bag, Te Anau), Milford Sound. © **03/249-8071.** Fax 03/249-8075. www.milfordlodge. com. 28 units, all with shared bathrooms. NZ$30 dorm bed; NZ$80–NZ$90 double; NZ$225–NZ$250 chalet. MC, V. **Amenities:** Bar. *In room:* TV (in chalets), fridge, hair dryer.

Dunedin, Southland & Stewart Island

Dunedin, the "capital" of Otago province; Southland; Invercargill; and Stewart Island have generally been lumped together as the south of the south; if visitors tend to overlook any part of the country, it would be this one. This is unfortunate because the area offers some of the most diverse and fascinating flora and fauna; some of the quaintest "real New Zealand" townships; and probably one of the least harried travel experiences of all.

Southland extends as far northwest as Lake Manapouri and as far east as Balclutha. It is the country's coolest and rainiest region, yet the even spread of its rainfall is the very foundation of its economy—the production of grass and grass seed, which in turn supports large numbers of sheep and dairy farms. Southland also has the longest daylight hours in New Zealand, and the Percy Burn Viaduct (near Tuatapere) is believed to be the largest wooden rail viaduct remaining in the world.

The area's coastline saw early settlement by Maori sealers and whalers. Today, the region's fishing industry is a major force—its contributions include those succulent Bluff oysters and crayfish (rock lobsters) you've devoured in your New Zealand travels.

Invercargill is a convenient central base for exploring the deep south. It lies an easy 2-hour drive from Fiordland and 2½ hours from Dunedin, via State Highway 1. It is the central focus of Southland—the only place in New Zealand where Scottish heritage has left a distinctive accent among the people, which you'll notice in the way many people roll the letter *r*. It is a place of incredible friendliness and hospitality, and the only spot in the world where people can see living tuatara, the only lizard left from the dinosaur age.

Stewart Island, the third-largest island of New Zealand, is an area of raucous birdcall, lush native vegetation, and unchanged Kiwi habits—which goes for both the human and the ornithological species. It is a rare treat and I haven't heard of one person who has regretted making the effort to get there.

Stewart Island and Southland both come under the umbrella of the Venture Southland/Destination Fiordland Sustainable Tourism Charter and participating tourism operators are listed at www.southlandnz.com.

1 DUNEDIN ★★

283km (175 miles) S of Queenstown; 366km (227 miles) S of Christchurch; 220km (136 miles) N of Invercargill

Dunedin is a southern gem—sometimes gray, bleak, and freezing in winter, but a gem nevertheless. I love the place for its dramatic scenery, its fine historic buildings, and most of all, for the immediacy of its funky university life, which lends an alternative air to what is inherently a strongly Scottish Presbyterian base.

With a population of about 123,000 (one-fifth of them university students), Dunedin
is New Zealand's fourth-largest city and the second largest in the South Island. The city
itself is vital, and you'll quickly notice that the streets are filled with young people. It's
the main business center for Otago province, and nearby Otago Peninsula is home to
several internationally recognized reserves, where some of the world's rarest wildlife can
be viewed year-round in their natural habitats.

The splendor of many of its grand city buildings reflects Dunedin's economic and
cultural preeminence in Victorian New Zealand, and today it has a justly deserved reputation as one of the best-preserved Victorian and Edwardian cities in the Southern
Hemisphere. The original 344 Scottish settlers, who arrived in the area in March 1848,
would be proud if they could witness the outcome of their early endeavors.

Things can be, and often are, a little different down here. Where else could you find
a kilt shop in New Zealand, plus a thriving population of alternative musicians, fashion
designers and artists, a castle, New Zealand's only whiskey distillery, a haggis maker, a
colony of albatrosses, a traditional Chinese garden, some of the best student pubs in the
country, and a chocolate factory? It's a slightly disconcerting mix that will charm the
socks off you.

ESSENTIALS

GETTING THERE   By Plane   Air New Zealand (www.airnewzealand.com), has
flights between Dunedin and Sydney, Melbourne, and Brisbane. **Air New Zealand,** at
the corner of The Octagon and Princes Street (© **0800/737-000** in NZ, or 03/479-
6594; www.airnewzealand.co.nz), provides service between Dunedin and Auckland,
Wellington, and Rotorua in the North Island, and Christchurch and Invercargill in the
South Island. **Pacific Blue** (www.flypacificblue.com) flies between Dunedin and Christchurch daily. **Stewart Island Flights** (© **03/218-9129;** www.stewartislandflights.com)
has flights to and from Stewart Island on Monday, Wednesday, Friday, and Sunday.

The Dunedin airport (www.dnairport.co.nz) is inconveniently placed 40 minutes out
of the city, and taxis charge approximately NZ$60 for the trip into town. You'd be well
advised to take one of the shuttles that run to the city at regular intervals. The **Dunedin
Taxis Airport Shuttle** (© **0800/505-010** or 03/477-7777) charges around NZ$25 to
NZ$30 to most parts of Central City. **City Taxis** (© **03/477-1771**) offers a fixed-fare
service from the airport.

By Coach (Bus)   InterCity (© **09/623-1503**) provides coach service between Dunedin and Christchurch, Invercargill, Picton, Queenstown, Te Anau, and Timaru. The
bus terminal is at 205 St. Andrew St. (© **03/477-8860**). **Bottom Bus,** The Octagon
(© **0800/304-333** in NZ, or 03/477-9083; www.bottombus.co.nz), has a range of
Southern tours including the 5-day In a Stew trip, which begins and ends anywhere you
like in this region and costs NZ$675. It includes a Milford Sound cruise and travel to
Stewart Island. It offers discounts to travelers with YHA, VIP, and BBH backpacker
cards.

By Car   Dunedin can be reached via state highways 1 and 87. It is 366km (227 miles)
and approximately 5 hours' drive south of Christchurch; 220km (136 miles) and
approximately 3 to 4 hours northeast of Invercargill; and 4 hours from Queenstown
inland through Central Otago. The Southern Scenic Route from Invercargill is another
alternative. It passes through the forested coastal Catlins area and is well worth the slight
diversion from State Highway 1.

DUNEDIN **DUNEDIN, SOUTHLAND & STEWART ISLAND**

17

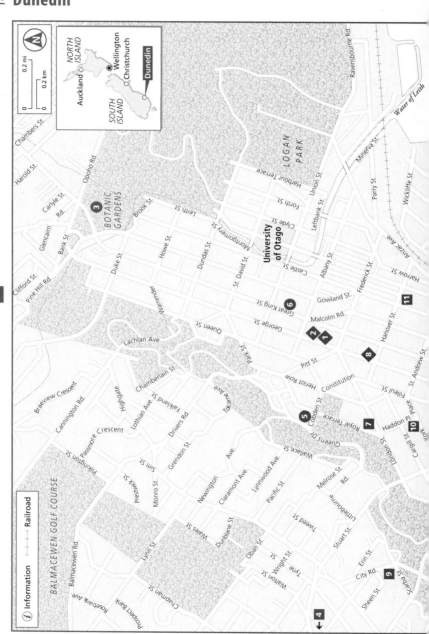

NORTH ISLAND

Auckland

Wellington

Christchurch

Dunedin

SOUTH ISLAND

0 0.2 mi
0 0.2 km

Water of Leith

Ravensbourne Rd.

Minerva St.

Parry St.

Wickliffe St.

Anzac Ave.

Harrow St.

Hanover St.

St. Andrew St.

Filleul St.

Haddon Pl.

London St.

Cargill St.

York Pl.

LOGAN PARK

Harbour Terrace

Union St.

Forth St.

Clyde St.

Leithbank

Albany St.

Castle St.

Frederick St.

University of Otago

Great King St.

George St.

Gowland St.

Malcolm Rd.

Leith St.

Montgomery St.

St. David St.

Dundas St.

Howe St.

Duke St.

Brook St.

Warrender

Queen St.

Park St.

Pitt St.

Heriot Row

Constitution

Royal Terrace

Cobden St.

Queens Dr.

Wallace St.

Chamberlain St.

Lachlan Ave.

Toome Ave.

Highgate

Lothian Ave.

Falkland St.

Drivers Rd.

Grendon St.

Newington

Claramont Ave.

Lynnwood Ave.

Pacific St.

Melrose St.

Rd.

Littlebourne

Stuart St.

Tweed St.

Braeview Crescent

Cannington Rd.

Passmore Crescent

Pilkington St.

Sim St.

Prestwick St.

Monro St.

Wales St.

Dunblane St.

Oban St.

Walton St.

Tyne St.

Wright St.

Lynn St.

Chapman St.

Rosebank

Prospect Bank

Balmacewen Rd.

BALMACEWEN GOLF COURSE

Erin St.

City Rd.

Sheen St.

Scarba St.

Clifford St.

Pine Hill Rd.

Glencairn

Bank St.

Carlyle St.

Harold St.

Chambers St.

Opoho Rd.

BOTANIC GARDENS

i Information   ┼┼┼ Railroad

3 · 6 · 2 · 1 · 8 · 11 · 5 · 7 · 10 · 9 · 4

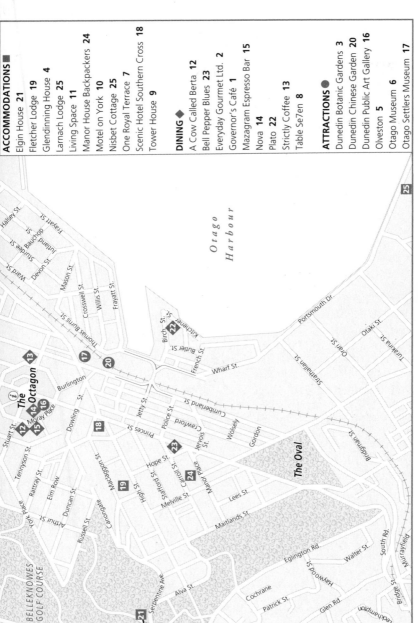

ACCOMMODATIONS ■
Elgin House **21**
Fletcher Lodge **19**
Glendinning House **4**
Larnach Lodge **25**
Living Space **11**
Manor House Backpackers **24**
Motel on York **10**
Nisbet Cottage **25**
One Royal Terrace **7**
Scenic Hotel Southern Cross **18**
Tower House **9**

DINING ◆
A Cow Called Berta **12**
Bell Pepper Blues **23**
Everyday Gourmet Ltd. **2**
Governor's Café **1**
Mazagram Espresso Bar **15**
Nova **14**
Plato **22**
Strictly Coffee **13**
Table SeZen **8**

ATTRACTIONS ●
Dunedin Botanic Gardens **3**
Dunedin Chinese Garden **20**
Dunedin Public Art Gallery **16**
Olveston **5**
Otago Museum **6**
Otago Settlers Museum **17**

Fun Facts   Scottish Roots

Dunedin is the ancient Gaelic name of Edinburgh in Scotland, and Otago University, the oldest in New Zealand, was modeled after Glasgow University.

ORIENTATION   All good cities have a heart, and Dunedin is no exception. Rather than a square, though, it has a tree-lined octagon, which acts as a central meeting place. This is where you'll find the visitor center, bus terminals, the main art gallery, and a host of cafes and bars. It boasts a statue of Scotland's beloved poet Robert Burns (whose nephew was Dunedin's first pastor), grassy areas under trees, and a giant chessboard. The Octagon divides the city's main street into George Street to the north and Princes Street to the south. A popular shopping area is to be found in the George Street section (see "Shopping," later in this section). The city center is at the head of Otago Harbour, and is encircled by a 200-hectare (500-acre) strip of land, the Green Belt.

GETTING AROUND   By Bus   Most city buses ((©) **0800/474-082** in NZ) leave from the vicinity of The Octagon. Four different companies provide service for the same prices, but all use different numbering systems and do different city runs. Your best bet is to get bus timetables from the visitor center on The Octagon or check www.orc. govt.nz. There is frequent service during the week, but it's a little spotty on weekends. The fares are by zone and range from NZ$2 to NZ$6 per section.

By Taxi   Taxi stands can be found at The Octagon, at all terminals, and near the Chief Post Office. Or call **Dunedin Taxis** ((©) **03/477-7777**) or **City Taxis** ((©) **03/477-1771**).

By Car   Once you familiarize yourself with the one-way systems and the interrupted street pattern around The Octagon, Dunedin is easy to negotiate. Most central streets have metered parking, and there's a municipal parking building near City Hall and a carpark in the Meridian Shopping Centre.

VISITOR INFORMATION   The **Dunedin i-SITE Visitor Centre,** 48 The Octagon ((©) **03/474-3300;** fax 03/474-3311; www.dunedinnz.com or www.dunedin.govt.nz), is set in the magnificently restored Municipal Chambers. It's open Monday through Friday from 8:30am to 5pm, and Saturday, Sunday, and holidays from 9am to 5:30pm. In summer, the office remains open until 6pm. You can also contact **Tourism Dunedin,** 193 Princes St. ((©) **03/471-8042;** fax 03/471-8021; www.dunedinnz.com).

SPECIAL EVENTS   Dunedin has an all-year program of festivals and events. To find out about them, check at the visitor center.

The **Dunedin Summer Festival** in February and March presents themed weekends, exhibitions, outdoor concerts, family activities, and sporting and cultural events. At the same time is the **id Dunedin Fashion Show** (www.id-dunedinfashion.com), where the city's many designers showcase their work on the Dunedin Railway Platform in front of international media. In May, the **Regent Theatre 24-Hour Book Sale ★** ((©) **03/477-6481**) offers up over 300,000 volumes in the country's largest sale of secondhand books. It all started as a way to raise funds for the theater's restoration, and it's become a successful, established event filled with fun, live entertainment, and great bargains. In the third week of October, **Dunedin Rhododendron Festival** celebrates the exotic beauty of Dunedin's most famous flower. A happy combination of soil and climate makes the city

one of the finest rhododendron-growing areas in the world. More information about
Rhododendron Week and its private garden tours is available by calling ℂ **03/474-3300**
or visiting www.rhododunedin.co.nz.

(Fast Facts   Dunedin

Area Code The telephone area code (STD) for Dunedin is **03.**

Automobile Association The **AA** is at 450 Moray Place (ℂ **03/477-5945,** or
025/386-122 after hours; fax 03/477-9760), and is open Monday through Friday
from 8:30am to 5pm. For breakdowns, phone ℂ **0800/500-222.**

Dentists Raymond J. George, Level 7, at The Octagon and George Street (ℂ **03/
477-7993**), provides 24-hour service.

Doctors Go to the **Travellers Medical & Vaccination Centre,** 169 Eglinton Rd.,
Mornington (ℂ **03/453-6121**).

Emergencies For police, fire, or ambulance service, dial ℂ **111.**

Internet Access A1 Internet Café, Level 1, 149 George St. (ℂ **03/477-5832**), is
open from 10am until late. The visitor center also offers Internet service.

Post Office The Chief Post Office is at 343 Princes St. (ℂ **03/477-3517**); there's
another at 233 Moray Place (ℂ **03/474-0932**).

Restrooms There are good public restrooms on Municipal Lane on the Upper
Octagon, between the visitor center and the public library. Open Monday through
Saturday from 8:30am to 8:30pm and Sunday from 9am to 5pm.

EXPLORING DUNEDIN

Swing by the visitor center to watch the half-hour video *Dunedin Discovered,* which will
give you an overview of the region. Also pick up a sightseeing map and look for the *Walk
the City* brochure (NZ$3). There are terrific scenic drives around the city and on the
peninsula, and the visitor center has plenty of maps and brochures to show you where to
go and what to look out for along the way. One of your first stops should also be the
Otago Museum (see below). Its gallery, "Southern Land, Southern People," will bring
more meaning to your visit.

Taking in the Views

There are three good lookout points from which to view the city and its environs: **Mount
Cargill Lookout,** 8km (5 miles) from the city center (turn left at the end of George St.,
then left on Pine Hill Rd. to its end, and then right onto Cowan Rd., which climbs to
the summit); **Centennial Lookout,** or Signal Hill (turn onto Signal Hill Rd. from
Opoho Rd., then drive 3km/1¾ miles to the end of Signal Hill Rd.); and **Bracken's
Lookout** (at the top of the Botanic Gardens), which was named after poet Thomas
Bracken, who wrote the words to New Zealand's national anthem.

Museums, Galleries & Historic Homes

Otago Museum ★★★ (Kids Established in 1868, this is New Zealand's fourth-
largest museum with over 1.7 million items; most people are surprised by the depth of

its large ethnographic, natural-history, and decorative-arts collections. It also has the best Pacific and Southern Maori collections in the country.

After a recent multimillion-dollar upgrade, it now has a new and improved foyer, cafe, and shop, a new special-exhibitions gallery, a stylish atrium, a new 6-minute introductory video (the best way to begin your visit), and a stunning gallery called **"Southern Land, Southern People"** ★★, which tells the human and natural-history story of the southern region. Allow an hour for this section and to get the best from it take a guided tour, which can be booked in advance.

Visitors can meet the extinct giant moa in a gallery that includes the museum's world-class collection of complete moa skeletons and one of the few complete moa eggs in the world; and fans of old-style museums should not miss the new **Animal Attic** ★, which replicates the Victorian timbered gallery of the museum as it was in 1868. It's my favorite museum space—unforgettable for its visual impact and zany collections of stuffed animals (which kids will love), birds, and New Zealand spiders. And don't overlook the fun factor of **Discovery World,** one of those terrific places for children where you end up playing yourself. The live butterfly experience that opened in 2007 is also a wonderful treat. Allow 2 hours for a good look around.

419 Great King St. (**03/474-7474.** Fax 03/477-5993. www.otagomuseum.govt.nz and www.discovery world.co.nz. Free admission to museum; admission to Discovery World NZ$10 adults, NZ$5 children. Southern Land Tour NZ$10 per person. Daily 10am–5pm. Closed Dec 25.

Otago Settlers Museum ★★   This is Otago's museum of social history, tracing the stories of those who have made the region home—from the original Maori inhabitants to the sturdy Scottish pioneers, the rough-and-ready gold miners to the business entrepreneurs who followed them. Exhibitions are comprehensive, presenting even the most detailed engineering and scientific facts in a readily accessible manner. There are also exhibits on the Kai Tahu Maori communities of Otago; an ever-popular transport collection (engine buffs will be in heaven); and a Penny Farthing cycle you can actually ride. A new gallery features the 19th-century settlers' shipboard experience, which includes a mock-up of the steerage of a sailing ship. Allow an hour for a quick overview. The museum also offers two very good 1- and 2-hour city walking tours, which include premium heritage sites. These can be booked at the visitor center.

31 Queens Gardens. (**03/477-5052.** Fax 03/474-2727. www.otago.settlers.museum. Free admission. Daily 10am–5pm. Research department Mon–Fri 10am–1pm NZ$12; 2-hr. walking tour NZ$20 per person; 1-hr. walking tour NZ$12 per person. Closed Good Friday and Dec 25.

Dunedin Public Art Gallery ★★   When the Dunedin Public Art Gallery opened in 1996, art lovers throughout the country celebrated. The new space is one of the best in New Zealand and has received acclaim for both its architecture and its collection—one of the best in Australasia. There are significant holdings of European art, Japanese prints, and French Impressionist works, along with a comprehensive collection of contemporary and early New Zealand art. The shop stocks a good range of art-related products.

30 The Octagon. (**03/474-3240.** Fax 03/474-3250. www.dunedin.art.museum. Free admission; charges for special exhibitions. Daily 10am–5pm. Special tours available by arrangement. Closed Good Friday and Dec 25.

Olveston ★★★ (Finds)   Olveston is one of New Zealand's best-known stately homes and if, like me, you have a passion for grand old homes, it should definitely be on your agenda. Designed by London architect Sir Ernest George, the 35-room, Jacobean-style mansion was built between 1904 and 1906 by the much-traveled and very prosperous

Kids Chocolate Heaven

Chocolate lovers and fans of *Charlie & the Chocolate Factory,* rejoice! The famous **Cadbury World,** 280 Cumberland St. ((© **03/467-7967;** www.cadburyworld.co. nz), is open. This unique, interactive chocolate-themed center offers daily guided tours of New Zealand's most famous—and favorite—chocolate factory every half-hour from 9am until 3:15pm. Immerse yourself in the process and sample treats along the way. A full tour takes about 75 minutes, but be aware that many of the most interesting processes are "secret" and you don't get to see them. I found that a little disappointing, and I suspect younger children may be less enchanted by the mechanical focus. It costs NZ$18 for adults, NZ$12 for children ages 5 to 15, and NZ$48 for families. A retail outlet here also offers special "tour only" prices, but you can't shop here unless you do take the tour.

Theomin family. It sits on an acre of tree-sheltered grounds, and since it was bequeathed to Dunedin in 1966, it has been carefully maintained in virtually its original state. David Theomin had a passion for Eastern decorative arts, and he filled his home with bronze, cloisonné, ivory, ceramics, jade, and over 250 paintings. On top of its unique interior finery, the house itself is a work of art and pays homage to the skills of 19th-century craftsmen. Those with reservations are given preference; house viewing is by 1-hour guided tour only. Reservations are required for the 2-hour painting tours.

42 Royal Terrace. (© **03/477-3320.** Fax 03/479-2094. www.olveston.co.nz. Admission NZ$17 adults, NZ$7.50 children ages 5–15. Guided tours given daily at 9:30 and 10:45am, noon, 1:30, 2:45, and 4pm. Closed Dec 25.

Other Highlights

Forgive me for not walking up **Baldwin Street,** which, according to the *Guinness Book of World Records,* is the world's steepest street. I couldn't face the 270 steps that take you to the top, or the footpath and its impossible gradient. Just minutes from the city center, this little street tricks you with a gentle beginning. It then rears dramatically skyward to come to a dead end on the hillside. If you're hale and hearty and have something to prove, this could be a good test, and I believe the views from the top are worth it. And if you want a certificate to prove to your friends back home that you had what it takes, then stop by the **World's Steepest Street Tourist Shop,** 282 North Rd. ((© **03/473-0923**). To get to Baldwin Street, take the Normandy bus to North Road; Baldwin is the 10th street on the right past the Botanic Gardens. And remember, if you drive to the top, there's only a very tight turnaround space and only one way out—down the way you came!

Dunedin's **Railway Station** warrants more than a cursory glance. This marvelous old Flemish Renaissance–style structure was designed by George A. Troup and built between 1904 and 1906. Troup won the Institution of British Architects Award for his efforts and was later knighted. Built of Kokonga basalt with Oamaru limestone facings, the station's most prominent feature is its large square clock tower. Equally impressive are the Aberdeen granite pillars supporting arches of the colonnade across the front, the red Marseilles tiles on the roof, and the colorful mosaic floor (more than 725,000 Royal Doulton porcelain squares) in the massive foyer depicting a "puffing billy" engine. Look for the replica of Dunedin's coat of arms and the stained-glass windows above the balcony.

> ## (Moments) Brew Stop
>
> Tours of **Speight's Brewery Heritage Centre** ★★, 200 Rattray St. ((C) **03/477-7697;** www.speights.co.nz), cost NZ$19 for adults, NZ$16 for students, and NZ$7 for children ages 5 to 15. For that you'll spend about 1¹/₂ hours looking at the brewing processes of this "Pride of the South," with tastings and a sample of the product at the end. Speight's has been favoring us with its fine ales since 1876, and the tour gives a good overview of the industry. Make sure you see the stunning Otago video presentation at the end—it made my little Kiwi heart burst with pride. Tours are limited to 25 people and run daily at 10am, 11:45am, and 2pm, with an extra 7pm tour Monday through Thursday. Ask about a combo deal that includes a Cadbury World chocolate factory tour.

Parks & Gardens

The 28-hectare (69-acre) **Dunedin Botanic Gardens** ((C) 03/477-4000; botanic@cityof dunedin.com) were the first to be established in New Zealand, in 1869. At the northern end of George Street, they feature the world-renowned Rhododendron Dell. Nestled into native bush with magnolia, cherry, and maples, the Dell features over 3,000 rhododendron plants and has spectacular masses of blooms from October to December. You can also see the comprehensive native-plant collection, an Edwardian conservatory garden, rock gardens, and rose gardens. The gardens are open daily from dawn to dusk, free of charge. A kiosk restaurant offers light snacks and morning and afternoon teas; a shop and information center are also on the grounds. All three are open daily from 10am to 4pm. Pick up the free gardens map from the visitor center.

For information on Dunedin's famous October **Rhododendron Festival,** go to www. rhododunedin.co.nz.

A new addition to the Dunedin garden scene is the magnificent and somewhat unexpected **Dunedin Chinese Garden** ★★★, corner of Rattray and Cumberland streets, Dunedin ((C) 03/479-0368; www.dunedinchinesegarden.com), which opened in 2008 and is said to be one of only three truly authentic Chinese gardens outside of China. The garden was created in authentic materials by Chinese craftsmen and artisans in Dunedin's sister city, Shanghai. It was then dismantled, shipped to New Zealand, and reconstructed on the current site under the supervision of the Chinese craftsmen. It was the brainchild of the Dunedin Chinese Garden Trust, supported by the local Chinese community, many of whom have roots back to the Chinese gold miners of the 1860s Otago gold rush. The garden is open daily from 10am to 5pm, with an evening viewing from 7 to 9pm on Wednesdays. Admission is NZ$8 for adults. Children 12 and under are free. A 1-hour guided tour costs NZ$20 per person.

EXPLORING OTAGO PENINSULA

Otago Peninsula is simply spectacular, especially on a clear day. It has some of the finest views of the southern coastline and is one of New Zealand's most renowned ecotourism areas, with several excellent wildlife centers. You can book tours of the peninsula through the visitor center, or pick up the free *Visitors' Guide to the Otago Peninsula,* which features a comprehensive map of attractions, arts and crafts, accommodations, and restaurants. The 33km (20-mile) peninsula curves around one side of Otago Harbour. It's an easy

road, although some portions are unpaved, and it takes you past quaint coastal boatsheds **487**
and quiet settlements. The listings below cover Otago's highlights. As most tourism
operations based on, or visiting this area, depend on the welfare of the peninsula's wildlife, you'll find most take a conscientious approach to environmentally safe viewing
practices.

Royal Albatross Centre ★★★ It seems a cruel irony that a magnificent bird such
as the royal albatross, which can stay in the air for weeks on end, should make such an
ungainly landing when it finally decides to come down to earth. But we can be thankful
that it has chosen to do so at Taiaroa Head, the only mainland colony of albatrosses in
the world. One-hour tours will show you the birds only; 90-minute tours add the tunnel
complex of the old Fort Taiaroa and the last working example of an Armstrong Disap-
pearing Gun. The best times to visit are January and February, when the chicks are
hatching; in late afternoon, you'll see courtship displays. After 6:30pm, the sea breezes
come up, and juveniles come in from the sea. It's important to remember, though, that
this is wildlife and there are no guarantees. Sometimes you can see birds as close as 3.5m
(12 ft.) away, sometimes much farther. But with binoculars and a telephoto camera lens,
you're bound to get good results. During the mating season, the main observatory is
closed, and viewing is from an alternative spot a little farther away. It's a 2-minute walk
up a path to the observatory; mobile carts are available for visitors with disabilities. A
souvenir shop, cafeteria, and wildlife displays are on the grounds.

Taiaroa Head. ✆ **03/478-0499.** Fax 03/478-0575. www.albatross.org.nz. Free admission to Albatross
Centre. Daily 1-hr. Albatross Tour, from NZ$40 adults, NZ$20 children 5–14; daily 90-min. Unique Taiaroa
Tour NZ$48 adults, NZ$24 children 5–14; Fort Taiaroa Tour, NZ$20 adults, NZ$10 children 5–14. Center
daily 9am–7pm. Closed Dec 25. Tour reservations required; call visitor center on The Octagon or the
Albatross Centre directly.

Penguin Place ★★★ When you consider that every yellow-eyed penguin has 200
feathers per square inch, you realize there's likely to be a whole lot of preening going on
in the heart of this excellent conservation project. The 1½-hour tour begins with an
informative talk and slide presentation; you're then driven 5 minutes across farmland to
an extensive network of tunnels and hides that took 8 years to build. Here you'll be able
to watch the world's rarest penguins at close quarters without disturbing them. Fifteen
years ago, there were eight breeding pairs; today, there are over 35 pairs in the colony,
which represents 20% of New Zealand's mainland yellow-eyed population. You'll need
sensible walking shoes, as there's at least 500m (1,600 ft.) of walking involved, much of
it uphill and steep. But you'll be rewarded with fabulous coastal views, colonies of
fur seals, possibly Hooker sea lions if you're lucky, and incredible, swirling tangles of
sea kelp—all fantastic photographic opportunities, but no flashes are allowed near the
penguins.

Pakihau Rd. ✆ **03/478-0286.** Fax 03/478-0257. www.penguinplace.co.nz. Admission from NZ$45 adults,
NZ$25 children 5–14. MC, V. Tours given Nov to mid-Mar 10:15am–7:45pm; reservations required. Tours
depart from the McGrouther Farm on Harrington Point Rd. It is well signposted and just 5 min. before the
Royal Albatross Centre.

Larnach Castle ★★ Larnach Castle may be small by European standards, but it's
clear William Larnach had more than a simple bungalow in mind when he set about
constructing this marvelous edifice in 1871. No doubt keen to impress his French heiress
wife, he hired 200 workmen for 3 years just to build the shell; a host of European master
craftsmen took another 12 years to complete the interior. The carved foyer ceiling alone

Moments   Close Encounters

If you're traveling with kids—or even if you're not—don't miss the **New Zealand Marine Studies Centre & Westpac Aquarium** ★★, Portobello, Otago Peninsula (© **03/479-5826;** www.marine.ac.nz). I can't keep my hands out of things, so I delighted in being able to delve into marine tanks—although it goes without saying that you should first see who's living in there. After all, there's no point in losing a finger to a lobster. You can help feed the sea critters every Wednesday and Saturday from 2 to 3pm; or take one of the daily guided tours at 10:30am. The center is open daily from noon to 4:30pm. If you're heading out to the view the albatrosses, it's on your way.

took three craftsmen 6½ years to finish. The Georgian hanging staircase is the only one in the Southern Hemisphere, and it sits comfortably with the best of everything that Larnach incorporated.

Larnach came to New Zealand from Australia in the late 1860s to set up the first Bank of Otago. He later became a Member of Parliament, but with three marriages behind him and a family history dotted with scandal and misfortune, he committed suicide in the Parliament Buildings in Wellington. (His first two wives both died at the age of 38, and his third dealt him a fatal emotional blow by dallying with the son from his first marriage.) After his death, the crown used the castle as a mental hospital. For the past 38 years, it has been the home of Margaret Barker and her family, who have committed themselves to its restoration. Pick up the self-guiding pamphlet at the reception area and wander as you wish. If you'd like to stay in the castle lodge or stables, see "Where to Stay," below.

Highcliff Rd. © **03/476-1616.** Fax 03/476-1574. www.larnachcastle.co.nz. Admission to castle and grounds NZ$25 adults, NZ$10 children; grounds only NZ$10 adults, NZ$3 children. Daily 9am–5pm. Closed Dec 25. Take Portobello Rd. 3km (2 miles) north of Glenfalloch Woodland Garden and follow the signs inland.

ORGANIZED TOURS

Dunedin is blessed with a number of excellent tour operators who provide enjoyable sightseeing the easy way. You'll find a profusion of pamphlets at the visitor center on The Octagon. During summer months, it pays to reserve early.

If you have food and wine on your mind, you should definitely hook up with **Zest Food Tours** ★★★ (© **0800/937-886;** www.zestfoodtours.co.nz), which will take you on a walking tour of the city, introducing you to the many gourmet tastes of the area. And if you join them on a Saturday, you'll also get a tour of the Otago Farmers' Market, which is held at the spectacular Dunedin Railway Station. Book your tour at the Dunedin i-SITE Visitor Centre and pay around NZ$180 per person.

Many of the operators are geared toward peninsula exploration. Outdoor types will find pleasure in the sea-kayak, rafting, walking, and mountain bike tours offered by **Wild Earth Adventures** ★★★ (© **03/489-1951;** www.wildearth.co.nz). Its **Ocean Discovery Kayak Tour** takes you along wild beaches and soaring sea cliffs to the albatross colony and offers amazing photographic opportunities. It costs NZ$99 per person.

Also popular is **Elm Wildlife Tours** ★★★ (© **0800/356-563** in NZ, or 03/454-4121; www.elmwildlifetours.co.nz); twice voted New Zealand's best wildlife tour, it gives

you a sound insight into the habits of various penguin species, fur seals, and sea lions.
Viewing hides give you a close encounter and options range from NZ$89 to NZ$134.

Coach (Bus) Tours

Citibus Newton Tours, Princes Street and Transport Place (© **03/477-5577;** www.
citibus.co.nz or www.time2.co.nz), conducts excellent tours of varying duration, all with
guides providing valuable insight into the area's highlights, along with the occasional
anecdote to liven things up. All tours may be booked directly with Citibus Newton or at
the visitor center. Pickups from your lodging can be arranged. The **First City** ★★ tour
departs five times per day from the visitor center. The fare for this double-decker bus ride
is NZ$20 per adult, NZ$10 per child 14 and under. They also offer and Otago Peninsula
Tour that includes Larnach Castle and others that include either the Albatross Centre or
Penguin Place.

Cruising the Peninsula

A number of cruise options can show you the wildlife delights of Otago Peninsula. The
visitor center has a comprehensive selection of brochures and a helpful staff to help you
sort out your priorities.

Locals are quick to tell you about the fantastic value offered through the family-owned
and -operated **Monarch Wildlife Cruises** ★★★, Wharf and Fryatt streets (© **0800/
666-272** in NZ, or 03/477-4276; www.wildlife.co.nz). Established in 1983 by owners
with degrees in biology and a wealth of experience on research vessels, Monarch won the
New Zealand Tourism Awards Natural Heritage category in 1994 and the Ecotourism
category in 1997. The crew are experienced Department of Conservation officers or have
degrees in zoology, so there's not much you won't be able to find out about albatrosses,
New Zealand fur seals, yellow-eyed penguins, and other species you're likely to pass. If
you're short on time, opt for the 1-hour albatross cruise from Wellers Rock, which costs
NZ$45 for adults, NZ$20 for children ages 5 to 16. (Remember that Wellers Rock is a

---

ⓘ Moments   Hair-Raising Fun

If you think ghosts don't exist, Andrew Smith's **Hair Raiser Ghost Walk** ★★
(© **03/477-2258;** hairraisertours@xtra.co.nz) might convince you otherwise. Get
behind the city's beautiful architecture and discover the truth behind many
famous ghost sightings, the wandering habits of the supernatural, and The Octagon fires. Based on fact, not fiction, it's not for the fainthearted and there's no
guarantee of a good night's sleep afterward. No garlic or crucifixes allowed. Tours
leave from outside the visitor center daily April through September at 6pm, and
October through March at 8pm; they cost NZ$30 per person. No credit cards.

Take the hedonistic approach to touring with **Top Hat Limousines** (© **03/
477-3900;** fax 03/477-3145; www.tophat.co.nz). They can tailor-make a tour to
suit your needs; they'll even drive you all the way to Queenstown or Christchurch
if you like (NZ$70 round-trip). Their standard hourly rate is NZ$100. **Classic Jaguar Limousines** (© **03/488-5961;** www.classicjaguar.co.nz) offers a very good
Dunedin City Heritage Tour for NZ$180 per person, or a tour of the city's heri-
tage homes for the same price.

45-min. drive from Central City.) Monarch also has full harbor cruises from Dunedin lasting just over 5 hours. Dress warmly and take your camera; if you're unsure about which option to take, note that the most popular is the cruise-and-bus trip that includes a guided tour of Penguin Place—it gives you a taste of everything. They run half-day tours from NZ$90 to NZ$130 and full-day options from NZ$210 to NZ$250.

OUTDOOR PURSUITS

BEACHES   New Zealanders don't often utter the two words "Dunedin" and "beaches" in the same breath, but the truth is, there are at least eight or nine magnificent, unspoiled, white-sand beaches within an easy drive of Dunedin. You may not always want to swim in the coolish waters, but from a scenic point of view, they're worth a visit. **St. Kilda** and **St. Clair** are probably the best known, made famous by a dedicated band of wet-suited surfers. A short drive north to the Port Chalmers area reveals **Long Beach, Aromoana,** and **Purakanui,** and on Otago Peninsula, **Pilot's Beach** (near the Albatross Centre), **Victory Beach, Sandfly Bay,** and **Seal Point** are all generally deserted and beautiful. Closer to town you have **Tunnel Beach,** which is accessed through private property and a tunnel. Ask the staff at the visitor center for driving instructions. You'll find great walks on **Brighton Beach,** a 20-minute drive south of Dunedin.

BIKING   Dunedin may be hilly, but there are great cycling opportunities, especially out on the peninsula. Rent a bike from **Browns,** Lower Stuart Street (✆ 03/477-7259).

If you're more into fat tires, the visitor center's excellent brochure *Mountain Bike Rides in Dunedin* outlines all the best tracks, including the very popular **Central Otago Rail Trail** ★★★ (✆ 03/474-6909; www.centralotagorailtrail.co.nz), a 5- to 6-day excursion that takes you into Middlemarch and Central Otago. It's an unforgettable trip through stunning scenery and dinky small towns.

FISHING   Nearby Port Chalmers is known for its stellar salmon and trout fishing from October to April. If you want to try your hand at shark fishing, deep-sea fishing, saltwater, or light-tackle sport fishing, call **Otago Harbour Salmon Fishing Charters,** 7 Henderson St., Mornington (✆ 03/453-6614), or inquire at the Dunedin visitor center for other options. **Wannabe Fishin'** (✆ 03/415-7146; wbfishing@xtra.co.nz), knows all the best local spots for trout fishing and hunting.

GOLF   The **Otago Golf Club Balmacewen Course** (✆ 03/467-2096; www.otagogolf club.co.nz) has been operating since 1896. It's an 18-hole championship course with a fully stocked pro shop. Affiliated members pay NZ$55, nonaffiliated pay NZ$75. **St. Clair Golf Club** (✆ 03/487-7076; www.stclairgolf.co.nz) is also popular; greens fees are NZ$50 per person.

(Moments   **Salt, Sea & Surf**

St. Clair Hot Salt Water Pool, at St. Clair Beach (✆ 03/471-9780), is a 25m (80-ft.) outdoor pool right beside the ocean and, if your bones are aching from too much walking, a soak in the therapeutic waters will do you a world of good. The pool's seawater is heated to a pleasing 82°F (28°C) and you can hear waves crashing on the nearby shore. It's open from late October through March daily from 6am until 7pm. Admission is NZ$6. Ask about their pool parties, which include fun activities, games, and a barbecue.

(Moments) A Train Trip to Taieri Gorge

The **Taieri Gorge Railway** ★★★ (© 03/477-4449; www.taieri.co.nz) is more than a small jaunt on a train—it is an award-winning journey through history and spectacular scenery that is otherwise inaccessible to the public. No matter what time of the year, you'll be impressed with both the scenic beauty and the sheer engineering feat of the railway's construction. The 75km (47 miles) of rail, including 12 tunnels, and the magnificent Wingatui Viaduct took 42 years to build, beginning in 1879. Make sure you get *Your Guide to the Taieri Gorge* when you board the train, so you can follow your progress through to the tiny township of Middlemarch, the final stopping point—a funny little backwater of a place where bachelors need hard-to-find wives. Once here, you can get off and, if you're not interested in finding the bachelors, you can link up to a coach to Queenstown; mountain bike, walk, or horseback ride—which will take you several days; or stay on the train for the return trip.

From October through April, the Dunedin-Middlemarch round-trip train runs Friday and Sunday morning. It leaves Dunedin Railway Station at 9:30am, has a 45-minute stop at Middlemarch, and returns to Dunedin at 3:25pm. (They offer reduced hours in winter.) It costs NZ$87 round-trip for adults. Students get a 20% discount; one child (ages 3–17) per adult rides free, with each extra child paying NZ$21. The shorter 4-hour trip to Pukerangi (19km/12 miles short of Middlemarch) runs daily at 2:30pm, returning 6:30pm, and costs NZ$76. Both trips include at least two photo stops, excellent ongoing commentary, and a buffet car for snacks and drinks. An adults-only car and a wheelchair-accessible carriage (book in advance) are available. For a coastal train experience, leap aboard the **Seasider,** which departs on selected Wednesdays and Saturdays in the summer season. I haven't tried this one yet, but I'm assured that the wild coastline on the trip north to Palmerston makes it more than worthwhile. You can make it a round-trip, or link with a gold-mine tour. It costs NZ$70 round-trip for adults, NZ$22 children ages 3 to 17.

SEA KAYAKING Otago Harbour is the perfect playground for sea kayakers. You can explore the spectacular sea cliffs teeming with wildlife, or turn your hand to a surf landing on an isolated beach. Contact **Wild Earth Adventures** (see above in "Organized Tours") for the best outings.

SURFING Head for **St. Clair** and **St. Kilda** beaches on The Esplanade. This is the center of Dunedin's surfer activity.

SWIMMING If the ocean seems too daunting, head for **Moana Pool,** Littlebourne Road and Stuart Street (© 03/471-9780). It has a terrific leisure pool, lap pool, and diving pool, and the water slides are fully enclosed tubes; you can opt for a slow or fast descent. Other watery options include scuba instruction, aqua-fitness classes, underwater hockey, and water polo. Or laze around in the cafe while the kids run wild in the play area. Admission is NZ$5 adults and NZ$3 children.

Dunedin provides the usual range of lodgings, from backpacker hostels to motels to fine hotels. But what I love most about the area is its very fine choice of heritage homestays and B&Bs, many of which are in exquisite Victorian-style buildings. At certain times of the year, midrange options are heavily booked because of university activities, so make your reservations early. Rates given below include the 12.5% GST and free off-street parking.

In Town
Expensive
Fletcher Lodge ★★★   This house is a stunning example of Dunedin's unique architecture. Built by one of New Zealand's leading industrialists in 1924, it features impressive detailing such as the Wedgwood ceiling and frieze in the music room and stained-glass inserts in almost every window. Keith and Ewa Rozecki-Pollard carried out major refurbishments in 2003; and they've more recently added two large suites in adjacent dwellings that are linked to the main house by boardwalks. All guest rooms contain desks and sofas, plus luxurious touches such as under-floor heating in the tiled bathrooms and sumptuous bedding that begs you to sleep in. Fletcher Lodge welcomes a wide range of overseas visitors, ambassadors, diplomats, and businesspeople. Definitely a place for the discerning traveler, but now more of a small boutique hotel than a B&B.

276 High St., Dunedin. ✆ **0800/843-563** in NZ, or 03/477-5552. Fax 03/474-5551. www.fletcherlodge. co.nz. 10 units. NZ$295–NZ$395 standard; NZ$450 premium; NZ$595–NZ$650 suite. NZ$50 each extra person. Long-stay rates. Rates include breakfast. AE, DC, MC, V. No children 11 and under. **Amenities:** Bar; airport transfers NZ$60; 4 nearby golf courses; free entry to nearby gym; Jacuzzi. *In room:* A/C, TV, hair dryer, small charge for Wi-Fi.

One Royal Terrace ★ (**Moments**)   From the hanging staircase and velvet-finished windows to the huge crystal chandelier in the entry hall, this big, two-storied Victorian beauty combines old-world charm with modern comforts. It's more ornate than the other old homes listed below, and if you're not happy here I'll eat my Victorian hat. Ian and Glenda Begg are passionate rally car drivers and you'll love the lavish touches they've added to their three big rooms. It's a more intimate experience than Fletcher Lodge, but it lacks their polished finish.

1 Royal Terrace, Dunedin. ✆ **03/479-0772.** Fax 03/479-0775. www.oneroyalterrace.co.nz. 3 units. NZ$350–NZ$450. Long-stay and off-peak rates. Rates include breakfast. MC, V. No children 11 and under. **Amenities:** Nearby golf courses and pools; Wi-Fi in reception. *In room:* TV, hair dryer, kitchenette (in apt).

Moderate
If you're looking for a smart motel close to town, **Motel on York ★**, 47 York Place (✆ **0800/006-666** in NZ, or 03/477-6120; www.motelonyork.co.nz), should do the trick. It's just two streets off The Octagon. Its 24 nonsmoking units offer all the comforts of a good little boutique hotel for NZ$155 to NZ$240.

Elgin House ★★   The very hospitable Roger and Carolyn Rennie live in the converted attic of their impressive three-story home, leaving the three luxurious bedroom spaces on the ground floor to you. The Inglenook is the biggest, with a fireplace and a romantic window seat overlooking a cottage garden. The Garden Room and the Oriel share a private bathroom and are let together to a single party. Drawing, dining room, and kitchen are all on the center floor and it's here you can unwind with the Rennies and a bottle of local wine after a big day of sightseeing. Rooms here are more contemporary than at One Royal Terrace.

31 Elgin Rd., Mornington, Dunedin. © **0800/272-940** in NZ, or 03/453-0004. www.elginhouse.co.nz. **493**
3 units. NZ$350. Rates include breakfast. MC, V. No children 11 and under. **Amenities:** Airport transport
by arrangement; nearby golf course. *In room:* TV/DVD, fridge, hair dryer, Wi-Fi.

Glendinning House ★★   I loved Jocelyn Robinson and Sandy Black's fabulous big
house from the minute I walked in to the smell of delicious things cooking. Jocelyn is a
former caterer, so expect a fantastic breakfast (and dinner if you give her 48 hr. notice).
The two upstairs rooms are huge and both open on to a big balcony. My pick here is the
two-bedroomed Blue Suite, which has an en-suite bathroom. The Yellow Room has a
private bathroom across the landing.

222 Highgate Rd., Roslyn, Dunedin. © **03/477-8262.** www.glendinninghouse.co.nz. 2 units. NZ$325–
NZ$385. NZ$95 each additional adult in suite; NZ$65 each additional child. Dinner NZ$95 per person.
Rates include breakfast, predinner drinks, and canapés. MC, V. **Amenities:** 3 nearby golf courses. *In room:*
TV/DVD, hair dryer, free Wi-Fi.

Scenic Hotel Southern Cross ★★★ ⓥ Value   This moderately sized hotel has always
been seen as the city's best, and after an NZ$8-million revamp in 2008, it has cemented
that reputation. It has the advantage of being centrally located; and rooms, in three wings
and across a range of prices, are very good value. I'm also happy to report that, after testing beds all over New Zealand, I've decided the Southern Cross has the best beds in the
country. Rooms in the Exchange Wing are the newest—they were added in 2000—and
the four corner rooms there are the largest. The premium apartment, with two bedrooms
and two bathrooms, is perhaps the best value of all. The Dunedin Casino is located
within the same building.

Corner of Princes and High sts., Dunedin. © **0800/696-963** in NZ. www.scenicgroup.co.nz. 178 units.
NZ$282 standard; NZ$428 junior suite and premium apt; NZ$535 executive suite. Off-peak rates and
special deals. AE, DC, MC, V. Valet parking NZ$15. **Amenities:** 3 restaurants (Ports of Call [Modern NZ];
Carlton [breakfast restaurant]; cafe); 2 bars; concierge; nearby golf course; gym; room service. *In room:* TV/
DVD, fridge, hair dryer, high-speed Internet, minibar.

Inexpensive

There are modest B&B digs at **Tower House,** 9 City Rd., Roslyn (© **03/477-5678;**
www.thetowerhouse.co.nz), where the price is from NZ$110 to NZ$140. Backpackers,
meanwhile, will be well taken care of at **Manor House Backpackers,** 28 Manor Place
(© **0800/477-0484** in NZ, or 03/477-0484; www.manorhousebackpackers.co.nz), where
dorm beds go for NZ$26 per person. There are also excellent, new, budget accommoda-
tions at **Living Space** ★, 192 Castle St., Dunedin (© **0508/454-846** in NZ, or 03/951-
5000; www.livingspace.net), which offers the nicest budget rooms in the city. Hotel
rooms are NZ$89 to NZ$109; studios NZ$99 to NZ$119; and premiums NZ$119 to
NZ$149.

On Otago Peninsula

There are certainly enough things to see on the peninsula to justify an overnight stay. At
ecofriendly **Nisbet Cottage** ★★, 6A Elliffe Place, Shiel Hill (© **03/454-5169;** www.
natureguidesotago.co.nz), hosts and nature guides Ralf and Hildegard Lubcke can advise
you on the area's natural history and unique bird life. They specialize in nature-based
accommodations packages that enlighten visitors to conservation issues and practices, in
which you tie up 2 or more nights' stay with guided wildlife tours of Dunedin, Otago
Peninsula, and the Catlins. There are two lovely suites with en-suite bathrooms and stunning views over Dunedin Harbor. Two-night tour packages start around NZ$600 and
include breakfast, tour, and picnic lunch.

Larnach Lodge ★ Larnach Castle (see "Exploring Otago Peninsula," earlier in this chapter) provides an imposing backdrop to the lodge's 12 spacious, themed rooms, which all have magnificent views. (There are no lodgings in the castle itself.) The Gold Rush Room features a king-size bed made from an old cart found on the castle grounds, complete with four huge wheels and the driver's seat and brakes attached to the end. There's a hint of the Wild West about it that doesn't quite fit the elegance of the rest of the lodge and castle. That aside, beds are divinely comfortable and bathrooms are generous. If you want to enjoy dinner in the castle's formal dining room, book by 5pm. Overall, an excellent place to base yourself for peninsula exploration, but a bit far out if you want town action.

Larnach Castle, 145 Camp Rd., Otago Peninsula. © **03/476-1616.** Fax 03/476-1574. www.larnachcastle. co.nz. 12 units. NZ$260 standard; NZ$280 premium; NZ$160 stable unit (with shared bathrooms). Rates include breakfast. MC, V. **Amenities:** Dining room; babysitting. *In room:* TV, fridge, hair dryer, Wi-Fi.

WHERE TO DINE

As a university town, Dunedin is home to many establishments that cater to students. Restaurants are therefore less stratified than in other New Zealand cities, and you'll find everyone—students, businesspeople, families, elderly couples—dining happily together in most places. There are plenty of budget options and quirkily named cafes and bars.

Plato ★★, 2 Birch St., Inner Harbour Warehouse Area (© **03/477-4235;** www. platocafe.co.nz), is a good restaurant choice for service and great original tastes, although the interior definitely lacks character and warmth. Take a cab, as it's easy to get lost in the wharf area. **A Cow Called Berta** ★★, 199 Stuart St. (© **03/477-2993**), is another that gets rave reviews for its cozy atmosphere and its fabulous meals. Mains here will set you back about NZ$36.

Expensive

Bell Pepper Blues ★★★ MODERN NEW ZEALAND Chef/owner Michael Coughlin and his wife, Marianne, have established an unpretentious restaurant with a focus on fine food—meals you remember long afterward for their flavor and stylish presentation. It's an intimate, award-winning, and heavily booked spot, so reserve ahead for such culinary pleasures as smoked duck terrine, or roasted fish filet with toasted fennel and chili rub. Make sure you save space for divine desserts like chocolate tart with a compote of nectarines, raspberry coulis, and vanilla cream. Widely regarded as one of Dunedin's best dining experiences, it also offers a delicious light lunch menu in the adjacent Chile Club, which doubles as a restaurant bar at night.

474 Princes St. © **03/474-0973.** www.bellpepperblues.co.nz. Reservations required. Main courses NZ$36–NZ$40. AE, DC, MC, V. Wed–Fri noon–2pm; Mon–Sat 6:30pm–late.

Table Se7en ★ INTERNATIONAL There's a slither of big-city style in this upstairs eatery that looks over the main shopping street. You can relax at the bar before tucking into more casual meals (than at Bellpepper Blues) like twice-baked pork belly on roasted root vegetables; or manuka-smoked beefsteak. If that doesn't tempt you, try beefsteak with a touch of chimichurri, or harissa-crusted, herb-smoked venison. It's not only their name they've gotten clever with—the menu is just as cool.

Level 1, corner of Hanover and George sts. © **03/477-6877.** www.tableseven.co.nz. Reservations recommended. Main courses NZ$25–NZ$32. AE, MC, V. Mon–Sat noon–3pm and dinner 6pm–late.

Moderate

Mazagram Espresso Bar ★ (Finds) ESPRESSO BAR One of my favorite Dunedin haunts, this place is a must-visit treat if you're a coffee connoisseur. You'll find yourself

(Finds) Gourmet Gifts

Everyday Gourmet Ltd. ★★★, 446 George St. ((℃ **03/477-2045**), provides instant gourmet satisfaction and the chance to find the perfect, unusual gifts for friends and family back home. Quite apart from the delicious counter food and light meals on offer, there are shelves bulging with products from near and far. I've decided it's easier to give into temptation than to resist. You'll find New Zealand–made items that will surprise and delight: the country's best olive oils, sauces, honey, preserves, chocolates, and cheeses, all presented in attractive gift packs. While you try to decide what to buy, enjoy the terrific coffee. It's open Monday through Friday from 9am to 6pm, Saturday from 10am to 3pm.

crammed into a tiny roastery with just four little marble tables (there are more tables outside). Mazagram supplies most of Dunedin's leading cafes. It does a mean brew and can also tempt you with a sweet to accompany your coffee.

Upper Moray Place. (℃ **03/477-9959.** Cakes NZ$6—NZ$12. No credit cards. Mon–Fri 8am–6pm; Sat 10am–2pm.

Nova ★★ ITALIAN/ASIAN   No trip to Dunedin is complete without a visit to trendy Nova. Step down off The Octagon into this smart, city-style cafe oozing ambience, and you'll find everything from delicious breakfast classics such as bagels and panettone to an easy mix of Italian and Asian dinner dishes. Seafood gumbo is a favorite—thick, spicy soup of seafood, bacon, and sausage served with toasted rye—or select from wok-fried vegetables, risotto of the day, steamed mussels, and lasagna, among others. Everyone comes to Nova, especially tourists and locals of an artistic bent, stepping in from the adjacent Public Art Gallery.

Dunedin Public Art Gallery, 29 The Octagon. (℃ **03/479-0808.** Reservations recommended. Main courses NZ$18–NZ$33. AE, DC, MC, V. Mon–Fri 7am–11pm; Sat–Sun 8:30am–11pm.

Strictly Coffee ★ CAFE   I almost got a chill up my spine when I discovered this cute, hidden-away place down a back alley. It's just my sort of place—slightly disheveled in a shabby-chic kind of way, unpretentious, friendly, and known to anyone who's anyone. On top of that, you get excellent coffee, fresh from their own roastery that you can huddle beside if you feel so inclined; sweet, savory treats; and good magazines. They've also wised up to the fact that opening early saves caffeine-deprived lives! And now they have a second location in the alley off George Street, opposite the Meridian Centre.

23 Bath St. (℃ **03/479-0017.** www.strictlycoffee.co.nz. Cafe food NZ$6–NZ$15. AE, MC, V. Mon–Fri 8am–5pm.

Inexpensive

For a firsthand taste of university social life, head for the **Governor's Café,** 438 George St. ((℃ **03/477-6871**), open daily from 8am to midnight, where the food is cheap, plentiful, and tasty.

Jizo Café/Bar ★ JAPANESE   I love to sit in this plain little restaurant and watch the chefs flinging my sushi together with an aplomb that leaves me breathless and hungry. This is the best place to sample cheap, authentic Japanese food in a casual environment. Service is snappy and the staff speaks both Japanese and English. It has a full sushi menu, *udon, katsu,* and seafood, vegetarian, and meat dishes, not to mention an impressive range of Japanese beers and sake. All this *and* jazz music. It could only happen in Dunedin.

56 Princes St. (C) **03/479-2692.** Main courses NZ$12–NZ$22. AE, DC, MC, V. Mon–Thurs 11:30am–9pm; Fri 11:30am–9:30pm; Sat 5–9:30pm.

SHOPPING

Dunedin offers excellent shopping, with most stores open Monday through Thursday from 9am to 5:30pm, Friday from 9am to 9pm, and Saturday and Sunday from 10am to 1pm (some later).

A good place to park your car and start browsing is the new **Meridian Shopping Centre,** George Street ((C) **03/477-1129**), which has over 40 specialty stores and an international food court. For a Kiwi memento to take home, check out the **New Zealand Shop** ((C) **03/477-3379;** www.upic.co.nz), in the civic center, next door to the visitor center on The Octagon. It's open Monday to Thursday 9am to 5:30pm, Friday 9am to 6pm, Saturday 9:30am to 4:30pm, and Sunday 10am to 4pm—and will even open just for you if you call ahead. It'll pack and post your order overseas, too.

If you want something with a "bonny wee Scottish" flavor, head for the **Scottish Shop,** 17 George St. ((C) **03/477-9965;** www.scottishshop.co.nz). It has a wide range of tartan and heraldic goods, right down to tartan ties. **Helean Kiltmakers,** 8 Hocken St., Kenmure ((C) **03/453-0233**), continues the theme with made-to-measure kilts.

Hides, 185 George St. ((C) **03/477-8927**), has top-quality Dunedin-made sheepskin and leather jackets, while **Glen's Leather & Accessories,** 192 Castle St. ((C) **03/477-3655**), offers good-value lambskin and leather products. **Kathmandu Ltd.,** 144 Great King St. ((C) **03/474-5178**), will see you right for all your outdoor gear.

For top-quality, one-of-a-kind New Zealand designer jewelry, you can't do better than **Fluxus Contemporary Jewellery,** 99 Stuart St. ((C) **03/477-9631**). This cooperatively run gallery exhibits the works of leading New Zealand jewelers such as Kobi Bosshard, Georg Beer, and Lyn Kelly. Exquisitely detailed pieces beg to be purchased!

The award-winning **University Book Shop,** 378 Great King St. ((C) **03/477-6976;** www.unibooks.co.nz), offers just about anything you're likely to want to read. It's just across the road from the Otago Museum and open Monday through Friday from 8:30am to 5:30pm, Saturday from 9:30am to 1:30pm. **Milford Galleries,** 18 Dowling St. ((C) **03/477-7727**), is the best dealer showing contemporary New Zealand art.

DUNEDIN AFTER DARK

Dunedin's nightlife ranges from its legendary university swill holes where drunken, animal-like behavior is de rigueur to smart, upmarket wine bars and a boutique casino. There are also two good theaters, a multiscreen movie theater, and several cafes that double as live-music venues.

THE PERFORMING ARTS The **Fortune Theatre,** Stuart Street and Upper Moray Place ((C) **03/477-8323;** www.fortunetheatre.co.nz), plays a major part in the cultural life of Dunedin with a wide range of performances, from Shakespeare to contemporary New Zealand works. The theater is in a historic late-1800s building. Its season runs from February to December. Tickets generally cost around NZ$35 for adults and NZ$25 for students.

The **Regent Theatre,** on the Lower Octagon ((C) **03/477-8597;** fax 03/477-4726), hosts a range of national and international performances. Check the local paper for the current schedule of concerts. Also look out for the Dunedin Sinfonia concert series brochure at the visitor center. Ticket prices vary.

(Moments) **Back Alley Pleasures**

Hunt for the *pièce de résistance* of Dunedin bars, the very suave, very hard to find gem **Pequeño** ★★★, Lower Ground Floor (they really mean "underground"), Savoy Building, 50 Princes St. (📞 **03/477-7830**). Alternatively, if you can find a friendly local to direct you, you can access it from a steep, dark alley off Upper Moray Place. I was taken here by Andrew of Hair Raiser Ghost Walk, so it stands to reason he would pick the darkest, seediest entry. Once inside, though, it is a salubrious and classy little den—all fur, leather, and artistic Dunedin types out for a good time. Definitely a place for grown-ups, and they have a terrific wine and cocktails list.

THE BAR, CAFE & PUB SCENE   We can thank the student population for much of the color in Dunedin's after-dark scene. Their favorite hangouts include the legendary **Gardens Tavern** (affectionately known as "The Gardies"), 697 Castle St., Dunedin North (📞 **03/477-6593**)—chance it if you dare! **ReFuel Bar,** 21 Frederick St. (📞 **03/477-2575**), has the Lounge and Fusion Bars, which provide a changing array of nightly entertainment.

The **Royal Albert Mine Host Bar,** 387 George St. (📞 **03/477-2952**), is a slight improvement for those in an older age group. The **Bennu Café & Bar,** 12 Moray Place (📞 **03/474-5055**), and the **Ra Bar,** 21 The Octagon (📞 **03/477-6080**), are currently deemed to be the happening spots for good food and a lively bar atmosphere for anyone over 25.

Bacchus Winebar, upstairs at 12 The Octagon (📞 **03/474-0824**), is a nice enough place overlooking The Octagon. It never really takes off in terms of a wild night out—it's more of a sedate place to savor good company and good wine in a smoke-free environment.

For a funky Dunedin night out, you can't beat the **Arc Café Bar,** 135 High St. (📞 **03/474-1135**). You'll find a wide cross section of society here, all blending amiably and listening to live music.

MOVIES   There are six big screens at the **Hoyts 6 Cinema,** 33 The Octagon (📞 **03/477-7019**). It has a licensed cafe and bar and plenty of parking at the rear. There is also a new **Rialto 3** theater complex on Upper Moray Place. The **Metro Cinema,** Moray Place, shows artsy movies.

EN ROUTE TO INVERCARGILL

You could drive from Dunedin to Invercargill in roughly 2½ to 3 hours via State Highway 1, passing through the small Southland townships of Balclutha, Gore, and Edendale. This pleasant drive will take you past farmland and mile after mile of grazing sheep.

But now that I've personally experienced the **Southern Scenic Route** ★★★ via the **Catlins** ★★★ for the first time, I urge you to consider taking an extra day to explore this rich, unspoiled coastline. I spent a leisurely 7 hours getting from Dunedin to Invercargill, taking as many side routes as I could, and I never regretted a second of it. The region contains the most significant area of native forest on the east coast of New Zealand, and walking tracks will take you through tall podocarps such as rimu and totara.

Keep in mind, though, that rain falls in this area 214 days a year, so chances are you're going to get wet. However, a lot of the rainfalls occur overnight and won't disrupt your sightseeing. Be sure to pick up the visitor center's brochure on the Southern Scenic Route (St. Hwy. 92), so you can make informed decisions about the stops you make. It is also important to note that many of the roads are unpaved, and if you're unfamiliar with this sort of driving, knock 20kmph (12 mph) off your speed, concentrate, keep in the road grooves, and don't overreact if you skid.

Leaving Dunedin, your first diversion should be to the wildlife-rich area of **Nugget Point** ★, signposted just south of Balclutha. Gloriously undisturbed coastline awaits, and from here all the way to Waikawa, you'll find a rich vein of scenic opportunity. Chief among them will be **Purakaunui Falls,** accessed by a 20-minute round-trip walk through beech and podocarp forest; **Cathedral Caves** ★, an 80-minute round-trip walk along the beach at low tide only; and the spectacular curve of **Tautuku Bay,** 2km (1¼ miles) south of Papatowai. If you see nothing else, the hilltop view of this bay alone makes the trip worthwhile.

Farther south, you'll find one of the world's finest fossil forests, which can be viewed at low tide at **Curio Bay.** This sea-washed rock terrace dates back 160 million years and is the original floor of a Jurassic subtropical forest of kauri trees, conifers, and other trees growing at a time when grasses had not evolved. At low tide, you can easily make out the stumps and fallen logs that were petrified after being buried in volcanic ash, then raised when the sea level changed.

Another worthwhile stop is **Slope Point.** As the name suggests, the strong winds here are responsible for the rather strange, bent-over form of the trees. Wear warm clothing, as the winds lash in off Foveaux Strait. This is the southernmost point of the South Island, and if you're here on a fine day, you'll be pleased with the views.

The Southern Scenic Route continues on to Te Anau—a total trip of 440km (275 miles) from Dunedin. The Catlins side of the journey is by far the most interesting leg, and it's easy to see why this area is one of the new frontiers of New Zealand tourism. There's a range of moderately priced motels, B&Bs, and backpacker accommodations along the way if you decide to stop over. There are brochures for many of these at the Owaka Information Centre. For more information on the route, call ✆ **0800/723-642** in New Zealand, or 03/214-9733, or go to www.southland.org.nz.

2 INVERCARGILL ★

190km (118 miles) S of Queenstown; 217km (135 miles) SW of Dunedin

Asked to name seven great things about Invercargill, most people hesitate and scratch their heads. The 53,000 residents of this southernmost city would be justifiably indignant. They'll quickly tell you that people from Invercargill are among the friendliest in the country, that the city has the best seafood, and that it makes a perfect base for exploring some of the country's finest scenery in Fiordland, the Catlins, and Stewart Island. Nor should we overlook the fact that Southland is the capital of country music in New Zealand; that it has the best cycle velodrome in the country; that it offers the lowest education fees in New Zealand; and it was the location for the hit movie *The World's Fastest Indian,* the story of Invercargill motorcycle legend Burt Munro.

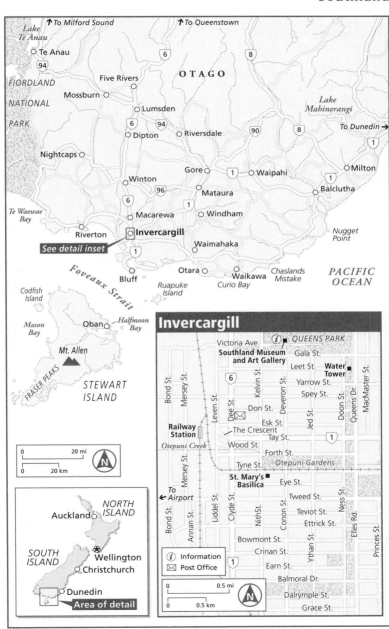

Originally settled by Scottish immigrants, the city's prosperity has been founded on the lush grasslands of Southland, and today several million sheep and cattle graze the flat pastures that surround it. Invercargill is the province's major service center, with more than 1,000 motel and hotel beds.

This once swampy bogland first attracted Europeans keen to establish a flax-milling industry. It was surveyed in 1856 by New Zealand's first surveyor general, J. Thomson, who wisely mapped out the main streets (named after Scottish rivers) 40m (130 ft.) in width, still giving the city its distinctive spacious character. Southlanders continue to be seen as a hardy, practical, gregarious lot, and they'll make sure your stay here is a memorable one.

ESSENTIALS

GETTING THERE & GETTING AROUND   **By Plane**   **Air New Zealand** (© 0800/ 737-000** in NZ; www.airnewzealand.co.nz) has service between Invercargill and Auckland and Wellington on the North Island, and Christchurch and Dunedin on the South Island. **Stewart Island Flights** (© 03/218-9129;** www.stewartislandflights.com) has daily scheduled flights to Stewart Island. The airport is 2.5km (1½ miles) from the city center. **Spitfire Shuttles** (© 03/214-1851) provides transport to and from the city. For more information, go to www.invercargillairport.co.nz. A cab to the city will cost around NZ$15.

By Coach (Bus)   **InterCity** (© 09/623-1503) has coach service between Invercargill and Christchurch, Dunedin, Queenstown, Te Anau, and Timaru. The bus depot is also on Leven Street. Look out for the **Freebie,** a free local shuttle service connecting inner city businesses. It runs Monday through Friday, every 15 minutes between 9:30am and 5:45pm. For information on connecting bus routes, call © 03/218-7108.

By Car   Invercargill can be reached on State Highway 6 from Queenstown or State Highway 1 from Dunedin. See the information on the Southern Scenic Route under "En Route to Invercargill," above. The **Automobile Association** office is at 47–51 Gala St. (© 0800/500-444).

By Taxi   Call **Blue Star Taxis Ingill Ltd.,** Tay and Jed streets (© 03/217-7777), or **Taxi Co.,** 200 Clyde St. (© 03/214-4478).

ORIENTATION   Invercargill's streets are laid out in grid patterns. The main thoroughfares are Tay Street (an extension of St. Hwy. 1) and Dee Street (an extension of St. Hwy. 6). Many of the principal shops and office buildings are found at their intersection. Queens Park is an 80-hectare (200-acre) green oasis in the center of town.

VISITOR INFORMATION   The **Invercargill i-SITE Visitor Centre,** in the Southland Museum and Art Gallery, Victoria Avenue (© 03/211-0895;** fax 03/218-4415; www. southlandnz.com), is open daily October through April 8am to 6pm, and in winter 8am to 5pm (closed Dec 25). The **Department of Conservation,** State Insurance Building, Seventh Floor, 33 Don St. (© 03/214-4589;** fax 03/214-4486; www.doc.govt.nz), is open Monday through Friday from 8am to 5pm. For more information on this area, check www.invercargill.org.nz.

FAST FACTS   The **Central Post Office** is at 1 Don St. **Southland Hospital,** Kew Road (© 03/218-1949), has 24-hour emergency care. You can get prescriptions filled at **UFS Dispensary,** 76 Tay St. (© 03/218-9393), or, for after-hours service, 90 Kelvin St. (© 03/218-4893). For information on **major events** check www.southlandnz.com.

Museums, Galleries & Architecture

It's hard to miss the big white pyramid of the **Southland Museum and Art Gallery** ★★ (✆ **03/218-9753;** www.southlandmuseum.com), on Gala Street near the main entrance to Queens Park. A wide range of exhibits brings the region to life. The biggest attraction of all, the **Tuatarium** ★★★, should not be missed. Here you'll find the fascinating tuatara—strange prickly reptiles that are descendants of the dinosaurs and now exceptionally rare. The museum breeding program is the only one in the world. As tuatara are nocturnal, they may be hard to spot during the day. The highlight is Henry, now over 100 years old, who, along with the successfully breeding Albert and his concubines, Mildred and Lucy, may show his face. Another excellent museum attraction is the comprehensive audiovisual program on New Zealand's **Sub-Antarctic Islands** ★★, an area of international importance because they have some of the world's last remaining areas of vegetation unmodified by humans. The museum is open Monday through Friday from 9am to 5pm; Saturday, Sunday, and holidays from 10am to 5pm. Admission is free but a charge may apply to some exhibits.

Anderson Park Art Gallery, 91 McIvor Rd., Invercargill (✆ **03/215-7432**) is housed in a fine Georgian-style residence set on 24 hectares (59 acres) of landscaped gardens. You'll find this architectural delight 7km (4⅓ miles) north of the city, just a short drive east along McIvor Road, which runs off North Road. It's open daily from 10:30am to 5pm. Admission is free, except during exhibitions.

Speaking of things old, ***Invercargill Heritage Trail*** is an excellent brochure produced by the New Zealand Historic Places Trust and available at the visitor center. It highlights 18 of the city's finest architectural specimens, including St. Mary's Basilica, on Tyne Street, and the town's famous 43m (139-ft.) red-brick Romanesque water tower. There is a similar brochure for nearby Bluff; and the ***Invercargill City Spirit Walk*** brochure details a 1-hour walk through the inner city, following history in sculptures, landmarks, and information panels.

Parks & Gardens

The main entrance to **Queens Park** is near Southland Museum and Art Gallery. This cool green 80-hectare (200-acre) oasis is a perfect place to wander and it features some beautiful trees. You'll find formal rose gardens, a rhododendron walk, an iris garden, a Japanese garden, a wildlife sanctuary, a walk-through bird aviary, duck ponds, a winter garden, tennis courts, and an 18-hole golf course. The aviary has a good parrot collection and is best visited in early morning or late afternoon, when the birds are most active.

Maple Glen Gardens and Nursery, in nearby rural Wyndham (✆ **03/206-4983;** www.mapleglen.co.nz), is a remarkable private garden and exotic bird haven that every gardener should see. It's open daily from 9am to 5pm. A guided walk costs NZ$5 per person.

Ⓣips   Picnic Time

Look out for the visitor center's handy green brochure that outlines *Invercargill's Picnic Areas*. It describes 16 ideal picnic spots and where to find them.

(Finds **Hidden Gems**

If you're looking for an interesting country drive out of Invercargill, go to **Cosy Nook** ★★, a delightful fishing settlement on one of the wildest coastlines in the world. Near Riverton, it's well signposted from State Highway 99. You'll find cute old fishing boats and cottages and some creative signage. **Riverton Rocks Beach** is also a treat, with gorgeous little green pebbles all over the place. It's about a 45-minute drive from Invercargill. Just over the hill to the southwest, you'll find **Colac Bay**—one big horseshoe swoop of surfing heaven, with a cluster of little cottages on the foreshore.

A Side Trip to Bluff

If time permits, take a drive to Bluff to find **Tiwai Smelter Tours,** NZ Aluminium Smelters Ltd. (② **03/218-5494;** www.comalco.com). This free tour is much more interesting than you might think and is available weekdays at 10am, with only three tours per week. Bookings are essential; there are special clothing requirements for safety reasons. Children 11 and under will not be admitted. **Bluff's Maritime Museum,** Foreshore Road (② **03/212-7534;** bluffmuseum@netscape.net.nz), is open 10am to 4:30pm Monday through Friday and from 1 to 5pm on weekends, and presents good coverage of Southland's maritime history. If you visit during oyster season, try and attend the annual **Bluff Oyster & Southland Seafood Festival** ★★★ (www.bluffoysterfest.co.nz), which is held in late April at the Bluff Events Centre on Gore Road. More information on this tiny town can be found at www.bluff.co.nz. Bluff is 27km (17 miles) south of Invercargill. In Invercargill, get on Dee Street, which becomes State Highway 1; the drive will take about 30 minutes.

ORGANIZED TOURS

If you haven't already explored the Catlins area (see "En Route to Invercargill," above), join the **Catlins Coaster** (② **03/437-0753;** www.catlinscoaster.co.nz), which offers a full-day Catlins tour, exploring wildlife and natural attractions for around NZ$155. **Lynette Jack Scenic Sights** (②/fax **03/215-7741** or 027/433-8370) has tours from 2 hours to a full day that explore not only the Catlins, but also Bluff, Riverton, and Western Southland. To sightsee in total comfort, contact **Ambassador Limousines** (② **03/ 217-4504** or 025/339-889). Both **Southeast Air** (② **03/214-5522;** fax 03/214-5520) and **Southern Wings Air Charter** (② **03/218-6171;** www.southernwings.co.nz) offer chartered scenic flights around Southland.

OUTDOOR PURSUITS

BEACHES   **Oreti Beach,** 9.5km (6 miles) west of Invercargill, out past the airport, is safe for swimming. This broad expanse of sand stretches from Omaui at the southern end right around to Riverton. There are surf patrols in attendance during summer.

BIKING   Single and tandem bikes can be hired from **Wensley's Cycles,** Tay and Ninth streets (② **03/218-6206;** fax 03/218-6368).

FISHING   There are numerous fishing opportunities in Southland, many within 30 minutes of Invercargill. The famous **Mataura River** offers some of the best trout fishing in the world. The season in most areas opens October 1 and goes to April 30. There are

exceptions, so check the regulation guide available at the visitor center. The team at
Outdoor World, Tay Street (☎ **03/214-2052**), can advise you on the best spots and the
best tackle. **Alan Wilson** (☎/fax **03/217-3687;** dryfly@southnet.co.nz) can help with
wilderness and heli-fishing.

WALKING There are numerous fine walks within an hour's drive of Invercargill. You
can read about them in the Department of Conservation's excellent brochure *Day Walks
from Invercargill,* available at the visitor center. **Sandy Point Domain,** 7km (4⅓ miles)
west of the city, has attractive walking tracks through totara forest and sand dunes. The
Foveaux Walkway in Bluff is a 2-hour walk around Bluff's rugged coastline. The track
begins at Ocean Beach Road and ends at Stirling Point, or vice versa. The 30-minute
Glory Track starts at Stirling Point and finishes at Gunpit Road. A little farther afield,
the **Tuatapere Humpridge Track** ★★, 31 Orawia Rd., Tuatapere (☎ **0800/486-774** in
NZ, or 03/226-6739; www.humpridgetrack.co.nz), is fast gaining a reputation as an
excellent 3-day walk for those of moderate to high fitness levels. Tuatapere is 86km (53
miles) from Invercargill and 100km (60 miles) from Te Anau on the Southern Scenic
Route.

WINDSURFING The best area for windsurfing is at **Awarua Bay.** Gear rental is available at **Anderson Wind and Surfing,** 204 Spey St. (☎ **03/214-4283**).

WHERE TO STAY

Most of the 1,000 or so beds available in Invercargill are in the budget and moderately
priced range, with little to offer in the bed-and-breakfast or expensive bracket. One thing
the area can boast, though, is its wide range of home- and farmstay options scattered
throughout the surrounding farmland, and plenty of reasonable motels. Pick up the
visitor center's brochure detailing home- and farmstays. The rates given below include
the 12.5% GST and free off-street parking.

Expensive

The Lodge at Tikana ★★★ You'll have to be in quick to secure the comforts of this
gorgeous rural stay 30 minutes from Invercargill. Sadly, it's single-party bookings only,
but if you're one of the lucky ones, you'll love this custom-built den on a working farm.
The stylish lodge accommodates four people only, and hosts Donna Day and Dave
Lawrence go out of their way to make sure you're well rested and well fed. Beautiful beds,
great meals, and all the mod-cons make this one of the best Southland stays I've discovered. The property also has a Qualmark Enviro-Gold rating and is a member of the
Southland Sustainable Tourism Charter.

374 Livingstone Rd., Browns, Winton. ☎/fax **03/236-4117.** www.tikana.co.nz. 2-bedroom lodge.
NZ$1,890; extra person NZ$810. Rates include breakfast, predinner drinks, gourmet dinner. Minimum
2-night stay. AE, DC, MC, V. No children 11 and under. **Amenities:** Bar; nearby golf course; Jacuzzi; room
service; spa treatments; grass tennis court; Wi-Fi in main lodge. *In room:* TV/DVD/CD, stocked fridge, hair
dryer, kitchenette, minibar.

Moderate

I'm very pleased to have discovered a very nice new bed-and-breakfast that should
suit travelers very well. **Beersheba Boutique Accommodation,** 58 Milton Park Rd.,
Invercargill (☎ **03/216-3677;** www.beersheba.co.nz), offers two very nice rooms in the
main house, plus a self-contained one-bedroom cottage in a private garden setting. The
whole property sits within a 4-acre landscaped garden with ponds and an abundance of
bird life.

Ascot Park Hotel ★★   This is deemed Invercargill's top spot, and although it's a bit too far out of town (4km/2½ miles) to be convenient, it does have silence on its side—unlike the Kelvin Hotel (see below). The four deluxe units are a good pick if you like heaps of space. The suites are perfect for two couples or a family. The motel units come complete with kitchens. The hotel is favored by sports teams, tour groups, and independent travelers, but it's plenty big enough for everyone to have a comfortable night. An additional 20 apartments and studios will come on stream in 2010.

Tay St. and Racecourse Rd., Invercargill. ✆ **0800/272-687** in NZ, or 03/217-6195. Fax 03/217-7002. www. ascotparkhotel.co.nz. 96 units. NZ$183 superior; NZ$195 deluxe; NZ$340 suite; NZ$115 motel unit. Extra person NZ$24. Long-stay and off-peak rates. AE, DC, MC, V. **Amenities:** Restaurant; 2 bars; airport transport; babysitting; children's play area; nearby golf course; small exercise room; Jacuzzi; heated indoor pool; room service; sauna. *In room:* A/C, TV, fridge, hair dryer, kitchen (in motels), minibar, Wi-Fi.

Kelvin Hotel ★   This hotel sits in the well-priced midrange bracket. It's pretty much a standard facility, but rooms are all fresh and light. Bathrooms are small but smart, all with combination tub/showers (and Jacuzzis in sixth-floor rooms). Room no. 601 is the corner honeymoon suite, with great views over the city. Molly's in-house restaurant has an Irish theme and is very popular with locals. This is a hard-to-beat central-city location, right in the middle of the main shopping streets, but unfortunately is also prone to a lot of noise, especially on weekends.

Kelvin and Esk sts., Invercargill. ✆ **0800/802-829** in NZ, or 03/218-2829. Fax 03/218-2827. www.kelvin hotel.co.nz. 60 units. NZ$145 deluxe; NZ$195 suite. Extra person NZ$24. Packages and long-stay rates negotiable. AE, DC, MC, V. **Amenities:** Restaurant (Molly's [Modern NZ]); 2 bars (Irish, casino); nearby golf course; nearby gym; room service. *In room:* TV, fridge, hair dryer, minibar, Wi-Fi.

Inexpensive

Backpackers will find comfortable beds at **Living Space** ★★, 15 Tay St. (✆ **0508/454-846** in NZ; www.livingspace.net), which has a colorful selection of studios and two- to three-bedroom apartments.

WHERE TO DINE

It's only been in recent years that Invercargill has come up to snuff on the dining scene. Restaurants are still few and far between given the size of the town, but there are some good eateries. **HMS Kings Restaurant,** 80 Tay St. (✆ **03/218-3433**), is consistently favored by locals for its seafood, although service can be erratic; and **148 on Elles,** 148 Elles St. (✆ **03/216-1000**), is recommended. **Soprano's Pizzeria** ★★, 33 Tay St. (✆ **03/218-3464**), has a lively atmosphere and tasty pizzas if you just feel like a quick bite. Of all the eateries here though, the one I'm most inclined to is **Rocks Café** ★★, Courtville Place, 101 Dee St. (✆ **03/218-7597**), which is tucked away off the main beat and is the most likely to deliver a reliable, tasty meal. If you like the safety of the familiar, you'll find **Starbucks** at 55 Esk St. (✆ **03/214-0117**)—supposedly the southernmost Starbucks in the world.

Zookeepers Café ★★ NEW ZEALAND/CAFE   Look out for the large elephant on the roof and you won't miss Zookeepers. The interior is just as zany, and there's always a chummy atmosphere that makes it one of the most popular places in Invercargill. Crumbed Stewart Island blue cod with Kumara fries, minced lamb kabobs, rib-eye steak, pastas, and salads are typical offerings. Come here for the mood more than the food. You'll find both young and old, locals and visitors.

50 Tay St. ✆ **03/218-3373.** Main courses NZ$12–NZ$28. AE, DC, MC, V. Daily 10am–late.

The **Lone Star,** Dee and Leet streets (ℂ **03/214-6225**), draws a crowd of mixed ages, and **Molly's,** in the Kelvin Hotel, Kelvin and Esk streets (ℂ **03/218-2829**), attracts Guinness fans and lovers of hearty Irish atmosphere. Sorry, Invercargill, but it must be said—you could do with some classier options.

3 STEWART ISLAND ★★

30km (19 miles) SW of Bluff, across the Foveaux Strait

Anyone who tries to visit Stewart Island in a day won't be giving this near-perfect place a chance. It is almost a cliché to call it one of New Zealand's best-kept secrets, but given that so few people are aware of its unspoiled tranquillity, it probably deserves this label more than any other place in the country.

New Zealand's third island is far bigger than most people imagine, and almost without exception, first-time visitors are surprised by its equitable climate and the range of activities it provides. Roughly triangular in shape, it is 65km (40 miles) long and 40km (25 miles) at its widest point, and with an area of 1,680 sq. km (655 sq. miles), it is about the size of Singapore or Fiji. Only 1% of the island is inhabited—the rest is given over to natural native bush, exquisite white-sand beaches, bird sanctuaries, and rugged mountains. All this makes it a naturalist's and tramper's paradise, and the perfect place for a remote yet accessible holiday. You need to be here only a few hours before the rest of the world melts away and you find yourself adopting the unhurried, laid-back approach of the locals.

The main fishing village of Oban is your landing point, and this is where the population of approximately 390 bases itself. Most permanent residents are involved in the commercial fishing or tourism industries, and a surprisingly small number of other smart New Zealanders have invested in holiday homes, or cribs, here.

Originally called *Te Punga o Te Waka a Maui* by the Maori, which translates as "The Anchorstone of Maui's Canoe," it is more commonly known by the Maori name Rakiura, which means "Land of Glowing Skies," referring to the vivid colors of dawn and the twilight skies.

Today, the island community jealously guards the amazing natural heritage that surrounds it. This is natural New Zealand the way it used to be—truly picturesque and serene, a place where native birds will land within inches of your teacup, a place you should not overlook.

ESSENTIALS

GETTING THERE   By Plane   Air transport to Stewart Island is provided by **Stewart Island Flights** (ℂ **03/218-9129;** www.stewartislandflights.com), which is based at Invercargill Airport. You get breathtaking views of the island from the nine-seat Britten-Norman aircraft, which takes approximately 20 minutes to cross Foveaux Strait. Shuttle buses then deliver you to your accommodations in Oban. The round-trip fare is NZ$185 for adults and NZ$105 for children 15 and under. Stewart Island Flights can also help you plan and book your entire Stewart Island holiday; and they have a number of day-trip specials that include a bus tour, walks, and short water-taxi trips. These are ideal if you're short on time but desperate to see something of the island. The five options are priced around NZ$300 for adults and NZ$150 for children.

> ## (Tips) Rough Going
>
> If you're taking the ferry, it is important to remember that Foveaux Strait is one of the most unpredictable passages in the world, and the water can be extremely rough. If you're prone to seasickness, come prepared and ask staff for comfortable sailing tips. They also sell homeopathic remedies at the check-in counter. It may be a short trip (1 hr.), but can be notoriously uncomfortable. Many people like to fly one-way and take the ferry the other. This gives you two perspectives, and eliminates a difficult water crossing if the weather is not fine.

By Boat The passenger-only ferry, operated by **Stewart Island Experience,** will have you on Stewart Island in an hour. It departs Bluff ferry terminal September through April daily from 8:30am until 4pm and from May through August 9:30am to 5pm. There's connecting bus service from Invercargill to Bluff; secure car parking (extra cost) is available near the Bluff ferry terminal. The round-trip fare is NZ$126 for adults and NZ$64 for children ages 5 to 14. There are very good, reliable coach connections that pick you up from your Invercargill or Bluff accommodations 1 hour before the ferry departure. Inquire at the time of ferry booking and expect to pay NZ$20 for adults and NZ$10 for children ages 5 to 14 for the coach trip. For inquiries and reservations, call ℂ **0800/000-511** in NZ, or 03/212-7660, or visit www.stewartislandexperience.co.nz.

GETTING AROUND Most things on the island are within walking distance, although a number of the accommodations lie farther out. To reach them, and some of the divine beaches, means a good up- and downhill walk. A shuttle/minibus operates around the island like a taxi service; and you can rent cars (NZ$65 for a half-day), mountain bikes (NZ$36 a day), and scooters (NZ$45 per 2 hr.), from both the **Stewart Island Visitor Terminal,** on the wharf (ℂ **03/219-0034;** www.stewartislandexperience.co.nz), and the **Stewart Island Flights Depot,** Elgin Terrace (ℂ **03/219-1090;** www.stewartisland flights.com). The **i-SITE visitor center** (see below) can also provide details and rates on these options. Charter boats and water taxis can be arranged for sightseers, hunters, divers, trampers, and fishermen. Make reservations at the **Stewart Island Visitor Terminal** (ℂ **03/219-0034;** www.stewartislandexperience.co.nz). If you prefer, reservations can be made directly with the operators; go to the i-SITE visitor center for information and brochures.

VISITOR INFORMATION The ferry will deposit you on the wharf at Oban within a few hundred meters from the center of the village. The village itself consists of the **Ship to Shore General Store** (ℂ/fax **03/219-1069**), which prides itself on supplying everything from a needle to an anchor; a hotel; a couple of restaurants; the Department of Conservation base; a small museum; a school and community hall; numerous homes; and various travel offices.

The **Stewart Island i-SITE Visitor Information Centre** is at 12 Elgin Terrace (ℂ **03/219-1400;** fax 03/219-1401; www.stewartisland.co.nz). It's open daily; summer hours are 9am to 7pm, and winter hours are 9:30am to 6:30pm. The **Rakiura National Park Visitor Centre** is in the Department of Conservation building on Main Road (ℂ **03/219-0009;** fax 03/219-0003; www.doc.govt.nz). All trampers must report here for walking-track and hut passes. The staff members here are extremely well informed about all aspects of tramping and exploring the island; since some of the tracks are challenging, it pays to ask their advice. Also take a look at the 4-minute tramping video, which gives you an idea of what you're in for. They're open daily in summer from 8am to 5pm, and in winter from 8:30am to 4:30pm. Both are closed December 25.

FAST FACTS   There is no full banking service available on the island. Credit cards are accepted by most businesses, but foreign traveler's checks and cash can be difficult to change, so it pays to arrive with New Zealand dollars.

EXPLORING THE ISLAND

Most visitors are drawn to Stewart Island's unspoiled beauty and unique lifestyle. Nowhere else in New Zealand will you find such ready access to fern-filled native forests and astonishing bird life (see "Walking & Tramping," below).

For those coming to simply unwind, there are lots of quirky activities that must be experienced. The **Rakiura Museum,** Ayr Street, Half Moon Bay (℮ **03/219-1049;** fax 03/219-1126), is worthwhile for those who want a glimpse at the island's past. It features photographs and exhibits tracing the island's history through sailing, whaling, tin mining, sawmilling, and fishing. It also has shell and Maori artifact displays. It's open Monday through Saturday from 10am to 1:30pm, Sunday from noon to 2pm, with extended hours during the summer holidays. Admission is NZ$5. The **Fernery,** 29 Golden Bay Rd. (℮/fax **03/219-1453**), is one of Stewart Island's crafts shops. It carries pottery, glassware, wood, silk, T-shirts, and souvenirs. **Glowing Sky Studio Shop,** Town Centre (℮ **03/219-1528;** www.glowingsky.co.nz), stocks some lovely merino wool garments. The **Rakiura Gallery** ★, 10 Main Rd. (℮ **03/219-1429**), is your best bet for work by local artists.

WALKING & TRAMPING

Stewart Island offers unparalleled walking and tramping opportunities. Trampers will go through undisturbed native vegetation and see hundreds of birds. It is important to remember that rain falls on Stewart Island about 275 days of the year, so bring good waterproof clothing. The weather is very changeable, often swinging from rain to warm sun in the space of an hour. Track surfaces are varied and include long sections of boardwalk, which protects the native vegetation. Some tracks also include long stretches of deep mud, so wear sturdy boots. You can get further information from the Department of Conservation.

Anyone staying in huts on Stewart Island must pay hut fees. You need to purchase a **Great Walks Pass,** hut tickets, or an annual hut pass from the Department of Conservation (see "Visitor Information," above). Comfortable huts are conveniently spaced along the tracks (ranging in size from 6 to 24 bunks), but they're packed in summer. There's a 2-night maximum stay in any one hut, and you can use tents as well. You will be fined a surcharge if you are found using the huts without a Great Walks Pass.

The **Rakiura Track** ★★★ is one of the Department of Conservation's eight identified Great Walks of New Zealand. The 36km (22-mile) track requires a moderate fitness level and can be comfortably hiked in 3 days, year-round. The circuit follows the open coast, climbs over a 300m (980-ft.) forested ridge, and traverses the sheltered shores of Paterson Inlet. Huts cost NZ$15 per person per night, campsites NZ$5 per person per night.

The **North West Circuit** ★★ requires a much greater level of fitness and is recommended for experienced trampers, who need to be completely self-sufficient and prepared for 7 hours of tramping a day for 10 days. This track has long stretches of mud and is dangerous once snow falls. It takes in the northern third of the island and the island's highest peak, Mount Anglem (980m/3,200 ft.). A North West Circuit Pass costs NZ$50 and allows 1 night in each hut on the North West Circuit Track, including the Great Walks huts at Port William and North Arm. Backcountry hut tickets (NZ$5 per night), or a Backcountry Pass (NZ$90), may be used on the North West and the Southern Circuit Tracks, but separate passes must be purchased for the Great Walks huts (NZ$15 per night).

The **Southern Circuit,** which can be added to the above or done separately, is more of a wilderness experience that requires 6 to 7 days of tramping. It requires a much higher level of fitness and some orientation skills.

Stewart Island Day Walks range from 15 minutes to 7 hours and spread out in a number of directions from Oban. They include comfortable walks to Observation Rock, Golden Bay, Lonneckers Bay, Lee Bay, and Ringaringa Beach (a great spot for shell hounds when the tide is right), and longer walks to Maori Beach (7-hr. round-trip) and Garden Mound (5-hr. round-trip).

Ulva Island ★★★ is one of the best soft-core walking experiences of all. The Department of Conservation recognizes Ulva Island as the "Showcase Project" for its Southland Conservancy, and you can see the results of successful pest-eradication and endangered-species enhancement projects at close quarters. Catch a water taxi to the island (NZ$25) per person round-trip for two or more people from Golden Bay, which is a 20-minute walk over the hill from Oban. It's a short boat trip to somewhere close to paradise—a protected place where you can see rare birds and plants up close without harming them. The island has an 11km (6¾-mile) coastline, and there are walks from 20 minutes to 3 hours. You can spend several hours on the island—and if you're a keen photographer or naturalist, you'll want to—and arrange your return pickup with the water taxi when you land. For information on organized walking treks, see "Other Outdoor Pursuits," below.

OTHER OUTDOOR PURSUITS

GOLF   Don't miss New Zealand's only registered 6-hole golf course at **Ringaringa Heights,** overlooking Ringaringa Beach. Greens fees are NZ$10 for two people, which may well make it the cheapest golf course in the world. Club rentals are available at **Stewart Island Flight Depot** (✆ 03/219-1090) for NZ$5.

HUNTING   The elusive American whitetail deer was liberated on Stewart Island in the early 1900s and now provides sport for the energetic hunter. Hunting parties may spend up to 2 weeks camped in isolated places during the winter "roar." **Southern Isle Charters** (✆ 03/219-1133; lhhansen@xtra.co.nz) can arrange water transport and hunting parties.

KAYAKING   **Ruggedy Range Wilderness Experience** ★★ (✆ 03/219-1066; www.ruggedyrange.com) offers six coastal and river kayaking adventures, including multiactivity options, priced from NZ$175 per person to NZ$950, around Stewart and Ulva Islands.

SKIN DIVING & FISHING   You'll immediately notice how clear the seawater is around Stewart Island, making it ideal for diving. Join Richard Squires on **Lo Loma** (✆ 03/219-1141; www.loloma.co.nz) for half- or full-day fishing and diving charters. Herbie Hansen of **Southern Isle Charters** (✆ 03/219-1133) offers diving and fishing charters. Fishermen should pick up the Department of Conservation leaflet called *New Regulations for Fishing in Paterson Inlet, Stewart Island.*

WALKING   Three companies offer excellent trekking options in various parts of Stewart Island. **Ruggedy Range Wilderness Experience** (✆ 03/219-1066; www.ruggedy range.com) has trips to Ulva Island for NZ$110 to NZ$190, a kiwi-spotting adventure

ⓂMoments Making a Date with a Kiwi

The nightlife on Stewart Island is a bit different from that on the mainland, and one of the strangest fellows you'll meet on your starlit adventures will be *Apteryx australis lawryi,* the Stewart Island brown kiwi. This bristly, brown flightless critter is a distinct subspecies of the brown kiwi found throughout New Zealand. It has larger legs and a longer beak, and females are generally bigger than males.

Everything you hear about this being the only place in New Zealand where you're likely to see a kiwi in the wild is true. They're often seen, day and night, foraging for sand hoppers among the kelp on the Stewart Island beaches. Just ask Phillip and Diane Smith—they're the experts at this kiwi-spotting game. Every second night, they gather up a bunch of curious, and hopefully fit, tourists and take them to the remote sandy beaches to find kiwis.

A shy creature at heart, the kiwi attracts a lot of attention, and in the interests of conservation, the Smiths limit their night tours to just 15 passengers (you'll have to book ahead). The evening starts with a twilight cruise on the 16m (52-ft.) MV *Wildfire,* leaving from Half Moon Bay Wharf. After a 35-minute boat trip to Glory Bay, you'll make your way to the jetty (with a ladder, not steps!) and, after a short bush walk, you'll spend the evening (or 3–4 hr. of it) prowling the length of Ocean Beach, looking for the ungainly bird that has won the hearts of so many. If you're lucky, you'll see its plump, feathered backside plodding along the sand as it absent-mindedly looks for its evening meal.

You can expect some rare nights out in New Zealand, but this one is sure to surpass the lot. You may never have envisioned yourself as a bird-spotter, crouching in the darkness on some strange southern coastline, but when you see this rare bird playing hard to get—plodding, darting, hiding, reappearing—you'll know you have experienced something unique. It could well be the best date you have in New Zealand—and you'll pay NZ$110 for the pleasure.

Gather up your sturdy footwear, warm clothing, and torch (flashlight) and contact Phillip and Diane Smith at **Bravo Adventure Cruises** ★, P.O. Box 104, Stewart Island (ⓒ/fax **03/219-1144**). The trip is subject to weather conditions and is not recommended for children 14 and under.

in Mason Bay for NZ$435 to NZ$835, and a 1-day coastal highlights hike on the Rakiura Great Walk for NZ$210 per person. **Ulva's Guided Walks** ★★★ (ⓒ 03/219-1216; www.ulva.co.nz) has half-day guided walks on Ulva Island for NZ$110, which includes the water-taxi fare. Ulva has a terrific sense of humor and an incredible local knowledge, and she'll give you a rare insight into the birds and Maori history of the area. She also offers a half-day Port William guided walk for NZ$120. **Kiwi Wilderness Walks** (ⓒ 021/359-592; www.nzwalk.com) has 5-day walks that depart from Riverton (near Invercargill) for Mason Bay on Stewart Island, including sea kayaking and kiwi spotting, priced from NZ$1,500 per person.

There are several options for organized sightseeing trips: water taxis, boat cruises, yacht charters, and scenic flights. Most of the following tours are subject to weather conditions and all have minimum-number requirements.

Stewart Island Experience ★★★ (✆ 0800/000-511 in NZ, or 03/219-1134; www. stewartislandexperience.co.nz), has an excellent adventure in an underwater submersible that enables you to see diverse fish species, sponges, sea quirts, and shellfish as you drift through crystal-clear water and kelp forests. It departs from the Stewart Island Visitor Terminal daily at 11:30am and 1:30pm all year, with an extra sailing at 4pm from November through March. It costs NZ$35 for adults and NZ$20 for children ages 5 to 14. **Village & Bays Tours** (✆ 0800/000-511 in NZ, or 03/219-0034), gives a 1½-hour tour of Oban village and the surrounding bays, with a good commentary on local history. It allows for photo stops and short walks along the way and costs NZ$42 for adults and NZ$20 for children ages 5 to 14.

I'd also recommend the pelagic seabird excursion offered by **Aurora Charters** (✆ 03/219-1126). Leap aboard their modern catamaran, and they'll give you up-close encounters with seabirds and mammals. Don't forget your camera, and if you have a day to spare take their cruise to **Port Pegasus** ★★★ (price on inquiry). It's the dramatic southern part of the island that you'll not otherwise see.

One wonderful way to experience the island from several perspectives is to indulge in the **Coast to Coast** ★★ option with **Stewart Island Flights,** Invercargill (✆ 03/218-9129), and **Seaview Water Taxis,** Stewart Island (✆ 03/219-1014). This trip involves a flight to the magnificent **Mason's Bay** and a landing on its 13km (8-mile) stretch of unspoiled white-sand beach, a 4-hour bush walk to **Freshwater Landing,** and a return boat ride. The excursion is very dependent on tides, and you should be prepared for an unexpected night out if the weather gets rough. It costs NZ$205 for adults and NZ$145 for children. And if you're a helicopter fan like me, you'll adore an outing with Zane Smith of **Rakiura Helicopter Services** ★★★, Fern Gully heliport, 151 Main Rd. (✆ 03/219-1155, or 027/221-9217; rakiheli@xtra.co.nz). He's a sixth-generation islander and there isn't a part of the island he hasn't explored. He knows the place like the back of his hand. This will be the highlight of your trip.

WHERE TO STAY

If there is one negative thing to be said about Stewart Island, it must be about the overall standard of accommodations. There are numerous small backpacker operations, but they generally have a reputation for being pretty grim. Midrange lodgings are scattered, and upmarket choices are virtually nonexistent. On top of that, some of the better offerings have recently closed down, so I cannot promise anything startling in the way of a base. There is, however, a good range of holiday homes available for rent. Remember that summer accommodations are often booked months in advance. **Bay Motel** ★, 9 Dundee St., Half Moon Bay (✆ 03/219-1119; www.baymotel.co.nz), is an addition that I would happily recommend. It has 12 modern units priced from NZ$165 to NZ$185, plus two two-bedroom apartments for NZ$200. The **South Sea Hotel,** Elgin Terrace (✆ 03/219-1059; www.stewart-island.co.nz), has modest rooms with shared facilities, plus some new, quieter, motel rooms, which I would recommend over the hotel rooms. Their rates range from NZ$85 to NZ$155, and they have the advantage of being right on the waterfront in the heart of the village.

Port of Call ★★ (Value)   Arriving at Port of Call is like finding pearls in the middle of the desert! If you've managed to beat out other desperate tourists, you can put your feet up and relax—which is the way of things on Stewart Island. Hosts Ian and Philippa Wilson run a thriving tourism business on the island, and if you combine their local knowledge with the comfort of their modern guest rooms and their self-contained studio, you have a great little operation. There's outdoor charm in large decks, barbecue areas, and courtyards. They also have a self-contained cottage surrounded by native bush, 5 minutes from the waterfront.

Leask Bay Rd., Stewart Island. (C) **03/219-1394.** Fax 03/219-1394. www.portofcall.co.nz. 3 units. NZ$320 main house; NZ$180–NZ$250 self-catering studio; from NZ$200 Turner Cottage. Long-stay and off-peak rates. House rate includes breakfast. MC, V. No children 11 and under. **Amenities:** Free airport transport; nearby golf course. *In room:* TV/DVD, fridge, hair dryer, kitchen (in studio and cottage).

Stewart Island Lodge ★★★   I'm thrilled to say that this secluded spot is now in the capable hands of Stewart Island Experiences and has improved tenfold as a result. Set in native bush (at the top of a steep walk), just above the village, it has great views and five smart rooms with en suites and king-size beds. All open on to balconies and guests have the use of a private lounge in the main lodge. As part of Queenstown-based Real Journeys' operations the property has a Qualmark Enviro-Silver rating and is a member of the Southland Sustainable Tourism Charter.

14 Nichol Rd., Oban. (C) **03/219-1085.** www.stewartislandlodge.co.nz. 5 units. NZ$390. Off-peak rates. Rates include breakfast and hosted predinner drinks with appetizers. AE, DC, MC, V. **Amenities:** Free airport transfers; nearby golf course; Internet. *In room:* Fridge, hair dryer.

WHERE TO DINE

Dining out on Stewart Island barely warrants a separate section. **Church Hill Café & Restaurant** ★★, 36 Kamahi Rd. ((C) **03/219-1323;** www.churchhillrestaurant.com), beside the Presbyterian Manse on the hill overlooking Oban, is not quite as consistent as we might like, but overall you'll probably get your best island meal here. I had no complaints about my recent meal there, and you can always bank on good seafood dishes. It's open daily 10am to late. You'll get cheaper meals at the **Wharfside Cafe,** upstairs at the wharf ((C) **03/219-1470**). It's nothing fancy, but you'll be right in the island fishing atmosphere and you get good sea views. I always find it a good spot to relax while you wait for ferries or boat cruises. It's open from 10am until late, or from 7am for breakfast during the summer months. Another source of cheap, tasty eats is the seasonal **KaiKart Takeaways,** a mobile caravan on Ayr Street, beside the museum and school ((C) **03/219-1225;** www.kaikartstewartisland.com). It's open daily from noon to 2pm and 5pm until late during summer, providing excellent-value fish and chips, hamburgers, and assorted takeaways. Their blue cod snacks are definitely worth trying. **South Sea Hotel Dining Room,** South Sea Hotel, Oban (C) **03/219-1059**), offers big, unimaginative meals that in my view, are seriously overpriced. But if you like plain and hearty, you won't leave hungry. It's open daily noon to 2pm and 6 to 8pm. Look out for **Bean Around Mobile Espresso** ((C) **03/219-1234**) for the best coffee. Their Fair Trade coffee is perhaps the southernmost in the world. As the name suggests, they're mobile, so when you see them, grab that coffee! **Just Café,** 6 Main Rd., Oban ((C) **03/219-1422**), is otherwise the best source of coffee. They serve delicious counter food and juices too; and they have an Internet service as well.

Fast Facts

1 FAST FACTS: NEW ZEALAND

AMERICAN EXPRESS The office is at 105 Queen St., Auckland (© **09/367-4422**). Other offices are located in Christchurch, Hamilton, Nelson, Porirua, Pukekohe, Queenstown, Rotorua, Wellington, and Whangarei. They accept mail for clients, forward mail for a small fee, issue and change traveler's checks, and replace lost or stolen traveler's checks and American Express cards.

BUSINESS HOURS Banks are open Monday through Friday from 9am to 4:30pm. Shops are usually open Monday through Thursday from 9am (sometimes 8am) to 5:30pm, and until 9pm on either Thursday or Friday. Increasingly, shops are open all day Saturday; many shops are also open all day Sunday, with others closing between noon and 4pm.

DRUGSTORES Pharmacies observe regular shop hours, but most localities have an Urgent Pharmacy, which remains open until about 11pm every day except Sunday, when there are two periods during the day when it's open, usually one in the morning and one in the afternoon.

ELECTRICITY The voltage is 230 volts in New Zealand, and plugs are the three-prong type. If you bring a hair dryer, it should be a dual-voltage one, and you'll need an adapter plug. Most motels and some B&Bs have built-in wall transformers for 110-volt, two-prong razors, but if you're going to be staying in hostels, cabins, homestays, or guesthouses, bring dual-voltage appliances.

EMBASSIES & CONSULATES In Wellington, the capital city, you'll find the United States Embassy, the Canadian High Commission, and the British High Commission (see "Fast Facts: Wellington," in chapter 12). In Auckland, you'll find consulates for the United States, Canada, Ireland, and the United Kingdom (see "Fast Facts: Auckland," in chapter 6).

EMERGENCIES Dial © **111** to contact the police, call an ambulance, or report a fire.

FILM Film is expensive in New Zealand, so if you're not using a digital camera, carry a lot of it from home. Most brands are available in larger cities.

INTERNET ACCESS Internet facilities are available in all major cities and in many smaller towns. Consult visitor centers for specifics, or go to www.cybercafes.com. Many establishments now offer broadband and wireless connections. See "Internet/E-mail" in chapter 3 for more information about traveling with or without your own computer.

LANGUAGE English is spoken by all New Zealanders. You'll hear Maori spoken on some TV and radio programs and in some Maori settlements.

LIQUOR LAWS The minimum drinking age is 18 in pubs. Children are allowed in pubs with their parents.

LOST & FOUND Be sure to tell all of your credit card companies the minute you discover your wallet has been lost or stolen and file a report at the nearest police precinct. Your credit card company or insurer may require a police report number or record of the loss. Most credit card companies have an emergency toll-free number to call if your card is lost or stolen; they may be able to wire you a cash advance immediately or deliver an emergency credit card in a day or two. Visa's emergency number is ✆ **0508/600-300** in New Zealand. American Express cardholders and traveler's check holders should call collect to the U.S. at ✆ **715/343-7977.** MasterCard holders should call ✆ **0800/44-9140** in New Zealand.

If you need emergency cash over the weekend when all banks and American Express offices are closed, you can have money wired to you via **Western Union** (✆ **0800/005-253** in NZ; www.western union.com).

Identity theft and fraud are potential complications of losing your wallet, especially if you've lost your driver's license along with your cash and credit cards. Notify the major credit-reporting bureaus immediately; placing a fraud alert on your records may protect you against liability for criminal activity. The three major U.S. credit-reporting agencies are **Equifax** (✆ **800/766-0008;** www.equifax.com), **Experian** (✆ **888/397-3742;** www. experian.com), and **TransUnion** (✆ **800/ 680-7289;** www.transunion.com). Finally, if you've lost all forms of photo ID, call your airline and explain the situation; they might allow you to board the plane if you have a copy of your passport or birth certificate and a copy of the police report you've filed.

MAIL New Zealand post offices will receive mail and hold it for you for 1 month. Have the parcel addressed to you c/o Poste Restante at the Chief Post Office of the town you'll be visiting. It costs NZ$3 to send an airmail letter to the United States, Canada, United Kingdom, or Europe. Overseas postcards cost NZ$2.

MAPS Get free maps from Automobile Association offices around the country by showing your home-country membership card. Rental-car firms also furnish maps with rentals. See "Mapping a Path" in chapter 3 for more sources of maps.

PASSPORTS For Residents of the United States: Whether you're applying in person or by mail, you can download passport applications from the U.S. State Department website at **http://travel.state. gov.** For general information, call the **National Passport Agency** (✆ **202/647-0518**). To find your regional passport office, either check the U.S. State Department website or call the **National Passport Information Center** (✆ **900/ 225-5674**); the fee is 55¢ per minute for automated information and $1.50 per minute for operator-assisted calls.

For Residents of Canada: Passport applications are available at travel agencies throughout Canada or from the central **Passport Office,** Department of Foreign Affairs and International Trade, Ottawa, ON K1A 0G3 (✆ **800/567-6868;** www. ppt.gc.ca).

For Residents of the United Kingdom: To pick up an application for a standard 10-year passport (5-year passport for children under 16), visit your nearest passport office, major post office, or travel agency or contact the **United Kingdom Passport Service** at ✆ **0870/521-0410** or search its website at www.ukpa.gov.uk.

For Residents of Ireland: You can apply for a 10-year passport at the **Passport Office,** Setanta Centre, Molesworth Street, Dublin 2 (✆ **01/671-1633;** www. irlgov.ie/iveagh). Those under age 18 and over 65 must apply for a 3-year passport. You can also apply at 1A South Mall, Cork (✆ **021/272-525**), or at most main post offices.

For Residents of Australia: You can pick up an application from your local post office or any branch of Passports Australia, but you must schedule an interview at the passport office to present your application materials. Call the **Australian Passport Information Service** at ✆ **131-232,** or visit the government website at www.passports.gov.au.

PRICE RANGES   Throughout this book, I separate hotel listings into several broad categories: **Very Expensive,** NZ$650 and up; **Expensive,** NZ$275 to $650; **Moderate,** NZ$150 to $250; and **Inexpensive,** under $150 for a double. *All rates given in this book include the 12.5% New Zealand Goods and Services Tax (GST).* Note that in the case of hotels, the category placement relates to the bulk of their room prices or their perceived status in the New Zealand accommodation sector. Some hotels have also opted to display dynamic pricing (a range) rather than individual room categories, so it goes without saying that you should always inquire about their best prices when you book.

I have separated restaurant listings throughout this book into three price categories, based on the average cost of a meal per person, including GST. The categories are **Expensive,** more than NZ$28; **Moderate,** NZ$20 to $25; and **Inexpensive,** less than NZ$20.

RESTROOMS   There are "public conveniences" strategically located in all cities and many towns. Local **Plunket Rooms** come with a "Mother's Room," where you can change your child's diapers. The Plunket Society is a state-subsidized organization that provides free baby care to all New Zealand families.

TAXES   There is a national 12.5% **Goods and Services Tax (GST)** that's applicable to everything. A **departure tax** of NZ$25 is assessed and can be paid by credit card or in cash in New Zealand currency.

TIME ZONE   New Zealand is located just west of the international date line, and its standard time is 12 hours ahead of Greenwich Mean Time. Thus, when it's noon in New Zealand, it's 7:30am in Singapore, 9am in Tokyo, 10am in Sydney; and—all the previous day—4pm in San Francisco, 7pm in New York, and midnight in London. In New Zealand, daylight saving time starts the first weekend in October and ends in mid-March.

TIPPING   Most New Zealanders don't tip waitstaff unless they've received extraordinary service—and then only 5% to 10%. Taxi drivers and porters are rarely tipped in this country.

VISITOR INFORMATION   To get started, contact the nearest **Tourism New Zealand office** for a complimentary copy of its *New Zealand Vacation Planner.*

Tourism New Zealand offices can be found in the **United States** at 501 Santa Monica Blvd., Ste. 300, Santa Monica, CA 90401 (✆ **866/639-9325** in the U.S., or 310/395-7480; fax 310/395-5453); in **Canada** at 888 Dunsmuir St., Ste. 1200, Vancouver, BC V6C 3K4 (✆ **800/888-5494** in Canada, or 604/684-2117); in **Australia** at Level 8, 35 Pitt St., Sydney, NSW 2000 (✆ **02/9247-5222**); in **England** at New Zealand House, Haymarket, SW1Y 4TQ, London (✆ **020/7930-1662**); in **Germany** at Rossmarkt 11, 60311 Frankfurt am Main (✆ **069/9712-1110;** fax 069/9712-1113); and in **Hong Kong** at Unit 1601 Vicwood Plaza, 199 Des Voeux Rd. (✆ **852/2526-0141**).

The official Tourism New Zealand website is **www.newzealand.com**. Click on your home country to see the latest deals, with contact information for travel agents. The site provides comprehensive details for every aspect of your trip and is a must-visit. Other useful sites include **New Zealand on the Web** (www.nz.com), which offers hundreds of excellent links; and for up-to-the-minute ski information, click on **www.nzski.com**.

When you arrive in New Zealand, you'll find 80 official **i-SITE Visitor Centres** scattered around the country. Friendly staff members can book accommodations, activities, and tours; provide maps; and sell stamps and phone cards. Each chapter in this book lists the particular district/city information centers, and you can pick up a list of i-SITE locations at Auckland and Christchurch international airports. Check www.i-site.org for more information.

WATER New Zealand tap water is pollution-free and safe to drink. In the bush, you should boil, filter, or chemically treat water from rivers and lakes to avoid contracting *Giardia* (a waterborne parasite that causes diarrhea).

---

2 AIRLINE, HOTEL & CAR RENTAL WEBSITES

INTERNATIONAL AIRLINES

Air New Zealand
www.airnewzealand.com
www.airnewzealand.co.nz

Air Tahiti Nui
www.airtahitinui-usa.com

American Airlines
www.aa.com

British Airways
www.british-airways.com

Cathay Pacific
www.cathaypacific.com

Emirates Airlines
www.emirates.com

Japan Airlines
www.jal.co.jp/en

Jetstar
www.jetstar.com

Korean Air
www.koreanair.com

Lan Airlines
www.lanchile.com

Lufthansa
www.lufthansa.com

Malaysian Airlines
www.malaysiaairlines.com

Qantas
www.qantas.com.au

Royal Brunei Airlines
www.bruneiair.com

Singapore Airlines
www.singaporeair.com

Thai Airways
www.thaiair.com

United Airlines
www.united.com

Virgin Blue
www.virginblue.com.au

MAJOR HOTEL & MOTEL CHAINS

Accor Hotels
www.accor.com

Crowne Plaza Hotels
www.ichotelsgroup.com/crowneplaza

Hilton Hotels
www.hilton.com

Holiday Inn
www.holidayinn.com

Hyatt
www.hyatt.com

InterContinental Hotels & Resorts
www.ichotelsgroup.com

Scenic Hotels Group
www.scenichotels.co.nz

Westin Hotels
www.starwoodhotels.com/westin

CAR RENTAL AGENCIES

Avis
www.avis.com

Budget
www.budget.com

Hertz
www.hertz.com

Payless
www.paylesscarrental.com

Thrifty
www.thrifty.com

Kiwi Terms & Phrases

Who would have thought the English language could be so confusing? New Zealand may seem like an easy place to negotiate, but it has developed some very distinctive language characteristics. Here's a guide to help you negotiate everyday colloquialisms.

For tips on the Maori language, see p. 28.

---

1 KIWI/YANKEE TERMS

Air-conditioning   Refers to both heating and cooling the air

All Blacks   New Zealand rugby team

Bach   North Island term for vacation house (plural: baches)

Bath   Bathtub

Bathroom   Where one bathes; bath

Biro   Ballpoint pen

Biscuits/bickies   Cookies

Bludge   Borrow

Bonnet   Hood of car

Boot   Trunk of car

Bro   Slang for "brother"; a friendly term used widely

Bush   Forest

Chemist shop   Drugstore

Chilly bin   Styrofoam cooler (U.S.), esky (Aus.)

Coach   Long-distance bus

Cocky   Farmer

College   High school

Cot   Crib (place where a baby or toddler sleeps)

Crib   South Island term for holiday house

Cuppa   Cup of tea

Cyclone   Hurricane

Dairy   Convenience store

Dish   As in "a bit of a dish"; a good-looking woman

Do   As in "a bit of a do"; a party

Doona/Duvet   Comforter, quilt (Aus.)

En suite   In-room bathroom

Fanny   Female genitalia; you'll shock Kiwis if you call the thing you wear around your waist a "fanny pack"

Flannel   Face cloth

Footpath   Sidewalk

Gallops   Thoroughbred horse racing

Get stuck in   Get started

Gidday   Hello

Grizzle   Complain

Grog   Booze

Gumboots   Waterproof rubber boots (U.S.), Wellingtons (Britain)

Hire   Rent

Homely   Homey

Hooker   Front-row rugby player

Hotties   Hot-water bottles

Housie   Bingo

Jandals   Thongs (Aus.), flip-flops (U.S./Britain)

Jersey   Pullover sweater (U.S.), jumper (Aus.)

Judder bars   Speed bumps (U.S.), sleeping policeman (Britain)

Jug   Electric kettle or a pitcher

Kiwi   Person from New Zealand; native bird of New Zealand

Knickers   Underwear, undies

Knock up   Wake up

Lift   Elevator

Loo   Toilet

Lounge   Living room

LSZ   Low-speed zone

Mate   Friend

Mossie   Mosquito

Nappy   Diaper

Pakeha   Anyone of European descent

Private facilities   Private bathroom

Pushchair   Baby stroller

Queue   Line, to wait in line

Rates   Property taxes

Return ticket   Round-trip ticket

Rug   Blanket

Serviette   Napkin

Shout   Treat someone (usually refers to a meal or a drink), buy a round

Single bed   Twin bed

Singlet   Sleeveless undershirt

Sister   Nurse

Smoko   Morning or afternoon break

Strides   Trousers

Ta   Thank you

Thongs   Brief underwear (not the Australian term for *jandals*—see above)

To call   To visit

Togs   Swimsuit (U.S.), cozzie (Aus.)

To ring   To phone

Track   Trail

Trots   Harness racing; in New Zealand the word also means diarrhea

Uplift   Pick up

Varsity   University, college

Yank   American

2   MENU TERMS

Afghans   Popular Kiwi cookies made with cornflakes and cocoa

ANZAC biscuits   Cookies named for the Australia New Zealand Army Corps; they contain rolled oats and golden syrup

Bangers   Sausages

Beetroot   Beets

Biscuits   Cookies

Blue vein   Bleu cheese

Capsicum   Green or red bell pepper

Chips   French-fried potatoes

Chook   Chicken

Courgette   Zucchini

Devonshire tea   Morning or afternoon tea, plus scones with cream and jam

Dinner   The main meal of the day; can be the meal eaten in the middle of the day

Entree   Appetizer

Grilled   Broiled

Hogget   Year-old lamb

Iceblock   Popsicle

Jelly   Gelatin dessert

Kumara   Kiwi sweet potato

Lemonade   7-Up

Lollies   Candy

Main course   Entree

Marmite   New Zealand–made yeast spread

Mash   Mashed potatoes

Meat pie   A two-crust pie filled with stewed, cubed, or ground meat (usually beef) and gravy

Milk shake   Flavored milk

Milo   A hot drink similar to Ovaltine

Pavlova   Popular meringue dessert named after prima ballerina Anna Pavlova, served with whipped cream and fruit

Pikelets   Small pancakes served at teatime

Pipis   Clams

Pudding   Dessert in general, not necessarily pudding

Roast dinner   Roast beef or leg of lamb served with potatoes and other vegetables that have been cooked with the meat

Rock melon   Cantaloupe

Saveloy   A type of wiener

Scone   A biscuit served at teatime

Silverbeet   Swiss chard

Silverside   A superior cut of corned beef

Snarlers   Sausages

Takeaway   Takeout

Tamarillos   Tree tomatoes

Tea   The national beverage; also a light evening meal, supper; see also "Dinner," above

Thick shake   Milkshake

Tomato sauce   Ketchup

Vegemite   Australian-made yeast spread

Water biscuit   Cracker

Weet-Bix   A breakfast cereal similar to shredded wheat

Whitebait   Very tiny fish, served whole without being cleaned

White tea   Tea with milk

INDEX